ARCHITECTS' DATA

Second (International) English Edition

Ernst Neufert

ARCHITECTS' DATA

Second (International) English Edition

General editor   Vincent Jones
Editorial consultant   George Atkinson OBE BA(Arch) RIBA
USA editor   Wm Dudley Hunt Jr BSc BArch FAIA
Editor   John Thackara
Deputy editor   Richard Miles

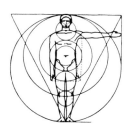

GRANADA
London Toronto Sydney New York

HALSTED PRESS
JOHN WILEY & SONS, INC.
New York

Granada Publishing Limited – Technical Books Division
Frogmore, St Albans, Herts AL2 2NF
and 3 Upper James Street, London W1R 4BP
Suite 405, 4th Floor, 866 United Nations Plaza, New York, NY 10017, USA
117 York Street, Sydney, NSW 2000, Australia
100 Skyway Avenue, Rexdale, Ontario M9W 3A6, Canada
PO Box 84165, Greenside, 2034 Johannesburg, South Africa
61 Beach Road, Auckland, New Zealand

Copyright © Granada Publishing, 1980

First published in Great Britain 1980 by
Granada Publishing Limited

Published in the U.S.A. by Halsted Press,
a Division of John Wiley & Sons, Inc., New York

British Library and Library of Congress Cataloguing in Publication Data
Neufert, Ernst
    Architects' Data. – 2nd ed.
    1. Architecture
    I. Title
    721   NA 2522   80-040644

    ISBN 0-246-11258-1
        0-470-26947-2 (USA)

Design and phototypesetting by Parkway Group London and Abingdon
Printed in Great Britain by William Clowes (Beccles) Limited, Beccles and London

Granada ®
Granada Publishing ®

Ernst Neufert

Professor Technische Hochschule Darmstadt

Ernst Neufert, born in 1900, in 1919 became the first student of architecture at the Bauhaus in Weimar. He left at the end of 1920 for a study tour in southern Europe but before long Gropius called him back as his assistant. In 1924 he became technical director of the Bauhaus offices in Weimar and then manager of the Gropius workshop during the rebuilding of the 'Bauhaus in Dessau' and also taught in the department of architecture at the Bauhaus.

In 1926 he became professor and director of the department of architecture at the newly founded Building Technical College in Weimar and shortly afterwards assistant director of the construction department. In 1930 he moved to Berlin to become head of the department of architecture at Itten, a private school of art, and started to work as a free-lance industrial architect. It was in Berlin that he brought out in 1936 the first edition of *Bauentwurfslehre*.

Following the war he was co-founder and member of the board of directors of the Bund Deutscher Architekten (Federation of German Architects), was appointed professor at Darmstadt Polytechnic and director of the Institute for Standardisation (Institut für Baunormung) and continued to work also as free-lance industrial architect.

Professor Neufert has lectured in many cities, such as Graz, Belgrade, Skopje, Thessaloniki, Athens, Istanbul, Beirut, Karachi, Rangoon, Hong Kong, in Japan's major cities and at Neutra in Los Angeles and F L Wright in Taliesin West Arizona.

He is honorary member of the Real Academica de Ciencias y Artes Barcelona and of the Royal Institute of British Architects, honorary professor and doctor at the University of Lima, Peru. He has been awarded the German Merit Cross with star, as well as various other German and foreign honours.

Ernst Neufert's other works include *Bauordnungslehre* (1943), *Ernst Neufert Industriebauten* (1973).

UK contributors

Peter Ackroyd Dip Arch (Poly) Reg Arch   *The Sports Council*
A G Aldersley-Williams MArch(MIT) RIBA   *Engineering Design Consultants*
Norman S Allanson Des RCS FSIAD   *John S Bonnington Partnership*
Robin G Booth MA MSc Dip Arch RIBA MRTPI   *John S Bonnington Partnership*
Jan Petr Čermák-z-Uhrinova BSc(Hons) TEng(CEI) MIAgrE   *Scottish Farm Building Investigation Unit*
J B Collins BSc(Eng) CEng MIEE FCIBS
Dr Francis Duffy ARIBA   *Duffy Eley Giffone Worthington*
Jolyn V P Drury MA(Cantab) Dip Arch RIBA MIMH   *Jolyon Drury Consultancy*
Nelson Foley RIBA   *Chief Architect Trust House Forte*
J A Godfrey ARIBA
David Jenkin   *Duffy Eley Giffone Worthington*
Eva M Jiricna Dipl Eng Arch RIBA   *Louis Soissons Partnership*
Geraint John Dip Arch(UCL) RIBA   *The Sports Council*
Geoffrey Jones BArch(Lvpl)
Olwen C Marlowe ARIBA Dip LD(Dunelm) Dip TP(Birm)
David L Medd OBE Hon DSc ARIBA   *Department of Education & Science*
Mary B Medd OBE ARIBA   *Department of Education & Science*
Alan Morgan Dip Arch RIBA
Dermot O'Brien FSIAD
Robert Payne *Duffy Eley Giffone Worthington*
Elizabeth Phillips Dip Arch RWA ARIBA
Dennis Sharp MA AA Dipl RIBA
Deyan Sudjic BSc Dip Arch
Richard E Theakston Dip Arch RIBA   *John S Bonnington Partnership*
P R Tregenza BArch MBdgSc PhD RIBA MCIBS
R E Vickers DLC CEng MICE   *British Lift Slab Ltd*
David Witham MA(Cantab) AA Dipl

USA contributors

Peter Frink BArch MSc MFA   *Principal Frink & Beuchat Architects*
Walter Hart AIA   *Architect*
Wm Dudley Hunt Jr BSc BArch FAIA
Margaret K Hunter BA AIA   *Architect*
Edgar H Hunter BA BArch AIA   *Architect*
Robert T Packard BArch AIA   *Director AIA Documents/Architectural Graphic Standards Division*
Mimi Ford Paul BA BSArch   *Architect*
Bradford Perkins   *Senior Vice President & General Manager Perkins & Will Architects*

Addendum to UK Contributors' list:

Nadine Beddington FRIBA FSIAD
[assisted by Dermot O'Brien FSIAD]

Acknowledgements

The Editors and the Publishers acknowledge with sincere thanks the kind help and information provided by many individuals and organisations during the preparation of this work. The Publishers have made every effort to establish and properly acknowledge the copyright owners of the drawings and plans used in this book and wish to apologise for any unintentional omissions that may have been made. Should any other acknowledgements be necessary the publishers will be happy to do so when the book is reprinted.

The works of individual architects are acknowledged throughout the text but particular thanks are also due to:

Henry Dreyfuss Associates for Fig. 2 on page 9;
The Architectural Press for Fig. 1 on page 19 and Figs 1 and 2 on page 22;
Sunset Books for Fig. 4 on page 77;
The Architectural Press for Figs 1-9 on page 83, Fig. 1 on page 84, and Fig. 5 on page 86;
Sunset Books for Figs 5 and 6 on page 113 and for Figs 6-11 on page 114;
Moriyama and Teshima for Fig. 4 on page 146;
Ahrends Burton and Koralek for Fig. 2 on page 148;
Powell Moya and Partners for Fig. 3 on page 150;
Watkins Gray Woodgate International (UK) for Fig. 1 on page 155;
R. Seifert and Partners for Fig. 5 on page 157;
The Nuffield Foundation for Fig. 1 on page 161;
Robert Matthew, Johnson-Marshall and Partners for Fig. 2 on page 161;
George Trew Dunn Beckles Willson Bowes for Fig. 1 on page 167;
Wilson and Wilson for Fig. 2 on page 168;
Robert Matthew, Johnson-Marshall and Partners for Fig. 2 on page 171;
The Oxford Regional Health Authority for Fig. 4 on page 171;
Donald A. Goldfinch Associates for Fig. 1 on page 175;
South East Thames Regional Health Authority for Fig. 2 on page 175;
The Nuffield Foundation for Fig. 2 on page 176;
Mehmet Konuralp for Fig. 3 on page 192;
Isabelle Hebey for Fig. 4 on page 192;

The Architectural Press for Fig. 2 on page 198;
The National Playing Fields Association for Fig. 7 on page 322;
The Architectural Press for Figs. 1, 4 and 5 on page 346 and for Figs 2-4, 7 and 8 on page 347;
Progressive Architecture for Fig. 3 on page 361.

The following are reproduced by permission of the Building Directorate, Scottish Development Department: Fig. 1 on page 82, Figs 10 and 11 on page 83, Fig. 2 on page 84 and Figs 1-4 and 6-8 on page 86;
Fig. 1 on page 148 is reprinted from Architectural Record September 1976 © 1976, by McGraw-Hill, Inc., with all rights reserved;
Fig. 2 on page 155 is reproduced with the permission of the Controller of Her Majesty's Stationery Office;
Fig. 1 on page 162 is reprinted with permission from the American Health Care Association Journal, Vol. 4, No. 4, July 1978. Copyright © American Health Care Association. All rights reserved;
Fig. 3 on page 162 is reproduced courtesy of Architects Derek Stow and Partners in association with the Regional Architect, South West Thames Regional Health Authority;
Fig. 2 on page 164 is reprinted from Architectural Record October 1979 © 1979, by McGraw-Hill, Inc., with all rights reserved;
Fig. 1 on page 171 is reproduced courtesy of Cullen Lochhead and Brown in association with the Chief Architect of Western Regional Hospital Board, T.D.W. Astorga, Esq., FRIBA;
Fig. 1 on page 174 is reprinted from Architectural Record August 1977 © 1977, by McGraw-Hill, Inc., with all rights reserved;
Fig. 4 on page 180 is reprinted from Architectural Record August 1977 © 1977, by McGraw-Hill, Inc., with all rights reserved;
Fig. 1 on page 201 is reprinted from Architectural Record June 1978 © 1978, by McGraw-Hill, Inc., with all rights reserved;
Fig. 5 on page 291 is the Zoology Extension, Edinburgh University and is reproduced by permission of the Designers, the Architecture Research Unit, University of Edinburgh;
Fig. 1 on page 361 is reprinted from Architectural Record June 1977 © 1977, by McGraw-Hill, Inc., with all rights reserved.

Foreword

Architects' Data first appeared in English in 1970, nearly thirty-five years after Ernst Neufert published his 'rules for building design' – *Bauentwurfslehre* – based on his lectures at the Building Technical College in Weimar. He had arranged in one book for convenient reference during design work, data on the spatial needs of man in his home, his work place and his leisure, and on his animals, tools and belongings. The book clearly met a need: in 1979 the 30th German edition appeared; it has also been published in Spanish (12 editions), Italian (5), French (5), Portuguese (3), Serbocroat (3), and in Russian, Greek and Turkish; but before the present, only one edition in English, which came late on the scene.

In the 1960s the book's international repute led the Professional Literature Committee of the Royal Institute of British Architects and many others to recognise the need for an English language edition; but to convert to imperial measures was a great obstacle. Conversion to the metric system in Britain and the Commonwealth changed this. An English edition became possible. It was edited by the late Rudolf Herz who had studied in Berlin and had practised many years as an architect in the United Kingdom.

He had no easy task. With so big a book translation alone was a major undertaking; furthermore much terminology and some practice details had to be modified. At that time, therefore, publishers and editor did not try to bring the whole book up to date; they concentrated on getting it out.

During the 1970s the need for a new edition thoroughly revised became more pressing: there were new imperatives of energy conservation, economic constraint and changing social needs to affect the design of buildings. More influential still for such a work: the 'information explosion', whose full force will be felt during the 1980s, changing the role of such a design handbook. When he wrote *Architects' Data* nearly fifty years ago Neufert provided a mixture of abstracted design, principles, hard data and examples. Today there is less need for illustration of construction details. Manufacturers increasingly distribute technical information which can be filed in uniform office systems; and with telephone line and video display unit an office can reach vast computerised and regularly revised data banks. To make sense of this mass of information the architect now needs even clearer guidance on the principles and bases of design.

Basis of the revision

Our aim, therefore, has been to simplify, rearrange and modernise. Requirements or advice contained in regulations, standards and codes have for the most part been left out: they change during the life of the book and vary from country to country; moreover for legal and codified data the designer should always look to the original source. Full references have been given. Information on construction elements (such as foundation, brickwork, roofs) can easily be found elsewhere; it has been left out or reduced to make more room for more fundamental work on building types.

At the beginning 'Basic data' summarises the essentials of the human scale in architecture and at the end 'Components' brings together some new European planning guidelines for the spaces needed to install, operate and maintain the often complex services now required in buildings; technical aspects of the internal environment; and practical criteria for such components as windows, doors, stairs and elevators. Though they are not directly applicable in a non-metric context we felt these pages to be of wide interest in their approach to the presentation of such information. In the body of the book the measure of what to leave out, what to put in or to expand has been: does this help the designer in solving her or his problems of spatial needs?

The sequence of sections has been rearranged. All parts have been reviewed, revised, brought up to date and in most instances expanded: this edition is twenty-five per cent longer and perhaps seventy-five per cent new in substance. Special attention has been given to new thinking on housing, education, hospitals, industrial construction and farm buildings. The section on sport and leisure has been made far more comprehensive. And throughout the implications of energy conservation, the needs of the elderly and disabled, and defence against fire have been stressed.

As the first international edition to be published the book contains several building types which are not common in some countries. Both British and American contributors liked this. In some instances, such as shopping precincts, more than a single building is involved; for these the information given is more general. In others, such as underground houses, projects as well as finished buildings have been given as examples, although this is the exception.

Units of measurement

The International System of Units (SI) is used for all units of measurement. A decision on how to apply the system faces architects and engineers when drawing plans: at what point to switch from the basic mm to the derivative m. There appears to be no ruling by authority on this. In *Architects' Data* it is solved in two ways. All linear measurements in text are given in millimetres up to 9 999, standing as here without indicator, and from 10 m upwards they are given in metres with the indicator m. On the other hand in the many small diagrams which form one of the book's most useful elements, four figure dimensions would often make for clutter: where there is this danger, for dimensions above 999 metres are used without the indicator m.

There has to be one exception to this rule. In sport international dimensions standards are given: some of these are still expressed in 'imperial' or US customary units. This section therefore presents an unavoidable mixture.

To meet the needs of users in the United States of America, who are mostly still using US customary or 'imperial' units, a set of conversion factors and tables is provided →p364–81 (with a simplified version on the bookmarker). In other appropriate instances the graphic scale may be used (see below).

Scales

Many of the plans and diagrams in the book do not need scales; their purpose is to express relationships or situations. In many others the practical needs of the user are best answered by giving dimensions on the drawing. Scales are used only in relation to plans or diagrams of specific buildings or installations and these are shown graphically in metres and feet.

Style

This book is not literature; it is a practical manual. The text is telegraphic and predicatory; in this it follows the practice of Ernst Neufert, who wrote in his first edition that his aim had been to 'reduce, schematise, abstract the elements of design basics so as to make simple imitation difficult and to oblige the user to create form and content out of data'. The size of many of the diagrams makes necessary the use of abbreviations: these are therefore used consistently in all plans and diagrams and in captions, the most common in the text also, the intention being that they quickly become familiar to the user. Abbreviations used in the book (→pxiii) are also listed for quick reference on the bookmarker which carries the conversion tables and factors.

Language is a usual problem in a book intended for users both

Foreword

sides the Atlantic, not to mention other continents. Sometimes it is possible to find a neutral alternative expression; at others we have risked annoying everybody occasionally by choosing a word from one or the other usage: thus the British have to accept 'aisle', 'elevator', 'truck'; North Americans must stomach 'foot-path', 'ground floor' for 'first floor' (and 'second' for 'first' . . .), 'cooker' for 'range' (which has a limited specific meaning in the United Kingdom). Only rarely have we fallen back on using a double expression such as 'trolley (cart)'. North American readers are also asked to accept that British spelling has been used all through.

Distantly related is the problem of the rule of the road. Quite a number of illustrations show access roads, car parking, turning circles and such details. Some have their origin in continental Europe, some in North America, some in the United Kingdom. Rather than try to convert all to one rule we have indicated on each relevant page whether it refers to left or right hand circulation.

Acknowledgements

The contributors in the UK and USA who have made this new edition possible are named →pv. Authors, publishers, architects, institutions and public bodies who have allowed the use of copyrights are listed on the page following. Warmest thanks to all.

Planning and execution of the revisions, changes, new concepts and improvements, while a cooperative effort, have been entirely the publishers' responsibility. But the work would not have been possible without consultant editor George Atkinson, whose experience, technical knowledge and practical outlook have been invaluable We are indebted also to Wm Dudley Hunt, whose professionalism and expertise, which are the basis of the respect he already enjoys in the USA, have helped enormously in the completion of the book.

Lastly we salute and thank Patricia Crowe, whose secretarial skills gave us a clear course through the seas of paper, and deputy editor Richard Miles, who stepped in to see things through in the later stages of the work. The formidable task of drawing or revising the many new or modified figures fell to Sheena Busby MSAT and the design and layout of the printed page to Tony Leonard, to both of whom our sincerest thanks.

Vincent Jones
John Thackara

How to use the book

Arrangement

The contents table →pix shows the grouping of subjects & sequence of the book: from basic data for man & his buildings, through man in his community, to buildings for commerce, industry & leisure, to some technical planning data & regulations. It can be used to find the pages referring to a given subject such as 'shops & stores'.

The index →p429 is a tool for quick reference to a point of detail *eg* 'access', 'shower', 'wheelchair'.

The bibliography →p413 is divided into 3 parts: a the main alphabetical (and numbered) list of publications for further reference, & extracted from this b a list of the most important regulations & codes of the UK & USA, c a list of references under subject headings *eg* 'airports', 'disabled', 'offices', 'schools'.

Abbreviations used →pxiii are also given on the bookmarker together with conversion tables from metric to USA customary or imperial measures.

Units of measurement: SI →p1, conversion →p364 & on insert.

Application

Suppose you have to prepare a scheme for a **college of further education.** Under 'education' in the contents there are page references for lecture rooms (134), schools of art (137), student hostels (140) dining rooms (142), libraries (145): these together give some of the main components needed.

On studying these pages you will find cross references (indicated →) to other sections such as accoustics (18 395), auditorium (350), cinemas (354), fire escape (44 91), kitchens (213), sanitary units (65), seating systems (351), shared accn (99), sight lines (351), space standards (44 48), workshops (288)

General information on proportions & human measurements is given →p9–24, on services, heating, lighting, sound ventilation & such components as elevators, stairs, windows →p383–412.

Regulations & codes should be studied before starting any design: →bibliography for a list of the most important.

Contents

Abbreviations

Abbreviations used in text and diagrams are listed below.
NB: plurals are not used in abbreviations

A	ampere
ar	area
AC	alternating current
accn	accommodation
admin	administration
arch	architect
ANSI	American National Standards Institute
ASTM	American Society for Testing & Materials
av	average
B	bed
b	bath
base	basement
bathr	bathroom
bedr	bedroom
balc	balcony
bldg	building
bldg reg	building regulation
BOCA	Building Officials & Code Administrators
BRE	Building Research Establishment
BS(I)	British Standards (Institution)
Btu	British thermal unit
BZ	British zonal classification
C or cpd	cupboard/USA cabinet
°C	degree Celsius
c/c	centre to centre/USA on centers
cd	candela
ch	children
CIBS	Chartered Institute of Building Services
CIE	Commission internationale de l'Eclairage (International Commission on Illumination)
ck	cooker/USA range
classr	classroom
clo	cloakroom
consult	consultation, consulting (room)
corr	corridor
CP	code of practice
CSSD	central sterile supply depot
d	day or depth
dayr	dayroom
dB	decibel
DC	direct current
deg	degree
dept	department
DES	Department of Education & Science
DF	daylight factor
DHSS	Department of Health & Social Security
dia	diameter
DoE	Department of the Environment
DPC	damp proof course
dr	dining room
dre	dressing room
E	illumination
el	electrical
eqp	equipment
exam	examination
°F	degree Fahrenheit
fdn	foundation
FFL	finished floor level/USA elevation
FHA	Federal Housing Authority
fr	fire resistant
ft	foot
g	gram
gal	gallon
gar	garage

GP	general practitioner
gu	guest room
h	height or high
ha	hall or hectare
hb	(wash) hand basin
hr	hour
HUD	Dept of Housing & Urban Development
hum	humidity
Hz	hertz
ICBO	International Conference of Building Officials
IES	Illuminating Engineering Society
IFLA	International Federation of Library Associations
ISO	International Organisation for Standardisation (Organisation internationale de Normalisation)
in	inch
J	joule
K	degree Kelvin
k	kitchen
kg	kilogram
kgf	kilogram-force
km	kilometre
l	litre, length, long
la	larder
lab	laboratory
lau	laundry
lav	lavatory or toilet
lib	library
liv	living room
lob	lobby
lx	lux
m	metre
mdr	maid's room (or au pair)
max	maximum
mech	mechanical
med	medical
MF	maintenance factor
min	minimum
MIT	Massachusetts Institute of Technology
mm	millimetre
m/s	metres per second
mur	music room
N	newton
NFPA	National Fire Protection Association
nur	nursery
off	office
oper	operating
OS	Ordnance Survey
OSHA	Occupational Safety & Health Act
P	passenger, patient, person, pupil
pa	parents room/USA master bedroom
pe	physical education
pto	power take-off
ptr	pantry
R	radius
radr	radiator
RC	reinforced concrete
reg	regulation
rh	relative humidity
RHA	Regional Health Authority
RIBA	Royal Institute of British Architects
rm	room
rsj	rolled steel joint

Abbreviations

s	second		USHB	United States Hospital Board
SBCC	Southern Building Code Congress		USPHS	United States Public Health Service
scl	scullery		uty	utility room
ser	servery			
SfB	system of classification (building literature)		V	volt
sho	shower			
sitr	sitting room		W	watt
SI	Système international d'Unités		w	width
sk	sink		wa	wardrobe/USA closet
st	seat		washr	washroom
sto	store (-age)		wc	water closet
stu	study		workr	workroom
			wp	working plane
t	tonne		wr	waiting room (or area)
temp	temperature			
T & G	tongued & grooved		yd	yard
ter	terrace		yr	year
			₵	centre line
UDC	universal decimal classification		∅	diameter
UF	utilisation factor		≥	greater than or equal to
UK	United Kingdom		≤	equal to or less than
USA	United States of America			

The human scale in architecture

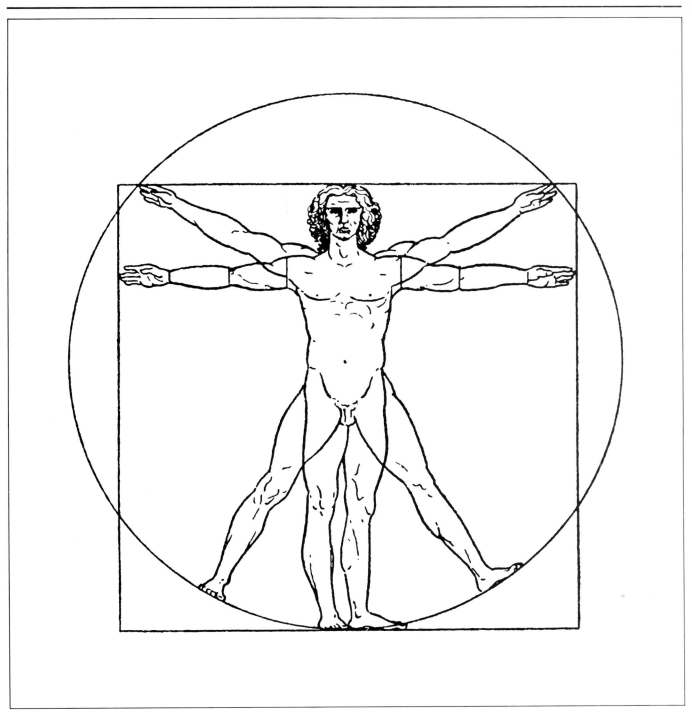

1   Leonardo da Vinci: rule of proportion

In the past dimensions based on the human body, and on man's daily activities, provided a natural basis for all units of measurement. Common units like the inch – twelfth part of the foot, palm, hand, span, cubit – length of the forearm, ell – outstretched arm, yard – pace are directly related to dimensions of the body. Other units (pole, furlong, mile – pound, stone, bushel etc) have their basis in human activities.

While trade was largely local and manufacture on a craft basis, local variations in measurements were of limited importance. The growth of science and technology, and the establishment of centralised states, typified in 18th century France, led to a demand for rationalisation of weights and measures. This the metric system, first adopted in 1790, met. It had a geodetic and decimal base, divorced from human dimensions and from the duodecimal bases of many earlier systems.

During the 19th and early 20th centuries, the metric system went through several refinements as scientific knowledge about the physical world progressed. Out of these refinements arose the 'Système International d'Unités' (SI) now almost universally adopted. *Architects' Data* is based on the use of SI units →p2.

Architectural design remains largely about man and his spatial needs. The aim of *Architects' Data* is to bring together in convenient form dimensional and spatial planning information relating to most human activities. The change to SI which took place in the UK – and many other English-speaking countries – in the 1970s stimulated a fresh look at user requirements and their dimensional framework. The introduction of SI in the USA during the 1980s will have a similar effect.

Use of SI units

quantity	unit	symbol	
length	metre	m	
mass	kilogram	kg	
time	second	s	note: practical unit for temp
el current	ampere	A	is degree Celsius (°C):
absolute temp	degree Kelvin	°K	temp intervals of Kelvin &
luminous intensity	candela	cd	Celsius are identical

1 Basic units

name	symbol	order of magnitude	expression
giga	G	10^9	1 000 000 000
mega	M	10^6	1 000 000
kilo	k	10^3	1 000
⌈ hecto	h	10^2	100 ⌉
deca	da	10	10
deci	d	10^{-2}	0.1
⌊ centi	c	10^{-2}	0.01 ⌋
milli	m	10^{-3}	0.001
micro	μ	10^{-6}	0.000 001
nano	n	10^{-9}	0.000 000 001

2 Multiples & sub-multiples of SI units

physical quantity	name	symbol	relation to basic units
force	newton	N	$= kg\ m/s^2$
work, energy, quantity of heat	joule	J	$= kg\ m^2/s^2$ (or Nm)
power or energy flow rate	watt	W	$= kg\ m^2/s^3$ (or J/s)
pressure, stress	pascal	Pa	$= kg/m\ s^2$ (or N/m^2)
el charge	coulomb	C	$= As$
el potential	volt	V	$= kg\ m^2/s^3A$ (or W/A)
el capitance	farad	F	$= A^2s^4/kg\ m^2$ (or As/V)
el resistance	ohm	Ω	$= kg\ m^2/s^3A^2$ (or V/A)
frequency	hertz	Hz	$= cycle/s$
magnetic flux	weber	Wb	$= kg\ m^2/s^2A^2$ (or Vs)
magnetic flux density	telsa	T	$= kg/s^2A$ (or Wb/m^2)
inductance	henry	H	$= kg\ m^2/s^2A$ (Vs/A)
luminous flux	lumen	lum	$= cd\ sr*$
illumination	lux	lx	$= cd\ sr*/m^2$ (or lm/m^2)

* sr steradian or solid angle subtended at centre of unit radius sphere by unit area of surface

3 Derived SI units

quantity	name	symbol	expression
length	kilometre	km	1 000 m
	metre	m	1 m
	millimetre	mm	0.001 m
area	square kilometre	km^2	1 000 000 m^2
	hectare	ha	10 000 m^2
	square metre	m^2	1 m^2
	square centimetre	cm^2	
volume	cubic metre	m^3	1 m^3
	litre	l	0.001 m^3
velocity	kilometre/hr	km/h	0.278 m/s
	metre/second	m/s	1 m/s

4 Space & time

quantity	name	symbol	expression
mass	tonne	t	1 000 000 g (1 000 kg)
	kilogram	kg	1 000 g
	gram	g	1 g
	milligram	mg	0.001 g
force (mass/acceleration)	meganewton	MN	1 000 000 N
	kilonewton	kN	1 000 N
	newton	N	1 N
	(1 lb force approximates to 4.5 N)		
pressure or stress (force/area)	pascal	Pa	1 N/m^2
	(sometimes expressed as N/mm^2)		

5 Structural design

The rationalised metric system 'Système International d'Unités' (SI) is a coherent system, nearly all the quantities needed being derived from only 6 basic and arbitrarily defined units →(1).

To avoid using large or small numbers a set of prefixes has been agreed for general use in the SI system. These are set out →(2). In selecting prefixes consideration should be given to orders of magnitude likely to be met with in practical situations. To reduce confusion preference should be given to multiples and sub-multiples chosen in steps of 1 000. Those multiples shown in brackets →(2) are not recommended.

SUPPLEMENTARY & DERIVED UNITS

From the 6 basic units others have been derived and mostly given special names →(3). For use in design of bldg these fall into 5 groups: space and time →(4); mechanics and properties of matter →(5); heat and energy →(6); acoustics and sound →(7); and illumination →(8). El units, already well established, are also reproduced →(3).

Some multiples and sub-multipes of basic units in common use also have special names:

litre $10^{-3}\ m^3$
tonne $10^3\ kg$
hectare $10^4\ m^2$

Conversion factors & tables →p364−81

quantity	name	symbol	expression
temperature	degree Kelvin	°K	0 °K
	[1]degree Celsius	°C	273.15 °K
energy (heat is only one form of energy)	megajoule[2]	MJ	1 000 000 J
	kilojoule	kJ	1 000 J
	joule	J	1 J
	millijoule	mJ	0.001 J
power or heat flow rate (energy/time)	megawatt	MW	1 000 000 W
	kilowatt	kW	1 000 W
	watt	W	1 W
	milliwatt	mW	0.001 W
conductivity	k-value	W/m °C	
transmittance	U-value	W/m² °C	
vapour pressure	newton/m²	N/m² (1 millibar = 100 N/m²)	
vapour resistance (reciprocal of vapour diffusion)		MNs/g	
vapour resistivity (reciprocal of vapour diffusivity or permeability)		MNs/gm	

[1] the absolute or Kelvin scale is used in science and is the official SI scale but for all practical purposes Celsius is used;
[2] 1 therm approximates to 105.5 MJ

6 Energy, heat & thermal insulation; technical data p16 393−4

quantity	name	symbol
frequency	hertz (cycle/second)	Hz
sound level[1]	decibel	dB
reverberation time[2]	second	T
absorption[3]	sabin	s

[1] sound levels recorded usually as A-weighted sound pressure in N/m^2 units: dB(A)
[2] reverberation time T = 0.16 V/A where V is volume of rm in m^3 & A is total sound absorption
[3] unit of absorption, the sabin, = a × S where a is the sound absorption coefficient of a material, S its ar

7 Acoustics; technical data p18 395−7

quantity	name	symbol
luminous intensity	candela	cd
luminous flux (flow of light)	lumen	lm
illuminance (light falling on surface)	lux	lm/m²
luminance (light emitted by source)	apostilb (candela/m²)	cd/m²

8 Illumination; technical data p25−6 398−9

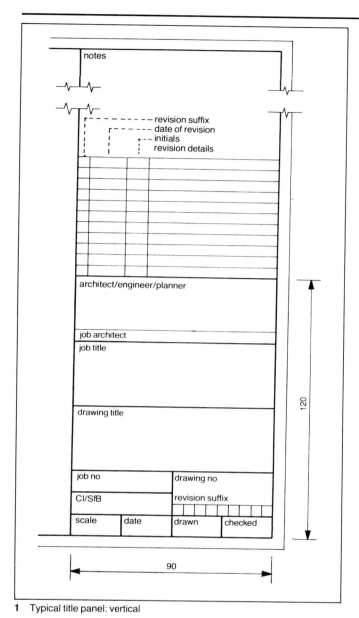

1 Typical title panel: vertical

LAYOUT & IDENTIFICATION

Layout: on every sheet filing margin, title and identification panel.

Filing margin: at left hand edge ⩾ 20 wide. Filing **punch marks** and **fold marks** printed as ticks at edges of sheet (microfilming →p7).

Title panel: place in bottom right hand corner of sheet to aid reference when prints filed or folded →(1)(2). Include: job title; drawing title; scale; date of drawing; job number; SfB and UDC reference if appropriate; name of architect. Panel may also give initials of person drawing, tracing and checking sheet. USA panels →(3).

Revision suffix should be changed each time drawing issued after revision; or list each revision as is USA practice.

Printed blank title panels or use of stencils, transfers or rubber stamps save time and labour.

Information panel: note nature and date of each revision, with architect's initials; start at bottom of panel and work upwards. If general notes included start at top and work down.

Key: on large projects give key diagram showing continuous drawing sheets, with appropriate part blacked in on each relevant drawing.

Orientation: show N point on every plan. When practicable all plans should have same orientation, except for site location plan. For this draw N at top of sheet to avoid identification with official maps.

3 Information & title panels in USA **a** vertical arrangement **b** horizontal

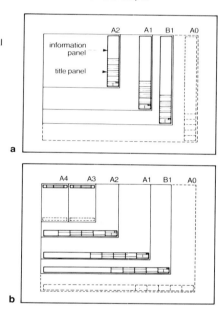

2 Typical title panel: horizontal

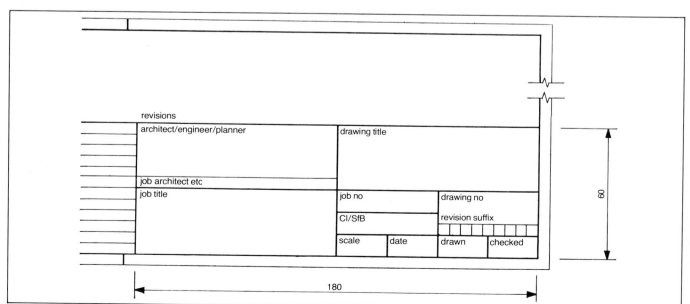

Drawing sheets

SIZES & FOLDS

Standard sizes
A0 841 × 1 189
A1 594 × 841
A2 420 × 594
A3 297 × 420
A4 210 × 297

These sizes all proportional, leading to simple reduction and enlarge-
ment: sheets may easily be folded for filing and despatch. Relatively
small sizes should lead to easier handling in drawing office and on site.
Keep number of sizes to min to ease binding and reference.

Original drawings and contact copies should each be of standard sizes;
therefore avoid trimming sheets to less than A sizes.

Folding
Prints may be folded to A4 size quite easily from any large A size.

When prints are to be filed necessary to fold in such way that punch
holes penetrate only 1 layer. Methods of folding →(1) and p5.

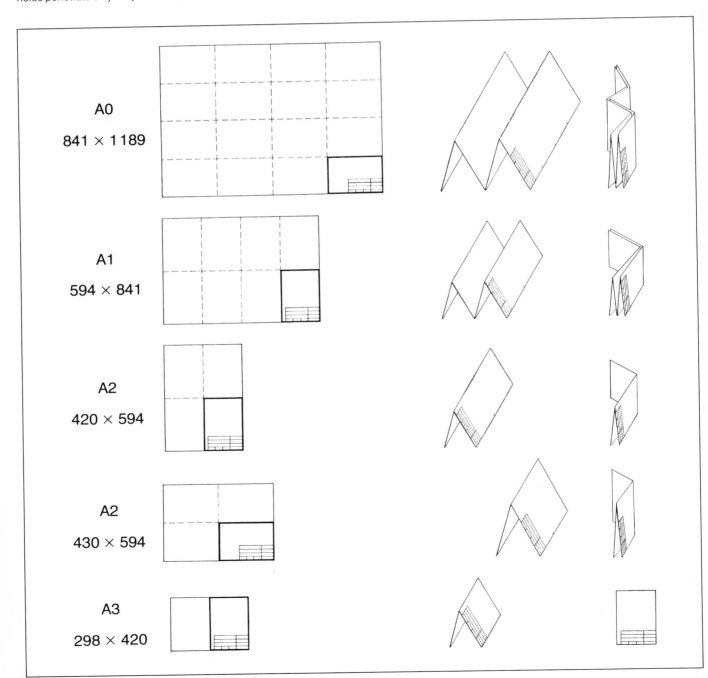

1   Simple folding of drawings

SIZES & FOLDS

A0 841 × 1189			
A1 594 × 841			
A2 420 × 594			
A2 430 × 594			
A3 298 × 420			

1 Folding of drawings for filing

Drawing practice

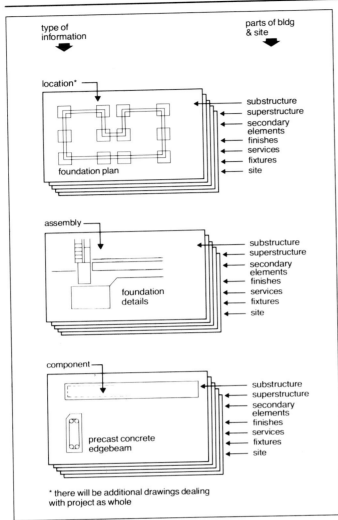

1   Arrangement of the set

Designer's principal language is through drawing and draughtsmanship. Drawings express his intentions clearly. They are internationally readable. Supplemented by schedules and specifications of materials and workmanship they enable quantities of materials needed and prices to be estimated, bids to be drawn up, work to be planned by builder and carried out on construction site. Drawings are principal means by which designer's intentions are discussed with client and authorities. On basis of architect's drawings designs of specialists (*eg* structural, mech, el engineer) and work of specialist contractors can be planned and coordinated.

In recent years much attention has been given to use of drawings and their coordination →p7. Draughtsman has available wide range of instruments and tools. Since first English edition of *Architects' Data* unprecedented developments in reprographic techniques and computer graphics.

WORKING DRAWINGS

Working drawings should convey bulk of technical information about bldg project. Builder needs to know 'shape', 'size' and 'location' of bldg as whole and of all constituent parts and must be told 'composition' of materials to be used and assembly and fastening methods (→ Bib 075 081).

Grids on plans and key reference planes on elevations improve quality of dimensional information on working drawings; when repeated on details they help to locate them in bldg. Composition best dealt with in bills of quantities or specifications. Drawings and schedules should indicate materials used; graphic symbols may be used for this purpose (→Bib142).

The set of drawings

Two facets of information used to classify information needed in structuring sets of drawings: first differentiates between location, assembly and component information; second parts of bldg and site →(1).

→(2) defines purposes of location, schedule, assembly and component drawings.

Not every type of these drawings will be required for 1 bldg project. Some types of drawings and some types of information may be in appropriate circumstances combined.

BRE tests favour elemental breakdown of bldg for systematic and convenient arrangement of information. →(3) shows universal list of elements with code numbers based on CI/SfB table 1 →p8 (→Bib563) (not used in USA).

location*	site & external works:	to identify, locate & dimension the site & external works
* there will be additional location drawings dealing with project as whole	building:	to identify, locate & dimension parts & spaces within bldg & to show overall shapes by plan, elevation or section to locate grids, datums & key reference planes to convey dimensions for setting out to give other information of general nature for which small scale is appropriate (eg door swings)
	element:	to give location & setting-out information about 1 element, or group of related elements
	cross-references:	to show cross-references to schedules, assembly & component drawings
schedule	element:	to collect repetitive information about elements or products which occur in variety to record cross-references to assembly & component drawings
assembly	element:	to show assembly of parts of 1 element including shape & size of those parts to show an element at its junction with another element to show cross-references to other assembly & component drawings
component	element or sub-elements	to show shape, dimensions & assembly (& possibly composition) of component to be made away from bldg to show component parts of an in situ assembly which cannot be defined adequately on assembly drawing

2   Type of drawing & purpose

(--) site, project								
substructure	superstructure			services		fittings		site
(1–) ground substructure	(2–) primary elements	(3–) secondary elements	(4–) finishes	(5–) mainly piped	(6–) mainly el	(7–) fixed	(8–) loose	(9–) external elements
(10)	(20)	(30)	(40)	(50)	(60)	(70)	(80)	(90) external works
(11) ground	(21) external walls	(31) external openings	(41) external	(51)	(61) el supply	(71) circulation	(81) circulation	(91)
(12)	(22) internal walls	(32) internal openings	(42) internal	(52) drainage, waste	(62) power	(72) rest, work	(82) rest, work	(92)
(13) floorbeds	(23) floors	(33) floor openings	(43) floor	(53) liquid supply	(63) lighting	(73) culinary	(83) culinary	(93)
(14)	(24) stairs, ramps	(34) balustrades	(44) stair	(54) gases supply	(64) communications	(74) sanitary	(84) sanitary	(94)
(15)	(25)	(35) suspended ceilings	(45) ceiling	(55) space cooling	(65)	(75) cleaning	(85) cleaning	(95)
(16) foundations	(26)	(36)	(46)	(56) space heating	(66) transport	(76) sto screening	(86) sto screening	(96)
(17) piles	(27) roofs	(37) roof openings	(47) roof	(57) ventilation	(67)	(77) special activity	(87) special activity	(97)
(18)	(28) frames	(38)	(48)	(58)	(68) security, control	(78)	(88)	(98)

3   Elemental breakdown (from CI/SfB table 1)

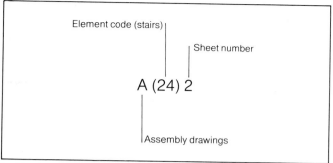

1 Simple numbering system

Title		Title
Assembly		Assembly
Stairs		Frame
Half landing staircase No 3		Beams on grid lines A & C

2 Titling

designation	nominal size of sheet	nominal border w	drawing frame size	preferred orientation*
A0	841 × 1189	20	801 × 11149	
A1	594 × 841	20	554 × 801	long
A2	420 × 594	10	400 × 574	horizontal
A3	297 × 420	10	277 × 400	long side
A4	210 × 297	10	190 × 277	vertical

* To facilitate automated printing on roll stock

3 Drawing sheet sizes & frame sizes

application	drawing sheet size	min character h
drawing number & title	A0, A1, A2 & A3	7
	A4	5
dimensions & all other characters	A0	3.5
	A1, A2, A3 & A4	2.5

note: it is stressed that recommendations in this table are min; however, when lower case letters are used they should be proportioned so that body h is approx 0.6 times capital letter h

4 Min character h for capital letters & numerals

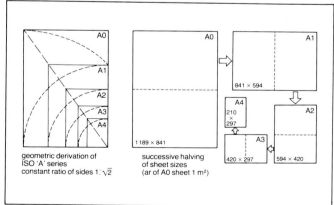

geometric derivation of ISO 'A' series constant ratio of sides 1 : √2

successive halving of sheet sizes (ar of A0 sheet 1 m²)

5 ISO A series of international paper sizes

WORKING DRAWINGS

Numbering, titling & coding

→(1) shows simple numbering system, (→Bib081). Other information, such as job number, or information relating drawing to particular block, zone or rm, best placed in separate but adjacent block.

Titles should be brief but comprehensive. If drawing shows particular feature of element, this should be stated in title. If detail applies at particular location, this too should be stated →(2).

Schedules of components, finishes etc can be used as convenient collecting centres for cross-reference.

Preparation of technical drawings for microfilming

Microfilming increasingly used for storing record drawings. Drawing sizes →(3) and min character height for capital letters and numbers →(4) (→Bib128).

Drawings should be on smallest standard sheet size compatible with clarity. Drawing sheets larger than 'A0' should be avoided. Centring mark in form of line should be shown at centre of each of 4 sides of drawing frame →(3).

Since size of copy printed back from microfilm usually different from size of original reference to scale used should be stated on drawing: *eg* (original scale 1 : 5).

International paper sizes

Derivation of ISO A series of paper sizes →(5). Drawing sheets sizes and folds →p4 5.

Scale ratios

Introduction of metric reduces number of scale ratios compared with USA traditional scales →(6).

traditional scales (expressed as ratio)		metric scales		remarks
		preferred	other	
full size	[1:1]	1:1		no change
half full size	[1:2]		1:2	no change
4'' = 1' 0''	[1:3]			
3'' = 1' 0''	[1:4]			
2'' = 1' 0''	[1:6]	1:5		
1½'' = 1' 0''	[1:8]			
1'' = 1' 0''	[1:12]	1:10		
¾'' = 1' 0''	[1:16]			
½'' = 1' 0''	[1:24]	1:20		
⅜'' = 1' 0''	[1:32]		(1:25)	(limited use)
¼'' = 1' 0''	[1:48]			
1'' = 5' 0''	[1:60]	1:50		
³⁄₁₆'' = 1' 0''	[1:64]			
⅛'' = 1' 0''	[1:96]			
1'' = 10' 0''	[1:120]	1:100		
³⁄₃₂'' = 1' 0''	[1:128]			
¹⁄₁₆'' = 1' 0''	[1:196]			
1'' = 20' 0''	[1:240]	1:200		
			(1:250)	(limited use)
¹⁄₃₂'' = 1' 0''	[1:384]			
1'' = 40' 0''	[1:480]			
1'' = 50' 0''	[1:600]	1:500		
1'' = 60' 0''	[1:720]			
1'' = 1 chain	[1:792]			
1'' = 80' 0''	[1:960]			
		1:1000		
total: 24		9	1 (2)	

6 Metric & traditional scale ratios compared

Drawing practice

LEVELS

General
Levels record distance of position above or below defined datum.

Datum
Property surveys refer site elevations to datum established by government on official maps. UK temporary bench mark (TBM), USA site bench mark, establishes plane to which all other levels related as positive if above and negative if below. Dimensions given in mm, or in USA normally in ft and tenths of ft, in relation to datum.

Levels on plan
On site drawings show existing levels differently from intended levels. Existing contours shown dotted new contours in solid lines. Spot elevations shown:

existing level: x 58.21
new level: | x 60.25 |

Exact position to which level applies should be indicated by 'x'.
Floor levels should be clearly indicated on plans:

UK Finished Floor Level   FFL = 60.25
USA Finished Floor Elevation   FFE = 60.25

Levels on section and elevation →(1).

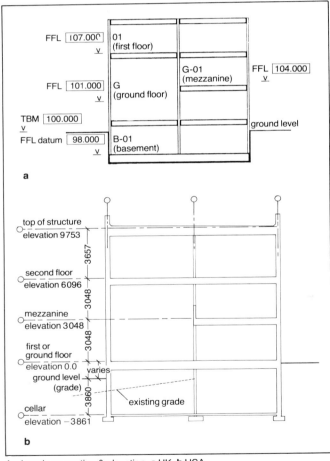

a

b

1   Levels on section & elevation **a** UK **b** USA

REFERENCING

Levels on section & elevation
UK practice uses same method as for levels on plan except that level should be projected beyond drawing with arrowhead indicating appropriate line →(1a).

Classification & coding
In USA practice drawings used to show locations and dimensions of bldg elements and materials identified in notes by generic terminology. Specifications accompanying drawings describe materials and workmanship. Widespread use of standard construction indexing system improved both coordination and reference between drawings and specifications and cost estimating and product data.

SfB system of classification and coding of bldg components and elements (applied in UK as Cl/SfB →Bib553) allows information be coordinated and correlated.

By means of SfB information contained within different kinds of documents (*eg* bills of quantity, drawings, specifications, texts, trade literature) can be coordinated and correlated for max benefit of user.

SfB is facet system of alpha-numerical symbols forming 3 tables which may be used individually or in combination to indicate concepts and terms required.

These tables list: building elements, components/products, materials; also →p6(3).

Each type of component or element shown on drawing may be identified by appropriate SfB notation *eg*:

concrete blocks   Ff2
concrete lintels   Gf2
aluminium sections   Hh4
hardwood sections   Hi3
manholes   (52)
external walls   (21)
windows   (31)
doors   (32)
radiators   (56)

Notations may be combined *eg*:

external walls, concrete block   (21)Ff2
windows, aluminium   (31)Hh4
doors, hardwood   (32)Hi3

Keep number and length of component and element notations to min compatible with rational system of identification for each particular job.

Specific component within any range may be identified by suffix giving nominal sizes for length, width, height:

concrete block   Ff2 400 mm × 100 mm × 200 mm

Alternatively, where principles of modular coordination are applied, such suffix may give nominal sizes for component or element in multiples of 100 mm (M) *eg:* concrete block   Ff2 4M × 1M × 2M

Drawing practice references:
→Bibliography entries 061 075 081 082 095 128 142 290 322 448 463 553 621 638

THE UNIVERSAL STANDARD

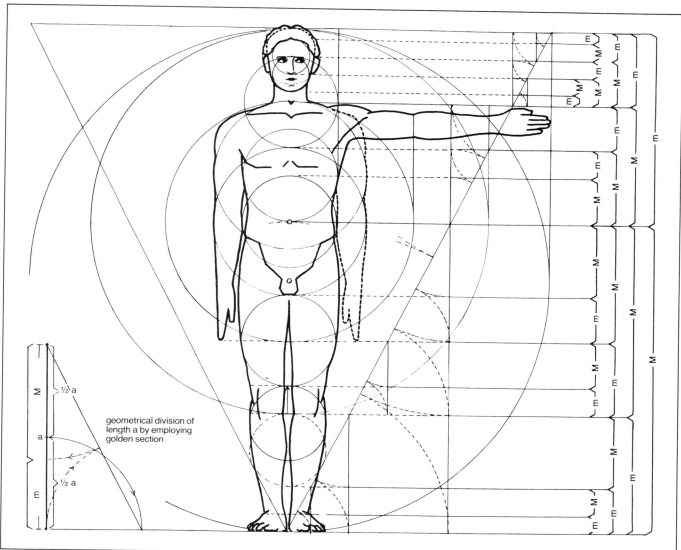

geometrical division of
length a by employing
golden section

1 Proportions of human body

Body and reach characteristics of people of key importance in architectural design: from early time artists and scientists have been concerned with dimensions and proportions of human body →(1). In such dimensional systems human body has been measured in terms of hand, foot, arm or head. Using data from anthropometrical survey one can plot graphs of measurements against their frequency of occurrence forming curved line →(2). Normal, or bell-shaped, curve obtained when adult standing heights or other measurements which depend on bone structure shown on graph. Curve is symmetrical if measurements of group normally distributed.

People by reason of age, sex, physique and, possibly, disability show wide range of body and reach dimensions. Anthropometry name used for science of measurement of human body and its movements in space. From studies of functional anatomy concept of effective work space has been developed. *Architects' Data* brings together much of this information. Although for purposes of design usually necessary to use av human dimensions as criteria, should be borne in mind that only half or less of population under consideration may be fully satisfied. In some circumstances, particularly when designing for young children, elderly or disabled, necessary to take account of special needs, and of variations from av. In stature adult females average about 5% less than adult males and elderly women up to 10% less.

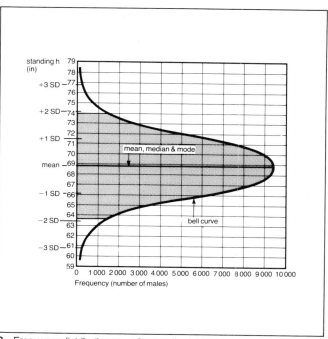

2 Frequency distribution curve for standing h USA males

Proportions

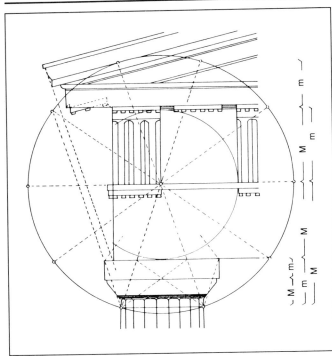

1   Corner of Doric temple based on golden section

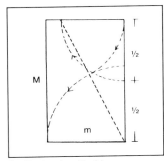

2   Rectangle with sides corresponding to golden section

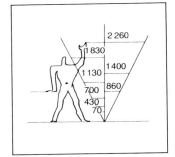

4   The modular

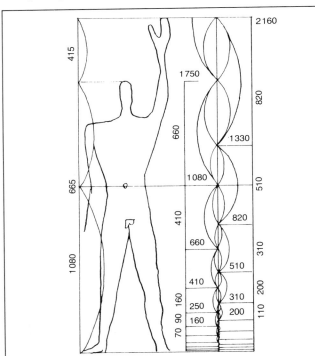

3   Human proportions

Systems of proportions have been used in design by architects throughout the centuries. Measurements of classical bldg show basis of geometrical proportion →(1).

One frequently used proportional relationship based on 'golden section': relationship M:m in which minor part m is to major part M as this is to sum of both *ie*:

$$m : M = M : (Mm) \rightarrow (2)$$

RELATION TO HUMAN SCALE

One architect to develop proportional system for use in design was Le Corbusier. His concept *Le Modulor* (Bib445) was first published in 1948, though he had been evolving the idea of combining human dimensions in a mathematical framework for some time previously in an attempt to use in his designs a measure related to the human scale which was universally applicable.

System uses Golden Section to mark out divisions of human body →(3)(4). First proposal for *Le Modulor* was based on man's height of 1 720 (approx 5 ft 9 in), giving with outstretched arm →(3) overall dimension of 2 160. Later height of 6 ft 0 in (or about 1 830) was adopted, giving overall dimension of 2 260. Based on these last dimensions 2 series, red progression and blue progression, were developed →(6). Each dimension is proportionally larger, or smaller, than its neighbour giving harmonious progression. Using dimensions from the 2 series a series of rectangular grids can be formed, based on Golden Section but related to human scale.

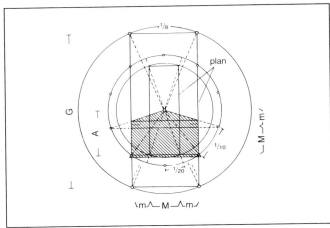

5   Greek temple in plan & elevation based, as in →(1), on golden section

dimensions in SI units in mm		dimensions in inches rounded to ½''	
red progression	blue progression	red progression	blue progression
952 807			
588 867	1 177 735		
363 940	727 880		
224 927	449 855		
139 013	278 025		
85 914	171 829		
53 098	106 196		
32 816	65 633		
20 282	40 563		
12 535	25 069		
7 747	15 494	306	609
4 788	9 576	188½	377
2 959	5 918	116½	233
1 829	3 658	72	144
1 130	2 260	44½	89
698	1 397	27½	55
432	863	17	34
267	534	10½	21
165	330	6½	13
102	204	4	8
63	126		
39	78		
24	48		
15	30		
9	18		
6	11		

6   Explanations of dimensions & working of Le Corbusier's modular

DIMENSIONS & SPACE REQUIREMENTS

Body measurements

→(1)–(20) show bodily measurements based on European data. → (21)–(26) show further body measurements based on USA data. School children →p129–30.

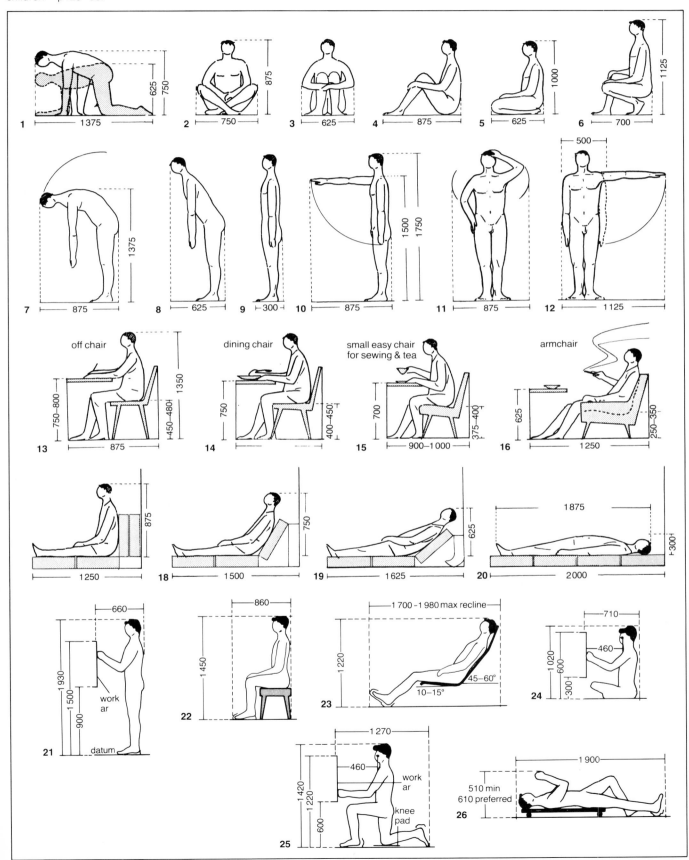

Man

DIMENSIONS & SPACE REQUIREMENTS

Min dimensions and space requirements of human beings in some
common situations, based on European measurements →also p11 13 14.

Space requirements between walls (for moving persons add ⩾ 10% to w)

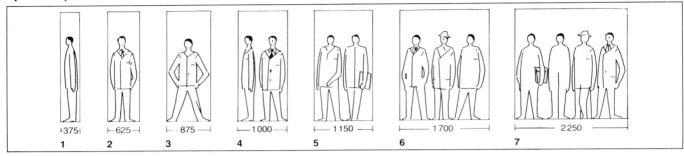

⊢375⊣	⊢625⊣	⊢875⊣	⊢1000⊣	⊢1150⊣	⊢1700⊣	⊢2250⊣
1	**2**	**3**	**4**	**5**	**6**	**7**

Space requirements of groups

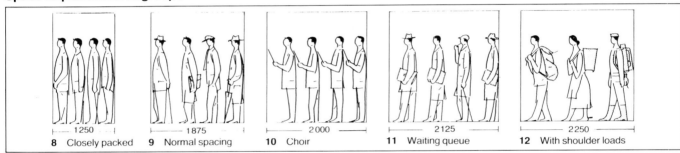

⊢1250⊣	⊢1875⊣	⊢2000⊣	⊢2125⊣	⊢2250⊣
8 Closely packed	**9** Normal spacing	**10** Choir	**11** Waiting queue	**12** With shoulder loads

Step measurements

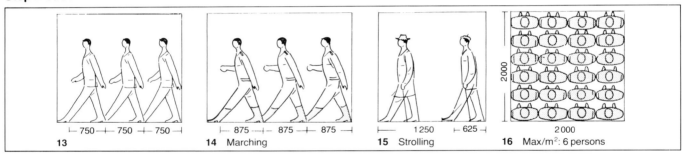

⊢750⊣750⊣750⊣	⊢875⊣875⊣875⊣	⊢1250⊣625⊣	2000
13	**14** Marching	**15** Strolling	**16** Max/m²: 6 persons

Space requirements of various body postures

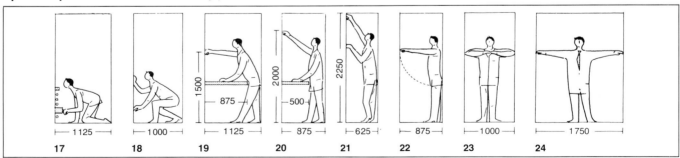

⊢1125⊣	⊢1000⊣	1500 ⊢875⊣	2000 ⊢500⊣	2250	⊢625⊣	⊢875⊣	⊢1000⊣	⊢1750⊣
17	**18**	**19**	**20**	**21**	**22**	**23**	**24**	

Space requirements for hand luggage

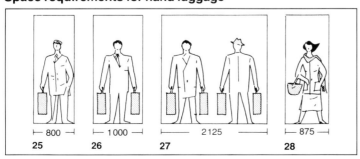

⊢800⊣	⊢1000⊣	2125	⊢875⊣
25	**26**	**27**	**28**

Space requirements with stick & umbrella

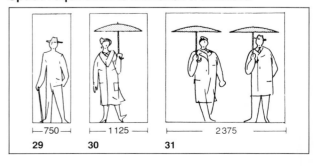

⊢750⊣	⊢1125⊣	2375
29	**30**	**31**

DIMENSIONS & SPACE REQUIREMENTS: ACCESS FOR WORK ON BUILDINGS

min 2450 · 450

1 Body clearance: prone

1000 · 800

2 Body clearance: crawl

700 · 1250

3 Body clearance: squat

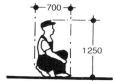

900

4 Body clearance: stoop

1100 · 1450 · 700

5 Body clearance: maintenance reach levels

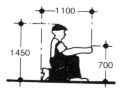

stand — 1550
kneel — 1220 · 920
sit — 600 · 300

6

650 dia
(800 square preferable)

7 Service access: crawlway

min 450 dia or square

8 Service access: hatch

min 600 h × 400 w

9 Service access: panel

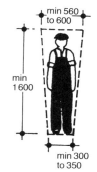

min 560 to 600
min 1600
min 300 to 350

10 Service access: catwalk

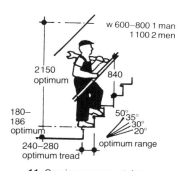

w 600–800 1 man
1100 2 men

2150 optimum · 840
180–186 optimum
240–280 optimum tread
50° 35° 30° 20°
optimum range

11 Service access: stairs

min entries for 1 man:
330–450 difficult
450–610 fair
610–920 good

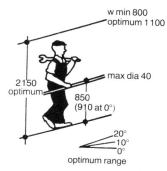

w min 800
optimum 1100
2150 optimum
max dia 40
850 (910 at 0°)
20° 10° 0°
optimum range

12 Service access: ramps

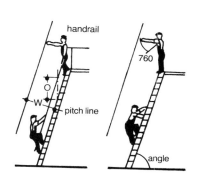

handrail · 760
pitch line · angle
O · W

recommended for angles 50° to 75°
handrails required on both sides if risers not left open or if no side walls
w: 500–600 with handrails
600 min between side walls

angle	W	O
50°–55°	1620–1570	880
57°–60°	1500–1450	900
63°–66°	1370–1320	910
69°–72°	1270–1200	920
74°–55°	1150–1050	950

recommended riser 180–250
tread 75–150
45 dia max for handrail

13 Service access: step ladders

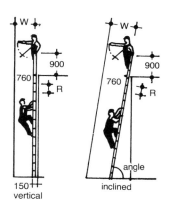

W · 900 · 760 · R · 150 vertical
W · 900 · 760 · R · angle · inclined

generally suitable for vertical movements 75°–90°
ladder frame should extend 900 above platform
w: 380 min, 450 desirable
600 min between side walls
150 toe space

angle	R	W
75.0°	330	1150
78.0°	335	1050
80.5°	340	1000
83.0°	350	950
85.0°	360	900
87.5°	370	850
90.0°	380 max	800
	300 min	

provide back guard over 6000 h

14 Service access: rung ladders

Proportions references:
Bibliography entries 075 081 082 445

Man

WALKING SPEEDS & FLOW CAPACITY

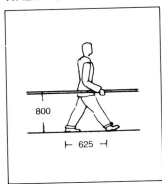

1   Normal pace of male adult on horizontal plane

2   On ramp pace reduced: desirable slope 10%–8%

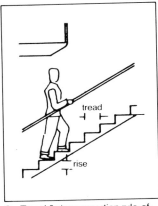

3   Tread & rise proportion rule-of-thumb: going + twice rise = 600

4   If stairs narrow or curved distance of walk line from outer string 450–400

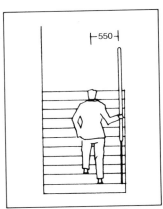

5   If stairs wide & straight distance of walk line from handrail 550

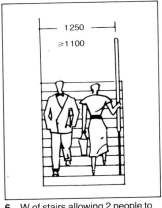

6   W of stairs allowing 2 people to pass

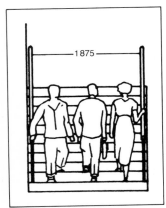

7   W of stairs allowing 3 people to meet & pass

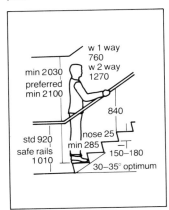

8   Stairs: USA dimensions

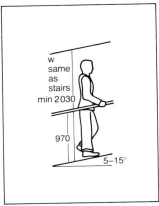

9   Ramp: USA dimensions

DIMENSIONS & SPACE REQUIREMENTS

Stairs

Relation between riser and going for most normal staircases: 2R + G where R = riser (not greater than 190, or for elderly and ambulant disabled not more than 170: external steps 145 preferred) and G = going (not less than 240, or for elderly and ambulant disabled not less than 250: external steps 370 preferred).

Av walking speeds on stairs lower than in corridors: generally faster down than up but in dense crowd down may be slower. Number of mis-steps increases as size of tread reduced; more accidents going downstairs than up. Design details →p87(5) 407.

Corridors & ramps

Factors affecting walking speeds on level footways (in or outdoors):
purpose of journey;
age and sex;
whether single person or in group;
air temp (quicker in cold);
floor surface;
whether carrying weight;
crowd density;
flow pattern.

Walking speeds vary within crowd; range between highest and lowest speed can be equal to mean value.

Limit of free flow conditions in corridors: approx 0.3 P/m²; higher densities limit individual's ability walk at natural speed and overtake. At density 1.4 P/m² (commonly adopted design max) most people will be walking at less than natural speed and feel some discomfort.

Short length of slope in level footway scarcely affects walking speed; similarly for low gradient ramps (≤ 5%). Steeper ramps can reduce speed markedly: *eg* by 20% with 10% gradient, 40% with 15% gradient. Elderly and disabled (→p85(2) 87(11)) generally walk more slowly down than up ramp (gradient ≤ 8%). Design details →p406.

Doors

With heavy traffic speed of flow through doors depends on type of user (*eg* old/young, carrying weight) and on density of traffic each side of door. For heavy 2-way traffic 2 separate openings desirable.

Design details →p400–1

Elevators

Traffic capacity determined by analysis of flow pattern →p409–11.

Man & his buildings

Bldg shelter man against unwanted effects of weather. A principal function of their design is to ensure within bldg environment conducive to well-being and efficiency. Several physical variables together involved in determining whether environment is, or is not, acceptable for 1 or more human activities. There are indices which combine in various ways physical variables which relate to human responses; 3 of these indices relate to: thermal comfort, visual efficiency, acceptable levels of noise →p16 17 18. Quality of air must be acceptable, not containing contaminants which may be unpleasant or even harmful.

constituent gas	% by volume
nitrogen	78.08
oxygen	20.94
carbon dioxide	0.03
argon & other gases	0.95

1 Composition of dry atmosphere

source	contaminants
physiological	CO_2, H_2O, body odour
combustion (fully burnt fuels)	CO_2, H_2O, SO_2
combustion (unburnt or partially burnt fuels)	CO, CH_4, petrol vapour
household activities	H_2O, odours
tobacco smoking	CO, odours, irritants

2 Common contaminants of air

activity	contaminant	
	CO_2(l/s/P)	H_2O (water vapour) g/s/P
resting	0.004	30
light work	0.006−0.013	40
moderate work	0.013−0.02	40
heavy work	0.02−0.026	40
very heavy work	0.026−0.032	40

3 Rates of production of physiological contaminants

activity	H_2O g/day/household
cooking	3 000
bathing	1 000
dish washing	1 000
clothes washing	500
clothes drying	5 000 (automatic dryers to be vented to outside)

4 Rates of production of water vapour (H_2O) from household activities

fuel	contaminant		
	CO_2 l/s/kW	water vapour (H_2O) g/hr/kW	SO_2 l/s/kW
natural gas	0.027	156	—
kerosene	0.034	96	8.9×10^{-6}
low pressure gas	0.033	130	—
tobacco	0.8 l/s/cigarette carbon monoxide (CO)		

5 Rates of production of contaminants by combustion & smoking

contaminant	limiting concentration %	
	toxicity	flammability
carbon dioxide	0.5	—
carbon monoxide	0.005	12.0−75.0
sulphur dioxide	0.0005	—
methane	30	5.0−15.0
propane	30	2.0−9.5
butane	30	1.5−8.5
acetylene	302	2.5−8.2
hydrogen	30	4.0−7.4
petrol (gasoline)	0.1	1.4−7.6

6 Limiting values of common contaminants

Quality of air

Fresh air in open country consists largely of nitrogen, oxygen, water vapour and small amounts of other gases. Amount of water vapour in air always changing. Composition of dry air →(1).

Outside air may be polluted by contaminants released from industrial processes, burning of fossil fuels for heating or transportation, dust etc. Indoor air may also be polluted →(2). Rates at which contaminants produced vary in part according to kinds of activity going on →(3)−(5). Limiting values of common contaminants →(6).

Odours, mainly body odour and consequences of tobacco smoking, present special problem: consist of large number of constituent chemicals in small but variable proportions. Attempts to define and measure odours chemically usually unsuccessful. In general tobacco odour masks body odour. With nearly all odours effects become rapidly less noticed after few minutes in contaminated space.

Fresh air supply needed to maintain body odour at satisfactory level depends upon standards of personal hygiene. Different for adults and children →(7).

For tobacco odour conditions, habits and patterns of occupancy vary greatly. Ventilation requirements for offices depend on whether office space small (when may be assumed all occupants smoke) or large open-plan (when on av only 50% or less will be smokers) →(8).

Air quality may be maintained in 3 ways: by controlling production of a contaminant, venting any residue to open air; by diluting contaminant by bringing in outdoor air through windows, ventilators etc; by replacing used and contaminated air mechanically through system of air conditioning.

For exact conditions check relevant codes and standards.

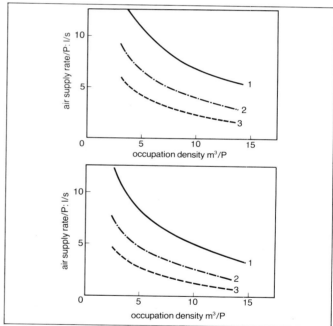

7 Air supply rate for odour **a** children **b** adults: 1 conditions regarded as good by occupants & acceptable to visitors 2 intermediate 3 conditions objectionable to visitors but still bearable by occupants

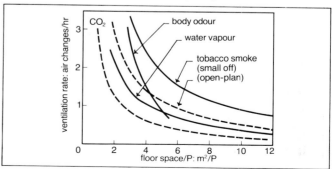

8 Ventilation requirements for off: vertical dotted line shows lower limit as defined by UK Offices & Shops & Railway Premises Act (assuming ceiling h of 2.7 m)

Man & his buildings

THERMAL COMFORT

Rm temp required for thermal comfort depends on occupant's activity and clothing worn. Also depends on speed of air movement and on hum of air (in temperate climates only to a small extent).

For purpose of specifying comfortable temp 4 levels of activity have been suggested →(1). Also convenient to divide clothing worn into categories according to insulation which it affords, this being specified in the unit 'clo': 1 'clo' = 0.155 m²°C/W. Except for bedclothing modern indoor clothing rarely exceeds insulation value 1 clo →(2).

In terms of comfort people affected almost as much by temp of surfaces which surround them as by that of air. 1 way of specifying combined effect of air and surface temp is by use of temp of globe thermometer →(3). However, if little difference in rm between globe and air temp (as happens in well insulated rm) air temp may be adequate measure of thermal conditions.

Important to distinguish between ventilation rates which affect air quality by diluting contaminants, and air movement which may affect thermal comfort. If air movement in rm exceeds about 0.2 m/s, higher rm temp required to provide equivalent comfort. In normal temperate environment effect of hum on perceived warmth very slight: but if people very hot (as during very active work or in very warm environment) high hum will aggravate discomfort. Air movement over skin will be beneficial.

No particular level of temp will be satisfactory for everybody. Not only will dress and degree activity vary, but people differ in requirements. Usually adequate maintain temp within 2°C of optimum. While no important general difference between temp preferred by men or women, young or old, there will be differences in part due to clothing and in part to activity. Old people usually less active. Children of secondary school age require similar temp to adults, but more tolerant of variations. Younger children even more tolerant and, being more active, prefer lower temp. 1 factor influencing clothing people wear is prevailing outdoor temp. For sedentary activities, carried out by people in their usual clothing, preferred indoor temp generally lie within bands shown →(4). Band A for bldg where heating, or cooling, plant operating; band B for 'free running' bldg *ie* where no artificial means for heating or cooling used; thermostat settings USA: C (cooling in summer) D winter. →(5) shows baseline thermal comfort chart based on USA data .

Heating systems →p385–91; ventilation 392

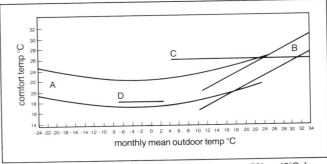

4   Preferred indoor temp: USA temp range greater, say −50°−+43°C; for interpretation →text

activity	description	rate of metabolic heat produced: W/m² body ar[1]
sleeping	body relaxed, lying down, reclining	40
sitting	reading, typing, clerical work	50–60
standing	little movement (*eg* serving at counter)	65–90
active	whole body moving: walking, bedmaking	90–130

[1] typical surface ar of male bodies 1.8 m²; female 1.6 m²

1   Levels of activity usual in bldg

clothing	description	insulation value: clo[1]
nude	naked or light underwear	zero
light	summer dress, trousers & shirt	0.3–0.7
normal	winter dress, skirt & jumper, 3-piece suit	0.8–1.2

[1] 1 clo − 0.155 m² °C/W

2   Categories of clothing worn indoors

clothing	activity			
	sleeping	sitting	standing	active[1]
nude	31	29	25	28
light	29	26	21	18
active	27	23	17	13

[1] estimates subject to degree of uncertainty

3   Comfortable rm temp in still air: °C in globe temp

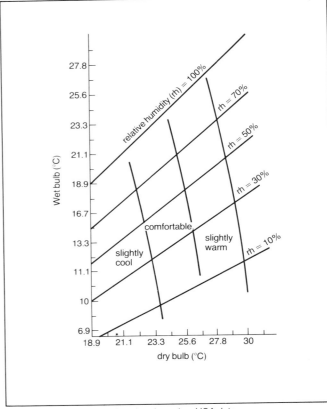

5   Baseline thermal comfort chart based on USA data

Man & his buildings

task	design illuminance	
	(lux)	(foot-candle)
circulation	150	13.935
casual work of short duration	200[1]	18.5806
routine work (young people)	300[1 2]	27.8709
routine work eg in off	500[2]	46.4515
demanding work eg in drawing off	750[2]	69.6773
fine work eg textile processing	1 000[2]	92.9031
very fine work eg hand engraving	1 500[2]	139.3546
minute work eg inspection of very fine assembly	3 500	278.7093

[1] if area windowless next higher level recommended
[2] where reflectances of surfaces unusually low or errors in task have serious consequences next higher level recommended: where task of short duration lower level may be acceptable

1 Design illuminances for common tasks: illuminance →p25 26

task	max value of glare index
demanding	16
routine	19
routine for short duration	22
casual	25
circulation	28

2 Recommended max values of glare index

task	min DF %
demanding	5
routine	2
casual & circulation	0.5

3 Min DF for certain types of task

VISUAL EFFICIENCY

Visual performance depends on total perception of space: involves quality of light as well as total amount. Indices to cover different aspects of lighting have been developed. They distinguish between artificial and day lighting.

Artificial lighting

Important are quantity of light (illuminance) and glare, also reflectances of surfaces being lit →p25–6 398. The task, and its relative importance against lighting its background and the whole space, determine illuminance. Design illuminances, ie mean illuminance over maintenance cycle of lighting system, for common tasks →(1).

Visibility of task depends on direction of incident light as well as quantity. Harsh shadows, and glare from bright or very bright light source or its reflection, undesirable. Glare can impair vision. But some shadowing helps perception of textures and shapes.

Discomfort glare arises when luminaires and other sources of light too bright in contrast with general background. Degree of discomfort indicated by glare index, recommended max values being determined by task: the more demanding the task the lower the value acceptable →(2).

Surface reflectances and colour of surfaces affect general brightness and distribution of light in rm.

Daylighting →p27–32

Windows in bldg have 2 main visual functions: to let light in during daylight hours and to enable people to see out – or in. They permit entry into a bldg of solar energy: direct, by absorption and reradiation by atmosphere, and by reflection from sunlit surfaces. Windows also source of heat loss. Choice of window basic to architectural design →p403–6.

As source of illumination daylight has many pleasant directional qualities. Its quantity varies with outside conditions and is specified in terms of DF; ie ratio of internal to external daylight levels →p26–7. For lighting tasks min DF specified, based on percentages of typical working year that required task illuminance will be exceeded →(3).

COLOUR

Colour in bldg is both aid to vision and means by which architect creates pleasant, stimulating appearance. Good colouring and good lighting interdependent.

Common practice of describing colours by arbitrary names deprecated. Several systems for classifying colours. One such, standardised by CIE, based on 3 physical attributes (wavelength, purity, luminance), widely used in colour lab but less suitable for architectural design than American Munsell system, based on 'value' (lightness), 'chroma' (saturation of pigment, or strength), 'hue'.

Munsell 'hue' scale includes 10 major 'hue' regions, each sub-divided →(4)(5). Major 'hue' regions denoted by initials, positions in region by numbers: eg 7.5RP denotes reddish red-purple hue. In UK attribute 'greyness' replacing that of 'value' or lightness. 5 distinct categories used: grey: nearly grey; grey-clear; nearly clear; clear.

For use in design of lighting possible to determine from Munsell value approx equivalent reflection factor independent of 'hue' or 'chroma' →(6). Hue planes →p18(1).

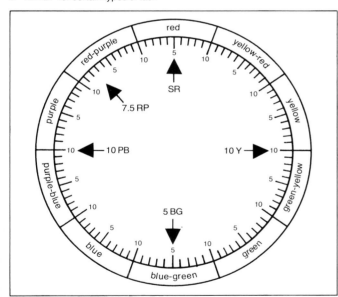

4 Munsell hue scale: 10 named hue bands with 10 steps in each (100 hue steps in all)

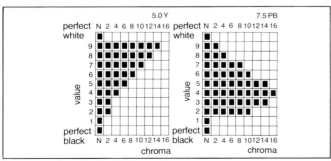

5 Vertical ½-sections through Munsell solid at a particular yellow (5Y) & particular purple-blue hue (7.5 PB) with neutral axis common to both: filled rectangles indicate approx scope of colour patches in Munsell atlas

	Munsell value	reflection factor %
very light	9–9.5	72–84
light	7–8	42–56
middle	5–6	20–30
dark	3–4	6–12
very dark	1–2	1.5–2

6 Reflection factor equivalents to Munsell value

Man & his buildings

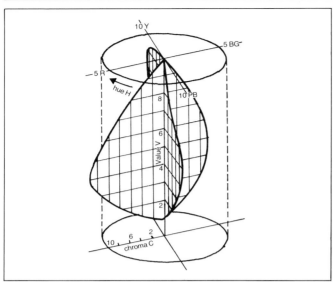

1   Diagram of Munsell solid with indications of 4 hue planes: →p17

distance between talker & listener m	normal voice dB(A)	raised voice L_{eq}
1	57	62
2	51	56
4	45	50
8	39	44

note: for telephone use level of 50 dB(A) L_{eq} satisfactory: 55 dB(A) L_{eq} may give occasional difficulty

2   Max intrusive noise level permitting reliable conversation

type of space & task	noise level dB(A) L_{eq}
auditoria requiring very good listening conditions	20–30[1]
small auditoria, conference & lecture rm	30–35[2]
bedr & for sleeping or resting	30–40
small off, classr & for listening to radio	40–45
large off, commercial premises, restaurants	45–50
typing pools, lab, machine rm	50–55[3]

[1] max peak level of intrusive noise: need for specialist advice
[2] max provided intrusive noise fairly steady
[3] higher intrusive noise levels may be accepted where there are high levels of machinery in space

3   Recommended max intrusive noise levels

PATTERN & TEXTURE

Many bldg materials have textured or colour-patterned finishes. Patterns large in scale, with clearly distinguishable elements, allow each element to be related to an individual colour. But if pattern small-scale, only dominant or composite colour stands out. As scale reduced, eg by increasing viewing distance, strong contrasts in colour lose effectiveness.

Changes in appearance with distance valued characteristic of such natural materials as marbles, grained timber, multi-coloured brickwork. Subtleties of colour and texture, apparent close to, give way to overall pattern viewed at middle distance. At still greater, become fused into 1 composite colour.

NOISE & ACOUSTICS

High levels of noise can lead to damage to hearing. At lower levels noise interferes with verbal communication. At still lower levels noise may be disturbing or annoying. Acoustic design controls intrusive noise and by choice of materials, dimensions and shape of auditorium speech and/or music to be enjoyed.

Many noise indices available for predicting noise effects. For many bldg and environmental situations equivalent continuous sound level (L_{eq}) expressed in dB(A) is adequate predictor. Exposure to high levels on noise results in hazard to hearing. Upper limit of 90 dB(A) L_{eq} has been suggested for 8-hour working day.

Interference with speech communication from intrusive noise depends on distance between talker and listener, and on whether voice normal or raised →(2).

Degree of annoyance from intrusive noise depends on number of factors, particularly type of use and task being carried out →(3).

Sound insulation →p395–7

SENSITIVITY TO VIBRATION

Frequencies of vibrations encountered in bldg lie mostly in range 5–50 Hz. When frequency exceeds approx 20–30 Hz passes into audible range. If energy sufficient, ie above threshold of audibility of sound in air, vibration will be heard as sound.

At certain frequencies amplitude small as 1 micron (0.001 mm) can be detected by human occupants though inaudible. Depending on frequency and amplitude vibration may be imperceptible or painful →(4).

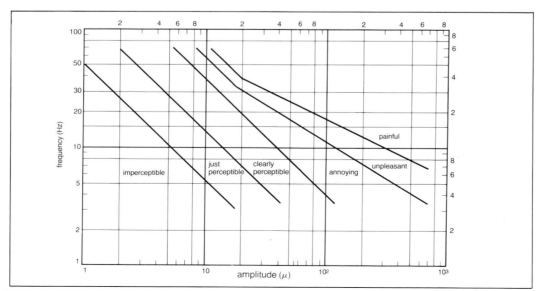

4   Human sensitivity: Reiher-Meister scale (vertical vibrations)

Man & his buildings

ACCESS & CIRCULATION

Space required around for access and circulation of people, prams, wheelchairs, trolleys (carts) etc. Access to bldg or groups of bldg also for private cars, delivery vans, moving vans, trucks etc. Space may be required for parking, short or long term. Separate space may be required for parking or sto of 2-wheel vehicles: bicycles, mopeds, motor cycles.

Shared surfaces

Usual to separate circulation of pedestrians and powered vehicles, but in certain situations (eg short culs-de-sac giving access to dwellings, car parks) shared surfaces may be adopted. Their design should be based on:

start of shared surface clearly distinguished from normal carriageway by change in texture or surface or change in level;
number of vehicles using shared surface should be limited;

design should ensure adequate visibility but discourage vehicle speeds;
parking spaces clearly marked;
provide clear zone free from parked cars to allow vehicles and pedestrians to circulate comfortably;
shared surfaces should be adequately lit after dark.

Footways

To design footways →(1)–(5) safe, convenient and secure necessary ensure that they:
provide shortest routes between dwellings and community services;
are kept separate from heavily trafficked roads;
have easiest practical gradients;
are protected from wind and driving rain;
are wide enough to avoid need for pedestrians when passing to step out into carriageway or on planted areas and, where necessary, for occasional access by emergency vehicles, eg ambulances.

Paths & sidewalks also →p43 85 106

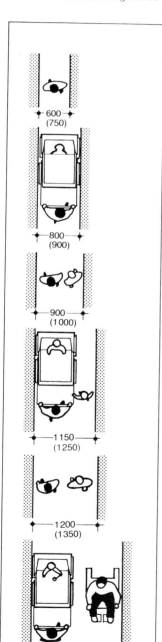

1 Spaces required for various types of pedestrian movement

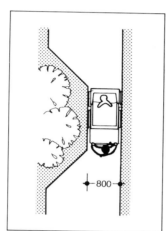

2 W of 800 allows prams or wheelchairs to pass through narrowest point; 1 800 allows passing on either side of narrowest point

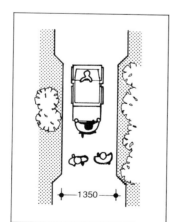

3 W of 1 350 allows prams & wheelchairs to proceed & pedestrians to pass each other in comfort; widening to 1 800 beyond narrowed point allows all users to pass in comfort

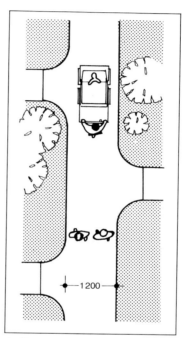

4 W of 1 200 allows prams & wheelchairs to proceed in comfort & pedestrians to pass each other; widening to 1 800 at entrances to curtilages allows all users to pass in comfort

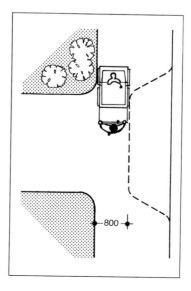

5 At entrances to private drives or parking spaces w of 800 carried through at footway level enables prams & wheelchairs to avoid ramps & dropped kerbs

Man & his buildings

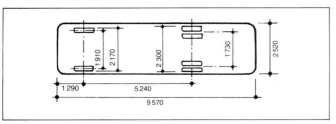

1 Furniture removal van

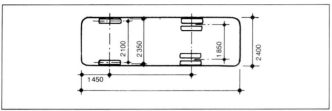

2 Refuse collection vehicle

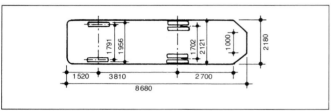

3 Fire engine

ROADWAYS

→USA standards p21
→access p41–2

Size and geometric characteristics of vehicles determine dimensions of roadways, junctions, turning and parking spaces. Special requirements for bldg serving commerce and industry. Not all types of vehicles likely to use residential roads. Those which do may not need access to all parts of site. In addition to private cars 3 types of vehicle may generally be expected in residential areas: furniture removal vans; refuse collection vehicles; and fire engines →(1)–(3) →p24.

Space required for these vehicles to move and manoeuvre depends on context within which they operate. For major roads national highway authorities lay down max permitted dimensions, axle loads and turning circles. They recommend road widths, sightlines and other characteristics of major urban and rural roads.

On residential roads traffic flows light and some tolerance in dimensions acceptable, *eg* to preserve existing features. Road widths narrower than 5 500 acceptable →(4)–(7).

Parking provision conditions adequacy of road width. Where roads give direct access to dwellings and parking spaces roadways likely to be used for casual parking. Where this does not happen widths largely determined by considerations of moving traffic. Narrowed sections may be used to discourage parking where there is danger at pedestrian crossing →(8) (rare in USA).

Allowance must be made for increase in width of larger vehicles at bends and for their turning and manoeuvreing →(9).

NB diagrams on this page apply for left hand circulation; for USA dimensions and reg →p21 250

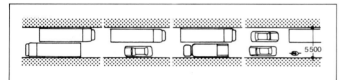

4 Normally max w for residential traffic 5 500: allows all vehicles to pass one another with overall tolerenance of 500 for largest vehicle

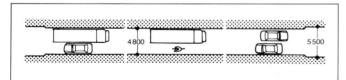

5 Carriageway 4 800 allows wide car & furniture removal van to pass each other with overall tolerance of 500 but is too narrow to allow free movement of large vehicles

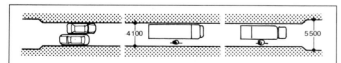

6 At 4 100 carriageway is too narrow for large vans to pass vehicles other than cyclists; cars can pass each other with overall tolerance of 500; below this w carriageway too narrow to pass each other comfortably

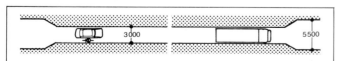

7 W of 3 000 min between passing bays in single-track system

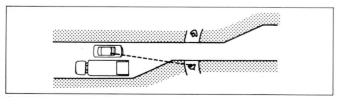

8 Parking should be discouraged at pedestrian crossing

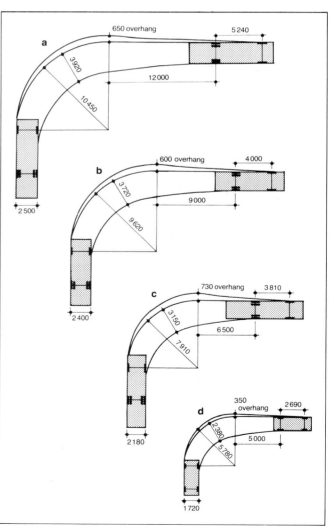

9 Vehicle turning through 90° **a** furniture van **b** refuse vehicle **c** fire appliance **d** private car

ROADWAYS

In USA roads described as follows:

Limited access freeways:
1 000–1 300 vehicles/lane/hr (high speed)
2 000 vehicles/lane/hr (slower speed)

Arterial highways:
600–800 vehicles/lane/hr (open road)
400–500 vehicles/lane/hr (with traffic signals, parking intersections)

Collectors:
100–250 trips/lane/hr
(6 206 min for 2 lanes residential)

Private roads:
6 706 for 2 lanes (5 486 min)
3 962 for 1 lane (3 048 min)
Note: city buses require 6 858 road for right angle turn from right lane.

Narrow road with passing bays →p20 not used in USA: occasionally on private sites. Single lane provided to remote service area (and turning space). Driveways for private houses recommended width 3 353.

Turning lanes frequently used to prevent back up of traffic at controlled intersections or for slowing down at exits from freeways.

Design of roads should include estimating traffic flows and impact of development on adjacent roadways.

Large vehicle dimensions →(1)

Garage entrances
→(2) shows dimensions for entrances to private garages and gradients for road to garage ramps. →(3) shows recommended dimensions for entrances to pay garages or car parks. Private garage →p100–2.

NB: diagrams on this page apply to traffic circulation on right

vehicle	l	w	overhang rear (OR)
intercity bus	13.7	2.7	3.1
city bus	12.2	2.6	2.0
school bus	12.04	2.4	3.9
ambulance	6.5	2.1	1.6
paramedic van	5.5	2.0	1.5
hearse	6.5	2.1	1.6
airport limousine	6.9	1.9	0.9
trash truck	8.6	2.4	1.8
UPS truck	7.1	2.3	2.5
fire truck	9.6	2.5	3.0

1 Large vehicles approx dimensions; exact sizes may vary

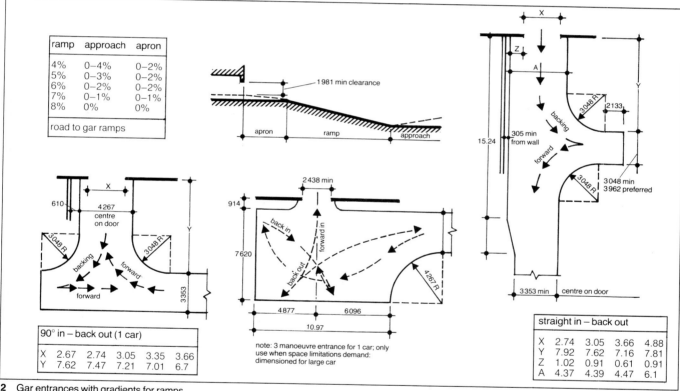

2 Gar entrances with gradients for ramps

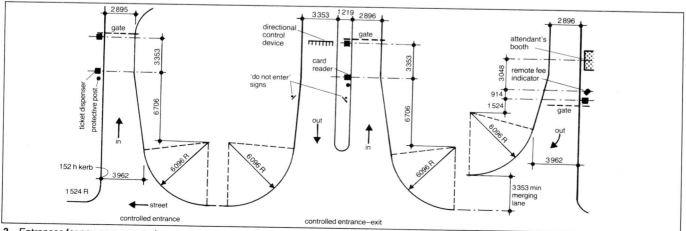

3 Entrances for pay gar or car parks

Man & his buildings

PARKING

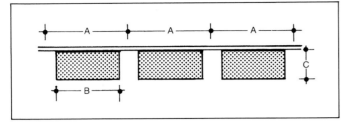

1   Parallel parking

	A	B	C
in bldg	5800	4600	2200–2300
in open	6100–6700	5500	2400

Basis or layout of vehicle parking spaces in parking bay ranges from 1800 × 4600 to 2400 × 6000. Larger bay dimensions usually adopted for open air parking, or where high proportion of larger cars and vans likely use. While 90° parking more economical in space requirement (20–22 m²/car) 45° parking (23–26 m²/car) more convenient →(1)–(3).

Vehicle lengths →p20 24

Vehicle parking spaces for disabled persons should be wider. For semi-ambulant persons bay widths should be increased to 2700 or better 2800; for wheelchair users 3000–3100 →p85 166.

USA parking spaces vary; depending on zoning ordinances.

NB diagrams on this page apply to traffic circulation on the left

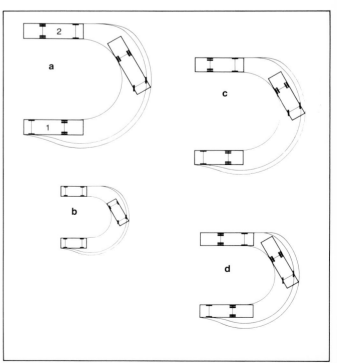

3   90° parking

	A	B	C	D	E	F
in bldg	4600	2300				6000
in open	5500	2400				6100–6700

2   45° parking

	A	B	C	D	E	F
in bldg	3000	4600	2300	3260	5000	2800
in open	3390	5500	2400	3890	5500	2800–3000

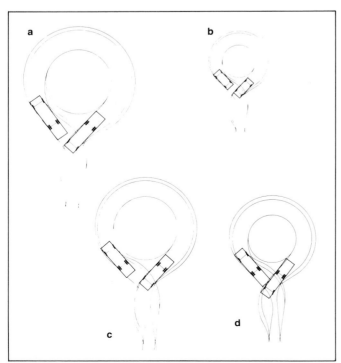

4   Full lock forward: a furniture van b car c refuse vehicle d fire appliance

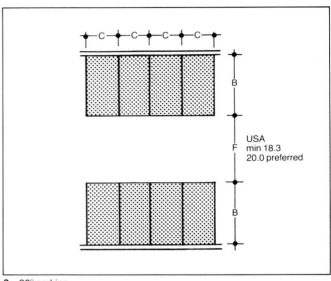

5   Full lock reverse: a furniture van b car c refuse vehicle d fire appliance

Man & his buildings

PARKING: VEHICLE TURNING SPACES
Vehicle lengths →p20 24

NB diagrams on this page apply to traffic circulation on the left

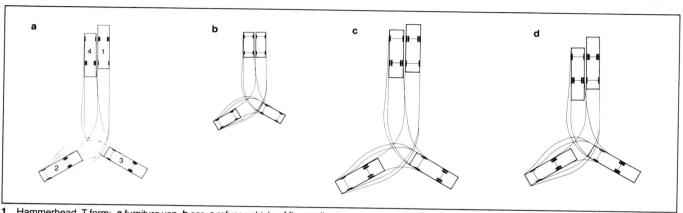

1   Hammerhead, T form: **a** furniture van   **b** car   **c** refuse vehicle   **d** fire appliance

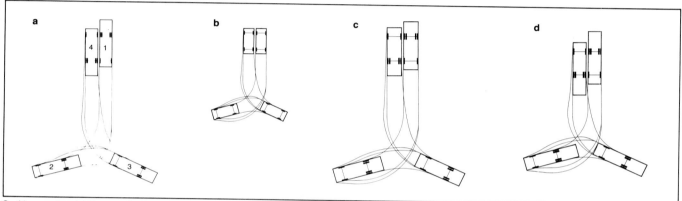

2   Hammerhead, Y form: **a** furniture van   **b** car   **c** refuse vehicle   **d** fire appliance

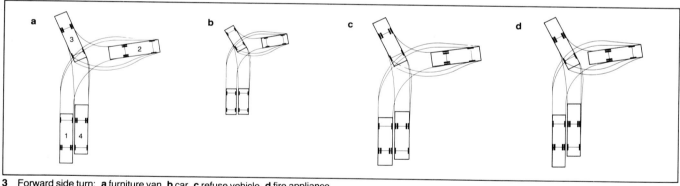

3   Forward side turn: **a** furniture van   **b** car   **c** refuse vehicle   **d** fire appliance

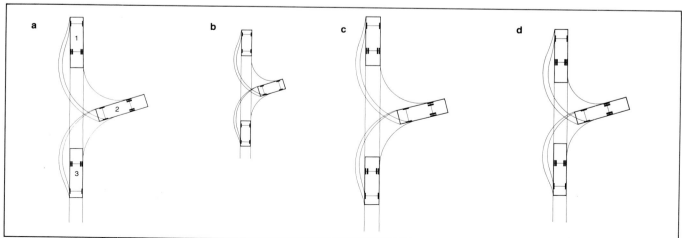

4   Reverse side turn: **a** furniture van   **b** car   **c** refuse vehicle   **d** fire appliance

Man & his buildings

ROAD VEHICLES   **Typical dimensions**

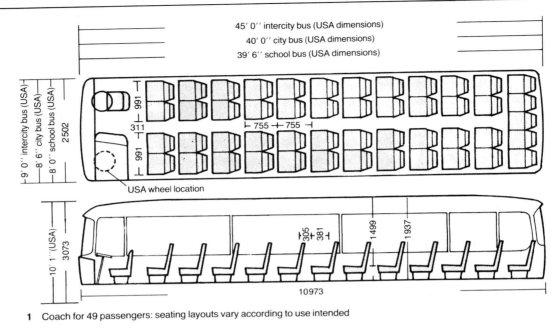

45′ 0′′ intercity bus (USA dimensions)
40′ 0′′ city bus (USA dimensions)
39′ 6′′ school bus (USA dimensions)

USA wheel location

1   Coach for 49 passengers: seating layouts vary according to use intended

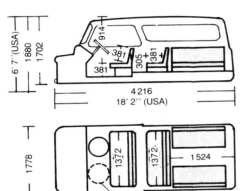

2   12-seater minibus/large van

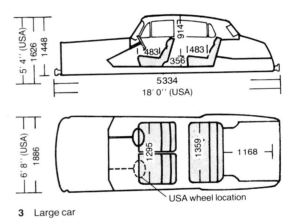

3   Large car

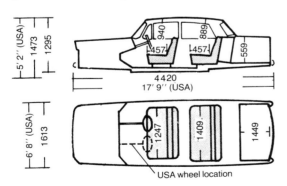

4   Car in middle range; USA standard

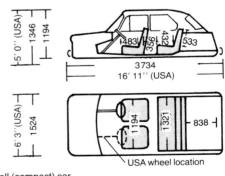

5   Small (compact) car

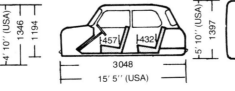

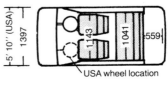

6   Mini car

Man & his buildings references:
→Bibliography entries 236 445

Lighting

Lighting inside a bldg must fulfil 2 functions: (a) to illuminate the interior and its contents; (b) where there is some task, *eg* reading, performing a delicate movement, walking up or down stairs, to illuminate the task appropriately and to appropriate extent so that visual mechanism can function at high level of efficiency.

When visual tasks might need to be carried out anywhere in interior bldg lighting and task lighting may be provided by same installation. Where tasks always carried out at some fixed location, *eg* work points on benches or at desks, less energy may be used by providing necessary task illuminance through bench or desk lights, or localised overhead lighting combined with lower illuminance from general lighting (but not less than 200 lux) to provide the surrounding visual environment →(1)(2). (For standard techniques and design rules →Bib383 387).

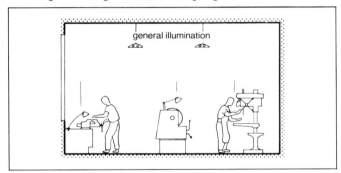

1 Arrangements of light sources for task lighting in off

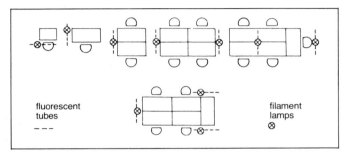

2 Artificial light

DEFINITIONS

Luminous flux: lumen
Radiant power emitted from source evaluated in terms of its visual effect is called luminous flux and measured in lumens. Effectiveness in converting input power (measured in watts) to lumens is called the efficacy and expressed in lumen/W. →(3) shows relative efficacy and some different lamp types.

Illuminance: lux
Amount of luminous flux falling on unit area of surface is called illuminance, measured in lux (1 lumen/m^2) (symbol E). Illuminance cannot be directly appreciated by eye, which sees effect of illuminance in making surface of object more or less bright according to magnitude of illuminance and reflecting power of surface.

Reflectance
Reflecting power expressed as reflectance (symbol ρ), on a scale on which 1 is max value achieved by perfect reflector, 0 value of perfect absorber and 0.2 reflectance of medium grey. Reflectance of coloured surface related to visual effect of light reflected. For reflectances of some typical surfaces →(4).

Some surfaces reflect light diffusely, *eg* blotting paper, some with very little spread (specularly), *eg* mirror. Most decorated rm surfaces reflect nearly diffusely with greater or less degree of gloss, so that brightness depends to some extent on relationship between angle of light and angle of viewing.

The higher the reflectances of surfaces in an interior the less the absorption of light and the lower the power to provide a given illuminance.

Light coloured curtains drawn over windows at night reduce loss of light.

A	good colour rendering lamps		
appearance of light	lamp type	efficacy relative to 'white' lamp	
warm	deluxe warm white, softone 27	70	similar to incandescent light and blend well with it; yellow emphasised: for homes, restaurants, hotels
	deluxe natural	65	good on all colours, emphasis on red: for shops, particularly food displays including meat
	colour 84, plus white	100	reasonably good on most colours, subdue deep red: for off, dept stores
intermediate	kolorite, trucolor 37	65	good on all colours: for display, shops, clinical areas in hospitals, museums
	graphic A 47	60	complies with BS 950 pt 2 for critical work in graphic arts
	natural	70	emphasises yellows: for off, dept stores, shops
cool	northlight, colour matching	65	similar to north sky daylight, emphasises blues: for blending with daylight but give 'cold' effect except at high illuminance
	artificial daylight	55	complies with BS 950 pt 1: critical colour matching

B	high efficacy lamps		
warm	warm white	100	blue distorted, red subdued, yellow & green emphasised: for factories
intermediate	white	100	similar to above but less 'warm'
intermediate	daylight	90	red subdued, yellow & green emphasised: blends acceptably with daylight

Notes
1 other types of lamp are made for special purposes, *eg* decorative colours: for reprography, horticulture, aquaria, ultra violet radiation;
2 circuit efficacy of 'white' lamp (*ie* including ballast) can be 45–65 lm/W depending on wattage; 3 properties of lamps change in consequence of developments by manufacturers who should always be asked for up-to-date information

3 Properties of fluorescent lamps giving substantially white light

ceilings	0.8	white emulsion paint on plain plaster surface
	0.7	white emulsion paint on acoustic tile
	0.6	white emulsion paint on no-fines concrete
	0.5	white emulsion paint on wood-wool slab
walls	0.8	white emulsion paint on plain plaster surface; white glazed tiles
	0.4	white asbestos cement sheet; concrete, light grey; Portland cement, smooth
	0.3	bricks, fletton
	0.25	concrete, light grey; Portland cement, rough (as board marked) timber panelling: light oak, mahogany, gaboon
	0.2	timber panelling: teak, afromosia, medium oak
	0.15	brick, blue engineering
floors	0.35	timber: birch, beech, maple
	0.25	timber: oak
	0.2	timber: iroko, kerning
	0.1	quarry tiles: red, heather brown

4 Approx reflectances of typical bldg finishes

Lighting

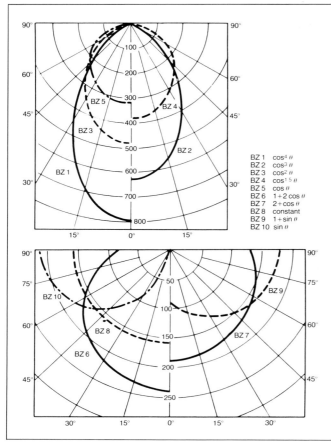

BZ 1 $\cos^4 \theta$
BZ 2 $\cos^3 \theta$
BZ 3 $\cos^2 \theta$
BZ 4 $\cos^{1.5} \theta$
BZ 5 $\cos \theta$
BZ 6 $1 + 2\cos \theta$
BZ 7 $2 + \cos \theta$
BZ 8 constant
BZ 9 $1 + \sin \theta$
BZ 10 $\sin \theta$

1   Intensity distribution curves with British Zonal (BZ) classification

	room index		
	1.0–1.6	2.5	4.0
direct & semi-direct lighting (BZ1–3, 25% upward light) floor cavity reflectance	0.1 0.2 0.3	0.1 0.2 0.3	0.1 0.2 0.3
$E_{(h)}/E_8$	2.8 2.4 2.1	2.6 2.3 2.05	2.5 2.2 2.0
general diffused lighting (BZ 4–10, 50% upward light) floor cavity reflectance	0.1 0.2 0.3	0.1 0.2 0.3	0.1 0.2 0.3
$E_{(h)}/E_8$	2.3 2.2 1.9	2.2 2.0 1.8	2.1 1.9 1.7

2   Conversion of scalar illuminance to illuminance on horizontal plane for interior with light ceilings & walls

DEFINITIONS (cont)

Colour: Munsell system →p17–18
Munsell system convenient and commonly used way of describing colour of surface in terms of hue (position in colour circle), chroma (paleness or fullness of colour) and value. Value corresponds to reflectance, approx given by:

$$\text{reflectance} = \frac{\text{value (value} - 1)}{100}$$

(→Bib100)

Luminance: apostilb or candela/m²
Mathematically physical brightness or luminance (symbol L) of diffusing surface is product of illuminance and reflectance, so that L = EP, and if E is in lux L is illuminance in apostilb. Alternative unit is candela per square metre (cd/m^2) which is SI unit →p2 and equal to π apostilb.

Note: calculation of luminance not needed in routine lighting design as standard methods (→Bib383 387) prescribe illuminance and reflectance separately.

Maintenance factor (MF)
Maintenance factor is proportion (expressed as decimal) of initial illuminance to which illuminance falls mid-way between cleaning and relamping periods. In design lighting design lumens are used for the lamp, which is av light output through life. MF therefore refers to dirtying of luminaires, rm surfaces and sources only: for interiors and installations maintained in av state of cleanliness maybe taken as 0.8. For those to be kept in specially clean condition take 0.9; for those which may be allowed to become dirtier than av take 0.7 →illuminance below.

Utilisation factor (UF)
UF is proportion (expressed as decimal) of luminous flux of light sources which falls on horizontal working plane in an interior: depends on shape of light distribution from luminaires, rm index →below and reflectances of rm surfaces. Light distribution characterised by shape of intensity distribution with respect to angle in vertical plane from downward vertical. These shapes commonly classified in UK by British Zonal System (BZ no); the 10 shapes and their mathematical descriptions are shown →(1). Most manufacturers now tabulate UF in their catalogues. Failing this they can be estimated by reference to tables (→Bib449).

Room index (RI)
RI relates to dimensions of rm: length l, width w, with luminaire height above working plane h_m.

$$RI = \frac{l \times w}{h_m(l + w)}$$

ILLUMINANCE

Where specific visual task exists illuminance is that on plane of task, whether horizontal, vertical or inclined. In places such as foyers and circulation areas 'scalar' illuminance is specified. This is a measure which is independent of direction and is related to illuminance on a horizontal plane in way which takes into account not only rm shape and luminaire light distribution but, most important, floor reflectance →(2).

Illuminance received from given lighting installation falls during use because there is gradual drop in light output of lamp during its life and luminaire and rm surfaces get dirtier between cleaning periods. (Shorter these intervals more efficiently el energy is used but more expensive maintenance cost becomes.) Recommended illuminance (→Bib383) is 'service' value ie av over period between cleaning; installed illuminance is higher than this by the reciprocal of the MF.

Lighting further detail →p398–400
Daylighting →p27–32; sunlight →p33–7

Daylight

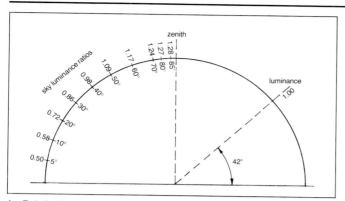

1 Relative luminance distribution of CIE standard overcast sky with av luminance taken as unity: conventional value at zenith to give 5000 lux illuminance on horizontal plane – 2050 cd/m²: illuminance →p25 26

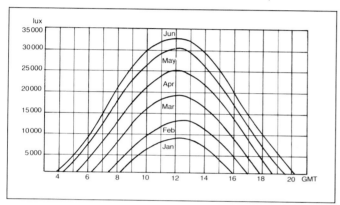

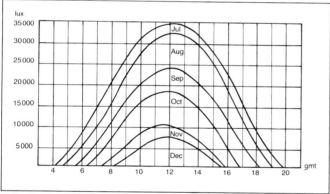

2 3 Illuminance in lux received from sky on horizontal surface out of doors averaged for each month & plotted against time

INTRODUCTION

Daylight factor

Because of varying intensity of daylight in countries with humid and temperate climates in practice most useful to base daylighting design on concept of daylight factor (DF), defined in simple terms as ratio of indoor illuminance →p26 (formerly known as illuminance value) to outdoor illuminance and given as percentage. (More exact definition →Bib123).

CIE standard overcast sky

To provide practical basis for estimation and measurement of DF in Britain and NW Europe has been found convenient to adopt standard overcast sky with sun obscured by cloud. This sky generally known as CIE standard overcast sky and assumed to have uniform luminance →p26–7, (ie physical measure of brightness), in azimuth with zenith luminance about 3 times that near horizon →(1). Zenith luminance depends on angular elevation of sun but conventional value of 2050 cd/m² was assumed originally, giving unobstructed illuminance of 5000 lux on horizontal plane outdoors.

Variation in outdoor illuminance over year

Conventional value of 5000 lux assumed for outdoor illuminance from overcast sky useful datum for initial calculations for daylight adequacy being representative of av conditions over much of day in mid-winter and significant periods in autumn and spring and wet days in summer. As this value exceeded for about 85% of time generally taken as critical value below which resulting daylight indoors would be considered inadequate. There are instances, however, where necessary to relate indoor illuminance to variation in outdoor illuminance values over specified period, especially in situations where it may be desirable to supplement daylight with artificial light. DF concept particular value in this context; for although outdoor illuminance will vary indoor illuminance will change with it and for all practical purposes DF will remain consistent. Seasonal and daily variations in daylight on horizontal surface outdoors, averaged for each month →(2)(3).

For indication of total working hr/yr for which indoor illuminance exceeds specified values in lux for a range of DF and for percentage of working hours when daylight illuminance in lux exceeds specified values, again for a range of DF, →(4)(5).

Average DF

Recommendations for adequacy of daylight have usually been made in terms of min DF. Recent studies have suggested use of av DF as better indication of adequacy of daylight over an interior. For side-lit rm, however, av daylight value on its own only general guide and needs to be associated with diversity index.

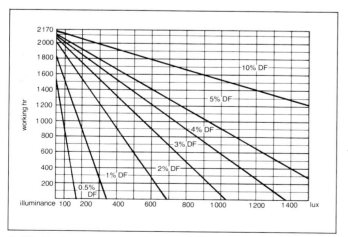

4 Working hr/yr for which daylight illuminances on working plane (wp) exceed specified values at various DF

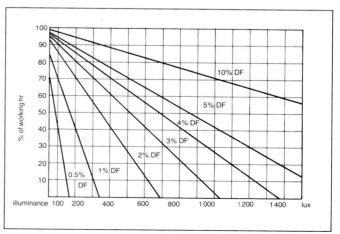

5 % of working hr when daylight illuminance on wp exceed specified values at various DF: graphs based on 5-day working week (0900–1700) giving yearly total of approx 2170 hr

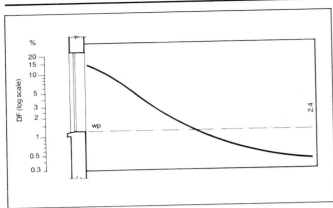

1 Gradient of illuminance on centre line of window

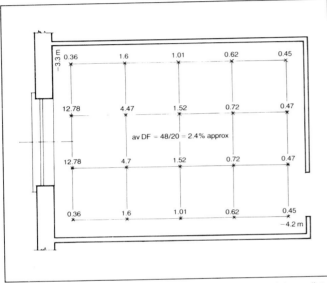

av DF = 48/20 = 2.4% approx

2 Distribution of daylight over horizontal plane: for clearness intermediate values have been omitted

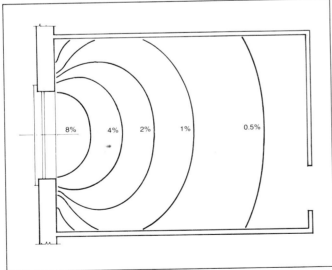

3 Distribution of daylight on horizontal plane shown by contours of equal DF

INTRODUCTION (cont)

Diversity of daylight

Diversity of daylight illuminance across rm can be shown as graph on cross section of rm, slope of curve indicating degree of diversity. Typical gradient of illuminance on centre line of window →(1). In line with artificial lighting practice diversity of illuminance can also be expressed numerically as uniformity ratio, *eg* as ratio of min to av DF. Thus

$$\text{uniformity ratio} = \frac{\text{min DF}}{\text{av DF}}$$

The greater the diversity, the lower the uniformity ratio.

For relatively simple window arrangements and for roof light systems index it has merit that it can show in general sense whether necessary to supplement daylight with artificial light. With complex window arrangements, however, may be preferable to examine distribution of daylight in some detail.

Distribution of daylight

Further refinement in assessing adequacy of daylight in rm is to calculate illuminance for number of points on regular grid. Contours of equal DF can then be drawn: distribution of daylight over working plane can be checked and areas where daylight is deficient be identified. If required av DF can be estimated by simply averaging values on reference grid. Where reference grid is taken right up to boundaries of rm values on boundary lines should be weighted, *ie* divide corner values by 4 and remaining boundary line values by 2 before averaging all values →(2)(3).

Comprehensive set of daylighting aids has been produced for UK by BRE; these give simple check between window size and proportional area of working plane within which specific values of DF equalled or exceeded. Aids thus give broad indication of horizontal distribution of daylight in rm →(4).

CALCULATION OF DF: GENERAL

Methods for predicting daylight illuminance at design stage range from simple formulas to sophisticated computer techniques (→Bib076 107 251 368 381 397 457).

Amount of design information required for predicting daylight factors in rm depends on complexity of method of calculation. For initial calculations, where window sizes not yet determined, useful if method of calculation can give area of glass required to provide particular standard of daylight.

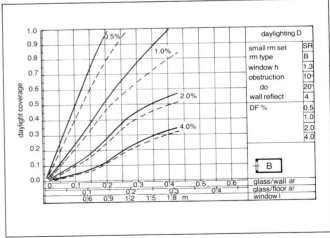

4 Typical daylighting aid

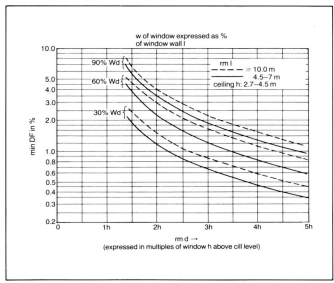

1 CIE method of daylight calculation: typical graph applicable to side-lit rm, unilateral lighting with no external obstructions

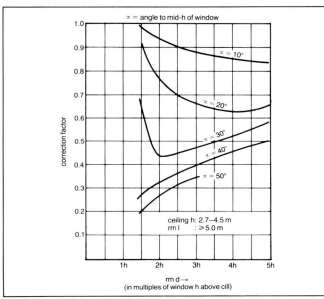

2 CIE method of daylight calculation: corrections to DF for angles of obstruction (to be read with →1)

angle of obstruction measured from centre of window (degrees above horizontal)	coefficient C
No obstruction	39
10°	35
20°	31
30°	25
40°	20
50°	14
60°	10
70°	7
80°	5

3 Variation of coefficient 'c' with angle of obstruction to be read with formula for av DF →above & IRC formula →p30

CALCULATION OF DF (cont)

Initial estimates: side-lit rm

Net area of glazing rough measure of amount of daylight admitted to rm. As first approximation, assuming side-lit rm of normal proportions with no external obstructions and with surfaces having av reflectance 0.4, av DF can be taken as equal about ½ of percentage ratio of glass to floor area. Thus windows on 1 side of rm with total glass area approx 20% of floor area will give av DF about 4%. Under same conditions min DF will be approx ½ av value, ie 2%. Conversely, to obtain av DF of 6% in rm with floor area 12 m² will require glazing area of approx 6 × 12 × 5/100 m² or 3.6 m².

For closer estimate of min DF in typical side-lit rm →(1)(2). These graphs give min DF related to rm depths for various rm lengths (parallel to window wall) and window widths, with corrections for angle of external obstruction to mid-height of window. Reflectances of rm surfaces taken as: ceiling 0.7, walls 0.5, floor 0.15. Min DF assumed be on centre line of window wall at point 600 from rear wall. Window widths (strictly window lengths) actual glass area widths given as % rm length. For more than 1 window widths aggregated and assumed windows regularly spaced along window wall. (Further details, including bilateral lighting →Bib397.)

Av DF calculations

Av DF over horizontal working plane can be calculated using formula put forward →Bib452

$$0.85 W \left[\frac{C}{A_{fw}} + \frac{CR_{fw} + 5R_{cw}}{A(1-R)} \right]$$

where w is glass ar
A is total ar of rm surfaces (including glass)
A_{fw} is ar of floor & of those parts of walls below mid-height of window (excluding window wall)
C is function of daylight incident on window & varies with sky luminance & angle of external obstructions →(3)
R is av reflectance of all rm surfaces including windows, expressed as decimal
R_{fw} is av reflectance of floor & lower walls below mid-height of window (excluding window wall)
R_{cw} is av reflectance of ceiling & upper walls above mid-height of window (excluding window wall)

Where window size not known glass area required give stipulated av DF can be worked out from basic formula restated as:

$$W = \frac{DF \text{ av}}{0.85 \dfrac{C}{A_{fw}} + \dfrac{CR_{fw} + 5R_{cw}}{(A(1-R)}} \ m^2$$

rm l (m)	rm d (m)	rm h (m)	window h (m)	av DF window l/rm l as percentages		
				30%	60%	90%
3.3	3.3	2.4	1.3	1.6	2.8	4.0
3.3	4.5	2.4	1.3	1.2	2.2	3.1
3.3	6.6	2.4	1.3	0.9	1.6	2.2
4.5	3.3	2.4	1.5	1.8	3.3	5.2
4.5	4.5	2.4	1.5	1.4	2.6	4.0
4.5	6.6	2.4	1.5	1.0	1.9	2.9
6.6	3.3	2.4	1.5	2.0	3.6	5.5
6.6	4.5	2.4	1.5	1.5	2.8	4.3
6.6	6.6	2.4	1.5	1.1	2.0	3.1
9.9	4.5	2.7	1.8	2.2	4.3	6.1
9.9	6.6	2.7	1.8	1.5	3.1	4.5
9.9	9.9	2.7	1.8	1.0	2.2	3.1

4 Basic assumptions: floor reflectance = 0.15, wall reflectance = 0.4, ceiling reflectance = 0.7, external obstruction = 20% at mid-h of window; no allowance for dirt on glass but 25% correction for window frame for 3300–6600 rm l & 15% for 9900 rm l

Daylight

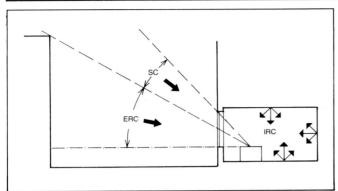

1   3 components of DF: SC = ERC = IRC = DF

ratio H/D = h of window above working plane: distance from window

ratio W/D	0.1	0.2	0.4	0.6	0.8	1.0	1.2	1.4	1.6	1.8	2.0	2.2	2.4	2.6	2.8	3.0	3.5	4.0	5.0	∞
0.1	0	0.1	0.2	0.4	0.6	0.7	0.8	0.9	1.0	1.0	1.1	1.1	1.1	1.1	1.2	1.2	1.2	1.2	1.3	1.3
0.2	0.1	0.2	0.5	0.8	1.1	1.4	1.6	1.8	1.9	2.0	2.1	2.2	2.2	2.3	2.3	2.4	2.4	2.4	2.5	2.5
0.3	0.1	0.3	0.7	1.2	1.7	2.1	2.4	2.7	2.9	3.1	3.2	3.3	3.4	3.4	3.5	3.6	3.6	3.7	3.7	3.7
0.4	0.1	0.4	1.0	1.6	2.2	2.7	3.2	3.5	3.8	4.0	4.1	4.3	4.4	4.5	4.5	4.6	4.7	4.8	4.9	4.9
0.5	0.1	0.5	1.2	1.9	2.6	3.3	3.8	4.2	4.6	4.8	5.0	5.2	5.3	5.4	5.5	5.7	5.8	5.9	5.9	5.9
0.6	0.1	0.6	1.3	2.2	3.0	3.8	4.4	4.9	5.3	5.6	5.8	6.0	6.2	6.3	6.4	6.6	6.7	6.8	6.9	6.9
0.7	0.2	0.7	1.5	2.4	3.3	4.2	4.8	5.4	5.8	6.2	6.4	6.6	6.8	7.0	7.1	7.3	7.4	7.6	7.7	7.7
0.8	0.2	0.7	1.6	2.6	3.6	4.5	5.2	5.8	6.3	6.7	7.0	7.3	7.5	7.6	7.8	8.0	8.2	8.3	8.4	8.4
1.0	0.2	0.8	1.7	2.7	3.8	4.8	5.6	6.2	6.7	7.1	7.4	7.7	7.9	8.1	8.2	8.5	8.7	8.8	9.0	9.0
1.2	0.2	0.8	1.8	2.9	4.0	5.0	5.9	6.5	7.1	7.5	7.9	8.1	8.4	8.6	8.7	9.0	9.2	9.4	9.6	9.6
1.4	0.2	0.9	1.9	3.1	4.3	5.4	6.4	7.2	7.8	8.3	8.7	9.1	9.3	9.6	9.8	10.1	10.3	10.5	10.7	10.7
1.6	0.2	0.9	1.9	3.2	4.5	5.7	6.7	7.5	8.2	8.7	9.1	9.5	9.8	10.0	10.2	10.6	10.9	11.1	11.6	11.6
1.8	0.2	0.9	2.0	3.3	4.6	5.9	7.0	7.8	8.5	9.1	9.6	10.0	10.2	10.5	10.7	11.1	11.4	11.7	12.2	12.2
1.9	0.2	1.0	2.0	3.3	4.7	6.0	7.2	8.1	8.8	9.5	10.0	10.4	10.8	11.1	11.3	11.8	12.0	12.3	12.6	12.6
2.0	0.2	1.0	2.0	3.3	4.7	6.1	7.3	8.2	9.0	9.7	10.2	10.7	11.1	11.4	11.7	12.2	12.4	12.7	13.0	13.0
2.5	0.2	1.0	2.1	3.3	4.8	6.2	7.4	8.4	9.2	9.9	10.5	11.0	11.4	11.7	12.0	12.6	12.9	13.3	13.7	13.7
3.0	0.2	1.0	2.1	3.4	4.8	6.2	7.5	8.5	9.3	10.0	10.7	11.2	11.7	12.0	12.4	12.9	13.3	13.7	14.2	14.2
4.0	0.2	1.0	2.1	3.4	4.9	6.3	7.5	8.6	9.5	10.1	10.8	11.3	11.8	12.2	12.5	13.2	13.5	14.0	14.6	14.6
6.0	0.2	1.0	2.1	3.4	5.0	6.3	7.6	8.6	9.5	10.2	10.9	11.4	11.9	12.3	12.6	13.2	13.6	14.1	14.9	14.9
∞	0.2	1.0	2.1	3.4	5.0	6.3	7.6	8.6	9.5	10.3	10.9	11.5	11.9	12.3	12.7	13.3	13.7	14.2	15.0	15.0
angle of obstruction	0°	11°	22°	31°	39°	45°	50°	54°	58°	61°	63°	66°	67°	69°	70°	72°	74°	76°	79°	90°

ratio W/D = effective w of window to 1 side of normal: distance from window

2   Sky components table (overcast sky) for vertical glazed windows: shortened version derived →Bib076

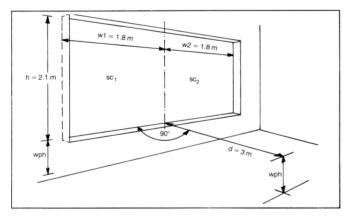

3   Example of simple case:
SC for section of window (W₁) is read →(2) against ratios H/D
& W/D; from drawing $\frac{H}{D} = \frac{2.1}{3} = 0.7$; $\frac{W}{D} = \frac{1.8}{3} = 0.6$

SC read against these ratios = 1.5; repeat section (W₂) & add SC₁ to SC₂ to give SC for whole window 1.5 + 1.5 = 3.0; for obstructions treat obscured section window & × 0.2 to correct for lower luminance; angle of obstruction on table gives appropriate H/D for obscured section

wall reflectance	to convert to floor ar of 10 m²	to convert to floor ar of 90 m²	to convert to av IRC
20	0.6	1.4	1.8
40	0.7	1.2	1.4
60	0.8	1.0	1.3
80	0.9	0.9	1.2

5   Conversion factors to apply to →(3)

CALCULATION OF DF (cont)

Point by point methods: vertical windows in side-lit rm

Basic assumption for most point by point methods of daylight calculation adopted in UK is to consider daylight reaching point in rm as consisting of 3 components:
sky component (SC)
externally-reflected component (ERC)
internally-reflected component (IRC)
How these 3 components operate is shown →(1). To give complete DF the 3 components are simply added together. Corrections for other than clear glass, area of window obscured by framing and window bars and effect of dirt on glass and rm surfaces can be made by applying correction factors to final figure →p31(4)(5).

SC & ERC

For preliminary calculations →(2) (Bib076). In use table gives data for effective width of window to right or left of line (normal to window plane) drawn to reference →(3). SC at any other reference point, also effect of external obstruction, can be found by adding or subtracting SC of hypothetical windows so that actual window remains. To allow for reduced luminance of obstructions values of equivalent SC for obscured sections of window are mulitplied by 0.8

Other methods of predicting SC and ERC include BRE DF protractors, Pilkington dot method, grid methods such as Waldram diagram. With all these aids ERC estimated by assuming that proportion of sky obscured by obstruction (as seen from reference point) has luminance which is some fraction of sky obscured. Unless luminance of obstruction known usual practice to assume obstruction luminance ⅕ av sky luminance.

IRC

For preliminary estimates min IRC can be obtained from →(4) if certain limitations on size of rm and reflectances of rm surfaces accepted. More comprehensive coverage →Bib076. Where relatively high accuracy required IRC for side-lit rm can be calculated using BRE inter-reflection formula:

$$IRC = \frac{0.85W}{A(1-R)}(CR_{fw} - 5R_{cw})\%$$

where
W is ar of glass in window
A is total ar of ceiling walls & floor including ar of glass
R is av reflectance of ceiling, walls including glass & floor, expressed as fraction
R_{fw} is av reflectance of floor & those parts of walls above mid-h of window (excluding window wall)
R_{cw} is av reflectance of ceiling & those parts of walls above mid-h of window (excluding window wall)
C is coefficient with value dependent on angle of obstruction outside window →p29(3).

Min IRC can be obtained by applying conversion factors related to av reflectance of rm surface:

av reflectance	conversion factor
0.3	0.75
0.4	0.7
0.5	0.8
0.6	0.85

window ar as % of floor ar	floor reflectance											
	10%				20%				40%			
	av wall reflectance (excluding window)											
	20%	40%	60%	80%	20%	40%	60%	80%	20%	40%	60%	80%
2	—	—	0.1	0.2	—	0.1	0.1	0.2	—	0.1	0.2	0.2
5	0.1	0.1	0.2	0.4	0.1	0.2	0.3	0.5	0.1	0.2	0.4	0.6
7	0.1	0.2	0.3	0.5	0.1	0.2	0.4	0.6	0.2	0.3	0.6	0.8
10	0.1	0.2	0.4	0.7	0.2	0.3	0.6	0.9	0.3	0.5	0.8	1.2
15	0.2	0.4	0.6	1.0	0.2	0.5	0.8	1.3	0.4	0.7	1.1	1.7
20	0.2	0.5	0.8	1.4	0.3	0.6	1.1	1.7	0.5	0.9	1.5	2.3
25	0.3	0.6	1.0	1.7	0.4	0.8	1.3	2.0	0.6	1.1	1.8	2.8
30	0.3	0.7	1.2	2.0	0.5	0.9	1.5	2.4	0.8	1.3	2.1	3.3
35	0.4	0.8	1.4	2.3	0.5	1.0	1.8	2.8	0.9	1.5	2.4	3.8
40	0.5	0.9	1.6	2.6	0.6	1.2	2.0	3.1	1.0	1.7	2.7	4.2
45	0.5	1.0	1.8	2.9	0.7	1.3	2.2	3.4	1.2	1.9	3.0	4.6
50	0.6	1.1	1.9	3.1	0.8	1.4	2.3	3.7	1.3	2.1	3.2	4.9

4   Min IRC (Bib076) based on rm of 40 m² floor ar with h to ceiling 3000 & window on 1 side; ceiling reflectance of 0.7 assumed and 20° angle of external obstruction; corrections can be made for other rm sizes & to convert min IRC to av IRC by factors in →(5)

CALCULATION OF DF (cont)

Roof light systems

Spacing, as well as size, of roof lights is important consideration for adequate daylighting: in general DF easier to predict than for side-lit rm but same variables apply, *eg* area and position of glazing, shape and size of space to be daylighted, reflectance of interior surfaces. Illuminance on horizontal working plane from correctly spaced roof lights nearer to distribution from overhead artificial lighting installations and usually sufficient to determine av DF.

CIE recommendations (→Bib397) include method for estimating av DF for various roof light systems at early stage in design, with graphs for flat and low-pitched roofs, sawtooth and monitor roofs, from which av DF can be ascertained. Typical curves for skylights in flat and 20° pitch roofs reproduced →(1)(2). By means of associated tables corrections can be made for various glass transmittances, for dirt on glass and for av surface reflectances differing from 20% (0.2) reflectance assumed for (3)(4)(5). For →(1)(2) av DF can be read direct given glass ar/floor ar ratios, length of bldg and height of walls above working plane.

Useful formula below with associated tables developed by Pilkington Brothers (1971) for prediction of av DF for roof lights in range of roof types, including shed, sawtooth and monitors.
Av DF on horizontal plane: D = 100.c.M.B.G.(g/f)%
where
c is coefficient of utilisation →(7)(8)

M is correction factor for dirt or aging of glazing →(3)
B is correction factor for window framing, glazing & internal obstructions, *eg* overhead supports for machinery: where details of framing not known typical value for B is 0.75 but figure could be less in factories with overhead pipework, ducting & structural members[1]
G is correction factor for type of glass other than clear glass
g/f is ratio of glazing ar to floor ar

Coefficient depends on roof light design, shape and size of interior space and reflectances of ceiling, walls and floor.

Rm index as tabulated $= \dfrac{1.w}{(1-w)h}$

where l = length of rm, w = width of rm and h = height above working plane to centre of glazing. To ensure fairly even spread of daylight spacing/height ratios should be kept within limits shown →(6).

Point by point methods: roof light systems

Where necessary to calculate DF at selected reference points with some precision, *eg* to test daylight distribution, SC and ERC can be obtained by using BRE protractors. IRC can be estimated by using BRE nomogram III →Bib076.

[1] *Note:* correction factor 'B' for large continous internal obstructions, such as ducting, can be worked out on cross section (by projection) for selected reference points.

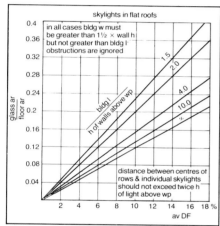

1 CIE method of daylight calculation: typical graph applicable to skylights in flat roofs

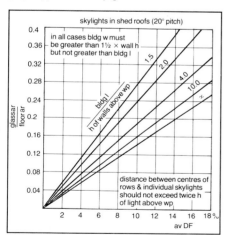

2 CIE method of daylight calculation: typical graph applicable to skylights in pitched roofs

av reflectance	correction factor
0.2	1.0
0.3	1.1
0.4	1.2

4 Correction factor to be applied to DF calculated from →(1)(2) to allow for av reflectances other than 0.2 assumed for tables

locality	vertical windows	roof lights	
		sloping	horizontal
clean *eg* country ar, outer suburbs	0.9	0.8	0.7
dirty *eg* built-up ar, light industry	0.7	0.6	0.5
very dirty *eg* heavy industry	0.6–0.5	0.5–0.4	0.4–0.3

3 Maintenance factor to be applied to calculated DF to allow for dirt on glass

glazing materials	vertical windows, steeply sloping roof lights		sloping & flat roof lights
	single glazing	double glazing	single glazing
glass: 4–6 clear or 6 polished wired	1.0	0.9	1.1
6 rough cast	0.95	0.85	1.05
wired cast or patterned	0.9	0.8	1.0
6 selectively heat-absorbing (pale green)	0.85	0.7	0.95
6 body-tinted heat-absorbing (bronze)	0.55	0.5	0.6
corrugated resin-bonded glass fibre reinforced roofing sheets: moderately diffusing	0.9	—	0.9
heavily diffusing	0.75–0.9	—	0.75–0.9

5 Correction factors to be applied to calculate for typical glazing materials: for precise details of proprietary materials consult manufacturers; for double glazing inner pane of clear glass is assumed

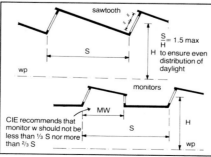

6 Max spacing of sawtooth roof lights & monitors as recommended for →(7)(8)

	reflectance			
ceiling	0.7	0.5	0.3	0
walls	0.5 0.3 0.1	0.5 0.3 0.1	0.3 0.1	0
room index	coefficient of utilisation			
0.6	.19 .16 .15	.19 .16 .14	.16 .14	.14
0.8	.25 .21 .2	.25 .21 .2	.21 .2	.18
1.0	.3 .26 .25	.29 .26 .24	.25 .24	.21
1.25	.31 .3 .27	.31 .29 .26	.27 .26	.24
1.5	.34 .31 .3	.32 .31 .29	.3 .27	.26
2.0	.36 .35 .32	.36 .34 .32	.34 .32	.29
2.5	.39 .38 .35	.38 .36 .34	.35 .32	.31
3.0	.4 .39 .38	.4 .35 .36	.36 .35	.32
4.0	.42 .41 .4	.41 .4 .39	.39 .38	.35
5.0	.44 .42 .41	.42 .41 .4	.4 .39	.36
inf	.49 .42 .49	.48 .48 .48	.45 .45	.42

7 Coefficients of utilisation for sawtooth roof with sloping glazing

	reflectance			
ceiling	0.7	0.5	0.3	0
walls	0.5 0.3 0.1	0.5 0.3 0.1	0.3 0.1	0
room index	coefficient of utilisation			
0.6	.15 .12 .09	.13 .12 .09	.11 .09	.09
0.8	.19 .16 .13	.19 .16 .13	.16 .13	.13
1.0	.23 .2 .18	.22 .19 .18	.19 .18	.16
1.25	.26 .23 .2	.24 .23 .2	.22 .2	.19
1.5	.27 .24 .22	.26 .24 .22	.23 .22	.2
2.0	.3 .27 .24	.28 .26 .24	.26 .24	.24
2.5	.32 .3 .27	.31 .28 .27	.28 .27	.26
3.0	.34 .31 .3	.32 .31 .28	.3 .28	.27
4.0	.35 .34 .32	.34 .32 .31	.32 .31	.3
5.0	.35 .34 .34	.35 .34 .32	.34 .32	.31
inf	.4 .4 .4	.4 .4 .4	.39 .39	.38

8 Coefficients of utilisation for monitors with vertical plus sloping glazing

Daylight

QUALITY OF DAYLIGHT: GLARE

DF is measure of daylight illumination: subjective aspects also help to determine essential appearance and character of interior. Of subjective lighting phenomena glare is one of most important. 2 distinctive aspects of glare recognised: *disability* glare, which impairs ability of people to see objects against glare source without necessarily causing visual discomfort and *discomfort* glare, which causes visual discomfort without necessarily impairing ability of people to see →p398.

Typical example of disability glare: window at end of corridor or top of staircase makes it difficult to see person or object silhouetted against window. Such cases usually resolved by common sense; little to be gained from calculation techniques.

Degree of discomfort glare can be assessed numerically and expressed as limiting glare index. (→Bib367 382). Main controlling parameter luminance of sky as seen through window; above low value of window/floor area ratio (1–2%) size of window not important. Recent studies indicate, for example, that if one assumes sky luminance of 8 900 cd/m^2 (exceeded for only about 15% of working year) predicted glare index for rm not exceeding 4 000 in height with av surface reflectances of 0.4 would be 26. For similar rm with av reflectances of 0.6 glare index would be 24. These figures apply to worst conditions, *eg* single window facing observer. For progressive reductions in sky luminance predicted glare indices would be reduced; *eg* with sky luminance of 6 400 cd/m^2 glare index would be reduced by 0.5 units and for sky luminance of 1 600 cd/m^2 by as much as 4 units, bearing in mind that incidence of glare would be increased because of higher proportion of working hours for assumed lower sky luminace. Conversely, for rm with higher ceilings (*ie* above 4 000) glare index may well be increased by 1–2 units.

As controlling factor is sky luminance, if values assumed for glare indices are greater than recommended values →(2) some amelioration likely to be required. Practical ameliorative measures include use of translucent curtains or blinds, louvred or slatted blinds, vertical or horizontal fins and high internal surface reflectances →p406. Other measures include placing windows so that immediate surroundings have high luminance, use of windows on more than 1 wall and detailed design of windows and their immediate surrounds so as to reduce contrast with view of bright sky.

location	DF %
liv (over ½ depth of rm but with min ar of distribution 7 m^2)	1
bedr (over ¾ depth of rm but with min ar of distribution 5.5 m^2)	0.5
k (over ½ depth of rm but with min ar of distribution 4.5 m^2)	2
dual purpose rm, *eg* k/liv to be lit to more exacting requirements	
following reflectances are assumed: walls 0.4, floor 0.15, ceiling 0.7	

1   Recommended min DF for dwellings extracted →Bib107

location	av DF %	min DF %	position of measurement	limiting daylight glare index
airport bldg & coach stations				
reception ar	2	0.6	desks	24
customs & immigration ha	2	0.6	counters & desks	24
circulation ar, lounges	2	0.6	working plane	—
assembly & concert ha				
foyers, auditoria	1	0.6	working plane	24
corr	2	0.6	floor	—
stairs	2	0.6	treads	—
banks				
counters, typing, accounting, book ar	5	2	desks	23
public ar	2	0.6	working plane	24
churches				
body of church	5	1	working plane (daylight glare index to be calculated for direction of view of congregation)	21
pulpit & lectern ar, chancel & choir	5	1.5	on desks	23
altar, communion table	5	2	on table (level depends on emphasis required)	23
drawing off				
general	5	2.5	on boards	21
general bldg ar				
entrance ha & reception ar	2	0.6	working plane	24
hospitals				
reception & wr	2	0.6	working plane	24
wards	5	1	innermost bedhead (min value refers to innermost bedhead)	21 21
pharmacies	5	3	working plane	21-
libraries				
reading & reference rm	5	1.5	on tables (additional el lighting will be required)	23
shelves (stacks)		1.5	vertical plane	23
museums & art galleries				
general	5	1	working plane	21
off				
general	5	2	desks	23
typing, business machines, manually operated computers	5	2.5	desks	23
schools & colleges				
assembly ha	1	0.3	working plane	21
classr	5	2	desks	21
art rm	5	2	easels	21
lab	5	2	benches	21
staff rm, common rm	5	1.5	working plane	23
sports ha				
general	5	3.5	working plane	21
surgeries (med & dental)				
wr	2	0.6	working plane	24
surgeries	5	2.5	working plane	21
lab	5	2	benches	22
swimming pools				
pool	5	2	pool surface (care should be taken to minimise glare & reflections from water surface)	23
surrounding ar	1	0.5	working plane	23
telephone exchanges (manual)				
general	—	2	working plane (avoid specular reflections: limit daylight on internally lit controls)	20

(further detail →Bib202 380 382 383)

2   Schedule of DF & glare indices

Daylight references:
→Bibliography entries 047 059 074 076 107 202 251 252 291 367 368 375 380 381 382 383 397 452 457 527 528 529 567

Sunlight

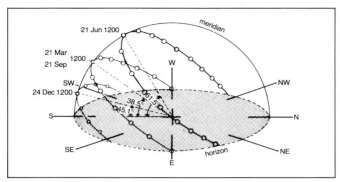

1   Altitude of sun in relation to bldg or observer (lat 51.5°)

CRITERIA FOR ADMISSION OF SUNLIGHT

Standards for UK
→BRE (Bib074)
→(Bib141)
→DoE Welsh Office (Bib251 252)

Standards for USA
→Ramsey & Sleeper (Bib549)
For USA latitudes →p34–6

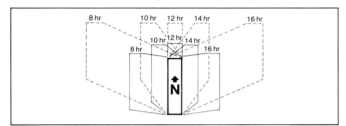

2   Block with main axis running N-S has long shadows cast to sides of bldg in early morning & late afternoon in Mar & Sep: small permanently shadowed ar to N of block in midwinter

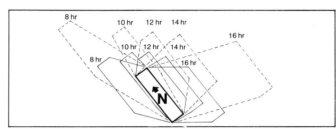

3   Block with main axis running NW-SE shadow pattern varies between am & pm: relatively small permanently shadowed ar in midwinter

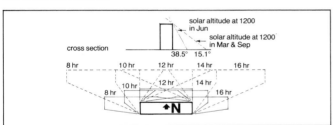

4   Tall block with main axis running E-W (favoured where main rm facing S are required) can give serious overshadowing of ground to N of bldg in Mar & Sep: comparatively large ar of site close to bldg receives no sunlight in midwinter

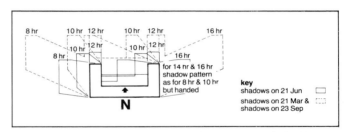

5   Where possible avoid siting high bldg with deep recesses facing N as comparatively large ar of ground receives no sunlight at all in midwinter

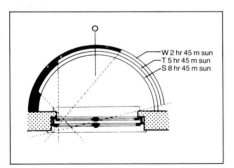

6   E & W windows receive horizontal sun rays at equinox; their angle of incidence becomes steeper towards summer solstice; W = shortest day of yr, T = equinox, S = longest day of yr

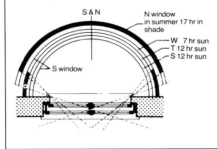

7   N windows receive only little direct sunlight round summer solstice; S windows receive sunrays with low angles of incidence in winter & steep in summer

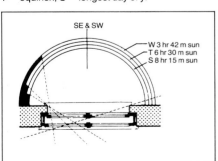

8   SE & SW windows receive fair amount of sunshine both summer & winter by low deeply-penetrating sunrays

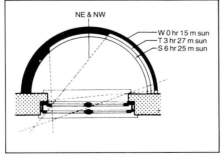

9   NE & NW windows receive no direct sunlight in winter but effective sunlight in spring & autumn

SITING, ORIENTATION & SPACING OF BUILDING

Check orientation of facades and spacing of bldg in relation to required standard of insolation →p34–6. Some compromise on ideal orientation of facades will be unavoidable on congested sites or in areas of mixed development. →Energy conservation houses →p79–81

INSOLATION OF OUTDOOR SPACES

Where possible site large bldg so that extensive and continuous shadowing of ground round them avoided; otherwise growth of vegetation will be inhibited. Problem dynamic and seasonal pattern of sunlight and shadow should be examined. For indication of extent of possible shadowing from tall bldg during summer and autumn (lat London) →(2)–(5).

ORIENTATION OF WINDOWS

Orientation, size and shape of individual windows may require checking on drawings by reference to sun path diagrams to determine sunlight penetration and effectiveness of required sun controls. For general indication of effect of various orientations on sunlight penetration at different times of year (UK) →(6)–(9).

Sunlight

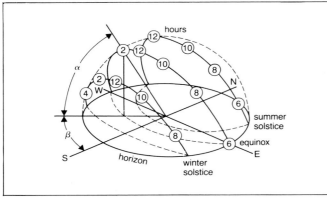

1 Diagram shows altitude (α) & angle of bearing (β)

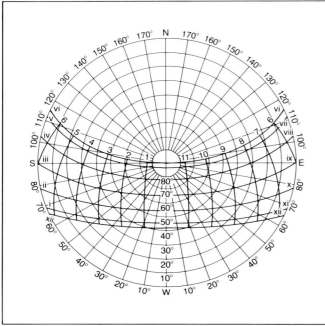

2 24°N latitude

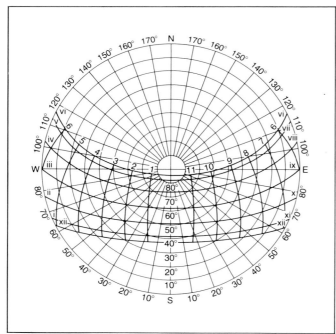

3 28°N latitude

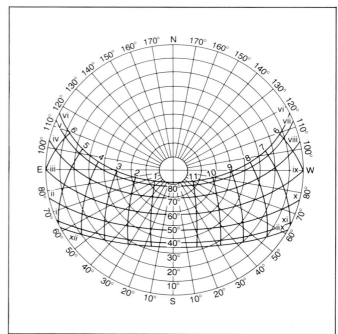

4 32°N latitude

METHODS OF FINDING SUN EXPOSURES OF BUILDINGS

3 ways of calculating position of sun relative to particular places, seasons, times of day:

use of models in conjunction with sundial allows visual observation but usefulness limited by obvious practical limitations;

calculations and tabular projections to afford high degree of exactness;

but graphic projection preferred by most architects since it allows measurement of both sun and shade.

SUN PATH DIAGRAM

Sun's position at any date or hour may be determined from sun path diagram which corresponds to latitude of observation point →(1) showing altitude (α) and angle of bearing (β). Diagrams for series of N latitudes →(2)–(4) p35(1)–(5).

On each diagram altitude angles shown at 10° intervals by concentric circles. Bearing angles shown at 10° intervals by equally spaced radii graduated along outer periphery of diagram.

Elliptical curved lines in diagram represent horizontal projections of sun's path, appropriate for 21st day of each month: months labelled in Roman numerals; crossed grid of vertically curved lines, labelled in arabic numerals, indicate hours.

Use of sun path diagram
Example:
Columbus Ohio at latitude 40°N on 21 Feb at 1400 →p35(2). Find elliptical curved lines for Feb (ii) and mark where it crosses vertical line of 1400 (2): these two lines intersect as sun's position; read altitude from concentric circle: 32°; read bearing angle from outer circumference: 35° 30′ W.

Example of use of diagram for approx latitude London England →p36.

Sunlight

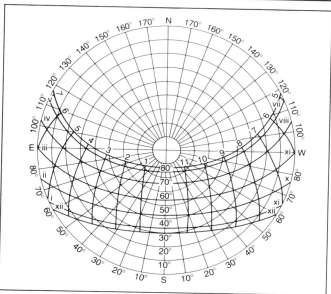

1   36°N latitude

SUN PATH DIAGRAM (cont)

Further examples of sun path diagrams →(1)–(5). For method of using diagrams →p34.

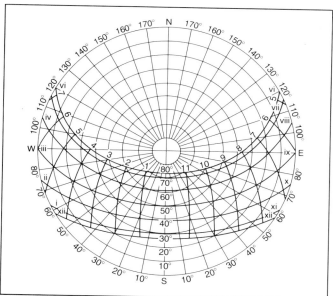

2   40°N latitude

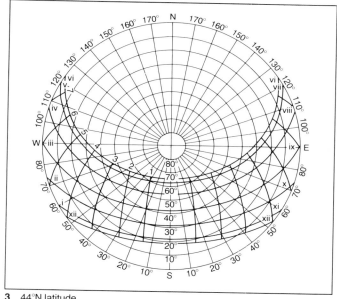

3   44°N latitude

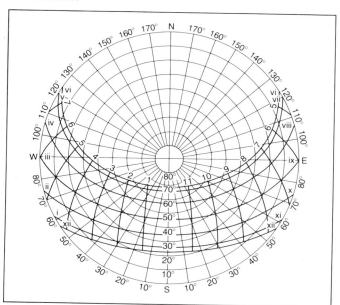

4   48°N latitude

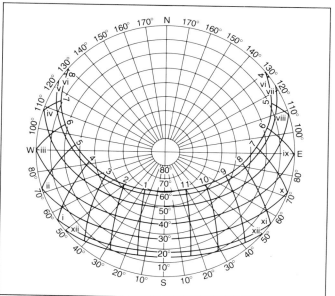

5   52°N latitude

Sunlight

USE OF SUN PATH DIAGRAM WITH BUILDING PLAN

Diagram →(1) shows path of sun on shortest day of year at approx latitude London England (51° 50′N); →(2) shows sun position at determining days of year; →(3)–(7) show method of finding amounts of sun and shadow on bldg.

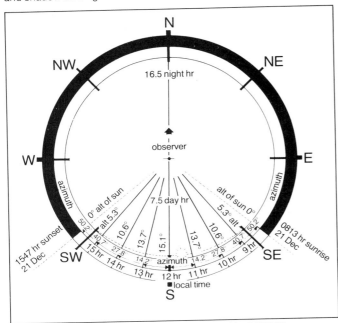

1 Path of sun shortest day of year (approx 21 Dec) lat 51° 50′N

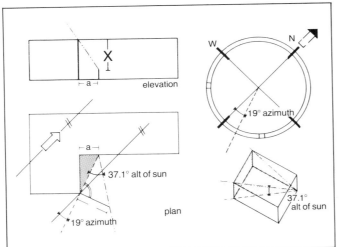

2 Sun position at noon at determining days of yr: distance of sun from observer equals radius of sun path diagram with dotted path of sun in plan, which represents plan projection of corresponding h of sun

3 4 To find amounts of sun & shadow on bldg at certain time of year & day (eg equinox 1100) azimuth angle (19°) is plotted in plan from corner of bldg in question; this shows limit of shadow cast in plan; angle of altitude of sun (37.1°) then plotted where this line intersects vertical plane of bldg further back; length x, found by intersecting line drawn at right angles to limit of shadow in plan with plotted angle of altitude, determines h of shadow cast in elevation; plotted to elevation at distance a from internal corner & linked with eaves of line of bldg gives limit of shadow in elevation

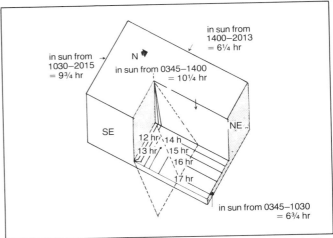

5 Shortly after 1100 at summer solstice NE elevation in shade; shortly after 1300 SE elevation also in shade; other elevations at corresponding times in sun

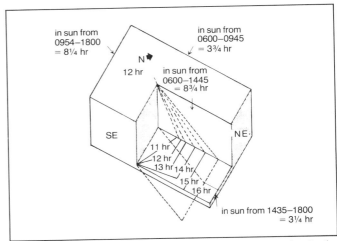

6 At equinox NE elevation in shade shortly after 1000, SE elevation shortly after 1500

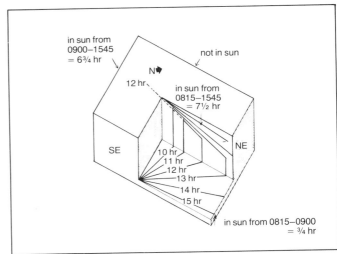

7 At winter solstice NE elevation receives sun for barely 1 hr, SE elevation in shade after 1500

Sunlight

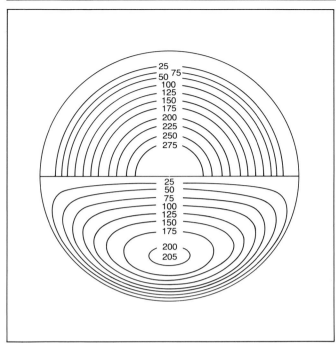

1 Radiation calculator: can be used at any latitude & any orientation; is in same scale & projection as sun path diagrams →p34–6; transfer calculator diagram to transparent overlay & superimpose on sun path diagram in desired orientation: radiation values can be read directly

solar altitude in degrees

5	10	15	20	25	30	35	40	45	50	60	70	80	90
67	123	166	197	218	235	248	258	266	273	283	289	292	294

Btu/ft²/hr

magnitude of solar radiation depends first of all on sun's altitude: tabulated values indicate direct radiation energies received under clear atmospheric conditions at normal incidence

CALCULATION OF RADIATION

Design implications of sun's altitude and bearing affected by actual amount of solar energy falling on exposed surface of bldg. Choice of orientation and selection of appropriate technical or passive devices for shading bldg will require this third range of data.

Graphic calculator →(1) (→Bib549) originates in USA therefore uses Btu/ft²/hr units. Upper half of diagram charts energies falling horizontal plane under clear sky conditions. Radiation lines at 25 Btu/ft²/hr intervals. Lower half shows amount of radiation falling on vertical surface. vertical surface.

For use calculator would be drawn to same scale and size as sun path diagram →p34–6. Superimposed on diagram with correct orientation radiation values can be read directly.

PREDICTING ACTUAL DURATION OF SUNLIGHT

Data on sunlight availability for any geographical location or climate should, in general, be sought from nearest meteorological station. Probability of sunlight unobscured by cloud or mist can be read off modified stereographic sun path diagram known as 'sunlight availability protractor' →(2) (→Bib074). Total number available hours sunlight obtained by adding small figures between hour lines and multiplying total, in this instance (latitude 51.5°N) by 30.4

In example →(3) by superimposing house plan on protractor total hours sunlight likely in February seem to be 1.5 × 30.4 = 45.

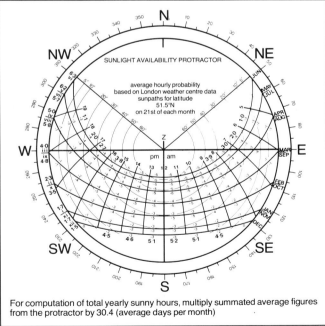

For computation of total yearly sunny hours, multiply summated average figures from the protractor by 30.4 (average days per month)

2   Sunlight availability protractor

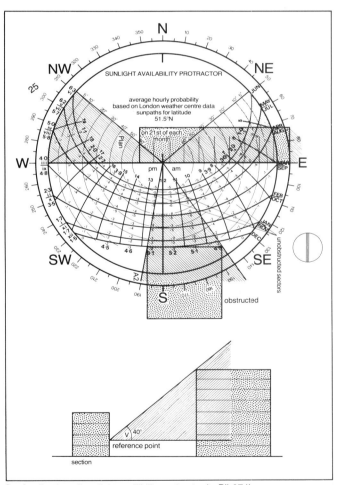

3   Application of sunlight availibility protractor (→Bib074)

Sunlight references:
→Bibliography entries 074 141 251 252

Design of houses

EXPRESSION OF PERIOD & CONVENTION

Access

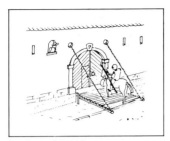

1   Around 1500 house or town was walled in & had heavy gates

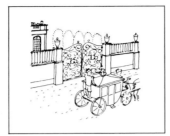

2   By 1700 wall & gate were only symbols through which glimpses of garden could be obtained

3   During 19th century secluded house was built in open surroundings with low fences

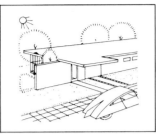

4   In 20th century there is no enclosure (especially in USA) & house stands unobtrusively in large communal park

Entrance

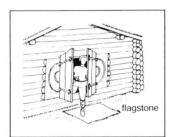

5   Around 1000 log houses had no windows, low doors & high threshold (light was admitted through opening in roof)

6   By 1500 there were heavy doors with door knocker & barred windows with bullseye panes

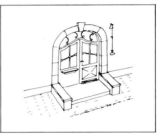

7   At about 1700 doors had attractive bars, clear glass & a bell pull

8   In 20th century covered way leads from car to entrance door (Georgian wired tempered plate glass) which electronic eye slides sideways at same time announcing visitor

Interior

9   At about 1500 there were low heavy doors, cells with sparse daylighting & floors of short, wide boards

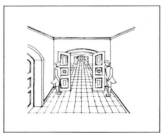

10   Around 1700 wide folding doors led into suites of rm with inlaid flooring

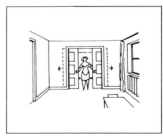

11   By 1900 sliding doors were fitted between rm, with linoleum, sliding windows & draw curtain

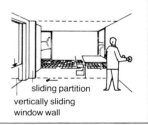

12   In 20th centurey rm are flexible, with el worked sliding walls & low unbarred windows of plate glass (tempered in USA): Venetian blinds or roller shutters provide protection against sun

Plans

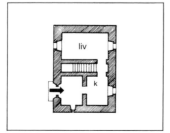

13   Timber (Walser) house of about 1500 was influenced by environment, method of construction & way of living (*eg* small windows)

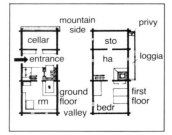

14   In stone house of c 1500 walls occupy same ar as rm so as to give protection against enemies & cold

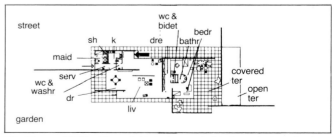

15   House of 2000 will have light steel supports & independent non-load bearing curtain walling & partitions whose composition provides protection against bad weather & affords sound & heat insulation: open planning probable, with no doors between liv ar, dr and ha

Between 1500's and present time science, technology and industry have transformed outlooks, forms and, not least, appearance of our society. House no longer fortress or crude shelter against climate; it is, or should be, a beautiful unobstructive framework for our lives – open to nature but protected from it.

Everyone has different concept; but the creative ability of the individual dictates how far he is able to transfer his experience into reality and express it through the material at his disposal. Some clients and their architects are still in the 16th century but a few of each have already arrived in the 20th; if the right centuries meet then a happy marriage between client and architect is assured.

House organisation

SUBDIVISION OF SPACE, FROM 1-ROOM DWELLING TO PALACE

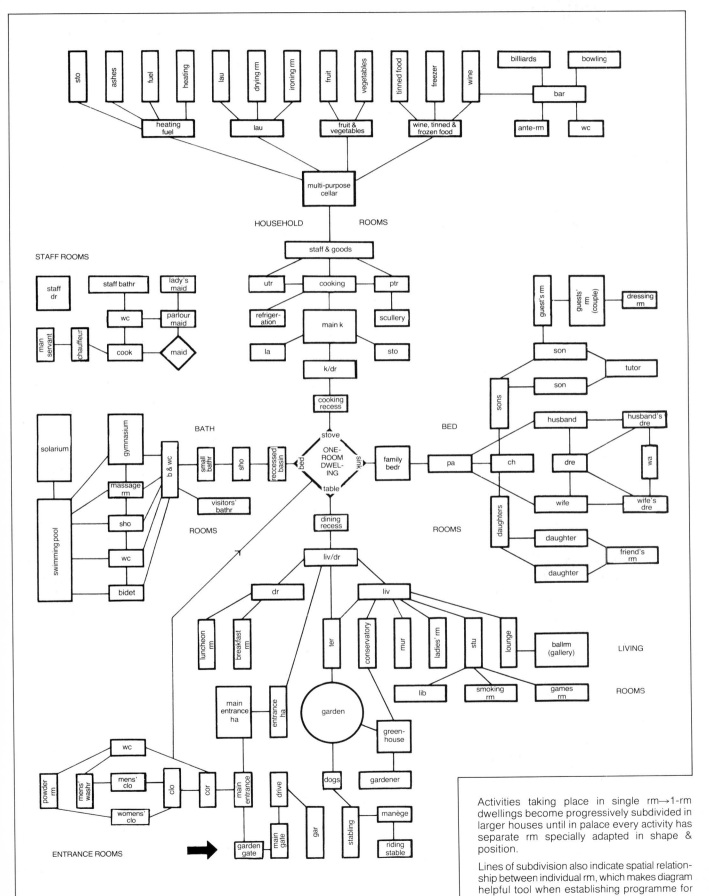

Activities taking place in single rm→1-rm dwellings become progressively subdivided in larger houses until in palace every activity has separate rm specially adapted in shape & position.

Lines of subdivision also indicate spatial relationship between individual rm, which makes diagram helpful tool when establishing programme for houses of all kinds.

Houses

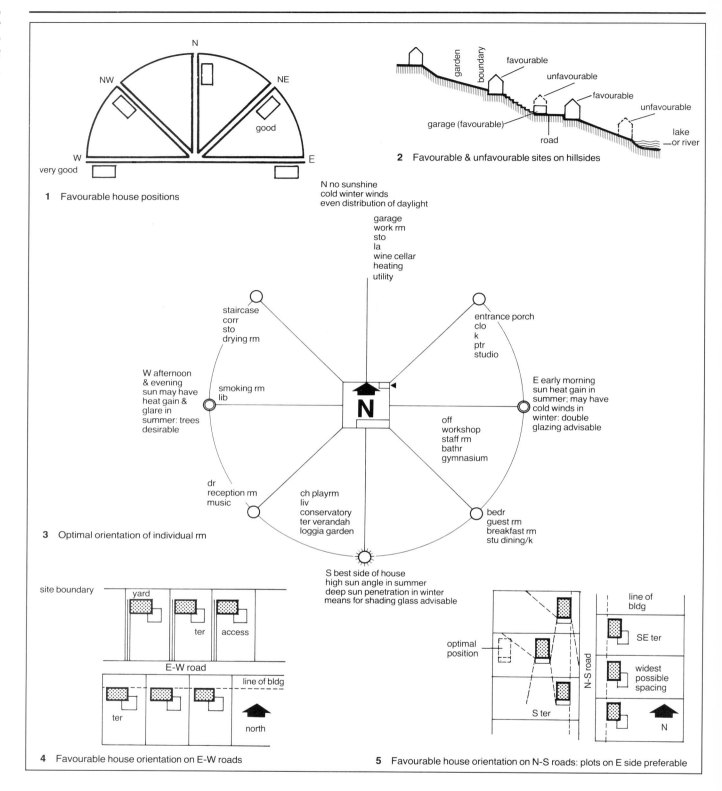

1 Favourable house positions

2 Favourable & unfavourable sites on hillsides

N no sunshine
cold winter winds
even distribution of daylight

garage
work rm
sto
la
wine cellar
heating
utility

staircase
corr
sto
drying rm

entrance porch
clo
k
ptr
studio

W afternoon
& evening
sun may have
heat gain &
glare in
summer: trees
desirable

smoking rm
lib

E early morning
sun heat gain in
summer; may have
cold winds in
winter: double
glazing advisable

off
workshop
staff rm
bathr
gymnasium

dr
reception rm
music

ch playrm
liv
conservatory
ter verandah
loggia garden

bedr
guest rm
breakfast rm
stu dining/k

3 Optimal orientation of individual rm

S best side of house
high sun angle in summer
deep sun penetration in winter
means for shading glass advisable

4 Favourable house orientation on E-W roads

5 Favourable house orientation on N-S roads: plots on E side preferable

EXTERNAL INFLUENCES ON HOUSE PLAN

Siting & orientation

Principles of positioning house on plot illustrated diagramatically →(1). For detached house plot on south side of E-W road most favourable, permitting entrance and services to be placed near road while living rm and bedr lie away from road, face sun and have access to garden.

Arrangements on E-W and N-S roads shown in detail →(3)(4). Houses on hillsides should generally be placed towards higher parts of their plots →(2). Prevailing winds for each site must be considered in planning for cold and heat protection.

Orientation also →p33–7

Rules for siting detached houses also apply to dwellings grouped in pairs or in rows. Some of factors considered on following pages, eg problems of access, which are most extreme in terrace (row) houses, apply to an extent to detached houses because of benefits, in road and service costs and depth of garden, which generally accrue from keeping plots narrow.

Safeguarding against obstruction

Where neighbouring plots already built on, position and plan of house can be adapted to known surroundings; otherwise possibility of future development must be taken into account. Architect has duty avoid undue obstruction of daylight over adjoining land likely to be developed for housing →p33.

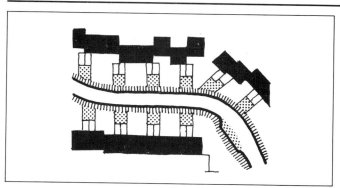

1   Residents' & visitor's parking within boundary of property: note service vehicle parking ar

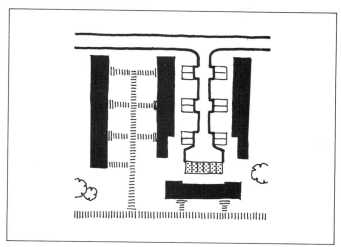

2   Residents' parking partly within boundary of property & partly communal

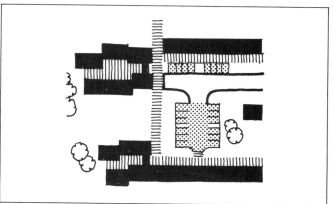

3   All parking communal

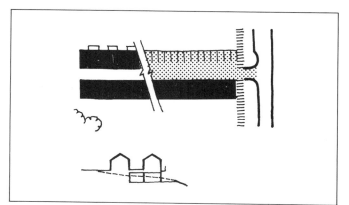

4   Parking ar off covered access below pedestrian deck

ACCESS

Access to dwelling

5 basic systems can be distinguished;

Houses and footpaths along road with no segregation of vehicular and pedestrian traffic: implies no through traffic, no on-street parking →(1).

Road and footpath on opposite sides of house: implies house design permitting access either side without loss of privacy; requires children's play area other than road →(2).

Vehicular access stopped short of houses: limited by access distance (46 m for most services: 61 m in USA); requires particularly well designed and maintained parking and garaging →(3).

Vertical segregation of vehicles and pedestrians: expensive, suits high density of steeply sloping sites →(4).

Primarily pedestrian access to small groups of houses shared with private cars and light delivery vehicles: requires careful design to enforce low speeds and restrict use to legitimate access →(5).

Access roads

Access roads to houses can be subdivided into 2 groups →p42.

General access roads: accommodate service vehicles, cars and, depending on layout system, frontage access or occasional visitor parking. Design to limit speed at junction with local distributor road.

Minor access roads: designed to allow slow speed vehicle penetration of pedestrian priority area, serve up to 25 houses, speeds kept low by width, alignment, surface texture and visibility provision, possibly hump or chicane at entrance. May be cul-de-sac with turning at end, short loop, or lead to restricted vehicle/pedestrian mixed courtyard.

Garaging the car

3 methods of garaging or parking car must also be considered; within or partly within house, adjoining house, separate from it. First 2 of these will affect house plan→p100–1 (→Bib225).

Design standards

National and local standards for zoning and subdivision reg should guide planner. Road widths and construction, footpaths, frontages, density, housing types usually established by codes and/or local reg.

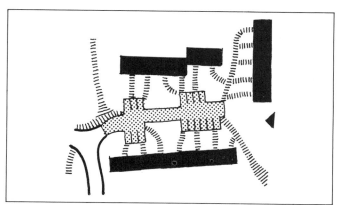

5   Access ar shared by pedestrians & vehicles

Houses

ACCESS

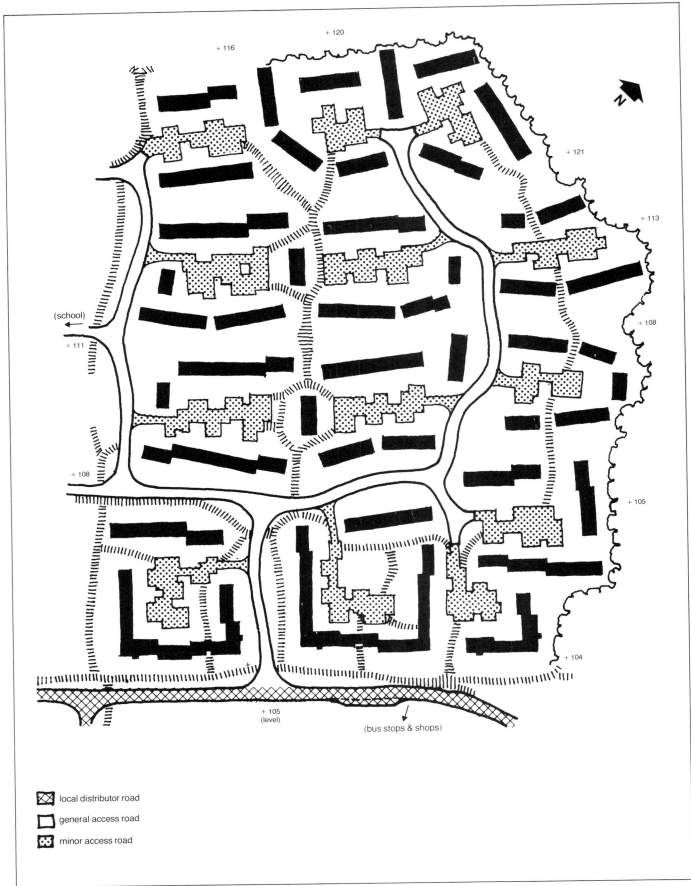

+ 116
+ 120
+ 121
+ 113
+ 108
(school)
+ 111
+ 108
+ 105
+ 104
+ 105
(level)
(bus stops & shops)

local distributor road

general access road

minor access road

Road hierarchy within housing ar: example makes use of shared pedestrian/vehicle courts as minor access roads

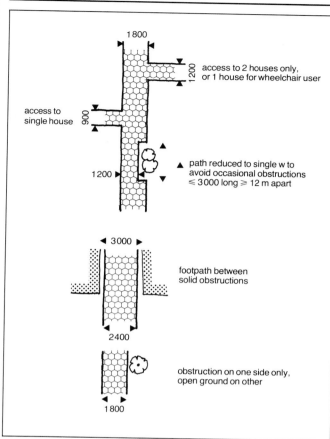

1 Pedestrian access & traffic routes

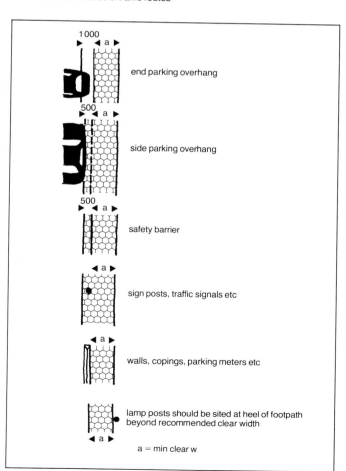

2 Footpaths: min clear w

ACCESS

Primary access

Footpaths should run as directly as possible to major attractions (schools, shops, bus stops) away from heavy traffic roads. Should be well lit and overlooked (for security), sheltered and avoid steep gradients. Use ramps rather than steps, or ramps as alternative routes where steps necessary. Critical design width should allow prams and wheelchairs to pass and clear obstructions. Min 1 800, but on pedestrian traffic routes generally allow 2400 on open ground, 3000 between bldg and fences. Footpaths between road or pedestrian traffic route and small groups of houses can be 1 800, 1 200 for 2 houses (USA min 1 220), 900 for single house →(1)(2). Max distance from road to door of house, 46 m.

Secondary access

Additional footways to serve garden side of houses, garage courts etc can be 900–1 000 between fences, 600 in open ground →p47(6) 106(21). Plan to discourage use as through routes.

SERVICES

Statutory utilities (*eg* gas, water, el, telephone) should be supplied with details of any proposed housing development at early stage in order to agree service routes between different interests and avoid later adjustment, which can be both time consuming and costly. In UK they will generally prefer to lay their services within public road, as this gives them certain automatic statutory rights of access; but in segregated layouts or those designed with narrow road widths this may prove inconvenient or uneconomic and alternative routes may need to be agreed. Perhaps preferable: rear-of-block service strips, easily accessible and surfaced with materials which may readily be removed and reinstated.

Television

Master aerials for television signal boosting often require licence or permit. Television cables below ground should be kept min of 300 from el supply or lighting cables and well away from telephone cables. Recommended depth for laying television cables: 450.

ACCESS FOR DISABLED

Housing for disabled →p85–7; internal access →p86. Spaces needed for wheelchairs →(3).

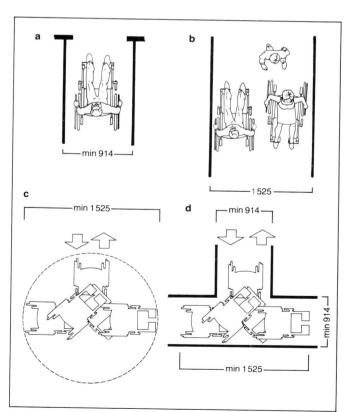

3 Min clear w: **a** for single wheelchair **b** for 2 wheelchairs **c** 1 525 dia space **d** T-shaped space for 180° turn

Houses

a

space[1]	min ar ft²					least dimension
	lu with 0 br	lu with 1 br	lu with 2 br	lu with 3 br	lu with 4 br	
lr	na	160	160	170	180	11'6''
dr	na	100	100	110	120	8'4''
br (primary)[2]	na	120	120	120	120	9'4''
br (secondary)	na	na	80	80	80	8'0''
total ar br	na	120	200	280	280	
ohr	na	80	80	80	80	8'0''

b

combined space [1]	min ar ft²					least dimension
	lu with 0 br	lu with 1 br	lu with 2 br	lu with 3 br	lu with 4 br	
lr-da	na	210	210	230	250	see note 3
lr-da-sl	250	na	na	na	na	
lr-da-k	na	270	270	300	330	
lr-sl	210	na	na	na	na	
k-da	100	120	120	140	160	

[1] abbreviations: br: bedr da: dining ar dr: dining rm k: kitchen lr: living rm lu: living unit na: not applicable 0 br: lu with no separate bedr ohr: other habitable rm sl: sleeping ar
[2] primary bedr shall have at least 1 uninterrupted wall space of at least 10'
[3] min dimensions of combined rm shall be sum of dimensions of individual single rm involved except for overlap or combined use of space

1   USA min rm sizes   **a** for separate rm   **b** for combined spaces

	ft	in
habitable rm	7	6
ha, bathr	7	0
luminous ceiling	7	0
sloping ceilings	7	6 at least for ½ rm with no portion less than 5' 0''
basements without habitable spaces	6	8

2   USA min ceiling heights

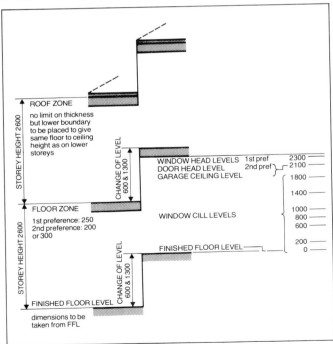

3   UK vertical controlling dimensions

STANDARDS & REGULATIONS

Controlling dimensions

Recommendations for horizontal and vertical controlling dimensions for housing have been developed in order to make use of dimensionally coordinated standard components. (Application in UK public sector housing →Bib228.)

Horizontal controlling dimensions should be, in descending order of preference, as follows:
first: multiples of 300
second: multiples of 100
third: multiples of 50 up to 300
For house planning to these dimensions a 300 grid is used.

Vertical controlling dimensions more closely defined. Heights of door openings and between floors differ over relatively small ranges. For dimensions for housing, with preferences for public sector in UK →(3). Min rm sizes USA →(1).

Ceiling heights

In USA FHA says ceiling heights must be such as not to create an unpleasant sensation and not to restrict physically movement of occupants and furnishings. Ceiling heights clear under beams or other obstructions →(2).

BUILDING REGULATIONS

Distinct differences in legal intention result in different degrees of control over housing design in different countries: *eg* reg in England and Wales limited to securing health and safety of occupants and other users; in Scotland designed to secure health, safety and convenience of occupants and public at large, imposing min space and eqp standards; in USA FHA, HUD reg and state and local codes apply (→Bib233).

Most houses built for sale in UK by private builders conform to standards set by National House-Builders Council (→Bib512); in USA generally conform to FHA standard min sizes and construction as may be required by financing: also consult state and local codes.

Fire escape

In houses of more than 2 storeys fire escape must be considered (consult codes).

Essentially single stairway in such house should be separated from all rm by fr construction and self-closing fr doors and lead to hall or passage giving access to outside air at ground level. This has effect of prohibiting open planning on ground or intermediate storeys unless alternative escape routes, *eg* by balcony to adjoining house, provided from rm on upper storeys.

Houses

RELATIONSHIP TO OTHER BUILDINGS

Daylight & sunlight →p27–37

Consult relevant reg and codes for daylighting standards in habitable rm; these also provide for protection of residential bldg and undeveloped sites from obstruction of daylight by new development. These provisions normally adopted in England & Wales by planning authority in development control (to some extent mandatory in Scotland). Proposed bldg can be tested for both distance from its own boundary and distance from other bldg by using permissible height indicators (→Bib251). USA →252 and city bldg codes.

So far as possible rm should receive sunlight at some part of day throughout most of year but this not generally enforced by reg or development control. Angles and direction of sunlight can be established hourly for any time of year at any latitude: examples for lat 51°50′ N →p36. Further orientation factors →p34–6 40 46.

Visual privacy

Many planning authorities seek to prevent overlooking of houses from neighbouring houses or across road (controlled by bldg reg in Scotland). Rule of thumb distance of 18 m often stated but is restrictive and ineffective since visibility affected by types of windows involved and their respective levels and incidence to one another. As with other environmental factors privacy must be considered in relation to competing benefits and in high density developments it is matter for careful consideration in design and layout.

Use of blind side or single-aspect house designs will help, *eg* on sloping sites or where footpaths pass close to houses; effective screening of private gardens also important →(1)(2). However, privacy should not be achieved at cost of isolation: ideally degree of screening for visual privacy should be within control of residents.

Privacy from noise

Houses built near distributor roads, or main highways best protected from noise nuisance by embankments or other land formation →(3). Privacy can, however, be improved by use of suitable house plans with rm facing away from noise source (→Bib240 254).

Spread of fire

Bldg reg generally restrict distances between houses built of combustible materials, such as timber, shingles or thatch, and their own plot boundaries; where non-combustible materials used extent of window and door openings in walls close to boundary might be restricted to prevent spread of fire to adjoining property by radiation.

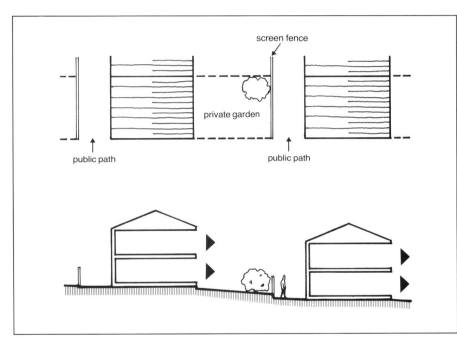

1 Privacy secured by use of single aspect houses

3 Noise attenuation: ar will be suitable for development with conventional house types

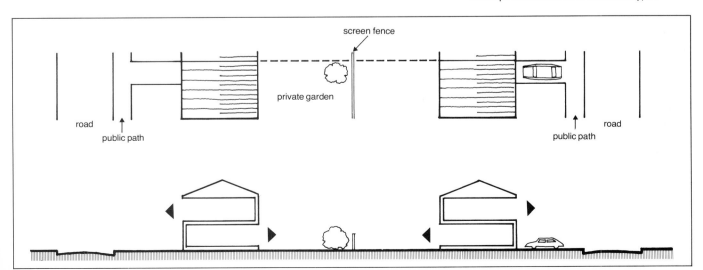

2 Privacy secured by use of reverse aspect houses: best orientation E-W

Houses

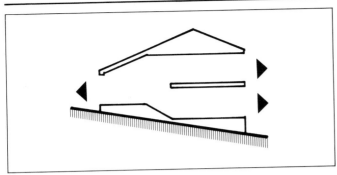

1   Split level

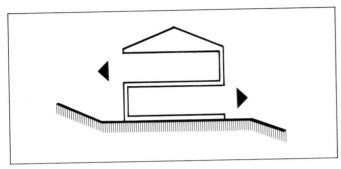

2   'Upside down'

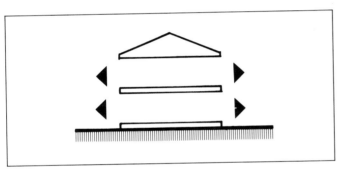

3a   Dual aspect

SITE TOPOGRAPHY

Effect of gradient

Where slopes moderate, choice of plan affected little by gradient; on steeper slopes some forms of plan can be used to greater advantage than others. Where houses run parallel to contours use of wider frontage houses minimises need for underbuilding or excavation. Savings thus made can counterbalance usually adverse equation between wide frontage and greater servicing and development costs. Very steep sites can, however, present opportunities for imaginative use of split-level plans or entry to upper floors →(1). Houses running across contours, especially in terraces (rows), should employ narrow frontage plans, stepping at each house or pair of houses.

North slopes

North slopes aggravate problems of maintaining density while providing adequate sunlight to each house and garden. Simple solution: reverse usual rule and place each house at lower end of its plot, with access on north side but on severe slopes spacing required might be excessive. Solution then might be to employ 'upside-down' section, placing living rm on upper floors where they can enjoy sun from south and views in each direction →(2). Houses running across contours can be particularly advantageous on north slopes, since no garden need be immediately overshadowed by houses and all rm will get sunlight.

Aspect

In considering orientation →p40, access, privacy and effect of gradient there has recurred the concept of aspect, an important characteristic relating house plan to conditions of its site.
4 models can be distinguished →(3);

Dual aspect: rm look out in both directions, to access and garden sides

Single, blind-side, or controlled aspect: rm other than kitchen and service rm look out in 1 direction only – usually garden side

Reverse aspect: rm on ground storey and upper storeys look out in opposite directions

Open aspect: ideal detached or semi-detached condition where rm can look out in 3 or 4 directions without constraint.

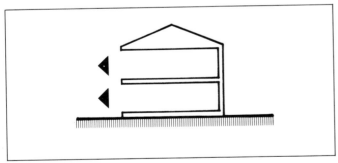

3b   Single aspect

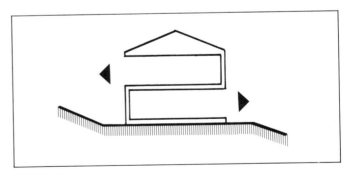

3d   Reverse aspect

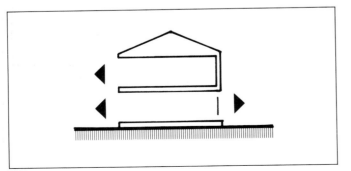

3c   Controlled aspect

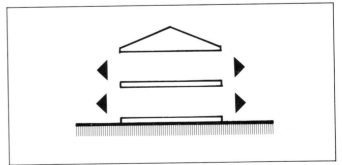

3e   Open aspect

HOUSE PLAN: INTERNAL INFLUENCES

Determining factors
Main internal factors affecting selection of house plan:

mode of horizontal circulation within house,
user requirements,
appropriate standards & regulations
site orientation & climate →p30 40 46

HOUSE PLAN: CIRCULATION

Circulation within house determined primarily by type of access appropriate to external conditions and layout →(1): 5 modes of horizontal circulation can be distinguished;

Through circulation
This →(2) provides circulation from entry to garden side by-passing all living and working areas. No secondary access to garden side needed. Through circulation suitable for all forms of entry and particularly appropriate where entry possible from only one side.

Through-storage circulation
In small terrace (row) houses through circulation though desirable can require excessive proportion of whole ground-storey area. Modification permits circulation from entry to garden side through hall and sto →(3). This arrangement suitable for all forms of entry.

Through-kitchen circulation
Provides circulation from entry to garden side through hall and kitchen →(4). Appropriate in layouts which provide secondary access to garden side; but can be used where there is none.

Single circulation
From point of entry garden can be reached only by passing through living rm →(5). This type plan should only be used in layouts which provide secondary access to garden side. Secondary access will normally be necessary only in mid-terrace houses but layout situations can arise when siting of other bldg imposes similar conditions on end-of-terrace, detached and semi-detached houses.

By-pass circulation
Garden side can be reached outside house but within property limits *eg* by path or through garage →(6).

Through atrium circulation →(7)

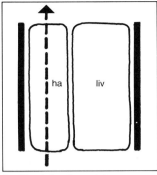

2 Circulation through ha

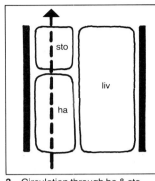

3 Circulation through ha & sto

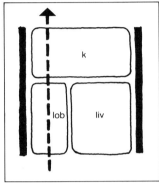

4 Circulation through ha & k

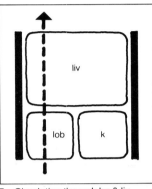

5 Circulation through ha & liv

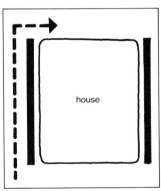

6 By pass circulation

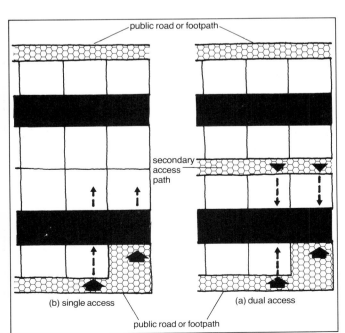

1 Access to property **a** from both sides **b** from one side only

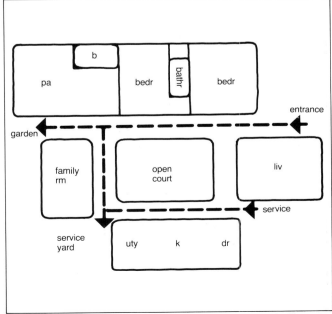

7 'Through atrium' circulation seen in USA single family detached house

Houses

HOUSE PLAN

User requirements

Where house not designed for known client, user requirements can most briefly be summarised in statement of number of rm (not counting kitchen, bathr etc) in house and number of people intended to accommodate. From normative standard of 1P/rm higher standards characterised by greater degree of specialisation →p39. Such specialisation has in past time reached astonishing lengths – one English Victorian country house said to have contained rm for ironing newspapers: nowadays degree of sub-division associated with palace unlikely to be reached. What does happen is that houses designed or adapted to meet special needs, whether, *eg* for musician, orchid enthusiast or disabled housewife, are more specialised, either by planning or by higher level of servicing, in 1 direction. This form of specialisation secured by adaptation: will not generally affect process of plan selection set out here.

User requirement check list →(1)

In absence of known client plans should be tested by list of questions about house that might be asked by user. In any such analysis all plans will not meet all requirements satisfactorily; it must be for designer to judge which priorities should be achieved (→Bib234).

STANDARDS & REGULATIONS

Housing standards

Consult reg. Standards for dwellings in public sector in Britain →(2) based on Parker Morris Committee's report (→Bib233). Mandatory only for new bldg by local authorities and housing associations these in practice provide quality platform against which new housing can be judged. Although min floor areas stated for various household sizes emphasis functional rather than quantitive. Rm layouts and house plans should be shown to be able to accommodate furniture and domestic activities that they can be expected to contain.

For USA standards consult reg (→FHA HUD) and state and local codes; min rm sizes →p44(1).

entrances	1 is protection from weather provided at entrances? 2 is there space in ha for receiving visitors? 3 is there convenient sto for outdoor clothing & pram? 4 can meters be read without entering living ar? (NB outside in USA)
living ar	5 is there space for required furniture in sensible arrangement? 6 is there sufficient space to seat guests in dining ar? 7 does liv face private garden?
kitchen	8 is there direct access, on same level, from k to dining ar? 9 is work surface adequate, free from interruption & obstruction? 10 is 'work triangle' (sink – cooker – frig/larder) compact & free from cross-circulation? 11 has possible use of k by elderly or disabled people been considered? 12 is there space for additional eqp, or larger items, likely to be used in furniture? 13 has k view of outside world – for callers, toddlers' play etc?
bedr	14 is there space for required furniture in sensible arrangements – consider use of single beds? 15 can bedr be used for child's homework, entertaining friends & hobbies?
bathr	16 is bathr convenient for bathing baby? 17 has use of bathr by elderly people, or invalids, been considered? 18 is there space for appropriate bathr eqp, hanging towels etc?
sto & accessibility	19 are refuse bin & fuel sto accessible, conveniently placed for collection & delivery? 20 can bicycles be taken outside, pram put in garden, & garden refuse removed, without passing through living ar?

1 User requirement check list

N = net space[1] S = general sto space[2]		number of persons (*ie* bed-spaces) per dwelling						
		1	2	3	4	5	6	7
houses				m²				
1 storey	N	30	44.5	57	67	75.5	84	
	S	3	4	4	4.5	4.5	4.5	
2 storey	N				72	82	92.5	108
(semi or end)	S				4.5	4.5	4.5	6.5
(mid-terrace)	N				74.5	85	92.5	108
	S				4.5	4.5	4.5	6.5
3 storey	N					94	98	112
	S					4.5	4.5	6.5
flats	N	30	44.5	57	70*	79	86.5	
	S	2.5	3	3	3.5	3.5	3.5	
maisonettes	N				72	82	92.5	108
	S				3.5	3.5	3.5	3.5
		*(67 if balc access)						

[1] Net space is ar of all floors in dwelling measured to unfinished faces; includes ar of each floor taken up by stairways, by partitions & by any chimney breasts, flues & heating appliances & ar of any external wc; excludes floor ar of general sto space (S), dustbin sto, gar, balc, any part of rm less than 1500 high because of sloping ceilings & any porch or covered way open to air; in single access house →p000 any space within sto required for passage from 1 side of house to other, taken as 700 wide, shall be provided in addition to ar in table.

[2] General sto space to be provided exclusive of any dustbin sto, fuel sto or pram space within sto ar, & in single access house, space within sto required for passage from 1 side of house to other; in houses some sto space may be on upper floor, separate from any linen sto or wa, but at least 2.5 m² shall be at ground level; in flats and maisonettes up to 1.5 m² may be provided outside dwelling; in some circumstances part of gar integral with or adjoining dwelling can count towards general sto space →Bib479 (also gives schedules of furniture to be accommodated)

2 Min ar for dwellings to accommodate various household sizes (UK standards: USA →p44)

1 Houses at Dundee Scotland: variations in simple basic plan   Arch Baxter Clark & Paul

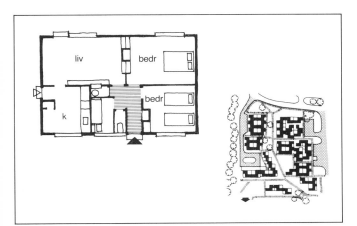

2 'Arcon' prefabricated house   Arch Arcon

SELECTING PLANS

Classification of plans

From external and internal determining factors set out in previous pages, basic characteristics of house plan can be stated under following heads:

levels: 1, 2, 3 storeys or split-level
aspect: dual, single, reverse or open →p46
horizontal circulation: through, through-sto, through-kitchen or single, core circulation through atrium →p47
number of rm and size of household: stated as *eg* (4 rm, 5 person).

These characteristics provide basis for classification of all house plans. To them is added vertical circulation when houses of more than 1 storey considered.

Plan development

Plan selection not initially affected by household size or specialised user requirements. First three heads of classification (levels, aspect and circulation) narrow choice to number of plan arrangements at this stage expressed in simplest possible terms →(1). This example shows how 1-storey house plans basically similar developed to accommodate different household sizes.

ONE-STOREY HOUSES

1-storey house gives greatest planning freedom, only planning determinants being aspect and horizontal circulation. Consequently both simplest and most luxurious houses often planned on 1 storey →(1)(2)(3)(4)p50–1.

Relationship between kitchen and bathr horizontal: economies in placing them together but savings in cost may not be great when weighed against user convenience →p51(6).

3 Old person's bungalow

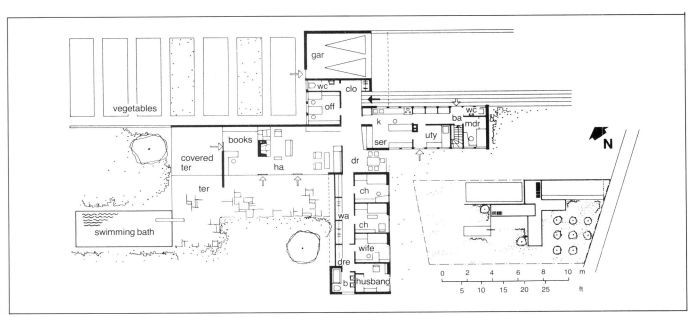

4 Large private house   Arch Biecker

Houses

PLANS: CLASSIFICATION

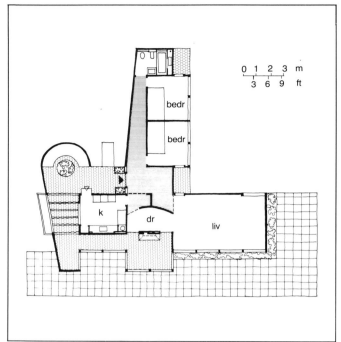

1   House at Whipsnade England   Arch Lubetkin & Tecton

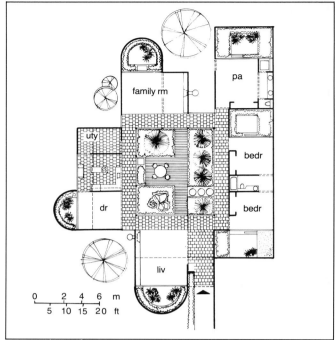

2   Single family detached house built round atrium Cleveland Ohio USA
Arch Hirum A Blunden

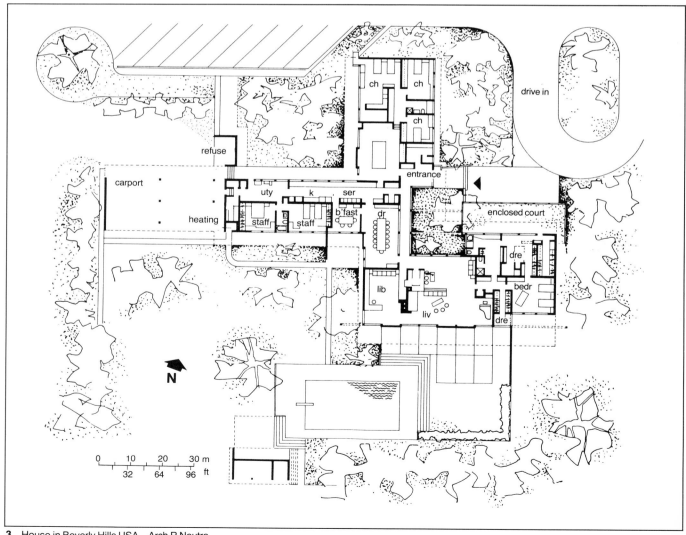

3   House in Beverly Hills USA   Arch R Neutra

PLANS: CLASSIFICATION

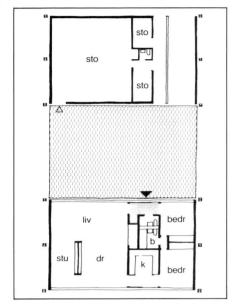

1 House for an artist   Arch Rogers

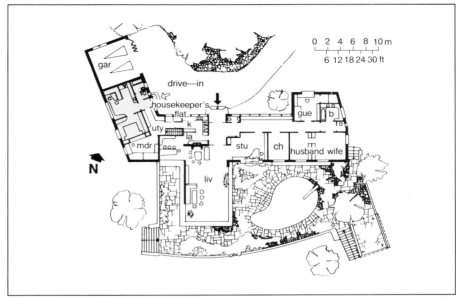

2 Bungalow with self-contained flat for house-keeper or chauffeur   Arch Neufert

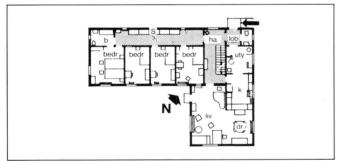

3 L-shaped house with day & night wings   Arch Kossler & Peter

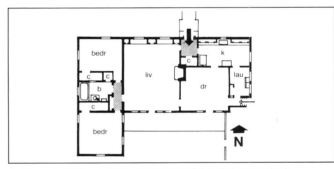

4 House in California USA with ter facing S & bathr between bedr
Arch Donald

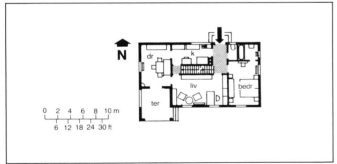

5 House for couple without ch: good relationship of ter, k & liv
Arch Erchmannsdorfer & Kindler

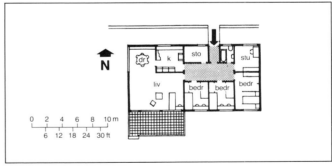

6 House to sleep 6   Arch L Hilberseimer

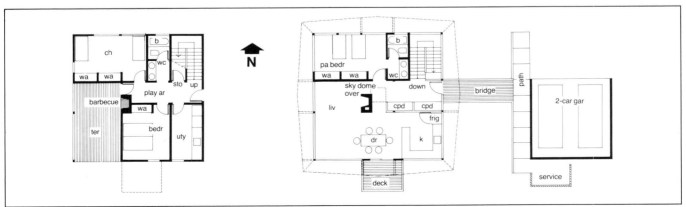

7 American 2-storey house with upper floor entrance (site is not flat)   Arch E H & M K Hunter

Houses

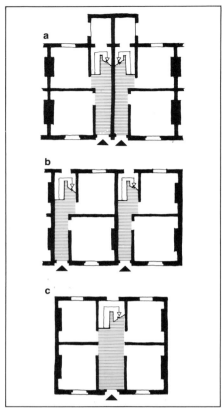

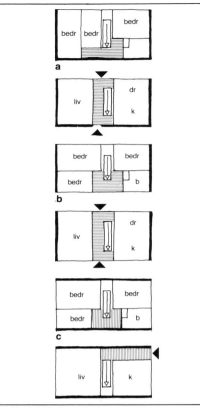

1 Dog-leg stair has great planning advantages & much used in traditional English house; note in ter house how access to small rm & services can be provided at half-landings **a** Victorian ter house **b** Georgian ter house **c** Georgian detached house

2 Straight flight at right angles to horizontal circulation often attractive in saving circulation space but divides plan rigidly: in some instances not disadvantage, particularly in blind-side planning **a** central stair through house, single aspect plan **b** central stair through house, dual aspect plan **c** central stair across house, dual aspect plan

MORE THAN ONE STOREY

New planning determinants introduced: vertical circulation, relationship between kitchen and bathr, which becomes vertical as well as horizontal, and balancing of ground and upper storey accn.

Vertical circulation: the stair

In all houses of more than 1 storey plan is influenced by position and design of stair. Stair and its location affect constructional system to be employed: in repetitive house design most important single standardising component.

Stairs differ in design (straight flight or dog-leg) and in position. These, in combination, impose different planning effects. To provide best circulation aim is to arrive on first storey as near as possible to middle of house; best choice of position and type of stair to achieve this related to plan shape →(1).

Kitchen & bathr

These comprise most heavily serviced part of house; economy in plumbing and water supply systems and problem of accommodating bulky soil and waste stack at lower level eased by placing one above the other →(4)(5).

Balance of ground & upper storey accn

In some house types, designed for both small and large households, total area required for bedr and related accn does not balance living, kitchen and other areas usually placed on ground storey: this because space allotted for common use does not increase proportionally to family size, as do number and sizes of bedr. Economic design for small houses, say for 3 or 4 persons, employs 1¼-storey arrangement, basically of 1-storey construction with open roof truss to enable roof space to be used for bedr. Such roof on 1-storey house can also facilitate future extension of small house. →p78.

Opposite problem occurs in 2-storey houses designed for more than 6 persons, where house plans can be adapted by providing bedr over pends, linking houses across pedestrian routes →(6)(7).

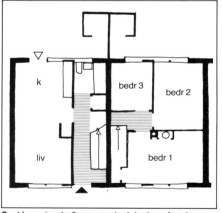

3 Very simple & economical design of ter house with 'farmhouse' k & bathr on ground floor

4 5 Economy achieved by placing bath over k

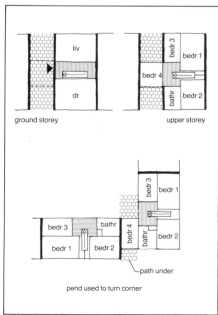

ground storey   upper storey

pend used to turn corner

6 7 Bedr over pends means of providing extra rm

MORE THAN ONE STOREY

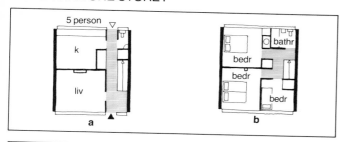

1 2 2 'through ha' type plans with solid fuel heating & chimney: note →(2) how wider frontage with straight flight stair on perimeter leads to long upper sto circulation   Arch National Building Agency (UK)

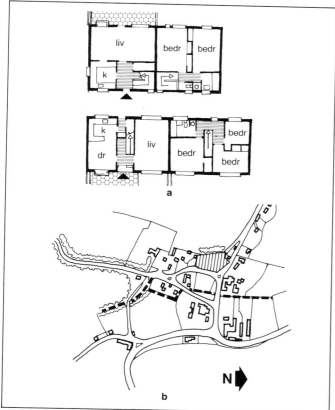

3   Houses at Moulton Yorkshire England: bedr insulated from one another by cpd & staircase; note influence of stair type on upper storey plan
Arch Butterworth

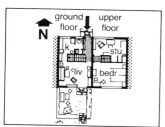

5   Small Swedish type with sho next to k on ground floor   Arch Swedish Architects Cooperative

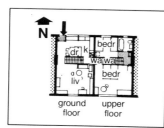

6   Larger type with dr next to k & centre stair   Arch W Kraatz

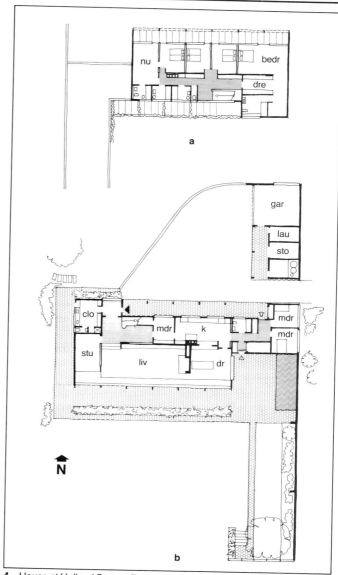

4   House at Halland Sussex England   Arch Chermayeff

7   Ter houses in Klampenborg Denmark: appearance of detached houses achieved by staggering   Arch A Jacoben

Houses

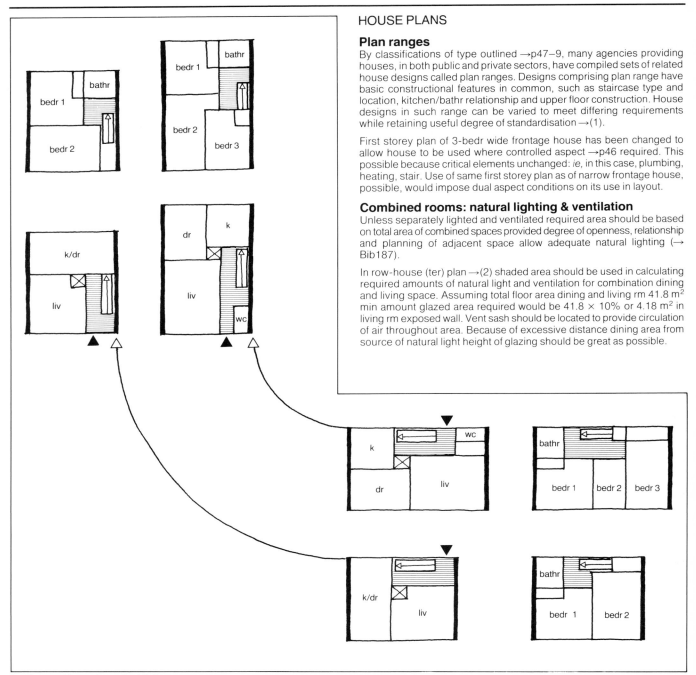

1   Range of house types for 4 & 5 person wide & narrow frontage houses   Arch NBA (Scotland)

HOUSE PLANS

Plan ranges

By classifications of type outlined →p47–9, many agencies providing houses, in both public and private sectors, have compiled sets of related house designs called plan ranges. Designs comprising plan range have basic constructional features in common, such as staircase type and location, kitchen/bathr relationship and upper floor construction. House designs in such range can be varied to meet differing requirements while retaining useful degree of standardisation →(1).

First storey plan of 3-bedr wide frontage house has been changed to allow house to be used where controlled aspect →p46 required. This possible because critical elements unchanged: *ie,* in this case, plumbing, heating, stair. Use of same first storey plan as of narrow frontage house, possible, would impose dual aspect conditions on its use in layout.

Combined rooms: natural lighting & ventilation

Unless separately lighted and ventilated required area should be based on total area of combined spaces provided degree of openness, relationship and planning of adjacent space allow adequate natural lighting (→ Bib187).

In row-house (ter) plan →(2) shaded area should be used in calculating required amounts of natural light and ventilation for combination dining and living space. Assuming total floor area dining and living rm 41.8 m² min amount glazed area required would be 41.8 × 10% or 4.18 m² in living rm exposed wall. Vent sash should be located to provide circulation of air throughout area. Because of excessive distance dining area from source of natural light height of glazing should be great as possible.

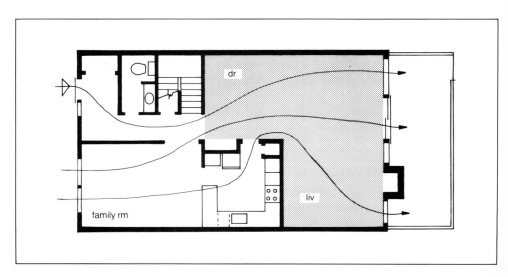

2   Combined rm: natural lighting & ventilation

KITCHENS

Kitchens best placed towards NE or NW of house and in small houses should ideally overlook entrance, front door and children's play area. Kitchen relates horizontally to front door (or tradesmen's entrance, if separate), dining rm or meal space, food sto, scullery and laundry areas, refuse sto or disposal, and outside clothes drying and toddlers' play spaces. It relates vertically to bathr, wc and other areas requiring water supply and drainage. In large houses functions of kitchen can be spread over several rm (eg laundry, utility, pantry, scullery) combined in household wing separated from rest of house to prevent spread of noise and cooking smells →p149(5).

Main activities for which kitchen designed: preparation, cooking and serving of meals and cleaning up afterwards. Ancillary activities can include clothes washing, general household mending and cleaning, eating, children's play, studying, hobbies, entertaining and general recreation.

WORKING SEQUENCE

Sequence of activities →(1) relates to sequence of fitments, worktop – cooker – worktop – sink – worktop, which is basis of modern domestic kitchen planning →(2): should never be broken by full-height fitments, doors or passageways.

Work triangle
Distance user has to walk between sink, cooker and refrigerator or larder critical in kitchen planning. Lines joining these 3 elements form what is known as 'work triangle' →(3). For normal family house combined length of sides of triangle should be between 5500 and 6000. Distance between sink and cooker should not exceed 1800; should never be crossed by through circulation.

Sinks
Sinks require good natural light: best placed under window; should not normally be more than 2300 from waste stack or external drain. Sinks should be kept away from corners →(4) and there should be plenty of room to stand in front of draining side, though in small kitchens washing bowl of double sink may be placed towards corner →(5).

Cookers & work tops
Cooker should never be placed in front of window but should, where possible, be provided with ventilating hood →(6). It should not be placed below wall cupboards and gas cooker should be away from doors where draughts might blow out burners. Worktop should be provided on each side; where cooker adjoins corner fitting return of at least 400 should be allowed for easy standing and access space. Low level cooker requires space of at least 1200 in front for access →(6). Adjacent worktops should be at same level as cooker top; if change of level required should be at point at least 400 from cooker →(7).

Split level cookers with separate hob and wall oven increasingly popular. May be 1 or 2 (stacked) above worktop height. No perfect location: if in continuous worktop interrupt work flow; if outside work triangle extra travel. Open door may be danger to children.

Space for casual meals to be taken should be allowed at worktop height in working kitchen, and ideally in working part of dining-kitchen.

Refrigerator
Most difficult of kitchen eqp to place. Important component of work triangle; should adjacent worktop space. Frig door should open away from work area for food access; should not block passageway or hit another door when opening.

Also →p58–9

DINING-KITCHENS

Kitchen may be associated with separate but related dining space to become dining-kitchen. Separation can be achieved by arranging fitments to provide degree of screening or by change in level of floor finish (undesirable). Dining area should be planned in same way as small dining rm.

Kitchen may also be enlarged to contain dining table and chairs, without separation, to form 'farmhouse kitchen': more economical in space than either separate kitchen and dining rm or dining-kitchen but offers less flexibility in use.

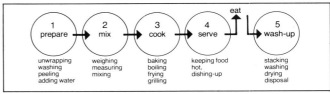

1 Sequence of activities

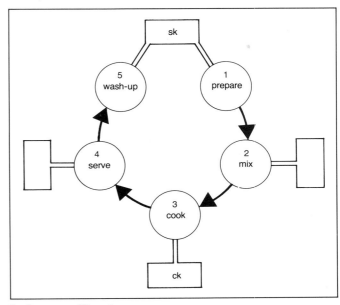

2 Sequence of fitments

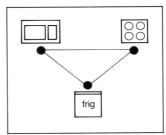

3 Work triangle (sk – ck – frig)

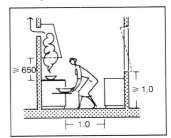

4 Single sk

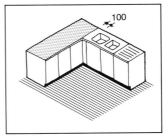

5 Double sk

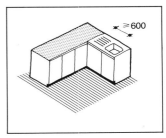

6 Low-level oven needs adequate space in front: note extractor hood over ck

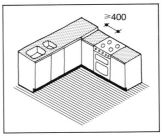

7 Change in level

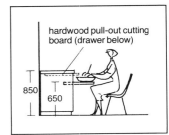

8 Provide place for working seated, preferably with pull-out worktop having drawer & cutting board above

Houses

work centre	no of bedr				
	0	1	2	3	4
	min frontages				
sk[1]	475	610	610	813	813
work top, each side	381	457	533	610	762
cooker or hob space[2 3 6]	533	533	610	762	762
work top 1 side[4]	381	457	533	610	762
frig space[5]	762	762	914	914	914
work top 1 side[1]	381	381	381	381	457
mixing work top	533	762	914	914	1067

Notes: [1] when dishwasher provided 610 sk acceptable [2] where built-in wall oven installed provide 457 w work top alongside [3] cooker shall not be located under nor within 305 of window; where cpd provided above cooker 762 clearance shall be provided to bottom of unprotected cpd or 610 to bottom of protected cpd [4] provide at least 229 from edge of cooker to adjacent corner cpd and 381 from side of frig to adjacent corner cpd
[5] frig space may be 533 when frig provided & door opens within own w [6] when cooker not provided 762 space shall be provided

1   Standards for fixtures & worktops

	number of bedr				
	0	1	2	3	4
			m²		
min shelf ar[1 2 3 4]	2.23	2.79	3.53	4.09	4.65
min drawer ar[5]	0.37	0.56	0.74	0.93	2.04

Notes: [1] dishwasher may be counted as 0.37 m² of base cpd sto [2] wall cpd over frig shall not be counted as required shelf ar [3] shelf ar above 1880 shall be counted as required ar [4] inside corner cpd shall be counted as 50% of shelf ar, except where revolving shelves used actual shelf ar may be counted [5] drawer ar in excess of required ar may be counted as shelf ar if drawer at least 152 d

2   k sto shelf ar

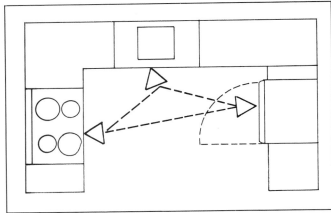

3   U shape k

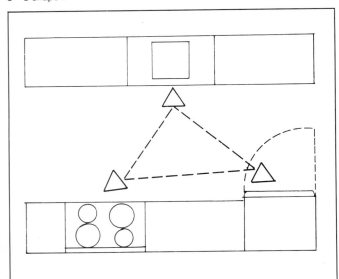

4   Corr plan k

KITCHENS

Fixtures & work tops

USA standards require kitchen area which provides for efficient food preparation, serving and sto, as well as utensil sto and cleaning up after meals. Provision of fixtures and work tops →(1); work tops approx 610 deep and 914 high. Clearance between base cpd fronts in food preparation area min 1 020

Required work tops may be combined when placed between 2 fixtures: cooker, frig, sink. Such work top shall have min frontage equal to that of larger of work tops being combined. Kitchen sto →p75.

→(2) gives recommended kitchen sto shelf area; min ⅓ required area to be located in base or wall cpd; min 60% required area to be enclosed by cpd doors.

Kitchen layouts

→(3)−(7) show various kitchen plans.

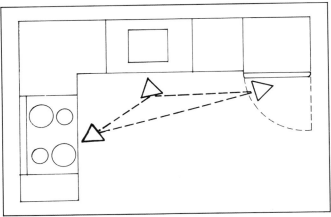

5   L shape k

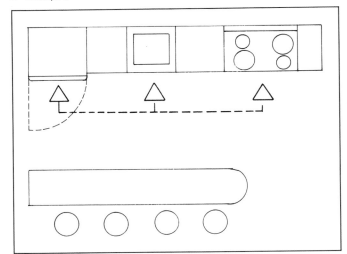

6   Straight wall plan k

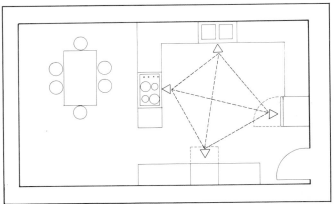

7   Square plan k with dining ar

KITCHENS: EXAMPLES

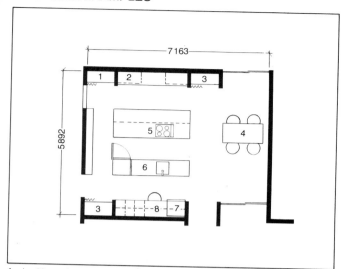

1 k with sewing ar & home off 1 ptr 2 sewing 3 cpd 4 family dining or off 5 hob 6 sk 7 freezer 8 home off files   Arch John R Peterson

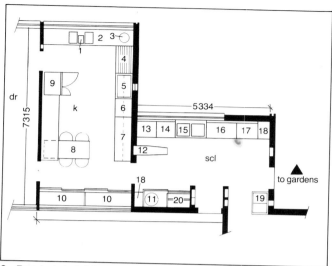

2 Farm k 1 sk 2 dishwasher 3 waste 4 cutting board 5 hob 6 oven 7 cpd over 8 family dining 9 frig/freezer 10 dry sto shelves 11 hot water 12 drop down ironing board 13 14 dryer-washer 15 sk 16 17 freezers 18 cleaning cpd 19 ventilated food sto 20 preserves, coat cpd   Arch E H & M K Hunter

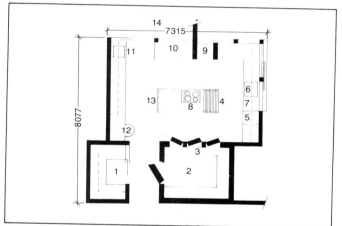

3 Gourmet cook's k 1 ptr 2 walk in frig 3 metal shelves 4 chopping block 5 marble slab 6 sk 7 dishwasher 8 hob 9 wall ovens 10 serving 11 warming tray 12 desk 13 hood ovr 14 dr   Arch Cliff May

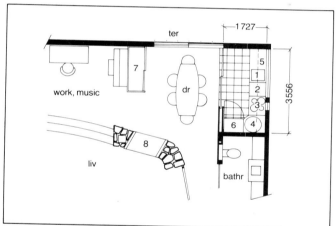

4 Efficient small k opens to or closes off from dr & ter 1 sk 2 dishwasher 3 ck 4 carrousel cpd 5 wall cpd 6 frig 7 china cpd 8 2-way fireplace Arch E H & M K Hunter

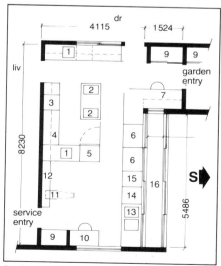

5 Combination k/uty with greenhouse 1 sk 2 hob 3 ovens 4 baking centre 5 frig 6 chest freezer 7 desk with books over 9 cpd 10 sewing 11 ironing 12 sto wall 13 lau sk 14 washer 15 dryer 16 greenhouse with sliding glass Arch E H & M K Hunter

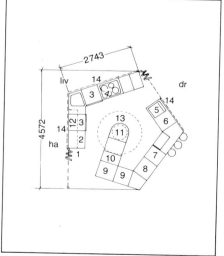

6 Home centre k *Life* magazine house 1 folding doors 2 frig 3 ovens 4 hob 5 sk 6 dishwasher 7 child's frig 8 freezer 9 washer-dryer 10 lift up mixer 11 rotating sto bin 12 cpd over 13 skylight 14 motorised wood slat blinds, lower from ceiling to worktop level   Arch M K Hunter

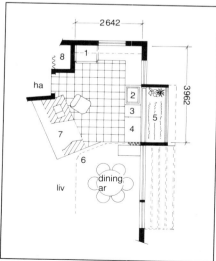

7 k shares fireplace with liv 1 frig 2 sk 3 dishwasher 4 ck 5 k herb garden 6 curtain 7 fireplace 8 cpd   Arch E H & M K Hunter

KITCHENS: EQUIPMENT

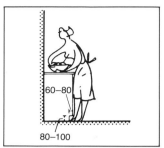

1   Correct toe space

2   Good & bad lighting

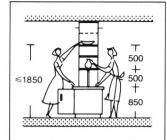

3   Hatch between k or ptr & dining ar or rm with 2-way sto cpd above

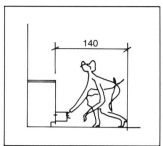

4   Space needed for bottom shelf

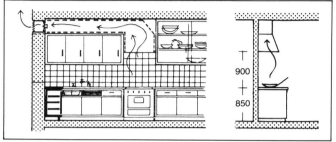

5   Where no vertical shaft planned, hood & duct to external wall advantageous

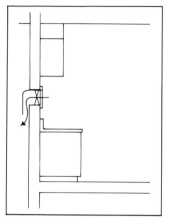

6   Outside wall exhaust fan

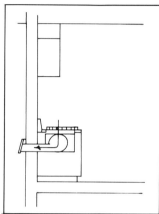

7   Self-venting cooker

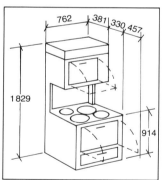

8   Cooker with high & low level ovens

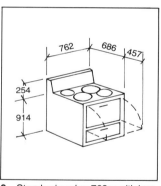

9   Standard cooker 762 w with low oven

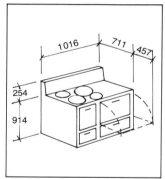

10   Range 1 016 w with low oven

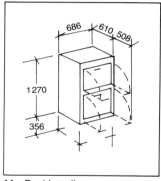

11   Double wall oven

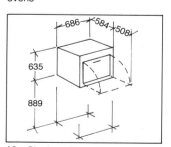

12   Single wall oven

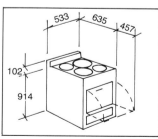

13   Small cooker 533 w with low oven

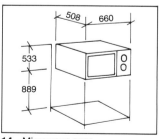

14   Microwave oven

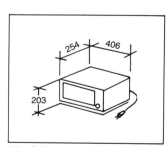

15   Grill toaster

refrigerators			
C (l)	b	t	h
500	550	550–600	800–850
750	550	600–650	850
1 250	550–600	650–700	900–1 000
1 500	600–650	650–700	1 200–1 300
2 000	650–750	700–750	1 300–1 400
2 500	700–800	700–750	1 400–1 500

built-in refrigerators			
C (l)	b	t	h
500	550	500–550	800–850
750	550	550–600	850–900
1 000	550	600–650	900

16   European dimensions for standard & built in frig: C = capacity

17   Frig with 0.65 m³ refrigeration & 1.17 m³ freezer

KITCHENS: EQUIPMENT

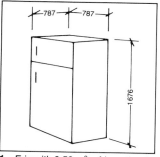

1 Frig with 0.59 m³ refrigeration & 0.2 m³ freezer

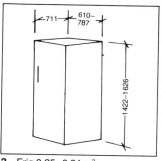

2 Frig 0.25–0.34 m³

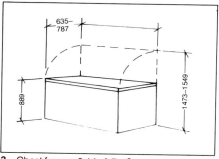

3 Chest freezer 0.14–0.7 m³

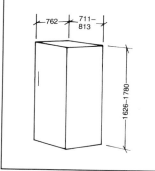

4 Upright freezer 0.31–0.7 m³

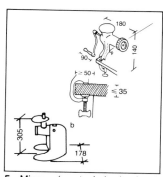

5 Mincers (meat grinders) **a** hand **b** el

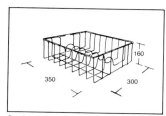

6 Metal & plastics plate rack

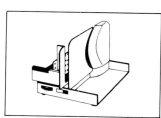

7 El slicer

8 Mixer

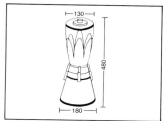

9 Blender

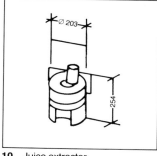

10 Juice extractor

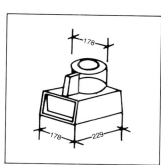

11 Food mill

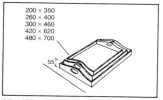

12 Coffee makers

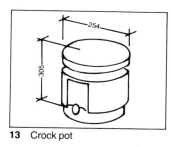

13 Crock pot

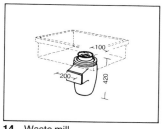

14 Waste mill

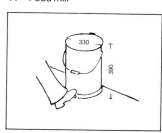

15 Pedal-operated waste bin

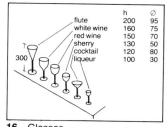

	h	∅
flute	200	95
white wine	160	75
red wine	150	70
sherry	130	50
cocktail	120	80
liqueur	100	30

16 Glasses

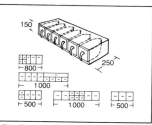

17 Glass or plastics food drawers

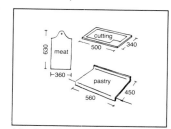

18 Boards

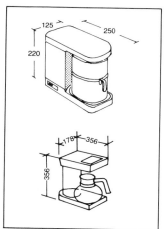

200 × 350
260 × 400
300 × 460
420 × 620
480 × 700

19 Wood trays

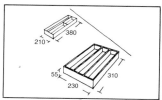

20 Cutlery boxes

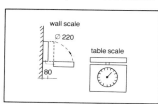

21 k scales

Houses

Habitat

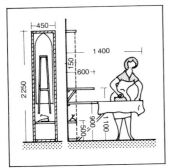

1   Hinged ironing board

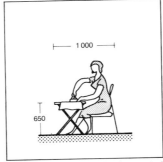

2   Space needed for ironing seated

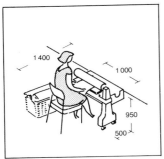

3   El ironing machine

4   How things used to be

LAUNDRY SPACES

Clothes washing may be done in kitchen, utility rm, bathr (not popular), back porch, garage or, in combination with wc, in downstairs cloakrm.

Laundry area needs space for washing machine and drier, for storing cleaning materials and, possibly, for storing dirty washing; may also have to accommodate ironing board or ironing machine and working surface for sorting. Although mobile washing machines available most models, automatic machines in particular, best plumbed in with permanent connexions to water supply and suitably trapped waste. Where washing machine not used, or in large houses where much hand washing done, sink 500 × 350 × 250 deep required and second bowl or tub desirable. Tumbler drier →(12) best placed against outside wall to allow direct extraction of water vapour: removable lint trap required by some models. Even where tumbler drier provided rack or line needed for drip-dry clothes. In small houses or flats this can be fixed above bath or shower; otherwise should be in ventilated drying cupboard or over trapped draining tray. Open-air drying preferred by many and makes no demands on energy resources. Open-air drying space should be easily accessible from laundry area and preferably in view from kitchen →p77.

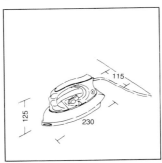

5   Twin tub washing machine (not available in USA)

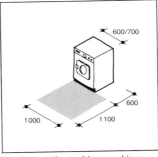

6   Automatic washing machine

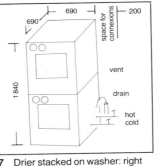

7   Drier stacked on washer: right hand connexions

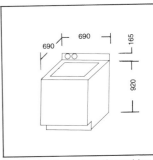

8   Top loaded automatic washing machine

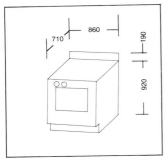

9   Combination front load washing machine/drier: back connexions (pull out)

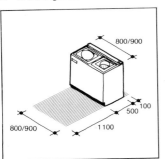

10   Water softener

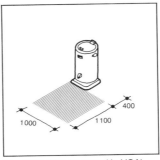

11   Spin drier (not used in USA)

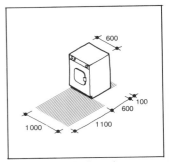

12   Tumble drier (must have space at rear for ventilation)

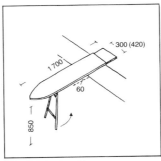

13   El iron

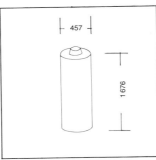

24   Ironing board

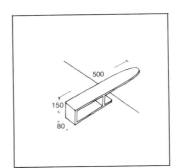

15   Sleeve board

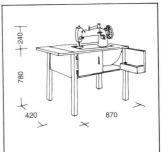

16   Sewing machine

Houses

BATHROOMS

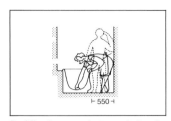

1 Recommended clearances

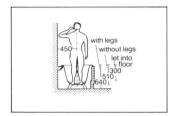

2 Min clearance between b & wall

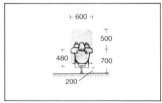

3 Space requirements for movement (h from floor)

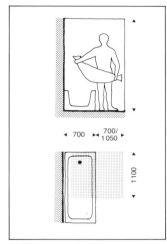

4 wc under sloping roof or stairway

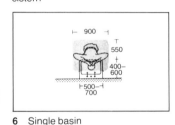

5 wc with flushing valve or h-level cistern

6 Single basin

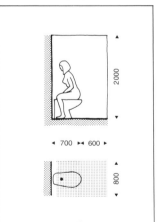

7 Bidet

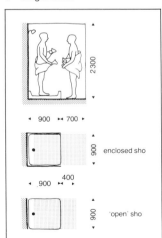

8 Sho

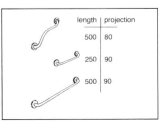

9 Grab rails

	length	projection
	500	80
	250	90
	500	90

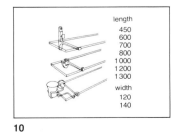

10

	length
	450
	600
	700
	800
	1 000
	1 200
	1 300
	width
	120
	140

Best daylight orientation for bathr SE–NW; for ease of installation (gas and water services) should be related to other rm requiring services (above or backing on to wc, kitchen, utility rm etc, →p52: will also minimise noise from pipes); for convenience should be close to bedr.

Internal wc and bathr fairly common: may be unavoidable where economical use use floor area important, especially in narrow frontage houses or in point blocks. Ventilation essential and must accord with appropriate reg.

Shower uses less water than bathtub; often considered more efficient because of its continuous flow; provides convenient alternative to full length where space limited.

Shower outlet may be fitted over bath where suitable wall or partition available at tap end for fixing, or combined bath tap and shower fitting with flexible hose may be used. For either bath activity space →(1) should be at tap end unless permanent shower screens fitted.

Showers in wall recesses have shower trays of enamelled cast iron, glazed fireclay or plastics with waterproof tiled walls or waterproof rendering and steamproof paint up to 2000: prefabricated shower units in enamelled sheet steel, aluminium or plastics also available →p64 65.

Fixed shower arms should be mounted at 1900: otherwise adjustable, hand shower with flexible hose should be used.

For ease of access, bathtubs sometimes partially sunk into floor with access to trap from rm below. Where bathtub parallel to wall distance from centre of bath to face of wall must be 450.

Where possible space should be available for at least 1 item of bathr furniture, such as stool or laundry box. Fittings such as towel rails and toilet roll holders should not obstruct activity spaces. Heated towel rails best fixed 750 above floor level, above height of small child's head. Medicine cabinets should be out of reach of children and fitted with safety lock. Exposed pipes should be fixed to allow sufficient wall clearance for cleaning.

Windows above baths can be difficult to open or to clean without standing in bath, common cause of accidents: may also limit privacy and cause draughts unless well insulated. Windows behind wash basins can also be difficult to reach; wall above wash basin best used for mirror or medicine cabinet.

UK practice does not allow el sockets in bathr other than specially designed shaver point, which should be out of reach of bath; enclosed light fittings with cord-operated switch preferred. USA practice: no el convenience outlets near water source; safest location as part of sealed light fixture over mirror with remote switching near doorway.

11

12 Heated towel rail

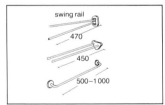

13

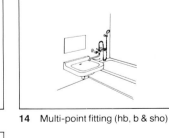

14 Multi-point fitting (hb, b & sho)

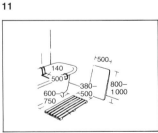

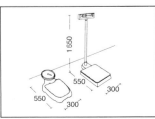

15

Houses

Habitat

1   Gas water heater fitted to hot water cylinder

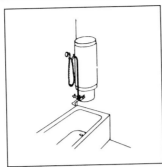

2   El sto heater for k or bathr

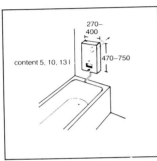
content 5, 10, 13 l

3   Gas water heater for chimney or outside wall

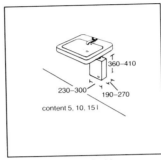
content 5, 10, 15 l

4   Gas water heat for hb

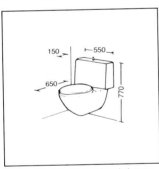

5   Wall toilet with low level cistern

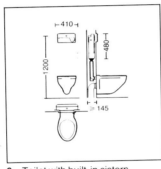

6   Toilet with built-in cistern

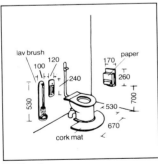
lav brush   paper   cork mat

7   Eqp for wc

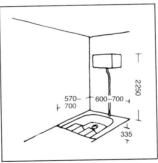

8   Squat wc

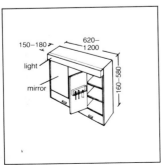
light   mirror

9   Bathr wall cpd

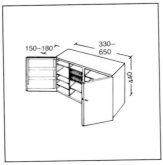

10   Lockable medicine cpd

BATHROOMS

Equipment

Movable baths of zinc or enameled mild steel suitable only for infrequently used baths, children's bath →p63(2), hip baths →p63(3) and use without main services.

Fixed baths →p63(4)–(8) usually enameled cast iron, pressed steel or plastics with various qualities of enamel (full gloss, acid resistant etc) or fireclay.

Free-standing baths →p63(5) usually have taps at foot end: sometimes joined to wall along 1 side to avoid water splashing behind bath.

Built-in baths →p63(6) with extended rim attached to surrounding walls & overlapping front: access panel necessary in UK.

Avon baths for use as built-in units →p63(4) have integral front panel; drain & overflow carried to outside in standpipe or trapped waste (USA).

Space-saving baths →p63(7)(8) installed where space restricted but do not necessarily save water; corner baths →p63(7).

Fireclay baths glazed inside and out beautiful and expensive but uneconomic as slow to warm up; pleasant for leisurely bathing, however.

Footbaths →p63(10) movable or fixed, usually installed in larger public baths; may be fireclay, earthenware or enamelled cast iron.

Showers →p63(11)(12) base may be cast iron or fireclay (terrazo); should preferably be sunk into floor & provided with tile or enameled sheet steel surround →also p64.

Polyban baths →p63(8) Spanish patent: can be used as hip baths, footbaths, bidets or shower (with flexible shower arm); require little space & save water (not used in USA).

Bidet →p63(9) earthenware or fireclay, many variations in design; mixer with anti-scalding device →also p61(7).

Basins with back skirting for plastered walls →p63(13); for washable walls →p63(14) many shapes & sizes, sometimes with separate mouthwash basin or as double basin →p63(15)(16); mixers for washing with running water, but wasteful.

Squat wc →(8) hygienic but uncomfortable; has either flushing cistern or flushing valve.

Wc →(5)–(7) siphonic more efficient but extravagant in water & prohibited by some water bye-laws. Low level cisterns flush with little noise; flushing valves more noisy →(5)(6) but use approx half as much water.

Water heaters (gas or el) →(1)–(4). El sto heaters →(2) use cheap night-time el & can be set to heat up at any time during day.

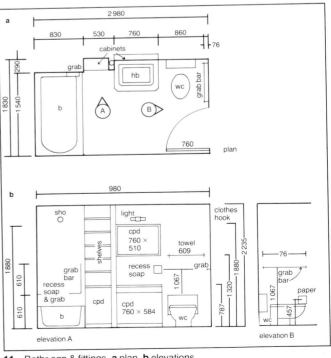

11   Bathr eqp & fittings **a** plan **b** elevations

BATHROOMS
Equipment

l	w
1500	
1600	700
1700	&
1800	800

1 Standard metric bath sizes

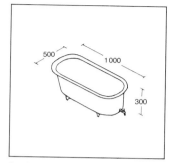

2 Children's bath

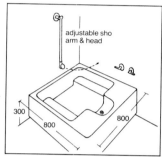

3 Hip bath

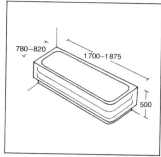

4 Enamelled cast iron bath

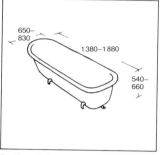

5 Parallel-sided cast iron bath

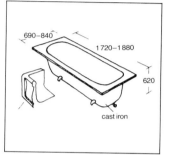

6 Bath for incorporation as built-in unit

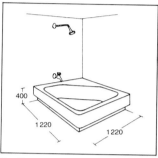

7 Economy American corner bath (enameled cast iron)

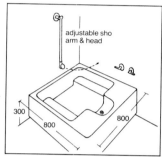

8 Polyban unit

Shorter baths require more water

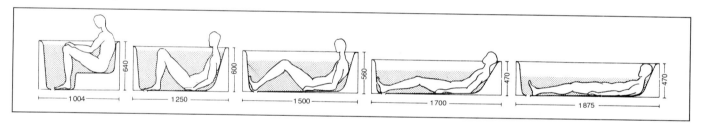

Shower requires approx 30 l water

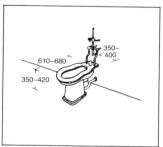

9 Bidet

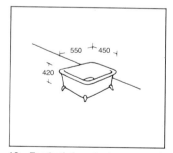

10 Footbath (may be incorporated as built-in unit)

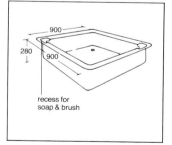

11 Sho b for incorporation as built-in unit

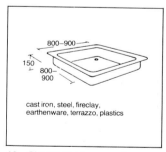

12 Sho tray for incorporation as built-in unit

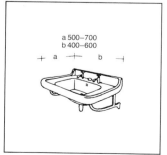

13 Hb with back skirting

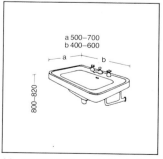

14 Hb without back skirting but incorporating mixer fitting

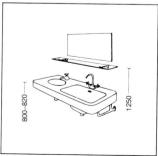

15 Hb with separate mouth-wash bowl

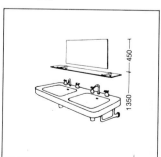

16 Double hb

Houses

BATHROOMS

Wc & washrooms

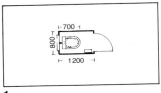

1

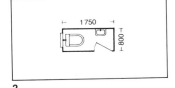

2

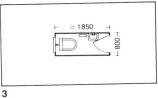

3

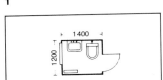

4

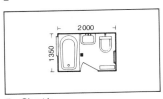

5 Short b

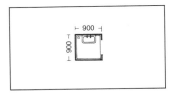

6 Hip-b (loose bowl in fold-up steel frame)

Wc with low-level cisterns under high-level windows →(1)–(3); wc with high level cisterns →(4)(6)(8): where cistern placed against exterior wall insulate against frost.

Bathrooms: smallest type of bath may be recessed into bedr wall →(7) with shower end screened off with glass partition and remainder curtained.

In general doors should be min 460 wide, should open full 90° and open inwards except in accn for elderly, when should open outwards.

Bathrooms

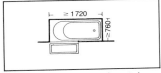

7 b in bedr, glass section at sho end

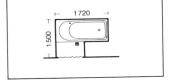

8 As (15) with drying space

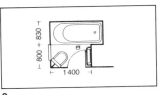

9

10

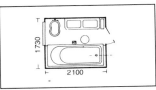

11

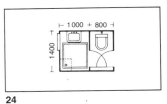

12

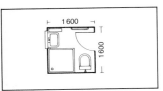

13

14

15

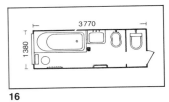

16

17 Divided bathr & dre

18 Double use bathr

19 De luxe bathr/dre

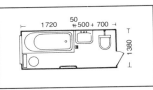

20 Divided bathr & dre between bedr

Showers

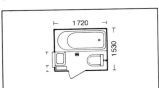

21

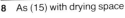

22

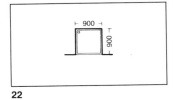

23 With fold-up hb

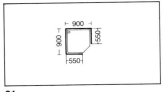

24

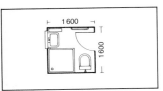

25

26

27 Standard American b

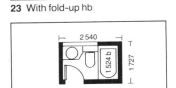

28 American square tub bathr

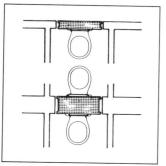

1 wc plumbing elements

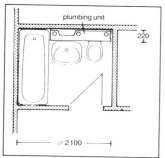

2 Plumbing wall

PREFABRICATED SANITARY UNITS

Standard lav and bathr fittings mostly fairly costly and take time to install. As requirements more or less uniform prefabrication preferable: in particular for terrace houses, maisonette houses and large scale blocks of flats, also for modernisation schemes and prefabricated housing.

Prefabricated items comprise complete plumbing units →(1)(3), plumbing walls →(2), complete elements storey or rm high, with pipe mountings and el leads, also items with accessories, flooring and, usually, ceiling →(4)–(9) (available without ceiling for old housing). Compact elements of fixed dimensions →(10)(11). Also individual elements with variable ground plan design →(5)–(9).

Construction: mainly sandwich with wood skeleton and chipboard, glass aluminium, aluminium, stainless steel, glass fibre reinforced polyester, reinforced concrete floor slabs →(10)(11) or new types of plastics.

Fittings and accessories similar materials. Basic essentials: anti-scratch surface finish and long service life (no material fatigue). Prefabricated plumbing units mostly for use internally in bldg →(13)–(16); proper through ventilation therefore necessary: possibly forced ventilation. Suitable for hotels →(14), hospitals, old people's homes →(13).

Connexion to 1-storey central heating system has proved successful.

3 Plumbing unit on wall

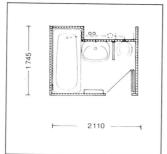

4 Self-contained wc elements & fittings

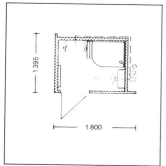

5 Self-contained wc element & fittings

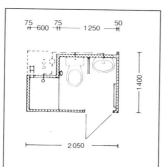

6 Sho element with plumbing shaft

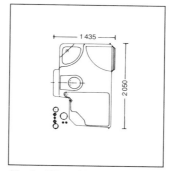

11 As **10** but with sho at side

12 Large unit comprising k, washr, heater

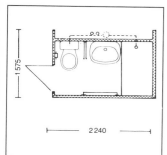

7 Small bathr unit

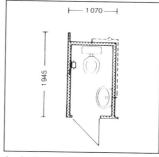

8 Bathr unit

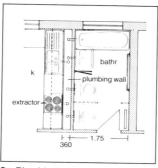

13 wc element in hospital

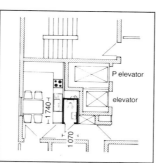

14 Sho element in hotel

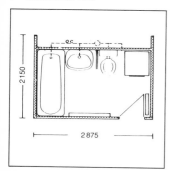

9 Bathr unit with washing machine

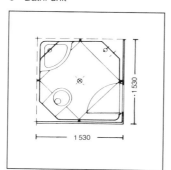

10 Compact unit

15 Sho element in small dwelling

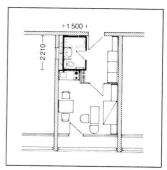

16 Prefabricated bathr with k partition wall

Houses

1   Min clearance from wall depends on method of serving (with or without servant)

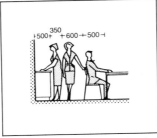

2   Space required between head of table & sideboard

3   Sideboard with drawers at head of table

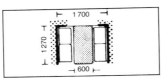

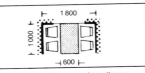

4 5   Min table space in railway dining car with tip-up seats **4**; little more space required in dining recess with loose chairs **5**

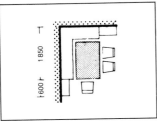

6   Space-saving arrangement of table with fixed corner seat & (possibly) small sideboards

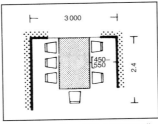

7   For more than 5 P access to all seats must be allowed for

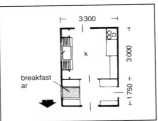

11   In America dining space near k with ample sto cpd & sideboard close at hand often considered adequate

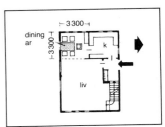

12   Dining recess in liv (with or without curtain) with access to k, intermediate stage to separate dr Arch Byrne

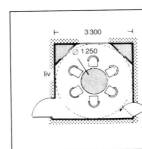

8   Smallest possible dr for 6 P without sideboard; door in corner preferable

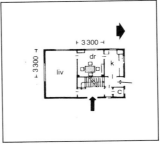

9   Smallest possible dr for 6 P with round table & corner cpd (double swing door to k)

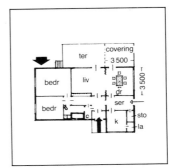

13   Separate dr between k & liv Arch Schwarderer

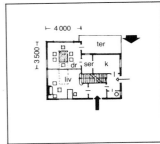

14   Dr between ter & liv (sliding folding doors allow combination)

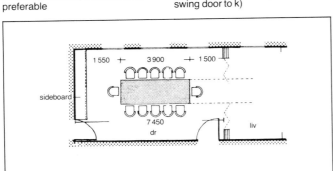

10   Dr for 12 P with sideboard & space for servants: may be enlarged into living rm with space-saving arrangement of sliding folding doors

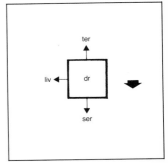

15   Dr & liv both opening on to ter, ensuring good daylight

16   Relationship of dr to other rm

PUBLIC ROOMS

Dining rooms

Position: breakfast area facing E →(11), dining area facing W →(12) (13)(15)(16); direct access from hall or corridor not necessary but from kitchen or pantry essential.

Space requirement: formerly largest rm dining rm has shrunk to bare essentials: very often utilises corner →(6), kitchen recess →p55–7 ante-rm or area in living rm →(4)–(7). Even in large houses dining rm kept modest →(8)(9), sometimes with provision to combine it with living rm for special occasions →(10). Doors in rm corners convenient.

Size of dr . . . ⩾ 6 to ⩽ 24 P
Table w . . . ⩾ 550 to ⩽ 1 100
Seating w/P ⩾ 550 to ⩽ 700
At head of table add . . . ⩾ 100 to ⩽ 200

$$\text{Dia of round table} = \frac{\text{seat w} \times \text{number of P}}{3.14}$$

$$eg\ 600\ \text{w and 6 P} = \frac{0.60 \times 6}{3.14} = 1040$$

Outside dining spaces (verandas, terraces): should lie on wind-protected sunny side of house in front of dining or living rm (ie in W Europe with prevailing SW winds should face E or SE). Since E sun shines at low angle roof can project quite prominently. Min width with bench seat along 1 wall 3 000: roof projection 2 000 sufficient.

PUBLIC ROOMS

Living rooms

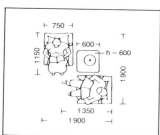

1 Comfortable low easy chairs beside table or standard lamp

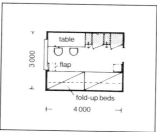

2 Table in front of fireplace off centre to allow access to fire

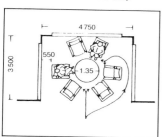

3 Easy chairs 350 h & table 600 h for taking tea in alcove

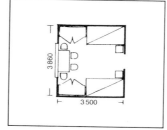

4 Seating group with settee: easy chair 380 h, table 600 h

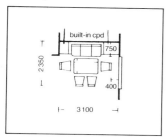

5 Seating group with settee & chairs: chair 420 h, table 650 h

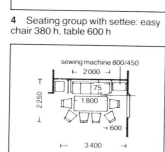

6 Seating arrangement in liv (may also be used for breakfast): chair 440 h, table 700 h

Music rooms

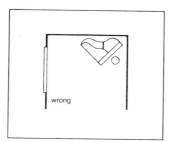

7 Incorrect grand piano often drawn by architects: long (bass) side is on left

8 Grand piano incorrectly placed: opening towards wall instead of rm

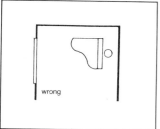

9 Grand piano well positioned in relation to seating group, wall & circulation, but window, heating & external door would be adverse factors

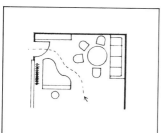

10 Grand piano against external wall, away from window & heating, well related to seating group & rm; daylight coming from behind player

Guest & children's rooms

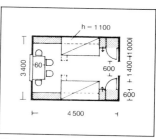

11 Narrow rm for guests or 2 teenage children, with joint work table, separate wa, fold-up beds

12 Similar rm to **11** with fold-up beds & built-in cpd but wider & with separate work tables on either side of window

13 Short rm with cpd 1500 h & fixed beds, primarily guest rm

14 Large rm with bunk beds in recess, large free ar, & hb & coat hooks near door

activity	furniture and eqp	specialised rm	combined rm
1 sitting	settee, low table, easy chairs	salon	
2 tea	tea trolley, sto of crockery etc, seating	ladies rm	
3 aperitifs, etc	sto of glasses, sideboard, liqueur trolley	bar	
4 smoking	smokers' table, pipe cpd, tobacco sto, smokers' requirements	smoking rm	liv
5 conversation	fire place, comfortable easy chairs, small tables	lounge	
6 dancing	parquet or linoleum dance floor, 2.5–3.5 m² per couple	ballrm	
7 playing	children's furniture, carpeted floor, toy sto	children's rm	
8 sewing	table, sewing machine, linen cpd, baskets	utility rm	
9 breakfast	breakfast ar towards E with ter, or between bedr	breakfast rm dr	dr
10 eating	dining ar, sideboard	dr	
11 writing	desk, chairs, filing, waste-paper basket	stu	
12 reading	shelves or cpd, easy chairs with headrest	lib	stu
13 music	piano, cpd for other instruments, music lib	music rm	
14 indoor sport	table tennis, billiard table, punch ball etc	games rm	

15 Living rm uses

Living rm usually multi-purpose; layout and furnishing vary widely with different uses entailing wide range of possible space requirements →(15). Therefore necessary define functions in detail before shape, space for furnishing and movement of users can be planned. For liv tables →(5) allow 650 space per person, for easy chairs →(2)(3) 866 and

dia for round tables $\dfrac{\text{persons} \times 866}{3.14}$ →(3)

Houses

LIVING ROOMS

Seating near windows

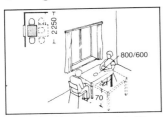

1   Work tables closely related to window

2   Avoid seating people with backs to window

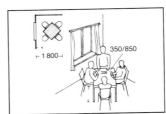

3   Diagonal arrangement preferable to **2** & requires less space

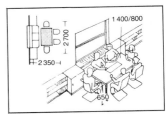

4   On built-in settee below wide window, however, several people can sit quite comfortably

Seating away from windows

5   Bench seat also satisfactory between 2 windows in light coloured corner with suitable carpet

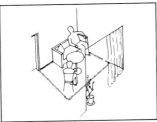

6   7   Seating against interior wall with view through picture window very relaxing, specially in front of french doors

8   Seating in middle usually uncomfortable from lack of relationship with rest of rm

Seating round fireplace

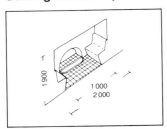

9   Ingle-nook   Arch Leusinger

10   Seating arranged to avoid draught from door to fireplace

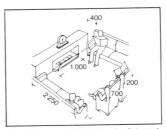

11   Chairs with high backs & 'ears' also protect against draught

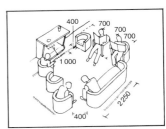

12   Larger groups should follow pattern of heat radiation

Seating round work desks

13   Colleagues working closely together should face each other; with large windows & light-coloured walls, daylight from right is tolerable for writing

14   Visitors usually sit in light at end of desk, face of interviewer being in shade

15   Assistants may work temporarily on flap at end of desk

16   Conference table unnecessary if desk top extensible

Correct arrangement of seating greatly enhances comfort of users. Relationship of daylight and artificial lighting important →(1)–(8). Give careful consideration to good combination of furniture elements, choice of independent heights and colours, well planned free area, correctly hung doors, kind of floor (direction of boarding) →(7), carpets →(5)(6)(8)(12), treatment of walls including pictures and siting of windows, radiators, fireplace and piano →p67. Seating area, however, will remain focal point of rm: everything else should be subordinated to it.

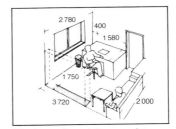

17   In small rm visitors may be seated against internall wall; small table should be provided

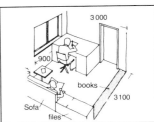

18   As alternative to **17** visitor may be seated behind host, who turns on revolving chair: door should be in front of desk

Houses

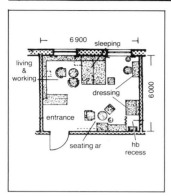

1 1-rm dwelling for 2 persons, with different activities well separated

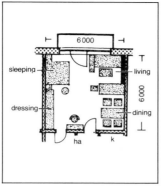

2 Square liv with seating ar near window & fold-up beds

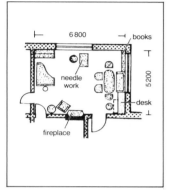

3 Mur & liv, with needlework table, fireplace, book-shelves
Arch Neufert

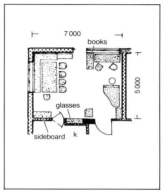

4 Liv/dr cum mur with built-in furniture, suitable for 10–12 persons
Arch Neufert

LIVING ROOMS

Living rm used for general daytime activities; serves mainly as focus of social activities of family round fireplace, tea or coffee table and for evening leisure activities. Orientation best between E, S and W. Windows →p404

Reception rm (salon): in larger houses often used as music rm or consult/waiting rm near entrance.

Conservatory (winter garden): usually facing S accessible from living or dining rm.

Music room: next to living rm; dimensions determined by size of audience and type and number of instruments; soft lighting from back or side of players. For acoustical reasons rm shape usually square with wood panelling; position of piano →p67. In large rm sound reflecting surfaces round players with absorbent surfaces behind audience.

Study: frequently serves as office or workrm. Near entrance and living rm with W or E aspect; fitted with desk, bookshelves, filing system, seating area (deep easy chairs, low table, cocktail cabinet).

Library: N orientation. 1000 shelf takes approx 30–40 books. Height between shelves 250–300, shelf depth 220–320. For approx, 120–150 books 1 m² of wall. Larger volumes, maps, folders etc in lower, deeper shelves. Height of top shelf approx 1700 from floor →p146.

Children's rm: away from living rm but easy supervision essential (from household rm) and preferably with access to garden or safe balcony; on sloping sites may be on lower ground to give garden access. Orientation E-W, low cill (guard rails outside), furniture to children's sizes. Washable wall finish (such as linoleum or plastics-covered panelling) to height of about 1500.

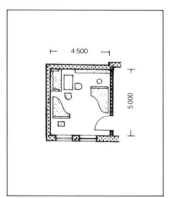

5 Small mur with grand & baby grand pianos & seating ar: avoid placing piano close to heating unit or in direct sun

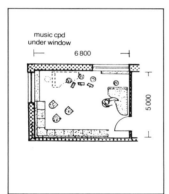

6 Mur for quartets, trios or 2 grand pianos & audience of 12 (daylight from behind pianists)

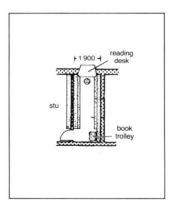

9 Book sto in long narrow rm with ample wall space: reading desk under window, small book trolley near door

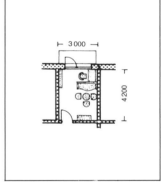

10 Small work rm with writing desk near window, bookshelves & seating ar

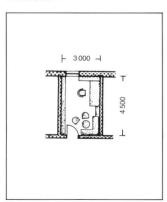

7 Small stu with bookshelves, desk & seating ar

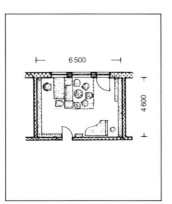

8 Large stu with bookshelves, seating ar in front of writing desk

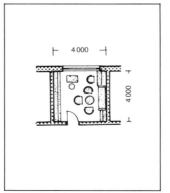

11 Work rm with whole wall for bookshelves, sewing machine (under bookshelves), writing desk, seating ar, chest of drawers

Houses

BEDROOMS

Position of bed

Bedmaking requires clear space of at least 400, preferably 700 (USA min), beside bed. In most small houses, therefore, choice of bed positions restricted by shape and size of bedr; to free as much floor space as possible single beds usually placed along walls and double or twin beds placed head to wall. Nevertheless, relation of bed to walls and to rm as a whole can also be important in contributing to feeling of security. While stable, self-reliant person may prefer free-standing bed →(4) less self-reliant person may prefer →(1)(2)(5) regardless of amount of space available.

Impression of restfulness depends on wall covering and colour, shape of bed, orientation (head towards N), relation to daylight (looking away from window) and relation to door (looking towards door). Relative position of 2 beds also important because where 2 people sleep in 1 rm different arrangements may be desirable, especially where head positions concerned, according to relationship between people →(9)–(12) (16). Also different arrangements for couples, depending on personal preference →(13)–(15). With separate beds change of direction may be preferable →(12)(15)(16). Separate beds for couples now common. Current fashion may also favour water bed, though well to bear in mind that, fully loaded, this may impose floor load of up to 2 or even 3 t.

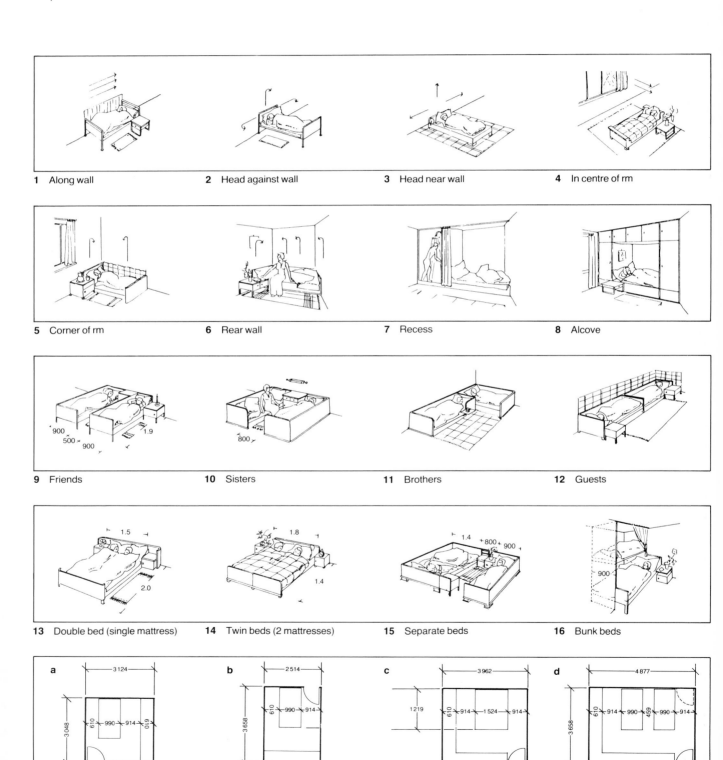

1 Along wall	**2** Head against wall
3 Head near wall	**4** In centre of rm
5 Corner of rm	**6** Rear wall
7 Recess	**8** Alcove
9 Friends	**10** Sisters
11 Brothers	**12** Guests
13 Double bed (single mattress)	**14** Twin beds (2 mattresses)
15 Separate beds	**16** Bunk beds

17 USA bedr sizes (main bedr min 11.15 m² least dimension 2845, secondary bedr min 7.43 m² least dimension 2438) **a & b** single **c** double **d** twin; USA bed sizes →p71

BEDROOMS

Today's reduced flat and house sizes call for most economical use of floor space and make built-in cupboards desirable. Best arrangement based upon enclosed wall recesses with flooring running into cupboard, walls papered or oil painted, and moth-proof doors. Ideal solution: complete cupboard walls between rm →(7)(11)(12): sliding, accordion or open out hinged doors.

Cupboards on exterior walls must be well insulated and ventilated to avoid condensation →p74(2); walk-in cupboards/dressing rm also require ventilation →(13). Cupboards can be located between bedr to reduce sound transmission.

	w	l	
single	762 914 1069 1219	bed l in UK vary according to manufacturer; 1905 is common size; other sizes 1880, 1981 and 2133	
double	1524 1829		

child's cot size usually 1219 long, 610 wide

USA mattress sizes

	king	also	queen	3-quarter	twin
l	1828	1828	2032	1905	1905
w	1981	1981	1524	1371	990

note: add 76 to each dimension for frame

USA water bed sizes

	king		queen		single
l	2133		2133		2133
w	1828		1524		1219

1 Bed, divan & mattress sizes

3 Elevation of double bunk-bed recess & built-in cpd

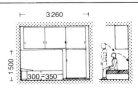

4 Elevation & section to plan **5** showing economical use of space

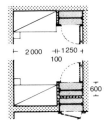

5 Bed recess formed by built-in cpd

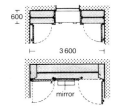

6 Cpd across full rm w, with window (above) & mirror on sliding door (below)

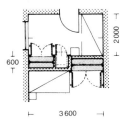

7 Built-in cpd related to position of beds

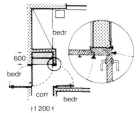

8 Linen cpd at end of corr, door frame serving 2 doors

2 Modern bedr fitment combining bedhead, bedside tables, fitted wa & sto space above

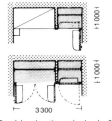

9 Double-depth cpd, single & double doors (opened)

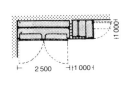

10 Double-depth cpd (with double doors) & corner cpd formed simply by doors; walls & floor of rm continuous

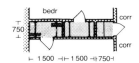

11 Cpd wall with walk-in cpd between 2 bedr: linen cpd opening to corr; wall thicknesses vary from 30 to 100 depending on materials used

12 Cpd wall with walk-in cpd & washr with sho between 2 bedr that are about 4000 deep

13 Walk-in cpd big enough to serve as dre

14 American example of window wall with cpd

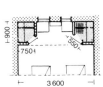

15 As **14** but with deep cpd on both sides angled at front to avoid obstructing daylight

16 Lowered ceiling & curtain will combine cpd of **14** & **15** to form dre

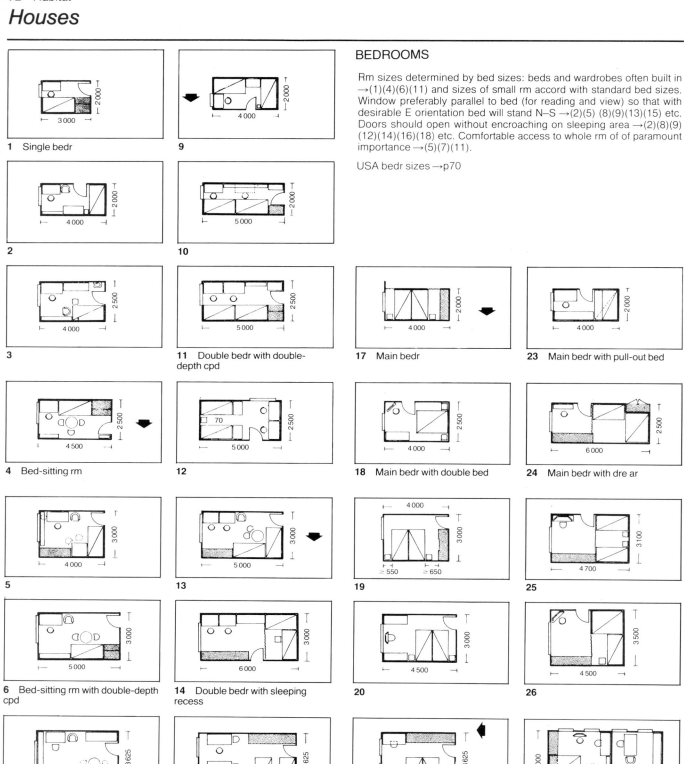

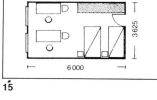

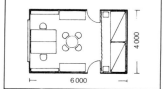

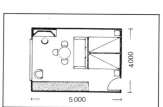

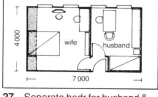

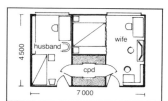

BEDROOMS

Rm sizes determined by bed sizes: beds and wardrobes often built in →(1)(4)(6)(11) and sizes of small rm accord with standard bed sizes. Window preferably parallel to bed (for reading and view) so that with desirable E orientation bed will stand N–S →(2)(5) (8)(9)(13)(15) etc. Doors should open without encroaching on sleeping area →(2)(8)(9) (12)(14)(16)(18) etc. Comfortable access to whole rm of of paramount importance →(5)(7)(11).

USA bedr sizes →p70

1 Single bedr

9

2

10

3

11 Double bedr with double-depth cpd

17 Main bedr

23 Main bedr with pull-out bed

4 Bed-sitting rm

12

18 Main bedr with double bed

24 Main bedr with dre ar

5

13

19

25

6 Bed-sitting rm with double-depth cpd

14 Double bedr with sleeping recess

20

26

7 Bed-sitting rm

15

21

27 Separate bedr for husband & wife

8 Bed-sitting rm with fold-up bed

16 Stu-bedr with sleeping recess

22 Main bedr-sitting rm

28 Separate bedr with walk-through cpd

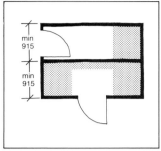

1 Entrance on long side of sto allows max use of shelving

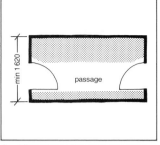

2 Allow space for passageway in 'through' sto

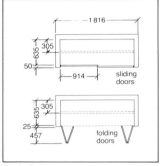

3 In line wa

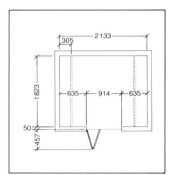

4 Walk-in wa

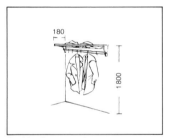

5 Hat & coat rack

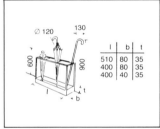

6 Umbrella stand

7 Clothes & linen cpd with doors put to additional use (for dimensions →(8))

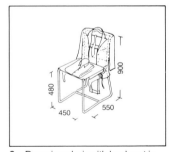

8 Dressing chair with backrest in coat hanger shape (copyright: Neufert)

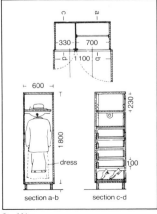

9 Wa

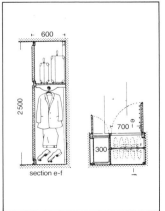

10 Built-in wa

STORAGE IN HOUSES & FLATS

Shape and position of sto space as important as its size. Sto should be provided within easy reach of activities to which related and shape should allow max use of wall area for shelving →(1). Sto generally more useful at ground level than on upper storeys. Family house will require at least 5 m² of general sto, of which at least half should be on ground floor (USA min 1.23 m²).

General storage

Sto rm require ventilation and those providing part of passageway through house should also permit natural lighting. In such cases allowance must be made for loss of usable space to circulation requirements →(2).

Garden tools, bicycles etc usually best in external sto or, if within house itself, in sto with direct access from outside →(3).

Hats & coats

Space required in or off entrance hall for hanging hats and coats and storing outdoor footwear, preferably in wardrobe or with racks to take hangers →(3). Additional space may be needed for storing working clothes and eqp →(11)(12).

The pram

In family houses space required for pram →p74(4): should be easy to manoeuvre pram indoors so that it can be used as cot (crib) during day if required.

Meters

Credit meters should be capable of being read without entering living area of house. Arrangements which can be read by inspector from outside →p74(3) available. Prepayment meters should be easy to reach from floor level but gas meters, especially, should be out of reach of small children.

Linen

Separate sto space should be provided for linen and bedding. At least 0.6 m³ required, fitted with slatted shelves. Must be dry and therefore not entered from bathr or kitchen or sited against outside wall (unless insulated). May be combined with suitably ventilated hot water cylinder cupboard (heater closet) but not with 'combination' water unit as condensation might occur.

Wardrobes

For clothing in particular, ease of access more important than sto space. Effective depth of built-in cupboard for clothes hanging 600 but deeper cupboards can be more fully utilised by attaching accessories to backs of doors →(7). As loads not great normal blockboard doors on strong hinges adequate; shelves can be supported by adjustable ladders and brackets. Walk-in cupboards →p71(2) take up little wall space, as door of 550 (USA min 610 preferred 660) will suffice for cupboard of any length; but floor space less efficiently used because of necessary access area. Walk-in cupboards must be ventilated and lighted and may be entered from, and used as access or escape routes between, adjacent rm.

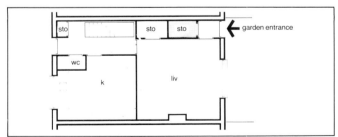

11 Internal sto accessible from garden without passing through living ar of house

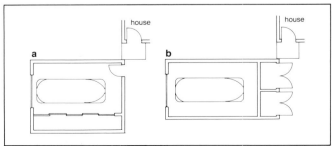

12 Gar sto **a** side **b** rear

Houses

STORAGE

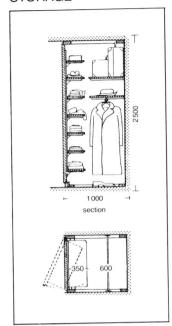

1   Built-in double wa (cheap & space-saving)

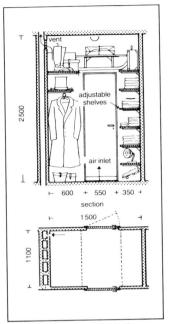

2   Walk-in wa between bedr →also p71

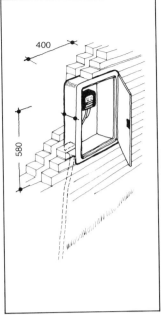

3   External el meter cpd

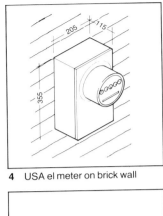

4   USA el meter on brick wall

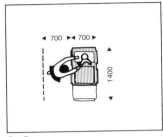

5   Pram

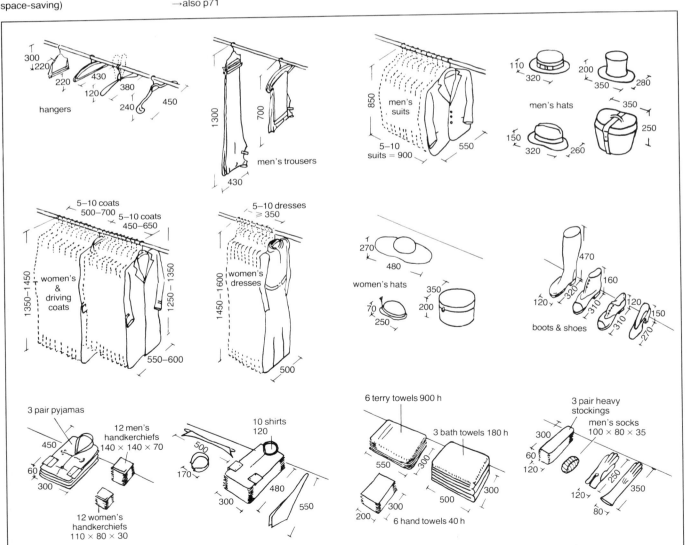

6   Dimensions of clothes

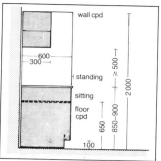

1 Section through worktop & sto

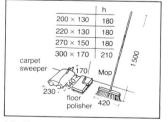

2 Eqp cpd

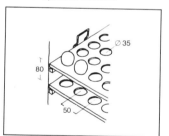

3 Cloths & towels

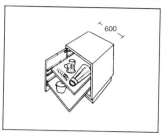

4 Space-saving vertical sto of dishes

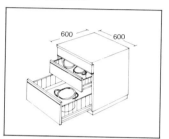

5 Dish cpd with drawers

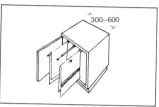

6 Glass or plastics containers

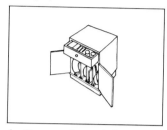

7 Egg rack for 100 eggs (500 × 500)

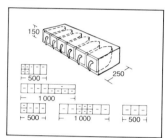

8 Slatted rack for fruit (800 × 420)

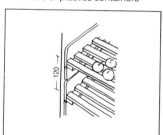

9 Potato rack

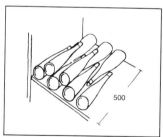

10 Bottles stored 'sardine fashion' in deep shelves

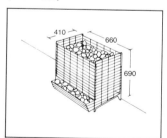

11 Bottles stored in drain pipes (64 bottles/m²)

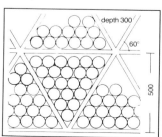

12 Bottles stored in overlapping pyramids

Kitchen storage

Space required in or next to kitchen for storing food and cooking eqp. Sto also needed for general cleaning and laundering eqp and materials. Dry goods should be enclosed and readily accessible from cooker and sink positions.

Floor cabinets best used for storing heavy or infrequently used articles. Wall cabinets economical in space and provide convenient sto for smaller and frequently used items: should be shallow enough to allow full use of worktops below →(1).

Larder ventilated to outside air and protected by fly proof screen desirable even when space for refrigerator and freezer provided: should not contain heating or hot water pipes nor receive direct sunlight. Should be provided with well fitting door, preferably with threshold, to discourage vermin.

Freezer need not necessarily be near kitchen: if placed in outside sto or garage must be locked against theft. Should be served by el power outlet on independent circuit.

Wine

Wine cellars should be clean, dark, dry, well ventilated (but avoid cold draughts) and in quiet position free from vibration and away from direct heat. White wines best kept at constant temp between 6°–8° C and red wines at between 10°–12°C. Bottle sto may be in racks or in unglazed clay drainpipes →(11).

Fuel storage

Solid fuel requires volume of not less than 1.13 m³ for fuel sto. Should be accessible from within house or from porch or other shelter. To avoid spread of dust arrange that bags can be tipped from outside without entering house.

In making provision for oil sto well be generous →p386–7. Fuel tanks up to 2000 l can generally be located adjacent to houses without restriction; if enclosed should be separated from remainder of bldg and provided with catch pit. Fuel inlet point should be positioned within 30 m of place where delivery tanker can conveniently stop. USA: oil tanks often buried if 2100 l or over.

Refuse

Refuse sto should be outside house, easily accessible from kitchen door. Simple, easily cleaned, covered stand required. Carry distance to collection vehicle access should not be more than 46 m and ideally less than 25 m.

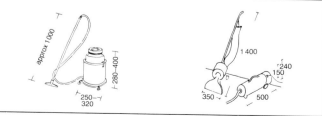

13 'Lazytongs' racking to fit available cpd spaces (80 × 80 × 80)

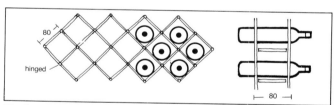

14 Brooms

15 Tubular steel ladder

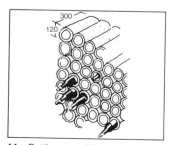

16 Vacuum cleaners

Houses

SECURITY

External security best served by good lighting and visibility. Access routes and entrances should never be dark or concealed, however romantic this might appear, and should if possible allow sufficient space to avoid unwanted encounter.

Avoid dense planting round entrances and ground floor windows (or use prickly shrubs!). In small blocks of flats entrance may be controlled by entryphones →(1)(2) but this may be inconvenient where many small children. For single people or working couples some provision needed for daytime deliveries.

For thieves ease of exit as important as ease of entry. Professional may be willing to break window to secure access but will be unwilling to rely on this as his means of exit. *All* external doors should therefore be fitted with deadlocks and openable windows, if possible, be fitted with window locks.

Free detailed advice, based on expert local knowledge, available from all UK police forces through their crime prevention officers.

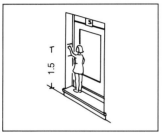

1 Bell-push & door microphone must be in reach of children

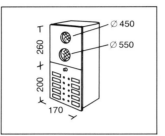

2 Typical dimensions of door transmitter with light button & bells for 5 floors

PRIVACY: PUBLIC & PRIVATE SPACES

Among most difficult problems in housing layout: striking right balance between need for privacy and need to avoid social isolation. Balance obviously varies according to individual character, temperament and age so no perfect solution possible but good layout will at least allow some degree of individual choice. Designs which opt strongly for either 'social' or 'private' approach unlikely to satisfy majority of occupants.

Dwellings opening directly on to busy public spaces and access decks designed to encourage social contact and neighbourliness may also suffer intolerable intrusion, while screening designed to provide 'defensible space' may result in roads and footpaths bounded by blank walls and fences. Either approach likely to lead to feelings of insecurity and dissatisfaction amongst residents.

In high density layouts, in particular, user satisfaction likely to be enhanced, and incidence of vandalism to be reduced, by sub-divison of large anonymous public areas into smaller spaces related to identifiable groups of dwellings.

For flats, transition between entirely public zone of street and entirely private zone of individual flat may be by way of both semi-public zone shared by all flats in block (elevator and staircase hall etc, possibly with some form of supervised access) and semi-private zone share by 2 or 3 flats with access under control of occupants →(3).

For houses, public access road may lead to mixed use pedestrian/ vehicle court →p42, with psychologically restricted entry, related to group of 20 or so houses and further transition zone provided by front garden to each individual house.

→also p77

Gardens →p103–14

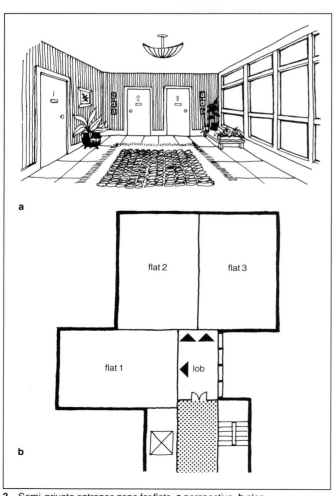

3 Semi-private entrance zone for flats **a** perspective **b** plan

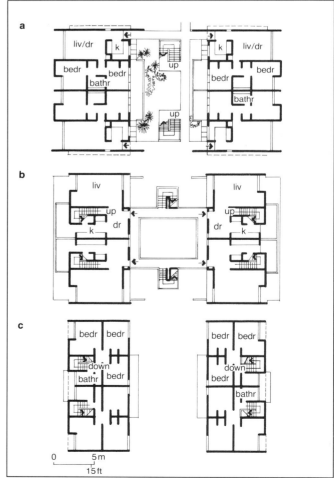

4 Hawaii Housing Authority; 2-storey units over flats: solves 3-storey public stair required for 3 floor flats **a** ground level **b** second level **c** third level Arch Akiyama/Kekoolani

Houses

PRIVATE OPEN SPACE

All family houses require some kind of related open space – whether garden, patio →(7) or balc →p88 – which is sunny and sheltered from wind. Should ideally be large enough to allow space for clothes drying →(5)(6), toddler's play, out-door hobbies and sitting out. Factors affecting location outdoor living areas →(3).

Gardens →p103–14
Enclosed garden enhances privacy. Walls, hedges and, to lesser extent, trees can provide natural protection from noise, wind and dust. Advantage if private garden can open out of liv, providing out-door extension of living space: but not necessarily best placed (UK) on S side of house since enclosed garden to N can provide sunlit view, though will need be deep to be effective because of overshadowing by house itself →(1).

Garden structures →p111
Tents and sheds in gardens do not usually rate as bldg in UK: not considered permanent living access when occupied only by day and not used for trade or business. Distance from site boundary or other bldg should not be less than 1 800. For frames and greenhouses →p111.

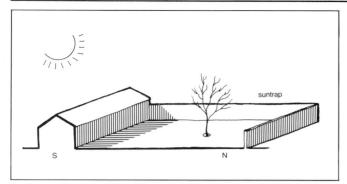

1 N face of house in shade & immediate foreground overshadowed but longer prospect on to sunlit garden & wall forming sun trap

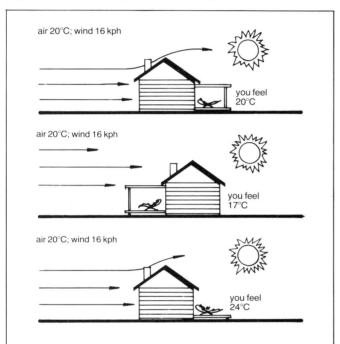

2 Wind effects

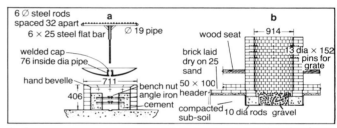

4 Built-in barbecues **a** adjustable grill can be raised to 305 above brazier on masonry base **b** barbecue firepit combination continuous unit with garden seat & patio paving: hard-burned firebrick liner; iron pins adjust h of grill   Design **a** A K Tobin **b** C Mason Whitney R Burton Litton Jr Robert J Tetlow

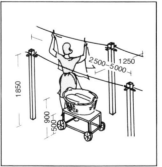

5 Washing lines

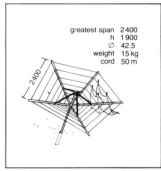

6 'Whirligig' clothes drier

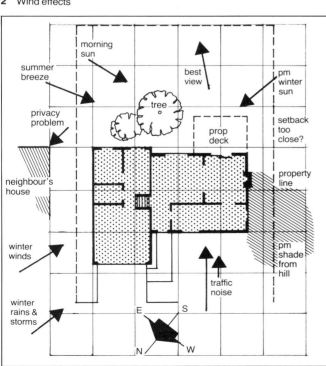

3 Factors affecting outdoor living ar locations: consult local reg

7 Pation & water's edge   Arch Lawrence Halprin

Houses

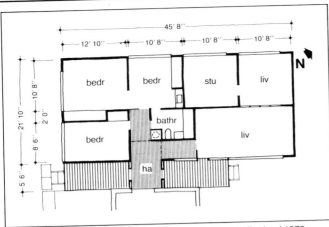

1 Self-contained extension to existing house in Sussex England 1970: external wall panels white glazed asbestos sheet outside, 50 woodwool slab core, plasterboard & laminate inside: flat roof overhangs at eaves; imperial dimensions retained to show how sizes relate to sheet materials, 2' 0'' panel w + 2'' joint & tolerance   Arch W Segal

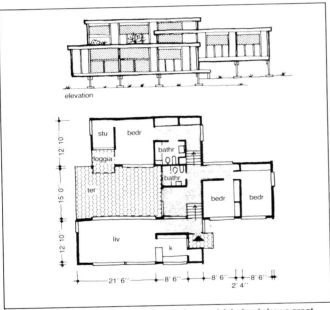

2 This larger house on sloping site at Ballycummisk Ireland shows great flexibility of system   Arch W Segal

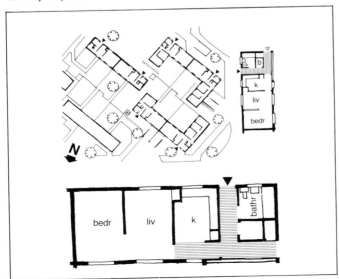

3 These 1-storey 1-bedr houses at Chatham England can be extended to provide up to 3 bedr but space required may mean high initial site costs   Arch W Cook Borough Architect

ADAPTABLE HOUSES

Two recent developments in house planning in Britain are intended to extend flexibility in meeting user requirements.

Walter Segal's houses

Architect Walter Segal has designed houses using sheet materials in standard panel sizes assembled in timber supporting construction. Column centres 3000–3600 apart give great planning flexibility with acceptable beam depths and accommodate most rm sizes. Bldg are raised above ground, with columns based on concrete pads. Planning readily adaptable and materials can be reused →(1)(2).

Extendible house

Extendible houses intended to permit first-home owners to enlarge their houses as family size increases. Examples illustrated represent 2 approaches, extension of 1-storey house to form patio →(3), and construction of rm in roof →(4).

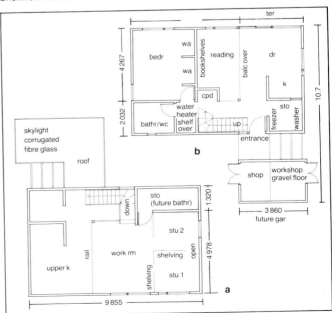

4 In this Scottish design house is extended upwards: no new foundations or brickwork needed   Arch National Building Agency Edinburgh

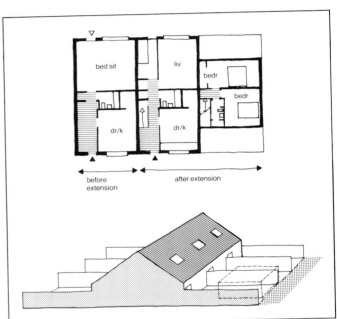

5 American design for low cost plywood panel house; roof panels & walls are built in flat position & hoisted or tipped up into place **a** ground floor **b** first floor   Arch E H & M K Hunter

Underground houses

Growing concern with safeguarding landscape from ill effects of intrusive development engenders greater interest in underground building for housing. Application to domestic house of techniques of construction devised for civil engineering or military projects: costs involved cut by recent refinements in bldg technology.

Energy conservation further factor tending to favour building underground, if only in part. Soil provides good insulation layer, keeping heat in during winter, out in summer →p80.

Underground housing still experimental. Designers must base predictions for such details as number of air changes/hr needed to keep up ventilation levels for preventing build-up of condensation on empirical calculations: not enough built examples see how different forms of excavated construction behave in practice.

In UK bld reg framed before underground housing became likely prospect; official approval therefore dependent on individual negotiation.

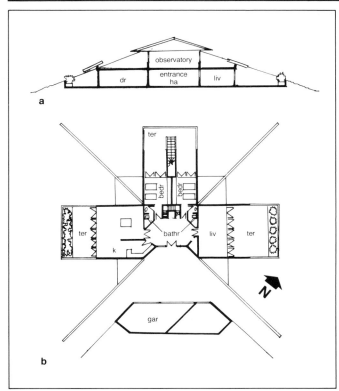

1 Hill top house Florida USA: sited for panoramic views but partly sunk in ground to reduce interference with natural contours; turfed roofs help rest blend in: upper level forms single space observatory **a** section **b** plan Arch William Morgan

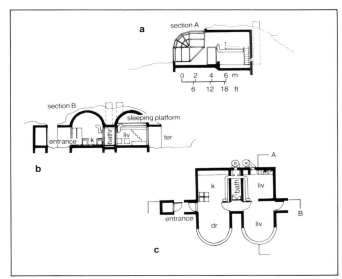

3 Holiday home Jutland Denmark: partly underground so as invisible from landward side with views seaward through 2 large glass domes; underground component concrete shell **a b** sections **c** plan Arch Claus Bonderup

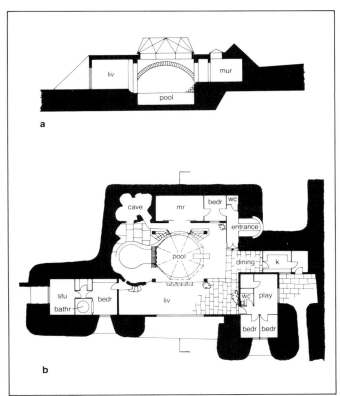

2 House in Pennines England: to avoid intrusion in aesthetically sensitive area partly underground, partly hidden behind earth mounds **a** section **b** plan Arch Arthur Quarmby

4 Twin beach houses Florida USA: underground so as not to interfere with views of houses on land side; built in pairs from shells cast in Gunite, cement mixture usually used for swimming pools; lower halves cast first into excavated sand then 100 thick roof shell built up over steel reinforcing rods; claimed costs approx ½ those of equivalent conventional structure thanks to layer of earth min 560 **a** section **b** plan Arch William Morgan

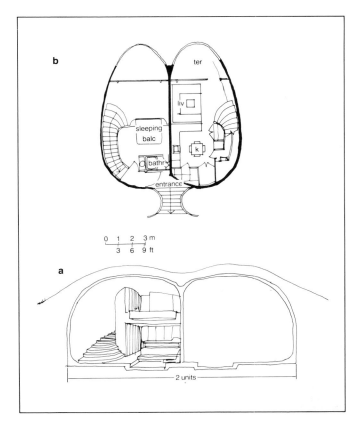

Houses

ENERGY SAVING BY PLAN SHAPE

Minimum perimeter house

Reducing exterior wall area can save energy. In theory dome or sphere ideal configuration but have obvious drawbacks: circular plan has smallest perimeter for given floor area →(1). Next best alternative: perfectly square plan of 1-storey house; minimises wall and window area and therefore energy loss →(2).

Entry locks

Enclosed entries, either within perimeter of house →(3a) or as appendage →(3b), can reduce energy consumption. Size of entry should allow access doors to open independently.

Atriums

Windows responsible for 15–30% total heating energy loss from house. Strategic placing reduces loss and maximises solar gain in winter. When windows face on to atrium this acts as passive solar collector →p81(1).

Sun planning

In many climates significant energy saving can be obtained by means of S-facing windows provided with overhangs, computed to restrict summer sun, and N walls buffered by sto areas. Sun trap with wind buffers can be very effective in cold climates →p81(2).

ENERGY SAVING: EARTH

→also p79

Check list:

gentle S slopes ideal for underground structures: can build into hill & still have benefits of southern exposures

avoid low-lying depressions: heavy, cold air will settle in them; increased danger from frost & damp

make sure no drain or leak into site area from surrounding construction such as parking lots & septic systems

identify ground water levels & seasonal variations in level before deciding location of bldg & excavation depth

assure adequate soil percolation for sunken courtyards & atrium areas; consider installing overflow drains

any structural system can be used, providing designed for proper loads; general rule: 290 kg/m² (150 lb/ft²) for grass-covered roofs & 1950 kg/m² (400 lb/ft²) where small trees are to be supported; snow & pedestrian loads must be added

wall design generally same as any below grade (ground level) construction; but insulation needed between earth & exterior wall of structure, allowing it to store heat, avoiding continuous loss to earth; best currently available material styrofoam (because of closed cell construction); insulation can be reduced in thickness as depth below grade (ground level) increases

when banking (berming) earth against existing walls advisable add cement plaster on metal lath between earth & insulation to prevent roots, insects & rodents from reaching existing walls

butyl sheeting good material for waterproofing; also serves as vapour barrier

to control dampness inside use dehumidification or circulating air

earth pipes (ducts buried in earth) may be used for cooling or for pre-warming outside cold air for winter fresh air supply

examine all local bldg codes, especially in relation to fire exits & ventilation; increased air circulation eqp may affect energy use

study lighting carefully: important for underground structures determine how this affects interior comfort & energy use

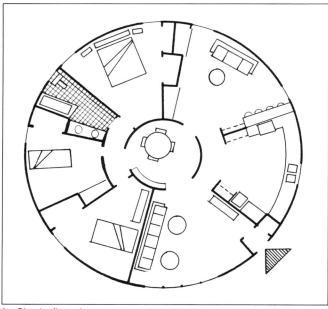

1   Circular floor plan

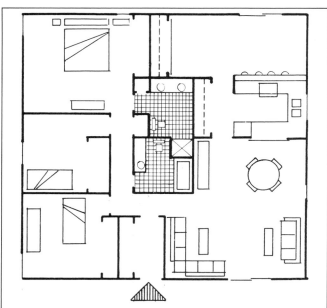

2   1-storey square floor plan

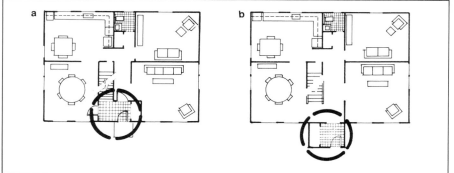

3   Entry lock: **a** within **b** added to (USA) standard practice house

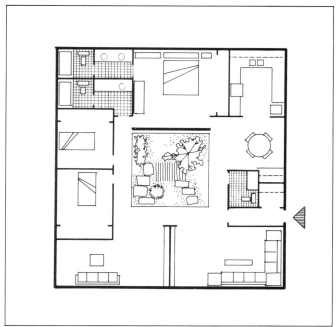

1 Square plan with atrium: windows face inwards; atrium covered by skylight

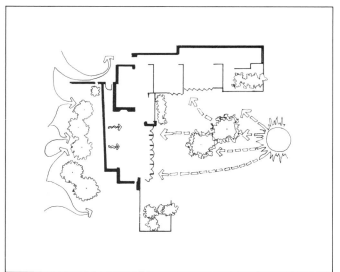

2 House planned to deal with climatic conditions of NW USA: sun trap with wind buffers   Arch Frank Lloyd Wright

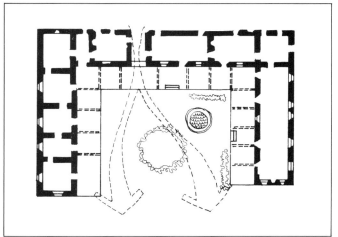

3 Bldg sited to accept prevailing breezes draws air quickly through portal, ventilating court & drawing cooling moisture from pool into air; massing reduces heat gain & provides evening warmth

ENERGY SAVING: VENTILATION

Effective passive approach to cooling: capture prevailing breezes and ventilate house naturally →(3). Ideal orientation for this places face through which breezes are to enter at oblique angle of 20°–70° to wind →(4). Instead of allowing wind pass straight through house this creates turbulence which makes for better ventilation. When wind velocity low internal velocity can be increased by use of wing walls next to window to create 'mini pressure zones' there. Casement windows or adjustable shutters can achieve same effect. Place windows where ventilation required with cills at desired cooling height: *eg* in bedr at mattress level. Window heights also →p404.

Plant evergreens on N and W sides of house to block cold winter winds →(2).

Use ground shape and any nearby ponds or lakes to improve natural ventilation. On sloping sites (particularly facing S) breezes move up hill during day, down at night. Near bodies of water cooling breezes move from water to land during day, from land to water at night →(5).

These guidelines may run counter to effective use of orientation to maximise solar gain →p80. Therefore for any design brief specify whether solar gain or natural ventilation should have priority.

In general consult local weather bureau for accurate information on solar radiation, solar altitude and bearing, cloud cover, rain and snow fall, direction and strength of prevailing winds.

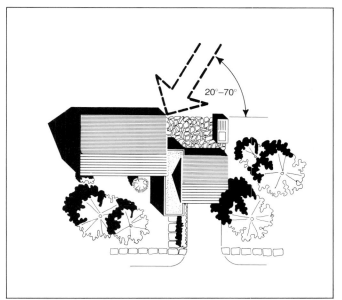

4 Orientation for natural ventilation

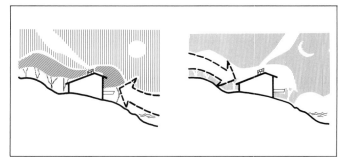

5 Influences of ground shape & bodies of water on natural ventilation

Housing: old people

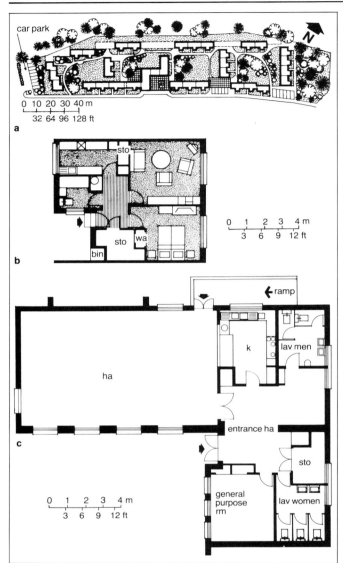

1 Housing for elderly at Cumbernauld Scotland has 31 cottages, warden's house & common rm, each cottage having warden call system with talk-back; meals provided at day centre **a** site layout **b** 2-person cottage **c** common rm/day centre layout plan   Arch Robert White Associates

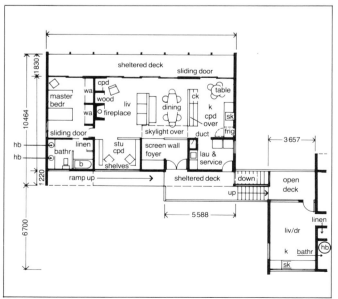

2 Private retirement house with adjoining unit for visiting children USA Arch E H & M K Hunter

Strong trend against putting old people in homes unless in need of special care and attention; →old people's preferences below. Limiting factor can be land values. In USA most low income housing for elderly has been high rise to allow use of expensive land near shops and recreation possibilities.

UK standards envisage 2 types housing:

self-contained for 1 or 2 more active old people →(2)
grouped flatlets for less active with some communal amenities and services →(1)(3)p84(2)

Old people's preferences
Check list of what old people want, based on USA experience:

view from living rm with 1 window low enough to see out when seated
'exterior personal territory' *ie* outdoor area for sitting and social contacts (porches, gardens)
close to shops
informal home-like scale
community outdoor area within easy walk
frequent resting places along walks
security and fire alarm systems
adequate sto
kitchen work tops lower than usual
separate bedr rather than efficiency design
choice of dining in or in community dining rm

Communal amenities
Common rm provided for self-contained dwellings may include sitting rm, tv rm, hobbies rm or workshop. Min floor space/P 0.95 m². Provide near common rm 1 wc and hand basin, tea kitchen or pantry with sink and hot water heater, space for hats and coats, cleaning cpd and sto ≥ 2 m².

For grouped flatlets provide warden's quarters, emergency alarm system →(1) connecting each dwelling with warden's, common rm with ≥ 1.9 m²/P and ancillary amenities as for self-contained above, laundry rm, telephone for tenants with adjacent seat, cpd for communal cleaning materials ≥ 1 m³. Provide access between all accn by enclosed and heated circulation areas and for direct goods delivery from door to door; delivery hatches or grouped lockers acceptable.

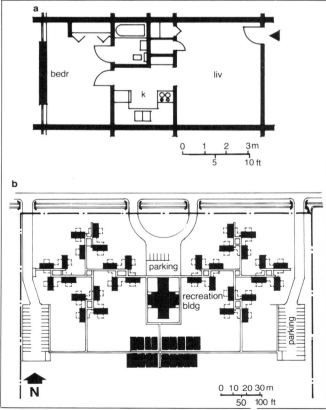

3 Low budget housing for elderly Florida USA **a** typical 1-bedr dwelling **b** site layout plan   Arch C Randolph Wedding

Housing: old people

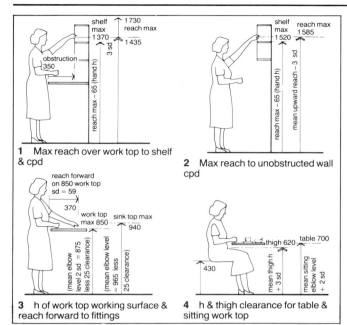

1 Max reach over work top to shelf & cpd

2 Max reach to unobstructed wall cpd

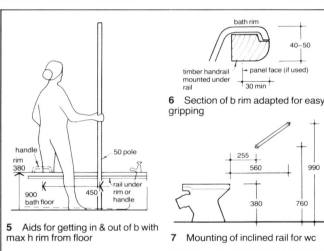

3 h of work top working surface & reach forward to fittings

4 h & thigh clearance for table & sitting work top

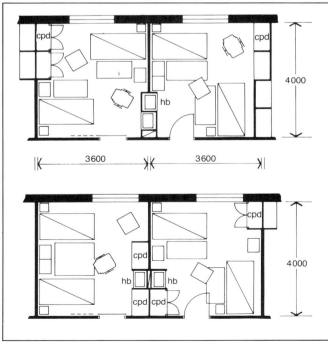

5 Aids for getting in & out of b with max h rim from floor

6 Section of b rim adapted for easy gripping

7 Mounting of inclined rail for wc

Planning factors

Access: if involves climbing more than 1 storey provide elevator: 2 elevators if more than 4 storeys high; access stairs should be enclosed. Stairs →p86(5) 408; ramps →p86 407. All dwellings should have hall or lobby with space for hanging outdoor clothes.

Doors →p401−2. Doors to wc and bathr must open outwards and be fitted with special locks which can be opened from outside.

Kitchen; work sequence →p55. Provide working surfaces both sides sink and cooker. Max height working surfaces 850; max height shelves 1 520 →(1)(2). Cookers specially adapted for safe use by old people. Min size frig 0.7 m³ (NB do not site underneath worktop). Min sto capacity 1.7 m³. Safety precautions →p84.

Heating: space heating living areas capable maintaining min 21°C; for circulation areas in grouped flatlets min 15.6°C when outside temp −1°C.

El socket outlets: generous provision of el socket outlets at convenient positions and levels important; min (UK) kitchen 4, living area 3, bedr 2, hall or lobby 1, bed sitting rm 5.

Living spaces: important provide adequate space for movement round furniture; consider use of built-in units (specially cpd, wa) but take account also of furniture which can afford hand holds when moving about rm. Remember in designing sto space old people tend accumulate treasured possessions.

Guest rm: preferable provide rm for visits from family in self-contained dwellings. For grouped flatlets guest rm may be provided; should be placed close to communal lav.

Bedr in self-contained dwellings follow standard design but note importance of room to move round; built-in wardrobe desirable. Bed sitting rm sometimes in grouped flatlets, usual in old people's homes →(10)(11).

Safety precautions for old people →p84

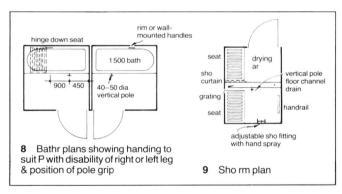

8 Bathr plans showing handing to suit P with disability of right or left leg & position of pole grip

9 Sho rm plan

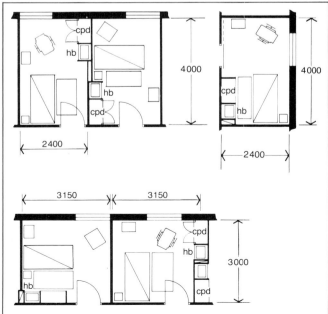

10 Double rm dimensions & data

11 Single rm dimensions & data

Housing: old people

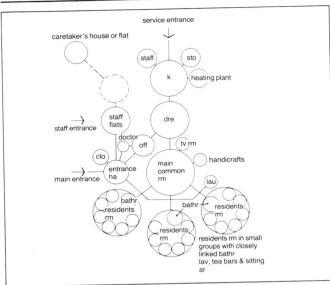

1   Relationships of elements in plan for home for old P

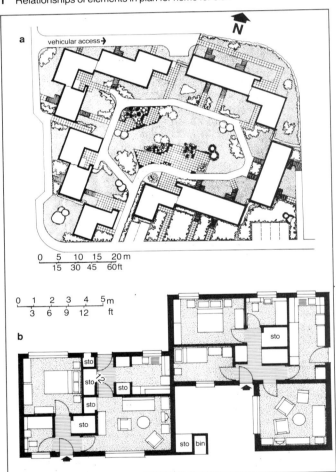

2   Amenity housing for elderly at S Queensferry Scotland: 15 cottages arranged round common gardens have external alarm bells but no warden service **a** site layout **b** house plans   Arch Marshall, Morison Associates

Safety precautions

Check list of safety precautions based on USA practice:

heating system should be designed to avoid burn injury
hot water system should hold water temp at 43°C or below
air conditioning should be designed to avoid draughts in sitting or sleeping areas
radiant floor heating plus air system preferred
door bells and alarms should have low pitch: high tones perception deficient in many old people
automatic shut-off for all gas eqp to prevent inhalation or explosion
place fire sensor over cooker
el cooking preferred for safety of old people
generous overall lighting: avoid glare or shadowed areas
avoid rough wall surfaces
avoid slippery floors; no 'scatter' rugs; wall to wall low pile carpets safest, especially in bedr, but NB strain on heart when vacuum cleaning carpet
no thresholds between rm

Bathroom, lavatory

Bathr large enough for undressing and dressing, if necessary with helper (especially in homes).

Handholds: at least 1 for getting in and out of bath →p83(5); at least 1 at side of wc pedestal →p83(7). Consider use of pole →p83(5). Bath rim should be adapted for easy gripping →p83(6).

Bath: low-sided, flat bottom; length limited so that user cannot be completely immersed: max 1 550. Consider seat at rim height for sitting to wash legs and feet.

Hand basin: rim between 800 and 850 high.

Shower →p83(9): compartment well heated with pegs for clothes on dry side, divided from wet side by shower curtain. Floor non-slip and free from hazards; if smooth with fall to drain, 1:40 tray with upstand to step over, not necessary. Provide secure handhold and wall-mounted seat. Water supply thermostatically controlled to give between 35° and 49°C (UK requirement but →USA safety precautions above). Adjustable spray outlet on flexible hose which can be clipped on in different positions.

Taps: must be usable by arthritic fingers; tops boldly colour-coded; keep hot and cold in same relationship throughout bldg.

Wc: seat height 380 →p83(7). In 1-P grouped flatlets hand basin should be provided.

OLD PEOPLE'S HOMES
Main areas

residents' rm with related bathr and lav
communal rm: *eg* dining, sitting, tv, handicrafts
kitchen, service, sto
admin, matron, med
staff accn, resident and day

Relationships →(1)

4-storey layout →(3)

Bedrooms: usually bed sitting rm. Typical layouts single p83(11), double →p83(10).

Furniture

Table heights: dining 700; gap between chair seat and underside of table top min 190 →p83(11); occasional tables in common rm not lower than chair seat height.

Easy chairs: not too low for getting out; low enough to keep feet on floor: 400–430; footstools for those with short legs; seat depth 410–470; arm rests 230 above seat. Back high enough to support head (consider adjustable pad) angled at 28° to vertical. Gap between under seat and floor for heels to draw back when getting up. NB too soft seat padding can put strain on tissues.

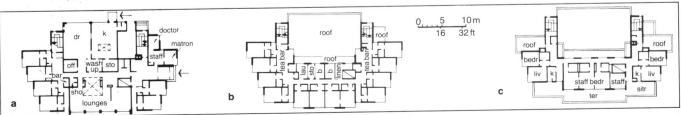

3   Layout plans of home for elderly Dorset England **a** ground plan **b** 1st & 2nd floors **c** 3rd floor

Housing: disabled

Housing for physically disabled traditionally in institutional centres. Now accepted as preferable provide accn in which disabled can live as members of general community, with their families or alone.

Particular requirements to be borne in mind when designing for physically disabled divide into those for
ambulant disabled
wheelchair users

Houses designed for ambulant disabled need not differ greatly from those designed for general use; detail and fittings principal concerns.

For wheelchair users particular attention needed to requirements of wheelchair circulation →(1) and to accessibility of fittings from seated position →p86(8). At initial planning stage allow approx 10% more floor area than for similar accn in general needs housing →p87(1)(3)–(5).

Choice of house type
Wheelchair users should preferably be accommodated in 1-storey houses or ground floor flats, though upper storey flat may be suitable on sloping site where level or ramped exit to place of safety can be provided. 2-storey house acceptable if bathr and at least 1 bedr on ground storey but this arrangement not ideal, particularly where disabled member of family is housewife.

Ambulant disabled may be housed in suitable upper floor flats of 2-storey houses; but seriously disabled, even if ambulant, should not be housed above third storey, max height for normal UK fire service rescue ladders.

In bldg more than 1 storey which houses disabled elevator location and design of critical importance. Lift doors must have 800 clear opening width. In USA cab must be min 1524 × 1524 with easy to push controls 1220 or less from floor and with raised or indented letters beside them →p412.

Escape stairs must have treads not less than 250 and risers not more than 175. Provide space within stairway enclosure on each floor for those with limited mobility to wait for help.

In 2-storey houses: 1 ground floor rm should be available as bedr and wc should be provided at ground storey level. Straight flight stair desirable.

Siting & access
Houses for disabled need to be within reach of shops, children's play spaces, church, pub, surgery. Access by level or ramped approach, min width 1200, max slope 1:12, preferably 1:20. Gradients greater than 1:12 need rest areas 1200 long at 9000 intervals (in USA rest areas also if ramp turns); those in excess of 1:20 at 18 m intervals →p87(11) 407. In USA platforms at doorways as for footpaths →below.

Kerbs should be lowered at crossings and driveways to not more than 25 above roadway; USA practice prefers kerb ramps →(2). Camber should not exceed 1:100. Slotted gratings should always be laid with bars at right angles to direction of wheelchair traffic →(3).

Footpaths →p19 43: where gradients exceed 1:20, or where drop to side more than 600, handrails required 950 high extending min 300 beyond beginning and end of ramp or ridge. Rails with smooth surface required for all ramps in USA on at least 1 side, 813 above ramp surface and extending 300 beyond beginning and end, with 1830 straight clearance at bottom. Avoid loose gravel, cobbles or setts, though materials with distinctive texture can be helpful, particularly to blind or partially sighted, in signalling approach to obstruction or change in level. Provide continuing common surface not interrupted by steps or sudden changes in level. Blend with levels of other paths or parking area lanes which may cross. At doorways level platform at least 1524 × 1524 if door swings out or 915 × 1524 if door swings in, stretching at least 300 each side of doorway (USA requirement).

Main access path to house should be at least 1200 wide and any garden paths min 900. Access from front to back garden should preferably by-pass house →p47(6), be kept clear of opening windows and similar hazards →(4) and, in wheelchair housing, provide turning space for chair →(1)p43(3). Width needed for wheelchair passing →(5).

Hazards: where such hazards as open manholes and access panels of open excavations occur protect by barrier min 2400 from danger point and mark with sound and sight warning devices.

Car parking: provide near house as possible, preferably within boundary of property. Ambulant disabled driver requires parking space min 4800 × 2700, wheelchair user min 4800 × 3000; USA requirement min 3660 extra on each side. In general car park handicapped should be nearest bldg and clearly marked. Disabled should not need travel behind parked cars. Garage space needed for wheelchair user →(6).

Parking for wheelchair users should preferably be under cover and linked to house. Car port particularly convenient: allows unimpeded access. Cross beam should be supplied to take stirrup grip or hoist. If garage provided should preferably be integral with house and give direct access. In this case floor should be laid to fall of at least 1:100 away from house; in UK relaxation from bldg reg requirements necessary to provide flush threshold.

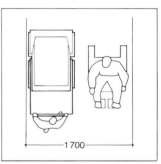

1 Turning ar required for wheelchair

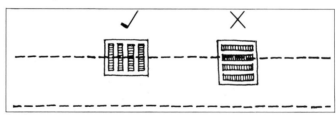

2 Kerb ramps should whenever possible make natural extension of alignment of footpath

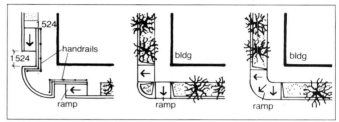

3 Slotted gratings should be laid at right angles to wheelchair traffic

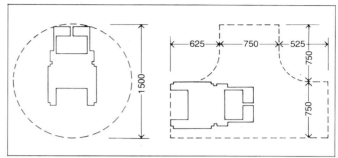

4 Opening window hazard

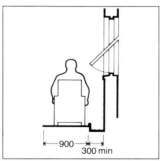

5 Footpath w for wheelchair passing

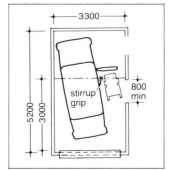

6 Gar space for wheelchair user (2800 w adequate for ambulant disabled)

Housing: disabled

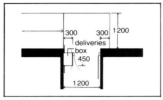

1 With double leaf doors design so that only 1 need open

2 Clear space beside door for ease of access to keyhole; shelf for parcels

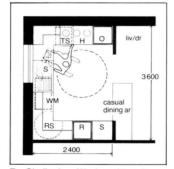

3 Deliveries box beside front door, inside box door lockable

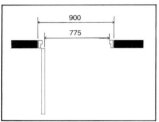

4 Doors for wheelchair users should be hung with hinges towards corner

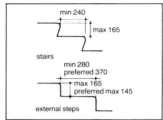

5 Stairs for ambulant disabled & elderly people

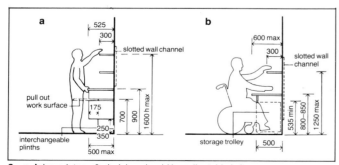

6 Standard k layout for ambulant disabled

7 Similar k →(6) altered to suit wheelchair user: O oven, H hob, C ck, T S trolley sto unit B broom cpd, WM washing machine, R frig, RS rotating sto unit, S sk

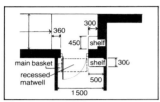

8 **a b** k work tops & shelving should be adjustable in h

Common access areas

In flats built to accommodate disabled and in other bldg likely to be used by them in any numbers at least 1 main entrance and any door giving access to emergency exit or external space likely to be used by disabled occupants must have:
level or ramped approach
flush threshold
clear width min 775

Elevator must be accessible to such entrance.

Double leaf doors should be designed so that only 1 leaf need be opened →(1). Automatic sliding doors operated by pressure pad most convenient but expensive. Where revolving doors used normal side hung door of suitable width should also be provided.

Internal planning

For ambulant disabled 900 wide enough for entrance halls and passages; will also allow enough space for occasional use by wheelchairs.

For wheelchair users entrance hall min 1 200 wide for depth 1 800, preferably 1 200 throughout. Lobby between 2 sets of doors will need be 1 500 × 1 500 clear of obstructions to allow freedom to manoeuvre chair. USA: floor level inside and outside for 1 524 from door in direction door swings.

Clear space min 300 should be provided alongside leading edge of front door for ease of access to keyhole and handle →(2): USA 300 each side of door. Shelf 300 × 300 useful both inside and outside to take parcels when opening or closing door →(2). Door closures should be suitable for disabled users. No sharp inclines or abrupt changes of level at door cill. If deliveries box provided →(3) inner door should be lockable. Mat wells should be fully recessed →(2).

All internal doors should have min opening 775. Thresholds should be flush. For wheelchair users doors should be hung with hinges toward corner →(4) or, in small rm, open out. Low hanging door closures must not obtrude into traffic ways. Floor should be non-slip. Each storey should be on 1 level or connected by ramp if level changes.

Stairs & steps →(5). Avoid abrupt nosing. Handrails 813 from tread at face of riser, 1 extending min 460 beyond top and bottom step (USA requirement). Ensure adequate lighting without confusing shadows. With low hanging ceiling lights or signs allow free-standing stair clearances ≥ 2 133 from floor.

Controls & switches for light, heat, ventilation, windows, curtains, fire alarms and others of essential use should be within reach of wheelchair user. Identification of switches important, specially for blind or partially sighted. Provide raised or recessed letters or numbers for rm identification at side of door at suitable height. Knurled handle or knob on doors leading to areas dangerous for blind person.

Living areas: additional space needed in wheelchair housing to manoeuvre chair in living rm, kitchen →(6)(7), bath →p87(1) and at least 1 bedr →p87(4)(5). Living rm windows should be designed allow seated person see out without difficulty. Bay window very suitable, especially in wheelchair housing →p87(6).

Kitchen work tops and shelving adjustable in height →(8). Knee space beneath fitments particularly important in wheelchair housing →(8). Cooker should preferably have separate oven and hob. Deep sinks difficult for most disabled people: max depth 150.

Bathr & wc should be equipped with basic support and grab rails →p87(7); seat 400 wide should be provided at head of bath. Hand basins best set into work tops cantilevered from wall; preferred height for use by ambulant disabled 850, by wheelchair users 750. Mirror, towel rails and shelves ≤ 1 016 above floor.

Wheelchair users need enough space round wc pedestal to permit both frontal and lateral approach, with space for assistance if necessary →p87(8); door should swing out. Dispenser and disposal units at side of wc not directly above. Bathr ceiling should be so constructed to allow for fixing hoist or track if necessary. If bathr planned open directly off bedr track can be fitted provide direct route between bed, bath and wc.

Sound warning signals should be duplicated by visual for deaf.

Internal planning

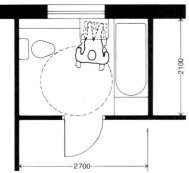

1 Standard bathr enlarged to provide space for wheelchair user

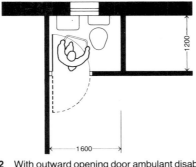

2 With outward opening door ambulant disabled can use normal wc compartment

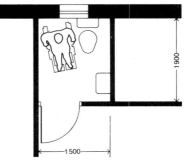

3 For wheelchair user wc compartment ar must be bigger

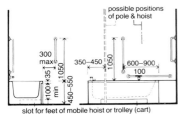

4 Single bedr large enough for wheelchair user

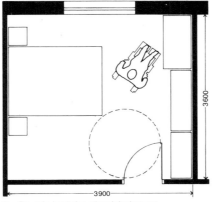

5 Double bedr for wheelchair user

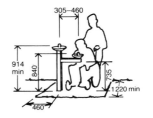

6 Bay window in liv can give pleasure to wheelchair user

seated eyelevel range
max h for control
1700 max ambulant
1350 max wheelchair
1000–1350
600

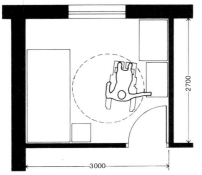

1600–1700 400
700–800
position of ceiling eye-hook
possible position of pole
1200
450
35
50
1800
possible line of hoist

possible positions of pole & hoist
1050
300 max
1100 35
1050 min
350–450
600–900
100
450–550

slot for feet of mobile hoist or trolley (cart)

7 Spaces & fittings for bathr for wheelchair user

External detail

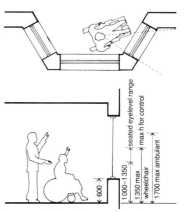

9 Public telephone suitable for handicapped & children; good lighting important; instructions in braille & push button dials for blind; volume control on headset

1980 min
1220
1524
762
762 min per phone
914

10 Drinking fountain for wheelchair user; should be operated by hand lever; paved ar round fountain to prevent mud & puddles

305–460
914 min
840
735
1220 min
460

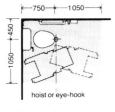

750 1050
450
1050

hoist or eye-hook

possible position of hoist or eye-hook for stirrup grip etc

flush handle
paper holder
900–1200
225
600–700
300
450–500

8 Spaces & fittings for lav for wheelchair user

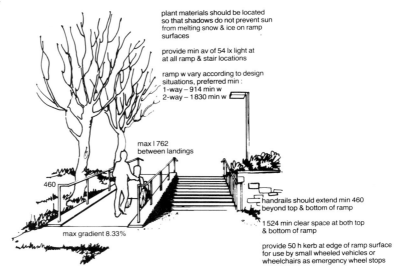

plant materials should be located so that shadows do not prevent sun from melting snow & ice on ramp surfaces

provide min av of 54 lx light at at all ramp & stair locations

ramp w vary according to design situations, preferred min :
1-way – 914 min w
2-way – 1830 min w

max l 762 between landings

460

handrails should extend min 460 beyond top & bottom of ramp

1524 min clear space at both top & bottom of ramp

provide 50 h kerb at edge of ramp surface for use by small wheeled vehicles or wheelchairs as emergency wheel stops

max gradient 8.33%

11 Outdoor ramp data: max gradient 1:12 →p407

Houses

BALCONIES

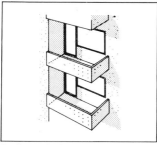

1   Corner balc

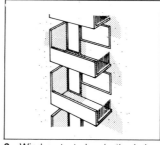

2   Wind-protected projecting balc

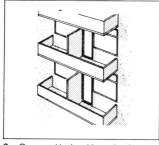

3   Grouped balc with projecting partitions

4   Grouped balc with separating sto for furniture

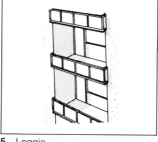

5   Loggia

6   Staggered balc

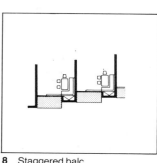

7   Balc staggered in plan & set at angle

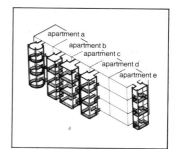

8   Staggered balc

Balcony desirable extension of living rm, especially for flats.

Corner balconies that cannot be overlooked and are protected from wind →(1) more comfortable than freely projecting balconies which have to be shielded on wind and weather side →(2). Grouped balconies should be suitably divided for privacy. →(3) or separated →(4). Loggias less economic as they create more exterior wall surface →(5). Balconies staggered vertically more difficult to protect from wind and from being overlooked →(6); balconies staggered in plan well protected and private →(7)(8).

Important considerations include orientation to sun, view, position of neighbouring flats and bldg and relationship of living rm, studio, kitchen and (sometimes) bedr. Other factors: appropriate size, privacy, protection from street noise, shielding from excessive sun, wind and rain. Suitable materials for parapets: frosted glass, plastics, asbestos cement, timber slats and steel sheets fixed to supporting structure of solid or tubular steel sections firmly attached to bldg; steel verticals (horizontal can be climbed by children) do not give protection against wind or being overlooked.

Draughts created between balcony floors and solid parapets →(9): better place parapet in front of floor →(10) or use solid parapet (not too high if 'bath tub' feeling to be avoided) with steel rail at byelaw height, possible room for flower boxes →(11).

Access balconies →p90 96 97

9   Parapet above balc floor level

10   Parapet in front of balc floor

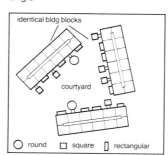

11   Solid parapet

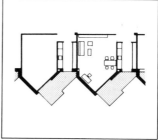

12   Prefabricated balc designed to be plugged on to apartment bldg to define & enhance exterior space Arch Kamnitzer

identical bldg blocks
courtyard
○ round   □ square   ▯ rectangular

apartment a
apartment b
apartment c
apartment d
apartment e

13   Apartment blocks at Cross Creek Village Playa del Rey USA have round, square & rectangular balc placed to modulate open space between bldg   Arch Kamnitzer

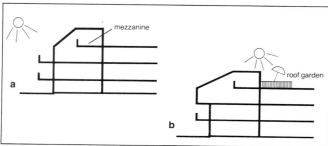

mezzanine
roof garden
a
b

14   **a** large top-floor apartments at Los Angeles USA have similar balc to those of smaller units **b** at apartments in Hollywood USA penthouse liv includes balc ar & roof garden mezzanine   Arch Kamnitzer

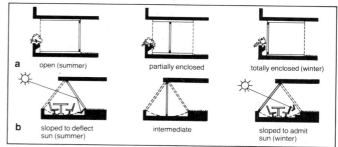

a open (summer)   partially enclosed   totally enclosed (winter)
b sloped to deflect sun (summer)   intermediate   sloped to admit sun (winter)

15   **a** Flexible balc created by using frame of sliding glass doors set on perpendicular runners **b** hinged glass creates balc adaptable to seasons Arch Kamnitzer

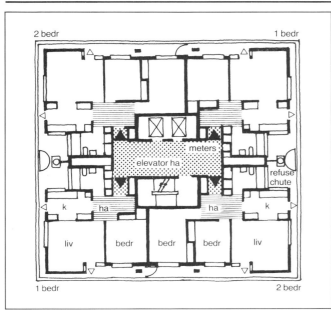

1 Upper floor plan of 12-storey point block at Battersea London England designed 1963: balc provide escape routes between flats   Arch George Trew & Dunn

BUILDING TYPES

This section discusses bldg divided horizontally to provide separate and self-contained dwellings which need not necessarily be on 1 floor only. Types can be distinguished as follows.

Low-rise or high-rise

In UK accepted max height of entrance door to dwelling normally reached by ramp or stairs 4 storeys from ground level or from main entrance to bldg. Beyond that limit elevator access must be provided: bldg containing such flats called high-rise. In practice low-rise flatted bldg often provided with elevators; in public sector housing these required where more than 2 storeys have to be climbed to any private entrance door. Such bldg, from 3 to 5 storeys, often called medium-rise.

Point block or slab block

In point block all dwellings share single vertical access system →(1). Vertical access must always include stairway; according to height and layout bldg might also have 1 or more elevators and secondary escape stairs. Slab block continous bldg in which dwellings reached by 2 or more separate vertical access systems →(2).

Maisonettes

Separate dwelling in low or high-rise blocks having rm arranged on more than 1 storey known as maisonettes: have been built in UK in 4-storey blocks →(3), in slab blocks and in combination with flats →(4). Such arrangements can show savings over flats of similar accn because common access space less. In USA similar 'skip floor' design halves elevator stops in high rise.

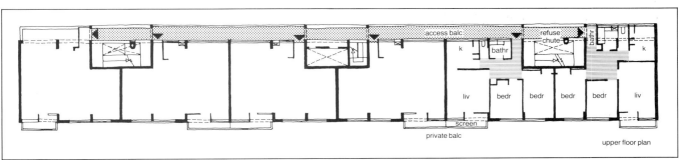

2 Slab block: 9-storey flats with balc access built 1953 at Pimlico London; *in-situ* rc construction: note use of sto to insulate bedr from stairwell   Arch Powell & Moya

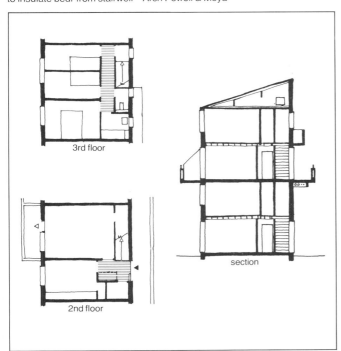

3 Maisonettes in 4-storey blocks in high-density development in London England; levels on site permit access at second-storey h & demand single aspect house plan: note screening of stair & escape balc at bedr storey in upper maisonette   Arch Yorke Rosenberg Mardall

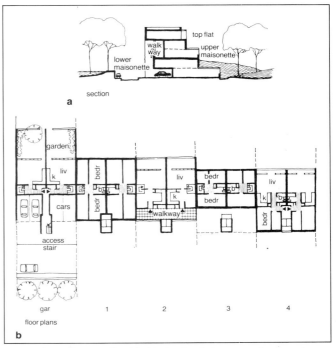

4 Housing at Runcorn Cheshire England on 5 storeys: section comprises 2 × 2-storey maisonettes, lower entered from ground level & upper from second-storey walkway, & top-storey flat approached by stairs from ground or walkway, connected by ramps & bridge to main shopping ar of town centre   Arch J Stirling

Flats & apartments: Access

TYPES OF ACCESS

Access can be classified as stairway, balcony or corridor.

Stairway access

Stairway access, with 2, 3 or 4 flats per landing allows grouping of services and can provide high degree of privacy: standard solution in point blocks. In slab blocks, however, disadvantages where more than 2 flats served from each landing: usually involves back-to-back planning and consequently some form of artificial ventilation →(1).

Balcony & corridor access

Balcony and internal corridor access, usually employed in slab blocks, permit savings in common access space. Exposure to weather obvious disadvantage of balconies, particularly in high rise, and internal planning constrained by potential lack of privacy on balcony side; window design can modify this constraint. Internal corridors escape weather but introduce new problems of sound insulation, lighting and ventilation and require higher standards of management in use. Open corridors or roof-streets avoid most of these difficulties. In medium rise development open corridors and sheltered balconies giving access to small flats over larger dwellings can accommodate wide variety of household sizes at high densities. →(2). Balcony and corridor access have been much used in conjunction with split-level flats and maisonettes. Such arrangements →p96 97.

Bridge access

For sites with steep or varied slopes bridge access →(3) offers flats with 1 storey at bridge level with 1 or 2 down and up. Stairs and landings covered but not enclosed in all but severest climates: if closed possible by orientation use them as passive solar trap.

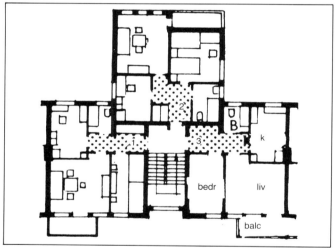

1   3 × 2-rm flats/landing achieve good daylighting & cross-ventilation but extra length of wall has to be weighed against economy of circulation
Arch E Gutkind

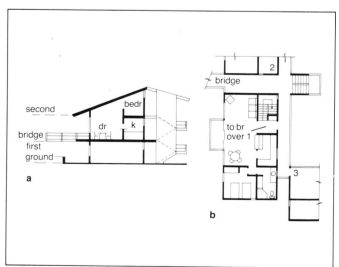

3   Bridge access **a** section **b** plan

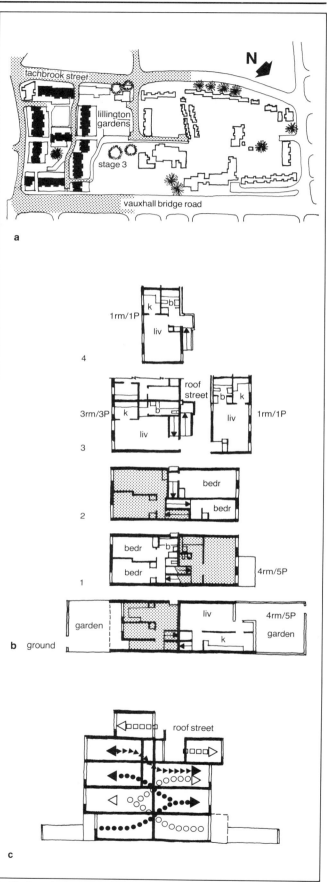

a

b   ground

c

2   Medium-rise housing at high density (618 B-space/ha) at Lillington Street London England: each family house entered at ground level through private garden; smaller maisonettes & flats have access from open corr or 'roof streets' which bridge between blocks & are served by elevators **a** site plan **b** floor plans **c** typical section   Arch Darbourne & Darke

FIRE PRECAUTIONS: PLANNING CRITERIA

Horizontal escape routes

Every storey containing entrance door to flat or maisonnette should be planned to ensure that fire in any 1 dwelling will not obstruct escape of other occupants from bldg. Problem related to type of access. Permissible travel distances in relation to access and plan arrangement given as designer's guide *ie* **planning criteria not code/legal information** →(1).

In USA national, state and local codes apply; inspections and approvals usually administered by local authority in cooperation with state departments: designers should seek early review of their proposals.

Protection of stairways

Every stairway serving flat or maisonnette more than 2 storeys above ground level should be enclosed and separated from remainder of bldg by fr walls and self-closing fr doors. No dwelling should open directly from such stairway but should be reached through intervening lobby, access balcony or corridor. Enclosure requirement does not apply to subsidiary access stairways serving small groups of dwellings from open corridors or access balconies, subject to conditons stated in (1) and in p93(1).

1 Travel distances in storeys containing flats & maisonettes: table has no legal authority but is designer's guide to escape requirements within bldg more than 2 storeys h which contain flats or maisonettes, based on various codes & reg currently applied in UK (1979); it gives max travel distance to storey exit which must either be door opening direct to open air at ground level or door to protected stairway as described →p93.

layout	conditions	travel distance from private entrance door to storey exit
flats & maisonettes entered from corr: no alternative escape route from each dwelling; a with smoke dispersal *ie* where corr is ventilated direct to open air b without direct ventilation to open air to secure smoke dispersal	corr has smoke outlets at each end, & at intervals not exceeding 60 m storey has 1 exit only with, i every entrance door not more than 4 500 from stairway approach lob, or ii every entrance door opening into ventilated lob & not more than 4 500 from self-closing fr door to corr leading directly to storey exit	i escape in 1 direction only: not more than 15 m ii escape in 2 directions: not more than 40 m not more than 4 500 not more than 15 m
flats & maisonettes entered from corr: each dwelling has alternative escape route	every private entrance door opens into corr with smoke outlets	i escape in 1 direction only: not more than 40 m ii escape in 2 directions: not more than 50 m
flats entered from lob in bldg up to 4 storeys with 1 stairway only	1 not more than 4 flats per storey, & net floor ar of flats above 1st storey not more than 380 m² 2 not more than 4 flats per storey, & net floor ar of flats above 1st storey not more than 720 m², & no private entrance door more than than 4 500 from storey exit or from self-closing fr door across lob, & every section lob ventilated to open air	not more than 4 500 not more than 15 m
flats & maisonettes entered from open access balc	floor of access balc constructed as compartment floor	not more than 50 m
flats and maisonettes entered indirectly from open access balc by subsidiary access stairway	each flat & maisonette has independent alternative escape route, or subsidiary stairway does not extend more than 1 storey above or below open access balc, & subsidiary stairway serves no flat at access balc level & not more than 3 flats at higher or lower level, & each flat entered & wholly contained within 1 level, & no flat entrance door more than 5 000 from head or foot of subsidiary stairway, & subsidiary stairway open to access balc & permanently ventilated at its head	not more than 50 m

Flats & apartments: Internal planning

European development

Development of flats in Europe between 1919 and 1939 largely dominated by concept of min dwelling. In extreme housing shortage dwellings of small floor area and few internal amenities were used to provide high-density housing in inner-city areas →(1)(2)(3)(4)(5). More generously planned flats used in suburban situations and for middle-class occupation →(6)(7)(8)(9).

Standards for flats & maisonettes

Modern flats not regarded as 'second-best' but should provide accn similar to houses for equivalent household size. Indeed space standards for flats in public sector in UK slightly more generous than for houses, recognising difficulties of providing for internal circulation and fire escape →p91 93.

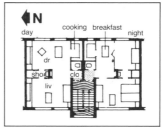

5 Convertible flat in day & night use with fold-away beds & screens; ar 40 m² Arch C Fieger

6 5-bedr flat in system bldg Stora Tuna Sweden Arch Y Johnsson

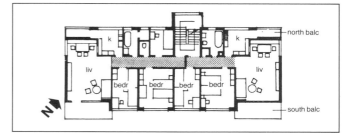

7 4 & 3-rm low-rise flats at Neubuhl Zürich Switzerland 1931 Arch M E Haefeli *et al*

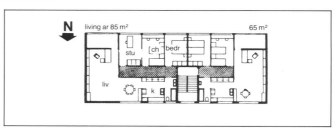

8 Classical German suburban flat; 4 & 3-rm S aspect flats with generous living ar & private balc Arch L Hilberseimer

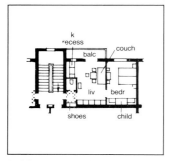

1 Viennese 2-rm flat of 1920s; 4 flats/landing Arch F Schuster

2 Small German flat with wc on inner wall; living ar 28 m² Arch Märkische Wohnungsbau

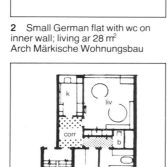

3 More generous 3-rm flat with wc & sho

4 Dutch 3-rm flat with internal bathr: compact plan with separated service Arch H Leppla

9 More tightly planned flats for E-W aspect Arch L Hilberseimer

10 5-rm flat at Highgate London England with bedr opening from internal lob (1936): this arrangement would now need secondary escape from bedr Arch B Lubtkin

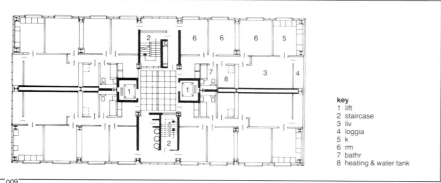

key
1 lift
2 staircase
3 liv
4 loggia
5 k
6 rm
7 bathr
8 heating & water tank

11 Flats in high-rise block Balornock Scotland Arch S Bunton & Associates

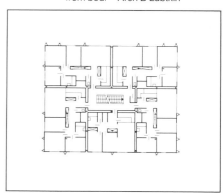

12 Apartment-size floor in block of flats Rouen France Arch Lods Depondt Beauclair Alexandre

Flats & apartments

layout	conditions	number of escape routes
all rm on same level as entrance door	1 bedr doors open into entrance ha: no bedr door more than 7500 from entrance door	1
	2 any other case	1 plus alternative escape route from every bedr with door more than 7500 from entrance door
all rm on level above entrance door	1 bedr doors open into passage at head of stair: no bedr door more than 7500 from head of private stair to entrance door	1
	2 any other case	1 plus alternative escape route from every bedr with door more than 7500 from head of private stair
all rm on level below entrance door	any case	1 plus alternative escape route from every bedr
bedr not opening from entrance ha or landing passage	bedr open from inner lob with fr construction & self-closing fr doors as required for private entrance ha	an alternative escape route from every bedr opening from inner lob
bedr on level above liv & k; entrance door at liv level	private stairway separated from upper lob by fr screen with self-closing fr door	1 plus alternative escape route from upper level
bedr on level above liv & k; entrance door at bedr level	private stairway separated from entrance ha by fr screen with self-closing fr door	1 plus alternative escape route from lower level
bedr on level below liv & k; entrance door at liv level	private stairway separated from lower lob by fr screen with self-closing fr door	1 plus alternative escape route from lower level
bedr on level below liv & k; entrance door at bedr level	no bedr door more than 7500 from entrance door	1 plus alternative escape route from upper level
alternative private stairway leads up or down to alternative escape route	liv & k separated from bedr by self-closing fr door	1 plus alternative escape route from level which is not entrance level
open plan maisonette	1 with private entrance ha & stairway separated from other storey by fr wall or screen & self-closing fr door	1 plus alternative escape route from every enclosed rm at entrance level not opening into private entrance ha, & alternative escape route from storey which is not entrance level
	2 with private entrance ha, but stairway not separated as in condition 1	1 plus alternative escape route from every enclosed rm at entrance level not opening into private entrance ha, & alternative escape route from every rm on storey which is not entrance level
any other type of layout		1 plus alternative escape route from every bedr & from every level which is not entrance level

1 Escape routes from flats & maisonettes: as →p91(1); this also has no legal authority but is designer's guide to escape requirements related to internal planning, based upon various codes & reg currently applied in UK (1979): where local differences exist they might be less onerous, but table should always provide guide to safe planning

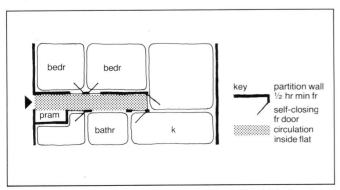

2 Conventional small flat plan, most safely arranged with liv & k furthest from entrance door

DETERMINING FACTORS

Privacy and fire escape principal determinants of internal planning of flats and maisonettes. Other user requirements summarised in Parker Morris standards →p44 48 Bib233.

Privacy →also p76 96 98
Privacy best secured by stairway access where only entrance door and possibly delivery hatch open to landing. In balcony access, bathr, wc and kitchen can be placed on access side, but note difficulty in providing natural light where high windows are below balcony.

Sound insulation presents greater difficulties in flats than in houses, and privacy best secured by planning. Avoid long separating walls to bedr, and avoid bedr beneath access balconies or adjoining elevators, stairs or refuse chutes. Where possible use cupboards (closets) to increase sound insulation of separating walls.

Fire escape
Bedr doors opening into private entrance hall should wherever possible be nearer to entrance door than living rm or kitchen. All doors other than bathr and wc should be self-closing and fr; walls enclosing entrance hall should have ½hr fr. In most other conditions plan for alternative escape routes from bedr above 2 storeys. Recommendations generally based on current codes of practice summarised in →(1) and illustrated → (2)(3)(4). But note: **always consult appropriate code.**

Services →p383–97
Attention should be paid to grouping of services and provision of adequate service ducts, especially where bldg incorporate variety of dwelling sizes and plans not repetitive. Standard location and arrangement of bath, wc and kitchen fittings facilitates design of ducts and service stacks. Internal bathr and wc require mech ventilation, either individually or by common ducting. Shared ventilation systems require smoke-stopping by fire dampers and stand-by fans to ensure continuous operation.

Check list for services in flats
water
el
drainage (+ rain water drainage)
gas(not in high-rise)
mech ventilation
TV/FM radio aerials
TV/radio relay
telephones
main entrance phone & control

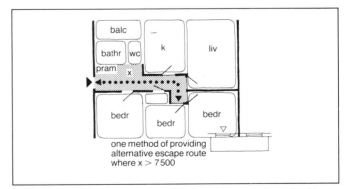

one method of providing alternative escape route where x > 7500

3 In larger flats distance between furthest bedr & entrance doors should not exceed 7500 unless alternative escape route provided

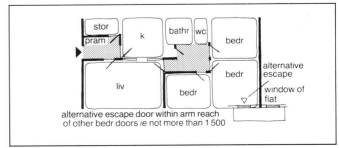

alternative escape door within arm reach of other bedr doors ie not more than 1500

4 Flat with inner lob, above 2 storeys, always requires alternative escape provision

Flats & apartments

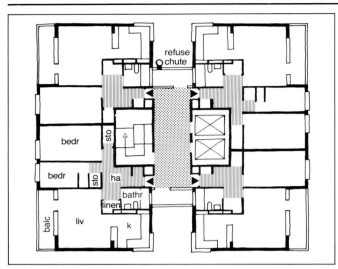

1   Point block at Thamesmead England: 12-storey system-built structure provides 4 flats on each storey   Arch GLC Architects Dept

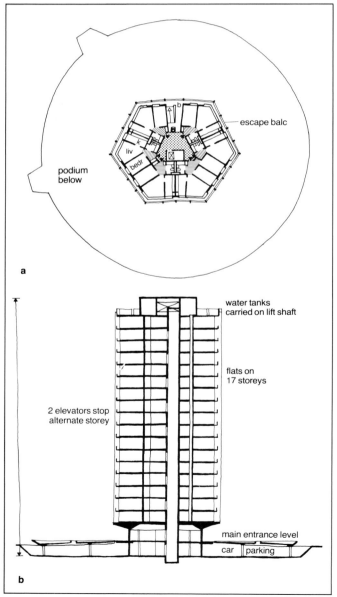

2   Point Royal Bracknell England: one of few British point blocks with more than 4 flats/storey; split hexagonal plan logically accommodates 6 flats & minimises circulation space & escape distances; car space for each flat under circular podium **a** upper floor plan **b** section   Arch Arup Associates

POINT BLOCKS

By ingenious planning up to 10 flats served by 1 vertical access system in some continental designs. Fire escape reg make such solutions difficult in Britain, unless flats very small or unless access balconies used, reducing convenience of point block arrangement.

Some point blocks built in Britain →(1)(2)(3)(4).

American and continental examples →p95

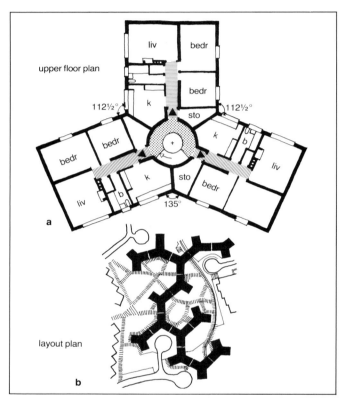

3   Y blocks have been developed in several countries, particularly in low-rise forms where they can be joined together without overshadowing: this example, built in 1957 at Cumbernauld Scotland, has arms at unequal angles, giving greater variety of layout arrangements & avoiding closed courts **a** typical upper floor plan **b** layout plan   Arch Cumbernauld Development Corporation

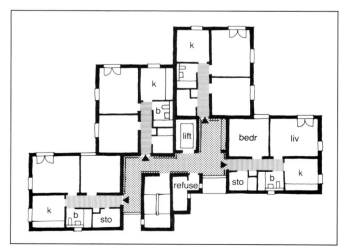

4   Low point blocks or 'stub blocks', with elevators, can provide suitable housing for elderly people, as in this London England 3-storey block of sheltered housing →p82   Arch Yorke Rosenberg Mardall

Flats & apartments

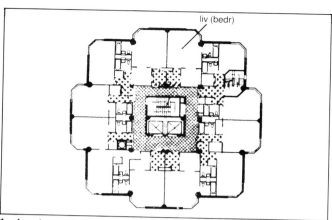

1 American apartments: small service flats surrounding 16-storey circulation core   Arch R C Reamer

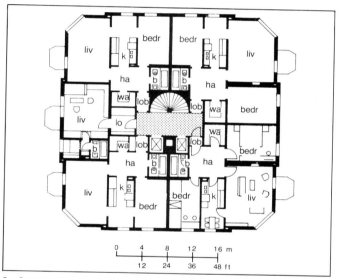

2 Swedish point block: fire precautions rely on containing fire in flat where it originates & preventing smoke penetration by double doors at flat entrance; escape hatches provided in balc floors: accepted that stairway & access landings might not be usable while fire being fought

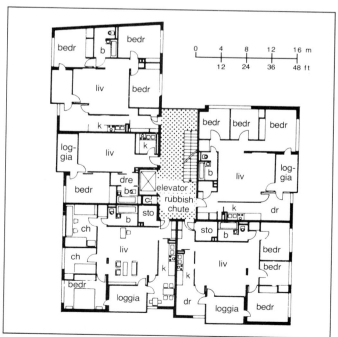

3 5 flats/landing Berlin Germany: flats have no corr but large loggias; liv acts as circulation ar   Arch A Aalto

POINT BLOCKS

Some American and continental examples, most of which would not meet British reg.

Flats in point blocks generally small, with kitchen and bathr planned as standard unit and often with artificial lighting and ventilation.

Point blocks can be planned as 2 blocks of flats connected by vertical access core. This twin plan arrangement improves daylight and sunlight to larger number of flats →(4).

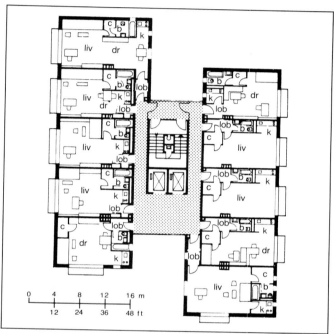

4 Twin plan: 10 flats/floor, escape stair well protected but travel distances would be too great for UK reg   Arch Müller-Rehm, Siegmann

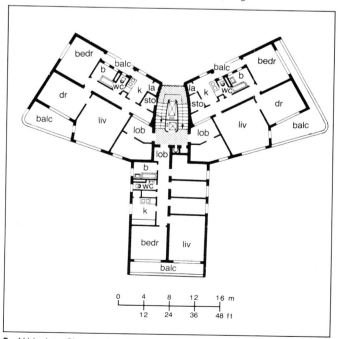

5 Y block on Siemens housing estate Munich Germany   Arch Freymuth

Flats & apartments

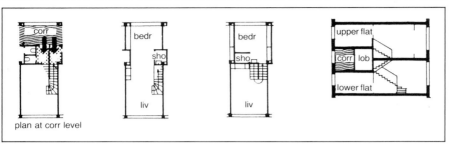

plan at corr level

DUPLEX & TRIPLEX SECTIONS

Designs for split level flats and maisonettes, with access balcony, deck or corridor every second (duplex) or third (triplex) storey, have been developed over many years. While some design problems solved, *eg* visual privacy, cross ventilation, others increased, such as sound insulation.

→also p97(1)(4)

1 Duplex: Russian type very small flat with limited sleeping ar but more spacious liv; access balc serves 2 storeys; wc off entrance lob   Arch M I Ginsberg

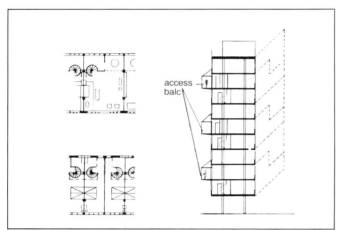

2 Triplex: early French type; lob opens from access balc with stairs up or down   Arch Pingusson

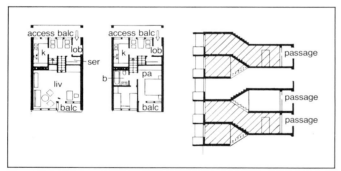

3 Split level flats with balc access: entrance, dining ar & k at entrance level, liv ½ storey up, bedr ½ down   Arch Hirsch

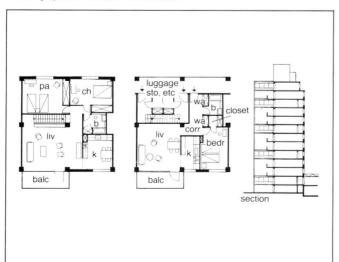

4 Triplex: Mareschal system, with access balc every third storey, Cambridge USA; separate entrances with private stairs for larger flats; all flats have cross ventilation   Arch Koch-Kennedy

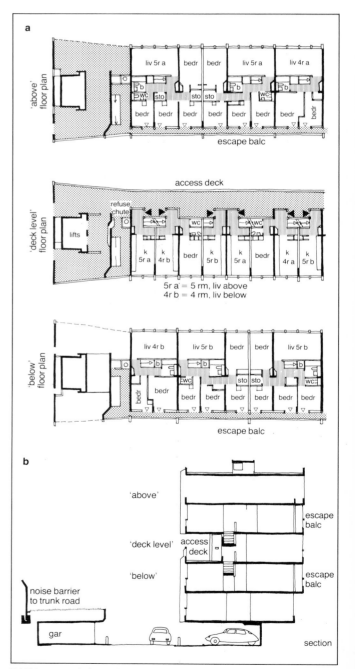

5 Wide access balc or 'deck' housing Robin Hood Lane London England: ½ bay partitions can be arranged to permit wide variation of dwelling sizes; stairs & blacked-in walls must be regarded as permanent structure; note escape balc at bedr levels   Arch A & P Smithson

INTERNAL ACCESS

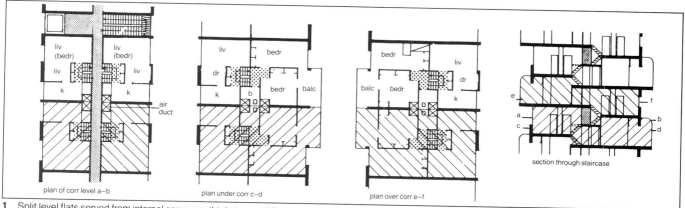

plan of corr level a–b   plan under corr c–d   plan over corr e–f   section through staircase

1   Split level flats served from internal corr every third storey: all flats have cross-ventilation →also p96   Arch Neufert

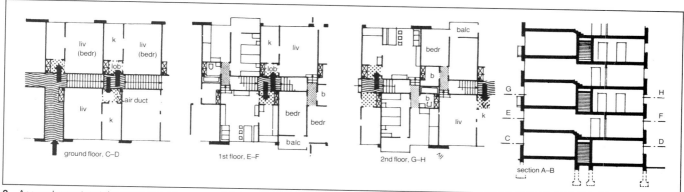

ground floor, C–D   1st floor, E–F   2nd floor, G–H   section A–B

2   Access by centre stairway; each landing serves 2 flats: again all flats cross-ventilated   Arch Neufert

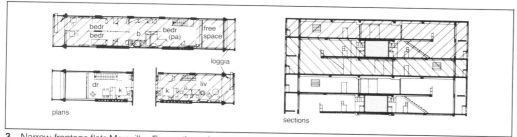

plans   loggia   sections

3   Narrow-frontage flats Marseilles France through extended through very deep block with private balc on each facade: double h liv allow sun & daylight penetration; access by wide internal corr every third storey   Arch Le Corbusier

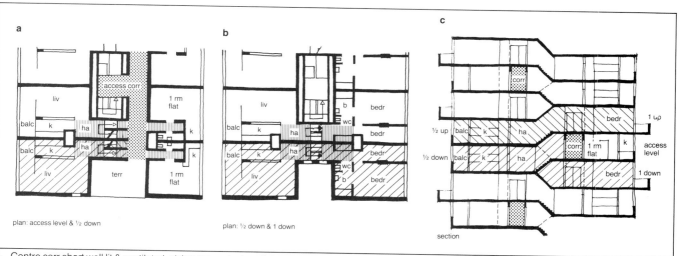

a   plan: access level & ½ down

b   plan: ½ down & 1 down

c   section

4   Centre corr short well lit & ventilated, giving access to 1-rm flats at corr level & 3-rm flats by short stairways up or down   Arch van den Broek

Stepped housing

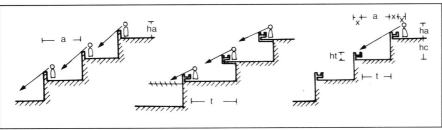

1 Garden troughs prevent overlooking of ter: necessary trough depth $x = \dfrac{a\,(ha - ht)}{hc}$

a = depth of ter ha = eye h hc = storey h ht = trough h

Steep slopes invite stepped form of construction. Rake (storey height to terrace depth) must relate to slope: can be 8°–40°. Min terrace depth of 3200 facing S will secure privacy while providing full sunlight and view. Garden troughs at front of terrace provide some advantages of private garden and prevent overlooking →(1). Other arrangements giving increased privacy →(2)–(5).

Advantages of stepped housing, with privacy and view at high densities, lead to use in special conditions, even on level sites in bldg of triangular or sloping section: can be in combination with different bldg use →(9) or in single aspect situation, to enjoy sea view or exclude motorway or railway noise →(8).

2 Ter overhang for extra privacy

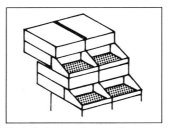

3 In 2-storey units upper floor overhangs

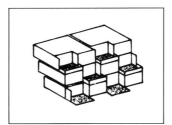

4 Staggered floor plans

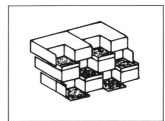

5 L-shaped flats with protected patios

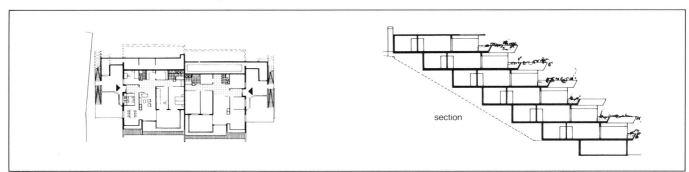

section

6 Hillside housing Arch Stucky & Menli

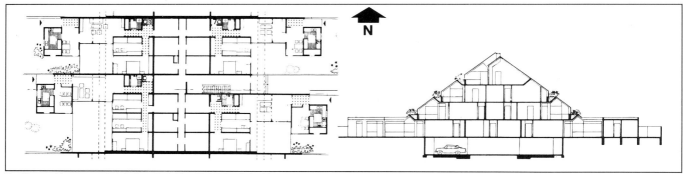

N

7 Stepped houses on level site Arch Frey Schröder Schmidt

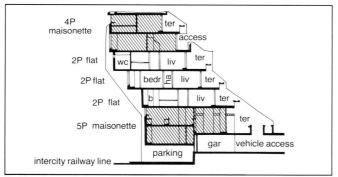

8 Housing at Alexandra Road London England: all dwellings enjoy S aspect & railway noise excluded Arch Borough Architect London Borough of Camden

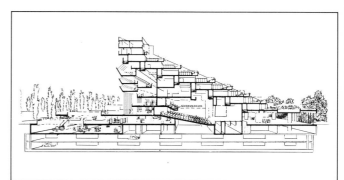

9 Section through conference centre Designed by E Gisel

Shared housing

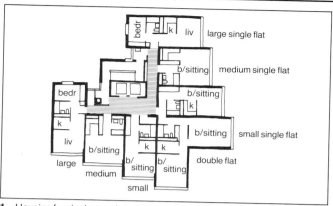

1 Housing for single people Leicester England: typical floor plan   Arch DoE

Needs of 1-person households normally very much like those of 2-person. In certain circumstances, however, single people may prefer share. May be provided in form of flats or houses, usually for between 4 and 8 people, containing 1-bed/sitting rm, bathr and farmhouse kitchen or separate living/dining rm and working kitchen.

Houses or flats used for sharing require more parking space than normal housing (at least 1 space/bedspace). Large private garden unlikely to be required though some out-door sitting out space should be provided. Generous provision should be made for sto of bulky objects, sporting gear etc.

Particularly advantageous if meters can be read from outside →p74(3) and if some form of external delivery box can be provided for use when occupants out at work →(5).

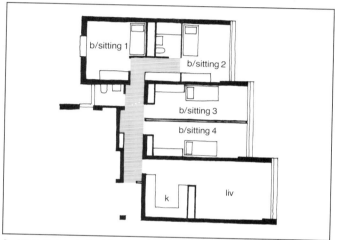

2 Variant of part of →(1) which provides large shared flat for 4 people instead of large, medium & small single flats

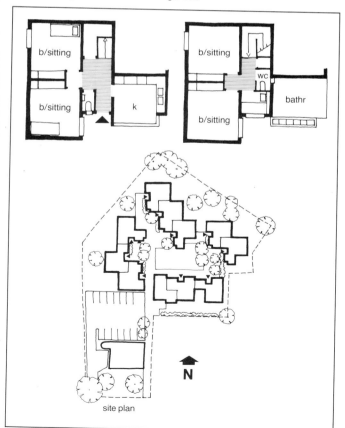

3 Bed-sitting accn with k common rm in small 4 person houses: note wc separate from bathr   Arch Manning Clamp & Partners

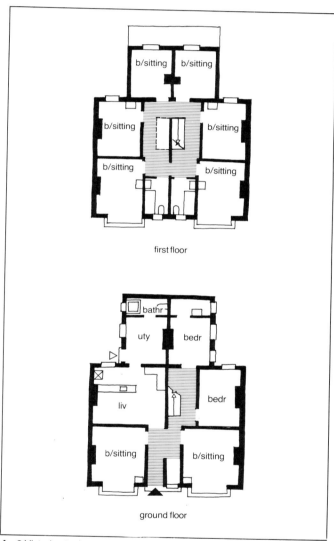

first floor

ground floor

4 2 Victorian ter houses adapted for sharing   Arch York (England) University Design Unit

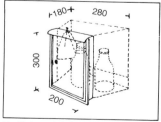

5 External delivery box

Housing references:
→Bibliography references 037 038 044 047 092 179 227 228 233 234 237 238 240 242 245 246 248 263 264 299 300 363 372 458 464 467 512 519 521 548 558 573 624 631 637 650

Houses

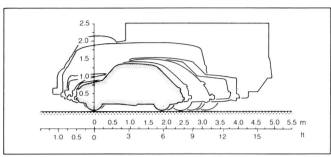

1 Typical vehicle elevations

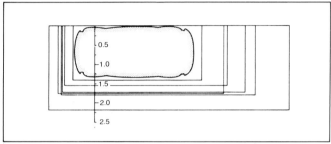

2 Plan views of typical vehicles

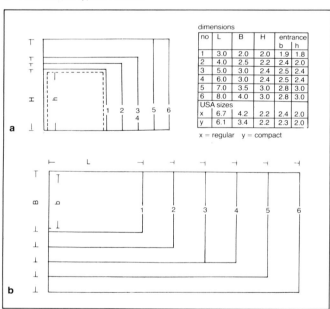

dimensions					
no	L	B	H	entrance b	h
1	3.0	2.0	2.0	1.9	1.8
2	4.0	2.5	2.2	2.4	2.0
3	5.0	3.0	2.4	2.5	2.4
4	6.0	3.0	2.4	2.5	2.4
5	7.0	3.5	3.0	2.8	3.0
6	8.0	4.0	3.0	2.8	3.0
USA sizes					
x	6.7	4.2	2.2	2.4	2.0
y	6.1	3.4	2.2	2.3	2.0

x = regular   y = compact

3 Standard garages **a** in elevation **b** plan sizes for: 1 motor cycle with side-car 2–4 cars 5 & 6 vans & trucks; usual materials for these dismountable garages asbestos cement or steel sheets, flat or corrugated, & timber

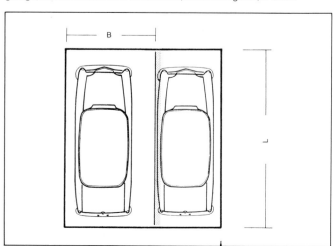

4 Garage in plan →(3)

PRIVATE GARAGES

Size

Avoid under-dimensioning garages. Clearance between car and side walls should be min 200–300 with margin in front min 500. For getting out allow at least door width between car and wall or between cars and never less than 700. For car cleaning, walls or other cars should be min 1 200 away.

Siting garages

Garage should be close to house entrance, though not necessarily front door, with easy access; actual distance from house will vary with size and number of vehicles. On steep slopes with houses above road, garage can be sited at street level (max driveway gradient 6%) but must be protected against ground water →(6). Where house is close to boundary garage can be set at angle or combined with next-door garage →(7)(8).

Access driveway should either be consolidated over its whole width or have concrete wheel-runs →(9). An apron in front of garage should be concreted full-width, 5 000–6 000 long and drained for car washing and to provide occasional off-street parking for another car. Garage floor should be raised 30–50 above washing area and slope towards it.

Integral garage →p101(1)(2)

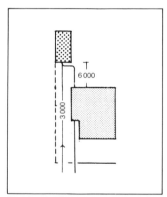

5 Usual siting

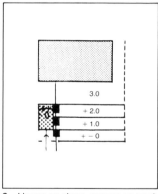

6 House on slope, garage on road below

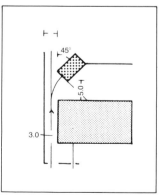

7 Boundary in close proximity to house, so garage at angle

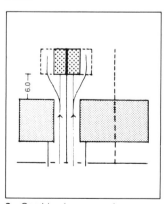

8 Combined garages where distance from boundary not stipulated

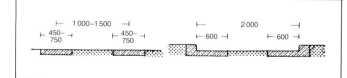

9 Access driveway wheel runs

PRIVATE GARAGES

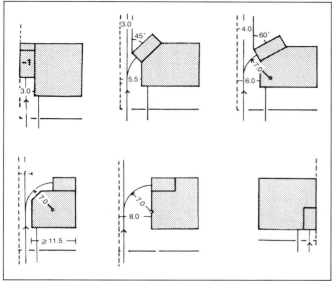

1   Garage in basement, various arrangements: w of garage doors & ramp = car + ≥ 1 000; garage dimensions 2 800 × 5 500–3 500× 6 500

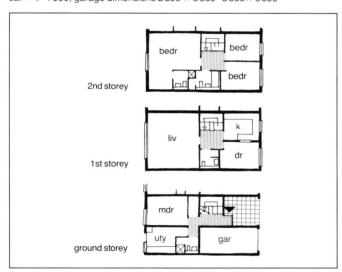

2   3-storey house with integral gar: can be sited directly behind pavement as gar & central porch provide privacy; access to garden through uty

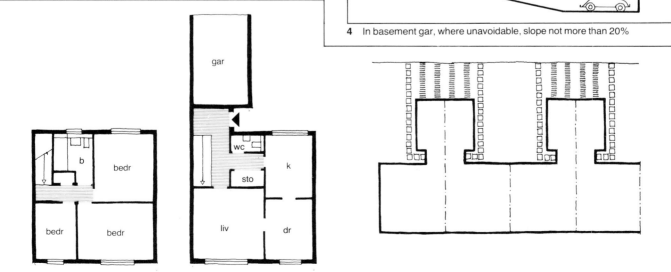

3   2-storey ter house with attached gar in front, screening semi-private entrance court: generally more economical (& attractive) than 3-storey house with integral garage →(2) but implies lower density

Incorporated within house

Garages have been placed in basement, sometimes under conservatory or similar annex to house →(1). Should be avoided if possible; should not be used in areas which have freezing weather: access slope not more than 20% →(4).

Driving up steep ramp with motor still cold shortens engine life, is noisy and can be difficult. Garage therefore better placed at ground level, driveway having slight fall towards road. On sloping sites ground floor or terrace may be raised sufficiently to allow basement garage at road level.

Direct access to garage from entrance hall or lobby via self-closing fr door usually permissible: threshold must be 100 min above garage floor. Otherwise access to garage can be provided under common canopy with entrance door to house.

Garage should be away from living rm and bedr, accessible from kitchen and side or service entrance. Car washing and driveway should be screened by shrubs and bushes, which will also muffle noise.

Carports →p102(6)

Doors →p102(7)–(10)

Up-and-over doors or roller shutters now usual: can be operated by el motors with remote control switch or by electronic devices, provide additional head-room for motor caravans and similar vehicles. Sliding-folding doors require additional width. Hinged doors opening outwards can be blocked by snow. When used should have provision for fastening in open position.

Folding doors also →p402

Windows and el light should be near car engine, with switches at garage door and any other entrance; spark protected socket outlet, well clear of floor, desirable. Heating best situated in front of or under engine, keeping garage above 5° C.

Water tap with hose attachment should be near door, in easy reach of washing area, with hose-reel mounted nearby. Garage should be ventilated near floor level.

Internal finishes

Walls can be fair-faced brick or blockwork, painted, or tiled. Floors usually cement screed, but oil stains hard to remove. Asphalt tiles dissolved by oil; best flooring material oil-proof ceramic tiles. For tyres, standing on hardwood timber inserts or woodblock is best if can be kept free from oil. Garage should have floor gulley, and floor should be 150–200 above ground level outside.

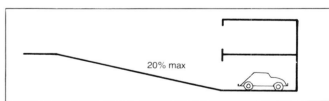

20% max

4   In basement gar, where unavoidable, slope not more than 20%

PRIVATE GARAGES: BUILDING REGULATIONS

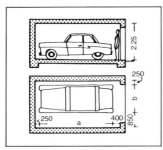

1 Single gar (for a b →p103(3))

2 Double gar

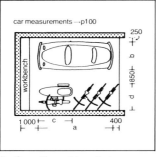

3 Gar with work bench, 1 car, motor cycle with sidecar & bicycles

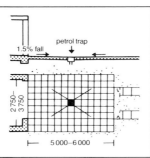

4 Gar with washing ar

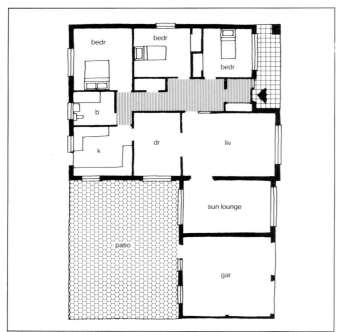

5 Double gar used to extend 1-storey house to screen patio; low density solution

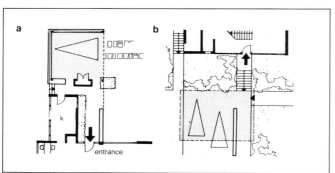

6 Examples of American carports well related to entrance **a** Arch-team Gropius **b** Arch H Seidler

Small garages

For domestic garages in England Wales →Bib650

Small garage defined as one which has floor area not more than 40 m². Such bldg subject to special rules (E15)

Where small garage combined with small open carport rules of E19 must also be studied.

Detached bldg consisting of small garage, or small open carport or both should be regarded as PG 1 bldg for purposes of Part E (E18).

Detached small garage which is 2000 or more away from any boundary must have roof covering complying with E15 (roofs) but need not conform to any other reg in Part E (E16).

Detached small garage within 2000 of boundary must have roof complying with E17 and any part of external wall within 2000 of boundary must be externally non-combustible. All its internal wall surfaces must be class O spread of flame (E18).

Detached small garage within 2000 of house must have roof complying with E17 and any part of external wall within 2000 of house must be externally non-combustible. All internal wall surfaces of garage must be class O spread of flame. However, if house wall is itself externally non-combustible and has ½ hr fr and no unprotected areas within the 2000 distance greater than 0.1 m² or nearer to one another than 1500 requirements on non-combustibility and flame spread do not apply to garage walls (E18).

Requirements on class O flame spread in E18 (3)(4) do not apply to exposed surface of frame member forming part of wall.

Small garage attached to or forming part of house must have roof to E17. If there is floor over garage floor must have fr of at least ½ hr. Any wall between house and garage must have at least ½ hr fr. Any opening in that wall between house and garage must have threshold at least 100 above level of garage floor and be fitted with self-closing fr door (½ hr fr) to E11. In all other respects such garage must comply with relevant requirements of Part E (E18).

Garage references:
→Bibliography entries 225 276 348 424 636 650

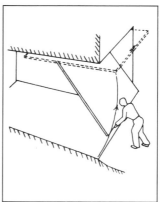

7 Overhead door (flyover)

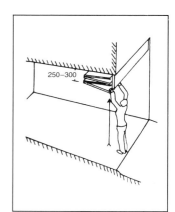

8 Overhead door (foldaway)

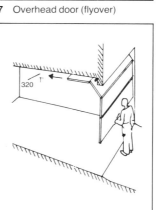

9 Overhead door, sectional (flyover trader)

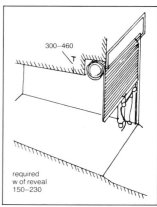

10 Roller shutter

Gardens

ENCLOSURES

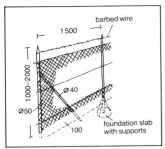

1 Simple chain-link fencing: iron posts with wire mesh

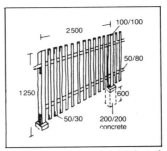

2 Concrete posts with framed-in wire mesh

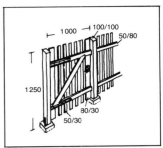

11 Prepared batten fencing (top of batten splayed)

12 Batten gate (from inside)

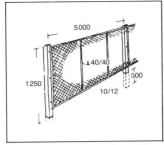

3 Wire netting gate with bracing

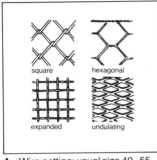

square   hexagonal

expanded   undulating

4 Wire netting: usual size 40–55

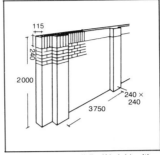

13 115 brick wall (half brick) with supporting piers

14 Close-boarded fence

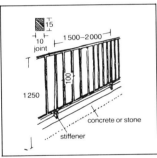

5 Wrought-iron railing rectangular section

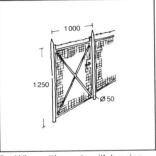

6 Angle-iron railing

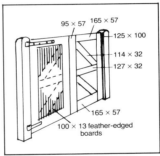

15 Framed, ledged, braced & boarded gates

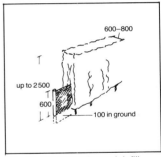

16 Hedge with link-mesh infill

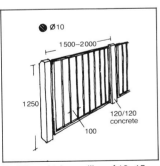

7 Wrought-iron railing of 10–15 sections & bars

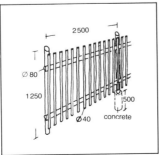

8 Wrought-iron gate between concrete or stone posts

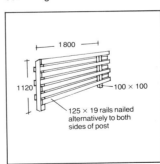

17 Horizontal boarded (ranch-type) fence

Design of fence and materials used in its construction should harmonise with surroundings. Show best side (fair face) of boundary fence outwards with posts visible from within site. On sloping ground fence should follow contours. Extend protective fences against animals 100–200 below ground, especially where hedge planted →(16). Hedges →p104.

Most timbers used for fencing require some form of protective treatment. Particularly important timber posts treated against decay below ground and at least 200 above ground. Concrete plinth helps prolong life of most timber fences.

Where termites present in ground very desirable use pressure-treated or termite resistant wood *eg* cedar.

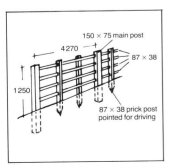

9 Timber post & rail (4 rail)

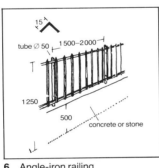

10 Fence of forest battens (top of battens weathered)

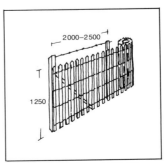

18 Wire-bound wood fencing available in rolls

Gardens

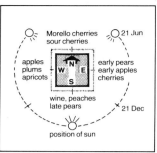

1 Suitable planting for house walls according to orientation

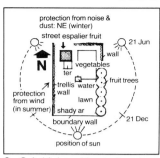

2 Suitable layout for small garden protected from wind with vegetables near k entrance

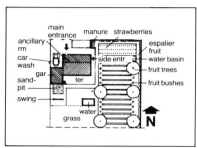

3 Layout for small site to give largest possible vegetable garden

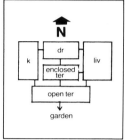

4 Orientation & relation of rm & ter to garden

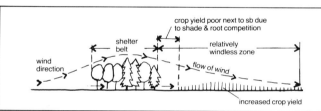

5 Effect of shelter belt on crop production

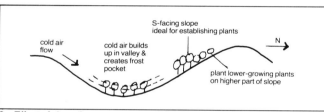

6 Effect of slope & exposure on establishment of plants

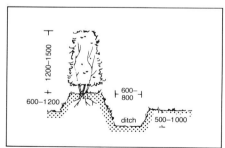

8 Hedge in northern Germany

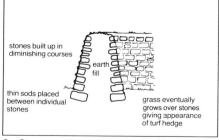

9 Stone used in construction of turf hedge

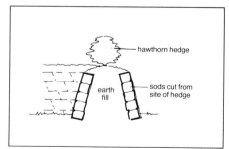

10 Turf hedge

SITING & LAYOUT

Siting

Aspect of ground and its angle of slope →(6)p105 have important bearing on amount of sun radiation it receives at different seasons:

S   slopes warmest during May and Sept
SW slopes warmest Oct – Apr
SE slopes warmest Jun – Oct

Orientation →p40

Layout

Plan landscape simultaneously with design of house so that levels of drives, terraces and entrances are coordinated. Where space permits provide turning area for vehicles and mechanised eqp.

Study position of sun and prevailing winds and avoid frost pockets when siting planting areas →(6). Plant trees and hedges to give protection from cold N and E winds.

Vegetable production: allow 55–75 m^2/P on best soil available.

Soil

Humus or sandy loam better than heavier loam, clay or loose sand. Conserve topsoil excavated from areas of paving or building for use elsewhere →p105.

Enclosures for gardens

Walls: brick or stone (use type which blends with materials used to construct house).
Fences: wood or metal (match surroundings) →p103.
Hedges →(7)(10): clipped foliage (formal) or flowering (informal). Allow sufficient space for ultimate width of hedge when established, 450–1 200. To produce thick hedge stagger plants thus:

Windbreaks

Planting of shelter belts has marked effect on soil temp, giving considerable increase in crop production →(5).

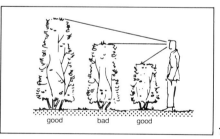

7 Hedge h

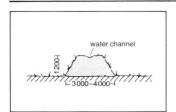

1 Top soil spoil heap

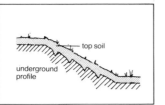

2 Fill on gentle slopes

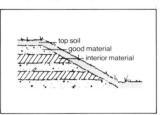

3 Building up in layers

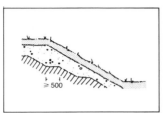

4 Cohesive material in core with slight stepping

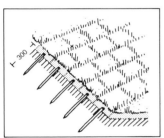

5 Turf bricks fastened with pegs: slope ≥ 1:2

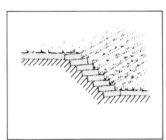

6 Binding with stepped turf

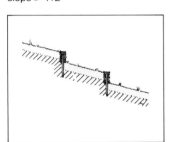

7 Dead wattle

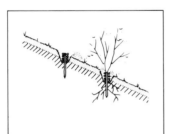

8 Live wattle

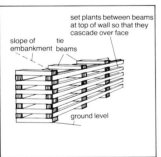

9 Crib structure

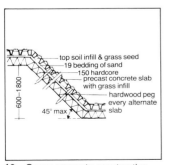

10 Grass-concrete construction

SOIL PREPARATION

Topsoil

Top layer of soil must be preserved: provides growing medium for plants.

On bldg sites store topsoil in temporary spoil heaps →(1). Keep free from weeds. If stored over long period use green manuring. Turn over heap at least once a year.

Spread topsoil after completion of earth moving. Allow 600–1 000 depth for planting trees, 500 for climbers and wall plants, 300 for shrub beds, 150 for grassed areas.

Soil compaction

Soil used as fill for hard landscaped areas should be spread in layers 300–400 deep and well compacted →(3) (not all soils suitable for this). Materials of different character should be deposited and compacted separately.

Banks

To prevent soil movement fill along slopes should be placed in layers. Form cuts in existing ground surface to create serrated profile to retain fill material →(2). On higher banks ground profile should be stepped to prevent sliding of fill material →(4).

Angle of slope should be considered in relation to maintenance operations required and top and bottom of bank gently rounded off. Provide drainage at both top and bottom of bank so that soil only receives moisture falling on its surface. Max gradient for mowing grass 1:3, for planting 1:2 (or 1:1 where no maintenance required). Turf laid on banks should be secured with wooden pegs →(5). On slopes steeper than 1:1 turfs should be thicker and laid stepped →(6).

Use wattle for steep banks where difficult establish plant growth. Distinguish between dead wattle →(7) and live →(8). In using live subsequent planting of shrubs necessary as willow acts only as pioneer.

On very steep slopes use retaining walls →p106(19)–(20). Crib structures →(9) and grass-concrete construction →(10) may also be used.

soil type		weight kg/m³	angle of repose (degrees)
earth	loose & dry	1 400	35–40
	loose & naturally moist	1 600	45
	loose & saturated with water	1 800	27–30
	consolidated & dry	1 700	42
	consolidated & naturally moist	1 900	37
loam	loose & dry (av for light soil)	1 500	40–45
	loose & naturally moist	1 550	45
	loose & saturated with water (av for med soil)	2 000	20–25
	consolidated & dry	1 800	40
	consolidated & naturally moist	1 850	70
gravel	medium coarse & dry	1 800	30–45
	medium coarse & wet	2 000	25–30
	dry	1 800	35–40
sand	fine & dry	1 600	30–35
	fine, naturally moist	1 800	40
	fine & saturated with water	2 000	25
	coarse & dry	1 900–2 000	35
broken stone, wet		2 000–2 200	30–40
clay	loose & dry	1 600	40–50
	loose & very moist	2 000	20–25
	solid & naturally moist (heavier soil)	2 500	70
dry sand & rubble		1 400	35

11 Weights & angles of repose for different kinds of soil

Gardens

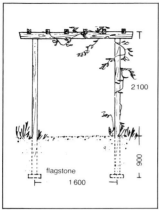

1 Climber support

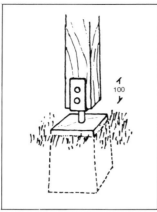

2 Insulation of timber against rot

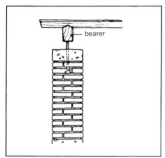

3 Pergola on brick pier

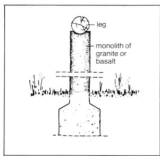

4 Pergola of monolith stone (common in Italy & Ticino)

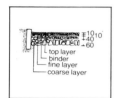

5 Gravel path

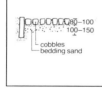

6 Cobbles: expensive but durable

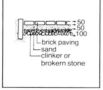

7 Brick paving

8 Paved path bedded & raised (easier keep clean)

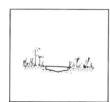

9 Paved path flush (prevents obstruction of lawn mower)

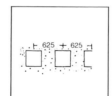

10 Spacing of slabs = length of stride: thickness ≥ 30

11 Wooden posts

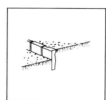

12 Flagstones on edge

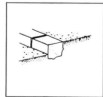

13 Stone with 2 sides finished

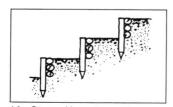

14 Steps with post supports

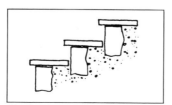

15 Steps with flagstone & support blocks

PERGOLAS, PATHS, STEPS & RETAINING WALLS

Retaining walls

Concrete construction cheaper than stone walling. Good form work detailing essential obtain pleasing appearance. Dry stone walling suitable for retaining earth up to 2000 high. Brick backing necessary for higher walls →(19)(20).

Paths

Width of ramped paths 1220–1350; length 6000–9000.
1 : 12 gradient necessary for easy negotiation by wheelchairs. For short pedestrian ramps 1 : 7 acceptable →p85. If stepped, max height of step is 125 →(11)–(13).
Paths also →p19 43

Steps

Tread width not less than 300. Risers 90–150 high →(14)(15)(17)(18). Detail of finish to end of steps important, especially where set in grass bank.

16 Walking more comfortable if path longitudinally concave:
a good, rise of steps concave **b** bad, rise convex

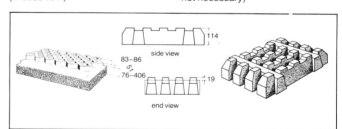

17 Steps with flagstones

18 Steps of natural or worked stone

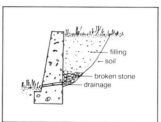

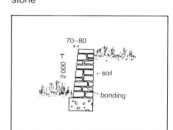

19 Concrete retaining wall (w base ⅓ h)

20 Dry walling (special drainage not necessary)

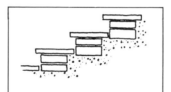

21 Turf & concrete pavers for drives, fire route round bldg, bank consolidation

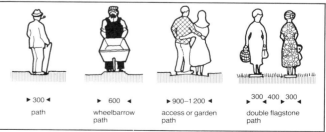

22 Dimensions of paths

Gardens: equipment

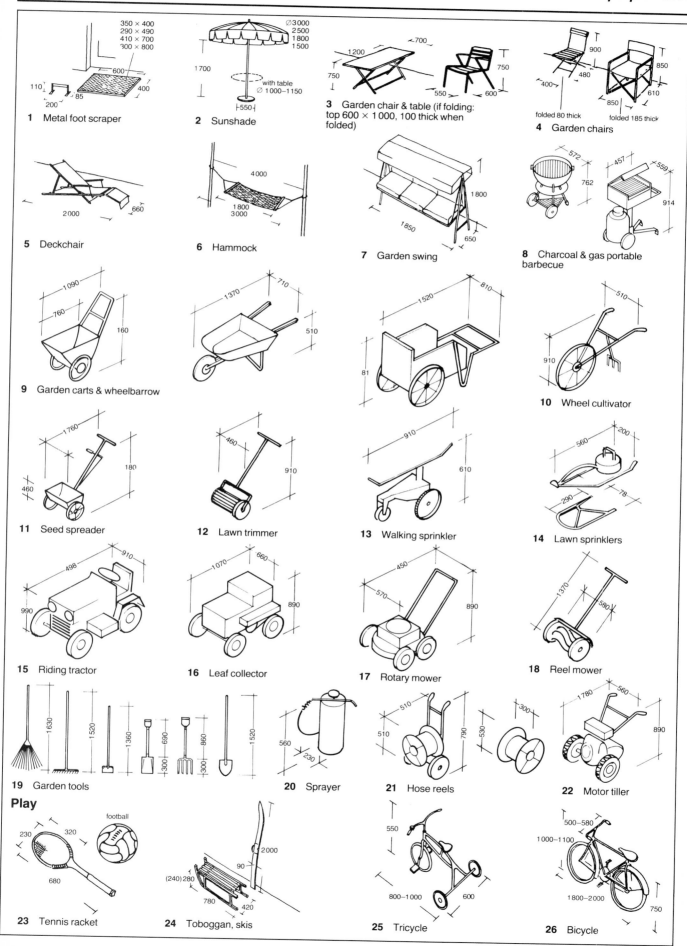

1 Metal foot scraper

2 Sunshade

3 Garden chair & table (if folding: top 600 × 1000, 100 thick when folded)

4 Garden chairs

folded 80 thick

folded 185 thick

5 Deckchair

6 Hammock

7 Garden swing

8 Charcoal & gas portable barbecue

9 Garden carts & wheelbarrow

10 Wheel cultivator

11 Seed spreader

12 Lawn trimmer

13 Walking sprinkler

14 Lawn sprinklers

15 Riding tractor

16 Leaf collector

17 Rotary mower

18 Reel mower

19 Garden tools

20 Sprayer

21 Hose reels

22 Motor tiller

Play

23 Tennis racket

24 Toboggan, skis

25 Tricycle

26 Bicycle

Gardens

TREES, SHRUBS

Trained fruit

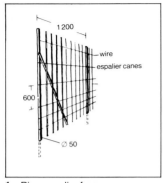

1   Pipe espalier frame

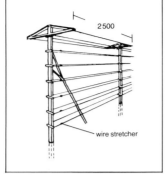

2   Frame for double espalier

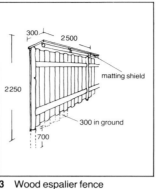

3   Wood espalier fence

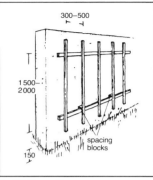

4   Wall espalier

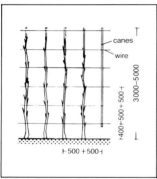

5   Upright cordon

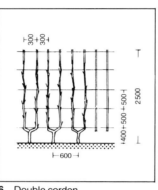

6   Double cordon

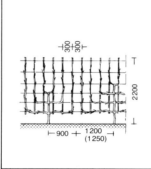

7   Palmette cordon 6 & 8 branch

(right image)

8   Chandelier cordon

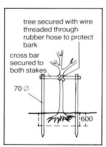

9   Horizontal cordon

Tree planting

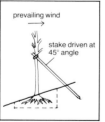

10   Heavy standard

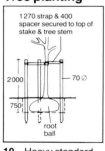

11   On exposed site

12   Normal situation

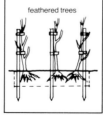

13   On exposed hillside

14   To form close group

15   Fruit bushes

Shrub planting

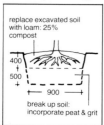

16   In poor soil

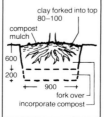

17   In sandy soil

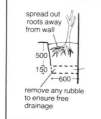

18   Against wall

fruit, tree shape, stock	enclosed site		in house garden & small-crowned varieties	
	planting interval	plant/ha	planting interval	plant/ha
standard apple	10 × 10	100	8 × 8	156
apple on strong EM stock	6 × 6	277–400	5 × 5	400–625
	5 × 5		4 × 4	
apple on weak EM stock	5 × 5	400–816	4 × 4	625–1120
	3.5 × 3.5		3 × 3	
standard pear	8 × 8	156	7 × 7	204
bush pear on pear stock	6 × 6	277	5 × 5	400
bush pear on quince	4.5 × 4.5	494	4 × 4	625
pear spindle on quince	4 × 4	625–1120	3 × 3	1120 × 1600
	3 × 3		2.5 × 2.5	
standard cherry	10 × 10	100	8 × 8	156
1/2 standard cherry on P mahaleb	6 × 6	277	5 × 5	400
standard bitter cherry	6 × 6	277	5 × 5	400
1/2 standard cherry on P mahaleb	5 × 5	400	4 × 4	625
standard & bush plum	7 × 7	204–400	5 × 5	400
	5 × 5			
peach bush	5 × 5	400	4 × 4	625
standard apricot	7 × 7	204–277	5 × 5	400
	6 × 6			
bush apricot	6 × 6	277–400	4 × 4	625
standard walnut	12 × 12	70–100	8 × 8	156
hazel nut bush	4 × 4	625	3 × 3	1120
gooseberry, red & white currant	2 × 2.5	2000–2500	2 × 2	2500–3333
	2 × 2		2 × 1.5	
black currant	2.5 × 2.5	1600	2 × 2.5	2000
gooseberry & currant cordon	1.5 × 1.5	4444	1 × 1.5	6666
raspberry & upright blackberry	2 × 0.5	10000	2 × 0.5	10000
rambling blackberry	2 × 4	1250	2 × 4	1250
annual strawberry cultivation	0.25 × 0.25	160000–	0.25 × 0.25	160000–
	0.3 × 0.3	111111	0.3 × 0.3	111111
perennial strawberry cultivation	0.5 × 0.3	66666–	0.5 × 0.3	66666–
	0.8 × 0.3	41666	0.8 × 0.3	41666

19   Planting distances: affected by soil & moisture conditions, manuring, strength of stock, variety & pruning, consequently greater or less variation from 'coefficients' possible; EM = E Malling

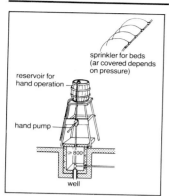

1 Hand-operated pump draws up to 7000 d, pumps up to 30 m h; output/min 40–80 l: for greater d larger pumps needed with suitably built deep-seated suction valves

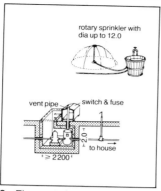

2 El-operated pump feeds water to pressure vessel until switch cuts out at approx 4 atm; after some loss of water pump starts up again at 2 atm

3 'Perrot' type sunken sprinkler: dug into lawn & centrally operated; coverage 8000–10000 at 1.5–3.5 atm; capacity/hr 0.5–1.0 m³/valve

WATER SUPPLY

Water essential for plant growth. If no mains (municipal) supply available trial holes should be dug to ascertain presence of water in soil.

Shallow wells

Sunk directly into water-bearing strata. Yield likely to fall off in dry weather.

To prevent contamination risk well should be at least 10 m (15 m USA) from any septic tank or sewer main and constructed with water-tight lining (steining).

Wells may be operated by hand →(1) or el pump →(2). Well house must be insulated, protected from frost and adequately ventilated if below ground. Recommended size: 2100 × 1500 approx. Switch and fuse box sited above ground level.

Reservoirs

Small pools may be constructed in variety of ways, depending upon site conditions and economics → (4)–(8).

Overflow should be incorporated →(10)–(12); make provision for emptying by either submersible el pump or siphoning →(12). Bottom of pool should be sloped to outlet if emptying to be complete.

Pool edges need concealing. Paving flags or coping more suitable for formal shaped pools → (7)–(12), and grass →(4)(5), marsh plants or rocks for informal layouts, according to ultimate effect desired.

Paddling pools

Recommended depth for children 200–400, 800–1000 for adults; for swimming pools →p114.

Water lily & fish pools
→p113

Irrigation

Simplest form consists of series of channels flooded with water →(13). Drains needed to remove surplus water →(13)–(16). Overhead watering by means of line or rotary sprinklers more efficient. Rate at which water delivered should be sufficient for soil absorption without forming puddles on surface.

Reservoirs

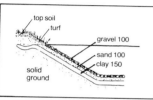

4 Waterproofing with clay, for watering only (not suitable for paddling pools): thick clay covered with layers of soil & gravel

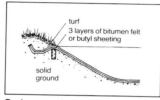

5 Inexpensive garden reservoir, incorporating felt, sheeting or continuous sealing with 3–4 layers of hessian stuck with bitumen; in case of impermeable sub-soil pan should be watered to diminish pressure on seal

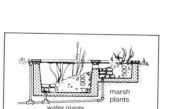

6 Reservoir with clay as seal, lined with stones: suitable for flower ponds

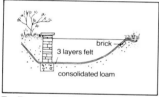

7 Reservoir with brick built banks

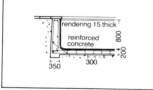

8 Swimming pool of reinforced concrete with damp-proof rendering or membrane; pool should be emptied in winter to avoid frost damage also →p000

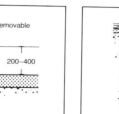

9 Marsh & water plant reservoir, showing varied combination of different plants: not suitable for hard water also →p000

Emptying

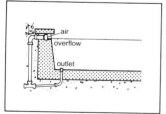

10 Overflow & outlet with plugs

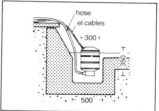

11 Overflow & outlet pipe combined

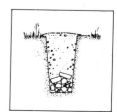

12 Floating el pump; further emptying by simple siphoning

Drainage

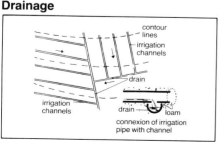

13 Drainage plan

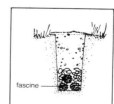

14 Open ditch with wattle

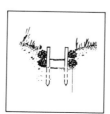

15 Covered wattle ditch with sand bottom

16 Covered ditch with flagstones & rubble

Gardens

Gardens for disabled

Height of raised bed suitable for wheelchair user 600 (must have knee space underneath →(3)); for ambulant disabled approx 860 →(4): varies according to individual height and physical state. For some elderly and handicapped outdoor gardening difficult; indoor garden can be designed suit special needs →(2).

Restrict width of beds to 1 200 so that work easily carried out from either side to cover whole area; comfortable total reach forward 750–965. Surround bed with hard paving →(1).

Important provide convenient supplies (eg water), sto and controls which make lifting and stooping unnecessary; rolling cart or trolley can eliminate much lifting and carrying.

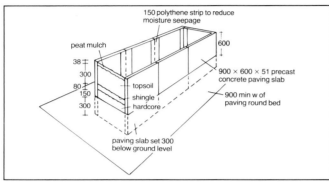

1   Raised garden for disabled gardener

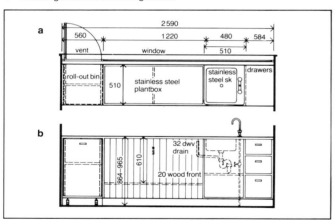

2   Stand-up garden plan **a** & elevation **b** with water, supplies, eqp close at hand, roll-out bin for fetching supplies

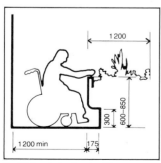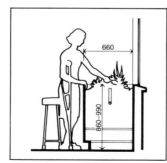

3   Raised planting bed for wheelchair user

4   Stand-up garden section

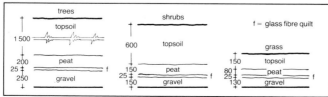

5   Roof garden construction

Roof gardens also →p112

Provide background of screens, walls etc to protect plants from effects of high winds.

To facilitate drainage finished surface of supporting roof structure should be laid to falls →(5).

Rock gardens

Undulating site with SE or SW aspect ideal. Simulate life-size outcrop (not mountain range in miniature) linked by irregular-shaped areas of stone chippings, alpine lawn or grass.

When placing rocks first select 1 or 2 specimens, min 500 kg, for key positions. Build up nucleus of rocks 250–500 kg round them. Place smaller rocks 150–200 kg towards perimeter →(6)(7).

Floodlit landscape features

To highlight foliage floodlights mounted on lower branches of tree and light beam projected upwards through foliage →(9).

If light-source can be concealed floodlights may be positioned at base of tree and beam projected vertically to illuminate full height of tree →(8b).

Light source placed some distance away from tree where foliage used as illuminated background and details unseen →(8a).

Sculpture may require only single floodlight but is enhanced by subdued lighting in surrounding area to give impression of reflected light.

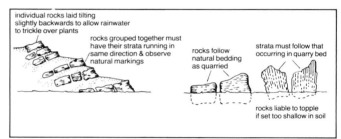

6   Positioning of rocks & method of bedding

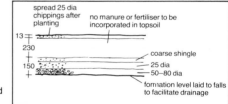

7   Construction of bed or rock garden

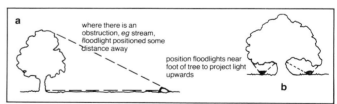

8   **a** floodlit landscape feature **b** light source below tree

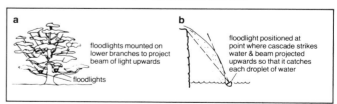

9   **a** light source located within tree **b** floodlighting waterfall

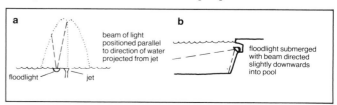

10   **a** floodlit fountain **b** underwater floodlighting

Garden structures

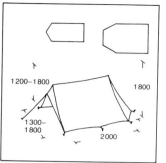

1 Small tent in 2 sections

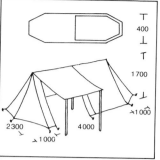

2 Larger tent in 8 sections with 2 end sheets

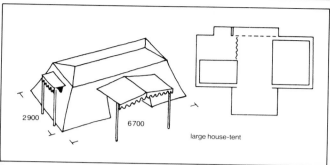

large house-tent

3 House tent

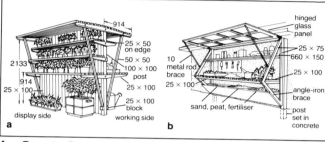

4 **a** Free-standing work centre as decorative screen **b** work centre attached to gar or house wall, closed with hinged glazed panel; sto bins under potting bench

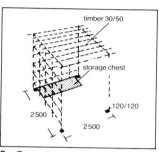

5 Open shed

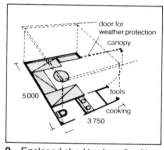

6 Open shed with roof & tool sto containing privy

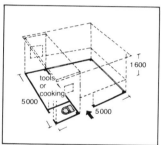

7 Similar to **5** but with solid separate tool sto & parapets to provide space

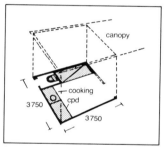

8 Enclosed shed to sleep 1

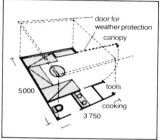

9 Enclosed shed to sleep 3, with separate cooking space

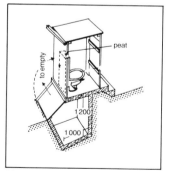

10 Peat privy (dry)

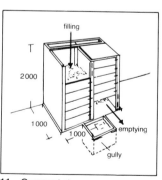

11 Compost sto

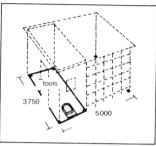

12 Frame

	a	b
	800	1 500
	1 000	1 500
	1 000	2 000

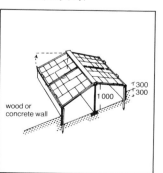

13 Small greenhouse

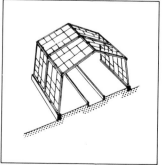

14 Dutch lights

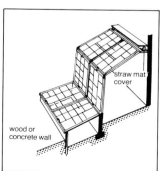

15 Hothouse against wall

GARDEN STRUCTURES

Tents & sheds

Not usually rated as bldg or considered as permanent living accn unless continually occupied or used for business purposes.

Should not be sited nearer than 1 800 to site boundary or bldg on same site, unless boat-house structure and waterway boundary. USA: check setback requirements in local zoning ordnance.

Barbecues →p77 107(8)

Glasshouses & frames

Specify glasshouses according to type and width.

Length adapted to suit conditions.

Roof ridge sited N-S. Frames face S.

Dutch-light →(14) built from ground level and often transferred to another plot after cropping. Other types may be set on dwarf wall.

Glass usually 680 g. Heavier weight 906 g or plastics sometimes used.

Temp of unheated glasshouses and frames 5–7°C, heated 12–15°C. Ventilation essential. Specify adequate number of vents. Hot or cold bed frame lights →(13) may be set on sliding tracks, completely removable or raised for ventilation.

Gardens

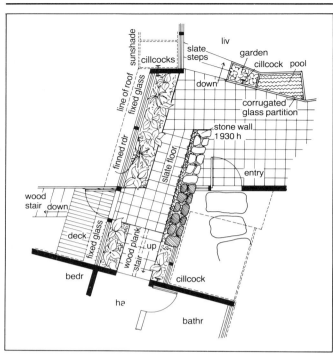

1   Corr garden plan

INDOOR GARDENS

Indoor gardens lend adjacent rm spacious feeling: plants freshen air, add hum, provide hobby, educate children. Ideal orientation in most climates for most plants S to SE. N to NE daylight should be augmented by special plant lights. W sun difficult control. Plan artifical lighting not only for plants' welfare but in relation adjoining rm. Studies show cool white fluorescents provide many characteristics needed by plants: also available specialised plant lights with greater range benefits. Ideal heating and cooling for plants very low velocity air system: other systems can be adapted.

ROOF GARDENS →p88

Consider shade from nearby bldg, wind and smog when choosing location and plants for roof garden. Weight of soil factor in roof garden design (0.03 m³ av soil equals 36 kg). If question of structural strength of roof consider hydroponic gardening using light weight holding medium such as perlite or vermiculite. Desirable set plants in planters or hanging baskets rather than beds for ease of plant replacement as well as weight considerations. Planters may be of wood, pottery or reinforced plastics.

Shade tolerant plants could include fuchsias, begonias, hardy ferns, impatiens, azaleas. Smog tolerant plants include ivy, oleander, azaleas, ginkgo, camellia, privet. Wind tolerant plants: holly, ivy, boxwood, euonymus (should be started as small plants to build up resistance).

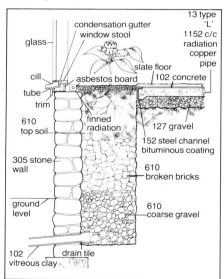

2   Section through corr garden

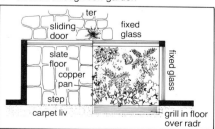

3   Add-on garden plan

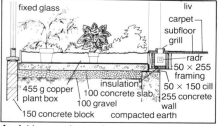

4   Add-on garden section

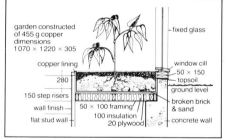

5   Entry garden section

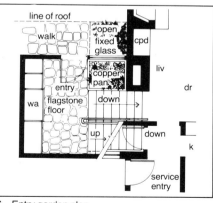

6   Entry garden plan

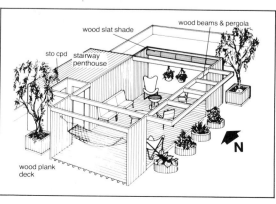

7   Roof deck outdoor rm; roof surface protected from foot damage by preservatives treated wood floor; design uses typical apartment house penthouse as part of plan   Arch E H & M K Hunter

8   Method of containerised hydroponic gardening

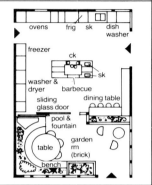

1 filter plate
2 filter tray
3 6 pipe fittings
4 pump fittings
5 under water pump
6 6 pipe fittings
7 hose to waterfall
8 cable with ground wire
H hose connexion to pump
G filter mat & gravel

water level 355

1 Filter system installed in pre-fabricated glass fibre pool

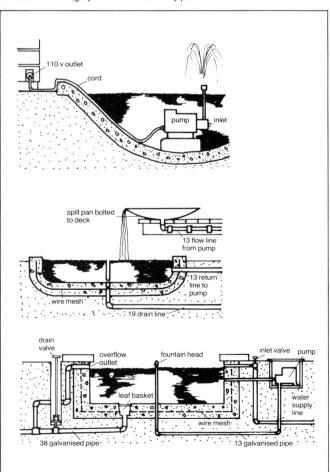

2 Garden ar largely devoted to fish & lily pool

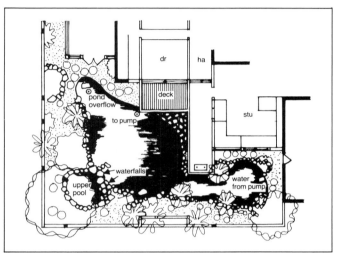

3 Plumbing & pumping systems

WATER LILY, FISH POOLS

Can be formal or natural in shape. Pre-fabricated pools usually glass fibre or other plastics. Built-in pools reinforced concrete, using rather dry concrete mix 127–152 thick, placed in wooden form or shaped excavation in firm soil lined with vinyl plastics before pouring concrete. Pools must be sited for max sun, high enough ensure ground water not enter pool in heavy rain, near water supply if no automatic supply. Depth water not less than 355 so that water lilies may be planted in boxes for ease of removal. Provide overflow pipe, removable for draining.

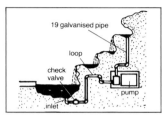

4 'Natural' pool with waterfall

ovens   frig   sk   dish washer
freezer
ck
washer & dryer   barbecue
sliding glass door   dining table
pool & fountain
table   garden rm (brick)
bench

5 Small pool & outdoor dining ar next k   Arch Stedman & Williams

chemical	characteristics
chlorine gas lowers pH	sterilising agent: form of chlorine which can be fed into water in continuous doses; inexpensive but highly acid & toxic: needs special handling, automatic feeder, constant alkaline adjustment
sodium hypochlorite raises pH	sterilising agent: popular chlorine form with high chlorine content; disperses quickly when added to water with no residue to make water harder; inexpensive but needs careful handling avoid splash, damage to clothes; tends deteriorate stored too long; needs frequent pH and adjustment; disperses fast in sunlight
calcium hypochlorite raises pH	sterilising agent: effective algae killer, specially for treating clinging algae; inexpensive; stores well; but dissolves slowly, leaving residue unless placed in basket or bag in water; can cause cloudiness & builds up hardness in water
iso-cyanurates no effect on pH	sterilising agents: dissolves completely, giving consistent, high residual; need less acid compensation than other forms; easy to use but cost more because must be used with conditioner; need special kit for periodic check of condition level
bromine lowers pH	sterilising agent: can be used in semi-automatic distribution system but is expensive, corrosive, toxic, difficult handle; less effective than chlorine
iodine lowers pH	sterilising agent: stable, odour-free but less active than bromine; does not cause pH fluctuation; easy to use but expensive; can turn water green; difficult test for residual; less effective than chlorine
sodium bicarbonate raises pH	corrects alkalinity: recommended for making extensive adjustments in alkalinity; long lasting; easy use; inexpensive but slower acting than sodium carbonate
sodium carbonate (soda ash) raises pH	corrects pH: effective, quick acting, stores well; inexpensive but has relatively short life in water; must be pre-mixed
sodium bisulphate lowers pH	corrects pH: generally considered best of dry acids; easier store than liquids; good for small pools needing small quantities but has to be pre-mixed and needs careful handling
muriatic acid lowers pH	regulates pH & alkalinity: readily available; most popular pH adjuster; stores well; needs no pre-mixing but can be very damaging to pool if not used properly; needs careful handling prevent splash on user; small amounts can cause significant pH change

6 Guide to common pool chemicals

Garden swimming pools

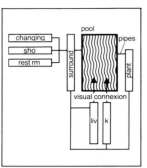

1 Layout diagram

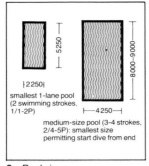

2 Pool sizes

smallest 1-lane pool
(2 swimming strokes.
1/1-2P)

medium-size pool (3-4 strokes,
2/4-5P): smallest size
permitting start dive from end

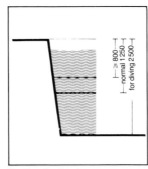

3 Depth of water

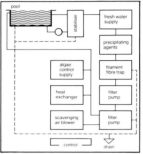

4 Layout of technical installations for fully equipped swimming pool

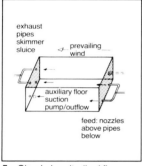

5 Simple longitudinal flow with suction pipes

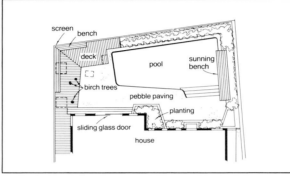

6 Deck at level of paving conceals filter eqp & heater below Design Armstrong & Sharfman

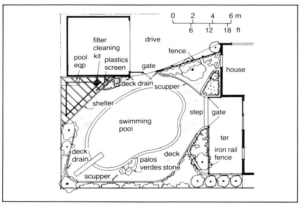

7 Perimeter fence at property line provides safety & background for plant materials, shelter

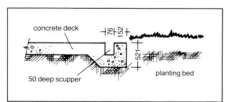

8 Scupper keeps chlorinated water out of planting beds

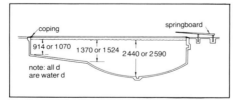

9 Section showing water d for 6100 × 12.2 pool with springboard

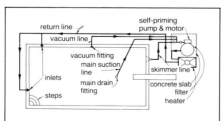

10 Plumbing system for sand or pressure diatomaceous earth filter with lines from main drain, skimmer & vacuum converging on 1 point (note valves) before entering pump & filter

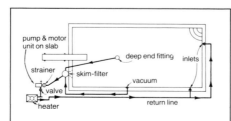

11 With skim filter all lines drain into skimmer; water filtered then drawn into pump for return to pool: pump & motor usually placed within 15.0 of pool

Siting

Protected from wind, close to rest rm (for use on cool days), within view of kitchen (children in sight) and living rm (for operation of automatic gate) ie within field of vision. No deciduous trees or shrubs by pool to avoid leaves dropping: provide means of preventing grass etc from falling into water; possibly raised coping (design decision).

Size

Width 2250. Length of swimming stroke approx 1500 plus body length: 4 strokes = 8000 length. Depth of water to chin height, of mother not children. Difference between height of pool and water level →(3) depends on skimming method adopted.

Shape

Simple as possible for reasons of cost and water circulation (→below: maintenance). Rectangular but with ladder or steps in corner. Circular pool shape also economical with welded steel plate construction.

Construction methods

Foil pool basin (foil = sealed outer surface) on supporting structure of masonry, concrete or steel (including above ground) or in excavated pit.

Basins made of polyester or glass fibre reinforced plastics, rarely erected on site, normally prefabricated; in general not self-supporting, backfilling of lean concrete necessary.

Waterproof concrete basins (on-site concrete double shells, cement-gun concrete single shells, prefabricated concrete components). Surface lining of pool usually ceramic mosaic, less often coated (chlorinated rubber or dyed cement) or cemented plastics sheeting.

Pool maintenance

Usually kept clean by means of recirculation system →(4): surface circulation →(5), with surface water kept clean by effective surface skimmers or preferably sluices. Types of filter: gravel or sand (bottom filters, some with scavenger blower), diatomaceous earth (surface filter), plastics foam.

Additional algae control by means of chemicals (chlorine, chlorine-free alginic agents, copper sulphate). Common pool chemicals →p113(6).

Water cleaning also →p337

Heating

By counter-current device or continuous-flow heater in boiler or solar collecting system. This prolongs bathing season for moderate additional outlay. In some places system using thermal heat economical.

Safety measures for children

Preferably not only through fencing off pool but by providing pool cover or self-operating alarm signal system (triggered off by wave formation).

Protection against freezing

With rigid pools by insertion of edge beams, heating or anti-frost outflow system. Do not empty in winter.

Open air pools also →p333

Private indoor pools

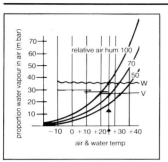

1 Evaporation limit in covered pool; top line: Pool in operation, bottom line: in state of rest; example: watertemp tw = 27°C, evaporation limit: in use 36 mbar (= 30°C/84% hum), resting 28 mbar (=30°C/65% hum)

water temp in use	relative air hum				
	50%	60%			70%
	air temp				
	28°C	26°C	28°C	30°C	28°C
24°C R	21	13	0	−1	0
24°C M	219	193	143	−1	67
26°C R	48	53	21	2	0
26°C M	294	269	218	163	143
28°C R	96	104	66	31	36
28°C M	378	353	302	247	227
30°C R	157	145	123	81	89
30°C M	471	446	395	339	320

[1] temp difference .4 K water/air not to be maintained for any length of time

2 Specific volume of evaporation in covered pool (g/m³h) in state of rest (R) & with max use (M)

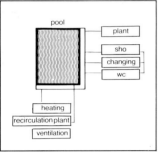

3 Layout of pool house

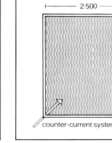

4 Smallest size pool

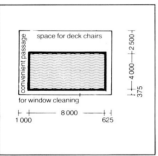

5 Standard dimensions of covered pool

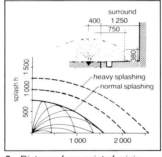

6 Distance from point of origin

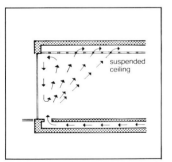

7 Bottom-top ventilation with mech plant for window heating

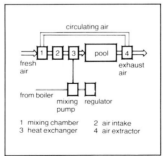

1 mixing chamber   2 air intake
3 heat exchanger   4 air extractor

8 Layout for heating plant

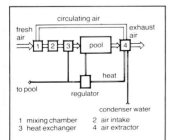

1 mixing chamber   2 air intake
3 heat exchanger   4 air extractor

9 Layout of ventilation plant

Standard

Water temp 26–27°, air temp 30–31°/60–70% relative hum; max airflow 0.25 m/s; water evaporation 16 g/m³hr (state of rest) to max 204 g/m³hr with pool in use. Main problem air hum: water evaporates from pool until evaporation limit reached →(1)(2). In state of rest evaporation stops even in low temp range, as saturated 'boundary layer' of water vapour remains over pool: pool should therefore not be 'blown at' with ventilation air. Expensive dehumidify pool house by ventilation (though essential, → below); with hum at level of up to 70° even small thermal bridge can cause structural damage in very short time.

Construction

Most common form fully insulated hanger-type bldg suitable for winter use (K_m max 0.73); less frequent form, uninsulated 'summer' pool house (can also be of kind which can be dismantled). Semi-retractable roof and other sliding parts make possible open pool house during fine weather, so can be used as open-air pool (all weather pool); however, this causes problems over thermal bridges.

Min size →(4); as part of pool house, in annexes if necessary: wc, sho, space for min 2 deck chairs. Width of pool surround depends on wall surface area (height of splashing →(6)); accessible passage round pool below floor level control leaks, full provision for leads and air ducts.

Location

In correlation with: a garden (ideal 'covered pool' open-air) and shallow feet-washing troughs: b master bedr (with pa bathr perhaps to be used for showering); c living rm: allocate 10 m² of plant rm for boiler.

Auxiliary areas for rest, galley, bar, massage, keep-fit apparatus, sauna →117, hot whirlpool (massage at 40°C).

Equipment

Mech eqp and installations: water treatment with filter plant, steriliser dosing system, splash water trap (approx 3 m²), water softener (from water hardness 7° dH), athlete's foot spray (particularly if floor carpeted round pool); ventilation system with either fresh air or secondary air →(7) with ducts in ceiling and in floor, or simple ventilation box and extractor (air flow not too fast, otherwise risk of draught); heating by radiators, convector heaters or warm-air heating, combined with air-conditioning, possibly solar collector system. Underfloor heating as extra comfort: only practicable with floor insulation K greater than 0.7 and surface temp less than 29°C.

Energy saving by means of heat pump (cost depends on that of current) or heat recovery heat-exchanger in air-conditioning plant, or by covering pool (roller blind or covering stage), or by raising air temp in between use (temp regulation by aquastat). Effective saving of 30% total heating requirement.

Other installation and eqp: starting block, underwater light (as safety element), reverse current installation, chute, solarium; diving boards require appropriate pool depth, and height of pool house. Sound protection (sound-absorbent roof, noise-damping with air-conditioning plant (white sound), protection against structure-borne sound in pool basin itself).

Technical specifications

In principle only corrosion-proof materials: pot-galvanised (hot dip) steel, corrosion-proof aluminium, no plaster, timber open-pore glazed. Heat insulation K_m, max 0.73 kcal/m²hr k.

standard w	standard l		h at centre
	min	max	
12.2	12.2	55.0	6.1
17.7	17.7	80.0	8.8
24.4	24.4	110.0	10.0
32.3	32.3	145.0	12.2
33.0	33.0	162.0	12.2
42.7	33.0	262.0	15.2
53.3	128.0	262.0	20.0

10 Air structure with air compressor, pliant multi-layered canopy & air lock
1 stress-relief design 2 cable system 3 skylight top view showing double cable system 4 anchor system 5 lighting system 6 HVAC systems 7 inflation systems 8 airlock 9 revolving doors 10 emergency doors 11 transparent plastics windows

Private indoor pools

Pool basins mainly reinforced concrete, in separate layers. Expansion joints not necessary with lengths under 12 m. Important: ground-water equalising valve essential to prevent damage to basin. Lining: ceramic, glass mosaic or paint on single layer of waterproof concrete or polyester, pvc film min 1.5 thick as sealing. Include in design skimmer or preferably overflow gully, bottom inlet, counter-current system, underwater flood-light, and build in with sealing flanges. Plastics pool basins, because of below level floor access surround, only possible in exceptional circumstances or with special structural reinforcement.

Floor lining: ceramic material or stone (must slope for water to run off): recently also water permeable carpet (so saving need for sound-absorbent covering). Provide for keeping out water from underneath lining and for sprays against athlete's foot. Floor heating pleasant addition but not essential.

Walls: surface lining material must be damp-resistant and unaffected by splashing.

Air conditioning essential.

Hotel swimming pools: basin of 60 m² normally sufficient. Exceptions: irregular periods of use, winter sports hotels. Important: generous rest area, deck chairs, holiday atmosphere, bar, keep-fit apparatus, sauna, direct communication between hotel rm and pool bldg (elevator or separate staircase); not many changing cubicles needed but clothes lockers with same locks as hotel bedr.

Bath attendant usually required. Extension of use throughout summer by means of additional open-air pool and connecting channel for swimmers (sun bathing lawns).

Indoor pools also →p329–32; changing rm →p335–6

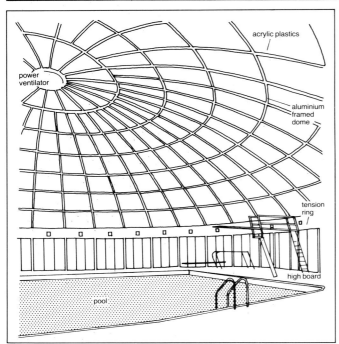

1   Pool roofed over with aluminium framed acrylic plastics dome

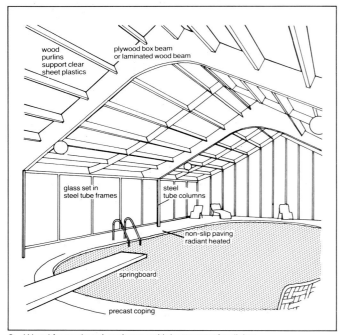

2   Wood framed pool enclosure with h at centre for diving

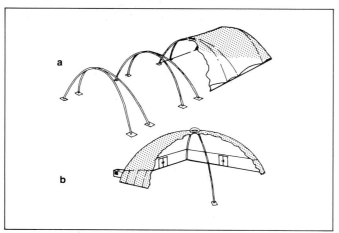

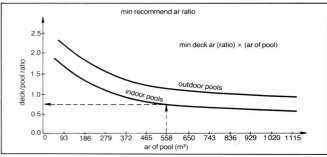

4   Ratio of deck space to pool area for indoor & outdoor pools

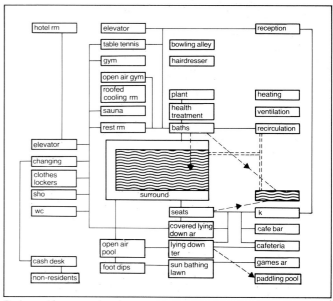

5   Layout for covered pool

3   a supporting framework of double metal arches spans 18–36 m rising to 7.4–12.3 m; pliant multi-layered canopy provides tension-stressed structure
b square domed structure with supporting framework of 4 metal ½-arch sections arranged 6.0–25.0 m/side; canopy of tension-stressed pliant multi-layered membrane

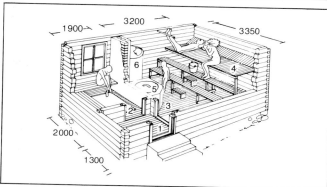

1 Sauna with lobby 1, changing rm 2, bathr 3, benches 4 →p338(5), water tank 5, bath stove 6

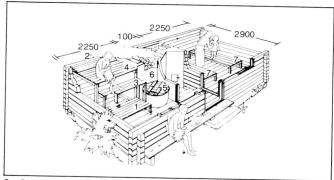

2 Sauna with lobby between bathr 1–6, & changing rm 7

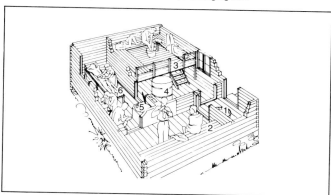

3 Larger sauna with lobby 1, changing rm 2, bathr platform 3, with stove 4, & massage rm with water boiler 5 massage bench 6, water basin 7

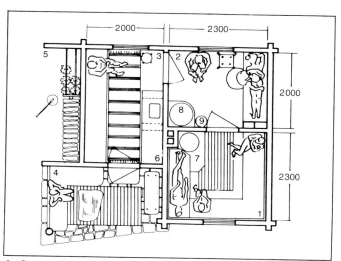

4 Sauna with bathr 1, massage & washr 2, changing rm 3, veranda 4, wood sto 5, cpd 6, bath stove 7, water boiler 8, & water supply 9

Sauna more than body bath: for many also method of mental cleansing. In Finland 1 sauna/6 P; used 1/week.

Bathing process: alternate application of hot and cold air, sweating in dry hot air, hot clean gusts of water vapour at 5–7 minute intervals by pouring on ¼ l water. Can be supplemented with intermediate application of cold water, followed by massage and rest.

Construction: usually blocks or timber: good heat insulation necessary for enclosing walls since heat difference between inside and outside can often be more than 100° in winter.

Bathing area small as possible, ≤ 16 m² ≤ 2500 high. Dark wooden lining to reduce heat radiation on ceiling and walls or solid wooden walls of soft wood, except for stove area. Plank beds of lattice (air circulation) at various heights for comfortable sitting and lying, top bed approx 1000 below ceiling. Plank beds demountable for cleaning, floors of gripping material, no wood frames.

Smoke sauna: layered stones heated to high temp by wood fire, smoke being sparingly drawn off through open door. When stones glowing fire removed, remaining smoke driven off by water and door closed. After short time sauna 'ripe' for bathing. Good smell of smoked wood and reliable vapour quality. 50% traditional Finnish saunas built this way.

Fumigating sauna: after heating with smoke removal, 'heated inwards' when stove bricks heated to about 500°C. Combustible gases burn out completely without causing soot. Stove doors then closed even if still flames in grate. Temp quickly rises by 10–20°C. Last carbon fog removed before bathing by quickly opening door etc and ladle of water splashed over stones.

Chimney sauna: brick stove clad in jacket of stone or tin sheet which guides smoke and gases to chimney. Heating by fire door to bathr or lobby. When stones hot fire door closed and upper air flap in stove jacket opened when required to let out hot air or pour water on stones.

City sauna: with special el heater; heat regulation of el heated stones with press button.

Temp: at ceiling 95°C dropping by 60°C down to floor.

Relative humidity: 5% or 10% at 90° or 80°C: 100–120°C also possible if sufficiently low air hum. Sweat then evaporates immediately.

Shower or water rm: where possible separated for initial washing and water cooling, 1½–twice size of sauna area, without wood if possible. Hip bath worth while 1000 × 1000, 1100 deep.

Air bath: for breathing in cool fresh air to balance hot air, cooling of body. Protect against peeping. Shower, spray and cold water basin desirable. If no open air bath possible, then well ventilated area.

Changing: open rm or cabins, twice as many as visitors at peak times (public sauna) →p338.

Rest rm: rest benches for half guests in sauna area, remote from functional area.

Massage rm: allow for 30 persons, 2 massage points (public sauna).

Details construction & eqp public sauna →p338

Garden references:
→Bibliography entries 002 021 032 066 087 155 161 166 167 171 263 264 320 376 410 411 430 431 466 482 550 562 563

Schools

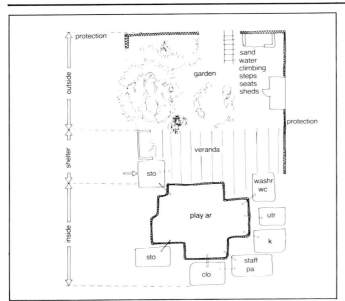

1 Planning ingredients: under fives

2 Activity zones: younger children

1 table work: eg using materials & objects not making much mess
2 acting: eg home play, camping, shops, hospitals
3 music: eg exploring sounds individually, singing & dancing together
4 messy: eg using clay, water, sand
5 quiet work: eg looking at books, writing, resting, story telling
6 moving: eg climbing, swinging, jumping, rolling
7 construction: eg building with blocks, small & large scale, undertakings such as engines, boats, houses

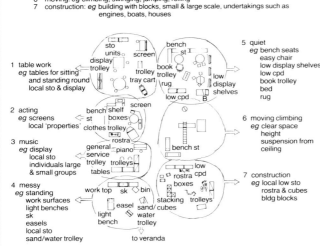

3 Nursery unit on site of associated primary school, built in 1922 for 60 ch from 3–5 years with 2 qualified teachers & 3 assistants: 30 full time, 30 mornings only, 30 afternoons (ie 90 on roll); play ar, carpeted/tiled, open to veranda leading to walled play court with views out but enclosed for safety

1 quiet ar
2 wc
3 sto
4 sk
5 rocker
6 basket
7 B
8 coats
9 st
10 water
11 dr
12 up
13 platform
14 shelves
15 rdr
16 sand bins
17 worktop
18 veranda
19 court
20 beams over
21 ropes
22 sand
23 railing
24 guinea pig
25 staff
26 home ar
27 mouse
28 head

PRINCIPLES

Since each country has its own tradition of school provision, governed by educational and economic circumstances, not possible give universally applicable data for school design. Information given largely derived from experience in England and Wales, but presented so far as possible in terms of widely applicable principles. These apply both to new schools and to adaption of existing ones, to industrial and to traditional methods of construction.

In last generation school planning has evolved in response to changing teaching methods and school organisation. Curricula have become increasingly diversified to meet needs of individual pupils; whole educational process more active and interrelated between its many aspects. Classrm and independent special subject rm no longer sole ingredients school design, particularly for younger and middle age ranges.

Age ranges for which schools designed vary widely in different countries: compulsory schooling may start at 5, 6 or 7 years, and end at 12 up to 16 years, with correspondingly different interpretations of pre-school, primary and secondary stages. These can usefully be studied in 3 age ranges: younger, approx 3–8 years; middle, approx 8–13 years; older, approx 13–18 years.

School furniture →p119 128–31

Boarding schools →p127–8

YOUNGER AGE RANGE: NURSERY LEVEL

For pupils of pre-school age, in nursery schools and kindergartens, learning process combines work and play. For main ingredients of planning, both for indoors and outdoors (which should be connected by covered areas to provide shade and shelter) →(1).

Work and play of very young children can be divided roughly into about 7 categories →(2). Indoors definition of zones mainly by arrangement of furniture, but appropriate surfaces important eg for messy work (clay, water etc) and for quiet work. Height also important for moving and climbing. Pre-school accn may be found as unit of school →(3) or as separate nursery school →(4).

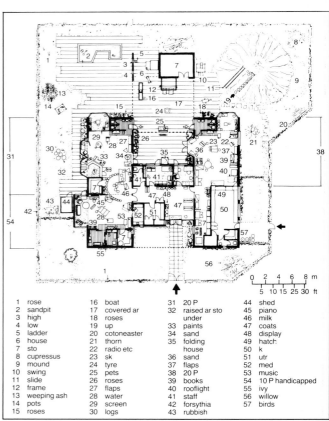

1	rose	16	boat	31	20 P	44	shed
2	sandpit	17	covered ar	32	raised ar sto	45	piano
3	high	18	roses		under	46	milk
4	low	19	up	33	paints	47	coats
5	ladder	20	cotoneaster	34	sand	48	display
6	house	21	thorn	35	folding	49	hatch
7	sto	22	radio etc		house	50	k
8	cupressus	23	sk	36	sand	51	utr
9	mound	24	tyre	37	flaps	52	med
10	swing	25	pets	38	20 P	53	music
11	slide	26	roses	39	books	54	10 P handicapped
12	frame	27	flaps	40	rooflight	55	ivy
13	weeping ash	28	water	41	staff	56	willow
14	pots	29	screen	42	forsythia	57	birds
15	roses	30	logs	43	rubbish		

4 Nursery school opened 1969 for 40 ch plus 10 handicapped, with head, 1 qualified teacher, 2 nursery assistants & auxiliary help; plan arranged for 2 groups of 20 & 1 as base for handicapped, giving scope for play, shelter, sto, animals & growing things in garden protected by hedges

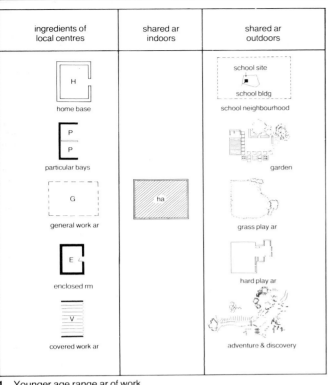

1 Younger age range ar of work

EARLY SCHOOL

In earliest years of compulsory school definition of spaces probably relies more on architectural planning: can be considered in 3 categories: ingredients of local centres, shared areas indoors, shared areas outdoors. Design of outside as place for work and play continues important →(1). Working groups vary considerably in size and may change from hour to hour as pattern of work changes.

Ingredients of 'local centres' can be assembled into centres of varying sizes and types according size and age range of school →(2): *home-base,* space for all pupils for whom 1 teacher responsible to be together, not necessarily at tables and chairs; *enclosed rm* for quiet concentration or noisy activity such as music-making; *particular bays* where special eqp, *eg* sink or cooker, can be installed and independent projects can be pursued with continuity by small groups; *general work area,* uncommitted space in which furniture can be arranged respond different needs; *covered work area,* to extend range of work by providing sheltered transition between inside and outside.

Change from standard classr planning to planning in terms of centres can be seen in adaptation of older school →(3)(4) and one designed on new principles →p120(1)(2).

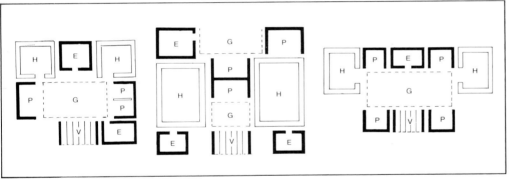

2 Diagrammatic examples of local centres each for 2 teachers working in collaboration: H home base, P particular bay, G general work, E enclosed rm, V covered work ar

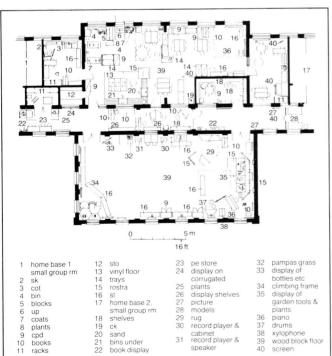

1	home base 1	12	sto	23	pe store	32	pampas grass
	small group rm	13	vinyl floor	24	display on	33	display of
2	sk	14	trays		corrugated		bottles etc
3	cot	15	rostra	25	plants	34	climbing frame
4	bin	16	st	26	display shelves	35	display of
5	blocks	17	home base 2,	27	picture		garden tools &
6	up		small group rm	28	models		plants
7	coats	18	shelves	29	rug	36	piano
8	plants	19	ck	30	record player &	37	drums
9	cpd	20	sand		cabinet	38	xylophone
10	books	21	bins under	31	record player &	39	wood block floor
11	racks	22	book display		speaker	40	screen

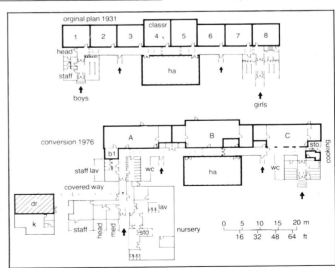

3 Conversion in 1976 of 1931 school built to standard classr planning; as reorganised there are 3 centres for 60 P & teachers, with corr furnished as additional work, reference & display space; ha & dr shown hatched are shared by all, nursery unit added

4 Detail of centre B from (3); furniture & fixtures have been arranged give adapted bldg greater flexiblity

Schools

RURAL SCHOOLS

Modernisation of rural schools has received widespread attention because many of smallest have fallen behind standards of their newer suburban counterparts, being economically hard to sustain. For 2 general trends in primary school design →(2): inclusion of nursery unit as integral part of design yet with degree of independence; contribution of money (and therefore space) from sources outside education service (here about ⅓ of total cost) so as to offer wider social service, both for school and for adult community, than could be provided independently.
→Bib215

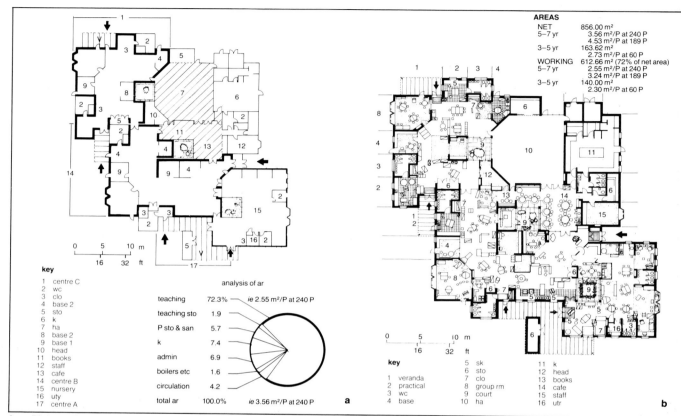

AREAS
NET   856.00 m²
5–7 yr   3.56 m²/P at 240 P
                       4.53 m²/P at 189 P
3–5 yr   163.62 m²
                       2.73 m²/P at 60 P
WORKING   612.66 m² (72% of net area)
5–7 yr   2.55 m²/P at 240 P
                       3.24 m²/P at 189 P
3–5 yr   140.00 m²
                       2.30 m²/P at 60 P

key
1 centre C
2 wc
3 clo
4 base 2
5 sto
6 k
7 ha
8 base 2
9 base 1
10 head
11 books
12 staff
13 cafe
14 centre B
15 nursery
16 uty
17 centre A

analysis of ar

teaching	72.3%	ie 2.55 m²/P at 240 P
teaching sto	1.9	
P sto & san	5.7	
k	7.4	
admin	6.9	
boilers etc	1.6	
circulation	4.2	
total ar	100.0%	ie 3.56 m²/P at 240 P

a

key
1 veranda
2 practical
3 wc
4 base
5 sk
6 sto
7 clo
8 group rm
9 court
10 ha
11 k
12 head
13 books
14 cafe
15 staff
16 utr

b

1 a Diagram **b** plan of infants & nursery school opened in 1979 for 240 P 5–7 years with nursery unit for 60; 3 centres, A & B each for up to 70 P with 2 teachers, C for up to 100 P with 3 teachers; hatched ar shared by all P of 5–7

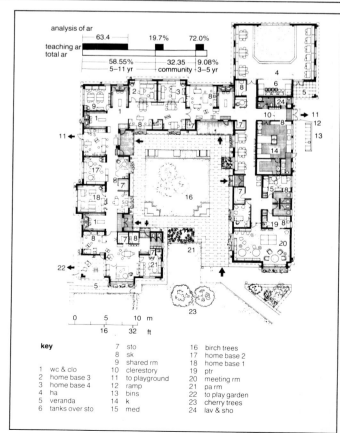

analysis of ar

	63.4	19.7%	72.0%
teaching ar total ar			

58.55% 32.35 9.08%
5–11 yr community 3–5 yr

key
1 wc & clo
2 home base 3
3 home base 4
4 ha
5 veranda
6 tanks over sto
7 sto
8 sk
9 shared rm
10 clerestory
11 to playground
12 ramp
13 bins
14 k
15 med
16 birch trees
17 home base 2
18 home base 1
19 ptr
20 meeting rm
21 pa rm
22 to play garden
23 cherry trees
24 lav & sho

2 In a Welsh country disrict 5 schools within radius about 2.5 km, with total enrolment 99 P, replaced 1976 by 1 new school for 120 ch of 3–11 years, with 2 local centres each for up to 50 P & 2 teachers & nursery unit; outside: pre-school garden, play ar, football pitch & illuminated hard-surfaced games ar for youth clubs & adults

MIDDLE AGE RANGE

In middle age range, as curriculum becomes more diversified, work in local centres increasingly supplemented by work in other spaces shared by everyone, indoors and outdoors, where scope of work can develop and deepen →(1).

Designs for such division of work shown by 2 schools →(2)(3)(4), each of which has centres grouped round common areas (hatched).

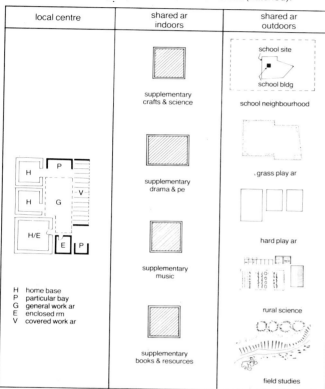

local centre	shared ar indoors	shared ar outdoors
		school site
		school bldg
	supplementary crafts & science	school neighbourhood
	supplementary drama & pe	grass play ar
	supplementary music	hard play ar
	supplementary books & resources	rural science
		field studies

H home base
P particular bay
G general work ar
E enclosed rm
V covered work ar

1 Diagram of ar of work for middle age range schools

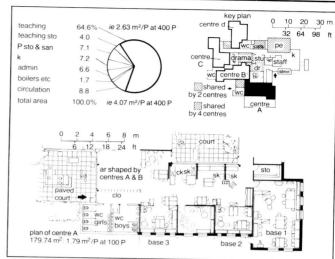

teaching	64.6%	ie 2.63 m²/P at 400 P
teaching sto	4.0	
P sto & san	7.1	
k	7.2	
admin	6.6	
boilers etc	1.7	
circulation	8.8	
total area	100.0%	ie 4.07 m²/P at 400 P

plan of centre A
179.74 m²: 1.79 m²/P at 100 P

2 Middle age range school with 4 centres & ar of common use (hatched); more detailed plan of centre ar is shown

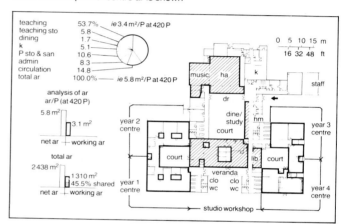

teaching	53.7%	ie 3.4 m²/P at 420 P
teaching sto	5.8	
dining	1.7	
k	5.1	
P sto & san	10.6	
admin	8.3	
circulation	14.8	
total ar	100.0%	ie 5.8 m²/P at 420 P

analysis of ar
ar/P (at 420 P)

5.8 m²   3.1 m²
net ar — working ar

total ar
2438 m²   1310 m²
45.5% shared
net ar — working ar

3 4 Diagram of organisation & furnished plan of school for 420 P of 9–13 years opened with 4 centres for approx 105 P, supervised by 3 teachers (other teachers being also involved in their work)

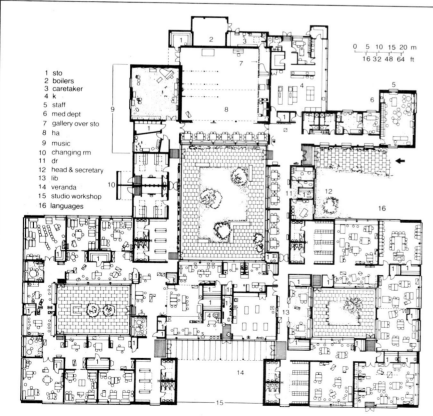

1 sto
2 boilers
3 caretaker
4 k
5 staff
6 med dept
7 gallery over sto
8 ha
9 music
10 changing rm
11 dr
12 head & secretary
13 lib
14 veranda
15 studio workshop
16 languages

Schools

MIDDLE AGE RANGE

Local centres not always planned as defined spaces. Another practice is to provide flexibility by means of uniform space sub-divisible by screens and panels, rather than variety of spaces for different kinds of work and grouping of pupils. These 2 approaches, to flexibility and to variety, represent 2 distinct trends in current school planning. →(1) shows shared working areas designed in terms of rm for specific subjects (as in conventional secondary school) and therefore do not imply integrated curriculum as implied in shared areas described →p121(3)(4). →(2) shows middle range associated with older range schooling in secondary school enlarged to comprehensive →block plan. 'Lower school' and 'upper school' share some areas such as pe, large scale music and drama, and dining.

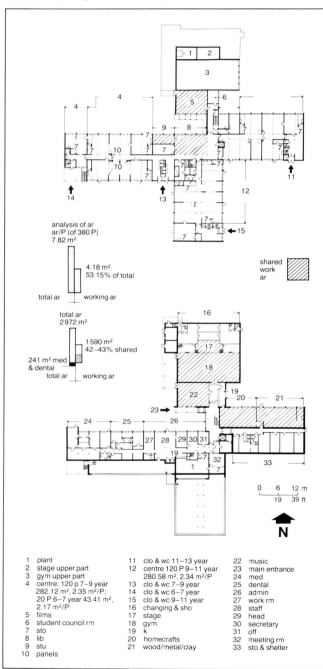

analysis of ar
ar/P (of 380 P)
7.82 m²

4.18 m²
53.15% of total

total ar   working ar

total ar
2972 m²

1590 m²
42–43% shared

241 m² med
& dental
total ar   working ar

shared
work
ar

N

1	plant	11	clo & wc 11–13 year	22	music
2	stage upper part	12	centre 120 P 9–11 year	23	main entrance
3	gym upper part		280.58 m², 2.34 m²/P	24	med
4	centre: 120 p 7–9 year	13	clo & wc 7–9 year	25	dental
	282.12 m², 2.35 m²/P;	14	clo & wc 6–7 year	26	admin
	20 P 6–7 year 43.41 m²,	15	clo & wc 9–11 year	27	work rm
	2.17 m²/P	16	changing & sho	28	staff
5	films	17	stage	29	head
6	student council rm	18	gym	30	secretary
7	sto	19	k	31	off
8	lib	20	homecrafts	32	meeting rm
9	stu	21	wood/metal/clay	33	sto & shelter
10	panels				

1 Norwegian school with 3 local centres sub-divided for different activities by screens & panels

2 Existing secondary school in Nottinghamshire England extended in 1971 to become comprehensive by adding 'lower school' (block plan) designed with 4 centres (key plan) & shared work ar; dining, pe & other large school activities shared with 'upper school'

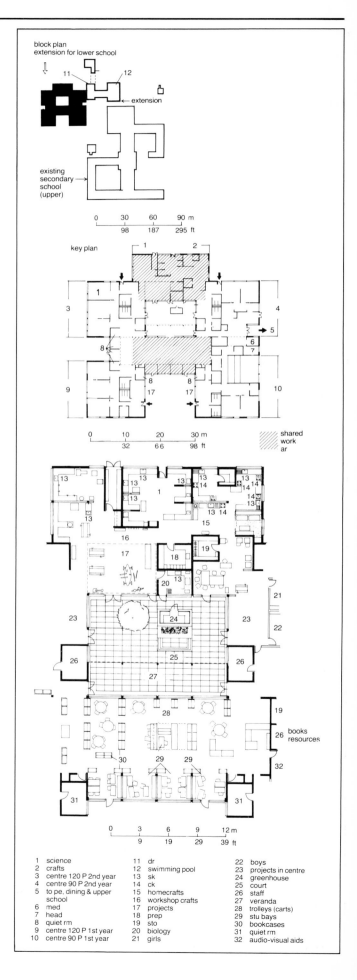

block plan
extension for lower school

← extension

existing
secondary →
school
(upper)

0	30	60	90 m
	98	187	295 ft

key plan

0	10	20	30 m
	32	66	98 ft

shared
work
ar

books
resources

0	3	6	9	12 m
	9	19	29	39 ft

1	science	11	dr	22	boys
2	crafts	12	swimming pool	23	projects in centre
3	centre 120 P 2nd year	13	sk	24	greenhouse
4	centre 90 P 2nd year	14	ck	25	court
5	to pe, dining & upper	15	homecrafts	26	staff
	school	16	workshop crafts	27	veranda
6	med	17	projects	28	trolleys (carts)
7	head	18	prep	29	stu bays
8	quiet rm	19	sto	30	bookcases
9	centre 120 P 1st year	20	biology	31	quiet rm
10	centre 90 P 1st year	21	girls	32	audio-visual aids

OLDER AGE RANGE

Designing for older age range more complex and less certain: educational policies at this stage increasingly affected by political attitudes, exam policies and demands of higher education and of adult society generally. Because of large numbers in schools and diversity and choices within curriculum, social organisation has to be considered more specifically within complicated pattern of time-tabling and accn. →(1) attempts bring into focus 3 essential elements: numbers, work and social organisation, taking as example 1 specific enrolment of 1035 pupils aged 11–18 years, with annual entry of 180 pupils and 135 students of 16–18 staying on after min school leaving age.

Characteristic principle affecting planning of schools for this older age range: work areas likely to be shared by all or most pupils, who move from 1 part of school to another according to their particular courses of work. Number of subjects and relative provision made for each depend on objectives of individual schools: some have predominance of academic provision, others of provision for scientific and engineering work, and so on. But many schools hope achieve certain balance, with wide range of choices →(2): usually common curriculum in lower years; preparation for examinations in middle years; diversification into many different courses in last few.

→(3) presents organisation of 3 schools, with 7 years age span horizontally, and numbers, work and social organisation vertically. Different stages also reflected in social organisation: in examples 1 and 3 some accn for work and for social bases exclusively for first and second year pupils; some planned mainly for third to seventh year pupils; and some (eg library) to be shared by whole school. In example 2 (largest enrolment) organisation, and consequently planning, divides school into 3 separate entities, except for workshop crafts and pe for which accn shared by everyone.

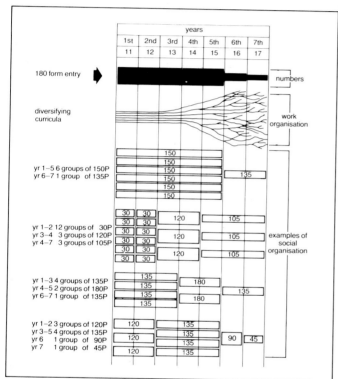

1 Older age range: school organisation

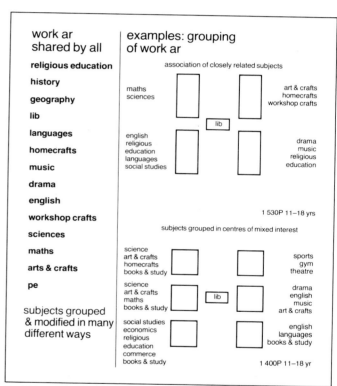

2 Older age: range of choices

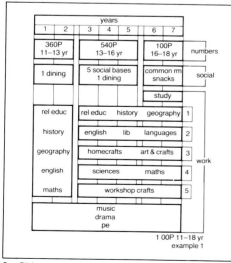
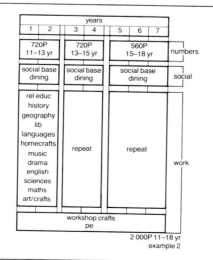
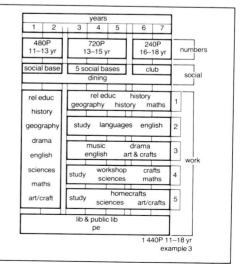

3 Older range: examples of school organisation

Schools

OLDER AGE RANGE

→(1)(2) illustrate diagrammatic grouping of subjects in centres of mixed interests →p123(2)(3).

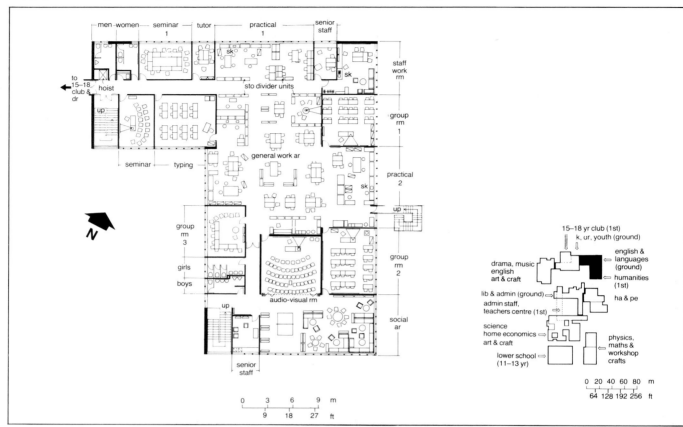

1 Mixed centre for humanities in Berkshire England comprehensive school for 212 P of 13–18 years, designed to provide working ar for all P in this group for history, geography, religion & philosophy, economic & social sciences; also provision for some to work on English, mathematics & commercial subjects

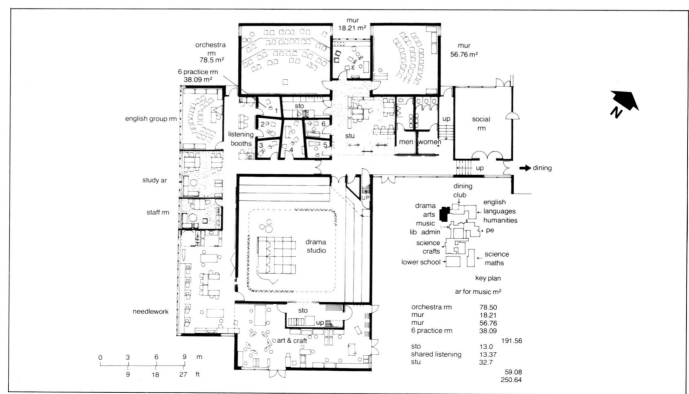

2 Centre in same Berkshire England school for music, drama, art & light crafts, needlework & associated studies in English, with practice rm, listening booths & other ar for individual work; designed for about 158 P to work there at 1 time & for 80 of 16–18 years to have social base there

OLDER AGE RANGE

1 aim in design of most schools for older age range mitigate institutional influences of size by finding ways in which individual and small group may retain sense of identity in large community. →(1)(2) show solution to this problem with school in 8 independent blocks, 7 of which (*ie* excluding largest, namely sports hall) planned as 'street community'. These, with 1 and 2 floors, linked by a gated wall and by sharing similar bldg materials but retain independence by shape, size and detail.

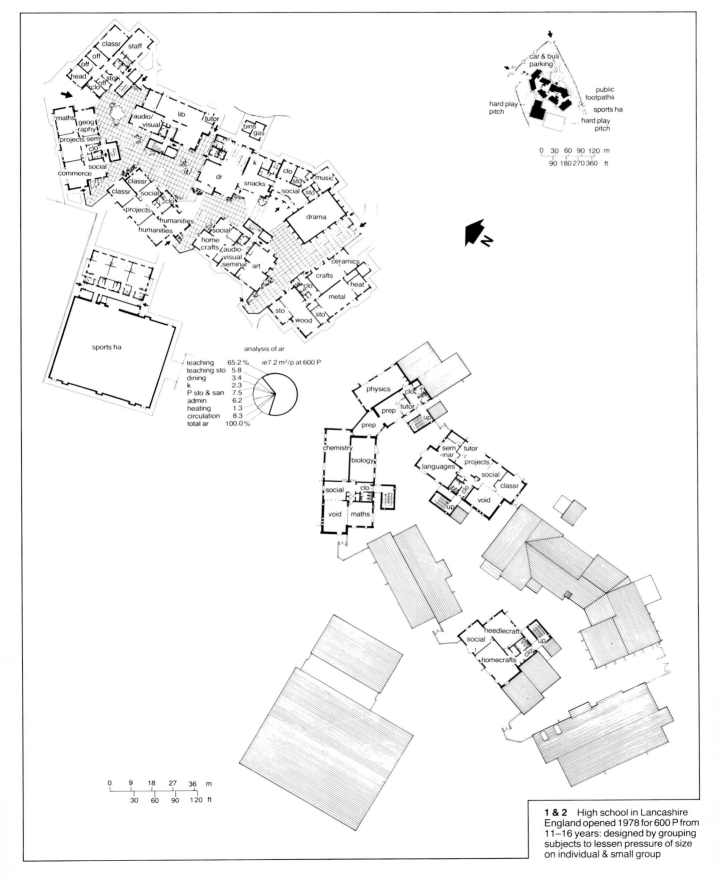

analysis of ar

teaching	65.2 %	*ie* 7.2 m²/p at 600 P
teaching sto	5.8	
dining	3.4	
k	2.3	
P sto & san	7.5	
admin	6.2	
heating	1.3	
circulation	8.3	
total ar	100.0 %	

0 9 18 27 36 m
30 60 90 120 ft

0 30 60 90 120 m
90 180 270 360 ft

1 & 2 High school in Lancashire England opened 1978 for 600 P from 11–16 years: designed by grouping subjects to lessen pressure of size on individual & small group

Schools

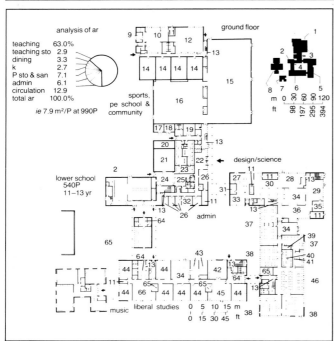

analysis of ar

teaching 63.0%
teaching sto 2.9
dining 3.3
k 2.7
P sto & san 7.1
admin 6.1
circulation 12.9
total ar 100.0%

ie 7.9 m²/P at 990P

key

1	sports, pe school & community	11	sto	25	k	39	optics	55	technical drawing
2	theatre	12	activities space	26	off	40	preparation	56	med
3	admin	13	up	27	pottery	41	seminar	57	mothercare
4	lib	14	squash	28	wood	42	lectures	58	textiles
5	design/ science	15	sports ha	29	engineering	43	classr	59	painting
6	liberal studies	16	gym, badminton	30	crafts	44	history	60	printing
		17	metres	31	kiln	45	lounge	61	languages
7	music school	18	el	32	head	46	practical	62	english
8	lower school	19	lau	33	sculpture	47	gallery	63	house rm
9	warden foyer	20	fuel	34	projects	48	dr	64	clo
10	teachers' centre	21	boilers	35	forge	49	needlework	65	staff
		22	foyer	36	metal	50	social	66	careers
		23	changing	37	advanced science	51	fabrics	67	lib work rm
		24	yard	38	general science	52	void	68	geography
								53	home crafts	54	

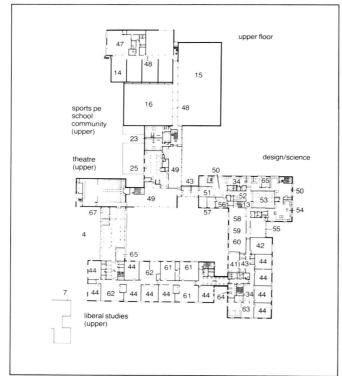

1 2 In this Nottinghamshire England school built on an industrial system lower school (block plan only) is for 540 P of 11–13 years, main school opened 1973 for 990 P of 13–18 years; central core for admin, dining, theatre, lib leads to 3 main 2-floor blocks; arts, crafts & sciences (design/science separate 1-floor bldg)

SYSTEM BUILDING

Industrial systems used build many schools: best offer sufficient flexibility in both plan and section meet educational needs all types schools, with quality that rates them first class permanent bldg. →(1)(2) show school built using such system (CLASP), also used →p120(1)(2). Financial contribution from non-educational sources made possible extended provision for sport available both to school and to community →p120(3).

→Bib200

REGIONAL INSTITUTIONS

Increasing diversity educational needs in 16–19 year age range encourages development separate institutions serve several schools in region. Some sited in association with 11–16 year school; some with college of further education →(3); some independent. At St Austell England →(3) provision of pe available in nearby borough sports centre. 6th form college and nearby college of further education share some teaching accn for linked courses. Generous provision for individual study both in library and elsewhere; this, together with small rm for seminars and tutorial work, of considerable importance for this age group.

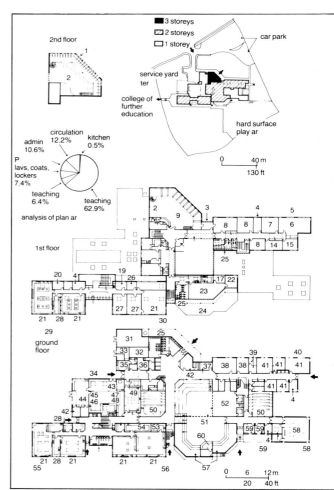

analysis of plan ar

admin 10.6%
circulation 12.2%
kitchen 0.5%
P lavs, coats, lockers 7.4%
teaching 6.4%
teaching 62.9%

3 St Austell England 6th form college, opened 1973 for 460 P 16–19 years, has dept for humanities (including drama), music, science & mathematics, social studies, & art & design centre, all related to ha, drama studio, lib & social centre

key

1	private stu gallery	13	projection	25	wc	39	tutorials	50	lecture rm
2	lib	14	private stu	26	computer	40	humanities	51	ha
3	careers	15	religious education	27	division rm	41	languages	52	drama studio
4	seminar	16	ha	28	preparation	42	seminars & heads of dept	53	optics
5	social studies	17	off	29	chemistry			54	science preparation
6	geography	18	head	30	mathematics	43	forge	55	biology
7	geology	19	head seminar	31	boilers	44	studio	56	physics
8	history	20	balance rm	32	design off	45	wood	57	students' social ar
9	control	21	lab	33	timber	46	textiles	58	music
10	rest rm	22	work rm	34	art & design	47	metal	59	tutor
11	deputy head	23	staff common	35	clo	48	pottery	60	k
12	gallery	24	ter rm	36	el	49	science projects		
				37	seminar off				
				38	english				

Boarding schools

Size varies from 50 to over 1000 boarding pupils. Proportion of day to boarding pupils also varies; many schools take only boarders. Few new boarding schools built recently but many extended, with new uses found for existing bldg. As school will be 'home' for two-thirds year aim for homely and relaxing ambience, allowing pupils develop own personalities and community spirit.

SITE LAYOUT

Requirements differ according to various factors: size of school, age groups to be provided for, integration or separation of living quarters from other school bldg, location, climate, inclusion of day pupils, education programme to be provided.

Design easy, quick access between bldg (in hostile climates protected); living, dining, recreational areas close together. In larger schools separate living quarters preferred, with communal dining. Integrated accn more suited to small schools with multi-use rm. Urban sites generally call for higher densities and multi-storey bldg, sharing amenities with community and using town services. On rural site school usually has to be self-sufficient, only classr and living quarters being multi-storey.

Boarding schools with many day pupils have living quarters integrated with other bldg. Larger schools require and can afford more and better provision for recreation, hobbies and cultural pursuits.

ACCOMMODATION

Sleeping
Preferable face E; separate rm for each sex over age 8; preferred same age group to each dormitory.

Open dormitory more usual in preparatory and junior schools (not in USA), uncommon in senior. ≥ 5 m² for first 2 beds, 4.2 m² each additional bed; 900 between beds. 6–12 beds normal but up to 20 can be accepted.

Dormitory cubicles each to have window ≥ 5 m².

Separate bedroom ≥ 6 m², preferably 9 m²; USA min 8.4 m², preferred 10.2 m².

Beds should not be arranged in tiers. Sto for each pupil's personal belongings and clothes beside each bed. Spaces to be adequately ventilated.

Sanitary
To be dispersed throughout bldg, accessible from sleeping quarters.

1 sho or b/10 P (50% baths)
1 hb/3 P up to 60 pupils then 1 hb/4 P for next 40 and 1 hb/each further 5: space 1 m²/P
1 wc/5 P
If day pupils' lav nearby requirements may be reduced.

USA: for details refer applicable codes and standards.

Sick rooms
In small schools placed near matron next to general sleeping quarters. In large schools can be in separate bldg with doctors and nurses quarters and dental suite. Provide separately for boys and girls. 1 sick rm/20 P. Allow ≥ 7.4 m²→/bed with 1800 between any 2 beds. Provide adequate rm ventilation. Provide separate sanitary accn for sick rm; separate isolation rm where pupils exceed 40; sufficient accn for nursing staff.

USA: for details refer applicable codes and standards.

Staff
Degree of supervision of pupils by staff depends on system adopted. Many schools divide pupils into houses, each with resident house master (often married), junior teacher(s) and matron; ancillary staff sometimes also accommodated. Some staff live in separate quarters.

Married teachers need living rm and bedr each 18 m², 3–4 smaller rm and kitchen each 11 m², larder, wc, bathr, sto. Total each approx 80 m². Larger areas normal in USA.

Junior teachers need study 12 m² near to day rm space, bedr 10 m² near to pupils' sleeping accn, preferably bathr and sto.

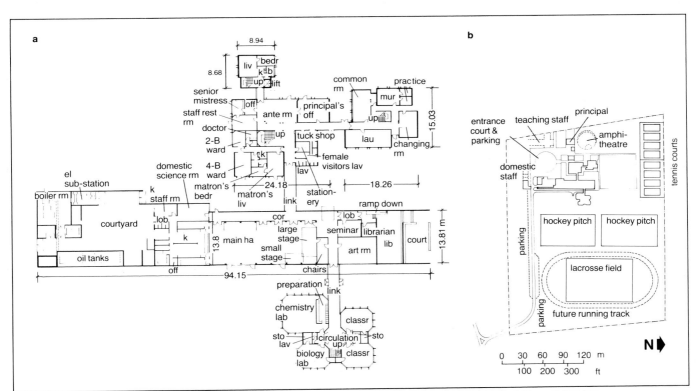

1   Carmel College Wallingford England: 120 pupils aged 13–18, integrated accn **a** ground floor plan, **b** site plan   Arch Hancock Hawkes

Boarding schools

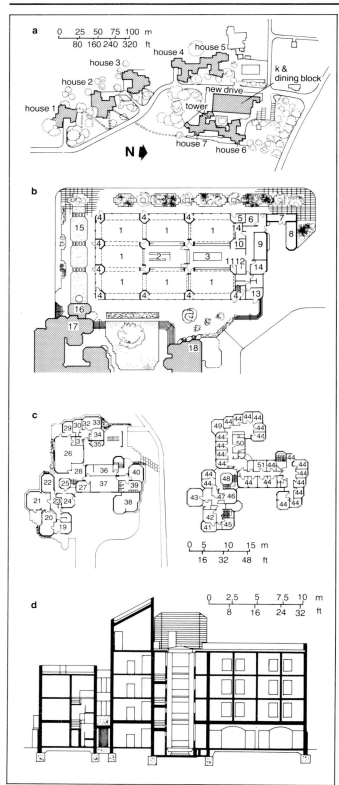

1   Charterhouse School Godalming England: separate accn for 462 pupils in 7 houses each with house master & family living in **a** site plan **b** dining block (7 dr round central k) **c** house ground & first floor plans **d** house section; 1 dr 2 wash-up 3 k 4 lob 5 lav 6 off 7 gas meters 8 bins 9 refrigeration 10 salad preparation 11 lift 12 pot wash 13 staff dr 14 sto 15 pool 16 tower block 17 house 7 18 house 6 19 house master's k 20 house master's dr 21 house master's liv 22 house master's stu 23 lift 24 service ar 25 stair well 26 common rm 27 monitors' common rm 28 entrance ha 29 hobbies rm 30 bedr 31 bathr 32 liv 33 k 34 bedr 35 tea rm 36 boot rm 37 games rm 38 gar 39 boys' lav 40 hobbies rm 41 ter 42 day nursery 43 bedr 44 stu/bedr 45 bedr 46 press 47 elevator 48 stair well 49 flat roof 50 washr 51 washr   Arch Sir Giles Scott Son & Partner

ACCOMMODATION (cont)

Day room
Provide ≥ than 2.3 m^2/P, preferably 4.5 m^2. Should consist of common rm, library →p129, hobbies rm, quiet rm, games rm, radio and tv rm.

Dining
Centralised dining normal: 1, 2 or 3 sittings, depending on school policy. Space can be sub-divided to be more intimate and to identify groups of pupils. In small schools space can be used for school assembly, concerts, drama productions.

Allow 1 m^2/P and adequate air space.

Kitchen
Allow 0.5 m^2/P with cafeteria servery, unit serveries for groups of pupils or mobile serveries to tables.

Ancillary
Adequate sto for pupils' luggage, bedding, clothes and eqp; laundry, ironing rm, airing rm, sewing rm.

Recreation
Depends on size of school and nearness to sports grounds, baths etc. Provide access to grassed areas for ball games, swimming pool, gymnasium, running track etc; suitable space and eqp for drama, art, music, films, lectures, crafts, religious worship.

Services
Provide adequate and suitable air space and heat or cool and ventilate according to climate. Services may be centralised or individual to bldg →p383–97.

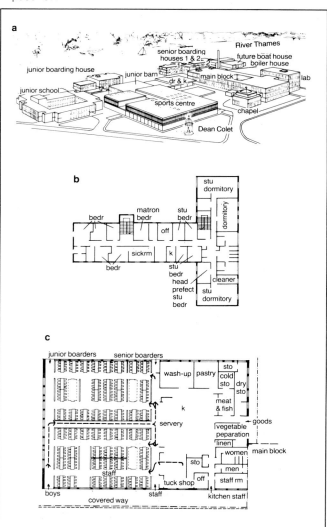

2   St Pauls School London England: 700 pupils, 60 junior & 122 senior boarding pupils in separate accn **a** axonometric view **b** senior boarding house first floor plan **c** dining/k block plan: 500 seats serve 1 200 2-course lunches in 3-queue cafeteria system   Arch Fielden & Mawson

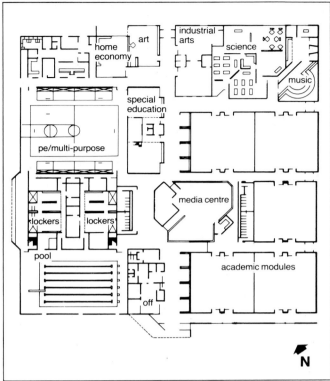

1 Middle school Westfield USA with media centre   Arch McGuire & Shook Corp

MEDIA CENTRES

Growth in use of instructional materials other than those of traditional lib coupled with new emphasis on individual study has promoted concept of media or resource centre. Such aids as microfilm, audio cassettes and film need viewing rm and study carrels wired for special technical eqp. Added to lib service space needs become larger; staffing and work areas needed give effective support for classr teaching needs. Student use suggests variety working and study options. Mutli-purpose spaces equipped with movable or stacking chairs.

Such centres include many of following:
chairs of several types, including cushions or carpet risers
tables
carrels, many wired for eqp →p177(3)
staff desks & chairs
special furniture: circulation desk, files, sto cabinets, display, photocopy
reading, browsing, listening, viewing
open access materials & stacks
small group listening & viewing
conference areas
group work projects & instruction
admin & work space
eqp sto
maintenance & repair
dark rm
professional collection for teaching staff
magazine & newspaper sto including microfilm

In larger school systems radio and tv studios and computerised learning resources may be included in centre. In some systems material may be distributed to several schools from 1 audio-visual sto centre.

Since such centres designed in response student input, local community needs and state guidelines variety of solutions found. Typical plan relationships to teaching areas indicated →(1)−(3).

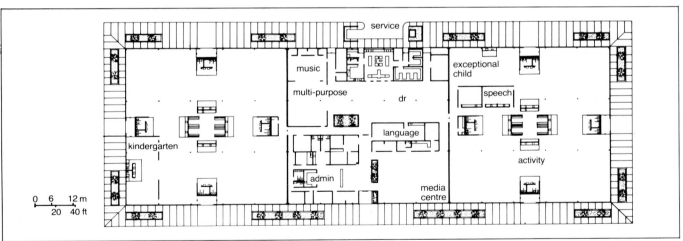

2 Elementary school Tampa Florida USA: media centre near language dept   Arch Rowe Holmes Associates

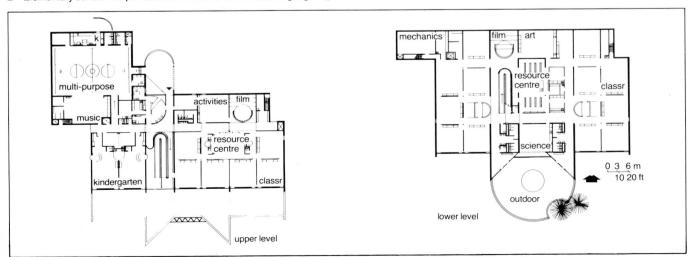

3 Elementary school on 2 floors Neola Iowa USA has recource centre at each level   Arch Dana Larson Roubal & Associates

Schools

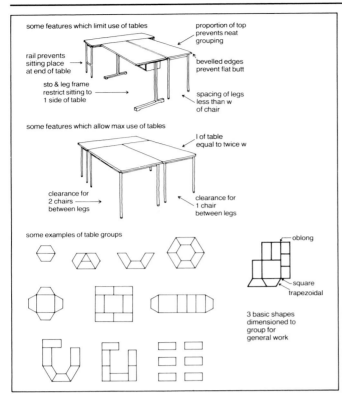

1   Grouping of tables

FURNITURE

General factors

Furniture governed by type of teaching for which provided and by size of pupils. In recent years learning and teaching involved greater variety of group sizes and wider range of activities. More mobility in schools and closer association of book work and practical work; both these affect design and distribution of furniture. →(1) shows common features which inhibit flexible use of tables and features which encourage efficient grouping and versatile use. Where tables required strictly for formal reading and writing work →(2) gives relevant data; but increasingly these proportions giving way to double square shown for grouping purposes →(1).

Modern UK furniture range will consist of sitting and standing height working surfaces in close association and of many forms of mobile sto and display. (→Bib197 207 208).

In USA typical work surface heights for educational use vary from 560–790, although lower tables used for very young. Recommended work depth varies from 330 for youngest children to 460 for 15 year olds or older. Width of work area varies from 530 for youngest children to 760 for 15 year olds or older →(3).

Sto under work surface not recommended unless at side of knee space or work surface increased in depth. Toe space min 610 for older children, who need varying work heights depending on task: typing tables 670, work tables 735, sewing tables 790. Work height for handicapped in wheelchairs must be adapted to their needs →p86.

Standing work surfaces for school age children should vary from 520–915 at age 15. Older children may find range 860–965 desirable depending on height and task to be done. Sinks set lower, high counters higher (1 015–1 120).

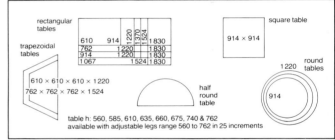

3   USA table sizes

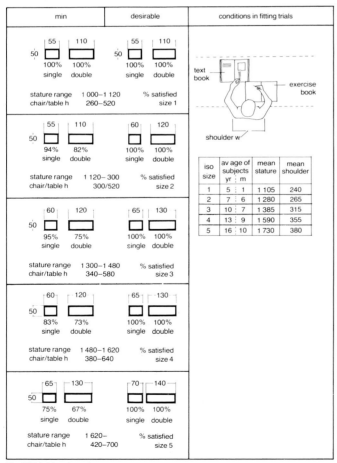

2   UK table plan sizes

iso size	av age of subjects yr : m	mean stature	mean shoulder
1	5 : 1	1 105	240
2	7 : 6	1 280	265
3	10 : 7	1 385	315
4	13 : 9	1 590	355
5	16 : 10	1 730	380

4   USA chairs & desks   a stacker **b** double entry study **c** tablet arm chair **d** lift lid table & chair **e** classr unit **f** desk with chair **g** classr typing table **h** desk **j** study carrels

FURNITURE

Stature data & distribution of furniture sizes

Mobility of pupils in schools and high degree to which working accn shared make increasingly impractical assign chair and table to single pupil. Furniture shared by many: each chair and related table size must therefore be designed suit max stature range rather than for individual pupils. This in principle means simultaneous satisfaction of 7 fitting criteria shown →(1), with clearance between top of chair seat and underside of table top.

Though sto decreasingly provided at work place, if sited at any sitting working plane adequate leg room can only be ensured if zones indicated for ISO sizes 1–5 →(2) free from obstruction.

UK view is that distribution of furniture should be based on pupils' stature rather than on pupils' ages →(3). Conversion of stature to age for UK school population in 1971 →Bib207. Current British standard specification for pupils' chairs and tables (→Bib134) now under revision to comply with ISO standards (→Bib407), sizes of which have therefore been shown.

ISO standards do not apply in USA: view held that student sizes vary so much 1 rm may need more than 1 chair/table height. Dimensions based on USA research (→Bib549) →(4).

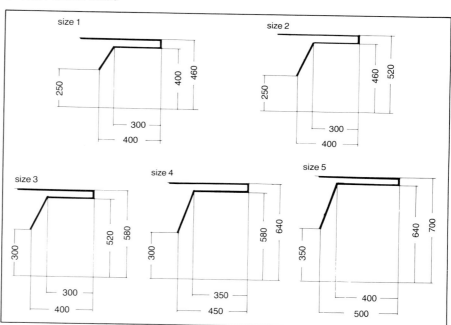

A   shod feet flat on floor
B   clearance between back of legs & front edge of seat
C   no press at front of seat between seating surface & thighs
D   clearance between thigh & underside of table for freedom of movement
E   elbows approx level with table top when upper arm vertical
F   firm support for back in lumbar region & below shoulder blades
G   adequate clearance between back rest & seat to ensure free movement of buttocks

P adopt many sitting postures but assessment of good fit is simultaneous satisfaction of above 7 criteria

1 Fit of P to chair & table

2 Min leg clearance zones

	ages	high reach A	low reach B	reach dist-ance C	high reach D	reach radius E	eye level F
HS	15	2085 1915 1765	815 730 665	735 685 635	1440 1374 1313	660 610 570	1215 1160 1100
Jr. HS	12	1880 1705 1545	705 630 560	665 620 565	1320 1250 1185	600 555 510	1100 1040 990
4th	9	1645 1510 1345	605 555 510	600 550 485	1175 1120 1040	535 495 435	975 925 880
2nd	7	1505 1370 1245	545 510 485	550 495 445	1080 1015 960	500 445 395	890 850 815
KDG	5	1330 1210 1085	500 465 425	480 435 390	970 915 865	430 385 345	815 770 720

up to ages	hat shelf h G	hb h H	work top J	work d K	table h L	seat l M
15	1675	760	915	460	550	370
12	1485	685	795	420	590	340
9	1320	635	695	380	525	300
7	1220	585	635	355	480	275
5	1090	485	570	330	445	250

ages	seat h N	seat to back-rest O	min back-rest h P	armrest spacing Q	seat w R	basic table w S
15	405	150	175	445	380	760
12	370	145	160	420	370	710
9	325	135	140	355	330	610
7	290	130	130	330	305	610
5	265	120	125	305	280	535

sizemark		0	1	2	3	4	5	6
chair/table h		220/400	260/460	300/520	340/580	380/640	420/700	460/760
stature range				1000 1120	1120 1300	1300 1480	1480 1620	1620
925 1 085	3		53%					
995 1 155	4		75					
1 045 1 215	5		38	18%				
1 095 1 285	6		10	61				
1 155 1 345	7			87				
1 205 1 405	8			77	22%			
1 245 1 465	9			47	53			
1 305 1 525	10			20	77	3%		
1 345 1 575	11				79	16		
1 395 1 645	12				57	40		
1 435 1 715	13				33	58	9%	
1 505 1 775	14				13	58	29	
1 535 1 815	15					40	57	
1 565 1 835	16					25	74	
1 565 1 865	17					15	84	
1 565 1 865	18					14	85	
						14	85	

UK statures 1971 (5–95% iles inc 25 for shoes)

3 Statures of UK school population

4 USA dimensions relevant to school furniture; HS = high school KDA = Kindergarten

Schools

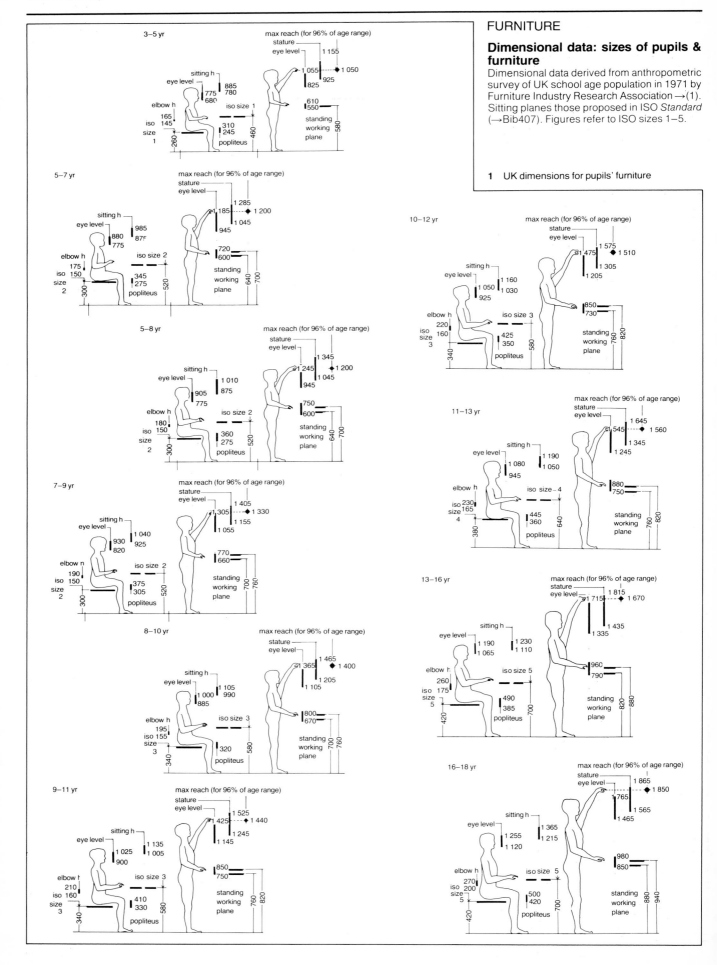

FURNITURE

Dimensional data: sizes of pupils & furniture

Dimensional data derived from anthropometric survey of UK school age population in 1971 by Furniture Industry Research Association →(1). Sitting planes those proposed in ISO *Standard* (→Bib407). Figures refer to ISO sizes 1–5.

1   UK dimensions for pupils' furniture

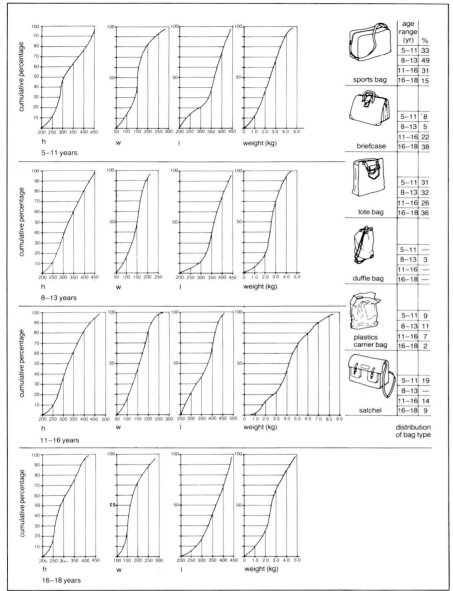

		age range (yr)	%
sports bag		5–11	33
		8–13	49
		11–16	31
		16–18	15
briefcase		5–11	'8
		8–13	5
		11–16	22
		16–18	38
tote bag		5–11	31
		8–13	32
		11–16	26
		16–18	36
duffle bag		5–11	—
		8–13	3
		11–16	—
		16–18	—
plastics carrier bag		5–11	9
		8–13	11
		11–16	7
		16–18	2
satchel		5–11	19
		8–13	—
		11–16	14
		16–18	9
		distribution of bag type	

1   Size, weight & distribution of pupils' bags

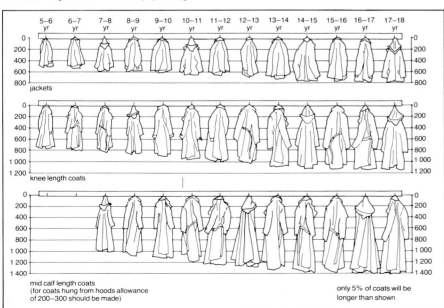

2   Lengths of pupils' coats

FURNITURE

Storage of pupils' belongings

In schools for younger children with less movement about school trays and individual containers at workplace suitable. Coats and small bags can be hung on pegs locally →p120(3). But greater movement of pupils in middle and older age ranges encourages widespread use of various kinds of bags in which books can be carried from 1 place of work to another. Central provision of lockers therefore of decreasing value since their dimensions and their location likely to be inconvenient. Provision of pegs and racks for bags associated with each work space becoming more convenient and more secure. For this dimensional data given →(1)(2) relevant. Data prepared by Furniture Industry Research Association as part of survey of sto of pupils' personal belongings.

In USA lockers →(3) still standard for older children, if only for security. In-rm sto provided for children up to 12 years old. Basket racks also used →(4).

Schools references
→Bibliography entries 134 191 192 193 194 195 196 197 198 199 200 202 203 204 205 207 208 209 210 211 212 213 214 215 265 267 275 314 446 451 476 484 526 530 575–81 607 652

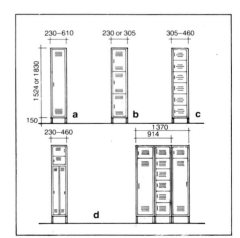

3   USA lockers **a** 1-tier **b** 3-tier **c** 6-tier
d combination units

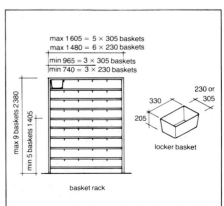

4   Basket rack; can be single row (d 305–335) or back-to-back

Colleges

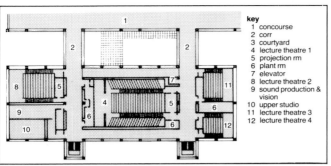

key
1 concourse
2 corr
3 courtyard
4 lecture theatre 1
5 projection rm
6 plant rm
7 elevator
8 lecture theatre 2
9 sound production & vision
10 upper studio
11 lecture theatre 3
12 lecture theatre 4

1 Lecture ha complex pre-clinical sciences bldg Southampton University England   Arch John S Bonnington Partnership

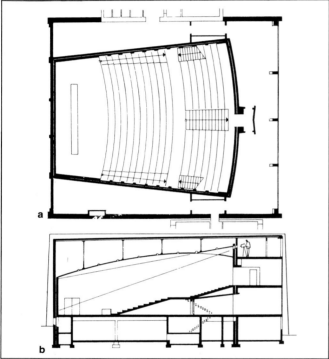

2 Physics lecture theatre with double walling to reduce sound & vibration Technical University Darmstadt Germany **a** plan **b** section

LECTURE ROOMS & THEATRES

Utilisation of lecture rm and theatres traditionally low in relation to space requirements and capital cost; therefore consider designing flexibility to accommodate various functions. Such spaces could suit lectures, stage productions, demonstrations and cinema. Large theatre could be divisible to accommodate different audience sizes; similarly, with retractable seating system →p135, large lecture rm can be converted into assembly hall or gymnasium. Number and extent of such activities will also determine need for adjoining ancillary spaces such as preparation rm, projector rm, workshops, changing rm, studios and sto.

If policy to hire lecture theatre to outside organisations during vacations consider improved space standards and environmental conditions to satisfy more sophisticated requirements of business world.

Min ar/P: 0.46 m² (based on moveable seats, armless 450 centre to centre)

0.6 m² (fixed seats with arms at 500 centre to centre)

Basic shape

Shape of lecture theatre becomes more important as size and volume increase. Square flexible but fan shape preferred for larger theatres where plan form relates to adequate sight lines for audio-visual presentations, cinema etc →p136. Consider rear projection →(3); tv data p136(1)–(3). Small capacity lecture rm up to approx 80 persons quite satisfactory with flat floor: larger halls require either ramped floor (max 1 : 10) or stepped floor, dependent upon achieving adequate sight lines. Uniform change of eye level should be achieved at each seat row, min being 60 and median 125.

Theatre auditorium →p350

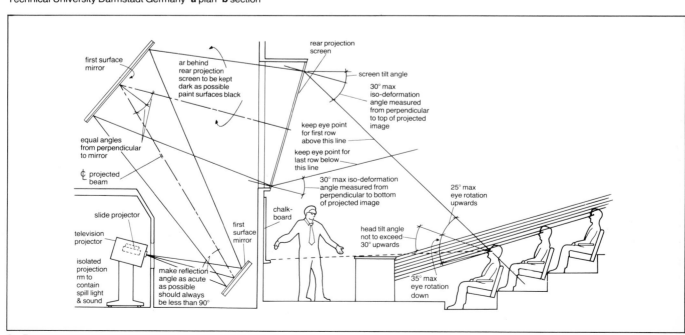

3 Rear projection of images for lecture ha: not so clear as front projection for large ha but more convenient for lecturer & allows higher light level in ha for note-taking

LECTURE ROOMS: SEATING

Seating types
Categories:

individual chairs capable of being linked together in rows, stacked and stored away, with or without arms, with or without writing tablets

fixed seating of various degrees of comfort with or without tip-up seats, with or without arms →(1)–(3)

retractable seating systems capable of folding down on to tiered staging (which usually includes aisles), whole arrangement being retractable and stored in relatively small area flat auditorium floor capable of being used for other purposes →(4).

Flexible seating →p351

Seating min dimensions
Back to back distance between rows of seats

(with tip-up seats)	750
Width of seats, linked, without arms	460
Width of seats with arms	500
Unobstructed vertical space between seats	300

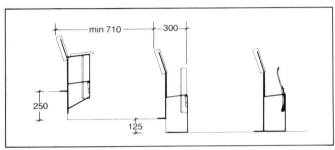

1　Fixed seating with tip-up seats

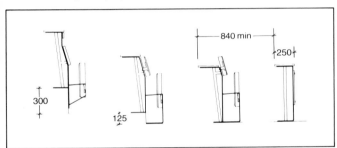

2　Fixed seating with tip-up seats & writing shelf

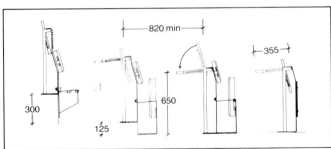

3　Fixed seating with tip-up seats & retractable shelving

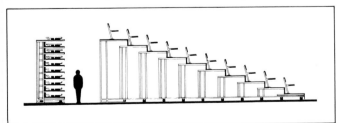

4　Basic principle of rectractable seating

SEATING ARRANGEMENTS

Relate to function of hall or theatre:

Lecture: audience should be able to see and hear lecturer. Where chalkboard or screens needed desirable viewing requirements affect seating plan. Increasing trend towards audience participation: implies students should be close as possible to lecturer. Can be achieved by U-shaped seating arrangement which reduces number of rows required and also give saving in total area.

Cinema: criteria for good viewing:

max horizontal viewing angle	30°
max vertical viewing angle	35°
critical angle of projector	12°
max viewing distance	6 × w of screen
min viewing distance	2 × w of screen

Demonstration: will usually require steeply raked floor to ensure good viewing to top of demonstration benches. Relative cost of such auditoria with heavily serviced demonstration benches, preparation rm and like should be compared with costs of normal lecture rm equipped with closed circuit tv →p136(1)–(3).

Seating can be set round demonstration area in semi-circular formation if no requirement for chalkboards or screens, as with anatomy demonstration theatres.

Sightlines →p136 351

Cinemas →p354–8

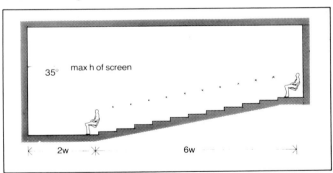

5　Section through orthodox lecture theatre

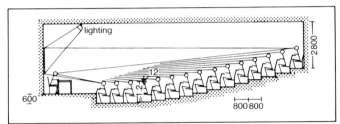

6　Preferred viewing distances for cinema projection

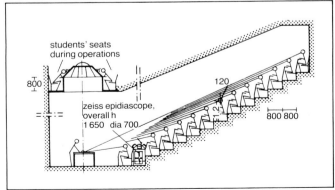

7　Lecture theatre with demonstration table (surgical clinic)

Colleges

LECTURE ROOMS: FIRE REGULATIONS

Design of lecture rm or theatre must conform to safety reg, in particular fire and means of escape. Number of seats permissible in any row →(4) dependent upon clear distance apart of rows (back to back dimension A), resultant clear section (dimension E measured between perpendiculars) and distance of seats from gangway (D = w of seat).

In turn clear width of gangways and number within hall must be related to number of persons to be accommodated.

ACOUSTICS →p18 395–7

Just as important hear distinctly as see clearly; lecture hall must be acoustically isolated from other noise sources.

No internal acoustic treatment should be necessary for rm less than 300 m^2 but as size and volume increases shape of hall becomes increasingly important.

Design of ceiling as reflector of sound from original source important factor in achieving even distribution throughout hall. Design of wall surfaces and finishes also important consideration in either reflecting or absorbing sound according to their relationship to stage or dais.

size of tv tube	seat row spacing		
	900	1300	1550
425	650	425	350
475	675	450	375
520	850	562	462
570	875	575	475
595	962	620	520

1 h of tv image in relation to size of tube & seat row spacing

size of tv tube	seat row spacing		
	900	1300	1550
425	1650	1250	1125
475	1700	1300	1150
520	2125	1625	1459
570	2150	1650	1475
595	2400	1825	1625

2 Min viewing distance from tv tube

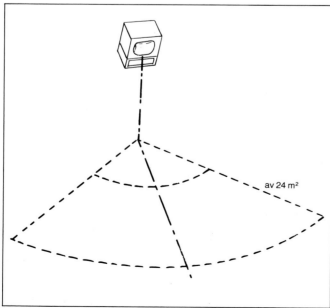

av 24 m²

3 Shape & square frontage of viewing ar for 520 receiver

a	min seatway (measured between perpendiculars) E	max distance of seat from gangway (500 seats) F	max number of 500 wide seats/row	
			gangway both sides	gangway 1 side
	300	3000	14	7
	330	3500	16	8
	360	4000	18	9
	390	4500	20	10
	420	5000	22	11

4 **a** distance of seats from gangways **b** plan of seating without arms **c** seating with backs & arms **d** part of auditorium

number of P accommodated on each tier or floor	min number of exits[1]	min w
200	2	1050[2]
300	2	1200
400	2	1350
500	2	1500
750	3	1500
1000	4	1500

[1] plus 1 additional exit of not less than 1500 for each extra 250 P or part thereof [2] would not normally apply to exit corr or staircases serving auditorium of theatre

5 Exit requirements

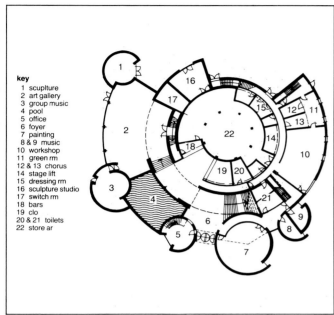

key
1 sculpture
2 art gallery
3 group music
4 pool
5 office
6 foyer
7 painting
8 & 9 music
10 workshop
11 green rm
12 & 13 chorus
14 stage lift
15 dressing rm
16 sculpture studio
17 switch rm
18 bars
19 clo
20 & 21 toilets
22 store ar

1   Gardner Centre for the Arts University of Sussex England   Arch John S Bonnington Partnership, formerly Sir Basil Spence Bonnington & Collins

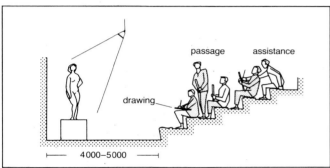

2   Tiers in life studio: seat ar/student 0.65 m²

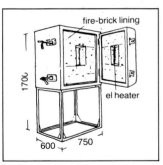

3   Small pottery kiln

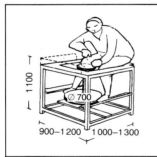

4   Ar needed for potter's wheel

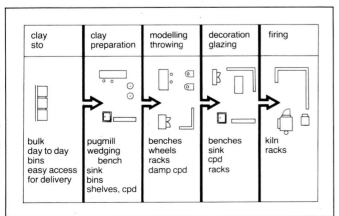

5   Sequence of operations: clay modelling & pottery

SCHOOLS OF ART, DESIGN, DRAMA & MUSIC

Scope and intensity of study in specialist art, design and drama subjects vary from college to college. Faculties likely include selection of:

drawing & painting: fine art
ceramics
sculpture
industrial design: engineering
furniture & interior design
theatre & television design
graphics & related visual arts including photography
silver & jewelry
textile design both print & weave
stained glass
drama
music

Schedule of accn for each will generally include design studio, work and practice rm, technical workshops and admin off. Communal lecture theatre or assembly hall usable also as exhibition centre often required but display areas for both 2 and 3 dimensional work should also be provided throughout college.

Design studios
Should be next to appropriate workr or workshop; consider exclusion of noise and dust. Sto space for plan sheets, wardrobes or clothes lockers, reference books and models should be included together with eqp for copying drawings and documents, although such may be centralised. Good lighting essential, both natural and artificial.

Drawing studios →p139

Fine art studios
Studios for painting and sculpture require large areas; must have good natural daylight with high level windows, equal to at least 25–33% of floor area, with N or E aspect.

Rooflights may provide ancillary light; all windows should be fitted with some form of daylight control. All surfaces should be durable and easy to clean.

Workshops
Siting will depend on type of work being done. Light work allied with graphics, silver and jewelry, photography and fashion may be placed on higher floor; metal, wood and plastics workshops where large machines may be installed best sited on ground or basement level.

Good workshop layout must conform to work flow and safety →p138(1)(2). Provide ample space round machines and for gangways to allow necessary movement without incursion on work space. Non-slip floor finishes should be specified; workshop technician should be able survey whole area from partially glazed off.

If each student provided with sets of tools space for individual lockers needed in workshop area.

Workshop eqp spaces →p288

Practice rooms
May be for individual study or group practice. Should be well insulated against passage of sound from one to another.

Stores
Methods of storing wide range of goods and materials needed support each activity should be closely studied, as should areas required house completed works before exhibition or disposal.

All sto should be sited next to appropriate workshop; consider proper conditions of heat and humidity where these may be detrimental to materials being stored if not held within reasonable limits, *eg* timber, clay, plaster.

Special racking needed for paintings and large canvasses; timber and timber-based board materials, plastics sheets, metal sections, rolls of textiles, glass and paper.

All such sto will require element of control and security.

Ancillary accommodation
Will include off for teaching staff, common rm, lav and possibly showers.

Colleges

SCHOOLS OF ART, DESIGN, DRAMA & MUSIC

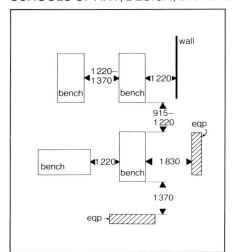

1 Clearances for layout of metal shops

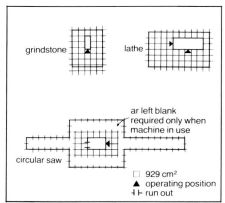

2 Working spaces round woodwork machinery

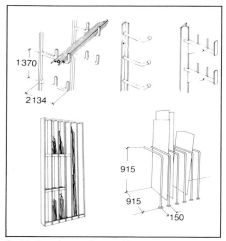

3 Various forms of sto racking

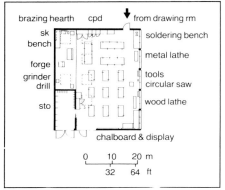

4 Layout for combined wood & metal shop

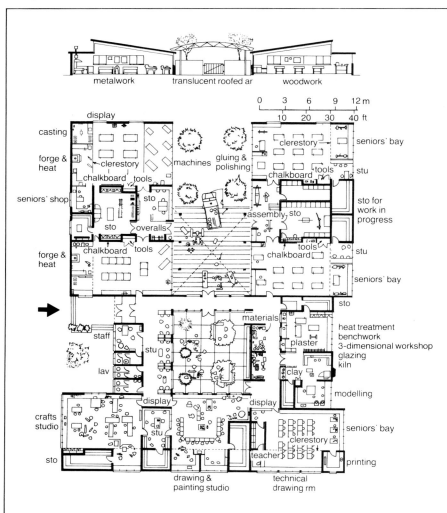

5 Arts centre layout for college

Colleges

DRAWING STUDIOS

Space requirements related to type of drawing and allied work, if any, to be undertaken →(1).

Work station sizes in part conditioned by eqp needed to accommodate drawing format to be adopted. Except in USA most offices committed to 'A' series of international paper sizes: smaller formats obtained by halving larger dimensions in each instance →p3–5. For most industrial, engineering and design consultants drawing requirements can be accommodated by A0 format; drawing boards and drafting machines sized accordingly.

Simplest form of work station: drawing board, eqp trolley (cart) and draughtsman's stool; where drafting work requires reference contained on other drawings either reference tables or vertical screens may be used carry this information. Screens have advantage of keeping floor area needed to min but at expense of controlled supervision. Reference tables, which may also provide plan chest drawing sto below work surface, either to side of draughtsman in parallel with drawing board or at right angles to it. Further possibility available with 'back reference' where reference table also support for drawing board behind. Where drafting function only part of job requirement and admin work also to be done reference area may double as off desk or, if space allows, desk may form additional element within work station.

Reference may not be confined to information contained on drawings; often need have comprehensive set reference books or manuals close at hand for draughtsman: may be housed communally or at each work station.

Further category of drawing studio that allied to workshops where full-sized setting-out drawings (USA shop drawings) (or workshop 'rods') prepared. Usually allied to construction industry, in particular joinery shops; such drawings prepared on rolls of paper set down at long benches. Draughtsmen work standing up at drafting surface which is horizontal and 900 from FFL. Original drawings stored in roll form rather than sheet as in other studios, for which housing may be either horizontal (plan chests with drawers) or vertical (plan file cabinets).

Layout of any studio therefore conditioned by type of work being undertaken and type of supervision required.

In all studios good lighting essential, both daylight and artificial; windows should have N to E aspect. If this not possible windows should be fitted with blinds to screen direct sunlight and prevent glare.

Ancillary areas may include printing and reprographic eqp; this may be housed in studio or, if sophisticated or large scale, sited in separate area. Archive sto for original drawings which may have to be kept for indefinite period should be properly conditioned for sto of paper and housings must be fire and flood proof. Present trend increased use of computer processes for production of working drawings; use of such eqp may influence spatial requirements of future drawing studios.

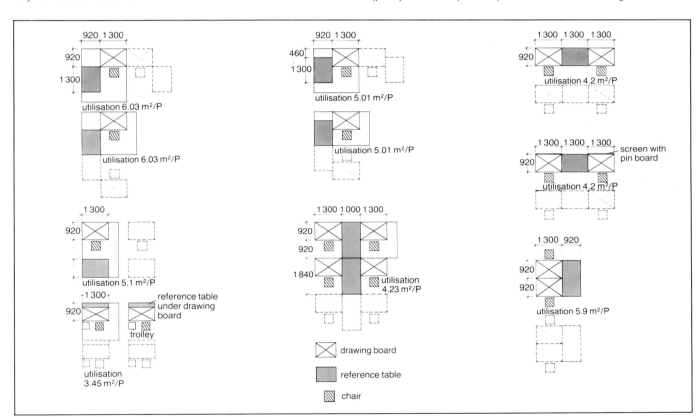

1   Various planning arrangements

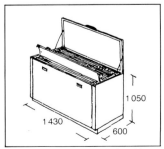

2   Drawings best kept in fr cabinets

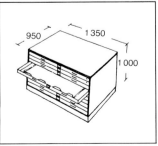

3   Steel chest for plans

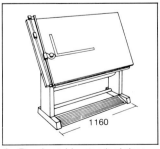

4   Drawing table: standard sizes 1 000 × 1 500 & 1 250 × 2 000; h 2 050 (USA 941 × 1 092–1 067 × 2 390; h 940)

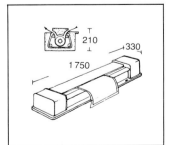

5   Typical small photocopying machine used in drawing off for reproducing plans

Colleges

STUDENT HOSTELS: PLANNING FACTORS

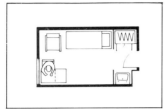

1   Single stu/bedr with hb: 10 m²

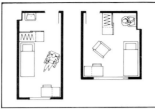

2   Single stu/bedr: longer shape provides more economical use of space

3   Single stu/bedr without hb

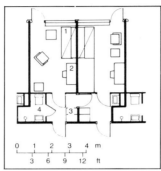

4   2-student unit, also used for conferences 1 B 2 desk 3 wa 4 bathr

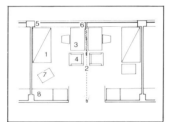

5   Double stu/bedr 1 divan B 2 curtain 3 desk with drawer unit 4 easy chair 5 heating convector 6 book shelf over 7 table with bookshelves 8 built-in wa

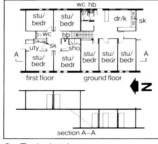

6   Typical staircase access

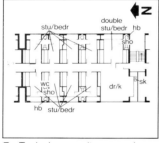

7   Typical composite access (corr access similar but continuous between staircase): note position of dr/k ar & shared washr & toilet

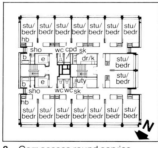

8   Corr access round service core; e = elevator

9   Composite access

10   Typical amenity ar

Hostel (USA dormitories) bldg usually financed by university or college from own funds, government grants or loans, open market loans: annual income raised has to cover interest, amortisation, running and maintenance costs. Some governments make grants to subsidise annual income. This can be supplemented by letting for conferences, educational courses, holiday visitors. In some countries educational establishments and student unions have formed businesses provide off bldg for letting so that income can subsidise hostels. Size of hostel rm and amenities to be provided therefore depend on uses bldg can be put to and on annual income obtained.

Single students generally need accn for 30–33 week/year. Married usually for 50–52 weeks. Accn should cater for children outside play space and be placed near shopping and social services and amenities.

Trend to house students in range of accn for all categories; many students prefer small independent units sharing some variety of accn to institutional residential communities. For social and admin reasons first year students usually placed in halls of residence with staff rm, area kitchen, laundry and ironing rm, toilets, sto etc, meals being taken in dining centre.

Dining rm →p142

Halls with shared dining and social services normally planned as large number of study bedr with central bathr and small kitchen: may also be rm or flat for staff member provide supervision. In recent residential bldg provision made for students prepare and take all meals independently in own social groups. Small groups up to 4 students need be self-selected; group of 6–8 socially large enough divide into sub-groups without being too big share cooking eqp successfully; 12 or more do not form cohesive group: shared kitchen with dining rm used for other activities could lead to problems.

Conference use requires min washbasin in each rm with good access car parking, lecture and dining rm: alternative accn for few students in residence during vacations and sto for possessions needed.

Independent housing or hostel units favoured by final year and postgraduate; can be in purpose-built groups, located in urban community or converted houses.

Shared accn also →p99

ACCOMMODATION REQUIREMENTS

1-bed/study space 9–15 m²; 2-bed/study space 13–19 m² (unpopular with UK students; liked in USA); self-catering unit total area 16–20 m²: areas may be slightly reduced in 'family' flats to allow more room for amenity space.

Rm to be furnished with bed/divan, desk and chair, shelves and hanging for clothes 0.8–1 m², open adjustable shelving and pin board, easy chair, small table, bedside table, mirror, bin, rm light and desk/bed lamp, 2 power points, rm heater, carpet, dense curtains/blinds. If wash basin included provide towel rail, mirror, cupboard or shelf, shaver point. Rm showers and wc sometimes included on individual or shared basis.

Some rm should be larger to provide for entertaining and meetings.

Provide proportion of rm suitable for physically handicapped.

Married student accn should comply with normal housing space standards →p44 48: some will have families.

Provide background heating supplemented by rm heater controlled by occupant.

Ensure good sound insulation, especially round service pipes.

Shared accn →p99

Sanitary

1 wc/6 students; 1 bath/6 students, or 1 shower/12 students (preferably 50% baths); 1 wash basin/3 students if not provided in rm.

Space standard 1.2–1.6 m².

USA: check applicable codes and standards for these details.

Prefabricated sanitary units →p65

Hot water heating local or centralised.

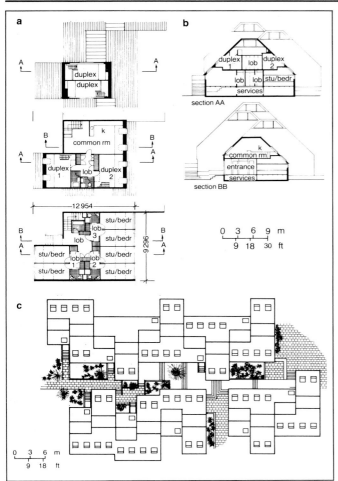

1 Student residence Guildford England **a** second, first & ground floor plans of typical unit **b** sections AA & BB **c** roof plan of court Arch Robert Maguire & Keith Murray

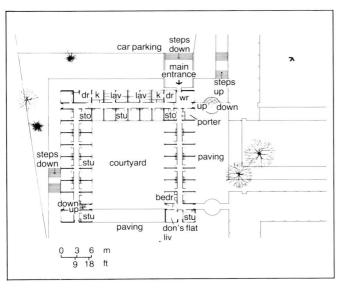

2 Hall of residence next campus Southampton England typical floor plan Arch J S Bonnington Partnership

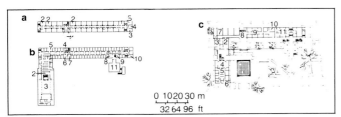

STUDENT HOSTELS: ACCOMMODATION (cont)

Amenity space

Dining kitchens not intended for full meal service with utility space allow 1.2–1.6 m²/student. With full meal service allow 1.7–2 m²/student (less for more than 6 students).

Where hostel close to other university bldg and communal service used, dining kitchen may be only shared social space. Cooking and dining areas should be separated with dining rm located where all students pass it.

New accn more likely provide self-catering. Eqp self-catering shared by 6: cooker and refrigerator, single bowl double-drainer sink, 2000–3000 work top with cupboards under and over (include individual food lockers), refuse with capacity 1 day's use. Provide eqp for washing, drying and ironing for each group of rm.

NB: above not normal practice in USA.

Residences on campus use communal amenities; where accn some distance from other university bldg allow within hostel m²/student:

large common rm	0.9–1.2
lib/reading rm	0.4–1.8
indoor games	0.2–0.4
hobby rm	0.2–0.4

Within these areas also coffee bar/shop, ante-rm/coffee lounge, place for debates and society meetings, television, music practice, lav for visitors as appropriate in accordance with local reg.

Offices

Large residences away from campus need some off with approx areas (m²): warden/supervisor* 20, secretary/archives 20, management committee/consult rm 30, housekeeper* 9, cleaner's changing rm* 9, porter* (next to entrance) 9, students' union 20.

* also needed when residence on campus.

Staff

Design to suit single, married and married with family categories. Some accn within residence provides supervision. Separate accn in houses or flats most economical. Warden needs (m²) 67–93; single academic staff and housekeeper each 56–67; single supervisory staff 46–56; single domestic staff as for students.

Ancillary

Allow baggage sto 0.3 m²/student. Provide adequate central sto for household and cleaning eqp, linen, furniture and refuse; on each floor sto for cleaners and eqp with sink and water supply. Provide laundry chute if appropriate.

Circulation areas and ducts account for 2–5.7 m²/student. Ensure passages adequate for trolleys (carts) and carrying suitcases. Provide entrance hall supervised by porter with space for notices, telephone kiosks and milk and mail delivery. Bell system or loudspeaker will serve to transmit messages in conjunction with some telephone points.

Finishes

Materials should be durable, hard and need little maintenance.

Layout & building form

Single row arrangement: width of bldg 5500, rm 3500, corridor 1500; double row arrangement: width 10 m, 2 rm each 3500, corridor 2000; triple row arrangement: width 14000, 2 rm each 3500, 2 corridors each 1500 with artificially lit and ventilated centre block for washr etc. Type of access available: by stairs to rm, by stairs and short corridors, by stairs to central corridors. Adequate means of escape in case of fire must be provided →p44 91. With 4 floors and more elevators required: more economical build up to 3 storeys.

Car parking: min ratio 1 space/3 students; sto for bicycles and motor cycles also.

Site footpaths away from ground floor windows and maintain privacy.

3 Quincy House Harvard University USA provides integrated communal services **a** second floor plan 1 single bedr 2 4-man duplex suite liv, bedr above or below 3 tutor liv 4 stu 5 bedr **b** first floor plan 1 k 2 servery 3 dr 4 janitor 5 4-bedr suites 6 liv 7 bedr 8 listening rm 9 workr 10 3-bedr unit 11 reading rm **c** ground floor plan 1 lower lob 2 grill rm 3 senior commons 4 junior commons 5 tutorial centre 6 superintendent 7 service & gar 8 entrance lob 9 house off 10 tutor suite 11 guest suite Arch Shepley Bulfinch Richardson & Abbot

Colleges

REFECTORIES/DINING HALLS

Can be provided in separate bldg within hostel (dormitory), within community activities bldg or as separate bldg. Space requirements depend on type of service (self-service from counter, self-service from dishes on table, waiter service) and seating arrangement but generally allow 1.2 m²/student, allowing for number of sittings. Long tables with benches →(1) preferable (not USA) to small with chairs: cheaper, durable, space-saving, easy clean and clear. Width of seat ≥ 600; width of table 600–(preferably) 700.

Space for cross passages: (500 × 1050/3 seats = 0.18 m²); add extra space for side passages and space in front of servery (service) and entrance. Benches should stand 80–100 away from this table; need be only 300 wide and 400–450 high (easy to step over). Benches near wall 400 wide, including 120 distance from wall to give access. More convenient enter from side but this means ≥ 4 students on wall bench.

For more elaborate furnishing →(2); where chairs and more comfortable tables desired dimensions are: width of seat ≥ 650; width of table ≥ 700–800. Space required (access from behind →hatched portion): 650 × 1150 = 0.75 m². Share of cross passages (550 × 1150)/3 = 0.21 m². Floor area/student with appropriate extra space as above: 1.1–1.2 m².

If space along wall behind chairs used as main passage width increased to ≥ 800.

Tables with seats at either end →(3) uneconomical, spoil communal feeling and equality among students. Space needed for tables in corners (→hatching): 5900 × 2550)/12 = 1.25 m². Space/student required

with all passages and appropriate extra space as above: 1.2–1.3 m². Seating also →p202–4; snack bars →p205

Circulation of diners should be 1-way only: can be achieved by correct disposition of tables and siting of columns at corners of tables to avoid waste of seating space →(4).

Kitchen, servery (service) and sto area between 40–50% of refectory; food preparation 20% of kitchen. Servery area for cafeteria service up to 20% kitchen area. Desirable design on 1 level with convenient stores delivery: avoid staircases and elevators if possible.

Kitchen should be big enough for work in uninterrupted sequence without opposing traffic flows from sto to servery. Sto at start of circulation followed by food preparation tables, sinks and eqp including area for pastry making, thence to cookers, ovens and boilers, then to warm cupboards and servery. Provide pot-wash near to cooking area. Off for chief chef should be positioned to provide supervision of stores and delivery points and also whole kitchen area. Crockery should be stored in servery area and after use go by trolleys (carts), dishwashers and drying cabinets back to servery.

Good ventilating system required to draw air from dining areas and kitchen and avoiding flow of air from kitchen to dining area.

Restaurant kitchens →p213→Bib217

Sanitary (USA: check applicable codes and standards): depending on location and proximity to other bldg should be provided next to dining rm; if already available nearby suggested provision: 1 wc/100 males, plus 1/250 males, 1 urinal/25 males; 2 wc/100 female plus 1/100; 1 wash basin/50 P.

Finishes: materials should be durable and require little maintenance.

Colleges references:
→Bibliography entries 039 040 041 063 096 097 113 114 147 168 176 200 217 226 261 377 413 437 441 446 472 476 485 526 556 569 581 612 629 630 652

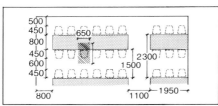

1 Long tables with free standing benches

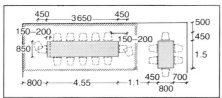

2 Long tables with chairs

3 Table with chairs at end

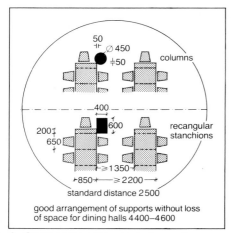

good arrangement of supports without loss of space for dining halls 4400–4600

4 Space saving arrangement of supports

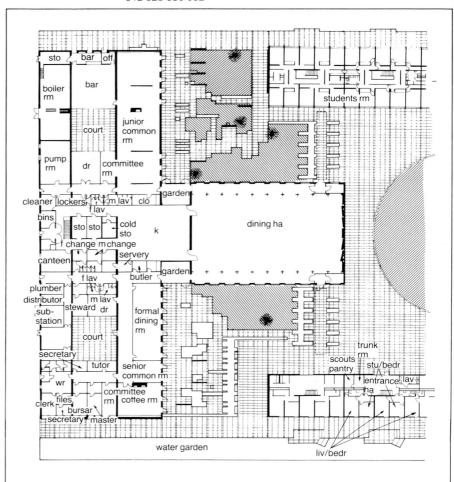

5 Integrated refectory services St Catherine College Cambridge England   Arch Arne Jacobsen

Youth hostels

Often conversions of existing bldg both because of shortage of money and because often in aesthetically sensitive surroundings; therefore Youth Hostels Association (YHA) reluctant lay down definitive plans for typical hostels. Nevertheless specifications and requirements particular and detailed, specially since tightening of fire reg →(1). In UK DES has also requirements for hostels for which it provides funds: more onerous on questions of space.

Bed spaces

3.1 m² floor ar/P in dormitories
1 wc/10 bed spaces
1 hb/6 bed spaces
1 b or sho/20 bed spaces

For purpose of computing floor area DES disallows any part of floor over which ceilings less than 2100 high.

YHA has lower standards, depending on grade of hostel: simple or standard. Simple (need not have resident warden) min 2.04 m²/bed space; standard (must have resident warden living within curtilage of hostel at all times when open to members) for dormitories min 2.32 m²/bed space, recommended 2.78 m². As double bunks normally used this means 6.31 m²/bunk if DES standards to be met.

Dormitories

YHA, ruling body for hostels in England and Wales (Scottish YHA has similar standards), lays down all hostels must have separate dormitories for men and women, with separate access. Layout of dormitories should be such that can be used by either sex as bookings demand: means that either sex must be able to reach appropriate lavatory. Most compact solution block of intercommunicating rm with appropriate door locked between sexes. YHA aims to switch to arrangement in many continental hostels with 4-bed dormitories, with sanitary accn reached from common corridor, motel style. DES pressing for degree of privacy in washing arrangements for women, satisfied by arranging washbasins in own cubicle with curtain at entrance.

Hosteller's amenities

As hostels closed during day arriving members need luggage rm to leave gear without having access to rest of hostel; may be combined with drying rm, where hostellers take off outer clothing before booking in at reception desk.

To allow to cook own meals members' kitchen provided in all hostels, in addition to kitchen of warden who will also cook for hostellers. Members' kitchens have combined double cooking rings and burners and grill units, fuelled by propane gas where mains services not available. Locker space also required, and also washing up space, in addition to that intended for those hostellers who take warden's meals who are required to wash up.

Warden's quarters

Hostels with more than 40 beds usually administered by married couples, possibly with children who will need living quarters. Largest hostels will have assistant wardens, provided with own sitting rm, staff dining rm, kitchens and recreation rm.

In larger hostels chief warden's quarters should be in form of self-contained house or flat, with 3 bedr, bathr, kitchen, dining rm and sitting rm. In these circumstances hostellers' accn should never be over or under warden's.

Fire safety

YHA increasingly concerned with application of more stringent standards of fire safety to both new and existing hostels. Sources of danger have been identified as primarily: interference with stoves or heaters, particularly in drying rm; el or gas faults; smoking; misuse of cooking stoves in members' kitchens. Provision of means of escape in old bldg difficult. Fr required for protected staircases difficult provide in bldg with timber floors. In smaller hostels, akin to domestic houses, distances travelled on fire escape routes not normally long enough to contravene reg. Generally 18 m travel distance to place of safety considered max where floors timber, or 30 m where non-combustible. Min of 2 staircases normally required, in such positions that no person on any floor has to go further than max travel distance to reach staircases or other point of access to place of safety.

place	ar m²	comment
entrance hall	14	with bench & shoe rack
off/reception/shop	11	hatch to entrance ha, reasonably close to warden's k
drying rm	14	preferably accessible from entrance ha without passing through principal rm: with racks or hangers heated
luggage rm	14	if combined with drying rm, laundries & wc 14–18.5 m² each
common rm	18.5–23	
dining rm	46.5	or 0.7–0.9 m²/P
member's k	16	with direct access as possible to dr
warden's k	16–23	if possible with hatch & door combined for direct service to dr; sk in k preferred to separate scl; access to dustbins
la	9.3	each
wash-up	11	with 1 or 2 sk; table space for dirty crockery; easy access from dr; if possible reasonable access to warden's k for return of crockery
warden's sitr	14	layout of these will depend usually upon balance of convenience, privacy, aspect
warden's bedr	11	
warden's 2nd bedr	9.3	
warden's 3rd bedr	7.5	
wardens bathr	3.25	
dormitories	158–167	ie 3.16/P
wc		for hostellers not less than 5, for warden 1
washing accn		for each sex 1 washrm with b (separated by partitions) or sho, 1 footbath, basins to DES standards
airing cpd	1	for warden's use
blanket sto	3.75	warmed
cycle sto	28	for about 30 cycles, preferably in racks: 1 machine/305

note: floor ar intended as min desirable but in alterations much will depend on existing bldg

1 YHA schedule of accn for 50-B hostel

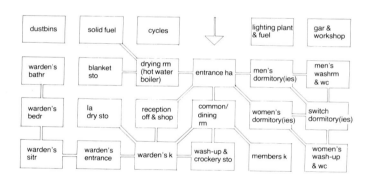

2 Schematic layout for 1-storey youth hostel

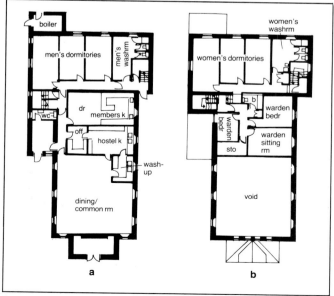

3 Youth hostel converted from existing house by YHA: **a** ground floor **b** 1st floor

Youth hostels

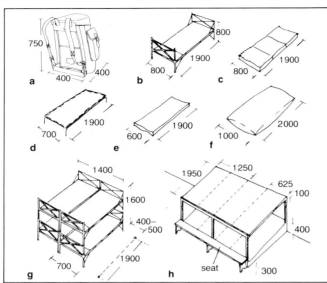

1 **a** rucksack **b** bed **c** mattress **d** camp bed **e** emergency mattress for sleeping lager **f** palliasse for blanket **g** double 2-tier bunks **h** plank beds

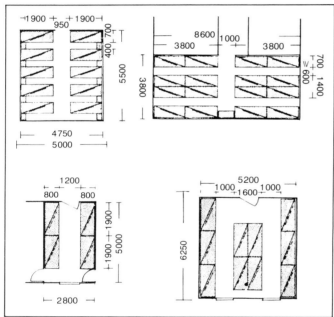

2 Typical sleeping rm; min ar between skirtings, 4-bed 16 m² (1 bed 4 m²), 8-bed 16 m² (1 bed 2 m²), 10-bed 30 m² (1 bed 3 m²), 20-bed 30 m² (1 bed 1.5 m²); in large dormitories 32 beds 32.7 m² (1 bed 1.02 m²)

GERMAN STANDARDS

Small hostel with dormitory 30–50 beds
Standard size 40–100 beds
Large 100–250 beds
Very large 250–600 beds
Optimum 120–180 beds, with 400 upper limit. Relate number of beds to av number visitors; design sleeping lager to cope with peak holiday demand.

Siting: open, sheltered from wind, main rm facing SE,S.

Space requirement: for standard hostel: in dormitory 2.2–2.8 m²/bed; for 2-tier bunks 1.8–2.0 m²; 1–2 large rm with 20–30 beds, or smaller with 4–12 beds; 8-bed rm much valued. Also rm for sick and accidents 1–2 beds.

Av occupation approx 40% girls 60% boys; sexes either on separate floors or segregated by partitions: some rm arranged to meet different balance up to 50/50. Av rm height 2800, not less than 2500.

Dormitory floor area 1.5 m²/bed.

Plank beds: single tier 1.2–1.5 m²/bed, 2-tier 1.1 m²/bed.

Common rm 1.0–1.5 m²/bed. Meeting/discussion rm sound-proofed and located away from other day rm.
Walls preferred wood lined, with rucksack stands and tip-up benches.

Kitchens: Both visitors' and warden's kitchens near entrance, preferably with light from 2 sides.
Visitors' kitchen fitted for self-catering; in smaller hostels can be in common rm, otherwise separated, also apart from warden's kitchen. Generous provision of cooking eqp; 100-l boiler and sk.
Rambler's kitchen big enough for group eat and also sit in winter.
Warden's kitchen: glass door or window allows supervision of coming and going; food hatch to common rm. Equipped double sk, low slop sk, 600 deep dresser under windows, lockable draw for money, power points for kitchen appliances; if gas-fitted, low rings for large pans. Sk and crockery cupboards next food hatch and apart from main kitchen: crockery washed by users.

Larder next kitchen, long narrow and cool.

Warden's quarters: min 3 rm each approx 16 m² including kitchen, which may be on same floor or separate, in which case on ground floor next to reception and with sitting rm, upstairs being 1–2 bedr next girls' section and bathr.

Assistants 7 m²/P

Entrance sheltered from wind or with porch; convenient approach, shelter canopy, easy for warden watch over. Focus of hostel hall and day rm, divided into noisy (workrm, table tennis, games, dancing), normal (common rm, dining rm), quiet (writing, reading, discussion, office, sleeping): noise control by separation on different floors.

Washrooms: area 0.35–0.4 m²/bed; 1 washbasin/4–6 beds; 1 footbath/15 beds, 1 shower/20–40 beds. Showers can be in basement, better next bedr. Ground floor washr for arrivals.

Lavatories: 0.3–0.35 m²/bed; 1 wc/1 urinal/8–10 boys; 1 wc/6–8 girls: lower proportion in larger hostels.

Laundry if possible related bathr, showers and heating; in large hostels machines and spin driers.

Ancillary rooms: sto for packs, bicycles, sports gear; drying rm; shoe cleaning; utility rm for hostel eqp, first-aid box; dark rm in larger hostels; warden's workshop.

Construction: suiting environment; resistant rough treatment; stone and timber mainly, min plaster.

3 Large hostel in Germany Arch Lauterbach

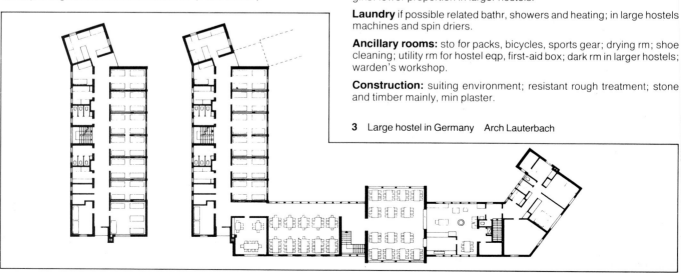

Libraries

INTRODUCTION

Essential that close rapport be established between librarian and architect; for largest schemes library consultant should be employed.

Types

Community: primarily lending books to adults and children and with general reference section. Current trend in UK towards larger central libraries with branch satellites; rural areas often served by mobile units.

Specialised: primarily used for reference, with small loan section.

National university: used for reference and research; continually growing collections.

See also school media centres →p129, hospital libraries →p177.

Increasing literacy and leisure time plus 'information explosion' make it important to plan for max flexibility and for future expansion. New techniques are changing methods of control/indexing/retrieval.

PATTERN

3 main elements, materials, readers, staff, are related in varying ways depending on organisation policy: eg community, school and hospital libraries require predominantly 'open access', ie readers have direct access to books; catalogue a necessary adjunct. At times large numbers of people circulate among spread-out shelving units and are attracted to browse.

Larger libraries including universities and colleges concentrate sto in 'open stack' and put reading spaces nearby rather than amongst shelving. Formal arrangement of this often used in USA.

Alternative 'closed acess' allows no contact between readers and books except through staff via catalogue. This method used for major sto in national, large city and county reference collections, for rare and valuable books and as 'back-up' sto in any library: 'closed stack'.

Specialised/large libraries may have separate subject dept each with enquiry service; catalogue should remain centralised unless computer based. Reference and loan section catalogues may be divided.

SPACE STANDARDS

Appreciable differences to be found among national and international authorities. Following generally based on IFLA standards:

Community libraries

population served	allowance per 1000 population	
10000 to 20000	42 m² total floor ar	Figures based on surveys, but can be useful check; include all general but not indirect services (meeting rm, lecture & exhibition spaces)
20000 to 35000	39	
35000 to 65000	35	
65000 to 100000	31	
over 100000	28	

allocation	percentage of total ar	
adult lending	27 (up to 40 in small units)	
reference	20	
children	13 (max ar 150 m²)	
circulation/ services/ ancillaries	40 (about half for staff rm)	in small libraries children's % A should increase & reference decrease

Adult lending

population served	total vol	floor ar in m²	
3000	4000	100	
5000	4000	100	
10000	6000	100	
20000	12000	180	open access accn; 15 m²/ 1000 vol (but min ar 100 m²); includes local circulation, catalogues, staff counters, informal seats for browsing at 1/1000 population, some display eqp
40000	24000	360	
60000	24000	360	
60000	36000	540	
80000	44000	660	
100000	50000	750	

Children

Floor ar 75–100 m² for populations up to 10000, and 100–105 m² for 10000 to 20000 people. Basis as for adults (see above); but does not include space for study/talks/'story hours'. Separate entrance sometimes provided; but control becomes difficult.

Reference

Allow 10 m²/1000 vol as less need for generous circulation. 1 study space of 2.32 m²/1000 population, with some degree of privacy to avoid distraction; these figures will cover any staff desks required.

None of the adult, children or reference figures include provision for periodicals, sto of audio-visual materials.

1 Relationships

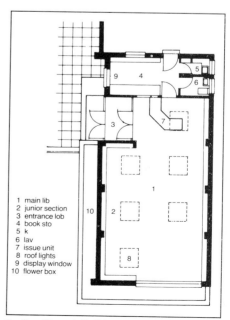

1 main lib
2 junior section
3 entrance lob
4 book sto
5 k
6 lav
7 issue unit
8 roof lights
9 display window
10 flower box

2 Small branch lib, Worcester England, 98 m²
5500 vol   Arch T Lewis

Libraries

ENTRANCE

Community libraries should clearly declare bldg function, and be wel-
coming. Lobby should reduce entry of noise/draughts. Provide visual
stimulation here. Adequate control needed to prevent high losses of
books etc through exit: some have had to use turnstiles or electronic
detectors. Remember needs of disabled people (ramps/elevator/
escalator →p86–8 406 411). Should lead to control/guide area →below,
with display *en route*.

CONTROL AREA

Close to or within sight of bldg entrance, and with space to absorb
congestion at peak hours, but located to allow max visibility for supervision. Function: to register new readers, issue and receive loan books,
deal with reservations and fines. In small libraries also handles reader's
enquiries →(1)–(3).

GUIDE AREA

Card index/book sheaves/computer print-out books, located near control
or enquiry, *en route* to all dept served, also close to catalogue work area.
If card index, allow say 12 m² covering 36 000 vol.

ENQUIRY DESK

Near catalogue guide and bibliographies. Can help to share supervision
with control.

MATERIALS

Books are, and will continue to be, primary material. Space may also be
required for: newspapers and periodicals, discs, tapes and music scores,
microfilms, maps and pictures; there may be more to add in future:
flexibility of layout necessary.

Shelving units
Most widely used type is metal shelving, individually adjustable, single
sided (along walls) and double sided (island). Unit height 2000 (loan
area), 1500 (children's area), 2300 (bookstack areas). Shelf depth
200–300 (children's books), 200 (fiction, literature, history, politics,
economics, law), 300 (scientific, technical, med). Width of unit generally
900 in UK and USA. Main routes in 'open access' areas 1800 clear
width, and minor routes 1200.

Book stacks
Optimum length of shelving 6 units (5400) to max 8 units (7200) but 4
units (3600) where accessible only from 1 end.

Centres of islands where 'open stack' are 1280–1520 (gives about 164
vol/m²); where 'closed stack' centres are 1060–1280 (gives 200–215
vol/m²). Choice between these limits depends on selection of shelf
depths and aisle widths.

Derivations from stack centre figures will give choice of economic
structural grid dimensions at centres of 5400, 6000, 6850, 7310, 7620,
7750 and 8350. Sub-divisions of these figures will relate windows, roof
lights, fixed elements, ventilation and lighting. Optimum column sizes
should be contained within 450 × 450 less finishes and tolerances,
clear ceiling height approx 2400.

Load-bearing stack units no longer favoured. Multi-floor 'closed stacks'
inhibit flexibility and require book hoist with staff captive on each floor.
Large area stack more flexible; max horizontal distance from bookshelf
to exit or book elevator approx 33 m: may need mech conveyors.

Variation for 'closed stack' sto: compact moveable shelving, of which
most common is 'right angle roller' type. Saves 50% of floor space
compared with static units but expensive and creates extra floor loading.
Space saving of 40% if aisles in static shelving were reduced from 900
to 550 wide.

Consider dividing into fr compartments of about 450 m². Use temp or
smoke detectors, not sprinkler system (causes more damage than fire).

Reading/study
Work table of 900 × 600/reader who should sit facing low screen
possibly with built-in light. Student should have 2.32 m² (which includes
circulation space), screened on 3 sides (open carrel); research worker

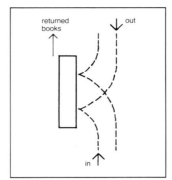

1   Small lib, staff of 1; snag: cross
circulation

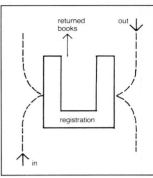

2   Island control, 1 staff at off-peak;
snag: separation from other staff ar

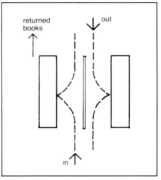

3   Large lib, can adjoin other staff
work ar; snag: min 2 staff all times

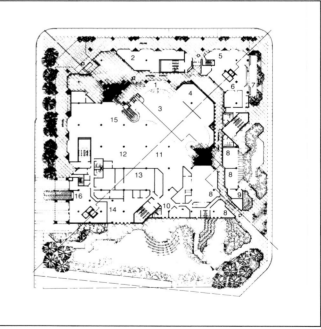

4   Metropolitan Toronto lib, largest public in Canada, houses over 1.25
million books, one third on display; space for over 800 readers to study mostly
in ar with some natural light
key
1 information 2 gallery 3 'synthesis' 4 extended hours reading 5 metro information services
6 newspapers 7 snacks 8 meeting 9 sto 10 audio visual services 11 general reference & information
centre 12 circulation 13 film stack 14 graphics 15 bibliographical centre 16 sending & receiving

3.0 m² or more screened on 4 sides (enclosed carrel). Aim give sufficient
privacy for mental concentration yet open enough to know if space
occupied and not misused. Lockable cupboards where books reserved
there for periods.

In community libraries trend away from formal reading rm towards small
scattered alcoves and nooks. In university libraries either large reading
rm separated from books stacks or, more commonly in UK, reading
areas round perimeter of stack areas, with further seating within stacks.

WORK AREAS

Unpacking and despatch, accessions and cataloguing, binding and repairs, photocopying and typing
Offices
Staff rest rm, lockers, lavatories
Mobile lending service: weather protected off loading, vehicle garaging, sto for book stock

ANCILLARIES

Study rm for reference materials
Typing/photocpy rm
Projection for slides, cine film, microfilm
Exhibition space, chair sto, rm for group meetings
Theatre (film, lecture, music)

Junior activity areas, group projects, story telling
Cloakrooms
Lavatories (locate to avoid use by general public)
Telephones

FLEXIBILITY

Larger the library greater the need for freedom of future change with interchangeability of major stack areas, reading areas, staff areas. Fixed elements (lavatories, staircases, major services etc) should be grouped. Best if floors can carry stack loading anywhere. Consider future expansion and possible effect on primary bldg. Partitions should be removable.

In medium and small community libraries some flexibility desirable (avoid 'built-in' fittings); but designer should beware lack of acoustic separation and loss of identity for areas of different function and mood. Consider changes of level.

FINISHES & SERVICES

Carpet general floor areas except stack and work areas; carpet or resilient flooring staff side of control; carpet all steps and stairs in quiet areas; sound absorbent ceilings to all areas. Pale colour floor in stack to reflect light to books on lowest shelves. Book spines highly decorative: for walls and columns consider natural wood/fabric/quiet paint colours.

Underfloor coil or ducted warm air heating; at least 3 air changes/hr. For older books and manuscripts hum controlled to 55%. In reading areas give temp of 20–22°C, USA: 18°C winter 26°C summer; but lending dept can be lower as most people wear outdoor clothes (add local heat in control and other work areas).

In larger bldg provide air conditioning at outset; or at least plan for future installation, especially for rare or valuable collections (contents of libraries often cost more than bldg itself). Air conditioning standard in USA. Avoid entry of direct sunlight; minimise solar heat gain (unless can be used for heating).

Lighting by fluorescent tubes generally but additional tungsten lighting to indicate changes of function/environment and to add sparkle and interest. Emergency lighting also required →Bib112.

Artificial lighting in lux →p2 25: control/enquiry 600 lx, reading tables 400 lx in lending, but 600 lx in reference, book stacks 100 lx on vertical surfaces, cataloguing and work rm 400 lx.

Shelf units in lending areas need special measures: consider illuminated canopy projecting about 500 from top of unit with sockets served by underfloor duct distribution.

Min DF →p17 27–9 10% with reflectance of 80% (walls and ceilings) and 30% (floors and furniture).

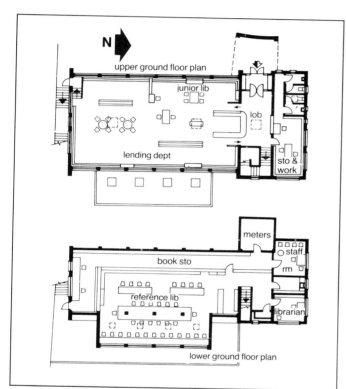

1   City branch lib, Durham England, 496 m² 17 000 vol   Arch A W Gelson

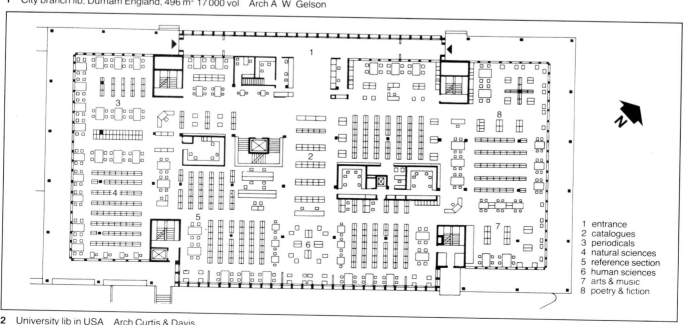

1 entrance
2 catalogues
3 periodicals
4 natural sciences
5 reference section
6 human sciences
7 arts & music
8 poetry & fiction

2   University lib in USA   Arch Curtis & Davis

Libraries

EXAMPLES

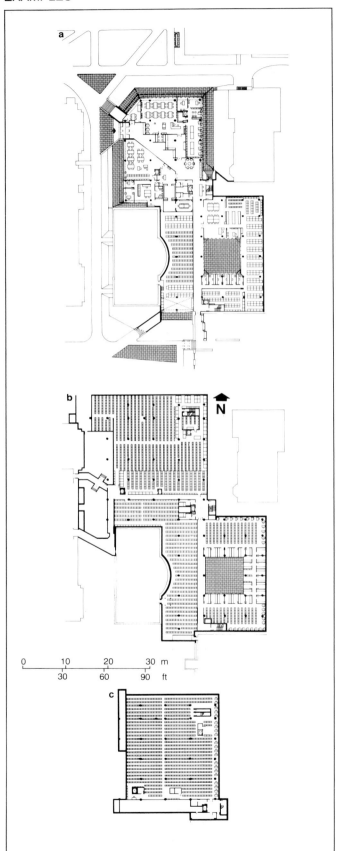

key
1 entrance
2 clo
3 wc
4 elevator
5 photocopy
6 catalogue
7 issue desk
8 carrels
9 seminars
10 reference inquiries
11 courtyard
12 cataloguing
13 subject inquiries
14 off
15 librarian
16 deputy librarian
17 despatch
18 machine rm
19 staff rm
20 book stacks
21 escape from floor
   above
22 escape stair
23 void

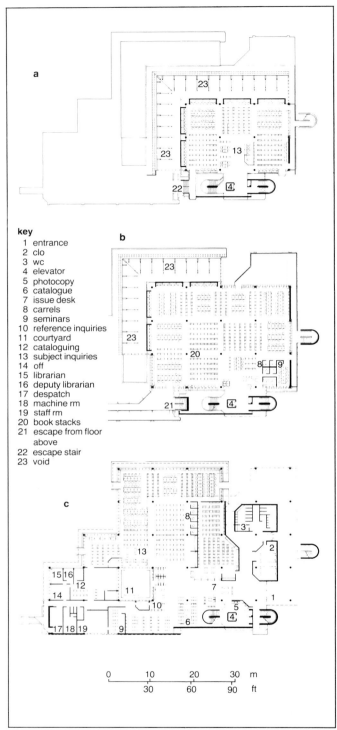

2 Polytechnic lib Portsmouth England provides sto for more than
320 000 volumes & 3 000 current journals on open access with reading
accn for 500 students **a** second floor **b** first floor **c** ground floor   Arch
Ahrends Burton & Koralek

1 Nathan Marsh Pusey lib Cambridge Massachusetts USA, an
underground sub-division which adds over 8 000 m² to Harvard College
lib, appears from outside as slanting grass-covered embankment; lawn,
trees, shrubs grow in stone-rimmed earth platform which forms roof
a level 1 **b** level 2 **c** level 3   Arch Hugh Stubbins & Associates

Libraries references
→Bibliography entries 065 073 314 323 353 399 437 455 471 472 474
476 625 641 652

HEALTH SERVICES STRUCTURE

Role and relationship to client of architect in designing for health care services affected by national differences in health care structure: wholly state organised, provided by private resources or organisations or community, or mixed.

In UK, though some hospitals, homes and clinics (and local family practice) still private, by far greater part, forming bulk of medico-architectural practice, now crown property administered by National Health Service (NHS). Under direction Dept of Health & Social Service (DHSS) or Scottish Home & Health Dept service organised into regional and area authorities and health districts. Broad planning, design and construction new bldg falls to regional authorities (RHA: in Scotland area health boards) while health districts (HD) serving 100000–500000 population have immediate control individual hospitals, clinics and health centres (HC). Area health authorities (AHA) deal with minor projects. During planning and design architect likely have contact with each these bodies.

Traditionally in USA health care industry much more varied with health services provided by private, educational and religious sources, community, state and federal bodies. More recently position modified by National Health Planning & Resources Development Act 1974 which greatly increased influence of federal agencies, providing for national guidelines for health planning and for setting up in each state Health Service Areas and Health System Agencies: as result architects's client more likely be state agency than individual institution.

Despite these differences, and with variations of emphasis, structure of health services in industrial countries essentially similar. Major elements:

Ambulant patient care: exemplified by group practice or medical office bldg, local or community clinics, health centres (HC), forming first contact between medical care and patient.

Small hospitals: range from 10–15 beds (UK 'cottage hospitals') up to 100 beds, offering basic inpatient services. In UK most private hospitals fall within this class.

Community hospitals (UK District General Hospitals (DGH)): medium-sized to large with 200–600 inpatient beds and most of all major diagnostic and treatment specialties. Also provide some teaching for med, nursing and para-med staff. Also provide specialist support for HC →p181.

Tertiary or teaching hospitals: usually have 600–1000 beds, house not only all basic services but sophisticated specialties. Most provide teaching for med students, nursing and para-med staff and post-graduate training and research.

Long stay: for elderly, chronically sick, children, psychiatric patients and some other special purposes p158 162–3 164.

In relation to all these continuing change of emphasis; general trend now shorter stay in hospitals, increase in specialist dept and services, greater stress on outpatient treatment and ambulant care, and development of such local services as health centres and clinics.

In many developing countries pattern and order of priority different, with greater stress on provision of local units for essential preventive medicine campaigns and techniques.

Building regulations
Whereas in UK national bldg reg apply to new and upgraded health bldg in USA federal, state and local codes and standards must be consulted.

INFORMATION SOURCES

In UK DHSS provides design information on specific areas, services and eqp: published as Design Guides; Building Notes (HBN), Equipment Notes (HEN) and Technical Memoranda (HTM); tendency now to provide more comprehensive and detailed information on Activity Data Sheets (ADB). Known as 'Red Pack', as yet incomplete, ADB sheets contained in 8 volumes divided into categories: 'A' describe activity space and list eqp required, together with appropriate physical and environmental standards; 'B' contain diagrams of individual pieces of eqp. 'A' sheets offer choice: decision rests with planning team. Sheets not computerised, have to be collated manually.

Other material is available from such sources as King Edward VII Fund for Hospitals in London, Nuffield Foundation, and SHHD and Central Services Agency (CSA); former Scottish Hospital Centre (SHC) produced small practical information sheets based on full-sized mock-ups of hospital rm. RHA, Welsh Technical Service and DHSS(NI) also produce guidance material.

In USA broad range of material, less organised, available. Sources: Robert Wood Johnson Foundation (Princeton NJ), sponsors studies on ambulatory care; Assistant Secretary for Health, Dept of Health & Human Services (Washington DC) for enquiries on all aspects of health services planning; Kellog Foundation (Battle Creek Mich); American Hospital Association (Chicago III) has extensive reference services; National Technical Information Services (Springfield Va).

PLANNING & DESIGN

Hospitals an amalgam of components, some simple, some extremely complex: each has time scale which covers useful design life, *ie* before it needs either major alterations or replacement. By careful planning and design components with similar characteristics can be grouped together so as to be adjacent to both those they serve and those with similar structural and service characteristics and life spans.

Large or medium hospital complex includes not only patient accn and medical/technical installations but large admin section →p179–80, electro-mech plant and engineering services, laboratories and pharmacy →p176 177, library p177, industrial installations for food services and laundry →p180, supply, service and disposal (sometimes in separate complex), lecture halls, staff hostels and restaurants, car parks.

Hospital essentially divided into 2 main units: inpatient care and outpatient care; further essential units; diagnosis and treatment, admin; frequent additional unit: education and research. In early planning relationship between these significant; diagnosis and treatment appears as linking function →(1)(2). Ideally these would all occur on 1 plane; however much site and other organisational factors impose multi-storey design ease of lateral movement remains prime consideration.

Before designer puts pen to paper brief must be prepared explaining operational policies of hospital, with description of activities to be carried out and resources required to do this efficiently. Successful design relies on effective and detailed brief: preparation must be joint venture between hospital users and architect with his design team.

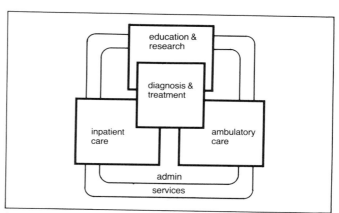

1 Hospital sectors: diagram of relationships

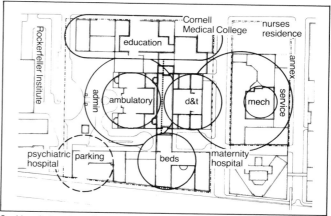

2 Hospital sectors diagram imposed on outline of New York USA Hospital: d & t = diagnosis & treatment

Hospitals

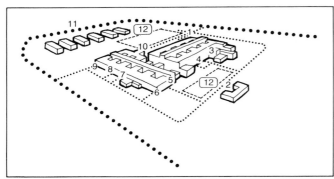

1   Typical 'harness' development plan for DGH

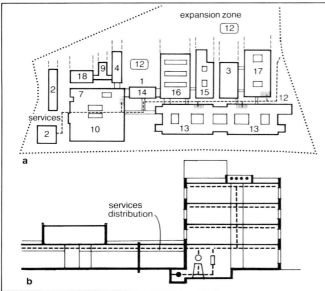

2   a & b Typical DGH: York England District Hospital 800-B
Arch Llewellyn-Davies Weeks Forestier-Walker & Bor

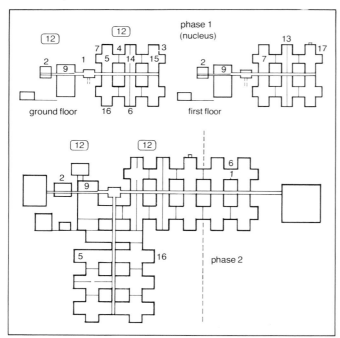

3   Typical 'nucleus' DGH: Maidstone England District Hospital
Arch Powell, Moya & partners

Key to **1 2 3**: 1 main entrance 2 industrial 3 A & E 4 pharmacy 5 non-
resident staff 6 geriatric day P 7 physical med 8 psychiatric day P
9 mortuary 10 k 11 residences 12 parking 13 wards 14 admin 15 x-ray
16 outpatients 17 operating theatres 18 isolation

MODULAR DESIGN

Both in USA and UK pressure to contain costs encourages use of
modular systems design →(1)–(4). DHHS in UK sponsored range of
standard designs for whole hospital:

'Harness' method
Range of dept based on common design module of 15 m selected as
required to meet operational needs and grouped in correct functional
relationship to 'Harness zone' of communications and services.

'Nucleus'
Evolved from Harness, Nucleus provides initial 300-bed serviced unit
within phased development.

'Best buy'
Standard hospital design providing complete package for 600-bed DGH.

TIME SCALES FOR HOSPITAL PLANNING

Multi-professional project teams make lengthy briefing, feasibility and
sketch design stages inevitable; inception of project to commissioning
can take 10–20 years: as result many new hospitals considered by
users outdated. To shorten pre-contract stage as much as possible
architect should produce carefully prepared time-scaled networks and
have these agreed by team before work started.

Once bldg handed over users should be given complete commissioning manual containing description of how bldg intended be used.
Instructions should be given for use and maintenance; where possible
full manufacturers' information should be included. Manual should be
compiled as work proceeds; this can do much to accelerate programme
and reduce criticisms made by users.

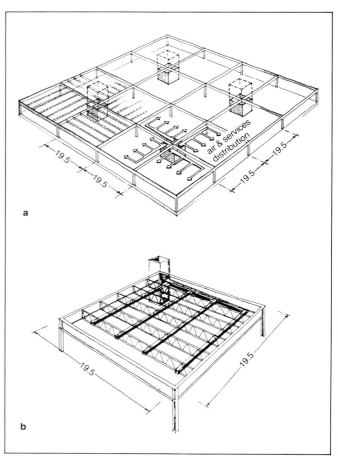

4   a Diagram of 16 modular units with air ducts & el/mech service shafts for
Armstrong Hospital Kittaning Pa USA **b** 1 modular unit with el/mech service
shaft

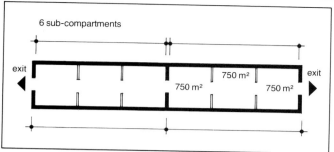

1   Compartments & sub-compartments

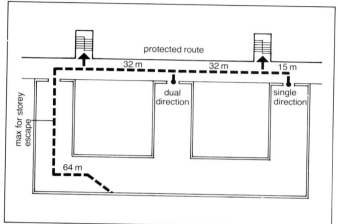

2   Travel distances for wards

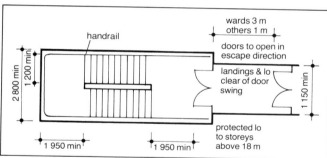

3   Escape stair dimensions

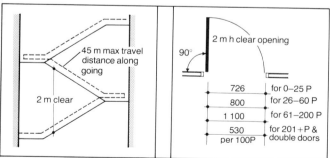

4   Vertical travel distance on escape stairs

5   Size of escape doors

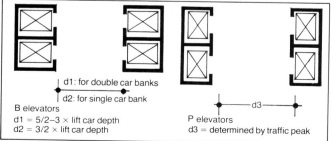

6   Bed elevators & P elevators

d1: for double car banks
d2: for single car bank

B elevators
d1 = 5/2–3 × lift car depth
d2 = 3/2 × lift car depth

P elevators
d3 = determined by traffic peak

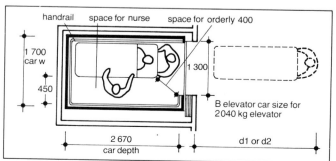

7   Bed elevator: detail

MEANS OF ESCAPE, FIRE PROTECTION, HAZARDOUS MATERIALS

Most bldg reg contain clauses on min allowable distances between adjacent bldg and type of construction acceptable to resist fire for given periods of time; some state distances and conditions for escape routes.

Up to 2 hours needed evacuate 600 patients from 2-storey, 4 hours from 11-storey bldg: exhausting exercise for rescuers. All health bldg which contain high proportion of bedfast, disabled and confused patients should be low rise, preferably with patients restricted to ground and first floors. High rise bldg should be confined to sites where no other solution possible. Because of their special problems health bldg in UK now have own more stringent fire safety measures based on fr compartments; system makes possible move patients short distances, if necessary in beds, to section sealed off by fire door from smoke or fire in adjoining section.

Design guidance on size of fire compartments and sub-compartments, together with max acceptable lengths of escape routes in wards, operating theatres, lab etc, can be found in official literature (→Bib216 218 219). As general guide following apply:

Fire compartments →(1)(2)(3)(4)
UK reg (USA →p152):
1-storey bldg must not exceed 3000 m²
Multi-storey bldg must not exceed 2000 m²
Horizontal distance to alternative routes must not exceed 64 m
Horizontal distance in single direction to exit must not exceed 15 m
Travel distance within escape stairway must not exceed 45 m along going

Fire sub-compartments (patient areas)
Floor area must not exceed 750 m²
Horizontal distance to alternative routes must not exceed 32 m
Horizontal distance to single directional exit must not exceed 15 m
Max occupancy 40 patients

Hazardous materials
Some eqp and substances used in examining, diagnosing and treating patients radioactive, explosive or highly inflammable. Take every care check that where these substances used design, construction, detailing and service installations comply with specific statutes and reg.

On fire safety and hazardous materials consult official publications and health authority concerned before making any decisions.

Hospitals

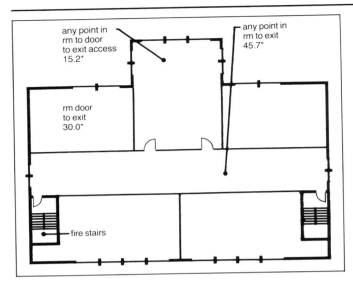

1   Travel distance to exits
* these distances or ar may vary in different bldg codes & can frequently be lengthened in bldg equipped with automatic fire extinguishing systems

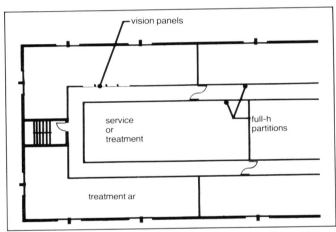

2   Corr walls: corr shall be separated from all other ar by partitions which shall extend full h from floor to under side of roof or floor slab above; vision panels in corr walls permitted with wire glass: size of panels limited unless whole bldg protected by automatic extinguishing system; interior stud partitions must be fire stopped to prevent fire spread both horizontally & vertically

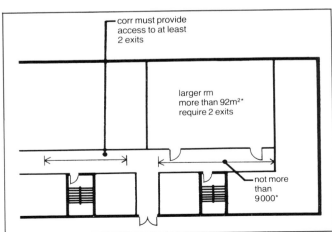

3   Arrangement of exits: all patient sleeping rm shall have exit door leading directly to exit corr which shall be at least 2 440* w in hospitals; rm larger than 93 m²* shall have at least 2 remote exits; exit corr shall lead to at least 2 approved exits; dead end corr shall not exceed 9 000*
* these distances or ar may vary in different bldg codes; travel distances can frequently be lengthened in bldg equipped with automatic fire extinguishing systems

MEANS OF ESCAPE (cont)

Typical USA requirements given →(1)–(4). For each design project necessary consult details of relevant state and local codes.

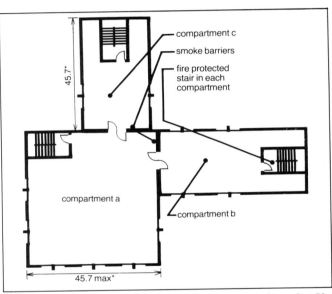

4   Subdivision of floors: floors used for sleeping or treatment of more than 50 patients must be sub-divided by smoke partitions and shall be divided into compartments not more than 2 090 m²* in ar; max l or w of compartments 45.7 m*; corr doors in smoke partitions shall be opposite swinging pair; doors shall have wire glass vision panels; ducts which penetrate smoke barriers shall have dampers must be fire stopped to prevent fire spread both horizontally & vertically
* these distances or ar may vary in different bldg codes; travel distances can frequently be lengthened in bldg equipped with automatic fire extinguishing systems

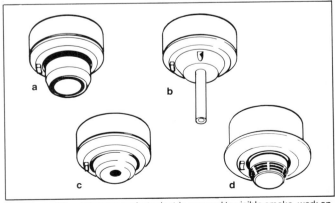

5   Types of fire detectors **a** photoelectric respond to visible smoke, work on obstruction principle (rising smoke tends obscure light beam & sounds alarm) **b** thermal respond to heat energy **c** infra-red respond to flame **d** ionisation respond to invisible combustion products

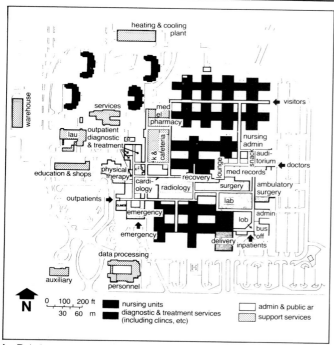

1 Relationships between major dept at proposed medical centre Tucson USA   Arch Perkins & Will

DESIGN/BUILDING CONFIGURATIONS

Ideal hospital design combines clear and simple traffic configuration with ability expand bed units and service base in future, growth and change within hospital structure being continuous. Beds do not always increase in same ratio as service programmes but each must contain master plan of direction. Bldg do not occupy major part hospital grounds; parking (1½–2 car/B) and multiple entry create larger land use.

Broadly hospital bldg made up of 2 parts: base and bed configurations.

Base concepts

Base services fall into 2 categories: ancillary services orientated to patient care and service dept such as sto, laundry, dietary, housekeeping. These 2 elements can be combined in 1 base structure or be independent. Different fire-rated enclosures may determine approach.

Bed concepts

Design should meet nursing concept of optimum organisation and staffing. B/staffing team usually 20–30 patients. Mix of private and semi-private rm also contributes to bed design. Min USA Health Dept standards also have controlling effect. Specialty and intensive care units have lower bed ratio; long term may contain more than 30 beds. Modular nature of bed design may conflict with structure of base. Concept of using long span trusses as mech-el route between hospital floors has developed. Question of additional initial cost as against life of bldg flexibility must be considered for each project.

By USA standards correct ratio beds to base for community hospital approx 37–46 m²/B for nursing units and 46–56 m²/B for base. Teaching hospital may range up to 140 m²/B, with university programmes and children's hospitals high as 185 m²/B.

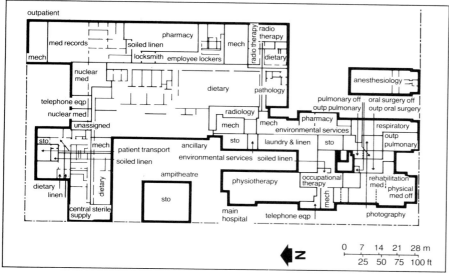

2 Master plan Temple University Hospital Philadelphia USA   Arch Perkins & Will

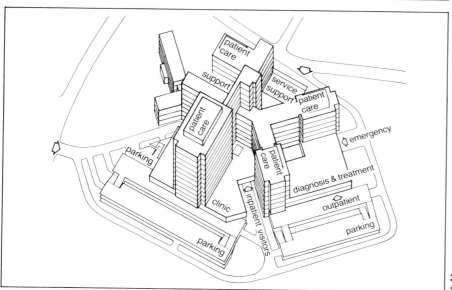

3 Relationships between patient care & support services & between bldg & site

Hospitals

WARD DESIGN: GENERAL

Outlooks on ward sizes subject rapid change. Main recent trend away from classical ward types (eg 'Nightingale': 12-B open ward with nurses desk at 1 end; 'Rigs': 24-B with nursing rm outside ward, beds set in clusters); preference now for 2–4 B. Despite this strong preference still controversial: very small wards give privacy and in theory more personal attention but can also be lonely, less often visited; ie society and staff supervision possibly better in larger ward. Patients need audio and visual privacy during med visits. Background noise and bed curtains provide some in large ward but lights disturb at night; small wards peaceful for resting patient but do not provide audio-privacy.

In USA most codes now give max 4-B/rm and design standards usually followed maintain mix of 2-B and 1-B. In UK small rm also common; but wards may consist of mix of different size rm →acute wards below.

Av stay in hospital for acute med or surgery has fallen, eg: major surgery 10–12 days, minor 2–3 days, max 6 weeks (mainly orthopedic). Wards for these purposes therefore designed for max efficiency of staff working. For physically and mentally handicapped and elderly – 'long stay' – ward design more domestic and social →p158 162 163.

Key problem of design for efficient ward system: relationship of nurse working rm to patient rm. Basic concept →(1).

WARD DESIGN: ACUTE

Acute wards contain 24–30 beds; where possible should be linked together to form admin unit of 2 or 4 wards, which also enables such service as day areas, doctors rm, disposal rm, sto etc be shared between 2 wards; but check against fire reg before design decision made. Possible breakdown of bed areas for 28-bed mixed sex wards include:

3×8-B rm $+ 4 \times 1$-B rm
4×6-B rm $+ 4 \times 1$-B rm
2×12-B rm $+ 4 \times 1$-B rm

Most acute med and surgical wards can be mixed-sex, argument being that it increases bed occupancy. 1-B wards need maintain occupancy at max of 85% or above: 1-B also required for patients liable to infection, or to infect others, those seriously ill or dying and those likely to disturb others. Mixed-sex ward may not be acceptable to all users: check before designing on this basis.

Walking distance: keep walking distances short as possible for nurses and ambulant patient. Max distance from bed to wc 12 m and from nurse working rm to furthest bed approx 20 m.

Observation: continuous observation of patient by staff essential part of nursing care: during day achieved mainly in course of walking from 1 duty to another, at night from nurses station. Good design aim: 50% of beds to be visible from nurses station. Patients gain confidence from seeing staff at work, dead-leg wards not popular for this reason; if staff have no duty perform less likely visit ward.

Control: patients, particularly children, adolescents and confused, need to be controlled; dayr must not be too isolated from rest of ward. Mixed-sex wards have own control problems. Staff need to control visitors and check that they do not overtire patients.

Noise: problem in large open areas; telephones and other el and mech eqp can be noisier than acceptable. Design for 40–45 dB by day and 35–40 dB at night in multi-B wards; 1-B wards should be 35–40 dB at all times. Courtyard designs can create problems of noise from adjacent windows to different rm.

Daylight & glare windows →p403–7 should not cause glare →p32 398 in bedfast patients' eyes; beds should be parallel to windows unless brise-soleil, external or between-glass blinds or similar devices fitted. Windows design important: confused patients may try get out; all opening lights should have device restricting accessible opening to 100.

Ventilation: mech ventilation often noisy and unsatisfactory, full air-conditioning expensive install and run. Normal sites away from air or traffic noise should rely on natural ventilation; 3 beds deep from window max before mech ventilation required. Central work rm require mech ventilation and suffer from heat build-up in summer.

Nurse call systems, closed circuit television (CCTV)
Devices of various grades of sophistication: all liable to abuse or failure. Seriously ill patients cannot operate call systems therefore unwise rely on these rather than personal observation; acceptable as auxiliary system.

A control access & egress to unit
B access & visual observation to P
C Convenient access to support activities

1   Diagram of nursing/P rm relationship

ACUTE WARD: SUGGESTED AREAS

1-B rm	10.0 m²	excluding wc & sho depending on amount of
multi-B bay (per B)	9.3–10.0 m²	day space provided in
dayr (per B)	0.75 m²	wards or as separate day space
lockers etc (per B)	0.5–1.0 m²	extra space for lockers etc
nurse station	4.0–10.0 m²	depending on position
clean utility	10.2–18.0 m²	of drug, linen bays etc
dirty utility & sluice	14.0–16.0 m²	if separate ar = 9 m² + 7 m²
treatment rm	14.0–16.0 m²	depending on sto provided
assisted bathr	10.25–12.0 m²	
sisters rm	7.0–9.0 m²	
doctors rm	7.0–9.0 m08²	
bathr	7.0 m²	for ambulant patients
washing & sho compartment	2.7 m²	
wc with hand rinse basin	2.0–3.0 m²	min for ambulant P max for wheelchair P
ptr	4.0–6.0 m²	beverage & snack point only
ward k	20.0 m²	for ward k service
flower bay	2.0–2.5 m²	
cleaner	5.0–8.0 m²	
sto (inc large eqp)	12.0–2.0 m²	may be shared with another ward
interview rm & overnight stay	10.0–12.0 m²	
circulation ar	25%–40%	depends on ward layout

Hospitals

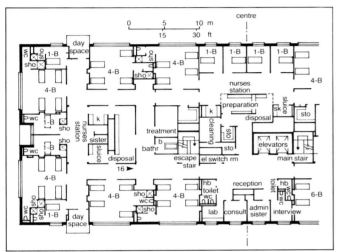

1 Guy's Hospital London typical ward floor, 2 × 27 B   Arch Watkins Gray International

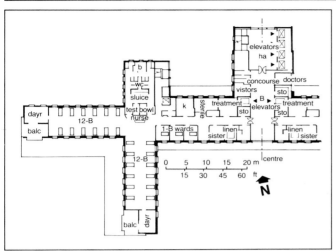

2 Falkirk ward; experimental, resulting from studies carried out by SHHD; built mid-1950's, 2 × 30 B; first & second floors

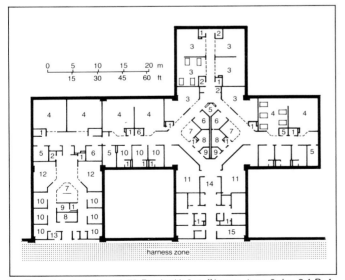

3 Typical 'harness' ward; 72-B unit with 3 staff bases 1 wc 2 sho 3 4-B 4 5-B 5 b 6 treatment 7 clean utility 8 dirty utility 9 sister 10 1-B 11 day/dining 12 3-B 13 sto 14 visitors 15 supplies

BASIC WARD TYPES

Linear ward →(1)

In past wards designed on linear form: large single space, 20–30 beds supported by nurse working rm at one end, sluices and wc at other, quite often large work table middle of ward. Main ward or wards and majority of spaces naturally lit and ventilated. Observation of patients good; patients had little or no chance of feeling neglected. Background noise problem but to some extent this gave greater privacy than in 4- or 6-B wards. Since 1950's different shapes have been used (also modifications of linear as at Guy's Hospital London).

Deep ward or race track →(2)

Design concept developed in late 1950's, complete contrast to linear: patients share nothing larger than 4-bed ward. Observation good so long as enough nurses to move round ward. Race track design prevents dead-legs where patients could feel neglected. Background noise reduced but as result audio-privacy for consultations not so good as in large linear. Wards placed on outside walls, naturally lit and ventilated; nurse working rm form central core, need artificial light and mech ventilation.

Courtyard plan →(3)(4)

Courtyard plan (harness, nucleus →p150) attempts reduce internal working rm and provide good patient observation. Success of this type depends on amount of daylight available and degree of privacy obtainable. All wards have some daylight but some mech ventilation may be necessary.

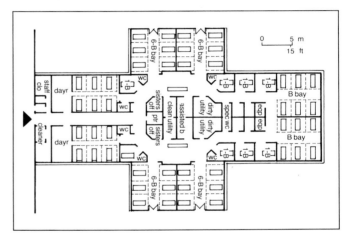

4 Typical 'nucleus' ward, 2 × 28 B

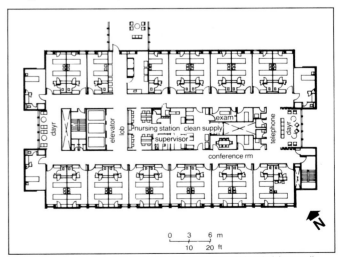

5 Typical nursing floor (48-B) Anne Arundel General Hospital Annapolis USA   Arch Metcalf & Associates

Hospitals

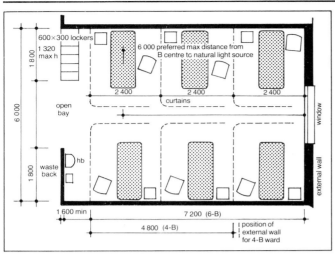

1   4- or 6-B ward, 8.4 m² & 8 m²/B: optimum privacy, each P having wall on one side; B parallel to window to reduce glare; curtains give each B visual privacy but centre B has less; max 3-B depth before artificial lighting & ventilation required

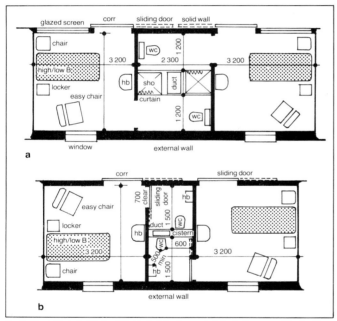

2   1-B wards suitable for P liable to infection or to infect others: **a** 13 m² with sho & wc, also suitable for other P needing special attention **b** 12.34 m² with wc, or could be without wc for bedfast P dying, needing special attention or likely to disturb others; NB 1-B wards for seriously ill must be close to nurses station

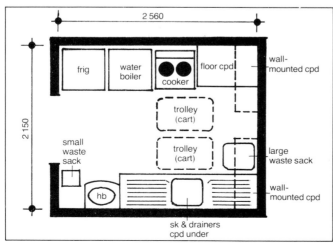

3   Small ward pantry, 5.5 m²: for beverages & snacks only

NURSE WORKING ROOMS

p156–7 show layout, dimensions and eqp required for main nurse working rm in standard ward. Variations in size and shape of rm may be dictated by ward plan, but work pattern and critical clear working spaces round beds and other eqp should be maintained.

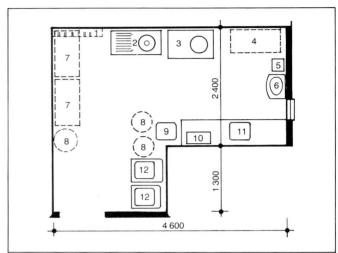

4   Dirty utility rm, 14 m², equipped for disposable bedpans: if non-disposable used washer replaces destructor, no disposable sto needed 1 rack for bedpan cradles 2 slop sk & drainer 3 bedpan destructor 4 space for disposable bedpan box 5 disposal bag 6 hb unit 7 space for disposable bedpan & urinal boxes 8 space for disposal bags 9 waste disposal bag 10 urine test cabinet 11 sk & work top, cpd under 12 sanichair

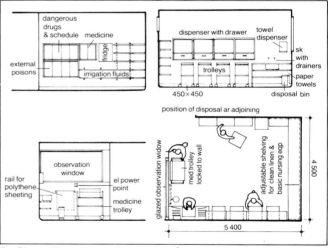

5   Clean utility or preparation rm, 24.3 m²; small dressing trolleys (carts) replace traditional fixed work tops, considered superfluous; linen stored on adjustable shelving & topped up to agreed level; no linen trolley required for clean linen

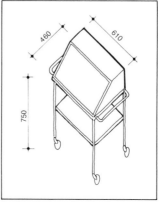

6   Medicine trolley (cart)

NURSE WORKING ROOMS (cont)

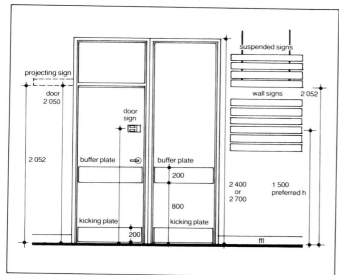

1 Doors & screens in ward corr

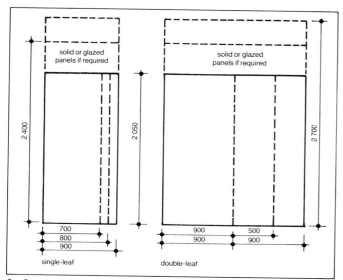

2 Standard door sizes for hospitals: where high/low B used standard 2 050 doors h enough to allow through B with balkan beams; min door w for wheelchair 800, preferred 900

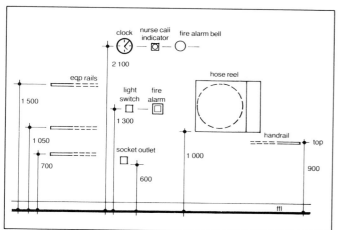

3 Fittings in ward corr

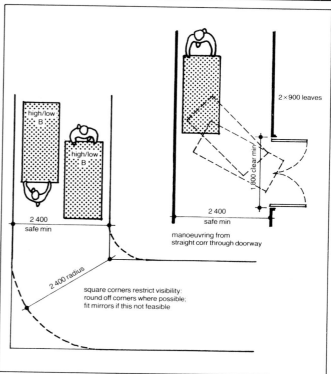

4 Min corr w for manoeuvring B

Princess Grace Hospital London

Small 136-bed hospital for private patients, majority from overseas. Visiting consultants and surgeons diagnose and treat patients; permanently employed nurses and support staff. Added need to attract patients by providing 1-B wards of domestic character and comfortable proportions (17 m²) with integral bathr, but as with NHS hospitals, prime importance to design best possible environment for diagnosing and treating patients.

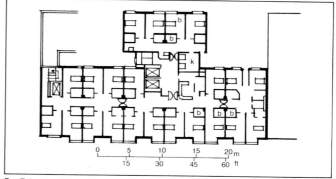

5 Princess Grace Hospital 22-B ward unit: private hospital   Arch R Seifert & Partners

DATA FOR DESIGNING WARDS: GERIATRIC

2 types; for assessment of elderly, for long term care.
For assessment patients normally housed in adaptation of standard acute ward within DGH, because access to full diagnostic and treatment services needed.

For long-term patients (assessed and found to be in need of long-term care) aim to provide homely environment in which basic nursing care can take place; emphasis on early ambulation and rehabilitation →p162. Often in separate bldg on hospital campus, within easy reach of diagnostic and treatment services.

In UK shortage of geriatric beds partially overcome by upgrading some wards in older hospitals (upgrading wards →p165). For details of geriatric bathr and wc →p163.

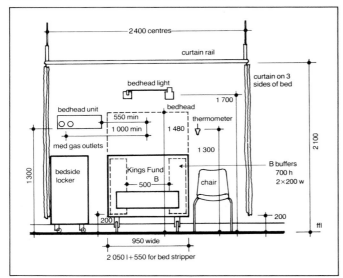

1   Multi-B ward: eqp & fittings in B ar

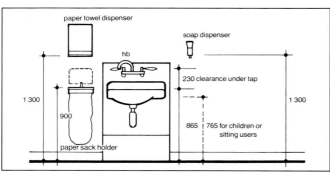

2   Staff hb unit in wards, nurse working ar etc

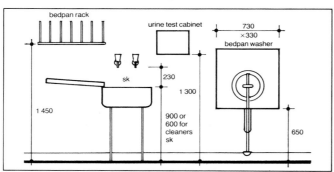

3   Dirty utility ar

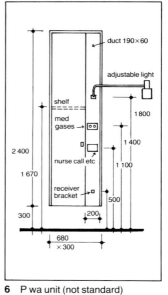

4   Bathr

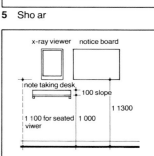

6   P wa unit (not standard)

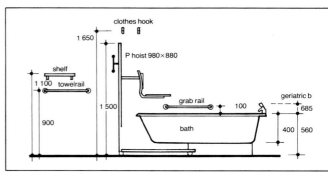

5   Sho ar

7   Nurses station

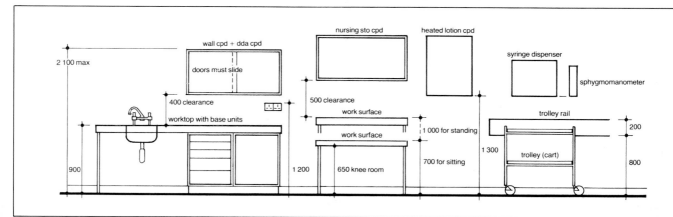

8   Clean utility or preparation ar (dda = Dangerous Drugs Acts)

DATA FOR DESIGNING WARDS (cont)

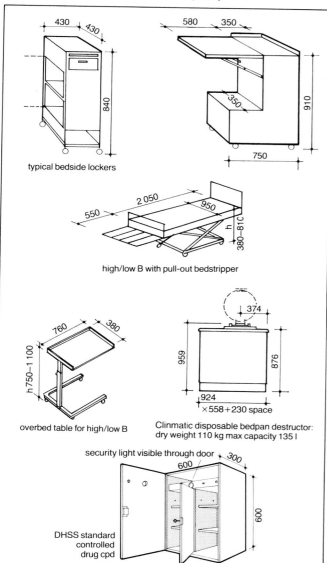

typical bedside lockers

high/low B with pull-out bedstripper

overbed table for high/low B

Clinmatic disposable bedpan destructor:
dry weight 110 kg max capacity 135 l

security light visible through door

DHSS standard
controlled
drug cpd

1 Typical ward eqp

3 Kings Fund B: 2 080 × 910 × 380 – 810 h

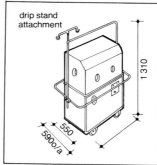

4 Orthopedic fracture frame: B
may be moved through doors
complete with frame

5 Childrens cot: 1 370 × 760 ×
610 + 690 h sides

drip stand
attachment

6 Typical incubator

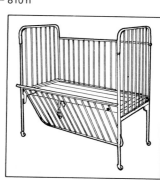

7 Bassinette for infants

2 Geriatric assessment ward
(upgraded Nightingale ward); 1
problem of elderly remain continent:
example shows how walking
distance from furthest B reduced
from 30 m to 8 m & day ar for
rehabilitation, dining & quiet
pursuits provided; B reduced from
28 to 22 & wc increased from 4 to 8;
total ar 2.25 m²/P 1 1-B rm 2 multi-
B rm 3 disposal 5 b (free standing)
6 preparation rm 7 hb 8 sluice
9 wc 10 k 11 staff clo/wc & hb
12 special bathr/cleansing ar
14 eqp sto 15 day ar 16 quiet ar
17 dining ar 18 nurses station
19 DSR 22 linen sto 23 wheelchair
sto 24 sanichair sto 26 sister
27 staff rm 29 switch gear/
calorifiers etc 31 P clothing sto
33 lecture rm 38 sho 39 special
couch 42 doctor 44 stainless steel
sk with laying shelf 45 la/ptr
46 free-standing bidet/wc

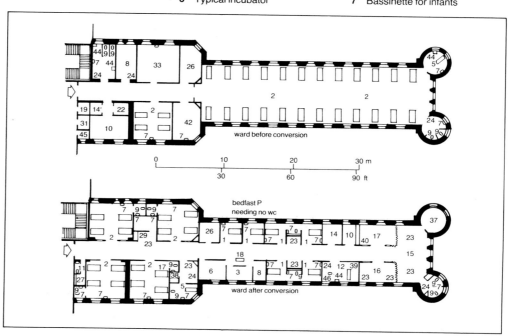

ward before conversion

0   10   20   30 m
30   60   90 ft

bedfast P
needing no wc

ward after conversion

Hospitals

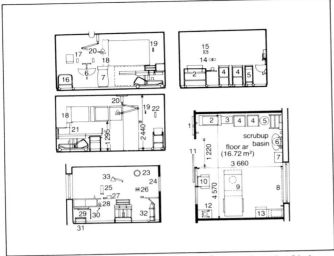

1   Combined first stage & delivery rm, 14.46 m² **1** caps & masks **2** baby cot **3** tray **4** trolley **5** single bowl stand **6** scrub-up hb **7** sack & stand **8** heating panel **9** obstetric B **10** chair **11** sliding door **12** writing shelf **13** bedside locker **14** time elapse clock **15** oxygen suction, child **16** sto rack **17** dispensers **18** curtain **19** coat hook **20** spotlight **21** drip pole on wall hook **22** wall thermometer **23** clock **24** observation panel **25** sphyg-momanometer **26** oxygen suction, mother **27** bedhead panel **28** cup & flask **29** overbed tray **30** towel rail **31** footstool **32** analgesia trolley **33** overbed light

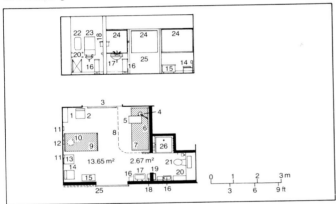

MATERNITY

Units normally attached to DGH or community hospital. Allow 0.5 B/ 1000 total population; 75 beds cater for 2700 deliveries/year, 100 beds for 3600 and 125 for 4500. Maternity clinics include ante-natal, post-natal, baby follow-up and family planning. Most units require normal backup for reception, admin, including records, and provision for education. In USA trend to set delivery suite alongside surgery suite or integrate with it.

Delivery suite includes: theatre, abnormal and normal delivery rm and assessment area. For 125 beds allow 17 normal first stage delivery rm, 10 observation beds, 4 abnormal delivery rm and 1 operating theatre. Obstetric theatre suite: theatre (28 m²) with full mech ventilation, hum and cooling control and antistatic flooring, oxygen and nitrous oxide and 2 vacuum points for mother, vacuum and oxygen for baby; scrub and gowning areas (9.5 m²), anaesthetic rm (16.5 m²), recovery beds for 2 patients (25 m²) and clean utility (8.5 m²). All delivery rm require pleasant daylit environment with privacy (blinds to windows), good lighting for suturing, sound attenuation, anti-static precautions, med gas, oxygen and vacuum outlets, and mech ventilation with hum and cooling installations. Abnormal delivery rm (24 m² plus scrub area 1.5 m²). Normal delivery rm (15 m²): 2 of these should be quiet with blackout eqp. Combined first stage/delivery rm →(2) enables patient stay in 1 place throughout labour, her first move being to post-natal ward after normal recovery period: provide 1 of these rm to 5 post-natal beds. Assessment area: 20% beds should be in 1-bed wards (13 m²) with oxygen outlet at bedhead, remaining 80% in multi-bed bays (9.5 m²/ bed) with oxygen outlet to each pair of beds.

Ancillary accn: sto, milk kitchen (14 m²) and flying squad sto (7.5 m²) – which may be in accident & emergency dept (A&E).

30-cot special care baby unit (SCBU) attached to this number of beds requires 22 multi-cot bays (4 m²/cot), 7 single-cot rm (5.5 m²) and 1 special-cot rm ((7.5 m²); 20 cots considered min size for viable unit. Entrance to SCBU must include gowning and handwash areas for visitors, and changing accn for staff: female, 11–14 m² male 7.5 m². Bedsitting rm for mothers with sho and wc →(2).

2   Mother & child rm, 16.32 m² **1** wa **2** visitor chair **3** window (curtains or blind) **4** mother's bedlamp **5** cantilever table **6** drawer unit **7** mother's B **8** curtain track **9** child's cot **10** overbed ceiling light **11** twin socket outlet **12** oxygen & suction **13** locker **14** child chair **15** toy box **16** waste sack **17** hb **18** towel dispenser **19** towel rail **20** shelves **21** wc **22** baby bath **23** mirror **24** glazed panel (with blind or curtains) **25** sliding door **26** sho

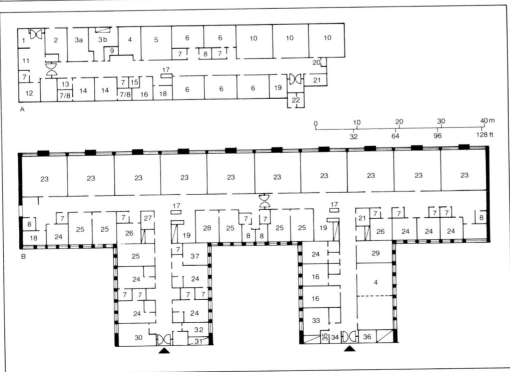

3   Obstetric dept Eastbourne England DGH:
A delivery suite **B** maternity ward
1 wr **2** seminar **3** staff changing: **a** female **b** male **4** dayr **5** first stage rm **6** multi-purpose **7** wc **8** b **9** lab **10** abnormal delivery **11** trolley (cart) & wheelchairs **12** overnight stay **13** dirty utility **14** exam **15** ptr **16** doctor **17** nurses station **18** charge nurse **19** clean supply **20** anaesthetic sto **21** dirty utility **22** transfer ar **23** 4-B **24** 1-B **25** 6-cot **26** assisted b **27** dirty linen **28** 6 incubators **29** k **30** central milk k **31** demonstration **32** obstetric tutor **33** nurse admin **34** reception **35** sto **36** mobile x-ray **37** 1-B toxaemia

PAEDIATRIC & CHILDRENS WARDS

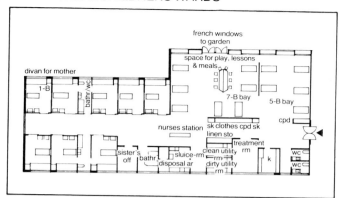

1 20-B childrens ward Arch Nuffield Foundation division for architectural studies

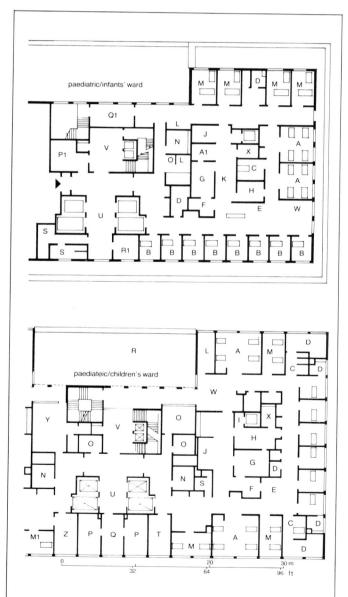

2 West Middlesex Hospital England **a** paediatric/infants ward **b** paediatric/children's ward A 4-B/4-cot ward A1 4-B – staff B 1-B/1-cot ward C wash/wc D bathr E nurses station F clean utility G treatment rm H dirty utility/sluice I disposal lift J ptr K trolley (cart) bay L sto M 2-B/mother & baby rm M1 clinical rm – staff N sisters rm O doctors rm P consult rm Q secretaries off R playground P1 milk k Q1 mothers si R1 relatives rm S staff clo T clinical rm U elevators V paternoster elevators & stairs W play ar X cleaners rm Y classr Z admission rm Arch Robert Matthew Johnson-Marshall

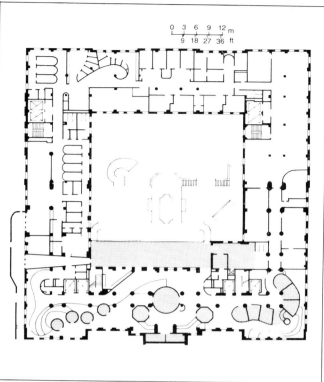

3 Diagnosis centre for school age children, converted from outmoded ar of older hospital in Jersey City USA; existing courtyard used as play rm & reception ar; sequence of rm provides both range of health tests & educational programme Arch Hillier Group

West Middlesex Hospital

Both wards →(2a,b) adapted from standard, part of 5-storey high system bldg. Paediatric/children's ward →(2b) contains 2 × 4-B wards, 6 × 1-B wards, 2 with wc and bath attached, and 3 × 2-B wards which can be used either for mother and child or for 2 patients. Classr for children in hospital for several weeks but fit enough attend classes, *eg* child with broken limb. Away from ward, area with adjacent toy sto where boisterous children encouraged play. Protected open air play area also provided. Paediatric/infants' ward →(2b) has 8 × 1-cot wards each fitted with baby bath and 4 mother and baby rm each capable of taking full-size bed and child's bed if necessary. Play space provided together with protected open air area. Milk kitchen provides for heated baby feeds and baby bottle washing: daily throughput 240 × 0.25 l milk, of which two-thirds kept under refrigeration; extra sto required to keep milk over public holiday periods.

Hospitals

LONG STAY WARDS

Long stay wards for elderly and infirm must be sited near public transport for easy visiting by relatives, often elderly themselves: need access to diagnostic and treatment services, so wherever possible should be built on same development as DGH (community hospital) or be grouped together to be able to support own services.

Patients could easily become institutionalised in wrong environment: accent on self-help and rehabilitation in setting as like home environment as possible without impairing quality of nursing care. Patients require sleeping areas which can identify as own, and must have ready access to personal belongings. Wc and washing places must be near to both sleeping and day areas. Design of day areas should allow patients follow therapeutic routine enabling them care for themselves and if possible return home to receive necessary community care either at day centre or by domiciliary visits.

Important provide variety of spaces for social meetings between patients and visitors and between patients, and for small group chats or games or larger group activities (corr alcoves, small separate rm). Dining arrangements also important for providing social and domestic atmosphere.

Clear marking of rm, corr, elevators essential; colour coding helps →(1).

Now few completely bedfast patients needing bedpans and bed baths during day: majority will be taken to wc and bathr even if incapable of attending to themselves →p163(2)–(7). Because incontinence prevalent extra wc required aid training (max distance from furthest bed or corner of day area: 10 m). Where space limited omit treatment rm and replace by cleansing rm with bath or wc each with thermostatically controlled sho handset →p163(2). Wc, sluices and cleansing rm must have efficient mech extract ventilation. Small utility rm with washing machine and clothes drier needed for patients' clothes.

Provide extra sto space for wheelchairs, walking aids and sanichairs, and for greater supply of linen, incontinence pads and, where used, disposable bedpans and urinals. Cpd also required for patients' suitcases and clothes not in current use, and for occupational therapy eqp.

All floor finishes should be soft, non-slip and washable: plastics flooring with welded joints suitable for wc, bathr and all nurse working areas. Carpets may be used in wards and dayr where number of incontinent patients limited. Patients can be confused and if allowed go outside more easily controlled in courtyards than in open hospital grounds. All doors wide enough for wheelchairs →p86; fire stop doors should be held in open position by automatic fail-safe devices for easy movement of patients in wheelchairs or using walking aids.

Term geriatric →p158 generally used to describe those over 65 years who develop several med problems at once and who may also suffer impaired mobility and be incontinent.

Mentally handicapped often also physically handicapped may also be noisy, aggressive, overactive and self destructive. Particularly important that furnishings be soft, spongeable and durable for these patients, and that ceilings have sound absorbent finish.

Psychiatric wards →p164

Long stay patients highly dependent on staff in cases of emergency: vital fire escape routes be easily identified, fire stop doors have automatic door closers connected alarm system and fabrics and finishes fr.

1 Elevator level coding system using colours & numbers; helpful to P with sensory defects; raised numerals aid near-sighted or blind

2 Mentally handicapped unit, plan of typical villa, Craig Phadrig Hospital Inverness Scotland 1 sister 2 visitors 3 P clo 4 sto 5 domestic service rm 6 5-B 7 4-B 8 1-B 9 wc 10 bathr 11 staff wc 12 preparation 13 linen 14 uty 15 disposal 16 hobbies 17 duty rm 18 TV 19 day space 20 dr 21 k

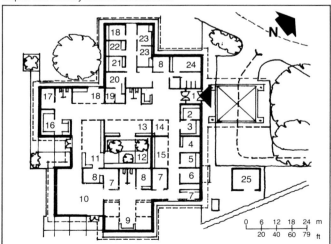

3 Geriatric Day Hospital Walton on Thames England: 35 P on basis of 5-day week; includes P assessment, med, para-med, nursing procedures, occupational & physiotherapy, training in aids for disabled & domestic routines 1 main entrance 2 reception 3 clo 4 interview 5 screen, dentist, optician, 6 hair, chiropodist 7 sto 8 off 9 individual therapy; physiotherapy duties 10 group therapy; physical exercises ar 11 occupational therapy dr 12 court 13 dr 14 interview 15 wr 16 k & servery 17 daily living unit bedr 18 rest 19 b 20 assisted b 21 treatment 22 dirty utility 23 consult/exam 24 staff rest 25 boilers & tanks   Arch Derek Stow & Partners

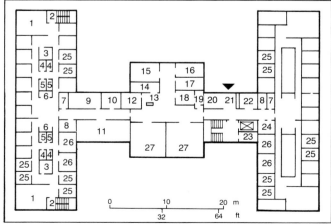

4 Hostel accn for P returning to hospital for rehabilitation courses (amputees & other physically handicapped P) 1 group dayr 2 fire escape stair 3 bathr 4 sh 5 wc 6 wheelchair bay 7 ptr 8 sto 9 doctors rm 10 sister 11 dr 12 duty rm 13 nurses station 14 preparation 15 treatment rm 16 assisted bathr 17 dirty utility rm 18 sluice rm 19 staff wc 20 wr 21 reception 22 off 23 porter 24 domestic service rm 25 1-B 26 large 1-B 27 4-B

Hospitals: long stay

EQUIPMENT

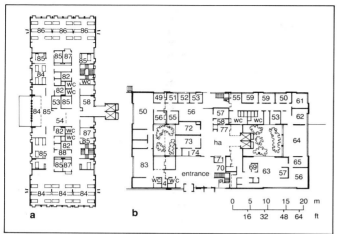

1   Liberton Hospital Scotland **a** first floor geriatric inpatients **b** ground floor geriatric day P 49 common rm 50 physiotherapy 51 dentist 52 chiropody 53 MD clinic 54 therapist 55 almoner 56 wr 57 hairdressing 58 dark rm 59 consult/exam 60 seminar interview rm 61 med staff 62 lounge 63 canteen 64 dining ar 65 servery 66 trolley wash 67 pot wash 69 cold sto 70 reception 71 reception 71 porter 72 admin & nursing staff 73 general off 74 shop 82 bathr 83 occupational therapy 84 ward ar 85 treatment 86 exercise & dayr 87 doctor 88 sluice

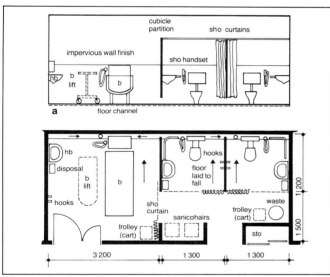

2   Incontinent bathr & wc, 8.6 m^2 + 7 m^2; may be planned as separate units; required in wards caring for elderly & handicapped where policy of early ambulation coupled with need to extend nursing care to non-bedfast P; both b & wc equipped with low-pressure sho handset to ease problem of cleaning incontinent P; good ventilation required: allow for 6 air changes/hr at peak times

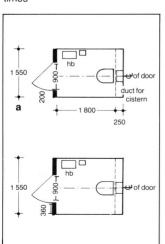

3   Assisted wc **a** for non-wheelchair P requiring assistance of 2 nurses **b** for wheelchair P requiring assistance of 2 nurses

4   Mobile b elevator

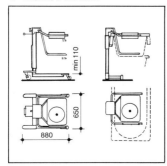

LIBERTON HOSPITAL →(1)

Geriatric hospital in grounds of existing hospital; has both in and day patients with total 184 beds mainly in 24-B units. Day patients can be examined in 1 of 2 consult/exam rm and have midday meal in dr; share physiotherapy, occupational therapy, dental and hairdressing services with inpatients. Wards contain dining area and 3 separate day spaces, 1 for exercising and 2 for sitting in.

Ward block

4-storey ward block: 3 floors 48 beds each, 1 of 40 beds on first floor used for hemiplegic patients. 48-B floors divided into 2 × 24 nursing units, each comprising 3 × 6-B bays, 1 × 4-B bay, 2 × 1-B. Bedside fittings include nurse call, radio and tv controls, bed light and curtains. Each 24-B unit has 2 bathr, 4 wc, clean preparation rm, dirty disposal rm, with small dining area for ambulant patients, and 2 small dayr. Each floor has ward kitchen, med officer's rm and sister's rm.

Ground floor

Entrance hall with reception counter and general waiting area. Lift hall with nursing and admin offices, hairdressing rm, porter and shop.

Occupational and physiotherapy, med social worker, dentist and chiropodist share patient waiting area. Day patients and dr for midday meals served from kitchen which also provides staff meals in small canteen. Consult/exam rm separated from therapeutic/social areas.

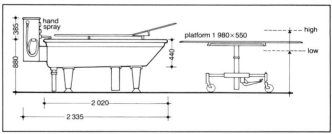

5   b & platform elevator

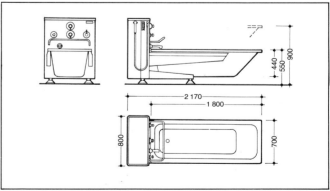

6   Fibreglass sitting b: dry weight 52 kg; av b 125 l

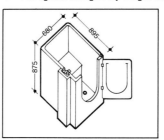

7   Elevating b

Hospitals

PSYCHIATRIC CENTRES

Present trend away from isolated sites for psychiatric hospitals in favour of places allowing easy access for day patients and visitors and enabling inpatients maintain close ties with their community. Community involvement often encouraged in USA both by making appropriate parts of centre available to public, *eg* gymnasium, children's play rm or craft studio, and by incorporating such amenities as art gallery or public lib.

Association with med centre desirable but important psychologically psychiatric centre maintain own identity and character. Environment contributes essentially to therapeutic process. Centre should be non-institutional as possible consistent with type of patient, need for security, protection from self-injury and vandalism; range from 'open door' to forensic institution for criminally insane.

Great size to be avoided; patients should be grouped into units (max 30 P), small enough facilitate development of community spirit (atmosphere nearer college dormitory than hospital).

Where climate allows common practice provide residential units in form of cottages in landscaped grounds. Even where restricted site imposes compact bldg form essential individual units be identifiable as separate entities.

Bedr should afford opportunity retreat and privacy: if 2-B, plan so that each patient has clearly defined individual area.

Conversely design and furnishing of public areas should encourage sociability, supplementing formal treatment with therapeutically beneficial, informal patient/patient and patient/staff meetings. Place nurse/security stations so that staff engaged in routine activities can observe patients casually. Unobstructive nature of such surveillance important psychologically in alleviating persecution complex.

Hierarchical arrangement of staff and patients in group therapy rm inhibits patient involvement. Square or circular seating space affording min distraction, with circular seating arrangement, probably ideal.

Mentally disturbed persons commonly show symptoms disorientation with regard to time and space. Views and contacts with outdoors and living plants aid patient's comprehension of time and season; direct and clearly defined circulation patterns, supported by such aids as graphics and colour coding, inculcate sense of security. Colour plays important role in therapeutic process: *eg* yellow and orange help dispel lethargy among geriatric patients.

Hospital psychiatric units

Similar considerations apply psychiatric units within general hospitals. Since patients generally ambulatory, day rm and therapeutic activity rm assume special significance. Although exigencies of hospital planning seldom allow direct access outdoor areas at ground level from psychiatric unit sunny outdoor roof terrace should form integral part, particularly for geriatric patients.

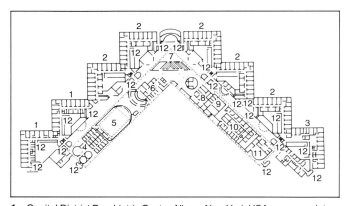

1 Capital District Psychiatric Center Albany New York USA accommodates 400 inpatients in 16 residential units each of which also serves 25 day patients: upper of 2 superimposed units set back from lower creates outdoor ter while lower has direct access to landscaped site; treatment, educational, recreational, admin, research & service dept housed in 4-storey chevron-shaped structure, joined to residential units by sky-lighted, brick-paved, indoor mall which has colourful banners, informal seating groups, beauty & barber shop, chapel, music & games rm, laundromat; plan at mall level
1 geriatric unit 2 adult unit 3 pediatric units 4 psychiatric outpatient clinics
5 consult 6 volunteers 7 dining 8 admissions 9 med records
10 emergency clinics 11 business 12 free-standing colour-coded stairs in mall each serve 4 residential units, supplemented by elevators for handicapped Arch Todd Wheeler & Perkins & Will Partnership.

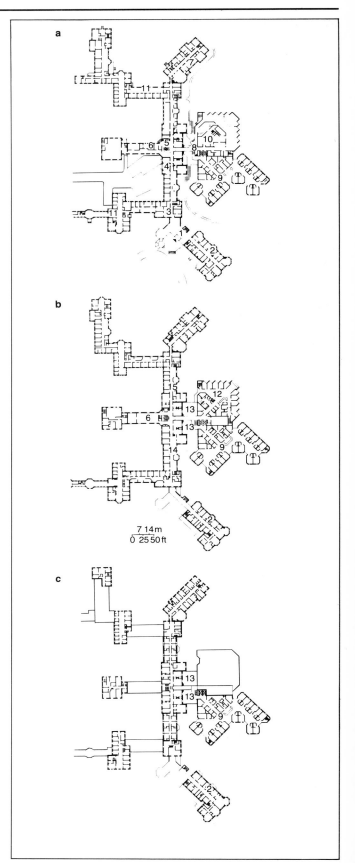

7 14m
0 25 50 ft

2 Hospital for mentally disturbed patients founded 1844 in Providence RI USA, which has been upgraded and expanded, stands in beautiful grounds by Seekonk river a first level b second level c third level
key 1 lob 2 admin 3 admission & testing 4 emergency 5 med records
6 activity therapy 7 day hospital 8 interior courtyard 9 inpatient units
10 food services & cafeteria 11 existing 12 intensive treatment unit
13 interior garden below 14 professional off 15 diagnostic/treatment
Arch Hillier Group

WARD UPGRADING

Although wards have always been designed for care of sick those built before 1940 were often intended for bedfast patients. Since then advance in technical nursing has allowed quicker throughput of patients most of whom fully ambulant for ²/₃ of stay; thus demand increased for nurse working rm and patient day areas, washing and sanitary services. Older wards, structurally sound but ill equipped for present day standards, therefore suitable for upgrading, particularly those with useful life of at least 15 years. Moreover, taking factors below into account, can be worth considering upgrading bldg scheduled to last only 5 years.

Factors

Number of patients to be cared for under sub-standard conditions if ward not upgraded, *eg* 28-bed ward with 80% occupancy and 5-day av stay has throughput of approx 1 680 P/yr and 8 400 in 5 years

Number of nurses to be trained in sub-standard accn, *eg* 28-bed ward with 6 students on duty during day and 2 at night for 6-week period equals 70 students/year or over 350 in 5 years

Proximity to ancillary supporting accn

Change of use from acute to long stay wards

Amount of money available

1 Reallocation & division of spaces, no extension to existing ward: existing 29-B, upgraded 25-B **2** small sanitary annexe added: existing 29-B, upgraded 28-B **3** corr & group of nurse working rm & wc added: existing 26-B, upgraded 30-B **4** extension added to long wall of ward: existing 31-B, upgraded 28-B **5** 2 wards joined with core of nurse working rm: existing 29-B each, upgraded 52-B total

Key to ward plans C or C'd – cpd Con – consult rm D – duty rm Disp – disposal rm Dr – doctors rm DR – dayr DSR – domestic service rm E or Equ – eqp sto fl flower rm I – incinerator k – kitchen L – linen sto Lab – laboratory & test rm NS – nurses station OP – outpatients wr PC – P clothes lockers Prep – preparation rm Rec – receptionist S – sisters rm Sec – secretary Sl – sluice St – sto Staff – staff wc T – treatment rm t – trolley (cart) tx – telephone V – verandah W – waiting ar for visitors

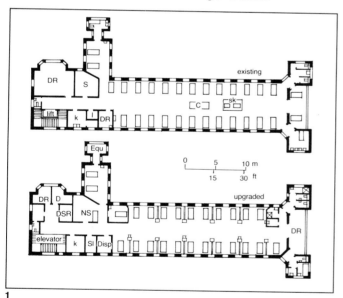

1

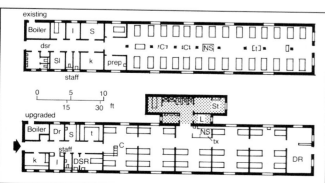

2

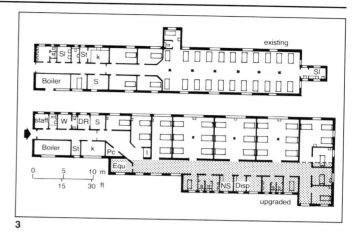

3

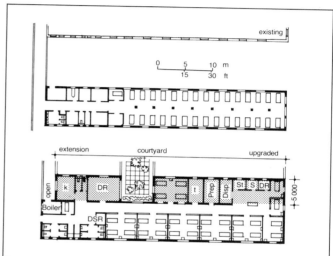

4

5

Hospitals

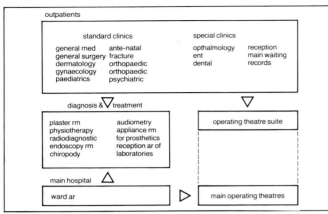

1 Relationship of clinics to other hospital functions

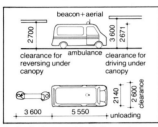

2 Ambulance critical dimensions, standard London England ambulance: turning circle 14.17 m, turning clearance circle 15.25 m

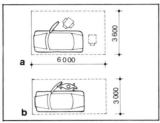

3 Car parking space for **a** wheelchair P **b** ambulent disabled P

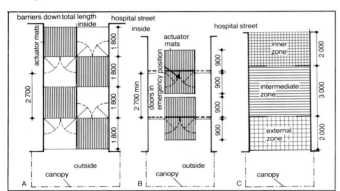

4 Automatic doors to P entrances layouts: A for set of 900 mm swing doors with safety barrier between each direction of traffic flow; B for set of sliding doors with parking space for doors in open position: max recommended size for each leaf 900 C 3 cleaning zones for dirt control: external zone should have open grid type matting suitable for wheelchair user, intermediate, matting with built-in scraper action, inner, non-slip dust control matting

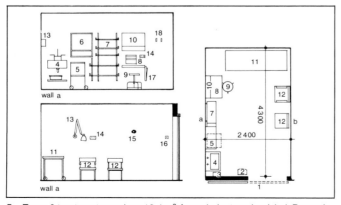

5 Exam & treatment rm or bay, 10.4 m², for ambulant or wheelchair P, couch intended only for P needing exam on flat surface, not designed for general anaesthesia 1 sliding door 2 waste sack 3 towel dispenser 4 sk 5 trolley 6 dispenser with drawer 7 shelving 8 writing surface 9 swivel stool 10 x-ray viewer 11 wheeled couch 12 chair 13 exam lamp 14 twin 13-amp point 15 emergency call button 16 light switch 17 x-ray film rack 18 coat hooks

ENTRANCES FOR NON-AMBULANT CASUALTIES & OUTPATIENTS

All patient entrances must be suitable for those disabled or in wheelchair →p86 and must provide dirt control zone. Doors to A & E →p168 must allow accident trolleys →p166(11) easy entry. In A & E and to lesser extent OPD standard practice to provide automatic opening doors →(4). Although these can be expensive and unreliable usefulness outweighs disadvantages in areas where wheeled access required. Two main types: both actuated by pressure mats or electronic devices. Some manufacturers supply outward opening swing operated mechanism to override normal operation in emergency.

Design area between 2 sets of doors to take trolley pushed by staff member, without obstruction from door swings etc (2 700 clear). Integrate 3 dirt control zones into design. Provide canopy or recess doorway to shelter doors. If ambulance required to back up to door allow 3 200 to underside of canopy →(2).

Outpatients dept (OPD) provide consultation, investigation, diagnosis and treatment for patients who require little or no recovery services afterwards and are not admitted to acute wards. Most patients requested attend session at specific clinic by appointment: receive initial diagnosis and treatment, *eg* injections. Sessions may be approx 3 hr long (10 per week) and held 0900–1800. Each doctor may use either 2 combined consult/exam rm or 1 consult with adjacent exam rm →(5)(7)p168(3) during 1 session. Rm use approx 9 sessions/week: formula for number of rm required:

$$\frac{\text{rm sessions/week}}{9} = \text{number of rm required}$$

After consultation patients may be sent directly or by appointment for further diagnosis and/or treatment to units within OPD, *eg* plaster rm, physiotherapy, operating theatre or endoscopy rm. Endoscopy rm → p167(2) requires accn available for patients under sedation and perhaps ante-rm for pre-medication and holding (NB fibre-optic cold light sources must not be used in conjunction with inflammable anaesthetic gases). Units may serve whole hospital; theatres and ancillary rm may be part of main hospital theatre suite.

Clinics which can use standard accn: general med, general surgery, dermatology, gynaecology, paediatrics, ante-natal, fracture, orthopaedic, psychiatry. Clinics which require special accn: opthalmology, ear, nose & throat, dental. Clinics should have own reception point and waiting area 36 m² (based on 1.4 m²/P).

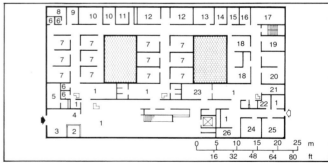

6 OPD Falkirk Scotland Royal Infirmary 1 wr 2 porter 3 trolleys 4 prams 5 hearing aid 6 wc 7 consult 8 clo 9 staff 10 sto 11 audio 12 treatment 13 recovery 14 disposal 15 CSSD sto 16 eqp sto 17 optician 18 eye 19 k 20 dental 21 off 22 dark rm 23 orthoptist 24 engineer 25 studio 26 technician Arch Wilson & Wilson

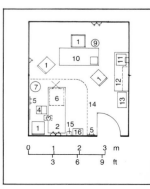

7 Combined consult/exam rm, 15.48 m² 1 chair 2 couch 3 scales 4 steps 5 hooks 6 couch-cover dispenser 7 disposal 8 exam lamp 9 wpb 10 desk 11 hb 12 work top, sto under 13 eqp trolley (cart) 14 curtain 15 sphygomanometer bracket 16 writing shelf

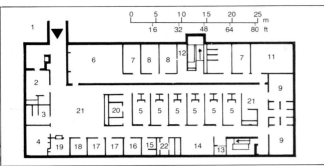

1 Ante-natal clinic Aberdeen Scotland Maternity Hospital **1** prams
2 children **3** P wc **4** sister **5** exam **6** lecture rm & mothercraft **7** tutor
8 study rm **9** consult **10** staff wc female **11** lecture rm **12** clo **13** elevators
14 work ar **15** staff wc male **16** typists **17** health visitor **18** nurse
19 reception **20** urine testing **21** waiting ar   Arch Trew Dann & Partners

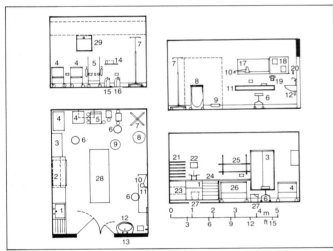

2 Endoscopy rm →p154, 17.28 m² **1** sk **2** work top **3** wall cpd for fibre
optics **4** trolley **5** anaesthetic trolley **6** stool **7** intravenous drip stand
8 linen holder **9** kick-about bucket **10** adjustable lamp **11** writing surface
with drawers **12** surgeons basin **13** warning light **14** shelf with light **15** low
pressure suction **16** high pressure suction **17** triple x-ray viewer **18** pin
board **19** telephone **20** coat hook **21** shelves for preset trays **22** towel
dispenser **23** cpd **24** drawers **25** shelving **26** alimentary trolley **27** bin
28 P trolley **29** DDA cpd

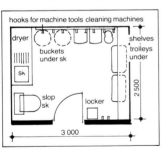

3 Domestic service rm, 7.5 m²

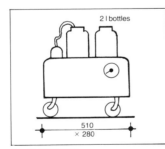

4 Suction unit

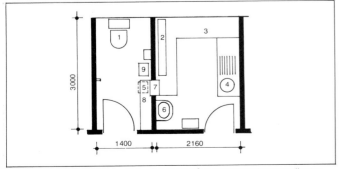

5 Clinette & urine test rm, 2.7 m² + 6.45 m² **1** urine specimens collector
2 reagent store **3** work top, sto under **4** slop hopper & drainer **5** disposal
6 basin **7** hatch **8** shelf **9** hand rinse

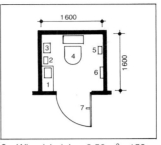

6 Wheelchair lav, 2.56 m²→152

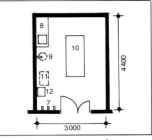

7 Cleansing rm, 13.4 m²

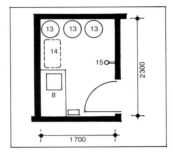

8 Disposal rm, 3.9 m²
key **1** basin with shelf **2** paper towels
3 waste **4** wc **5** toilet paper **6** mirror
7 hook(s) **8** sk **9** gulley **10** P trolley
11 hose point **12** disposal **13** sack
holders **14** trolley **15** stapler

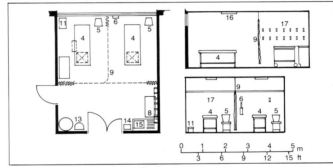

9 Plaster removal rm, 22.3 m²

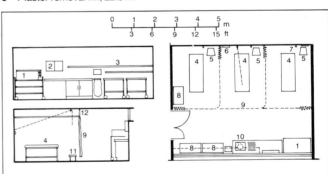

10 Plaster application rm, 33.5 m², serves OPD & A & E; not suitable for
general anaesthesia because more than 1 P space
key **1** oven on trolley **2** double x-ray viewer **3** sto shelves **4** plinth **5** chair
6 plaster-saw mounting **7** clothes hook & mirror **8** trolley **9** curtain **10** sk &
drainer with plaster trap **11** steps **12** ceiling hook **13** plaster cast disposal
14 waste **15** sk & drainer **16** plaster dust extractor **17** wall hook(s)

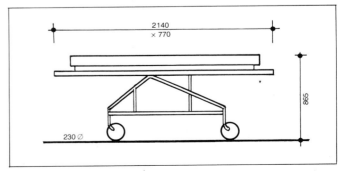

11 Tilting accident trolley

Hospitals

ACCIDENT & EMERGENCY

Accident & emergency dept (A&E) provide 24-hr 365-day/year service for accidents and med emergencies occurring in home, at work, at sports or travelling. Patients normally taken to DGH (community hospital) with A&E resources. Dept provides resuscitation, reception and first stage exam; patients can then be discharged, sent to another part of hospital for further investigation and treatment, admitted as inpatients, or sent by ambulance to hospital containing regional specialty, *eg* burns unit, neurosurgery →p173–5. Patients dead on arrival taken to small rm near entrance before being removed to hospital mortuary. For dept close to potential sources of accidents (airports, motorways) extra provision for resuscitation needed.

A&E need to be on good access roads with drive-in entrances for ambulances, sheltered from wind and rain by covered ways and baffle walls. Entrances should have 2 sets of automatic fail-safe doors to prevent draughts, with enough space to manoeuver stretchers and trolleys →p166(4). Dept must have direct access for patients on trolleys to all parts of hospital, particularly radiology →p169 170, plaster rm →p167(9)(10), surgical (OPD) →p171 172 and short stay wards. Resuscitation rm must be fully equipped with med gases and be close to entrances. Doctors, often on duty for long periods, require comfortable duty rm. Relatives of patients need access to public telephone. Interview rm required by doctors for interviewing relatives and by police for interviewing witnesses. Generous sto required for stretchers, blankets and trolleys. For benefit of patients, relatives and escorts, who may be in severe state of shock, all waiting spaces as well as clinical areas should be heated to min 21° C.

CASUALTY DEPARTMENT

Casualty dept provide 24-hr 365-day/year service for casual attenders and patients referred by GP for immediate examination and treatment; generally linked to A&E; can share some nurse working rm and staff services. But combined only for convenience: specific functions very different. Patients arrive on foot or by car, usually accompanied by relative or escort. Casualty dept should have separate entrance, preferably with double set of automatic fail-safe doors →p166(4).

Patients come without appointment and may have to wait some time before being examined and treated; provide generous waiting space, with beverage point and at least 4 wc, 2 suitable for wheelchair users p167(6).

Full snack bar can be provided if shared by OPD →p166. Patients who return for further dressings or treatment given appointments outside morning and evening rush hour for casualties so can use same accn. Exam and treatment rm preferable to cubicles for patients requiring audio and visual privacy (can undress and be seen in comfort); casualty doctor will work set of rm. Cubicles suitable for small cuts and abrasions which do not require patient to undress. Separate provision may be requested for cleansing patients and dealing with infected wounds.

Peak periods for both A&E and Casualty dept invariably coincide with weekends and public holidays: essential that sufficient stores and nursing eqp be available either by providing extra sto at point-of-use or by giving staff access to central sto during holidays and off-peak periods.

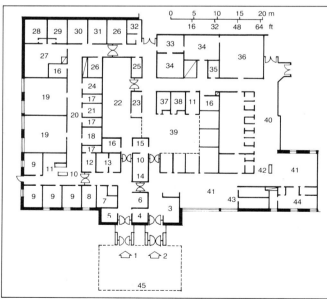

1   A & E Eastbourne England DGH 1 ambulance entrance 2 casualty entrance 3 trolleys, wheelchairs 4 porter 5 flying squad 6 trolleys 7 staff clo 8 rest rm 9 1-B 10 nurses station 11 clean supply 12 duty doctor 13 cleaned interview 14 reception 15 doctors station 16 charge nurse 17 wc 18 assisted b 19 6-B 20 outpatient B ar 21 dirty utility 22 resuscitation ar 23 disposal rm 24 k 25 surgeons changing 26 sto 27 dayr 28 P changing male 29 P changing female 30 doctor 31 nurse admin 32 housekeeper 33 anaesthetic rm 34 minor operating 35 crutch sto 36 plaster rm 37 ear, nose & throat (ENT), eyes, noisy children 38 septic treatment 39 treatment ar 40 fractured & orthopaedic clinic 41 waiting 42 clinic reception 43 P lav 44 appliance fitting 45 canopy over

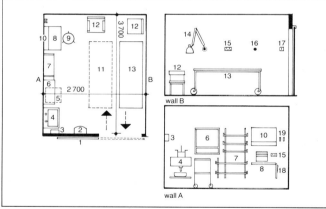

2   A & E Falkirk Scotland Royal Infirmary 1 ambulance 2 ambulant P 3 prams 4 eqp 5 trolleys 6 treatment 7 interview 8 sister 9 duty 10 wc 11 to theatres 12 disposal 13 preparation 14 to shared x-ray 15 visitors 16 exam 17 resuscitation 18 reception 19 plaster 20 sto 21 clo

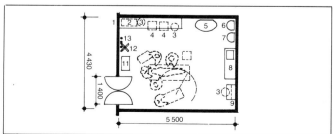

3   Exam & treatment rm or bay, 10.15 m². designed to allow for trolley exchange system; P on emergency trolley can take place of trolley in rm 1 sliding door 2 waste sack 3 towel dispenser 4 sk 5 trolley (cart) 6 dispenser with drawer 7 shelving 8 writing surface 9 swivel stool 10 x-ray viewer 11 emergency trolley 12 chair 13 trolley 14 exam lamp 15 twin 13-amp point 16 emergency call switch 17 light switch 18 x-ray film rack 19 coat hooks

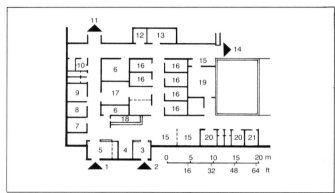

4   Resuscitation rm, 24.36 m² 1 work top 2 suction unit 3 stool 4 trolley (cart) 5 surgeons sk 6 linen sack 7 waste sack 8 work top with sk 9 writing surface, shelves over 10 mobile x-ray 11 anaesthetic trolley 12 drip stand 13 oxygen suction gas

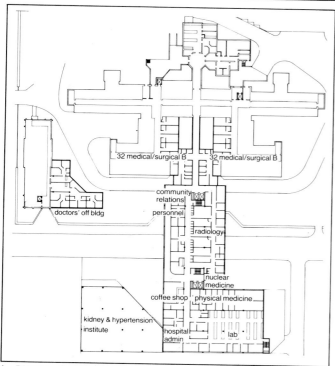

1 Diagram of relationships between radiology & other dept in representative USA hospital

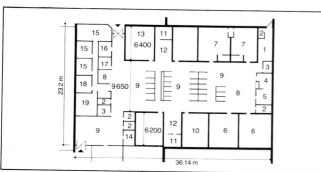

2 Eastbourne England DGH x-ray dept 1 lavage & disposal 2 wc 3 sto 4 clean supply 5 recovery 6 x-ray rm special 7 x-ray rm barium 8 bed holding 9 waiting 10 x-ray rm general purpose 11 dark rm 12 sorting & viewing 13 x-ray rm A & E 14 cleaner 15 reporting rm 16 film sto 17 disposal 18 superintendent radiographer 19 staff rm

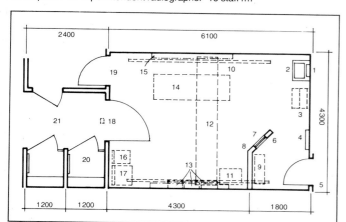

3 Diagnostic x-ray rm designed by American Health Facilities/Medical Planning Associates Malibu USA 1 dispenser unit 2 step-on waste receptacle 3 surgical/instrument dressing cabinet 4 apron & glove rack 5 to daylight processing ar 6 intercom 7 lead glass vision panel 8 partition 2100 h 9 x-ray control unit 10 ceiling tube mount 11 generator 12 tube carriage 13 3-size film dispenser 14 radiographic table with tomographic attachment 15 fluorescent light fixtures wall mounted 16 footstool with handrail 17 side chair 18 warning light 19 to lav 20 mirror 21 corr

RADIOLOGY DEPARTMENTS

X-ray or radiology has 3 major sub-divisions: diagnostic, which may include ultra-sonics, fluoroscopy etc; radiation; nuclear medicine. Depending on admin pattern or on physical/functional relationships with other dept these may be arranged contiguously or separately.

Diagnostic radiology

Provides internal images of patient either on film (radiography) or on cathode ray tube (CRT – fluoroscopy). Must be provided for outpatients and inpatients both for routine examinations and for emergencies. Dept therefore has relationship to OPD, medical, intensive care and surgical units.

Separation of inpatient, typically on trolley, stretcher or wheelchair, from outpatient in street clothes and often bloody, should be maintained long as possible, certainly through entrance, reception and waiting: if dept large enough also through radiographic procedure and exit.

Arrange x-ray procedure rm so that patient's travel path does not cross that of radiology technician until they meet in procedure rm. Easy trolley/stretcher acc s to x-ray table essential. Plan dept so that technician travel time kept min particularly between rm and film processing.

Simple x-rays to locate fractures or position of catheter take less than 10 minutes; more complex or intermittent procedures involving barium swallows or radio-opaque injections may take up to 3 hr to complete while patient waits in or near dept. Design for following requirements: separate rm for ultrasonography and for thermography; wc next to 2 x-ray rm for patients who have had barium enemas; bench with drinking water, bottle-trapped sink with sto cpd over exclusively for barium preparations: should be next to 2 x-ray rm; rm and viewing bay to process and check accuracy of films (normally completed within 15 minutes of being taken): automatic plumbed-in processors need special drainage; forward waiting area on basis of 1.3 m²/P plus 1.0² for relative or escort; extra screened space for 2 patients' trolleys; 2 wc suitable for patients in wheelchairs →p167(6).

Each x-ray rm must be screened from other parts of bldg either by barium plaster or by lead sheeting, both very dense heavy materials. All glazing should be in lead glass. X-ray eqp heavy and requires ceiling heights between 3100 and 4000; extra moveable structural beams suspended from ceiling will be required. Design floors and ceilings to take extra high loads. Entrance doors to x-ray rm should be 1400 wide in 2 leaves 900 + 500.

In addition to above mentioned areas support spaces for film sorting, film reading by radiologists and filing necessary, also spaces for transcribing reports, sto for eqp and supplies, admin off and often conference rm.

X-ray beam carries inherent danger to living cells: proper shielding of all procedure rm essential; must be designed and supervised by radiation specialist.

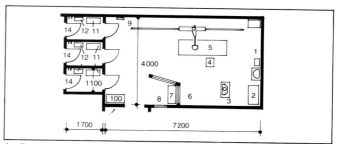

4 Radiodiagnostic rm/changing cubicles, 28.8 m² 1 transformer 2 eqp trolley 3 chest x-ray 4 steps 5 bucky table 6 safety screen 7 control unit 8 cassette hatch 9 clock 10 sto unit 11 bench seat 12 shelf & mirror 13 hooks

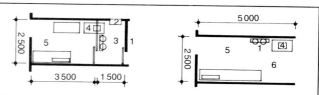

5 Viewing & processing rm, open & closed layouts 1 tanks & water installation 2 cassette hatch (from radiodiagnostic rm) 3 dark rm 4 processor 5 sorting & viewing 6 processing

Hospitals

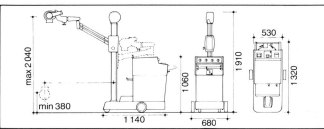

1 Mobile-x ray unit; can be power or hand driven: weight 460 kg

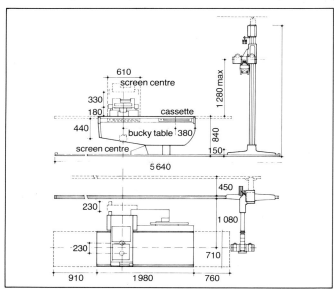

2 Bucky table: rm h required with floor/ceiling tube stand min 3 000 max 4 000

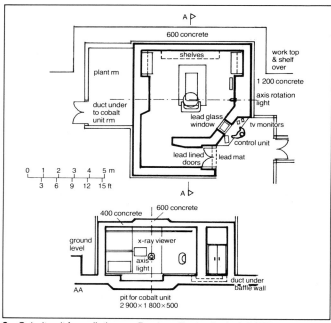

3 Cobalt unit for radiotherapy Pembury England   Arch S E Thames RHR

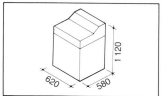

4 Typical cyclotron

RADIOLOGY DEPARTMENTS (cont)

Radiation therapy

Technique whereby radiation used reduce or eliminate carcinogenic cells: generated either by natural source such as radioactive cobalt or by man-made as in linear accelerator. Because of massive quantities of radiation used extremely heavy shielding required contain it: so heavy that some reg require this dept be placed at ground level.

Whole unit constructed of dense concrete: walls, ceiling, floor pit thickest (approx 1 200) within 360° arc of eqp, remainder approx 600. Design all steelwork, conduit, piping to prevent radiation leakage. Viewing porthole double-skinned with highly corrosive fluid infill (zinc bromide solution); door locks controlled from console in adjoining rm.

Procedure rm with their shielding mazes must be large enough accommodate eqp plus access for patient on stretcher/trolley. Spaces required for patient reception and waiting, examination, treatment planning, mould making for shielding needed for patient during treatment, off and work space for staff. Off and lab space also needed for physicist for calibration and radiation safety of eqp.

Patients taken into rm containing eqp and so positioned that all 3 sources of radiation converge on diseased part of body; attendant then retires to control rm from which patient can be observed through heavy lead glass porthole or by tv. Procedure can be very frightening for patient: ventilation, temp and general environment control of utmost importance. Pastoral photomural or fresco on walls and ceiling within view of patient during treatment, together with false window with pastoral 'view' opposite entrance, will help alleviate fears.

Nuclear medicine

Diagnostic procedure involving ingestion by or injection into patient of radioactive materials which then traced by scanning eqp. Rm used for scanning require some shielding; must be large enough accommodate eqp, patient on stretcher/trolley, console and technician. In contrast to diagnostic or therapy procedure rm level of radiation low enough allow 2 or more patients scanned simultaneously in same space. Support spaces include reception and waiting, off, sto, well shielded 'hot lab' beside procedure rm for sto and preparation of radioactive materials.

CAT scanning

Relatively new method of non-invasive imaging of internal organs; although diagnostic procedure, often in separate suite with own procedure rm, control rm, computer eqp space and support areas.

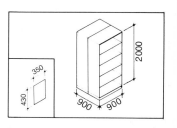

5 X-ray film cabinet; will hold approx 10 000 envelopes (360 kg), 26 000 x-ray films (1 040 kg): total floor loading 1 728 kg/m²

6 Standard x-ray film very heavy (155 kg/m run): max unsupported w of shelf 900; each radiodiagnostic rm produces approx 625 envelopes/ month

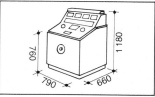

7 Transformer: weight 380 kg

8 Radiodiagnostic control unit

Hospitals

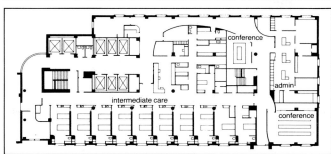

1 Typical floor of surgical & special services bldg Massachusetts General Hospital USA   Arch Perry Dean Stahl & Rogers

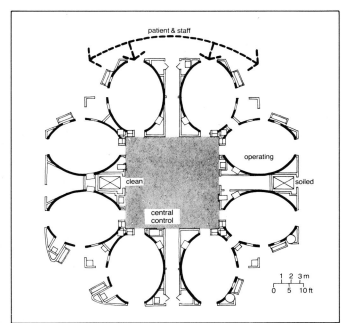

2 St Joseph Hospital Tacoma USA has elliptic oper rm arranged round central control rm   Arch Bertrand Goldberg Associates

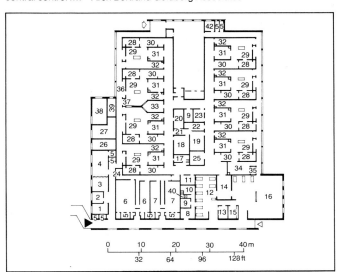

3 Stobhill oper theatre suite: 8 standard theatres with clean & dirty corr
1 consult anaesthetist off 2 anaesthetist secretary's off 3 duty anaesthetist
4 student lecture rm 5 wc 6 male changing 7 female changing 8 porter
9 cleaner 10 workshop 11 theatre superintendent 12 reception ar
13 dirty utility 14 transfer 15 clean utility 16 recovery ar 17 dark rm
18 nurses rest rm 19 surgeons rest rm 20 technicians rest rm 21 tea k
22 eqp sto 23 theatre sister 24 lab 25 endoscopy 26 calorifiers
27 refrigeration plant 28 preparation rm 29 oper theatre 30 exit lob
31 anaesthetic rm 32 scrub-up ar 33 monitor rm 34 plaster rm 35 plaster
sto 36 disposal bay 37 disposal lob 38 el gear 39 med gases 40 stair to
air-conditioning plant 41 TSSU 42 staff rest rm   Arch Cullen Lochhead & Brown

OPERATING THEATRES

Surgical and delivery suites increasingly considered centres to which patients brought for procedures too complex for handling in physician's off or treatment area. Unlike traditional suite with different rm for different services (*eg*, ENT, orthopedic) suites now collection of multi-purpose rm. In large institutions more than 1 suite likely be provided, based on usage: short (1–3 hr) procedures, such as ambulatory, frequently separated from general, av length (2–4 hr) and very long (6–8 hr) procedures. Delivery suites, formerly completely separated from surgical, today commonly alongside or integrated.

Design elements
Consider patient flow: entrance, control, holding pre-anaesthesia, operating, recovery. Consider staff: control, clean-up. Consider eqp, particularly instruments and other goods which must be sterilised between each use: done locally (within suite) or centrally (for hospital)? Let volumes guide. Consider sharing: like types of procedure rm can share supplies, cleaning etc. Consider testing functions: 'quick' lab tests, x-ray etc: how will they be done?

Space needs
Space suites need per inpatient bed varies greatly, depending on whether ambulatory surgery offered, whether hospital has teaching programme and other such factors: generally 28–46 m² for each operating theatre. Space for circulation, nursing and medical staff and non-functional bldg elements such as air-conditioning eqp usually high ratio in this setting, perhaps 80% above individual rm needs. If reprocessing goods due within suite 28–37 m²/operating theatre or delivery rm must be added. Locker rm, showers and rest rm for staff should be provided based on number staff expected.

Circulation
Crucial to design of high technology operating and delivery suites; 2 basic types: single corridor and double corridor or 'racetrack'. Single has 1 corridor leading to all operating/delivery rm, used for patients, staff and eqp: sterility maintained in each user of corridor and within theatre itself; each rm preceded by scrub-up ar and has provision for sterilisation within it or between 2 rm. 'Racetrack' arranges rm in 'circular' fashion with outside corridor or rm for staff and eqp, presumed sterile; locker rm 'bridge' corridors; staff and eqp leave with patient; staff 'bridged' back through locker rm and showers.

Cleanliness
Also critical in operating/delivery suite. All materials, surfaces, joints etc must be easily cleanable and durable for repeated washings: sealed joints to prevent infection. Anti-static materials should be used where patients likely be connected anaesthetic machines. Check requirements with technical literature.

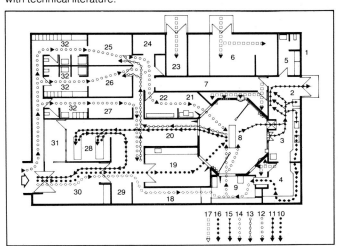

4 Vedesta system modular oper theatre uses basic standard octagonal to form series of units for use in new hospitals or for upgrading; 10 sizes available, ar from 23.22 m² – 43.6 m² 1 domestic staff change 2 disposal
3 sluice 4 inspection/sto 5 generators/batteries 6 air-conditioning
7 emergency corr 8 theatre 9 sterile rm 10 P in 11 P out 12 surgeons nurses orderlies in 13 surgeons nurses orderlies out 14 sterile supply
15 soiled instruments/disposal 16 cleaned instruments 17 access to services 18 sterile supply 19 anaesthetic rm 20 exit 21 gowning
22 scrub-up 23 med gas 24 instrument sto 25 nurse staff rm 26 surgeon staff rm 27 orderlies staff rm 28 recovery 29 mobile eqp 30 transfer
31 sister 32 change – NB servicing of lighting eqp completed from outside theatre

Hospitals

OPERATING THEATRES (cont)

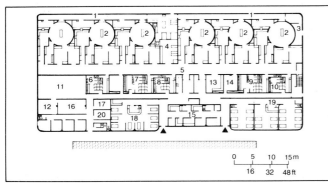

1 Oper theatre suites Ninewells Hospital Dundee Scotland, designed for teaching 1 service corr 2 oper theatre 3 x-ray 4 TSSU 5 access cor 6 female surgeons 7 male surgeons 9 nurses 10 students 11 anaesthetic dept 12 surgeons rest 13 sto 14 nurses rest 15 research lab 16 lecture rm 17 junior staff 18 recovery ward 19 reception ward 20 senior staff Arch Robert Matthew Johnson Marshall

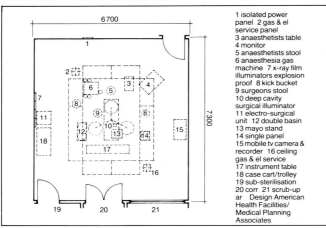

1 isolated power panel 2 gas & el service panel 3 anaesthetists table 4 monitor 5 anaesthetists stool 6 anaesthesia gas machine 7 x-ray film illuminators explosion proof 8 kick bucket 9 surgeons stool 10 deep cavity surgical illuminator 11 electro-surgical unit 12 double basin 13 mayo stand 14 single panel 15 mobile tv camera & recorder 16 ceiling gas & el service 17 instrument table 18 case cart/trolley 19 sub-sterilisation 20 corr 21 scrub-up ar Design American Health Facilities/ Medical Planning Associates

2 General oper rm

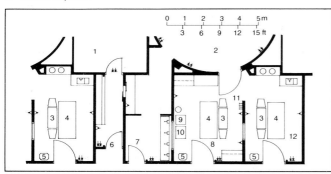

3 Anaesthetic rm, exit rm, scrub-up rm, sterile sto: el outlet points in anaesthetic & exit to be sparkless & hoseproof, in sterile sto & exit hoseproof only 1 sterile rm 2 oper theatre 3 table 4 B 5 hb 6 sterile sto 7 scrub-up rm 8 anaesthetic rm 9 anaesthetic trolley 10 anaesthetic machine 11 service points 12 exit rm

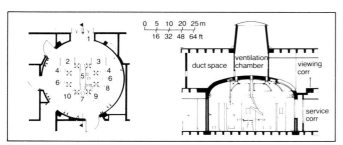

4 Oper theatre, 36.10 m²; all el outlet points in anaesthetic & exit rm to be sparkless & hoseproof, in sterile sto & exit rm hoseproof only 1 control panel 2 dressing trolley/cart 3 instrument trolley 4 basin stand 5 table 6 kick basin 7 stool 8 switch stand 9 anaesthetic machine 10 anaesthetic trolley

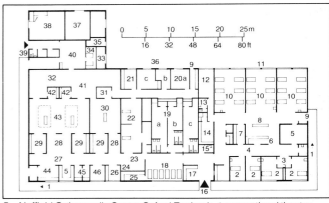

5 Nuffield Orthopaedic Centre Oxford England: 1 conventional theatre, 2 'clean-air glass enclosures' with filtered air & special suits with air intake & exhaust for staff 1 ramp 2 1-B 3 nursing 4 intensive care ar 5 sto 6 clean utility 7 dirty utility 8 nurses station 9 fire exit 10 6-B 11 intensive care 12 seminar/rest rm 13 staff 14 locker rm 15 visitors 16 from wards 17 waiting 18 B park 19 changing rm a surgeons b orderlies c nurses 20 rest rm a nurses b orderlies c surgeons 21 theatre sisters 22 plaster rm 23 transfer zone 24 orderlies bay 25 linen 26 monitor eqp station 27 oper dept 28 exit bay 29 anaesthetic rm 30 oper theatre 31 gown/scrub-up 32 forward holding 33 switch rm 34 sterilisers 35 battery rm 36 service ar 37 med gas 38 plant rm 39 loading dock 40 TSSU 41 preparation 42 scrub-up 43 oper rm 44 disposal bay 45 dark rm 46 mobile x-ray

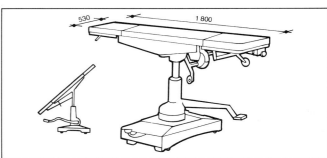

6 Typical oper table in standard position: will tilt in both directions; also designed take various attachments; small wheels used put very high rolling loads on floor: weight approx 230 kg, min h approx 700, max h approx 1 040

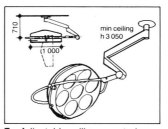

7 Adjustable ceiling mounted exam lamp, weight 4.5 kg

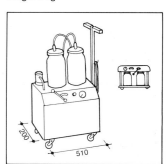

8 Suspended operating lamp weight 8 kg

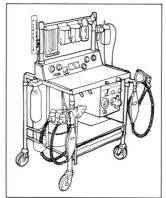

9 Anaesthetic machine

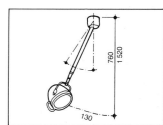

10 Mobile suction unit: this type also available without castors or pull handle; units for connexion to piped systems do not have lower part of control box

Hospitals: special units

INTENSIVE CARE

Hospitals contain 2 basic types bed accn: 'hotel' for patients not needing continuous direct visual supervision or life-sustaining eqp; 'critical' (UK intensive) for patients whose survival depends on constant attention and/or complex life-support eqp. Proportion of critical to hotel and of number of types of special care units increasing.

Special units include cardiac, spinal injury, burn, transplant, respiratory, neurosurgical, limb fitting, physical medicine. Usually form part of larger hospitals (regional specialties in UK); very large hospitals may have all of them.

Design considerations
Will patient be conscious, require privacy, toilet, constant nursing attention? Will location or configuration of unit help or hinder patient's recovery? Can staff see all patients easily? Is ratio patients/staff station appropriate? Can staff get help quickly? Can they reach services (medications, uty etc) and support (lab tests etc) quickly and easily? Can they examine patient easily? What about infection control? Can special eqp be brought quickly bedside in emergency? Can monitors, pumps, screens be easily read by staff? Can eqp be stored handily when not in use?

Bed unit basic space module: number beds related to unit, decided by usage or projected usage: 6–7 usual max. Unit must be sized for bed (larger and larger as new features added or structured), eqp (respirators, pumps, monitors), people (many as needed during resuscitation): common today 11–15 m^2/unit.

Access from entrance to bed unit and between critical. Spaces required include: nurse/physician for supervising monitors, charting, consult; support for medication station, uty; special use, *eg* treatment, procedure, x-ray, based on patient plus staff/eqp 11–15 m^2; amenities such as rest rm, locker, wc.

Keep distance from control station or viewpoint to patient small so that eqp can be read and patient actually seen. Bed unit may be enclosed in rm (*eg* coronary care, where patient conscious, or where infection control or separation patient from noise necessary) or open (*eg* for max visibility and quick access where patient unconscious).

Staff changing arrangements similar those for operating theatres; visitors if allowed, may be required change shoes, wear gowns and masks.

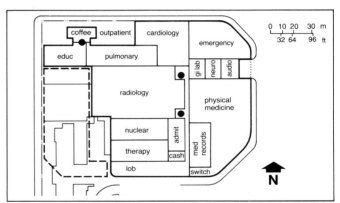

1 P unit intensive care pavilion Long Island Jewish-Hillside Medical Care Center USA

2 Master plan Temple University Hospital Philadelphia USA showing relationship between specialty units Arch Perkins & Will

NEUROSURGERY

Because of length of each operation and its exacting nature neurosurgery units rely heavily on support services. Ratio of population to beds 1:100000. 2 theatres shown →(3) serve 60 beds. Theatres egg-shaped to promote smooth flow fully conditioned air (21 changes/hr). Heat-filtered theatre lamps set in ceiling and 1 wall. Monitoring eqp and viewing gallery in mezzanine with viewing ports in domed ceiling. Each theatre equipped with 5-panel x-ray viewing box, oxygen, nitrous oxide, suction, nitrogen for pneumatic tools, electro-encephalograph (EEG) connexions, and CCTV for transmission of encephalograph recordings. Anti-static flooring and flashproof el outlets required. X-ray rm attached to theatres heavily equipped for cranial and spinal radiography. Separate lab for electro-encephalography and special eye exam. Support measures include physiotherapy with hydrotherapy pool.

Wards attached to neurological theatres: mixed sex 20 beds (4 × 4-B, 4 × 1-B). Early ambulation of patients in need of observation reflected in size of day and sun rm; patients encouraged to have visitors who can help return normal life by using these and adjacent flower bay.

SPINAL INJURY

Care for young people, who suffer from paralysis as result of accidents, *eg* motor cycle. Require 100% care: nearly always doubly incontinent; because of shock to system can be aggressive towards staff and visitors. Occupational therapy, physiotherapy and study form vital part of rehabilitation. Patients may take months recover; care can be divided into 3 stages: patients bedfast: can only be moved for bathing and treatment in horizontal position; patients spend part of waking hours in wheelchair: therefore more mobile (after this stage some patients go home and return for stage 3); patients begin move round on crutches or with walking aids.

Stages 1 and 2 require 20–24 beds, stage 3 28–32 beds. Provide approx 20% beds in 1-B wards and remainder in 4- or 6-B. Beds wider than normal (1000); allow min bed centres of 3500. Provision of nurse working rm similar to that for physical/mental handicapped units, →p163(6)(7).

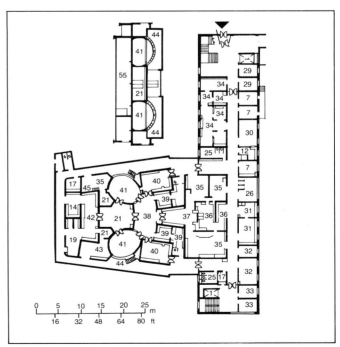

3 Neurosurgical oper theatres Western General Hospital Edinburgh Scotland 1 elevator 7 med staff 12 k 17 domestic service 19 eqp sto 21 sterilising annexe 25 staff toilets 26 wr 29 secretaries 30 staff conference rm 31 plaster rm 32 eye rm 33 dept/theatre sister 34 EEG 35 x-ray rm 36 dark/work rm 37 theatre ha 38 scrub-up ar 39 changing rm 40 anaesthetic rm 41 oper theatres 42 preparation rm 43 scientific observation 44 stair to viewing gallery 45 stair to theatre EEG 55 engineering plant

Hospitals: special units

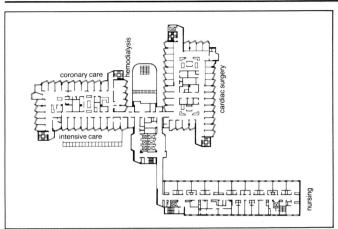

1   Relationship between cardiac surgery unit, intensive care, coronary care, nursing rm at St Vincent Medical Center Los Angeles USA   Arch Daniel Mann Johnson & Mendenhall

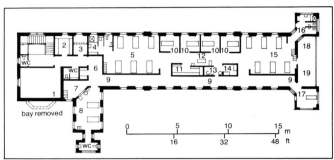

2   Cardiac surgical unit Stobhill England General Hospital; conversion of existing ward to surgical unit 1 off for registrars/research fellow 2 k 3 sister 4 wc/sho 5 womens ward 6 domestic service rm 7 eqp sto 8 isolation B 9 corr 2 000 w 10 intensive care B 11 preparation rm 12 nurses station 13 disposal 14 sluice 15 mens ward 16 wc/sho 17 treatment bathr 18 day rm 19 dining ar   Arch E Phillips

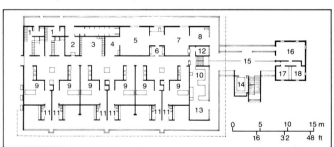

3   Nuffield transplantation surgery unit Western General Hospital Edinburgh Scotland; mech ventilation to aseptic ar, 1-B wards, clean corr, auxiliary rm, twin oper theatres, (designed for close control of air movement pattern) & pressurisation to min infiltration 1 changing 2 k 3 sterile supply 4 anaesthetic 5 recipient theatre 6 scrub-up 7 donor theatre 8 decontamination 9 P rm 10 lab 11 P bathr 12 disposal 13 eqp sto 14 elevator 15 entrance ha/waiting ar 16 conference rm 17 secretary 18 director   Arch Peter Womersley

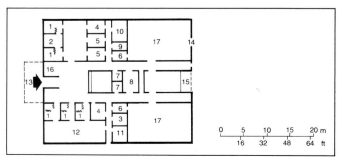

4   Limb fitting centre 1 consult rm 2 prosthetist 3 prosthetist off 4 plaster rm 5 fitting rm 6 rectifying 7 toilets 8 treatment 9 domestic service rm 10 staff/seminar rm 11 med social worker 12 walkway 13 entry P/staff/ambulance 14 entry plant/large materials 15 entry goods/materials 16 wait 17 workshop 18 sto service   Arch E Phillips

CARDIAC SURGICAL

2 stages of care: intensive therapy and intermediate care. Patients vulnerable infection: 2 out of 6 or 8 beds should be in isolated bays with full height walls. Patients most vulnerable at immediate post-operative stage when in transit and not attached to electrically operated ventilators or monitors. Intensive care units must therefore be close to operating theatres.

Example illustrated →(2) also shows area to be upgraded as coronary care unit. Requires bio-chemistry lab; some research and staff areas can be shared. Provide for relatives' overnight stay close to but not in unit.

TRANSPLANT

For replacing damaged or diseased organs (usually kidneys) by direct transplant from donor: need paired operating theatres, one for donor, one recipient. Patients nursed in 1-B wards in carefully controlled environment (liable both to infection and to infect others). When donors not available kidneys may be obtained from cold store bank (may hold other surgical spares required for transplant surgery such as skin, eyes, bone marrow, bone and blood).

LIMB FITTING CENTRE

Considered advisable hold clinics in DGH (community hospital) save patients, often elderly and diabetic, from having travel long distances. All patients require rehabilitation for everyday living; walking training should be provided for, either in centre or within wheelchair distance. If centre provides early post-operative walking training hostel type beds may be required in or close to it. Patients come to centre for consult, assessment, stump casting and limb fitting, and return for stump dressings, limb adjustments and walking training. Provide workshops for making limbs: if modular limbs mainly assembly process. Cosmetic covers made on vacuum-forming machines from highly inflammable material; special sto required for this and for paint. For workshops and sto areas refer to factory legislation.

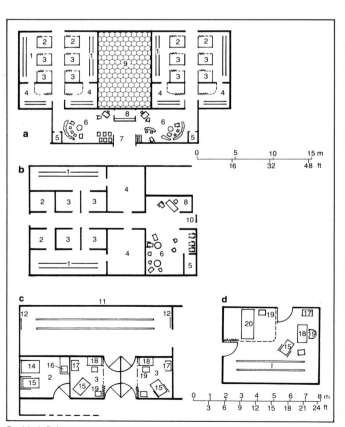

5   Limb fitting centre consult rm layouts **a** for 4 suites **b** for 2 suites **c** consult rm **d** walk, fitting rm, plaster rm 1 walkway 2 plaster rm 3 fitting rm 4 consult rm 5 wc 6 wr 7 entrance 8 admin 9 courtyard 10 from OPD 11 window wall 12 long mirror 13 walking rails 14 plaster chair 15 P wheelchair 16 sk 17 hb 18 desk 19 chair 20 couch   Arch E Phillips

Hospitals: special units

BURN UNITS

Seriously burnt patients arrive by ambulance; nursed on special beds in carefully controlled environment. Patients liable to infections which prevent acceptance of skin grafts. Each has 1-bed ward with scrub-up and gowning lobby for staff and wc and hb for patient. Visitors not allowed enter ward: view patient through fixed observation window. Unit has own theatre suite for treatment and skin grafting.

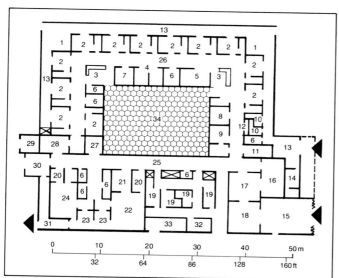

1 Burns unit Queen Victoria Hospital E Grinstead England **1** wr **2** 1-B with wc **3** nurses station **4** clean utility **5** k **6** sto **7** weighing rm **8** clinical lab **9** doctor off **10** visitors wc **11** sisters off **13** visitors ha & corr **14** relatives rm & wc **15** ambulance bay **16** resuscitation **17** assessment **18** admission rm **19** staff clo **20** surgeons scrub **21** anaesthetic rm **22** oper theatre **23** sluice **24** treatment rm **25** theatre corr **26** nursing corr **27** rest rm **28** dirty utility **29** med gases **30** air lock **31** disposal corr **32** interview rm **33** entrance to plant rm under **34** courtyard Arch Donald Goldfinch & Partners

2 Dept of physical med Southern General Hospital Govan Scotland **1** plant rm **2** heavy workshop **3** timber sto **4** light workshop **5** eqp sto **6** duty rm **7** utility rm **8** finished articles sto **9** bathr **10** bedr **11** k **12** senior occupational therapist **13** female staff changing **14** male staff changing **15** hydrotherapy pool **16** gym sto **17** apparatus gym **18** P changing **19** active treatment rm **20** apparatus sto **21** preparation bay **22** linen sto **23** paraffin wax rm **24** female students changing **25** female staff changing **26** male students changing **27** students common rm **28** staff rm **29** passive treatment male **30** passive treatment female **31** interview rm **32** reception/records **33** waiting space **34** trolley (cart)/wheelchair bay **35** consult rm **36** med officer **37** principal's off **38** upper gym **39** tank rm Arch Keppie Henderson & Partners

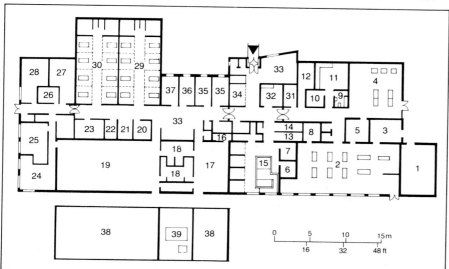

PHYSICAL MEDICINE

Provides med, domestic and often industrial rehabilitation to fit patients, either return work or for active domestic life. Provide for inpatients as well as outpatients: min population for viable unit 150 000. Accn related to type of population to be served; activities include physiotherapy, remedial gymnastics, hydrotherapy, occupational therapy, heavy and light workshops, consult and clinical resources, together with provision for speech therapists, disablement resettlement officers and social workers. Because most attenders disabled accn should be on ground floor with car parking close by (3 000 wide bays allow disabled manoeuvre wheelchair from car) →p166(3). Special provision children up to age 10, usually within children's ward. Some patients attend for half or whole day, others for 1 session/day; may be need for hostel accn for those who have to travel long distance.

Gymnasium should be 10 × 20 × 7.6 m h (for ball games) with bay 1 500 deep off one side for stacking apparatus, and changing rm and wc (1.5 m^2/P). Physiotherapy also involves individual treatment cubicles, walking and other exercise areas, wax treatment rm (high fire risk) and splint rm, with offices, interview rm and linen sto. Part of treatment area should have suspended below ceiling, at approx 2 000 above floor, reinforced metal grid for connecting slings and pulleys necessary to support patient's paralysed limb during treatment or training.

Hydrotherapy pool →(3) requires changing accn with clothes lockers and sho, including 1 for wheelchair users, recovery areas with couch (1 700 × 2 200 deep), utility area for drying costumes and gowns, and possibly washing machine and drier. Provide apparatus bay for floats, cradles etc.

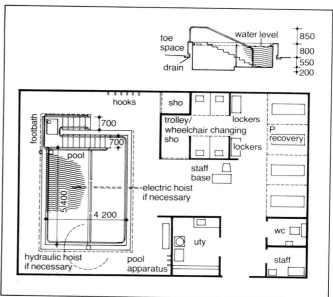

3 Hydrotherapy pool

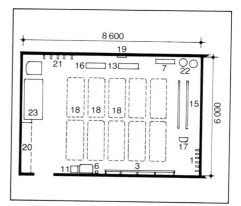

4 Physiotherapy & rehabilitation, 51.6 m^2
1 coathooks **3** wall bars **6** paper towel dispenser **7** bench seat **11** disposal bin **13** fixed bicycle **15** parallel bars **16** exercise steps **17** mobile mirror **18** mat **19** clock **20** adjustable shelving **21** wall hooks **22** stool **23** trolley (cart)/mat sto box

Hospitals

PATHOLOGY LABORATORY, POST MORTEM ROOMS

Pathogens classified in UK in 4 categories: A, B, B2 and C

Category A extremely hazardous: includes lassa fever and smallpox. Specimens as soon as identified must be sealed into special containers and sent to regional lab assigned for purpose.

Category B include brucella spp, hepatitis B, m tuberculosis: all work on these must be carried out in exhaust protective cabinets. Lab should not be less than 18 m², must have lockable door with glazed observation panel and also contain handbasin with bi-flow wrist operative taps, paper towel dispenser and bin near door. Other eqp includes frig, deep freeze, sto for disposable gloves, tissues, encasing jars etc, row of pegs near door for protective clothing. Discarded specimens must be sent for autoclaving. Waste drainage from most of these areas required to be in separate runs.

Categories B2 and C do not require special accn but advisable design all lab to category B standard.

Provision for changing vital to safety of staff: each lab must contain pegs for lab coats and each unit must store 6 sets protective clothing including boots for each staff member. Discarded clothing must be put in receptacle for autoclaving. Each workr, off and reception area must have handbasin near exit. Staff lockers for outer clothing and personal belongings must be in separate cloakroom. Staff visiting wards must wear separate lab coats for this and these must be stored away from lab. If tea

and snacks not available nearby, rest rm where these can be made must be provided.

Reception area must have bench with impervious disinfection proof finish and handbasin set as in lab (above), with racks for delivered specimens and sto for spare racks etc. Specific area, not within reception or lab, must be provided for patients sent to give blood samples.

Note: pathology lab must not be designed without reference to pathologist in charge.

Laboratory benches

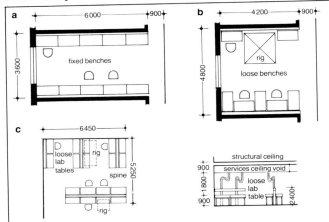

2 **a** 'Nuffield', 24.8 m², fixed benches with fixed service spines along partitions: has been criticised for inflexibility **b** 'Darwin', standard 1 200 × 500 tables associated with 150 × 2400 movable service spine: services & drain have flexible connexions to ceiling & floor points **c** 'Edinburgh', 24.5 m², provides free benches & fixed service spines supplied from vertical ducts: gives greater flexibility of layout

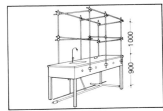

3 Typical bench with rig & built-in service

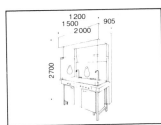

4 Fume cpd

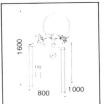

5 Autoclave

6 Deioniser

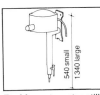

7 Manesty water still small size: output 1.1 l/hr, weight 13.5 kg

1 Pathology dept Eastbourne England DGH 1 escape stair 2 fire escape 3 films 4 lab off 5 pathologist 6 hb & particle mixing 7 coagulation & electrophoresis 8 ante-natal 9 grouping 10 pathologist 11 manual & special 12 sto 13 packing 14 centrifuge 15 blood bank 16 reception 17 wc 18 wr 19 exam 20 clerical 21 chief technician off 22 sterilising 23 outfit preparation rm 24 stacking 25 mech section 26 balance rm 27 chromatography & toxicology 28 chemical sto 29 disposal 30 workshop 31 microbiology lab 32 media preparation 33 print rm 34 dark rm 35 studio 36 records 37 med photographer 38 wc **a** female **b** male 39 staff rm 40 fluorescent microscopy 41 cold rm 42 hot rm 43 histology sto 44 pathologist off 45 serology lab 46 cytology lab 47 Specimen cutting 48 histology lab 49 staining & sections 50 pathology gas sto 51 mechanised section 52 wash-up

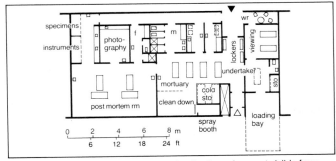

8 Mortuary & post mortem rm: locate loading bay where not visible from main P or visitor ar; viewing rm not clinical in character; hospital chapel sometimes used for this purpose; good ventilation needed

PHARMACY

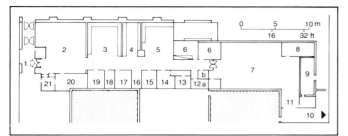

1 Pharmacy Eastbourne England DGH 1 staff entrance 2 issue ar
3 dispensary 4 wash-up ar 5 bulk preparation ar 6 dangerous drugs &
poisons sto 7 bulk sto 8 chargeable empties 9 inflammable liquids
10 incinerator 11 goods entrance 12 clo **a** female **b** male 13 aseptic rm
14 sterile preparation rm 15 quality control 16 sterilising rm 17 staff rm
18 deputy pharmacist 19 chief pharmacist 20 general off 21 reception lob

Many large hospitals manufacture pharmaceuticals as well as dispensing them. Some hospitals serve satellite hospitals, health centres, clinics and individual outpatients: check policies before starting design.

Because goods delivered can be bulky and heavy main loading dock should be used; but because can be inflammable, explosive, corrosive, fragile, require special environment for sto: if (UK) Dangerous Drug Act (DDA) drugs, poisons, or other poisons liable to misuse, must be delivered to specially designed protected area with access for authorised persons only; DDA drugs must be transported in locked containers at all times.

Sto areas should provide floor sto for large items, adjustable shelving for smaller items (300 for normal, 100 for small). Inflammable sto may contain items from other dept: must be isolated from main bldg (refer to current legislation controlling design and use). Cool sto for drugs must be kept remote from any heat source, including sun; these sto often within security sto: should be internal with controlled access (refer current legislation for design and use). Bulk sto: divide into liquid and dry powder areas; allow for storing heavy items on floor; pallet and fork-lift systems suitable for some items; allow ample room for manoeuvring fork-lift.

Preparation areas include large floor-mounted mixers and steam-heated pans for manufacture; small lab may be required for quality control. Required also: machine to reduce items to unit packs; sterile area to prepare and package material for autoclaving, which requires inspection, labelling and sto areas. Install autoclaves (large floor mounted machines) against walls so can be maintained from outside sterile area. Stills for manufacturing distilled water require piped connexion to sterile preparation area. All sterile areas require special dust-free finishes comply with stringent requirements of med inspectorate. Wash-up area requires sink, washing eqp, drying cabinets and shelving for clean and returned containers.

Dispensing and messenger service area with ante-rm for empties should have counter and security sto for pharmacy boxes awaiting distribution. Hospitals which dispense to individual outpatients need separate counter and waiting area for this.

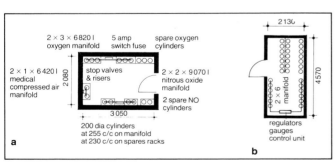

2 **a** Manifold rm for small hospital **b** combined manifold & sto rm; gases normally sto: oxygen, nitrous oxide, nitrous oxide/oxygen, compressed air – *must not be put with hydrogen or acetylene;* sto must be on ground level for access for delivery vehicles from open air, not from cor; single storey, non-combustible, 1 hr fr min, 2 brick walls or equivalent; sto normally takes manifolds & racks for spare cylinders; typical automatic manifold with 2 duty & 2 reserve cylinders: 1 630 × 610 deep: 1 extra cylinder each side gives 510 extra l; 2 × manifold – 3 600

LIBRARY

2 types of hospital lib, professional for med and nursing staff, lending for patients; libraries also →p129 145–8.

Professional normally attached educational areas; med and nursing lib traditionally separate. Both require bookstacks (16 books/m) with space for browsing, work tables and, if requested, study carrels →(3) and security barriers at entrance and exit. Area 140 m² for general hospital with post-graduate med training and similar space for nurse training school lib. Hospital without these activities will require approx 46 m² for each profession.

Patients' lib will serve both ambulant and bedfast and open for limited periods during day. 600-bed hospital may have 5000 books in area 65 m². Provide bookstacks (26 books/m), chairs and tables usable by elderly and disabled →(4)(5). Bedfast patients served at bedside from book trolley (cart) →(6). Adjustable shelving needed take large print books. Permissible floor loading in these areas should be checked as books can weigh up to 30 kg/m run of 5 shelf stacks. All lib need small workr (10 m²) and book sto with shelving (5 m²).

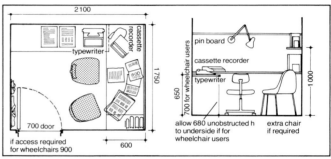

3 Study carrel, provided for med & nursing staff; also suitable for P studying for exam

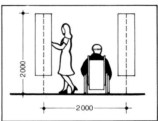

4 General lib: recommended min space between bookstacks

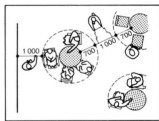

5 General lib: informal layout of table & chairs

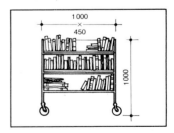

6 Lib trolley (cart) for taking round wards

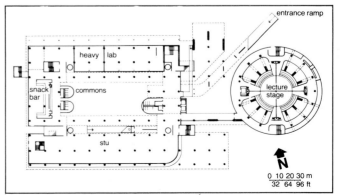

7 Layout of teaching centre Knight Campus University of Rhode Island USA

Hospitals

NON-RESIDENT STAFF CHANGING

As proportion of part-time staff to full-time increases percentage of total staff on duty at any 1 time tends to decrease. In all instances estimate of av number of staff on duty at any 1 time approx 20% of total employed. If hours worked by part-time staff reduced, eg to 30 hr/week, percentages of staff on duty slightly lower.

staff on duty	% of total staff
full-time staff only	19
1 full-time : 2 part-time	18
1 full-time : 4 part-time	17.5
1 full-time : 10 part-time	17

1   Max percentage of staff on duty at any 1 time: only immediate circulation ar included; entrances & main corr vary according to location & number of staff involved

basis of allocation	approx total ar/P m²
a lockers allocated on permanent basis, changing & sto combined	
i locker 300 × 550 × 1800	0.8
ii locker 200 × 550 × 1800	0.72
b lockers allocated on temporary basis, changing & sto combined	
i locker 300 × 550 × 1800	0.43
ia with small permanently allocated lockers adjacent	0.5
c hanging baskets allocated on permanent basis: sto of baskets behind counter, changing separate or adjacent	
i single tier hanging baskets	0.84
ii 2-tire hanging baskets	0.63
d hanging baskets allocated on temporary basis: sto of baskets behind counter, changing separate or adjacent	
i single tier hanging basket	0.48
ia with small permanently allocated lockers adjoining	0.55
ii 2-tier hanging baskets	0.34
iia with small permanently allocated lockers adjacent	0.41

2   Space required by each employee for storing & changing clothes

	acnn provided	ar m²
female staff	3 wc with hb 2 separate hb 2 sho 1 chemical disposal bin	25.92
male staff	2 wc with hb 3 urinals 5 separate hb 2 sho	25.92
waiting ar (peak use by 20 staff)	informal arrangement of comfortable seating & low tables	23.23

3   Ancillary accn provided on peak use figures (peak use by 36 staff)

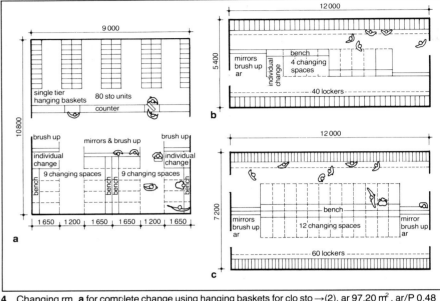

4   Changing rm **a** for complete change using hanging baskets for clo sto →(2), ar 97.20 m², ar/P 0.48 m², ar/P with personal locker 0.55 m²; **b** for staff required to change down to underclothes; locker 300 × 500 × 1800; 1 changing space: 8 sto lockers; **c** for staff required to remove outdoor clothing; locker 200 × 550 × 1800; 1 changing space: 5 sto lockers

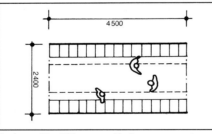

5   Layout for 150 personal lockers near user's work station

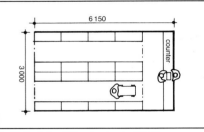

6   Bulk sto for 384 sets clean uniform

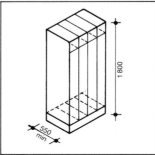

7   Bulk sto for supply & disposal bags from lau: 10–12 disposal bags cater approx 300 staff/week

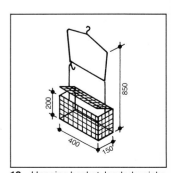

8   Clearances for lockers

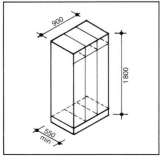

9   Locker for staff required to remove outdoor clothing only

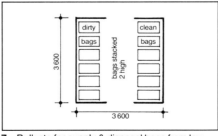

10   Locker for staff required to change down to underclothes eg nurses

11   Small personal lockers near user's work station

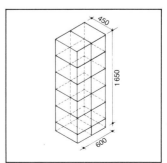

12   Hanging basket: loaded weighs about 8 kg

Hospitals

code no	space	unit ar m²	spaces	total ar
1	business off: clerks	65	1	65
2	business off: manager	11	1	11
3	staff lockers	3	1	3
4	staff lounge	7	1	7
5	credit/collections off: credit manager	9	1	9
6	credit/collections: off	7	1	7
7	accounting off: comptroller	11	1	11
8	accounting off: secretary	7	1	7
9	accounting off: accountants	9	3	28
10	accounting off: payroll	9	1	9
11	accounting/audit: conference	15	1	15
12	cashier: office	9	1	9
	net ar total			181
	grossing factor (50%)			90
	gross ar total			271

1 Off space allocations

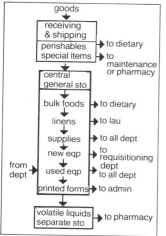

2 CGS allocations

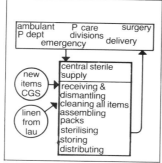

3 CGS functional relationships

Commodity	number of B served								
	2000	3000	4000	5000	6000	7000	8000	9000	10000
sto ar									
dry provisions	90	125	145	170	190	215	245	270	295
cold sto provisions	25	35	50	60	70	85	95	105	120
staff uniforms	45	65	80	95	105	120	140	155	170
P clothing	5	10	10	10	15	15	15	20	20
cleaning materials	20	25	35	40	40	45	50	55	60
hardware & crockery	25	35	45	50	55	60	70	75	85
bedding & linen	15	20	25	30	35	40	45	55	60
printing & stationery	95	130	155	175	195	220	245	275	300
dressings (exc CSSD)	45	60	70	80	85	95	105	115	125
CSSD dressings	20	25	30	35	35	40	40	45	50
med & surgical sundries	60	75	95	110	125	145	160	180	195
disposables	50	65	85	95	110	130	145	160	180
disposable bedpans & urinals	60	75	100	110	130	155	175	185	210
ex-local authority items	65	90	105	125	140	160	180	200	215
total sto ar	620	835	1030	1185	1330	1525	1710	1895	2085
non-sto ar	370	390	425	465	475	490	520	555	565
basic total sto ar	990	1225	1455	1650	1805	2015	2230	2450	2650
recommended total sto ar	1050	1310	1560	1770	1940	2170	2400	2640	2860

4 DHHS guide to planning central sto: required sto ar in m² with working h between 6000 & 6500 & sto up to 5 pallets h

OFFICES

As in other industries and services demand for admin space grows alarmingly. Can be thought of as having 2 components, 1 which processes information and 1 which uses it. Processors: such dept as med records, data processing, accounting; users: such dept as hospital admin, med staff, financial control. Admissions combine both.

Space requirement for each component different: for processing dept factors: volume and type of information and eqp used or projected to be used: input changing rapidly as data processing advances; for user dept people determine spaces.

Individual office spaces similar commercial offices →p235-8.

People form prime design consideration: admin workers generally spend all day at their posts; pleasant environment accordingly important. Patient and med staff interface crucial. Privacy of interviews, particularly about things med and/or financial must be considered.

Typical space allocations for hospital offices in USA →(1).

SUPPLY STORES & DISPOSAL

Nearly all goods, except sometimes pharmaceuticals and often food, received and disposed centrally. UK figures suggest daily av weight goods handled in hospital 30 kg/B, waste produced 19 kg/B.

Considerations relating to central general stores (CGS):

Function: receiving sto, distribution of goods, supplies and movable eqp; inventory control.

Main planning options: use of disposables or reusables? Systems for materials handling, conveying and transport; remote sto possibilities.

Key space: service court for vehicles, sized for separate access to bldg entry points for various types service traffic →(2). Receiving dock with levellers. Warehouse: special/secure sto areas.

Main design issues: separation of incoming goods from outgoing material (supplies, eqp, perishables, trash, refuse, soiled goods); separate receipt and handling of foodstuffs; internally segregated sto and control of goods (central supply sto (CSS), pharmacy, engineering); special sto requirements: med gases, volatile liquids.

Items classified as fragile, or needing light, moisture or dust control, need special arrangements. Items with high security risk (eg radioactive material, dangerous drugs, inflammable gases, volatile material) must be stored in accordance with legislation and reg. Guide to UK areas required →(4).

Sto areas at point-of-use must allow for extra space required during public holiday periods when portering staff not available. Usual holiday (UK): 72-hr period 4 or 5 times/year →(5).

Conveying methods vary from hand-pushed trolleys (carts) to automatic conveyor systems; UK experience suggests automated system, needing trained maintenance engineers, cannot be justified on savings expected in labour costs: such systems vulnerable to mech failure or industrial action.

CENTRAL STERILE SUPPLY

What happens: centralised receipt, cleaning, packing, sterilisation, sto and distribution of reusable supplies (UK central sterilised supply depot (CSSD)). Special sterile processing of goods used in patient care dept, particularly surgery, obstetrics, emergency. Functional relationships →(3).

Main planning options: closeness of relationship to other materials handling functions: CGS, lau against traditional ties to certain users: surgery, obstetrics. Means of conveyance for sterile goods (dedicated or general use systems).

Key spaces: decontamination, sterile processing preparation, sto and issue.

Main design issues: strict separation of dirt and clean work areas, use of steriliser bank to form separation; location of sterilisation function for surgical instruments.

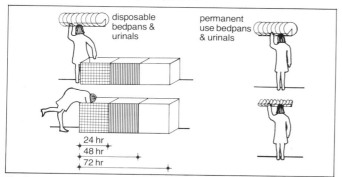

5 Sto requirements at point-of-use over 72-hr holiday period for disposable & permanent use items: disposable items increase space required

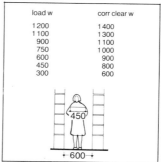

load w	corr clear w
1200	1400
1100	1300
900	1100
750	1000
600	900
450	800
300	600

6 w of load carried related to w of corr on sto ar

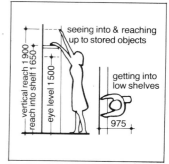

7 Reach & space requirements for av woman collecting sto

Hospitals

HOUSEKEEPING

What happens: regular, thorough cleaning all parts hospital with special emphasis on infection control in patient care areas and with respect related materials flow; refuse disposal. Option: linen handling. Relationships diagram →(1).

Main planning options: determine effect on work load of cleanliness standard desired, extent of air-conditioning/air filtration, ease of cleaning and maintaining interior finishes. Manual or mech means of conveying trash (*eg* pneumatic tube system)? Manner and means of trash disposal (→lau/linen services).

Key spaces: housekeeping materials sto (*ie* maids/janitors cpd, eqp sto); staff training area/admin.

Main design issues: size and distribution of cpd; centralisation of eqp/materials sto.

LAUNDRY/LINEN SERVICE

What happens: dirty linen collected at points of use, conveyed to centralised sorting stations; washed, extracted, dried, mended, ironed, stored. Clean linen distributed user dept according quantity and time schedules. If outside commercial service used linen counted and weighed when sent and received; dirty collection and clean distribution functions remain unaffected.

Main planning options: linen load: operating policies on linen use depend upon disposals against reusables →p179(5). Dirty linen collection system: handling and accumulation at points of use, means of conveyance to sorting station, infection control, volume of cart/trolley traffic, overall cleanliness. Clean linen distribution: cart/trolley system to user dept, sto system in units. Inventory control: preventing wasteful use, excessive wear, loss from pilfering.

Key spaces: dirty collection and holding: hamper packing, chutes and vestibules. Lau: area, shape and height for efficient handling of material and for employee comfort. Clean linen distribution and sto: cart/trolley parking, shelf-cabinet sto.

Main design issues: degree of decentralisation in bed units of nurse work areas and supplies/linen sto. Pneumatic system expense against general cleanliness in patient units and corridors. Functional relationships →(2).

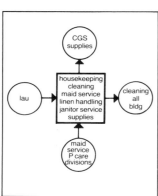

1 Housekeeping relationships

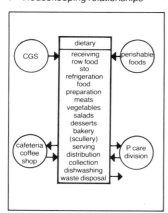

3 Food service relationships

DIETARY SERVICES

Most space-consuming of all service elements.

What happens: meal service to several hospital populations: inpatients, staff, ambulant patients, visitors. Procurement, diet planning, food preparation, distribution to inpatients by transport means, others by serving line and dining rm; dishwashing and cleaning of dirty returns.

Main planning options: form of distribution: bulk transport from central kitchen to local stations in patient units against centralised tray make-up →(4).

Key spaces: central kitchen: receiving and sto, preparation, cooking, dish-washing, scullery, waste, trash and garbage disposal. Dining (for staff, visitors, ambulant patients); service line, table seating; local distribution stations; nursing floor kitchens or pantries.

Main design issues: means of distribution of inpatient meals. →Functional relationships food services →(3).

In UK trend towards tray service from kitchen as opposed bulk supplies to ward →(5): patients can choose menu day before. Food may travel several km before reaching destination: insulated trays and plates on heated carts/trolleys essential. Diet kitchen provides both med and ethnic diets.

Machinery noise and vibration can be disturbing, particularly potato peelers, food mixers and central wash-up machinery. All ventilators and grilles removable and washable. Floors and walls: impervious easy clean finish; floors non-slip; floor drains must have grease traps.

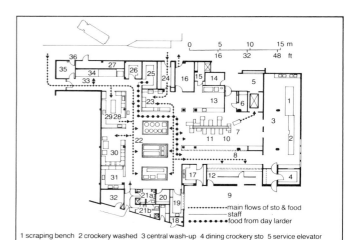

1 scraping bench 2 crockery washed 3 central wash-up 4 dining crockery sto 5 service elevator to wards 6 eqp sto 7 cart/trolley 8 dining servery 9 staff dr 10 conveyor belt 11 ward servery 12 barrier rail 13 diet k 14 diet off 15 la 16 refuse sto 17 still rm 18 sto 19 tea bar 20 chef off 21 clo **a** female **b** male 22 main k 23 vegetable preparation 24 vegetable sto 25 day la 26 dry goods sto 27 plant rm 28 fish preparation 29 meat preparation 30 pastry preparation 31 pot wash 32 domestic supervisor 33 corr 34 meat fresh 35 catering officer 36 ramp Arch Derek Shaw & Partners

5 Kitchen area Wycombe DGH England, serves 650 meals/sitting; individual food plates prepared for P on conveyor belt; filled tray taken by trolley to wards by lift; used trays & crockery washed centrally

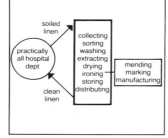

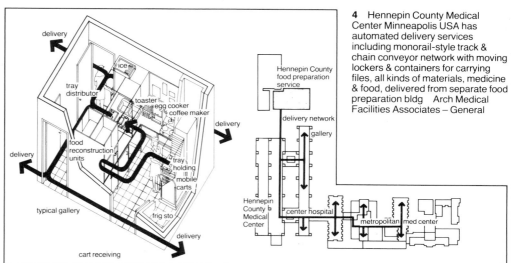

2 Lau/linen service relationships

4 Hennepin County Medical Center Minneapolis USA has automated delivery services including monorail-style track & chain conveyor network with moving lockers & containers for carrying files, all kinds of materials, medicine & food, delivered from separate food preparation bldg Arch Medical Facilities Associates – General

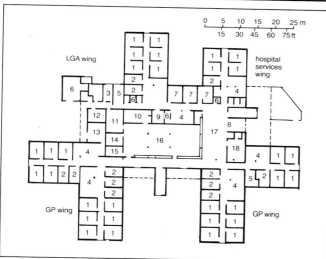

1   Clydebank Scotland HC ground floor with wings for local health authority, hospital services & GP, some amenities being shared 1 consult 2 interview 3 dispense 4 waiting 5 staff 6 wc 7 treatment 8 lob 9 test 10 typist 11 sterile sto 12 sto 13 leisure eqp 14 switchboard 15 secretary 16 records & reception 17 entrance 18 play centre

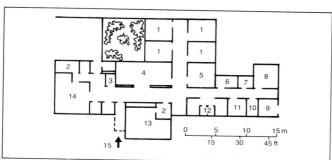

2   Crieff Scotland HC 1 consult 2 sto 3 clo 4 wr 5 health visitor 6 telephone 7 k 8 staff 9 boiler 10 dispense 11 clo 12 toilets 13 reception 14 treatment 15 entrance

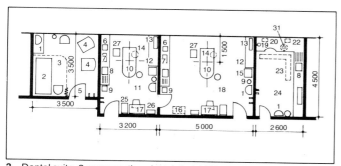

3   Dental suite, 2-man practice; dental chair (165–200 kg), dental unit (51 kg) need firm fixing to floor; services required: water, waste, gas, el, compressed air 1 hb 2 couch 3 curtain 4 armchairs 5 recovery rm 6 steriliser 7 aspirator 8 sk 9 disposal 10 dental chair 11 small dental surgery 12 worktop 13 dental eqp cabinet 14 operating lamp 15 cart/trolley 16 anaesthetic cart/trolley 17 desk 18 large dental surgery 19 gas outlet 20 bench with bench pin 21 waste hole bin below 22 dust extract 23 duckboard 24 dental workshop 25 filing 26 DDA cpd 27 dental unit

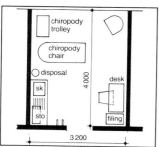

4   Chiropody rm, 11.0 m²

COMMUNITY HEALTH CARE

Community health care in UK, alongside general practitioner (GP), now principally provided by health centre (HC). In USA 'free-standing' ambulatory units fall into several categories, in addition to physician's office, generally with twofold aim providing preventative medicine and making available health care at lower cost than involved in full hospital treatment. Each such unit starts with programme worked out meet market needs within service area, community or region. Various types unit include Health Maintenance Organization (HMO), founded some 40 years ago as alternative insurance programme for industrial workers, primary care centres in rural areas for emergency exam and treatment (include pre-hospital beds), community health and social centres usually founded by local or regional government. Each of these may contain some, all or more services than UK HC. Larger ones often attached hospitals.

HC primary activities: consult, exam and minor treatment backed by med records, reception, waiting and sto areas. Basic amenities must include: pram and car parking, wc for patients and staff, changing areas, rest rm with kitchenette for staff.

Secondary activities for large HC may include diagnostic and treatment services – physiotherapy, chiropody, dentistry, radio diagnosis and pharmacy – and health clinics for education and assessment, off for health visitors, domiciliary nurses, social workers etc.

Viable size for HC consulting resources for not less than 6 GP, but as vital to place HC near population served may be smaller and less well equipped in rural areas.

On basis 1 GP has approx 2500 patients, centre for 6 GP will serve population of 15000 and for 12 GP 30000. Assume health visitor can cover approx 3500 and district nurse 2500 people.

Sites must be near public transport routes; access from roads and car parks must be designed for wheelchair →p19 43 166 and pram users. Entrances should be protected from rain and prevailing winds and have covered and well supervised pram park. Allow for protected disposal area for waste: check with local authority or health authority how to be collected. Large centres may require separate staff and service entrance; patients entrance may need canopy high enough take ambulance →p166(2). HC grounds should be attractive but simply landscaped for min maintenance.

Many rm in HC serve same purpose as equivalent rm in OPD: same layout can be used with minor adaptations. Main difference: HC do not deal with such large numbers of patients; nor do they deal with acute med and surgical cases needing sophisticated diagnostic and treatment eqp. Rm which can be adapted for HC are set out →p166–7; most important are: wheelchair wc p167(6), disposal rm, p167(8), clinette & urine test rm, p167(5), ambulance dimensions, p166(2), automatic doors, p166(4), disabled patients car parking, p166(3).

Waiting
Provide general waiting area. Small forward waiting areas required for each group of consult rm. Assuming appointment system, allow 7.0 m² waiting area for each suite. Seating should be comfortable and informal.

Med records
Med records in 2 sizes: standard 175 × 125, new A4 in folders 310 × 240. Sto may be in shelves, filing cabinets or rotary filing units. Including access these methods require floor space 1.5–2.0 m²/1000 records. Shelves cheap but offer no security; cabinets expensive but secure and adaptable; rotary not secure and expensive. Allow for increase in numbers of records.

Dental clinic →(3)
Dental clinic for 2-man practice consists of 2 surgeries (1 large enough for principal surgery), recovery rm with couch and basin for post-anaesthesia patients, dental workshop and waiting area plus normal central records and reception area. Allow 9.5 m² waiting area for 2 surgeries. Surgeries should have NE aspect if daylight needed but trend towards theatre-type operating lamps and more mobile eqp. Obscured glazing required for windows.

Chiropody room →(4)
Should be on ground floor or accessible by elevator.

Hospital references:
→Bibliography entries 013 014 017 020 022 024 025 054 218 219 220 262 294 296 303 315 336 337 341 349 354 362 419 420 421 478 525 547 551 559 560 576 577 578 647

Churches

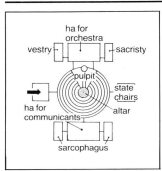

1 Design for Berliner Dom (Lutheran) Germany Arch Schinkel

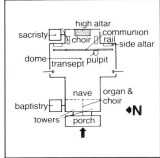

2 Typical Roman Catholic church layout

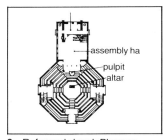

3 Reformed church Planneg Germany Arch T Fischer

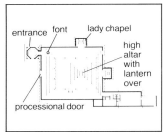

4 St Paul Bow Common (Anglican) London England Arch R Maguire

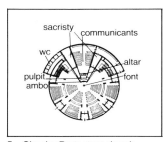

5 Circular Protestant church Essen Germany Arch O Bartning

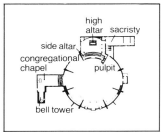

6 Roman Catholic church Cologne-Riehl Germany Arch D Böhm

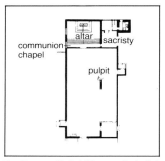

7 Corpus Christi (Roman Catholic) church Aachen Germany Arch R Schwarz

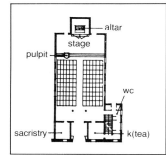

8 Church & parish ha (Reformed) Hanweiler Germany Arch R Krüger

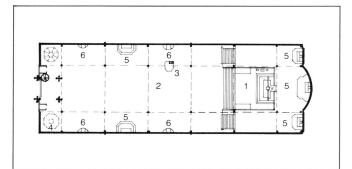

9 Notre Dame du Raincy (Roman Catholic) Paris France Arch A Perret
key 1 sanctuary 2 nave 3 pulpit 4 baptistry 5 secondary altars
6 confessional

GENERAL ARRANGEMENT

Main divisions of Christian churches today: Orthodox (principally Greek and Russian), Reformed, Roman Catholic, separation between Orthodox and Roman dating from earliest history of Christianity, break between Reformed and Roman Catholic from 16th century.

In Roman Catholic churches emphasis now placed on mass in common tongue; altar usually raised. Reformed order of service depends on whether 'high', 'low' or 'free'. Some likeness between forms of Roman Catholic, High Anglican and High Presbyterian (Scotland and USA). Free follow Calvinist and Lutheran origins with emphasis on preaching and communion carried out round 'Lord's Table', usually centrally placed with nearby pulpit either behind table or to left hand side. Baptists need large heated water tank usually under removable floor for inititiation by total immersion. Fonts used almost universally for initiation into main groups and dedication into others. Many newer religious sects have idiosyncratic requirements related to special forms and musical performances. In USA Protestant churches have approx 70 million members, Roman Catholic 50 million, Orthodox 4 million.

Churches throughout world now have strong community concern; planning often relates to weekday uses; keyword flexibility. Ancillary accn, according to programme, may incorporate, eg coffee rm, counselling rm, meeting rm, radio station. Car parking must be taken into account. Centralised plan popular; but ritualistic, processional and oblong forms also used. However, importance of priest, pastor or leader should not be lost; liturgical functions carried out by individual churches of great importance in design.

More recently new factors have emerged, among them security of church property, adequate acoustic design (for music and voice) and provision for disabled.

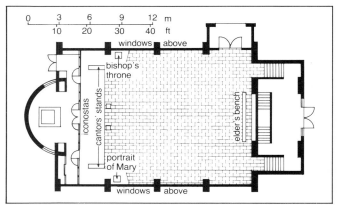

10 Orthodox church of St Sava McKeesport USA Arch Pekruhn

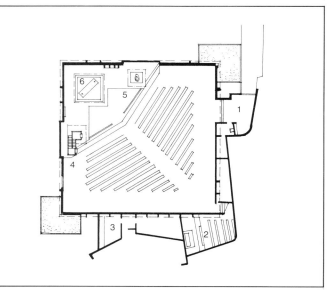

11 St Michael Hatfield Hyde (Anglican) Welwyn Garden City England Arch Clarke Hall Scorer & Bright
key 1 entrance 2 chapel 3 vestry 4 pulpit & lectern 5 baptistry 6 altar with baldachino

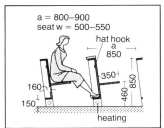

a = 800–900
seat w = 500–550
hat hook
a
850
350
160
850
460
150
heating

1 Seating without knee rail

a = 850–950
b = 50–140
seat w = 500–550
a
900
100
160

2 Seating with knee rail

INTERIORS, FURNISHINGS

Seating

In some churches provision for worshippers to kneel not necessary →(1); in others simple hassock or kneeler incorporated in bench →(2). Most important measurement for benches with kneelers: distance of outside edge of kneeler, when folded down, from perpendicular dropped from arm rest: approx 175–200.

Area/seat required: without kneeling rail 0.4–0.5 m² →(1); with kneeling rail 0.43–0.52 m² →(2).

Aisles

Dimensions →(3)–(6). Cold radiation from external walls makes side aisles advantageous. Central aisle useful for processional entry and exit in larger churches. In UK aisle should be provided for every 8–10 persons length of bench (benches more than 10 persons long need aisle at each end – in USA more than 7 persons). Including aisles allow 0.63–1.0 m²/P. For standing allow 0.25–0.35 m²; on crowded occasions wall space and rear aisles may be used. Width of exit doors and stairs should comply with reg for places of assembly →p401.

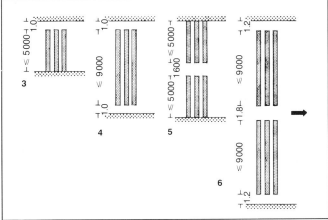

3–6 Aisle w

Pulpit

Requirements vary from church to church →(7)(8)(10). Usually raised with steps; but growing practice also place on level of sanctuary or raised 1 step. In Roman Catholic churches pulpit now likely be replaced by 2 ambos or reading desks, 1 at each side. In 'free' churches pulpit of central importance. In all churches essential preacher be visible to whole congregation.

Altars →(9)

In Reformed churches altar usually placed close rear wall; may have passage at back. Many Roman Catholic and some Anglican churches now have altar in centre of sanctuary: priest or celebrant stands behind to face congregation for purpose of worship.

Roman Catholic and some Anglican churches have sacrament house or tabernacle (small decorated cupboard with lockable doors, bolted down and immovable: →catalogues of church furnishers): may be in side chapel or on plinth behind main altar, some 2000 away. Separate side chapel sometimes desired.

Font

Used for baptism; often symbolically placed in or near entry of church, though in Protestant churches in USA sometimes placed conveniently for baptism to form part of main service. May be 1 or 2 steps lower than, and separate from, main body of church (baptistry →p182(2)(9)(11)), with room for up to 30 people to stand during baptism. For Baptist churches immersion tank →p182.

Confessional boxes

Best placed in aisles: separate compartments for priest and penitent →(13). Construction must be sound proof.

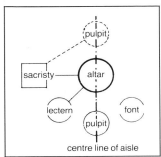

pulpit
sacristy — altar
lectern   font
pulpit
centre line of aisle

7 Pulpit & altar in same axis

sacristy — altar
pulpit   lectern
font
centre line of aisle

8 Pulpit sideways to altar

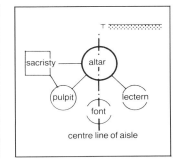

1000 800 2000
950
150   50
1000   250

9 Altar table for small reformed churches

⌀ 2200
⌀ 1000 1100
light   1050

10 Pulpit (microphones have made sounding board unnecessary)

350 550
1100

11 Lectern

⌀ 600
900

12 Font

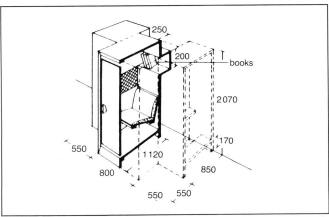

250
200 — books
2070
170
550
1120
800   850
550 550

13 Confessional box

Churches

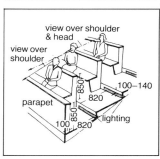

1   Gallery seating tiered, risers with lighting: must be possible see altar or at least pulpit over heads of occupants of second row in front

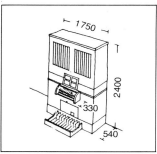

2   Small organ (Walcker type) with 15 stops for church ha & smaller churches

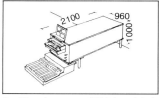

3   Chamber organ (Walcker-Jahn) with about 275 pipes for ha

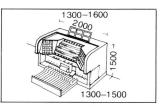

4   Organ with manual closed by roller shutter

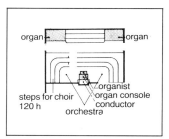

5   Organ & choir: organ console in front of conductor, organ divided

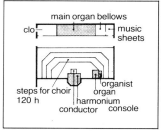

6   Organ & choir with harmonium & organ placed to each side, otherwise as **5**

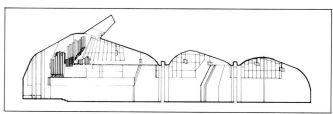

7   Section through Vuoksenniska church Imatra Finland with gallery & organ   Arch Aalto

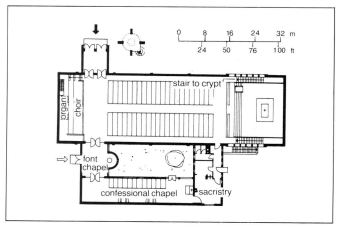

8   Roman catholic parish church with organ & choir gallery at W end   Arch Schwarz

GALLERIES, ORGAN

Galleries

Increase seating capacity for same area; also improve acoustics if suitable distance from pulpit: common in Reformed churches. Have tiered seating so that congregation at back may see and hear better. Convenient positions: opposite altar wall (for organ and choir) or sideways opposite pulpit. Height of gallery determined by necessary free sight of congregation beneath it in relation to altar and pulpit. Stairs and exits from galleries must comply with reg for assembly halls. Requirement/P 0.7–1.0 m² inclusive of gangways →(1).

Choir galleries

In front of organ →(5) have 100–150 high steps (increasing front to rear) and are 1 000–1 200 wide. If desirable choir on loose chairs arranged in semi-circle in front of conductor; if necessary organ console can also be in front of conductor with orchestra seats built up behind to achieve unity between organ, orchestra and choir. Next to conductor's desk and organ console large cupboard for music sheets; outside gallery suitable cloakrm for choir members.

Organs

Specialist should be called in for organ installation (acoustic specialist also important). Size of organ (number of voices and stops) not simply relative to size of church as volume variable, but generally:

smaller churches 200–300 m³/voice
medium churches 300–400 m³/voice
larger churches 400–500 m³/voice

Each voice needs width of 2 000–3 000 and 250 depth. Each voice weighs 200 kg therefore 10-stop organ needs area (if 3 000–4 000) h of 10 (3 × 250) = 7.5 m² and weighs 10 × 200 = 2 000 kg, therefore approx 300 kg/m². But organ specialists ask for ≥ 750 kg/m². Height determined by length of pipes. Largest: 32 ft open voice pipe 11 m high with sounding board; is passed through several storeys or may be bent. Determining factor: 8 ft pipe, 3 000 high with sounding board. Therefore storey height for smaller churches may be 3 000–4 000, for larger churches 4 000–5 000. Organ may be divided →(5). Bellows best in separate rm if possible. Organ builder should be consulted at planning stage, also regarding appearance of visual pipes.

In USA organs often electronic.

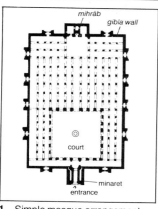

1 Simple mosque arrangement: Tlemcen Mosque of al-Mansur 1303–1306 AD

2 Friday Mosque Isfahan: 8th–17th centuries AD

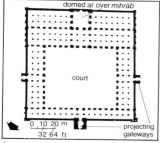

3 Mosque of az-Zāhir Baybars: 1266–9 AD

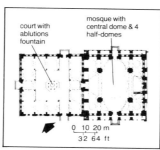

4 Mosque & court Sehzade Mehmet Istanbul: 16th century Arch Sinān

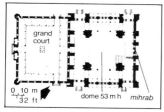

5 Süleymaniye complex including mosque Istanbul; covers 60 000 m² & includes numerous ancillary bldg Arch Sinān

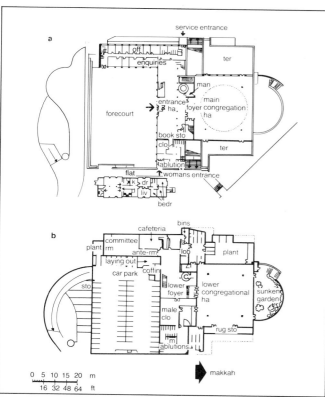

6 London central mosque **a** ground floor **b** lower ground floor Arch Gibberd & Partners

Mosque place of prayer for Muslims: not necessarily bldg. Term derives from *masjid,* meaning prostration. Prayer as community act not mentioned in *Quran* but derives from prophet Mohammed's Friday communal meetings. Friday sermon (*khutba*) set piece, made from top of stairs (*minbar*), often incorporated as feature.

Early mosques characterised by wide and shallow shape →(1)(2) to enable ranked formation of beilievers face *mihrab* wall. (*Mihrab* itself is niche resembling door: highly decorated feature in later examples.)

Holy mosque at Mecca, most holy sanctuary of Islam, to which all mosques should preferably face (arrows in illustrations), houses *ka'bah*. *Ka'bah* stands in huge courtyard surrounded by arcaded precinct which forms pattern for many subsequent examples. However, mosques vary extensivey throughout Islam from square village hall types to great historical examples in Egypt, Syria, Spain, Iran, Turkey and India. Few purpose built examples in W: many sects, with varying needs, adapt or rent existing bldg for Friday prayers and for the two *id* celebrations, for Islamic new year and end of Ramadan.

3 main types of traditional mosque: early open plan, usually to be found in desert regions; central court, patterned after Mohammed's house at Medina; open court, with 4 vaulted halls (*iwans*) 1 on each side of court.

Mosque bldg have followed climatic needs for shade through use of arcades, colonnades and courtyards incorporating areas of water – most important for ablutions but also for cooling. These elements often used symbolically in designs and heavily ornamented or planned as landscape features round mosques. Main architectural feature *mihrab* basic to all mosques: set in wall facing Mecca (*kibla* wall), often emphasised by windows or by dome above. Monumental grandeur of mosque came largely through need to enclose activities in harsher northern climates but also related to advances in vault construction in 11th and 12th centuries AD; thus domed *mihrab* area was enlarged by single vault prayer hall or 4 vault *iwans* or *liwans* arranged symmetrically around court. Tendency use this pattern with open or closed courts according to climate.

Minaret
'Call to prayer' tower often attached to mosque: name derives from 'lighthouse'. After introduction of loudspeakers little used for calling. Types vary from none to cylindrical needle minarets in glazed tile with 1 high gallery, common in Iran; type with 2–3 galleries capped with wood cones and based on polygonal plan in Turkey; often 2–6 minarets per mosque in some countries, depending on size.

Segragation
Male worshippers only in most mosques although gallery for women often found. Some sects, eg Ishmailis, fully integrated.

Ablutions
Requirement of the faith; modern western examples →(7) include these with other toilet arrangements in part of bldg next to nearby congregation hall.

Planning
Because of ranked formation allow 680–1 250/standing P in congregation hall. Carpets and other floor coverings required as faithful are barefoot: sto space for shoes required. Axial layout common but open courtyard for prayers useless in W climates.

Decoration
Accepted generally should be non-representational although not decreed. This rigidly observed tradition, however, allows free use of calligraphic devices from *Quran* which forms valuable counterpart to plain surfaces and basic architectural forms.

Synagogues

No formal architectural precedent for synagogues (literally 'assembly'); tend to follow architectural style of country in which built. Dual function of place of worship and of social or community meetings tends demand complex of bldg. 3 divisions of Jewry all require space for prayers; conservative and reform Jews use choir and organ but orthodox Jews do not use instrumental music.

Liturgical furniture consists of: *ark,* focal point generally at E containing scrolls; *paroches,* curtain-type covering; candelabrum to right; pulpit for rabbi and cantor. Furniture mounted on *berna,* raised platform at centre (orthodox) or end of hall (conservative, reform).

Second commandment proscribes 'making of graven images', so ornamentation floral or geometric.

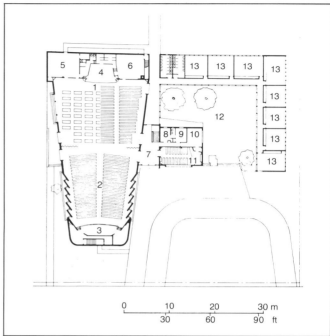

3   Beth Israel Synagogue & school Omaha USA: seats 650 in sanctuary & extra 800 in congregational assembly ha; courtyard provides additional multi-use flexibility 1 congregational h 2 synagogue 3 rostrum 4 stage 5 k 6 sto & uty 7 foyer 8 cantor 9 rabbi 10 off 11 chapel 12 court 13 classrm   Arch Kivett & Myers

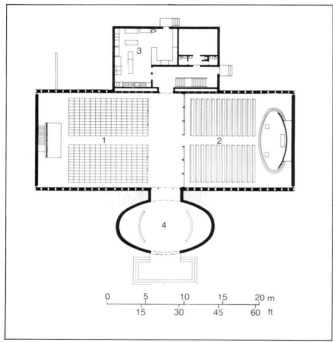

1   KTI Synagogue New York: accommodates up to 1 000; note flexible space for social and/or religious use 1 social ha 2 sanctuary 3 k 4 entrance foyer Arch Philip Johnson

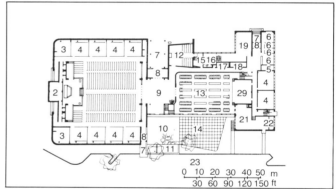

4   Temple Beth El USA: normal seating 1 000 can be extended to 1 600; bldg includes provision for religious education, lib & dramatic presentations 1 temple 2 retiring rm 3 chair sto 4 classr 5 supply & mimeograph rm 6 off 7 covered entrance 8 vestibule 9 lob 10 temple garden 11 pool 12 chapel 13 social ha 14 social garden 15 ante-rm 16 rabbi off 17 women 18 men 19 lib 20 stage 21 k 22 dressing rm 23 driveway   Arch Percival Goodman

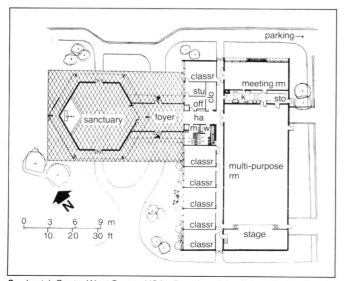

2   Jewish Centre West Orange USA: all week social, religious & educational use; chapel seats 250–350; multi-purpose rm up to 750 on high holy days Arch David Brody Juster & Wisniewski

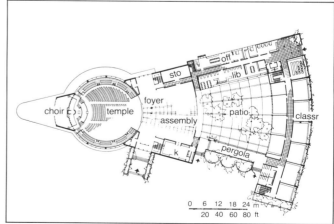

5   Plan of main floor Park Synagogue & community centre Cleveland USA Arch Erich Mendelsohn

Mortuaries and crematoria

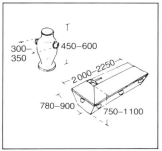

1   Urn & coffin

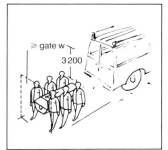

2   Min w needed by bearers

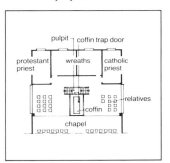

3   Mortuary layouts

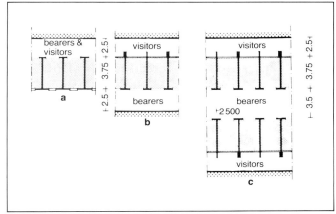

4   Plan of installation with furnace below chapel

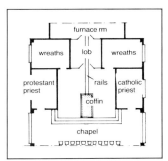

5   Furnace rm behind chapel with intervening lob

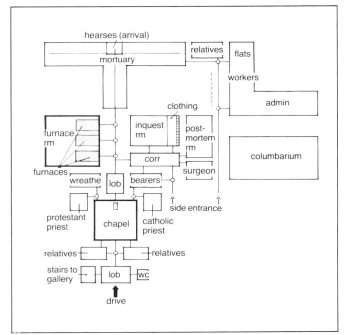

6   Layout of mortuary with crematorium and ancillary rm for large cemetery

MORTUARIES

Dead kept in cells separated by partitions (usually sheet metal, sometimes plants) →(3). In larger mortuaries gangway for bearers separated from visitor's →(3b), from which relatives may see dead through airtight glass panes before funeral service. Protruding piers between cells prevent inconvenience to different groups of mourners →(3b). Usual dimensions of cells:

2200 × 3500
2500 × 3750
3000 × 3500

Temp in mortuary: ≥ 2° to ≤ 12°C; if it fell below min figure frost could expand corpses. This temp range maintained by central heating, air conditioning and, specially in summer, ventilation. Floors mut be impervious, smooth and easy to cleanse; walls best lime washed (frequent renewal advisable). Larger mortuaries also need rm for guard and bearers 15–26 m² inclusive of toilets and lavatories. Stand for hearses also needed.

In city morturaries special rm may be set aside for unidentified bodies with sto for their clothing, next to which locate post-mortem rm and surgery →(6).

CREMATORIA

Furnace room

Should be either on lower floor with lift for coffins →(4) or behind chapel, separated from it by lobby →(5)(6). Horizontal transport with hand-operated winches easiest, hydraulic lifts being necessary for vertical movement. Lobby door or floor trap designed to shut slowly as coffin disappears through opening.

In furnace rm coffin taken from transport carriage and transferred to chamotte grating in furnace. Cremation performed by special coke, el or gas-fired furnace consuming 45 kW per cremation. Height of 2-storey furnace 4300. Cremation completely dust free and odourless by means of 900–1000°C dry air; no flames reach deceased. Furnace pre-heated for 2–3 hr and cremation itself lasts 1–1¼ hr after which ashes gathered in iron box for sto in urn. Cremation supervised through peep-holes.

Chapel

Cremation installations should if possible lie at rear of cemetery chapel, which serves all denominations. Size of chapel varies: must be at least 100 seats and 100 standing places; also 1–2 rm for relatives (which may be added to chapel rm) and such ancillary rm as may prove necessary →(6).

Administration

Conveniently close by chapel should be admin rm: 1 for director, 2–3 offices, coffin sto, flats for cemetery keeper and boilerman etc; nursery can be located nearby, with greenhouse →p105, rm for gardener and landscape architect, worker's rm, sto for eqp and seeds, and toilets.

Urns & gravestones

Often limited in size by cemetery reg →(1); wall niches in columbaria usually 380–400 wide and deep, and 500–600 high.

Shops & stores

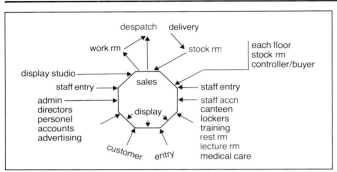

1   Plan analysis of rm & routes of customers & goods

2   Free standing modular shelving units make up major part of furniture in modern establishments

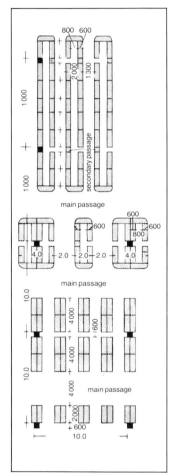

3   Functional display stands for different types of merchandise with units running between equal column centres

SITUATION

Prominent sites in population centres served by convenient public and private transport. Car parking standards in UK, 3.5–5.25 car spaces per 100 m² gross retail area (3–4 changes day). In USA max 150 cars/acre.

Access

Pedestrians, vehicles and delivery traffic should be kept separate; shopping centre best restricted to pedestrians, short connexions (covered to protect from sun and rain) linking parking area and shops. Bus stops or underground railway stations may be adjacent to shopping centre with direct access. Max distance between shopper's car or bus stop or station and principal shops should be 201 m and should be within inner distribution road system.

Space allocation →(1)

Large stores may have lecture and demonstration rm, restaurants, cafes, kindergartens, banks, post office, travel agencies, cinema and garden area →p199–201. Small shops often grouped in shopping centre. Design begins with allocating space to units, conforming to fire and other reg, followed by subdivision into sales areas, internal service areas, joint services etc.

Sales areas

Should be immediately above one another and as near entrance floor as possible. Basement better for selling than additional upper storey, so stock rm and staff rm best located on upper storeys, with offices on highest floor.

Storey heights

For large units, 4000–5000; for small units, 3000 dependent on services (UK practice). Unnecessary floor to floor heights deter customers and are tiring to staff. Shop units do not rely on natural light but on artificial lighting with mech ventilation.

Structural grid

Column dimensions and centres determine lay-out of fittings. Recommended structural grid: large units, between 7300 and 9000 width on frontage and 9150 depth; small units between 5300 and 6000 width on frontage, 18 to 36 m depth front to back.

Aisles

Recommended min aisle width: 1980, subsidiary aisles 990. Counter heights generally 920. System modules vary according to type of shelving and bracketing used.

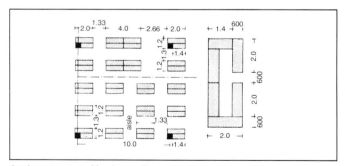

4   Arrangement of furniture units

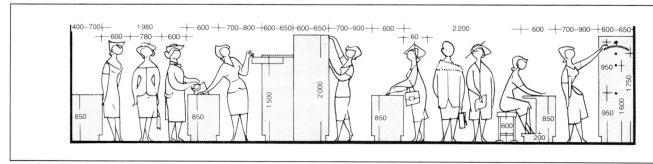

5   Section through shop sales floor with aisle w which have proved practical in use for personal service

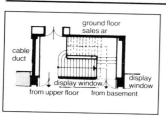

1 Separate exits from basement & upper floors in stair well

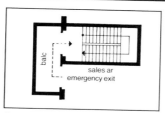

2 Emergency stairs in multi-storey bldg

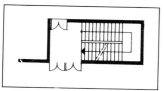

3 Unimpeded exit from stairs

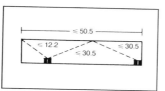

4 Max distance from enclosed staircase in UK

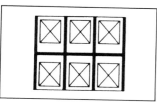

5 Back-to-back arrangement of elevators

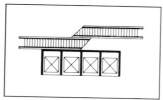

6 Combination of elevators & escalators

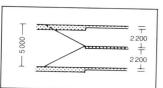

7 Ancillary rm on mezzanine level

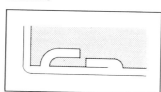

8 Goods delivery in parking bays

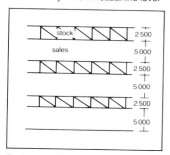

9 Intermediate stockrm floors which take floor structure (in USA stock delivered from ground floor or basement)

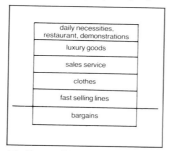

10 Favourable arrangement of goods for efficient selling on sales floor

MOVEMENT BETWEEN FLOORS

Number and widths of staircases →p408 Bib501 628 and exits prescribed by reg. In UK number of staircases related to travel distances, widths of staircases and exits related to occupancy, eg UK practice calculates load as follows: ordinary consumer goods 1.9 m² gross floor area/P; specialised shops 7 m² gross floor area/P.

Different reg govern multi-storey stores and shops, and 1-storey small shops. Except for 1-storey units UK reg require shop bldg to be divided into compartments not exceeding 7080 m³ →fire reg. This prevents use of very large staircases, makes use of escalators difficult and restricts features such as open wells between more than 2 floors →(1)–(4).

In USA determine total occupancy, consult national and local codes: bldg classified by use and fire ratings; open floor areas subject to sprinkler systems, fire curtains, specified exits etc.

Most customers use escalators; elevators available for express service. Numbers of customers to be transported from ground floor estimated from density × storey area × number of storeys (80% on escalators, 20% elevators); this figure must be divided by capacity of transport chosen to give number of elevators and escalators required.

Elevators →p410–2
Should be in groups visible from entrance; in large stores in centre of bldg not more than 50 m from any part of sales floor. May be arranged in groups back to back or in combination with escalators →(5)(6).

In USA elevators only used for carrying goods; not common in new dept stores: nearly all have escalator bands, parallel or scissor.

Escalators →p409
Essential when min of approx 2000 P/hr must be transported; should run in successive series (return flights) to all sales floors, both directions. Best placed in centre of floor visible from all entrances: pitch 30°. In UK may need to be enclosed to comply with fire reg; normally open in USA.

Refreshment rm often on top floor with kitchen and hoist to sto.

Ancillary rm
Wc, telephone booths, staff cloakrm and lavatories commonly placed on mezzanine floor →(7); often placed in basement in USA, also bargains →(10).

Goods delivery
Separated from customer circulation, frequently in goods yard or by delivery ramps. Delivery may be made to goods sto connected to general sto, perhaps with automatic conveyors. If delivery difficult in busy street, parking bays recommended →(8). Circulation through receiving rm, sto rm etc, to selling positions →(10). Refuse and waste has to be handled from dept back to despatch through waste disposal area.

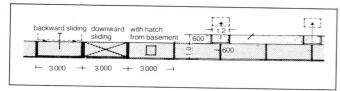

11 Single display window **12** Continuous display window with movable cpd units

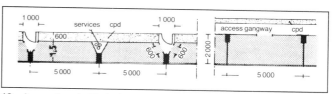

13 Access from behind columns **14** With access gangway

Shops & stores

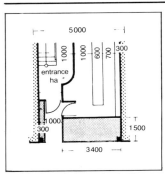

1 Display window extended by having shop entrance behind it & staircase to upper floors set back: internal w of shop min 2600

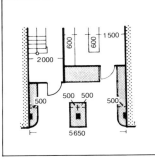

2 Very deep shops often permit extensive display windows, impressive even if shop itself quite small

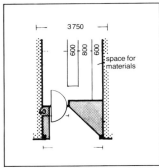

3 Deep shops may have wide vestibules with display windows at angles to entrance, attracting customers away from street traffic

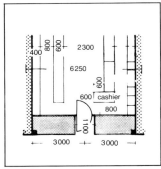

4 Central doors suitable for shops ≥ 6000–6200 wide; counters may be installed on both sides; should be cash/wrap near door

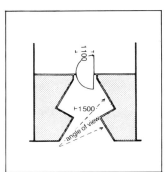

5 For narrow frontage recess entrance to provide larger display area & angles of view through offsets

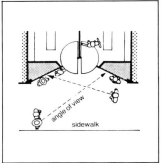

6 By slanting entire window ar & having doors in same line, idea of (5) is developed to its logical conclusion

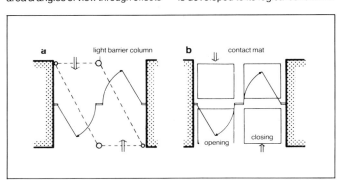

7 Automatic installation for opening & closing doors (1-leaf door with 2-way passage, entrance & exit coupled): **a** photo-el cell & light barrier; **b** contact mat

SERVICE DETAILS

Back-up stock

Either on 1 floor, preferably top sales floor, or on each floor in separate back stock rm area or on low mezzanine floors →p189(9).

Goods transport

By trolley (cart), goods hoist, chute, roller conveyor, conveyor belt, ramp conveyor, spiral chute, fork-lift, palleted trolley.

Display windows

Interchangeable fitments usual in dept stores. In designing window space important give easy access to display, with min loss of display space at back.

Staff entrance →(1)–(8)

Separate from customers, if necessary in conjunction with goods delivery; own stairs to cloakr, which should be 0.4–0.5 m²/P. Staff rm preferably on top floor.

Staff wc

Should be at min rate of 1 for 25 females, 1 for every 25 males up to 100 and 1 for every 40 thereafter; however, ratio of 1:15 recommended, with wash basins *pro rata*. Staff should be provided with drinking water, rest rm, locker rm, drying arrangements for outdoor clothes, control of temp, ventilation and lighting, seating (UK reg).

Building regulations

Consult reg on construction, eqp and finishes of shops and stores. In UK: openings in wall must be of appropriate fr construction and comply with appropriate bldg reg. Division floors must be of approved fr construction with all vertical communication between floors cut off. Floor heights usually governed by general bldg height limits laid down by reg. Sales areas should be min 3000 high.

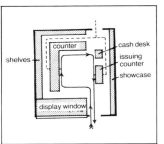

8 Properly placed fittings allow customers to move from entrance to sales counter, cash desk, issuing counter & exit without reverse circulation

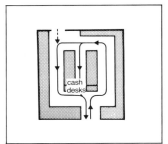

9 No separation between customer & sales staff: whole rm at disposal of customer (self-service)

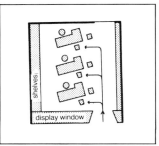

10 Shop for individual consult, fitting tables, *eg* for trying on spectacles in optician

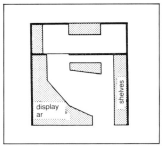

11 Flower shop with large window & display ar: rear of shop for arranging flowers

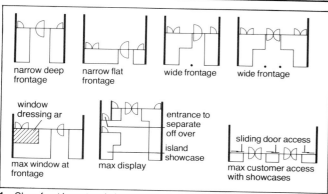

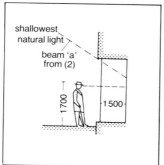

narrow deep frontage

narrow flat frontage

wide frontage

wide frontage

window dressing ar

max window at frontage

max display

entrance to separate off over island showcase

sliding door access

max customer access with showcases

1 Shop front layout variations: deep window plans suitable for fashion, furniture etc, shallow for jewellery, books, stationery etc

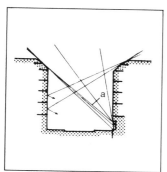

2 Insufficient day or artifical lighting reflects lighter bldg opposite or viewer

shallowest natural light

beam 'a' from (2)

1700

1500

3 Reflection substantially reduced if strong light strikes back on display above eye level of viewer

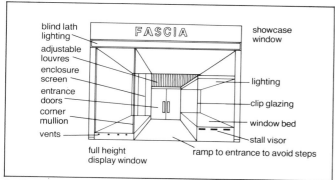

blind lath lighting

FASCIA

showcase window

adjustable louvres

enclosure screen

entrance doors

corner mullion

vents

full height display window

lighting

clip glazing

window bed

stall visor

ramp to entrance to avoid steps

4 Typical shop front components

SERVICE DETAILS

Stock & despatch rooms

Sto and workshops to be separated from sales areas by fr walls and floors (UK reg), these to be treated as separate sto areas and to comply with restrictions on compartment size.

Entrance & exits

In bldg of over 1 500 m^2 usable floor area all yards should have entrances and exits sited as far apart as possible. Entrances and passages: min height and width clearance 3 700 on level ground →UK reg: access for fire appliances. Turning circle for appliance 17 m. Roads to take laden weight of 10.1 t. Distance of any point from entrance max 25 m. On ground floor exits and main aisles for customers to be 1 070 wide for first 200 people, additional 152 for each additional 30 people. Where 2 exits required each opening to be wide enough for full number of occupants. Exit doors to open outwards: no sliding doors →BSI 19xx. Amounts and type of glazing controlled by reg.

Stairs →p408

Preferably on outside walls with direct exit to open air or through entrance hall etc (UK reg). From each part of upper floor min 2 stairs, within distance of 30.5 m. Rm in vicinity of 1 staircase only must be no further away than 15 m.

Width for first 200 people 1 070; additional 152 for each additional 30 people. Rise/going 125–250 min (UK reg). Stairs to basements enter direct from open air or separated from stairs to other floors by lobbies.

All rm for staff and customers must have emergency lighting independent of main lighting. For circulation areas, stairs, exits etc special emergency-lit direction signs.

WINDOWS

Shop window's impact determines its value. Almost useless: dazzling, reflecting panes, deep dark windows near bright pavements: goods for sale can only be seen with effort →(1)(2).

Shop windows now rely for impact on artificial light.

Sun blinds necessary to protect goods on all aspects except N facing. Fascia to take sign: integral to shop front and relative to sun blind.

Cold

Condensation and ice on frosty windows can be avoided for windows connected with shop by warm air circulation over whole area, if necessary by ventilator; for enclosed cases ventilation slots in shop front windows required.

Provision may be needed for fresh air intake into slip through louvres or mech intake over shop window or over doors.

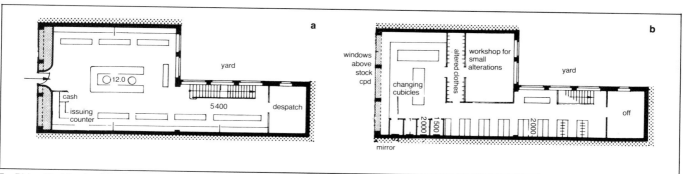

a

yard

12.0

cash
issuing
counter

5 400

despatch

b

windows above stock cpd

changing cubicles

altered clothes

workshop for small alterations

yard

off

2000   1500   2000

mirror

5 Bldg with side wing & back yard (typical layout of rented accn in German cities) suitable for shops: goods for passing trade on ground floor, on upper floor workshops for alteration, fitting rm, stock rm etc; in basement clo, wc & ancillary rm for staff **a** ground floor **b** upper floor

Shops & stores

Commerce

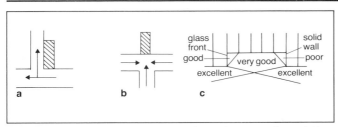

1 Impact siting: **a** max frontage & display; **b** good impact; **c** effects of siting

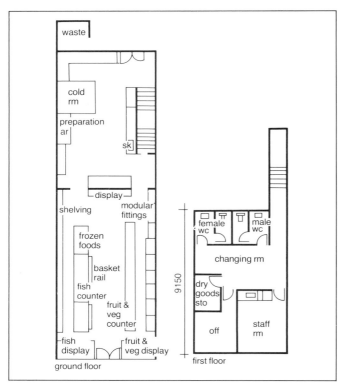

2 Typical shop layout (fish, fruit & vegetable sto)

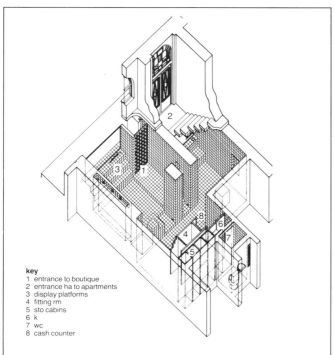

key
1 entrance to boutique
2 entrance ha to apartments
3 display platforms
4 fitting rm
5 sto cabins
6 k
7 wc
8 cash counter

3 Boutique Istanbul Turkey: example of troglodytic illusionist interior; reflecting ceiling makes h appear greater, visitor left guessing about shop's extent   Arch Mehmet Konuralp

Fire

Special fire precaution installations: smoke detectors, automatic warning systems, sprinklers. Compartment size →p189 can be doubled where sprinklers supplied.

Temperature & ventilation

16°C min after first hour of occupancy (UK requirement). Ventilation by extract/intake fans or air-conditioning in larger units. Necessary design for heat build-up from artificial lighting and occupancy loading.

Shop layout

As with display shop itself should be easy to take in at glance. Space for customer and sales staff depends on commodity and number of customers; aim at smooth quick procedure. Big store organisations develop system planning to suit their particular requirements.

Location of shops

Varies according to type of business: determined by custom, *eg* convenience shopping and consumer durables. Trade of smaller units will be affected by location of dept stores, variety stores and supermarkets which act as magnets. These larger units should be sited to draw shoppers past as many shops as possible. Shops should be situated for max impact related to trade potential and should be seen from as many angles as possible.

Shape of frontage, shop sign (integral component) and protection from weather should draw customers. Corner shops 30% more valuable than shops in row. Each type of shop has its individual shop window shape (shoe shops need different displays from butchers and jewellers). Dept stores usually have flat frontages. Sizes of window vary with local conditions even in new bldg. Size and design of display windows and height of stall-riser related to goods displayed, *eg* jewellery or furniture →p191(4).

Boutiques

Examples of 2 different concepts →(3)(4)

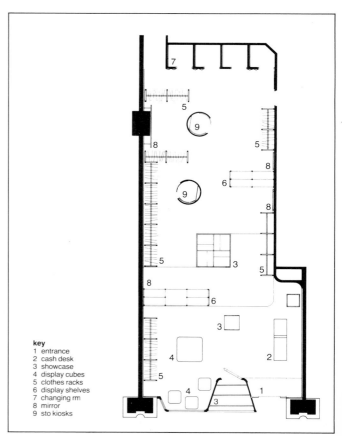

key
1 entrance
2 cash desk
3 showcase
4 display cubes
5 clothes racks
6 display shelves
7 changing rm
8 mirror
9 sto kiosks

4 Boutique Champs Elysèe Paris France: reflecting glass sets goods off against complex background; artificial lighting directs eye to most rewarding points   Arch Isabelle Hebey

Shops & stores

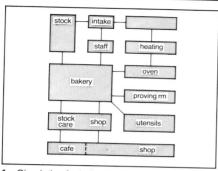

1 Circulation for bakery: shop well ventilated, if possible with steam extractor

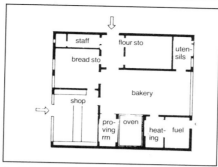

2 Plan of small bakery: bread sto with good connexion to bakery, shop & despatch

BREAD & CAKE SHOPS →(1)–(4)

Generation ago small bakeries produced approx 85% of household requirements of bread and pastries, factory bakeries remaining 15%: these percentages now more or less transposed in UK.

Sales in personal service shops mainly over counter, which may contain refrigerated display. Freshly baked goods require good air circulation.

FRUIT & VEGETABLE SHOPS →(6)–(9)

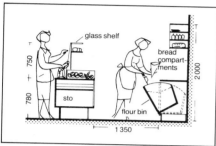

3 Sales counter with screen: bread compartments →(4) vary with loaf size

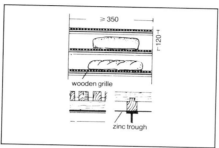

4 Shelf arrangement: bread on slatted shelves (air circulation) with tins below to catch flour

Fresh vegetables should be stored cool but not refrigerated: potatoes in dark rm, carrots & root vegetables in sand, fruit in dark rm at temp 1–5°C & 85–95% hum. Deep freezers for deep frozen supplies. Walls tiled or washable.

Sale often from delivery containers (baskets, crates, boxes) →(7)(8). Dirt traps below sto racks →(8). Fruit & vegetable shops usefully combined with flower shops.

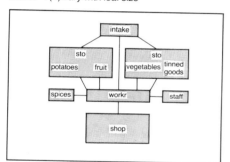

5 Circulation for greengrocery: small stock as most goods delivered daily

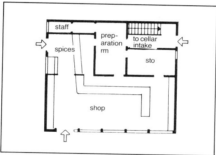

6 Plan of fruit & vegetable shop: rm with machines for cutting & preparing vegetables

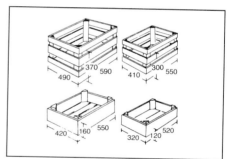

7 Typical boxes for fruit & vegetables

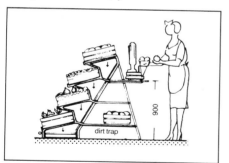

8 Counter with stands for boxes & wire baskets, drip pan & dirt trap

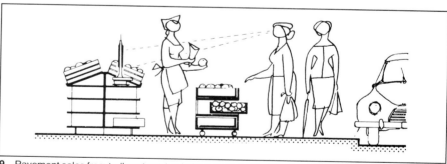

9 Pavement sales from trolleys (carts) or in front of shop with attractive display

Shops & stores

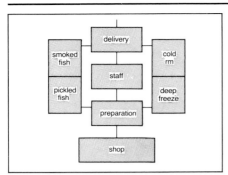

1 Circulation for fishmonger

2 Sea food specialty shop without allied sales

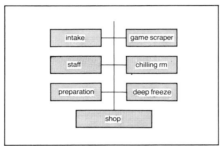

3 Fish counter with cooling compartment & drain

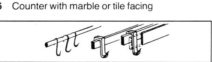

4 Circulation for poultry & game shop

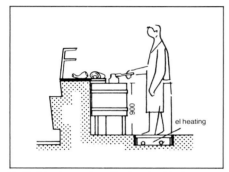

5 Butcher's counter with chopping block

6 Counter with marble or tile facing

7 Hooks & rails for hanging meat

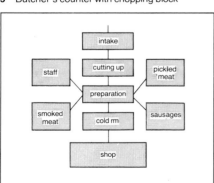

8 Circulation for butcher's

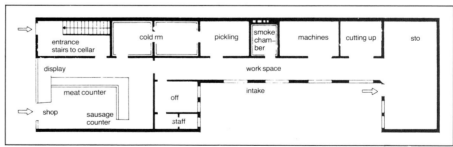

9 Large butcher's shop

FISHMONGERS →(1)–(3)

Fish need cool sto (often marble) for display, cold rm for overnight sto and deep freeze cabinets in shop for deep frozen products. Smoked fish must be stored quite dry in contrast to fresh fish.

Shop must be well equipped with ventilation devices. Walls and floors washable. New UK reg may require glazed shop fronts.

Arrangements for receiving large deliveries and for refuse disposal.

If desired, aquarium for eye appeal →(2).

BUTCHERS →(6)–(10)

Work procedure: 1 delivery, 2 cutting up, 3 manufacturing, 4 refrigeration, 5 selling.

Preferably on 1 level, if possible with rail and wheel carriages as pig halves and beef quarters heavy: 75–100 kg. Manufacture and cold rm 1.5–2 times size of shop.

Walls: tiles, mosaic etc, washable.

Table tops: marble, glass, ceramic.

GAME & POULTRY →(4)

Often together with fish. Similar in requirements. Workr with plucking machine and game scraper.

Poultry absorbs smells so must be stored separately from fish in shop and cold rm. Table tops and walls washable: marble, tiles, mosaic, plastics.

Spacious refrigerated compartment or show cases.

10 Counter in butcher's shop →also (5)

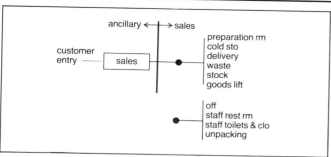

1 Circulation for self-service shops

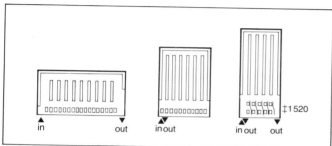

2 Typical self-service shop layouts showing checkout points related to frontage w

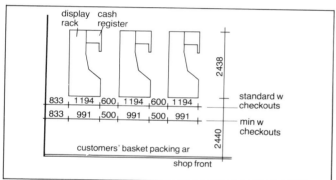

3 Layout of checkout points showing dimensions

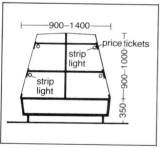

4 Sales display with stacking compartments & concealed lighting

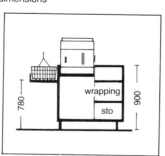

5 Section through small cash desk

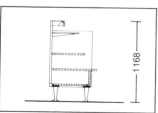

10 Self-selection unit: l varies; special merchandise needs special inserts

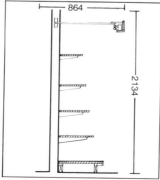

11 Back fixture with shelves only

SELF-SERVICE

Self-service stores mostly for food shops, drug stores and increasingly for other types of convenience goods. Staff mainly for advice, assistance, checking out, replenishing, possibly for quick service of meat and dairy foods. All goods prepacked and clearly displayed and ticketed (except sometimes fresh foods).

Proportion of ancillary accn may vary between 60% sales 40% ancillary and 48% sales 52% ancillary. Width of aisles 2200–2500. Entrance via basket stands or trolleys (carts); exit via checkout points. Replenishing by assistants.

Wall shelving up to reaching height (top shelf 1650, bottom shelf 300 above floor level) →(8)(9). Free-standing sales display suitable →(4). Checkout points →(5)(6) laid out to suit frontage of unit with counter top for purchases, cash register, wrapping space with paper bags, space for parking basket or trolley. Surveillance point essential.

Number of checkout points varies with unit scale and is related to turnover/m², as controlled by trading policy →(2)(3).

For each 100 m² shop area: 50–100 baskets and 10 trolleys.
For each 200 m² shop area: 50–200 baskets and 30 trolleys.

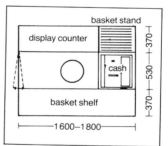

6 Plan of cash desk with min dimensions

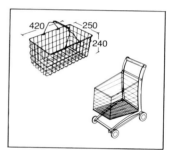

7 Stackable basket & trolley

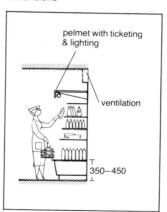

8 Wall shelves for bottles

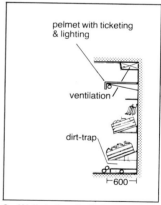

9 Wall shelves for fruit, vegetables & unpacked goods

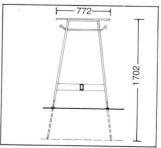

12 Free-standing hanging rack; hanging rack l 1525

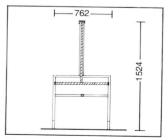

13 Millinery table

Shops & stores

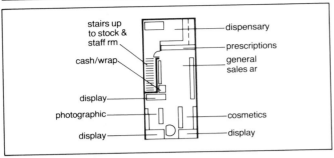

1 Plan of chemist shop

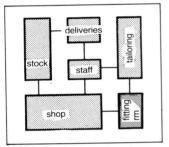

2 Space-saving arrangement round service core in hairdresser

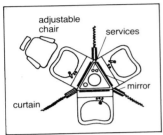

3 Standard shampoo unit with back wash for beauty parlours & hairdressers

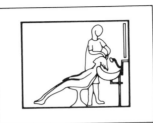

4 Organisation of a tailor' shop

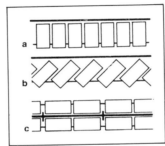

5 Arrangements for sto of cloth:
a shelf same w as l of bale
b oblique staggered system (for shop) **c** paired shelves, each of bale w

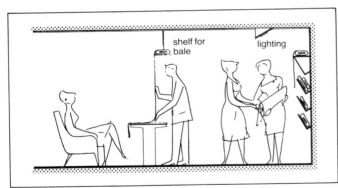

6 Display counter with shelf above for materials

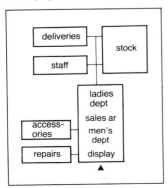

7 Organisation of shoe shop

8 Shoe shop

CHEMIST →(1)

Frequently self-service except for prescription counter. Will include other merchandise, *eg* photographic eqp, cosmetics. Min requirements for accn and fitments usually laid down in special chemists' manuals. Dispensary (with reg-type double-locked cupboards for poisons and narcotics) subdivided according to activities. Prescription counter and customers' section of shop provided with seats for waiting.

Dispensary of paramount importance; must allow undisturbed work with good view over drug shelves; must be well ventilated with fr ceilings, acid-resistant table tops and floor coverings and washable wall surfaces. Ancillary rm and workrm ≥ twice size of dispensary. Med supply basement must not be connected with other basement rm; spirits, ether, phosphorus etc must be kept in secure recesses or in cellars with steel doors.

Night dispensary may serve as office in daytime; alternatively night counter may be provided in recess with illuminated sign and night bell.

MENSWEAR & FASHION SHOPS →(4)

For self-selection clothes displayed in free stands or wall racks; for personal service in glass-fronted and hanging cabinets with special displays. Arrangement must be flexible, with movable eqp and fitting rm 1500 × 2000.

SHOE SHOPS →(7)–(9)

Medium size shop, personal service: 8000–16000 pairs; polish, stockings, socks, tights also available. Allow 1 footrest/2 seats, 1 stool/2 footrests for sales assistants →(9). Carpeting desirable; low level and wall mirrors should be provided. More convenient if stock and sales on same floor. Forward open stock or hidden stock at rear. Adequate forward open stock preferable for quick service but self-service shops follow general pattern, with special display racking.

FASHION FABRICS →(5)(6)

Often sold in conjunction with ready-to-wear clothes, lingerie, fashion accessories, woven goods, haberdashery. Merchandise required to be attractively arranged with lighting to show true colours →p25 398.

Shelves not higher than 2200 so that they may be reached without steps; optimum height 500–1500. Surfaces smooth so that material slides easily and does not catch. Counters for standing customers 850–950 high, for seated customers 550–700; counter width 700–850.

For ready-to-wear clothes dept provide changing cubicles 1100 × 1150 and fitting rm →(10)(11).

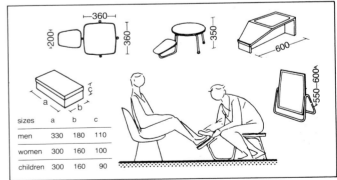

sizes	a	b	c
men	330	180	110
women	300	160	100
children	300	160	90

9 Combined foot-rest & assistant's seat

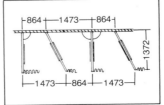

10 Typical fitting rm

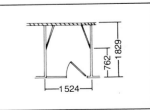

11 Better dresses fitting rm

SUPERMARKETS: EXAMPLES

1 oil heating
2 air-conditioning plant
3 air shaft
4 refrigerating plant
5 cold sto fats
6 deep freezing
7 cold sto meat
8 minced meat
9 ante-rm
10 meat
11 cold meats
12 fish
13 deep freeze
14 coffee
15 fats

16 vegetables
17 fruit
18 checkout
19 flowers
20 trolleys (carts)
21 wr
22 changing rm, women
23 changing rm, men
24 wc women
25 wc men
26 fruit & vegetable preparation
27 fruit & vegetable cooling
28 empties
29 bottle reception
30 heating oil tank

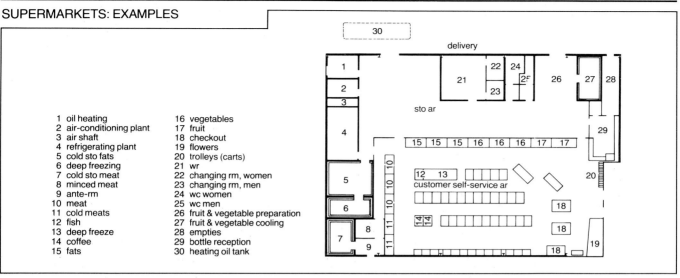

1   German supermarket   Arch Peter Neufert

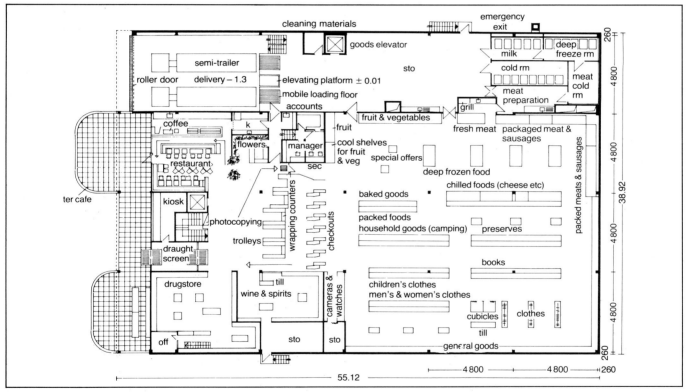

2   Swiss supermarket

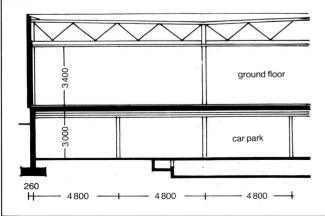

3   Cross-section of (2)

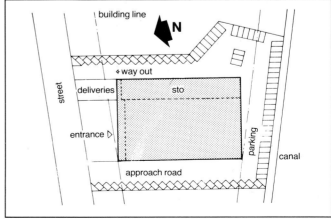

4   Site plan of (2)

Shops & stores

HYPERMARKETS

Basically single volume transfer shed, gross area 10000–50000 m²: 1 trader under 1 roof, using self-service methods to sell max range of convenience and durable merchandise at low prices; goods delivered direct from manufacturers to large on-site warehousing areas.

Location

Out of town on perimeter of city, town or district centre. Min catchment area 80000 population; 25 minutes driving time out of town; 10–15 minutes from inner zone: siting related to road pattern to allow this.

Car parking

5.25 cars/100 m² gross area (av shopping trip 1 hour). Provision for trolley (cart) collecting. Separate provision for service vehicles and refuse collection (perhaps with incineration or compaction). Discount petrol and tyre service for customers only.

Planning

Up to 50% gross area for warehousing, cold sto, food preparation, offices and staff. Main sales on 1 floor, mezzanine could house restaurant, hairdressing, offices, toilets, staff accn and some warehousing. Staff numbers related to sales area: say 3 staff to 350 m² sales, with shift working.

Warehousing & ancillary accn

Sto will be open 24 hr/day for restocking out of hours, cleaning, servicing etc. Deliveries and restocking using mech aids, eg forklift transfer in warehouse to palleted trucks for restocking shelves; warehouse racking may be high (groceries) or low (textiles). Large food preparation areas needed for fresh foods, butchery, baking, preferably visible by customers.

Sales area

Self-service principles apply generally →p195. Aisles must be designed for palleted trucks, with 1800–3500 between racking.

Construction

For flexibility wide spans and max column spacing (say 8 m × 12 m). First floor must be designed for heavy loading if used for warehousing. Compartmentation of warehouse areas essential: controlling factor in design may be insurance requirements. Waivers may be needed to allow max open sales area.

Service

Air-conditioning, high intensity artificial lighting, throughout. Cold sto refrigerator.

Services →p383–97

Floors must be hard wear, easily cleaned tiles.

Fire regulations

Consult reg. Subject to distance of bldg from boundary, fr and compartment reg do not apply in UK to 1-storey hypermarkets: means of escape provisions must be approved by local authority. In 2-storey areas normal compartmentation reg do apply, subject to possible relaxation by appropriate authority. Sprinkler essential.

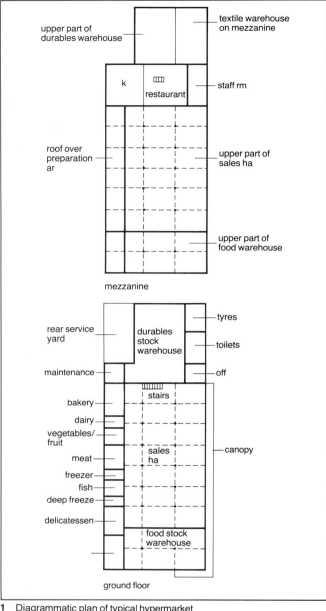

1   Diagrammatic plan of typical hypermarket

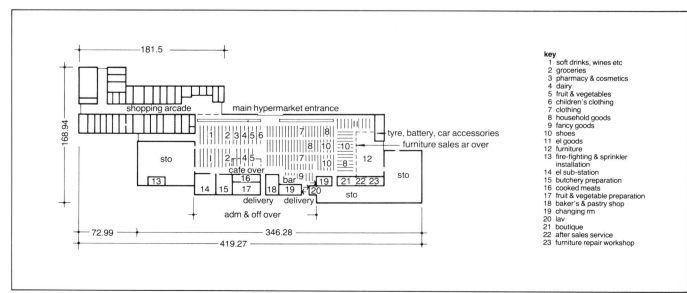

key
1   soft drinks, wines etc
2   groceries
3   pharmacy & cosmetics
4   dairy
5   fruit & vegetables
6   children's clothing
7   clothing
8   household goods
9   fancy goods
10   shoes
11   el goods
12   furniture
13   fire-fighting & sprinkler installation
14   el sub-station
15   butchery preparation
16   cooked meats
17   fruit & vegetable preparation
18   baker's & pastry shop
19   changing rm
20   lav
21   boutique
22   after sales service
23   furniture repair workshop

2   Layout of typical hypermarket with approx 20 000 m² selling space

Shopping centres & precincts

Increasing trend in Europe and USA during 1970s plan large retail complexes in inner city areas. Despite their large size restricted space forms primary design factor. High site rents often mean these complexes incorporate office space; also sometimes residential flats and condominiums but less frequently. As with convention hotels →p221–3 large internal spaces allow separation of interior circulation of public from that of service and store personnel. Traffic patterns which maximise retail display and access to retail units generally mechanism by which high rent units let.

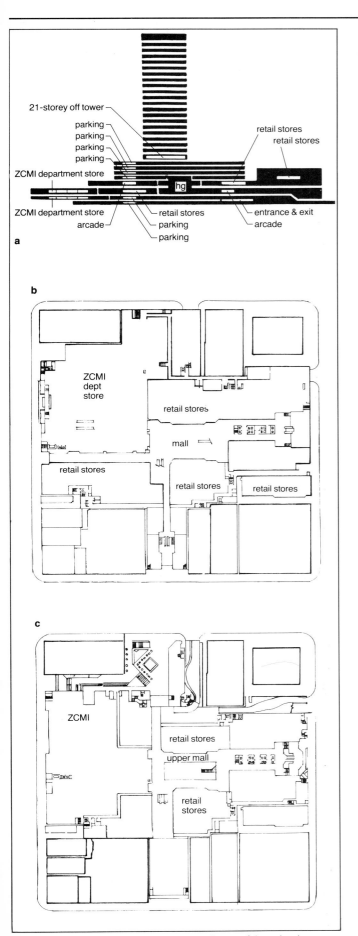

1   ZCMI Centre Salt lake City USA **a** section diagram **b** lower level **c** upper level   Arch Gruen Associates

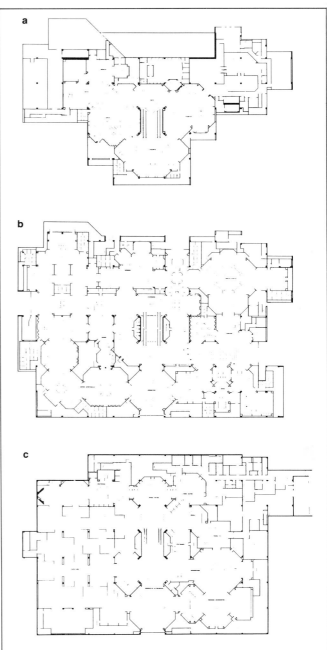

2   Bullock's South Coast Plaza Costa Mesa California USA **a** second floor **b** first floor **c** ground floor   Arch Welton Becket & Associates

Shopping centres & precincts

EXAMPLES

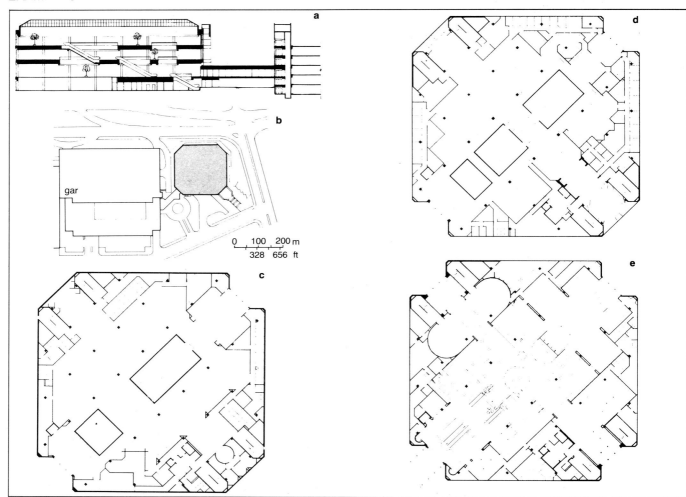

1 Bergdorf Goodman shopping complex White Plains USA **a** elevator with escalators in court or 'street' **b** site plan **c** third level **d** second level **e** main level   Arch John Carl Warnecke

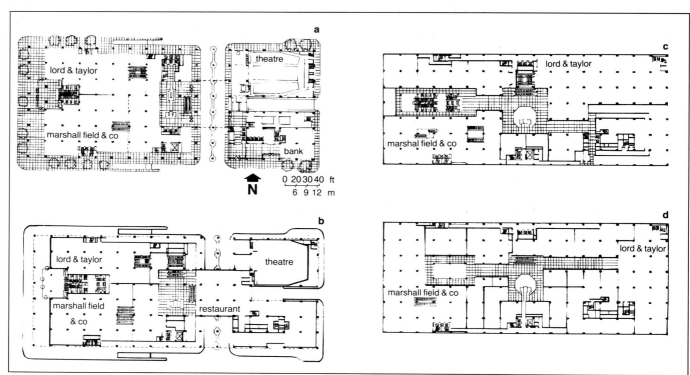

2 Water Tower Place Chicago USA **a** ground floor **b** mezzanine floor **c** first floor **d** second floor Consult arch Warren Platner Associates   Arch Loebl Schlossman Bennett & Dart

EXAMPLES

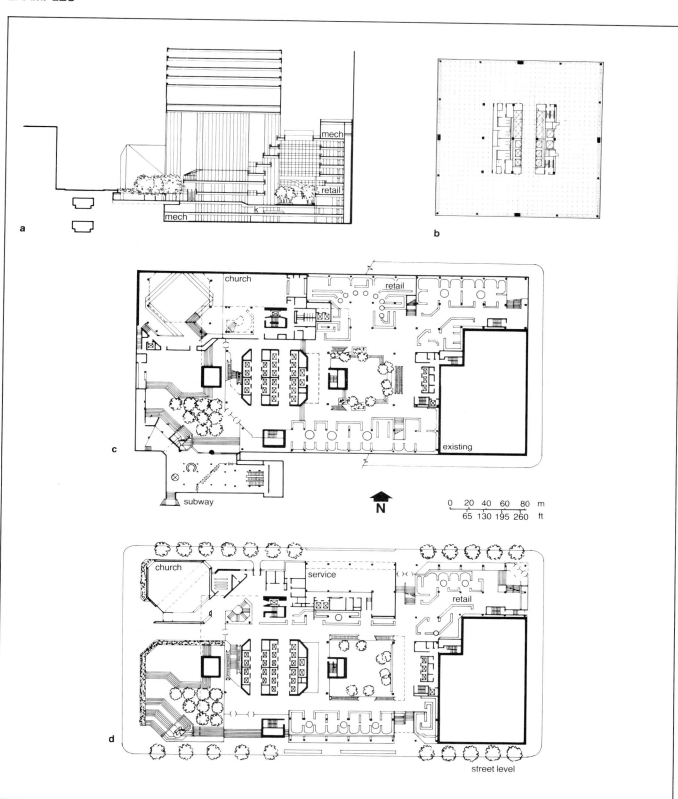

a section b typical mid-rise tower floor

church   retail

mech

retail

k   mech

existing

subway

N

0   20   40   60   80   m
65   130   195   260   ft

church   service

retail

street level

1   Citicorp Center New York USA   **a** section   **b** typical mid-rise tower floor   **c** concourse level   **d** street level   Arch Hugh Stubbins

Shops and stores:
→Bibliography entries 116 117 340 341 369 374 450 477 552 601

Restaurants

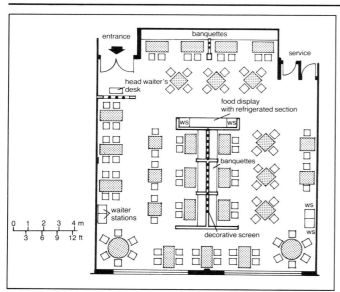

1 Traditional restaurant: 110 seats

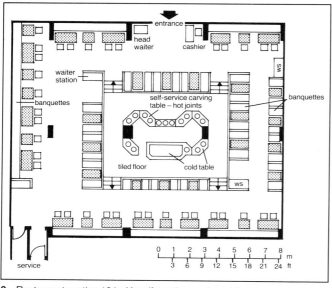

2 Restaurant seating 124 with self-service carving table

SPACE ALLOWANCES (EXCLUDING COOKING AREAS)

Snack bar service
Usually restricted to light meals, served at counter or taken by customer to table. Food normally cooked within counter area but back-up preparation, wash-up and sto required. 1.50–2.20 m^2/P including counter and cooking.

Cafe service
0.83 m^2/P: limited menu, usually family type of business, designed on traditional lines with kitchen separate from dining rm. Food may be collected by waitress from small service counter or hatch to kitchen.

Self-service cafeteria
1.4–1.7 m^2/P, long self-service counter, provide good circulation space. Space for clearing trolleys required.

Coffee shop service →(3)
1.2–1.4 m^2/P, usually waitress service, often from forward cooking area with counter which may be decoratively screened. Main preparation and wash-up at rear. Counter service sometimes included.

Specialty restaurant
Space requirements vary widely. Display cooking, grill, dance floor, special decor effects may be required. Bar may be included within restaurant.

Traditional restaurant →(1)
1.3–1.9 m^2/P according to type of business. Should have space for display table, flambé work, generous seating and spacing of tables.

Carving table restaurant
1.6 m^2/P including space for carving table. Display table with hot and cold positions for self-service of joints, vegetables and sweets. Preparation, cooking and wash-up done in main kitchen.

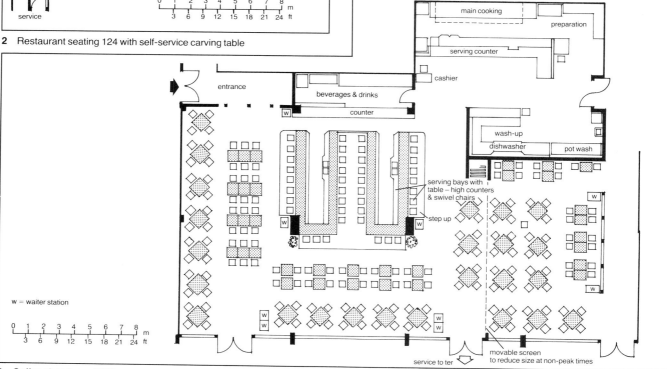

3 Coffee shop to seat 200

PLANNING FACTORS

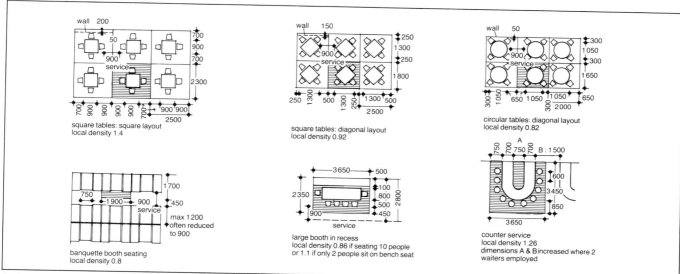

square tables: square layout
local density 1.4

square tables: diagonal layout
local density 0.92

circular tables: diagonal layout
local density 0.82

banquette booth seating
local density 0.8

large booth in recess
local density 0.86 if seating 10 people
or 1.1 if only 2 people sit on bench seat

counter service
local density 1.26
dimensions A & B increased where 2
waiters employed

1 Layout arrangements

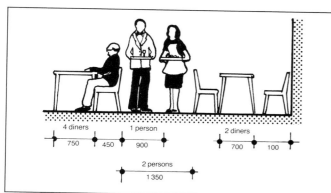

4 diners 1 person 2 diners

2 persons

2 Aisle w

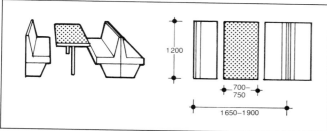

3 Typical banquette seating

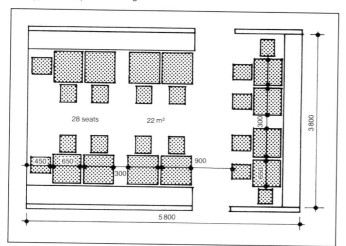

28 seats 22 m²

4 Min layout for part of restaurant: local density excluding main circulation & waiter stations & service areas

Restaurants should be planned so that variety of seating arrangements can be achieved, *eg* tables for 2 and 4 and placing together of tables to provide 6, 8 and 10 places. Consider also banquette or booth seating →(3)(6); but these should be supplemented by normal tables to give flexibility.

→(1) shows typical table and counter layouts and local densities. Columns best situated near group of tables or at corners of table. Provide acoustic lobby to service doors between restaurant and kitchen. Access for guests should be planned so that not confused with service.

Service aisles →(2) not less than 900–1350 if to be used by both trolleys and guests.

Waiter stations should be located so as not to disturb guests: number will vary according to standard of service but following may be used as guide:

restricted menu : 1 waiter/waitress per 12–16 covers
typical menu : 1 waiter/waitress per 8–12 covers
à la carte & de luxe : 1 waiter/waitress per 4–8 covers

Ambience an important factor in restaurant design: decoration, lighting should be integral part. Large regular spaces should be broken up into smaller more intimate areas, if necessary by means of screens of various heights or decorative features. Changes of level not usually favoured by caterers but acceptable providing they make positive contribution to design, do not involve more than 2 or 3 steps and main part of restaurant on same level as kitchen. Where changes of level occur seating areas should be protected by balustrades. Cash desk may be at entrance or by service doors or within kitchen area depending on cashing system operated by management.

Provide head waiter stand in à la carte or de luxe restaurants. Hard wearing floor service in area around service doors. Traditional and specialty restaurants frequently have aperitif bar associated with them for waiting customers and drinks before meal. Such bar should be planned so that head waiter can take orders and call forward customers when tables ready.

Dance floor in restaurant: allow 1.0–3.5 m²/couple.

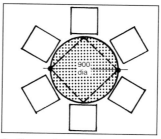

5 Banquette seating booth: table must be moved to gain access or top may be movable

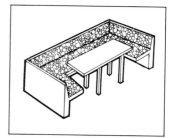

6 'Staadtler' table to seat 4: with flaps extended seats 6

Restaurants

TABLE SIZES

Table sizes vary according to type of restaurant; min for cafeterias etc: 2 persons 600 × 600, 4 persons 600 × 1100. Diagrams show tables for good standard of restaurant.

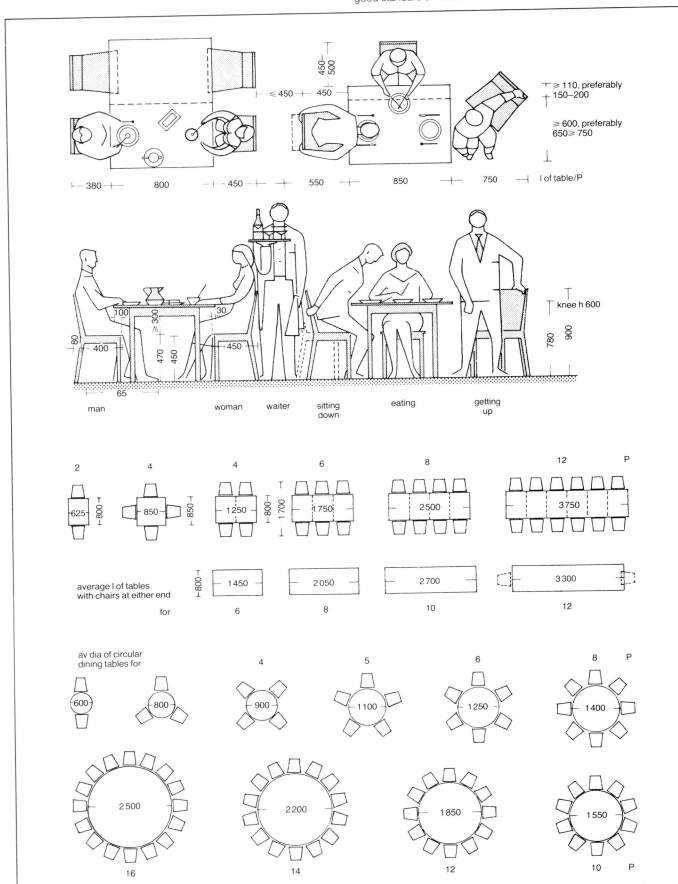

man   woman   waiter   sitting down   eating   getting up

average l of tables with chairs at either end for

av dia of circular dining tables for

SNACK BARS

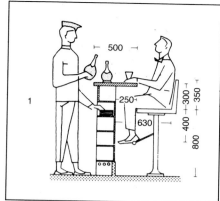

1 Bar stool

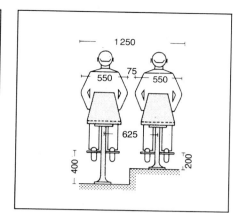

2 Bar stools: normal distance

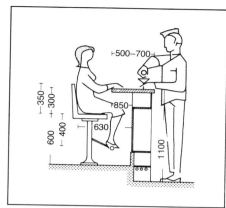

3 Medium h bar stool

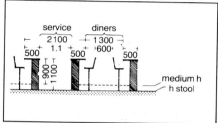

4 High density arrangement with small tables

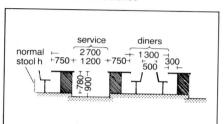

5 Wider tables with more space

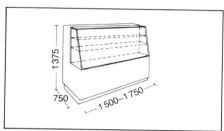

6 Refrigerated showcase

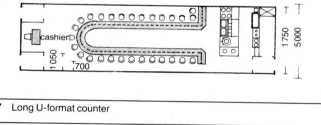

7 Long U-format counter

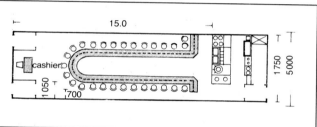

8 Short U-format counters

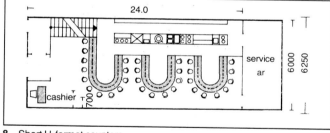

9 Paired U-format counters

Situation

In centres of cities where accn expensive must be max turnover of customers. Counters with stools less economical of space than closely spaced tables but ensure speedy service and quick turnover. Av sitting time 20 minutes: 3 occupants/hr compared with perhaps 1/hr in normal restaurant.

Format

Typical U format with 12 seats min length 600/P = 7200. This length may be served by 1 waiter if meals pre-cooked; if meals and drinks have to be prepared at counter further 1–2 waiters necessary →(7)(8)(9).

Areas required

Per seat 1 480–2 150
Ratio of service area to total area 25–50%
Net kitchen area 15–25%

Kitchen & wash-up

Preferably at same level as restaurant, kitchen area divided into:
servery
area of cooking, frying, grilling and preparation of soups and vegetables
cold buffet (meat, salads, fruits, fish, sweets and desserts)
wash-up area
→Bib217

Other requirements

Toilets for customers, staff toilets, staff cloakrm, small office, food sto including refrigerator and deep freeze, liquor sto, boiler rm, air-conditioning plant if required. For scale of sanitary fittings →reg. Public cloakrm not normally required for this type of restaurant, hat and coat stands or coat rack on wall sufficient. In large snack bars separate entrance and exits desirable. Cashier near exit.

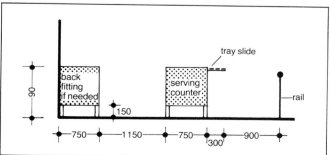

10 Self-service cafeteria service

Restaurants

DRIVE-IN & SELF-SERVICE RESTAURANTS

Drive-in restaurants supply food and drinks direct to cars so that guests may eat without leaving vehicles. For access and serving provide canopies and covered ways; dining hall should be separate, with parking space close to drive-in service. 1 waiter can serve 6 cars.

Self-service advantageous for snack bars and to overcome staff shortages. Smooth-running system (entrance-trays-counter-cashier-dr-exit) more important than comfortable atmosphere because diner's stay much shorter than in ordinary restaurant.

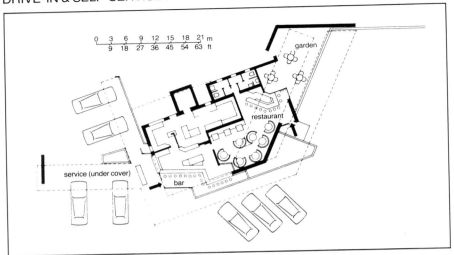

1 Drive-in restaurant California Arch Lauter

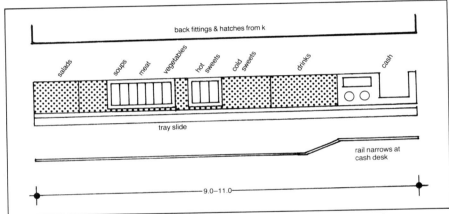

2 Typical self-service counter to serve range of 2/3 choices to 80/90 customers in 10 minutes

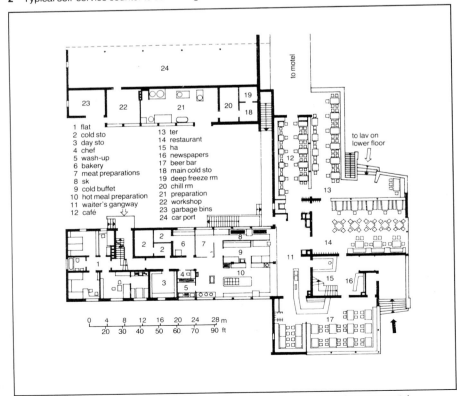

1 flat
2 cold sto
3 day sto
4 chef
5 wash-up
6 bakery
7 meat preparations
8 sk
9 cold buffet
10 hot meal preparation
11 waiter's gangway
12 café
13 ter
14 restaurant
15 ha
16 newspapers
17 beer bar
18 main cold sto
19 deep freeze rm
20 chill rm
21 preparation
22 workshop
23 garbage bins
24 car port

4 Restaurant on main highway: rest rm & lav on lower floor, where they can also serve motel
Arch Neufert

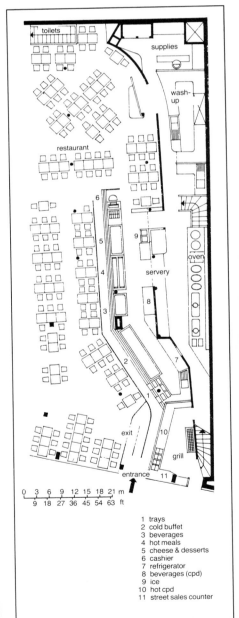

1 trays
2 cold buffet
3 beverages
4 hot meals
5 cheese & desserts
6 cashier
7 refrigerator
8 beverages (cpd)
9 ice
10 hot cpd
11 street sales counter

3 Self-service restaurant Paris Arch Prunier

Restaurant cars: minimum use of space

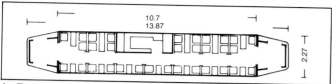

1 Tram restaurant car of Rhineland Rail Company

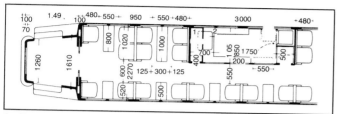

2 Details of **1**; dining tables only half as wide as in restaurant cars: no serving pantry; kitchen located almost in middle of vehicle where springing most effective to lessen jolting

Space needed for dining services in long-distance trams and motor coaches →(1)(2) modest compared with train dining cars →(9). Dimensioning of German dining cars result of many years experience; present system after numerous design changes. Diagonally placed tables tried out in recent years found unsatisfactory and not illustrated here.

Kitchen arrangements represent max use of available space; this applies both to width of doors and service hatches and to refrigeration units, which are exceptionally large →(8).

All dishes have to be washed up in kitchen between 2 meal services (main and snack lunch). Service in dining car made easier because number of customers limited to number of places →(8).

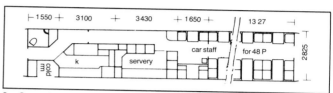

9 Ground plan of German restaurant car →(6)(10)

3 Section A-A →(8)

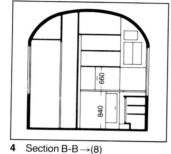

4 Section B-B →(8)

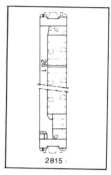

10 Ground plan German restaurant car →(6)(9)

11 Ground plan German sleeping car →(10)–(14)

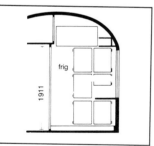

5 Section C-C →(8)

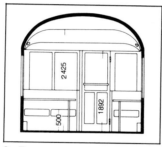

6 Transverse section →(10)

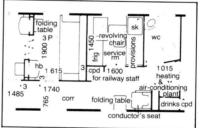

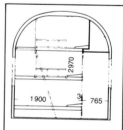

12 Sleeping car ground plan detail →(13)

13 Cross section →(12)

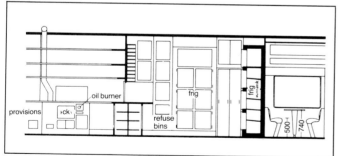

7 Section D-D →(8)

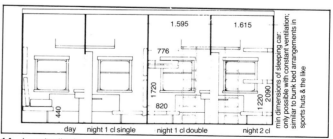

14 Longitudinal section

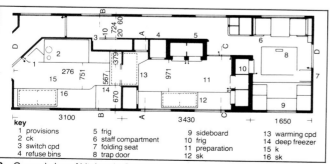

key
1 provisions	5 frig	9 sideboard	13 warming cpd
2 ck	6 staff compartment	10 frig	14 deep freezer
3 switch cpd	7 folding seat	11 preparation	15 k
4 refuse bins	8 trap door	12 sk	16 sk

8 Ground plan of kitchen in German restaurant car: section (3)–(5)(7)

15 'Comet' articulated train double compartment

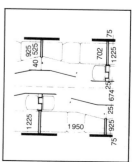

16 Special 'Comet' compartment with berths along axis of train

Hotels

Location is one of most important factors for commercial success. Depending on market orientation hotels should generally be conspicuous and sited near main road or motorway intersections, airports, commercial and business centres or resorts.

Site

Following points should be considered: height and plot ratio requirements, ease of access, adequacy for parking either on ground or within bldg, views and aspect, relationship to adjoining bldg, levels.

Types

Market orientation will dictate type of hotel. Construction of new hotels of less than 70–80 bedr hardly viable unless they can be run on family basis.

City centre: include luxury, convention and city tourist hotels. Characterised by high plot ratio, high rise construction, frequently large function accn, inclusion of shops →p222 or offices →p223 in development to improve viability.

Motor hotels: cater mainly for people *en route* by car or motoring locally, therefore sited at important road junctions and on outskirts of cities. Land cheaper therefore sites fairly large allowing large car park and low or medium rise construction. Generally contain all usual hotel services but on modest scale. No rm service.

Airport hotels: similar planning to motor hotels but catering specifically for air travellers therefore require all night reception and possibly some night catering. Sometimes have convention services for convenience of international companies.

Resort hotels: at seaside or mountain resorts or spas. Usually planned to cater for package holidays with reception arrangements for large intake at weekly or fortnightly intervals. Restaurant should accommodate all guests at 1 sitting. Require spacious lounges, games rm, bars, possibly also swimming pool, beach and sports installations. Conference rm can also be included encourage off-season business.

Motels: →p219 220

Convention hotels: →p221–3

Condominium: development involving joint ownership where individual owner has full benefit of rm, suite, villa for own use or letting but shares costs common to whole development which may include all usual hotel services.

Functional relationships

Diagram →p209 shows typical relationship of parts of medium size hotel. Points of principle to note are:

separation of guest and service areas: no cross circulation; distinction between front and back of house

all catering outlets if possible be on same level as kitchens: if not, main. restaurant directly related to kitchen; other restaurants and banqueting rm should have service rm connected by elevators and stairs main kitchen where bulk cooking is undertaken

organisation of back of house such that staff and goods are separate far as possible and control can be maintained over both.

Space allocation & standards

→(1) guide to gross ar/rm for various types of hotel.

(2) shows space allocation for 2 typical contrasting hotels: figures assume most economical layout. Quality of hotel mainly dependent on service and finishes; de luxe hotels have larger service areas, more service elevators etc; in economy hotels these areas reduced, sometimes to bare min of reception, office, breakfast rm, bar and supporting services.

type	m²/rm gross
convention hotel with large conference rm, night club, shopping	55–65
city centre hotel	45–55
motor hotel	35–45
resort hotel	40–55
low-medium tariff hotel with private bathr but min catering	20–30
hostels: single rm & min service	18–20

1 Gross ar/rm for various hotel types

section	a 20 bedr motor hotel		b 500 bedr city centre hotel	
	m²/rm		m²/rm	
residential				
bedr	24		26.5	
corr, elevators, stairs	3.2		9.3	
service ar	0.6		0.7	
total residential		27.8		36.5
public & service ar: front of house				
lob & circulation including P elevators	1.6		1.8	
reception, clo, reservations off, switchboard, luggage	0.4		0.5	
admin	0.3		0.4	
restaurant	1.1		0.6	
coffee shop	0.6		0.5	
bar 1 including counter, sto	0.8		0.4	
bar 2 including counter, sto	0.5		0.3	
lounge	0.5		0.3	
toilets	0.4		0.3	
function rm	1.1		1.3	
pre-function ar	—		0.5	
furniture sto	0.1		0.2	
private dining/meeting rm	0.4		0.9	
shops	—		0.2	
total front of house		7.8		8.2
public & service ar: back of house				
k & k sto	3.8		2.5	
sto	0.9		0.9	
workshops & maintenance	0.8		0.4	
lau, linen sto etc	0.3		0.7	
staff canteen, lockers, toilets	1.0		1.1	
off for personnel, accounts, control, housekeeper etc	0.3		0.5	
circulation, service elevators etc	0.8		0.9	
total back of house		7.9		7.0
total		43.5		51.7

boiler houses, plant rm & car parking excluded

2 Space allocations

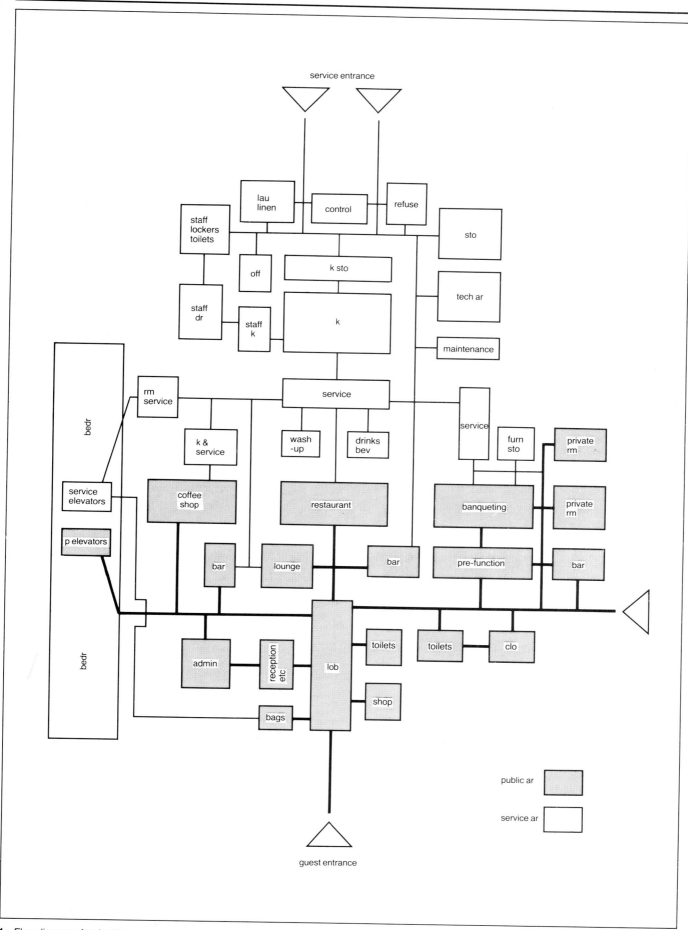

1 Flow diagram of typical hotel

Hotels

PLAN FORMS

Bedroom accommodation

As bedr forms greater proportion of hotel construction key to economical design largely in layout of bedr block. →(1) shows some possible arrangements:

Double-loaded block (A) capable of development into L U courtyard plan; requires only 2 stairs; considered most economical layout.

Double-loaded T shaped block (B) capable being developed into cross; also economical but 3 stairs required.

Single-loaded block (C) capable of being developed into L U or courtyard plan: not economical solution but may be desirable, perhaps combined with A take advantage of site conditions; if developed form centre courtyard can be used provide atrium effect.

Square block (D) with central core containing all vertical services, maids' rooms etc, compact and useful for small sites where tower development may be required.

Y plan (E) requires 3 staircases and has more complicated structure than straight blocks; structural system may cause problems in public areas.

Triarc (F) similar to E but more space taken up by circulation; concave curve results in bedr wider at bathr end providing opportunity for larger bathr and dressing area.

Circular (G) requires careful handling avoid awkward and inward facing rm; not capable of extension.

Circular with central core (H), similar to D; also requires careful handling avoid awkward rm. Convex curves in G and H result in bedr narrower at bathr end, causing cramped space for bathr.

Relationship of bedroom block to public room areas

Many ways in which bedr block may be related to public rm and circulation but can be illustrated by 3 basic arrangements shown →(2). Likely that combinations or variations of these arrangements would have to be adopted.

A Compact development of bedr block superimposed on podium. Suitable for high rise development on city site. Problems arise from bedr services having to pass through public rm and from probable need carry bedr block over wide spans.

B Bedr block adjacent to public rm block: considered to be economical because optimum structure and services can be designed for each part. Suitable for motor hotel development on large site.

C Open layout with public rm and service block completely separate from bedr which may be in groups scattered about large site. Suitable for motel and resort type hotels where plenty of land available and landscape conditions dictate.

VERTICAL CIRCULATION

Hotels of more than 2 storeys should be provided with passenger and service elevators (→(3) →p410–2). Except in small hotels all elevators should be duplicated provide efficient service and standby in case of breakdown or repair. Number and speed of elevators will depend on height and population of bldg and for large installations should be based on traffic study by specialist.

Service hoists or dumb waiters not advised owing need have 1 person each end: better make service elevators large enough take trolley (cart) plus personnel.

If possible plan all elevators in 1 bank or tower with service elevators opening to kitchen area and passenger elevators opening directly to guest lobby. Separate baggage elevators not required except in de luxe hotels; but may be desirable to have 1 elevator available for manual control if large amount baggage handled. In high bldg much depends on quality and speed of elevator services as regards both guest elevators and service elevators: not wise to skimp this aspect.

In addition goods elevators may be required in back areas: should be of large capacity and of sturdy, easily cleaned construction.

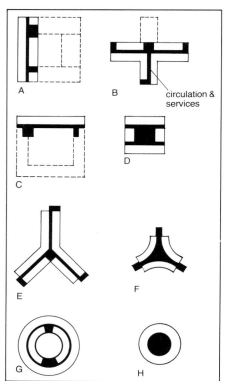

1 Plan forms for bedr accn

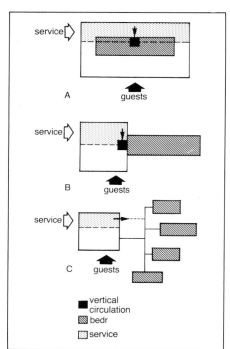

2 Relationship of bedr to public rm

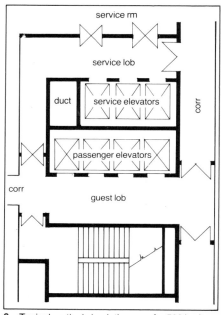

3 Typical vertical circulation core for 500 bedr hotel

Hotels

PUBLIC ROOMS

Restaurants

In medium and large hotels common to provide more than 1 restaurant give customer choice menu and price. Cheaper restaurant usually coffee shop or cafeteria: more expensive à la carte. Large hotels may have additional specialist restaurants. In certain situations, *eg* city centre hotels, cheaper restaurant may be accessible from both hotel and street to attract non-residential business.

Seating capacities restaurants vary according size hotel, amount potential outside business, location in relation other restaurants, duration stay guests, amount breakfast rm service to be provided.

In resort and other suitable locations provision should be made serve meals in open air either by extension of 1 restaurant or by separate service.
Further details →p202–7; kitchens →p213

Bars

Cocktail or aperitif bar (if required) should be planned as comfortable intermediary waiting area between hotel lobby and main restaurant; service may be by waiter: long bar counter may not be required.

Main bar will provide chief drink service of hotel. May have external entrance to encourage non-resident business. Fairly long bar counter supported by bar sto with ice making machine and bottle cooler should be provided: section may be required for service of simple meals.

Possible other bars: roof top, pool side, beach, club areas.

All bars capable of being shut securely during non-opening hours either by grill or shutter at bar counter or by closing rm. Former has advantage rm can be used as lounge when bar closed. Should be possible service bars without passing through public rm. Bars should comply with licensing laws.

Space allowance for bars excluding counter:

cocktail lounge (comfortable)	1.8–2.0 m²/P
general bar (some standing & on stools)	1.3–1.7 m²/P

Lounges

Reasonable provision should be made for people waiting and relaxing either in relation to lobby or circulation areas or to revenue-earning areas such as bars. More lounge space required in resort hotels than others. Service of drinks, tea and coffee should be provided from dispense or from main kitchen. Separate residents lounges not normally required.

Recreation rooms

Card rm, table tennis, billiard rm etc should be considered for resort hotels.

Function rooms

Multi-purpose rm for meetings, banquets, balls, parties, exhibitions valuable asset. Design considerations include: separate access if rm large; divisible by movable partitions; separate access for guests and service desirable; audio-visual eqp to be provided. Large span required precludes this rm being planned beneath bedr block except on costly city sites.

Space allowances:

banquet style seating	1.1–1.3 m²/P
meetings: table groups	0.9–1.1 m²/P
theatre style seating	0.5–0.6 m²/P

Other requirements for function rm:
ante-rm, preferably approx ⅓rd area of function rm, with dispense bar

furniture store 0.5 m²/seat easily accessible from function rm

cloakrm and toilets (depending on proximity of hotel toilets): provision of wc and urinals as for public areas →p212 unless music and dancing licence required, in which case should be as for concert halls, theatres etc.

Movable partitions should be full height and fold completely away into pockets. Av dB reduction of 45–50 sould be achieved through partitions and between function rm and kitchen.

In large function rm consider separate access for heavy exhibits. Allow 510 kg/m² floor loading.

Meeting rooms

In addition some meeting rm, preferably associated with main function rm, may be required. May vary in size; should all be capable being serviced from either main kitchen or pantry.

Fire precautions

Alternative exit routes must be provided for all public rm. Travel distances to exits, flame resistance of materials, fire and smoke resistant compartmentation must be in accordance with regulations →p216 408.

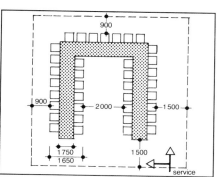

1 Space required for banqueting for 37 allowing for service

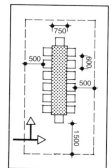

2 Space required in dr for 14 allowing for service: 2.0 m²/cover

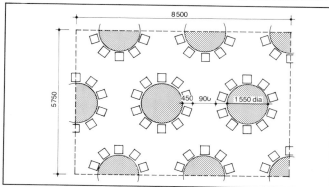

3 Banqueting seating at tables for 10: typical arrangements for large banquets: 1.2 m²/cover

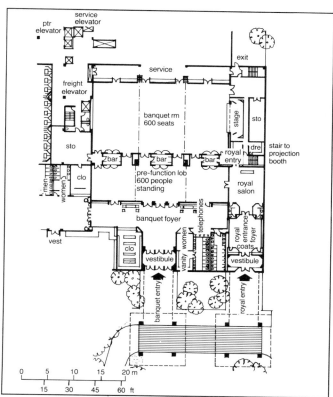

4 Example of banquet suite for large hotel

Hotels

FRONT OF HOUSE

Entrance

Arrange drive-in so cars can pull off road and with space for waiting cars and taxis: waiting space for coaches sometimes needed. Provide canopy. In exposed positions provide draught lobby or revolving doors (require pass doors for fire escape and baggage). Where traffic heavy with guests carrying own bags automatic doors. Separate door to baggage rm in high class hotels. Special provision for baggage handling for hotels expecting people in large groups.

Reception area

Reception desk →(1a) near and visible from entrance with porter, receptionist, cashier close by. In large hotels separate desk for porter (mainly supervising baggage handling).

Hall porter's desk

Length of counter arranged so porter can go freely into entrance hall. Depending on size of hotel should be fitted with alphabetical guest list, message waiting indicator, working shelf, drawers. Site key rack →(3) with slots for keys and letters corresponding with number of bedr in easy reach receptionists. Rm behind for short term sto small items, post box and slot.

Receptionist's desk →(1a)

Fitted with sloping rack not visible by guests for rm states (usually manual card system but may be electronic in large hotels), worktop and counter top for guests registration, section at normal height for clerical work, shelving, cupboards. Provide alphabetical list. Behind reception desk reservations office with direct access for receptionists: should have wall space for charts and telex (if any).

Cashier's desk →(1b)

In small-medium size hotels may be part reception desk. In large hotels normally partitioned-off section of main reception desk with small office at rear for chief cashier. Desk office for: 1 or 2 cash registers, bill tray spaces alongside registers, lockable cash drawers, shelves and drawers, guest safe deposit boxes →(4), deposit boxes for staff floats, telephone meter display board, airtube system terminal if required, safe.

Telephone switchboard →(3)

Often placed near reception counter so receptionists can operate at off-peak times. Otherwise in separate rm, possibly with hatch to public lobby and public telephones nearby.

Fire alarm panel: at reception desk or some other point where all night attendance.

Typical counter lengths for different sizes hotel:

no of rm	counter length
50	3000
100	4500
200	7500
400	10.5

Hotel lobby

Consider supplying in or near lobby: house telephone, public telephones, television security monitors, clocks and calendars, news teleprinters, information desk, travel agents, airline and car hire desks, kiosks and shops, lounge and waiting areas, guest secretarial and business services, public toilets.

Cloakroom & toilets

In small–medium hotels where not economical employ cloakrm attendant space may provided for coats and bags under eye of porter or receptionist. Otherwise provide cloakrm for main lobby, restaurants, function rm: sited discreetly, if possible together for ease of supervision. Plan cloakrm for large function rm so as ensure easy flow and quick issue of coats. Provide recessed area at least 1200 in front of counters to avoid encroachment on main circulation. Counter lengths: generally 1000/100 P.

Public toilets: number of wc, urinals, wash basins usually determined by local reg. For women's toilets vanity top, mirrors, good lighting. 1 wc for each sex for disabled persons.

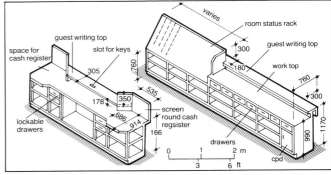

1   Reception & porter's desk for 400-bedr hotel: receptionists, porters, cashiers not normally seated, therefore work top height for standing

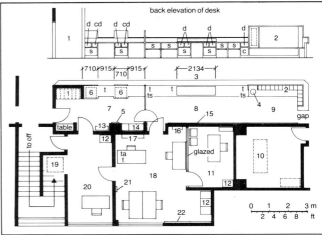

2   Typical cash desk for 400-bedr hotel

key
1 safety deposit boxes
2 key & message rack
3 rm status rack
4 rotary alphabetical index
5 currency information
6 cash register
7 cashier
8 reception
9 concierge
10 switchboard
11 front off manager
12 filing
13 telephone switches
14 telephone meters
15 tapestry & decorative clock
16 paging reciever charger
17 fire alarm panel
18 reservations off
19 safe
20 chief cashier
21 clock
22 advance reservations rack
23 taped music & paging eqp
t normal telephone
ts service station telephone
ta airport telephone
d drawer
cd cash drawer
s shelf
c cpd

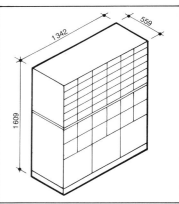

4   Typical bank of safety deposit boxes: various sizes should be provided

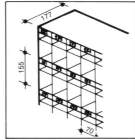

3   Key & letter rack

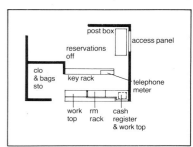

5   Typical front off for 120-bedr hotel

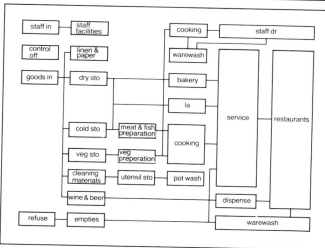

1 k & food sto flow diagram

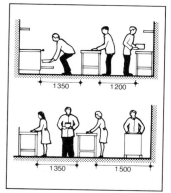

2 Min spaces between eqp to allow for circulation

3 Limiting h for sto shelving

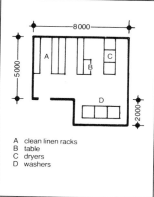

A clean linen racks
B table
C dryers
D washers

4 Non-iron lau for 120 bedr hotel

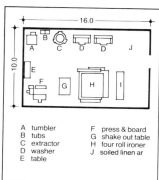

A tumbler
B tubs
C extractor
D washer
E table
F press & board
G shake out table
H four roll ironer
J soiled linen ar

5 Lau for 200 bedr hotel

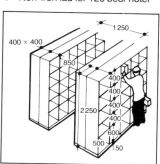

6 Stands with open shelves for goods

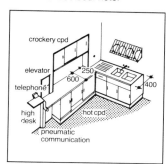

7 Waiter's servery & sk

KITCHENS & FOOD STORES

Should be planned on one level if possible to serve all catering outlets. If not possible main kitchen should be on level with main restaurant with preparation and sto on different level. For economy 1 wash-up desirable. Banqueting and any other food service area not next to kitchen should be linked by service elevators (preferably not hoists) and stairs and have own forward service eqp. Kitchen, cold rm and food sto area should be planned to be locked off from staff when not in use. In large hotels food and drink sto should be under control of storeman.

Approx space allowances for kitchen planning including food sto, cold rm, wash-up, chef's office:

main restaurant kitchen area $1.4 \text{ m}^2 \times$ no of covers
banquet kitchen & service area $0.2 \text{ m}^2 \times$ no of covers
coffee shop kitchen $0.3 \text{ m}^2 \times$ no of covers
separate independent coffee shop $0.45 \text{ m}^2 \times$ no of covers

Increase or reduce these allowances according whether fully traditional or convenience food operation envisaged.

Allow approx 50% extra for staff toilets, changing rm, canteen and other sto (see below).

Specification notes for kitchen areas: floors non-slip tiles, draining to gulleys with wide radius coved skirtings; sloping floors to have gradient not more than 1:20. Recessed area at restaurant doors for ribbed rubber matting or other non-slip cleanable material. Plinths required for some eqp. Grease traps outside kitchen if possible. Gas, water and plumbing supplies to be run to within 1 000 of appliance: final connexion by specialist. Walls in kitchen tiled up to 1 800. In sto walls fairfaced or plastered and painted. Dwarf walls tiled with inclined top surface. Corners protected. False ceilings of fr tiles with access panels to inspection covers, fire dampers etc. Openable windows to have fly screens. Where mech make-up air provided windows non-openable except for cleaning. Doors to have vision panels and metal kick plates or automatic opening devices.

Main cooking eqp should be either in island or against wall with extract canopies extending about 250 over. Extract velocity usually 7.7 to 10.2 m/s. Should preferably have vertical sides extending to ceiling. Height to underside 2 150.

Sizes of kitchen sto will depend on type of hotel, location, frequency of deliveries, type of food, *ie* whether convenience food. Cold rm temp: deep freeze − 20°C, chill rm 2 to 3°C.

Other stores

Furniture sto with adjacent workshop, paint shop etc: 0.2–0.3 m²/rm depending on amount in house maintenance
Cleaning materials: 0.2–0.4 m²/rm
Glass, silver, china: 0.1 m²/rm
Liquor: 0.2 m²/rm, divided into areas for beer and mineral bottles, kegs, red wines 14–16°C, white wine 10–12°C and spirits
Empties: close to loading dock

Refuse: planning will depend on method of sto and collections *ie* bins or compactor. Allow space for vehicle back up to receptacles. Provide for washing down refuse area, bins etc. In warm climates provide refrigerated refuse sto.

Linen: area depends on type of hotel. Typically 0.4 m²/rm: may be less if inhouse laundry provided. Shelves at least 600 wide open lathed. Allow space for sorting and work table for repairs.

All above areas for 200 bedr hotels, do not necessarily increase or reduce *pro rata* according to number of bedr.

Laundry

For 200 bedr hotel space of approx 140 m² required excluding line sto, steam boiler, chemicals sto, office. If non-iron linen used space can be reduced to 40–59 m². Ventilation ratio should be 15–20 air changes/hr with separate extraction for steam eqp and dry cleaning.

Service bay

Should be arranged in such way that incoming goods can be kept separate from outgoing refuse and preferably with separate entrance for staff all under supervision of control office. Vehicles back up to loading dock. Provide wash down, weighing scales, staff clock-in. Allow sufficient height and turning space for large vehicles. Columns and corners to be protected from damage by vehicles.

Hotels

KITCHENS & STORES

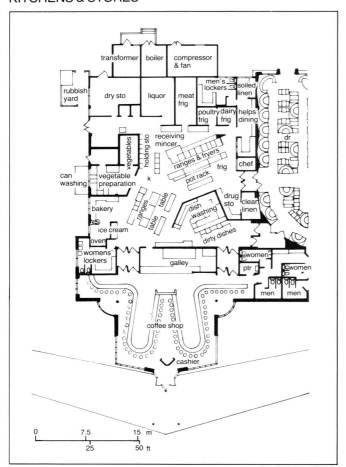

1 Kitchen layout of large roadside restaurant California USA

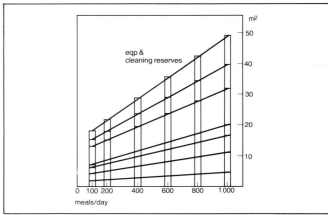

2 Total sto requirements for conventional k based on number of meals prepared/day

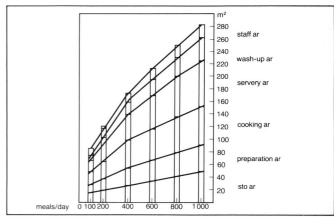

3 Ar required for sto k, servery & staff ar using conventional methods of food preparation

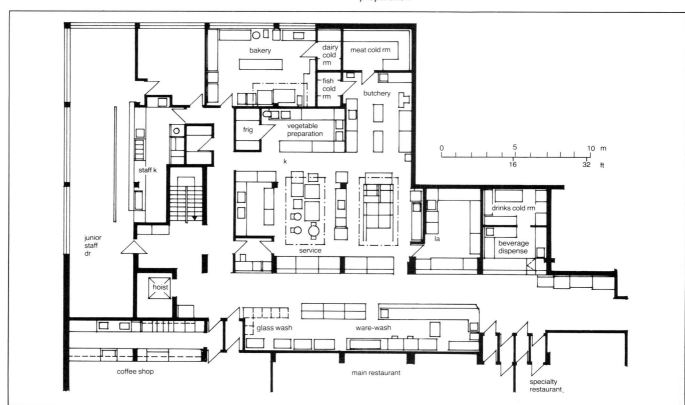

4 Example of k to serve 4 restaurants: coffee shop 120 covers; main restaurant 100 covers; specialty restaurant 100 covers; staff dr 80 covers; main food sto in basement, also service & k to function rm

ADMINISTRATION

In small hotels office accn may be limited to general office behind reception desk, manager's office and chef's or control office at rear. Larger hotels will require all or some of following:

At front of house associated with reception: reservations office, front office manager, chief cashier, sales manager, secretary.

General admin (preferably near reception but can be elsewhere): general manager, 2 or 3 assistant managers, secretaries, chief accountant, accounts' dept, duplicating rm, archives.

At back of house: control office at service bay, storeman, personnel office, secretary and clerk, waiting rm, chief engineer, security officer, chef (within kitchen), housekeeper, training rm.

Space allowance for offices (UK): $0.3–0.4 \, m^2/rm$ or in accordance with statute (→Bib346 347).

Staff accommodation

In large hotels provide staff canteen for approx ⅓rd staff with own kitchen. Canteen should be accessible without staff having to go through kitchen. Senior staff dining rm may be required. In small hotels senior staff may use restaurant and junior staff dining rm may be supplied from main kitchen. Provision of staff toilets →Bib341 480.

Lockers: 1 full height locker for each member of staff should be provided: space allowance $0.36 \, m^2/P$ excluding bench space: ½ height lockers may be used for certain grades of staff. Assume equal number male and female staff unless otherwise informed.

Staff sleeping accn depends on location and management policy. Manager's flat may be required.

Technical areas

Maintenance engineer's workshop and sto required adjacent plant rm. May include, according to size of hotel, furniture sto, engineering eqp sto, carpenters shop, paint shop, printing dept. All under chief engineer's eye. Access for replacement of heavy plant to be allowed for. Space also required for el sub-station and switch rm.

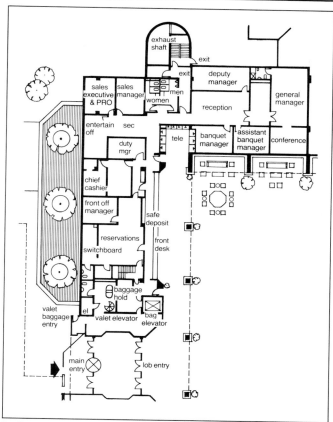

2 Example of admin off for large hotel: except for front desk, reservations & cashier these may also be sited elsewhere, *eg* on mezzanine

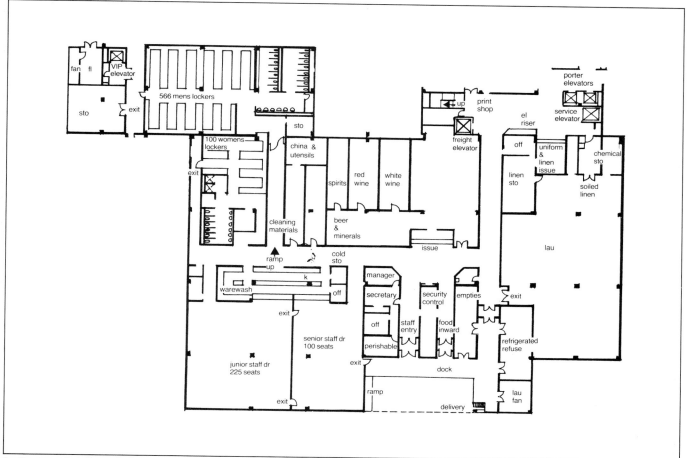

1 Service ar & staff accn for large hotel

Hotels

GUEST BEDROOMS

Bedroom sizes →(1)

In medium tariff hotels 2-B rm typically approx 15–17 m². High tariff hotels may have rm up to 28 m², excluding lobby and bathr but including sitting area.

American size bed: twin 990 × 1900; double 1370 × 2030; queen size 1520 × 2100; king size 1830 wide.

Most hotel organisations build bedr sized to take twin or double beds in order provide flexibility and avoid built-in obsolescence as standards raised in future. Some rm may have fold-away beds so that they may also be used as sitting rm or small meeting rm →(2). Murphy beds fold vertical closed with wall panel.

Floor to ceiling height 2500 (min 2300) with lower ceiling of 2000 over entry to allow for mechanical services.

Except at resort hotels balconies not usually favoured by hoteliers because of cost and maintenance problems.

Proportion of rm (approx 20%) with communicating doors. Should be 2 doors, preferably with rubber or neoprene gaskets to reduce sound transference. Sound transmission between bedr and between bedr and corridors should be minimised by dB reduction of 45–50. Where external noise from heavy traffic or aircraft provide double glazing for reduction 40–42 av dB.

For greater privacy and sound insulation additional door may be placed between entry lobby and bedr.

Private bathrooms

Bathr normally contain wc, wash basin or vanity unit with mirror over, bath with shower. In some de luxe hotels and in most S European and S American hotels bidet necessary. Showers in place of baths save little in cost or space, therefore not often provided. Shower compartment in addition to bath sometimes provided in de luxe hotels, as also separate or screened off wc.

Bathr should be carefully planned in relation to plumbing and ventilation ducts. These should be located in relation structure and ease of access for maintenance.

Following additional features should be included: glazed tiling round bath tub (at least), grab handles for bath shower and bath, shower curtain and rail, soap tray, removable bath panel for access to plumbing, shower mixer valve preferably thermostatically controlled, adequate towel racks in accordance with class of hotel, good shelf space if vanity top not provided, el shaver connexion, bath mat and non-slip surface to bath/shower, toilet roll holder, clothes hooks. Other items to be considered: tissue dispenser, bottle opener, hook for shoe duster, waste basket, sanitary bin, stool. Good lighting over mirror essential.

Bedroom corridors & stairs

Corridors not over-long; may be 1200–2000 wide according type of hotel. Corridor flow capacity →p407. Where width less than 2000 consider modulating corridor by recessing bedr doors. Ceiling void often used to house engineering services: height to ceiling not less than 2250.

Direction signs and numbering of doors to be clear and well lit. Protect corners from damage. El socket outlets at 12 m intervals. Provide emergency lighting. Carpet floor for quietness. Space for shoe cleaning machines, drink dispensers and ice machines may be required in corridors or lobbies.

Fire precautions →(4)

Follow national and local fire codes.

Doors to bedr to be self-closing with min half hour fr. Partitions separating guest rm from corridors to have 1 hour resistance unless automatic sprinklers installed. Min fire ratings for separation of exits such as staircases normally: bldg up to 3 storeys 1 hour, 4 storeys or more 2 hours.

In UK self-closing smoke stop doors should be provided every 18 m in corridors and at all exit staircases. Max travel distances to exit stairs shown in diagram. Linings to corridors and stairs should have class A or B rating for surface flame spread.

All exit stairs must be at least 1050 wide, be of fr construction in fire protected enclosure having 2 hour rating. Access must be through vestibule fitted with self-closing doors at least 1000 wide. Locked doors should be provided with panic bolts or break glass system.

Floor service

Number of rm per floor should ideally be related to number of rm which can be serviced by 1 maid: will depend on class of hotel, productivity of staff and size of rm, but will come within the range of 12–18 rm per maid.

Maids' rm should be centrally located and close to service elevators. These should contain space for service trolleys (carts), soiled linen hampers, clean linen racks and rubbish sacks. Depending on class of hotel and rm service system pantry may also be required: should contain shelves for setting out breakfast trays, sinks and work top, refrigerator, ice maker, boiler, toaster, space for trolleys.

There are arguments for and against linen and rubbish chutes. Need should be checked with operator.

Every floor should also have sto space for cots, extra beds and spare tv sets.

In hotels where maids cannot get from bedr to staff toilets without passing through public rm, eg in motor hotels and motels, provision may be made for staff toilets and changing rm in bedr block.

	bed size	rm ar
single bed	1000 × 2000	8.75 m²
double bed	1500 × 2000	12.5 m²
twin beds	1000 × 2000	13.5 m²

1 Basic min rm sizes (excluding lob & bathr)

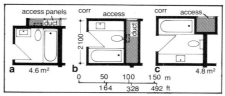

3 Typical arrangements of bathr & ducts: access panels to ducts should be ½ hr fr; ducts should have fire stops between floors; sizes vary with height of bldg; 'a' is best for access to duct but 'b' & 'c' provide more space for vanity top

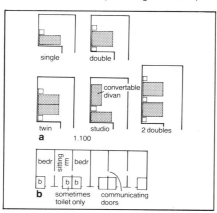

2 **a** basic bed requirements **b** arrangement of sitting rm between bedr provides max flexibility for suites; suites can also be formed at corners of bldg or where standardisation of structural grid not possible; luxury suites may also be planned as penthouse or villas in grounds

4 Fire: max travel distances

1 max allowable travel distance from most remote corner of rm to doorway
2 in multi-rm suites no single cross-rm dimension should exceed 9 m
3 in multi-rm suites any associated private corr should not exceed 7.5 m in length
4 stage 2 escape; no further than 18 m allowed from exit door of rm to entrance of protected route
5 dead end portion of any escape corr should not exceed 7.6 m

5 Typical service ar for 50–60 rm/floor; note: **a** provision of ptr depends on class of hotel and rm service arrangements in k **b** local linen sto or cpd may be required depending on method of control **c** floor sto for beds, cots not shown

GUEST BEDROOMS

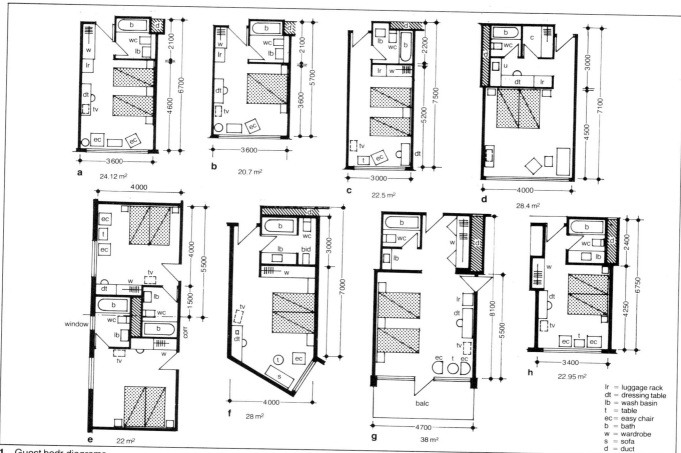

1   Guest bedr diagrams

lr = luggage rack
dt = dressing table
lb = wash basin
t = table
ec = easy chair
b = bath
w = wardrobe
s = sofa
d = duct

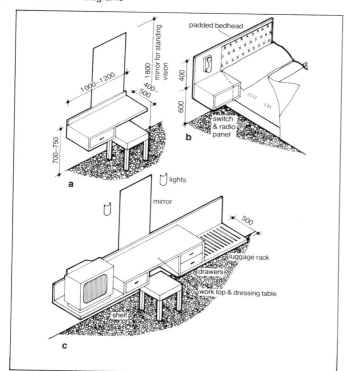

2   **a** dressing table unit **b** night table & bedhead with wall hung telephone to leave table clear: table may be splayed to allow easy movement of bed
c combined dressing table, luggage rack & tv unit; may be cantilevered for ease of cleaning but if so must be firmly anchored to take P sitting; upstand should be provided at back of fitment to prevent dirt marks on wall; luggage rack may be replaced by tea making unit; lights should be placed to illuminate work top & both sides of face evenly

Diagrams →(1)(2) show configurations for bedr and bathr. Most new hotels planned with private bathr attached to bedr; examples without private bathr therefore not included.

a Typical twin bedr in common use: 3600 rm width optimum for economy/comfort; wardrobe in lobby
b Similar but reduced in depth for single or double bed
c Narrow frontage scheme against bathr
d Width of rm increased allow possibility of dressing area & walk-in closet
e Bathr placed between bedr allow one bathr have natural light
f Layout provides for separate wc compartment with bidet if required; angled window can be applied to any of these schemes & allows for extra sitting area & directional view
g Luxury bedr with vanity unit separated from bathr
h Staggering wardrobes in partition wall can save space

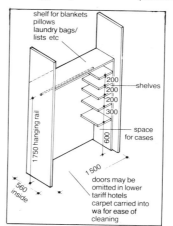

3   Typical combined unit wa: where hanging space only allow 500 rail/P; some luxury hotels have walk-in closets & dressing rm

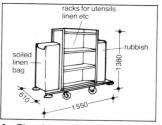

4   Chambermaid's trolley (cart)

5   Linen trolley (cart) with removal fabric

Hotels

BUILDING SERVICES

→(1) shows salient features of bldg services design (→p383–97) but following additional points should be noted:

Emergency electrical supply

Certain essential services must be maintained in event of failure of mains supply. Generator will be required maintain following: fire exit and emergency lights, approx 20% of public area lighting, cold rm and refrigerators, fire pumps, cash registers, fire alarm indicator systems, telephone communications, sump and sewage pumps.

Fire alarm systems

Following essential: manual break-glass contacts and automatic smoke or heat detectors with audible warning throughout bldg; automatic recessed hose reels throughout, hoses to be capable of reaching every bedr; external fire hydrants; portable fire extinguishers at strategic locations; asbestos blankets in kitchen; fire dampers.

Air conditioning

Central system generally preferred to individual rm units. Should be capable of being controlled by guests in bedr. Public areas must be zone controlled to cope with peak loads and for economy when certain areas not in use. Good maintenance access to all units essential.

Central heating

If air-conditioning (normal USA) not adopted bedr should be heated by radiators with individual controls designed for quick response. Public rm, particularly restaurants, should be provided with controlled mech ventilation to balance kitchen extract. Bars should have extract fans.

Bathroom ventilation

Generally extract system should be ducted to fans on roof with individual bathr connected to main riser by shunt ducts to minimise sound transmission between bathr.

Lighting

Bedr lighting systems to be arranged so that at least 1 main light switched from door and bedhead. More elaborate switching arrangements may be adopted according to type of hotel. Fluorescent lighting in bathr to be of 'quick start' type. Each bedr or pair of bedr to have consumer unit with isolating switches. Corridor lighting should be time switched so that sections can be turned off at certain periods for economy. Public rm should be switched in zones and special consideration given to decorative effects. Main switches should be located where public cannot reach them.

Shaver sockets

There should be dual voltage (single voltage USA) shaver sockets in all private bathr and male public toilets.

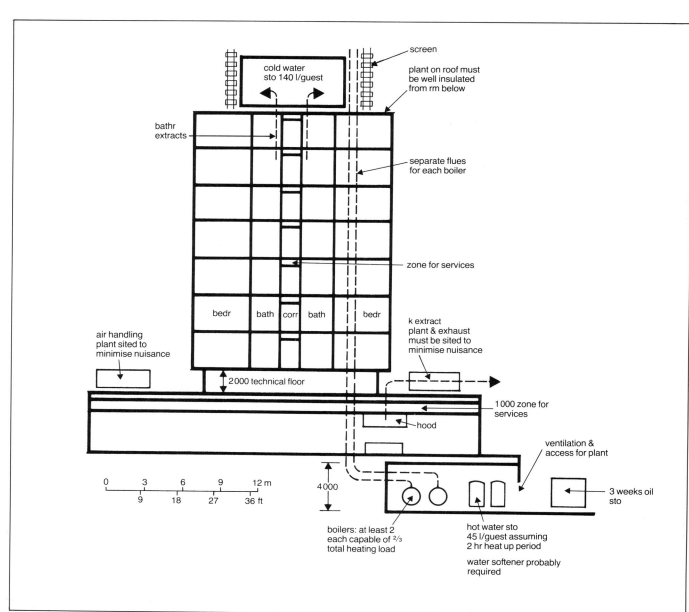

1 Section showing salient features of bldg services design for hotel

Motels

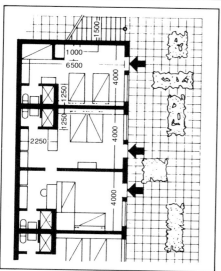

1 Unit open to 1 side only; 3 different layouts Arch Polivnick

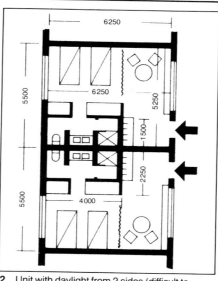

2 Unit with daylight from 2 sides (difficult to control) Arch Roberto

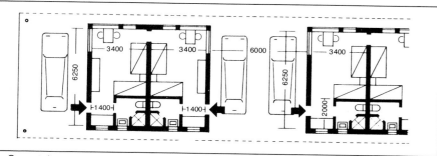

3 Carports between groups of 3 or 6 units Arch Duncan

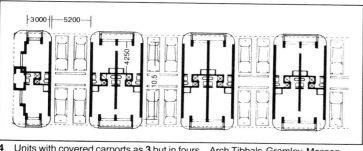

4 Units with covered carports as **3** but in fours Arch Tibbals-Gramley-Masson

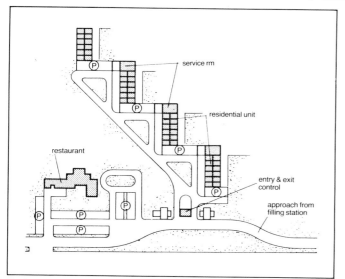

5 Layout of motel with parking ar for each block & restaurant as independent establishment Arch Fried

Location

On major highways, often near large towns, excursion centres and holiday resorts, and convenient for supplies (water, el, gas, fresh food and laundry). Restaurant, petrol and garage services need not be connected to motel but should be available nearby.

Sited so that passing headlights do not sweep bldg: avoid hilly terrain because of noise of vehicles braking and changing gear.

Approach

Take into consideration stopping distance of cars: 100 kph ~ 150 m.

Entrance: leads to reception (short stop), then to parking area (carport or garage) near as possible to rm. Exit through reception (control and return of keys).

Size

Motels generally 1-storey and spread out since land relatively cheap.

If run by couple without help 10–12 units practicable; 1 helper required for every additional 10 rm.

If affected by seasons, divide motel into smaller groups of 4–8 rm with stop-cocks for water, el, gas etc. Single bldg cost more than terrace housing.

If trucks to be excluded construct low canopy over passage at reception.

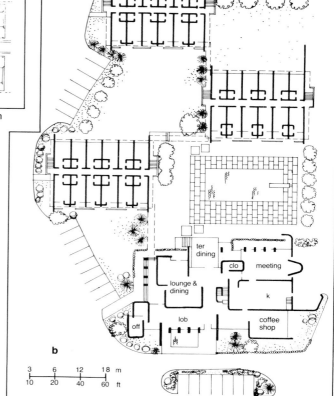

6 Motor hotel Revere Massachusetts USA **a** units in blocks of 12 with access to parking at end each bldg **b** catering & admin bldg provides for entertaining, dining, conferring Arch Salsberg & Le Blanc

Motels

1   Staggered layout of residential units with reception & caretaker's flat   Arch Williams

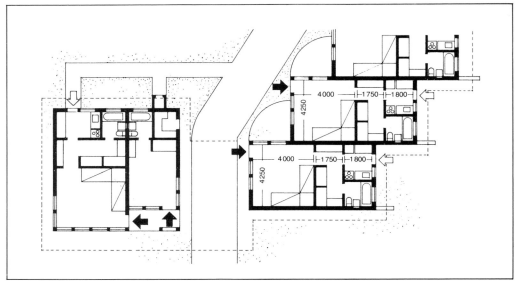

2   2 double rm with lob (for cold season) and cabin (for ch) which can be used separately or with either rm

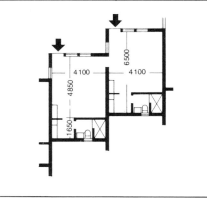

Provide large central rm for all guests, with recesses for writing and reading, card tables, radio, television, souvenir shops etc.

Telephone boxes should have provision for sitting and writing, and have maps, directories etc available as mostly used for long-distance calls.

Room size

Large than for city hotel: approx 4000 × 4000 up to 5000 × 5000, with bathr and if necessary kitchenette, even if only 1 bed.

Provide inter-communicating doors between units so that suites may be formed.

Since 90% guests stay only 1 night cupboards and chests unnecessary: provide large coat racks on wall instead, where belongings hang visibly, so less likely to be left behind.

Ancillary rooms

1 centrally situated linen rm with 5 sets linen/B (1 being used, 3 in sto, 1 in laundry). Cleaner's rm accomodates trolley (cart) with compartments for clean and dirty linen, soap, bath salts, toilet paper, vacuum cleaner, broom, floor polish etc.

If possible direct access from rm to car park. Efficient drainage of approaches, parking areas and paths, as guests enter rm straight from outside.

Play areas some distance away to avoid disturbing resting guests.

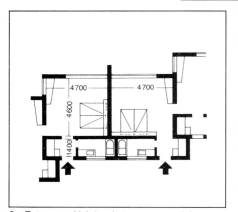

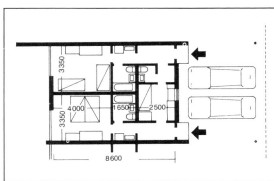

3   Entrance with b/wc, between car park & guest rm for sound insulation   Arch Hornbostel

4   Staggered layout with approach from 1 side only   Arch Thompson

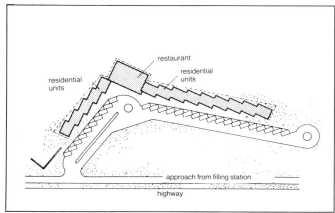

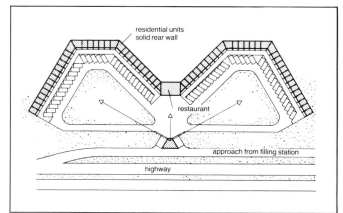

5   Layout of **3** with restaurant   Arch Hornbostel

6   Establishment with efficient entrance & exit control

Convention hotels

a

restaurants	m²	occupancy	
main lob:			
main restaurant	595	425	
coffee shop	280	400	
lob bar	185	185	
mezzanine:			
gourmet restaurant	370	200	
lower lob:			
snack bar	175	185	
ice cream parlour & cafe	93	75	
night club	520	375	
convention space		meeting	banquet
small ballrm 1	520	800	400
small ballrm 2	390	600	300
grand ballrm	3750	5785	2900
guest of honour rm	540	758	880
total 3 adjoining ballrm	4660	7148	3580
preconvention foyer space	740		
total ar contiguous meeting rm	5390		
21 additional meeting rm: av size 75–100 P	70		
exhibition space (convertible to parking)	7930		
shops			
main lob floor	58		
mezzanine	520		
lower lob	432		
total	1010		

Planning and design concept which absorbed large proportion of hotel investment in USA during 1970s, often as part of efforts regenerate inner city areas. Basic characteristic: large amount of space available for convention business activities such as meetings, exhibitions, seminars. Conventions entail dense traffic: 400-rm hotel can have population 800 or more at height of convention or conference.

Flexibility of space essential →(1)(2). Spaces for eating capable of being served independently at all times but kitchens should utilise same central supplies (*eg* water, gas, drainage).

Staff servicing guests or working behind public spaces should not cross or impede public areas →(2). In addition to segregation of personnel, main public and meeting areas require large outside halls for security, check-in by conference organisers, provision of coffee, literature and exhibition stalls etc.

Large numbers involved make necessary control of traffic in and between main convention spaces. Use of atrium as unifying design concept →p223(1) groups ballrm, meeting rm, exhibition spaces, shops, bars, restaurants on 4 levels. Service functions of offices, laundry, sto, loading thus contiguous with space they serve but out of sight; segregation of vehicles also obtained.

Conferences and conventions generate need for bedr with space and eqp for daytime business meetings. Small kitchen, tables, easy chairs, adequate lighting required →p222(1d). (Rm thus equipped termed suites in some hotel chains.)

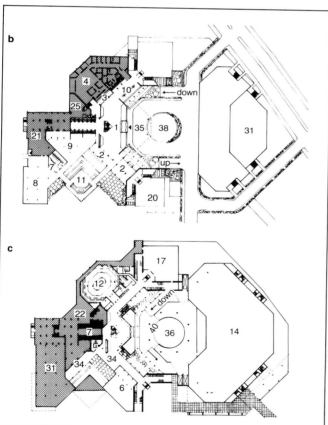

1 Phoenix of Atlanta Hotel USA **a** breakdown of public ar (total of 2058 guest rm) **b** main lob floor **c** lower lob floor   Arch Alan Lapidus

key 1 main lo 2 lo lounge 3 registration 4 admin 5 luggage holding 6 shops & agencies 7 check rm 8 restaurant 9 coffee shop 10 news stand 11 bar/cocktail lounge 12 discotheque 14 grand ballrm 17 meeting rm 20 receiving k 21 main k 22 k 25 rm service 30 maintenance & sto 31 mech 34 snack bar 35 main entrance 36 convention foyer 37 reception & control 38 open light well 40 convention entrance

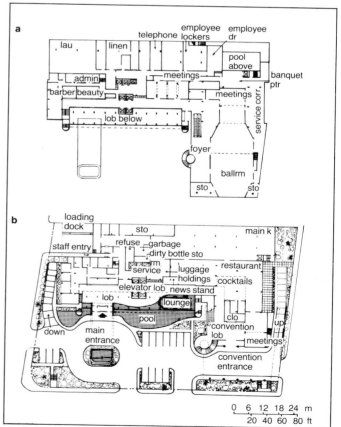

2 Small convention hotel (400 rm) **a** second floor **b** main floor: showing segregation of hotel & convention business vehicle traffic & tight control of service & personnel traffic inside

Convention hotels

EXAMPLES

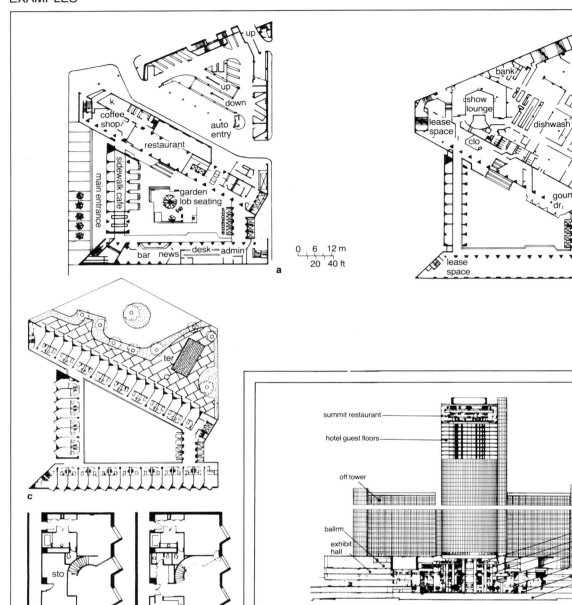

1 Hyatt Regency Hotel Houston Texas USA
a lob floor **b** first floor **c** typical guest rm floor
d examples of bedr suites showing provision of
meeting space; note possible use of dividing walls
to create smaller rm   Arch JVIII

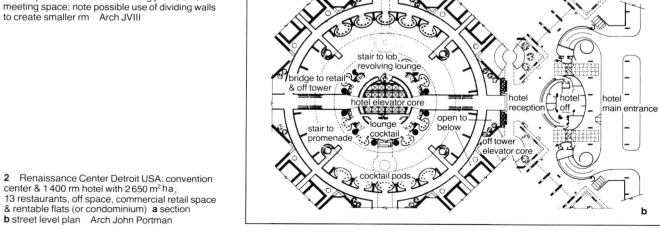

2 Renaissance Center Detroit USA: convention
center & 1 400 rm hotel with 2 650 m² ha,
13 restaurants, off space, commercial retail space
& rentable flats (or condominium) **a** section
b street level plan   Arch John Portman

EXAMPLES

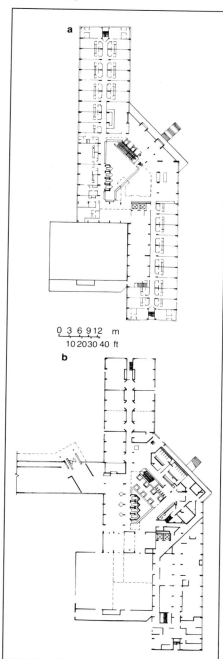

1 Hyatt Hotel Boston USA: atrium design with added feature of orientation over river providing view from public spaces & guest rm **a** ground floor **b** typical guest rm floor   Arch John Portman

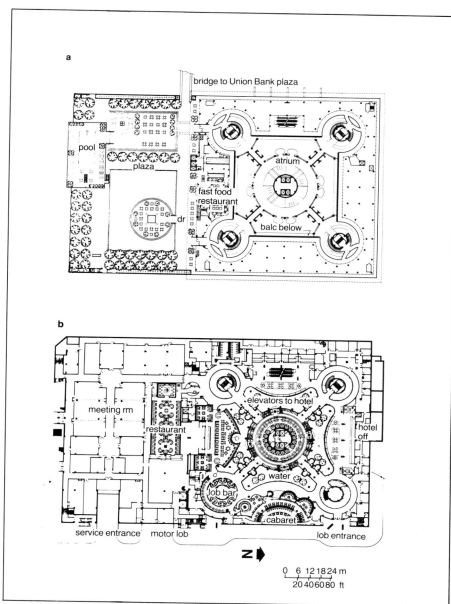

2 Bonaventure Hotel Los Angeles USA: atrium design incorporating 4 cylindrical towers & central tower **a** retail floor **b** lob floor Arch John Portman

Hotel references:
→Bibliography entries 001 011 043 050 147 176 223 255 272 273 274 319 324 341 346 347 363 377 440 477 480 583 645

Public houses

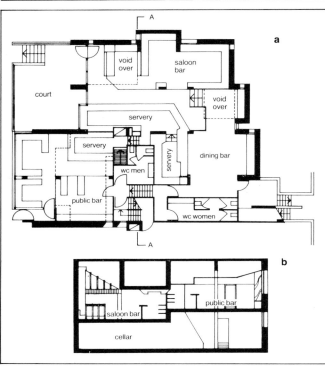

1 Lord High Admiral London England: entirely modern pub which recreates atmosphere of traditional English design, contained within large scale housing scheme; bars separated, varying in design & comfort: **a** ground floor **b** section   Arch Darbourne & Drake

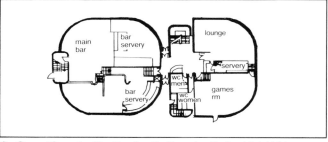

2 Ground floor plan The Fanciers Northampton England; bright & breezy working men's club; colourful use of materials, striped glass panels & curved corners   Arch Roscoe Milne Partnership

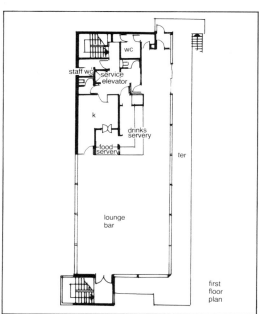

3 1st floor plan Foxhills golf club Chertsey England   Arch Building Design Associates

English pubs famous as social institutions throughout world: very difficult create afresh. Being increasingly copied as special attractions in large European and American towns. (Even prefab pubs available for export.)

Few modern designs have satisfactorily caught right atmosphere; many originals have been brutally altered, often first to so-called modern design, then back again to spurious Edwardian. Constant feature of successful pubs seems to be breaking up of space into small intimate rm which nevertheless retain feeling of bustle all round. Traditional way do this central servery with bars radiating round. Good pub has something of theatre about it: good taste should be used sparingly; brashness and vulgarity have place in interior fittings.

Regulations

Apart from statutes, for purpose of fire safety UK pubs mainly controlled under liquor licensing law. Applicants opening pub must apply to local magistrates for licence. Must also notify fire authority, which has power inspect premises on questions of adequacy of fire separation, between such areas as kitchens and bars, and means of escape. Fire authority inspector has power object granting of licence if dissatisfied.

For pubs catering for less than 50 people 1 exit generally considered enough when pub 1-storey. Elaborate formula, takes into account travel distances, door widths and numbers of people, to calculate number of exits needed for pubs serving more than 50 people.

Unless pubs employ more than 20 little affected by (UK) Shops & Offices Act; but if parts of larger structures full rigour of bldg reg apply: could dictate, *eg,* provision of sprinklers at base of multi-storey block. Finishes on walls and ceilings also controlled by reg to prevent flame spread.

Amenities

Scale, siting, quality, cleanliness of lavatories most important aspect of successful pub; can be decisive in keeping or losing customers: particularly important when renovating old pubs.

Most pubs now also provide some snack bar service though not usually with stools →p205; provision of heating and cooking eqp suitable for bar counter important. Quick restaurant service for lunch time trade now common in town pubs, necessitating some kitchen and food preparation area.

Do not forget provision for pub games, generally darts, dominoes but some highly localised.

For modern cellar techniques and installations consult client and/or (in UK) Brewers' Society.

4 Markham Arms Chelsea England; sympathetic conversion of existing Victorian pub; original bow front remains; addition has been tacked on at back; geometry of bow repeated in built-in seating: **a** ground floor **b** section   Arch Roderick Gradidge

Office buildings

BUILDING TYPE

Office bldg either custom built to meet particular set of requirements or speculatively to attract largest possible range of tenants. This distinction has led to wide differences in bldg form. In theory should be no difference at all because same fundamental principle applies to all office design: organisations change far more rapidly than bldg. Distinction managed by distinguishing between design for 4 scales of time:

Shell last at least 50 years: must be designed to meet wide variety of organisational needs →(1).

Services become obsolete as office technology changes and must be replaced at least every 15 years →(2).

Scenery: fitting out of office interiors to meet precise organisational needs; scenery need last only so long as lease, usually 5–7 years →(3).

Sets: positioning and repositioning scenery elements such as desks, chairs, screens and partitions to meet immediate organisational needs perhaps even every 3 or 4 months →(4).

2 fundamental developments in office bldg in recent years. First, significance of long term **shell** diminishing as short term **scenery,** particularly furniture, absorbs more and more functions. Carrying services, visual and acoustic separation and decoration now frequently achieved by furniture. Second, becoming increasingly difficult distinguish office function from allied activities such as lab, industrial processes, education →(5).

OFFICE FUNCTION

Most employees in advanced economies work in offices. Office work primarily involves handling information and making decisions based upon information. This definition hides enormous variations in size of office organisations, office technology and styles of management.

Range includes multi-nationals which employ thousands of people in only 1 of many bldg to 1-man enterprises.

Much office work sedentary but offices also include spaces for machinery, canteens, meetings, filing, libraries and other ancillary activities which can take up ⅓ of space needed by organisation →(6).

Office organisations changing rapidly and in every respect. Extreme care should be taken to avoid building obsolescence into new bldg.

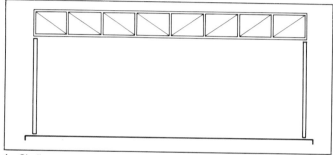

1   Shell

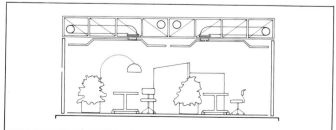

2   Shell & services

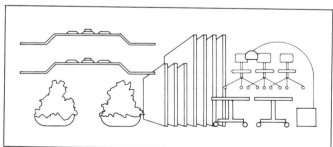

3   Scenery

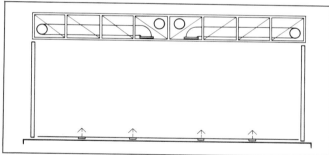

4   Sets

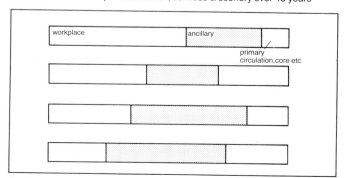

5   Relative cost comparison of shell, services & scenery over 45 years

6   Comparison of space requirements in 4 bldg showing various relationships of workplace/ancillary needs

Office buildings

	gross floor ar – for planning purpose in UK equivalent to GOA used for costing purposes in USA	gross floor ar – for costing purposes in UK	net usable ar	rentable ar lettable ar (British practice)	lettable ar (USA & European practice)	bldg core	service ar
each off floor							
thickness of external walls	●	●					
columns	●	●					
staircases	●	●		●		●	●
lifts	●	●				●	●
lav	●	●			option	●	●
ducts	●	●				●	●
plant rm	●	●				●	●
circulation within core	●	●				●	●
public corr	●	●	●				
private corr			●	●	●		
internal walls required for bldg purposes–not influenced by space use	●	●					
internal walls – tenant's own subdivision			●	●	●		
floor reception		●	●	●	●		
off space/desk ar	●	●	●	●	●		
whole bldg							
bldg plant rm	●	●	●	★	■		●
bldg reception	●	●	●	★	★		
covered parking	● (if enclosed)	● (if enclosed)		†	†		
sto for whole building eg in basement	●	●	●	★	★		

★ option if single letting ■ partially included
† subject to separate rental calculation ● wholly included

1 Definitions of terms used to describe office ar: precise definition sometimes difficult because of different usages, variations in bldg design (*eg* slab & centre core), difference between letting floors, parts of floors & whole bldg

DEFINITIONS OF OFFICE AREAS →(1)

Efficiency of office bldg usually measured in terms of ratio of usable office area to gross area of bldg. Real estate definitions vary but basic units always same:

Work place area (or useable area): spaces in which possible for people to work at desks; includes secondary circulation.

Primary circulation: circulation essential to provide access and means of escape to work place areas.

Special areas: space which cannot be used for office workers but is dedicated to particular function, *eg* archives, restaurant.

Core: space needed for support of bldg, *eg* lifts, stairs, ducts, lavatories.

Gross outside area (GOA): →(2a)(2b) sum of all constituent office areas including core, structure and perimeter walls.

Net usable area (NUA): →(2c)(2d) what remains when core, structure and perimeter walls subtracted from GOA.
Core in multi-storey office bldg should occupy no more than 20% of GOA →(2e). Obviously smaller core more efficient bldg →p228–9.
Primary circulation usually takes up between 10 and 15% of net usable area. Special areas vary enormously depending upon function of office organisation →(3). NB in multi-tenanted bldg primary circulation sometimes excluded from 'rentable' area.

Special areas should be convertible to work place area. Not all work place area equally valuable. Common design faults →(4) which result in insufficient use of space:
columns too close to perimeter walls
wasteful modules
dominant columns fixing primary circulation routes
space of wrong depth
provision of services only at perimeter

2 a for planning purposes gross floor ar is total of bldg measured from outside edge of exterior walls **b** for cost purposes gross floor ar total of bldg measured from inside external walls **c** NUA: UK practice excludes all corr between tenancies **d** NUA: USA practice excludes only circulation in core **e** bldg core: example has major & minor core

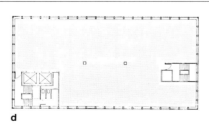

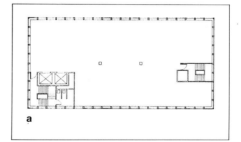

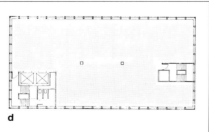

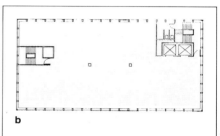

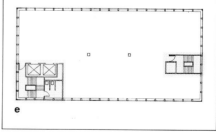

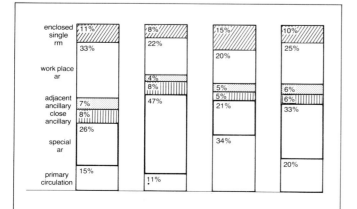

3 Analysis of space use in 4 projects showing varying space requirements

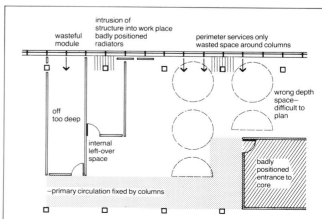

4 Common design faults

Office buildings

TYPES OF OFFICE SHELL

3 factors determine shape of floor of office bldg →(1):

Depth of space: depth of any work place area measured between perimeter or core and primary circulation.

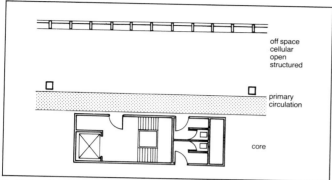

1 Determinants of shape

Positions of primary circulation: fixed? does it serve to 1 side or 2 (single or double loaded corridors)?

Position of core: placed centrally, or at 1 end, or detached.

3 major bands of office space depths can be identified →(2):
narrow, 4000–6000: suitable for single office rm or for 2–3 open plan work places
medium, 6000–8000: suitable for enclosures larger than single rm or for 3–5 open plan workplaces
deep, 8000 + : more than 5 open plan work places deep

These depths can be combined in various ways and together with position of core and circulation generate wide range of office shell configurations →(3).

CELLULARISATION

Greatest test of office bldg capacity to accomodate various kinds of organisation: degree to which can be divided up into rm of various sizes. Not all organisations require large number of small rm and not all can use high proportion of open plan space successfully. In life of organisation demand for cellular and open spaces will fluctuate. Consequently capacity of office bldg shell to provide range of rm arrangements must be measured. Should be remembered that small rm not just required for individual office but increasingly for other functions, eg noisy or confidential machines such as terminal printers or telexes. Capacity can be measured by number of rm of various sizes which can be provided in given shell →(4): this can be matched with demands of typical organisations for rm of various sizes →(5).

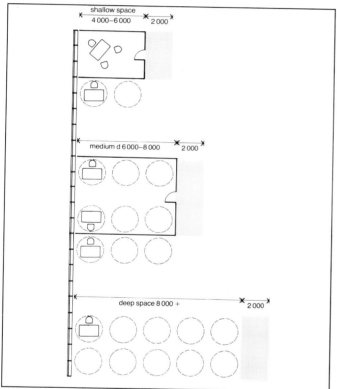

2 Space d

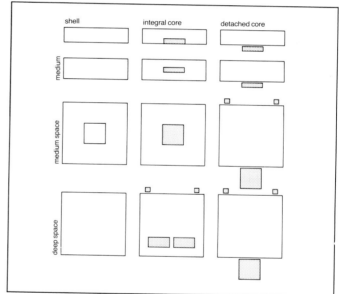

4 Shell array

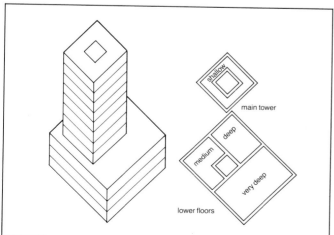

3 Space d

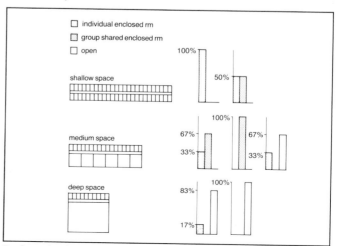

5 Capacity of 3 shells, showing max amounts of individual cellularisation and different ways of organising space

Office buildings

CORE

Office bldg core →(1)(2) p229(1)(4) must provide for:

Elevators: number and size depend upon population of bldg, number of floors, and required waiting time. Elevators should be grouped so that availability of any elevator in bank on any floor can be easily observed. In tall bldg elevators usually grouped to serve 10 or more floors →p410–12.

Ducts: vertical ducts required for heating, telephone, electrics, drainage and water supply; also in air-conditioned bldg for air movement. Provide on generous scale, particularly for increasingly important electrics and telecommunications. In large multi-storied air-conditioned bldg allow for:
vertical air movement
el
telecommunications & telephone
drainage
water supply
Services →p383–97

Lavatories: Proportion men and women on each floor may change: desirable that male and female wc be adjacent so that replanning possible using same ducts →(3).

Cleaners' cupboards: on each floor of multi-storey office bldg provide cleaners' cupboard (min 2 m²) containing sto and slop-hopper.

Stairs: width of stairs determined by reg on means of escape and in particular by numbers of staff to be provided for →p407–9.

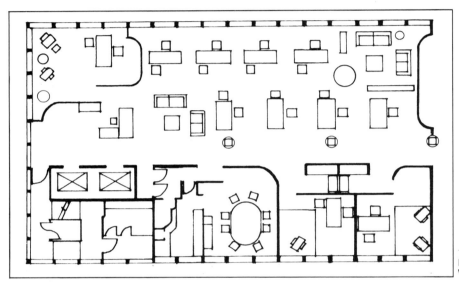

1 American Express Banking Corporation London England   Arch Duffy Eley Giffone Worthington

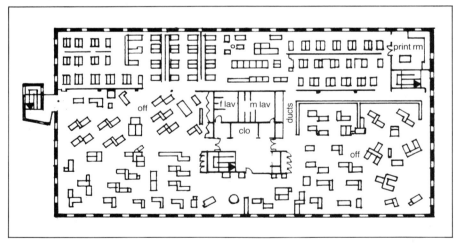

2 S W Electricity Board Bristol England   Arch SWEB Property Section

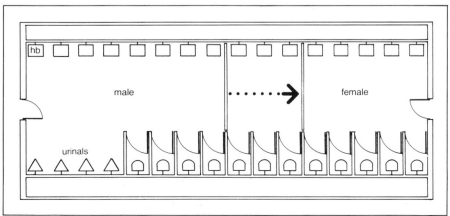

3 Grouping lavatory provision to allow for changing proportions of men & women

CORES: EXAMPLES

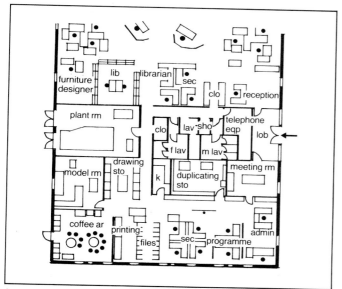

1 Dobson House Killingworth New Town England Arch Faulkner-Brown Hendy Natkinson Stonor

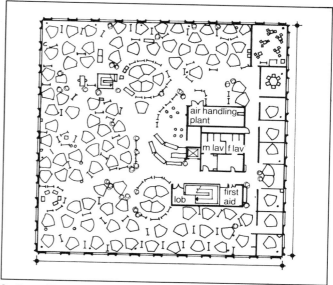

2 Dept of Environment London England Arch Property Services Agency

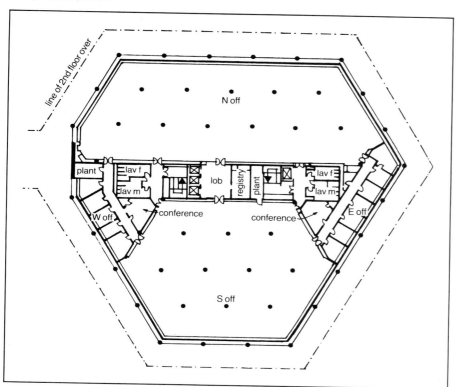

3 Greater London Council island block London England Arch GLC Architects Dept

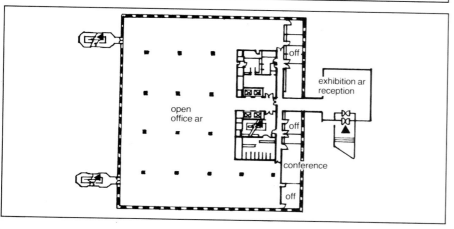

4 Europa House Stockport England Arch John Caytten & Partners

Office buildings

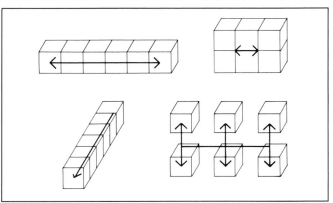

1   Connexions

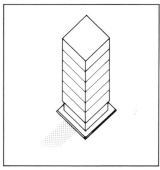

2   3   Organisation's interface with outside world reflected in how approached & degree of penetration allowed to public

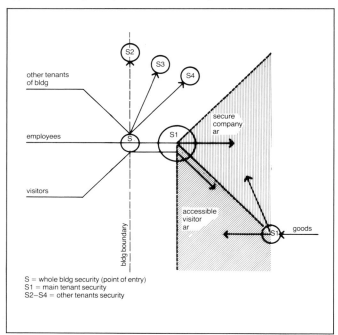

S = whole bldg security (point of entry)
S1 = main tenant security
S2–S4 = other tenants security

4   Types of access: depending on type of organisation, boundary shown between visitor & company ar may fade & 2 spaces become 1

RELATIONSHIPS

Office bldg can be designed provide best relationship between parts of organisation; travel distances both horizontal and vertical can be reduced; visual links between component parts can magnify sense of close relationship. Other bldg forms can be used to achieve precise opposite: max autonomy of component parts →(1).

INTERFACE WITH OUTSIDE WORLD

Ideally office bldg, whether speculative or custom built for 1 user, designed with 1 entrance so that contact with outside world controlled for security, to present united face to visitors, and to make finding one's way inside bldg obvious as possible →(3). However, different policy which allows for more than 1 entrance can be adopted if organisation does not value security so highly and wants to allow free access to several internal functions →(2). Another condition when major user wants sublet space. Proportion of sublet space may change: could cause severe design problems. Third problem: when office bldg designed to be let to very large number of small users and easy public access to all parts of bldg becomes a major objective.

Office buildings

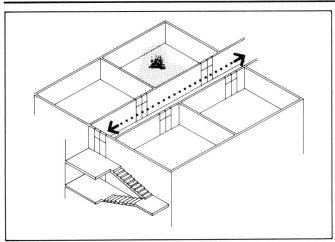

1 Alternative escape routes with limited travel distance must be available from fire to protected zone

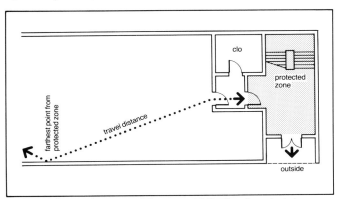

2 Travel distance from any point on ground & first floor to protected zone must not exceed 30.5 m

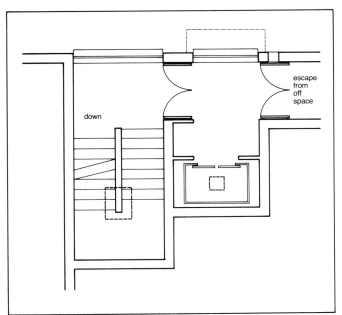

3 In some bldg over 18.3 m h some staircases should be constructed as fire-fighting staircases, with smoke outlets, vents & fr self-closing doors

MEANS OF ESCAPE

Means of escape important determinant of office bldg shell. In bldg over 2 storey travel distance from any point on office floor to escape stair strictly regulated (30 m). Alternative means of escape on each floor usually demanded. Design of access from bldg to street controlled. Reg also affect scenery planning: *eg* rm may not open off rm. Each space must have direct access to means of escape →p(1)–(3) →p91 → Bib346 347.

Office buildings

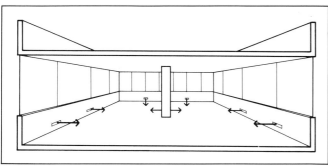

1 Perimeter servicing

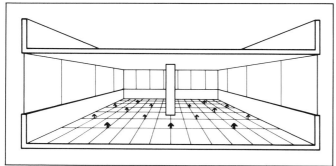

2 Floor grid

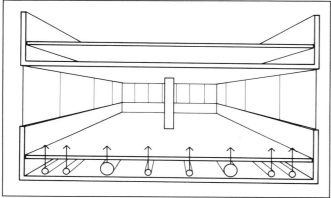

3 False floor servicing

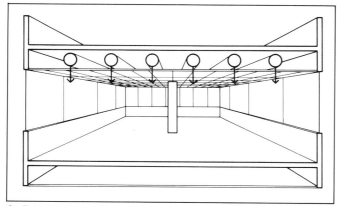

4 False ceiling servicing

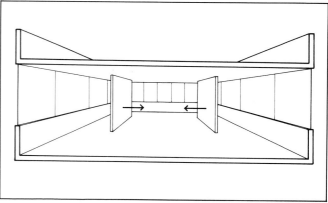

5 Distribution through fin walls

OFFICE SERVICES

Demand for services in offices increasing. Each work place must be next to outlets for power and telephone. Coaxial cable access for terminals frequently required: with increasing automation and tele-communications will become common see work stations with 6 or even 8 wires of various kinds. Already some organisations provide 1 terminal for every 2 work stations. Precise need for connexions cannot be predicted: essential provide grid to which each work station can have easy access without dangerous, trailing wires. Such grid can be provided in following ways:

distribution at perimeter and through partitions
distribution through floor grid (usually 1 800–2 000 centres)
distribution through false floors (height should be 50–500)
distribution from ceiling (NB problem with safety)
distribution through fin walls (points at desk top height)

INTERNAL ENVIRONMENT

Quality of internal environment become major consideration: rising energy costs mainly responsible, leading to reconsidering design of:
ventilation (natural – mechanical – air-conditioned)
lighting (high general levels – task lighting)
heating (single source – optional source)
→(1) for difference in energy use before and after energy crisis (c 1974). Environmental system should allow for:

Adaptability: servicing systems may be expected to have life of approx 15 years. System should be adaptable to:
varying degrees of cellularisation and screening as occupant changes
possible changes in fuel sources
changing expectations and standards

Control: individuals may be able control their immediate environment according to nature of work: providing some control over lighting and ventilation can help. Acceptable level of lighting and ventilation in 1 location must not create glare or draughts in another. Solution must recognise no 2 people equally comfortable in single environment.

Management & maintenance: environmental systems should be simple, maintenance free, easy to change. Depending on size, bldg manager/supervisor·will probably be needed, ideally appointed during construction and before commissioning.

Economic fuel consumption: flexibility to adapt to alternative economic fuel sources in future. →(2) for comparison of energy use in 4 generic bldg:

A shallow, 12 m deep, naturally ventilated
B shallow, 12 m deep, mech ventilated
C medium, 14 m deep, mech ventilated
D deep, 50 m deep, mech ventilated

Each bldg form has same gross floor area, construction and amount of glazing, with vertical dimensions adjusted to suit each.

Requirements for heating each plan form shown separately. Can be seen that relatively little difference in energy consumed with respect to variations in form, increased energy going into lighting as depth of space increases, compensating for reduction of energy for mech plant because of more compact shape of bldg.

Each plan form tested for 2 different overall lighting levels: 400 lux, 700 lux. Can be seen lighting and fan power can account for approx 70% of energy consumed.

If prime objective conserve energy attention must be paid to reducing artificial lighting requirements by:
providing min overall lighting level of 400 lux for office work
reducing lighting further and introducing task lighting
making greatest use of natural daylight and providing localised switching

Fan energy use may be reduced by attention to design of mech systems and by using low pressures and velocities for distribution of air.

Any economic environmental system must be designed for specific bldg to ensure energy usage kept low as possible.

However, first 2 questions any user must ask are:
what office plan form is required?
does this form or its location make air-conditioning necessary?

before energy crisis
high overall illumination levels (1 000 lux) min task lighting complex centralised control min external glazing heat recovery high thermal capcity excess heat sto single energy source deep plan bldg

after energy crisis
lower overall illumination levels task lighting more individual control more external glazing heat recovery lower thermal capacity excess heat sto possibility of additional energy sources variety of bldg forms

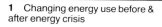

1 Changing energy use before & after energy crisis

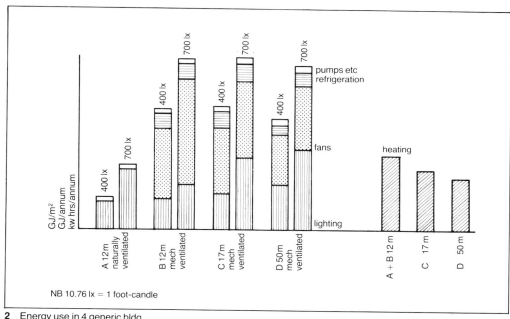

2 Energy use in 4 generic bldg

Office buildings

OFFICE CONSTRUCTION

3 critical constructional elements affect office layout: partitions, ceiling, window module. 2 basic choices: complete modular integration and its opposite, avoiding precise modules →(1).

Test of any office planning: how well range of small rm sizes can be accommodated. Small rm usually found in following approx sizes: 15 m², 20 m², 25 m², 30 m² (smallest size USA: 7.4 m²). Single rm depth should not exceed 6000 otherwise unusable space created towards back of each rm. Acceptable rm proportions should not exceed ratio of 1:1.5. Thus if strict modular grid thought necessary, 1500 min feasible grid →(2) (USA 1220–1524).

Ceiling grid can affect single rm design in similar way. Single most critical dimension: standard size of fluorescent tubes (1200, 1800, 2400; USA 1220, 1830, 2440).

Wide variety of possible types of ceiling: light fittings set in ceiling diagonal patterns
movable fittings
waffle grids
large coffers

All can be made compatible with planning small rm. Discipline of ceiling grid relaxed when task lighting used because fewer lights needed in ceiling.

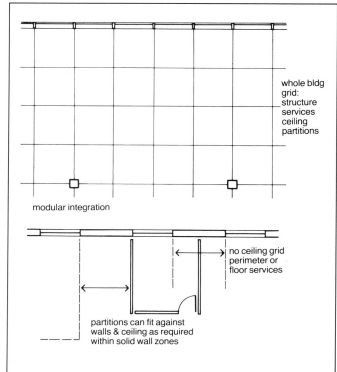

whole bldg grid:
structure
services
ceiling
partitions

modular integration

no ceiling grid perimeter or floor services

partitions can fit against walls & ceiling as required within solid wall zones

1   Non-modular & modular integration

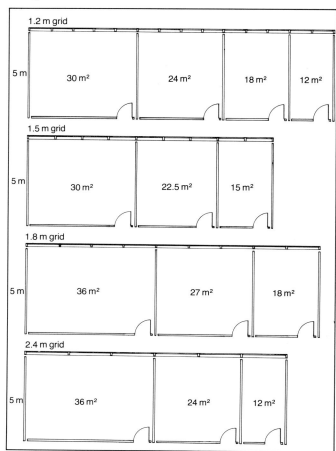

1.2 m grid

5 m | 30 m² | 24 m² | 18 m² | 12 m²

1.5 m grid

5 m | 30 m² | 22.5 m² | 15 m²

1.8 m grid

5 m | 36 m² | 27 m² | 18 m²

2.4 m grid

5 m | 36 m² | 24 m² | 12 m²

2   Range of rm sizes at constant 5000 depth with various window grid modules

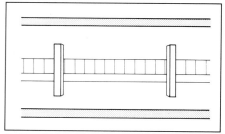

3   No grid, smooth finish, exposed concrete slab or direct finish ceiling, surface mounted light fittings

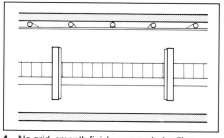

4   No grid, smooth finish, suspended ceiling, surface mounted light fittings

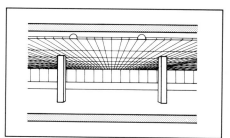

5   Linear grid, dry suspended ceiling, continuous 1-directional recessed light fittings

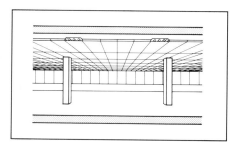

6   2-way gridded suspended ceiling with recessed light fittings

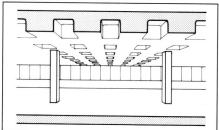

7   2-way small structural waffle grid

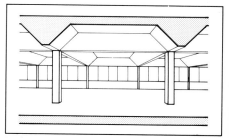

8   Large coffer/bay grid

Office buildings

SPACE STANDARDS

Rm sizes determined by space standards which allocate area and enclosure to different levels of staff. Many companies use such standards but wide variation in:
number of levels of staff
at which level enclosure required
allocation of space to levels

These factors, and even greater degree of variation in ancillary needs, make extremely difficult predict amount of space/head which should be used to calculate roughly amount of space needed to accommodate given number of staff. Certainly 10 m² NUA/head very low; 25 m²/head high. Any figure in between could be relevant to given organisation.

UK statutory min of workplace area excluding any ancillary approx 4 m². (No statutory min USA.)

CALCULATING SPACE REQUIREMENTS

Office area requirements calculated in 2 parallel ways:
people space (ie individual space standard × numbers) + allowance for immediate ancillary + factor (usually 15%) for primary circulation;
non-people space, eg machine rm, libraries, which depend more on eqp than on staff numbers for their area should be calculated by informed estimates based on existing good practice or comparable examples: again factor must be added for primary circulation.

CALCULATING RELATIONSHIPS

To prepare stacking plans ie relating 1 department to another in an existing bldg, or even to work out configuration of new office bldg, interconnexions between parts of organisation can be studied by more or less detailed surveys of communications.

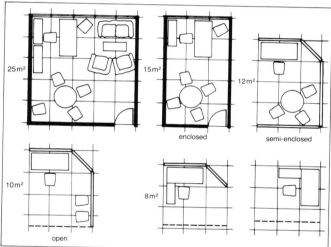

1 Examples of space standards

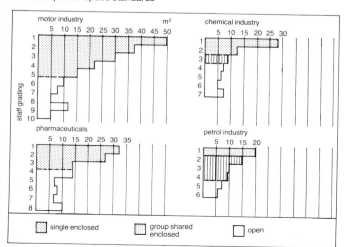

2 Comparative space standards in 4 companies

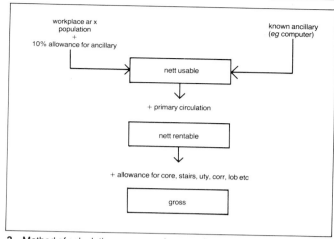

3 Method of calculating space requirements for whole bldg; adjustments should be made for shared common spaces in multi-tenanted bldg

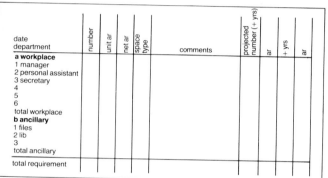

4 Example tabulation sheet used for recording existing space requirements & future predictions

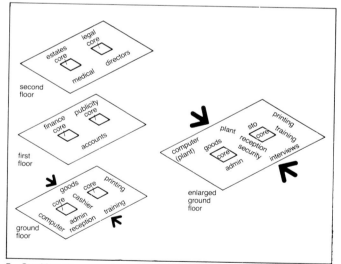

5 Stacking plan example

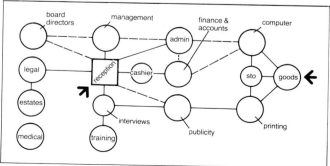

6 Interrelationships

Office buildings

	ventilation	loading	servicing	access
computer	★	★	★	★
lib	★	★	★	★
meeting	★	★	★	★
presentation	★	★	★	★
k	★	★	★	★
restaurant	★	★	★	★

1 Requirements of special ar

SPECIAL AREAS

Offices contain large number of special areas which may need:
ventilation (or air-conditioning) →p392
superior floor loading
to be placed away from windows in centre of bldg
special servicing even to extent of suspended floors
greater height than normal office dimensions
special access to public or goods

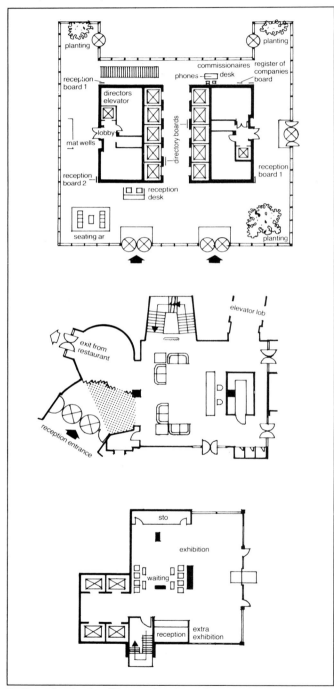

2 Examples showing different styles of reception

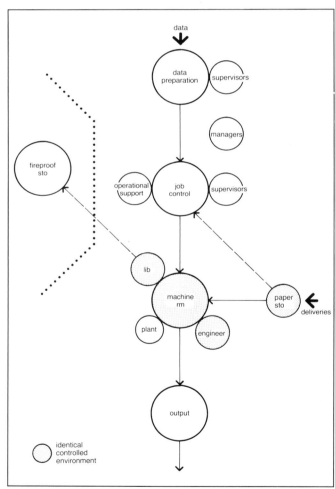

3 Computer rm

SPACES FOR MEETINGS
also →p238

type of space	number of P	typical space required per P	type of use	provision of eqp	location
provision at workplace meeting at desk	2–3	m² 2.0–2.75	short discussions briefing subordinates, personal interviews	1 or 2 visitor's chairs at work station	located in screened ar if in planned open off environment
meeting ar	4	1.5–2.5	working discussions with members of staff or visitors	conference table & chairs; related eqp: pinboard, chalk board	
provision for group of workplaces meeting ar	6–8	1.5–2.5	working sessions between members within group of personnel from outside involved with some project: may last several hr	conference table & chairs with some screening from surrounding work stations; related eqp: flip charts, pin up space, chalk board; provision of permanent notice board or chart board for use of group	located in group ar adjacent to primary circulation, to limit disturbance of individuals
provision for all members of staff interview rm	2–3	1.5–2.0	interviewing personnel or sales representatives; discussions with members of public: short periods of use up to ¾ hr	aural & visual privacy required	close to main entrance & dept with major usage; may require waiting ar adjacent if used frequently
rm	8–12	1.5–2.0	meetings with outside visitors or internal policy making & planning meetings: 2–3 hr meetings	slides, overhead projector, flip charts, dimmer lights, good ventilation; sto for drinks, audio-visual eqp	ease of access to all dept: easily serviced with refreshments; access for outside visitors without going through work ar; coats ar close by
rest ar	12–18	2.25–4.0	primarily used for refreshment breaks, but may also be ar where general notices, scheduling charts etc can be displayed; may become important point for exchange of information & ideas; used throughout day for short periods	vending machines, stand-up counters, low tables & easy chairs; display board; screening from work ar	adjacent to clo, wc & rest rm; equally accessible to all personnel on each floor
assembly ar	100–150		infrequent meetings: involvement of all staff		may use cafeteria or recreation space
board rm	16–24	1.5–2.0	formal board meetings; signing of contracts; management meetings; business lunches & entertaining: 2–3 hr meetings	formal layout; audio-visual eqp: good ventilation essential; telephone extension; space & eqp for stenographer	anterm (for refreshments & leaving coats) attached: easy access for refreshments: 2 visits
conference rm	15–20	1.5–2.0	presentation; working discussions with outside visitors	audio-visual eqp; dimmer lights & black out; sto for eqp & furniture: allow sufficient space for alternative layouts	easy access for visitors
lecture rm	50–100		large conferences, presentations, lectures & training sessions	closed circuit tv system; control rm for projector, lighting, curtains, tv & audio systems; sto space for furniture display systems	adjacent ar for audience to assemble before meeting; several entrances

1 Types of meeting places, characteristics & requirements

Office buildings

SPACES FOR MEETINGS

also →p237

support spaces	space allocation expressed as % of total net ar			
	av of all off	av of off using 'Kew' furniture	av of other 'general' off	av of drawing off
	%	%	%	%
meeting spaces	3	3	4	2
sto	4	4	6	2
refreshment/rest	5	3	6	—
clo	2	2	2	—
general services	7	7	4	8
circulation	18	15	19	15
total support spaces	31	34	29	31

1 Percentage of space allocated in open plan off for meeting ar as percentage of total net ar

	meeting ar at work place	meeting ar serving group of workplaces	meeting rm 6–8 P	lounge/ rest ar	meeting rm 12–16 P	meeting rm 16–20 P	conference rm 22–28 P	lecture rm 100–150 P
headquarters accn for engineering organisation (population 1 200)	1 per 15 office staff	1 per 10 office staff	1 per 80 office staff	1 per 280 office staff	1 per 120 office staff	none	1 per 1 200 office staff	1 per 1 200 office staff
manufacturing admin organisation (population 400)	1 per 40 office staff	1 per 12 office staff	1 per 45 office staff	1 per 80 office staff	none	1 per 60 office staff	1 per 200 office staff	none
headquarters accn for clerical organisation (population 1 400)	1 per 18 office staff	1 per 26 office staff	1 per 55[1] office staff	1 per 400 office staff	1 per 280[1] office staff	1 per 230[1] office staff	1 per 1 400 office staff	none
consultancy organisation (population 80)	1 per 16 office staff	1 per 20 office staff	none	none	none	1 per 80 office staff	none	none

2 Meeting ar provision for different types of organisation

[1] apportioned to separate companies on each floor

seating arrangement & condition

1 informal situation with both parties working on equal basis

2 informal situation probable difference in status between parties

3 involved interview or brief with subordinate

4 formal interview

3 Meeting table space requirements

Office buildings

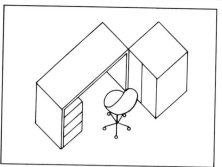

1 Typical clerical work station

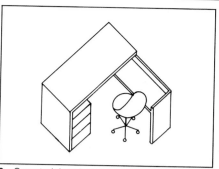

2 Secretarial work station

OFFICE FURNITURE

Once simply element in work stations for clerical staff and managers office furniture has become more specific and also means of controlling use of space, *eg:*
screens to separate
linking units to allow workplaces to be ganged in various ways
services carried by furniture
use of vertical surfaces for sto
use of sto to sub-divide
fin walls

These developments have been basis for many proprietary furniture systems. Many types of layout possible but principal controlling factor density. Densities in open office planning at 8 m²/head, 12 m² and 16 m² →p240(3)−(5) give some idea of range of possibilities.

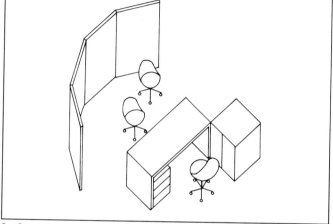

3 Supervisor's work station

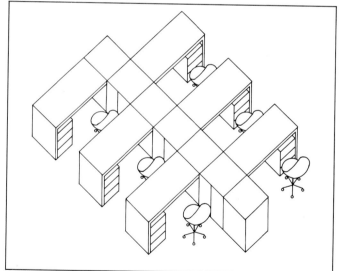

4 Ganged work stations: open

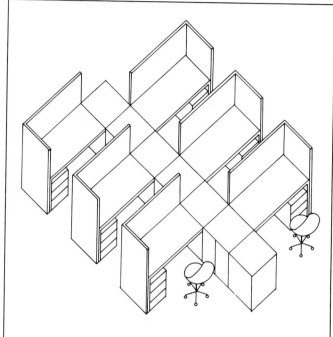

6 Ganged work stations: screened (carrel)

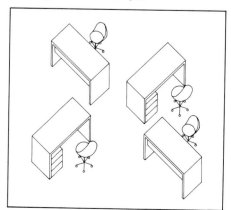

5 Free standing furniture

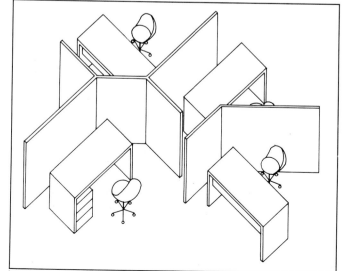

7 Free standing: enclosed

Office buildings

OFFICE FURNITURE

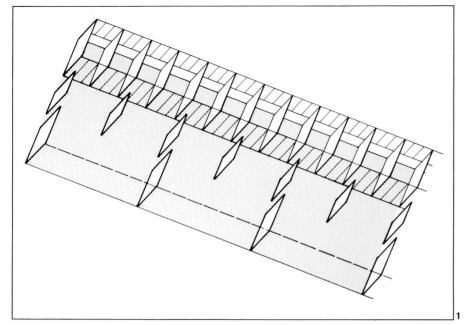

1 Furniture used to control space: fin walls

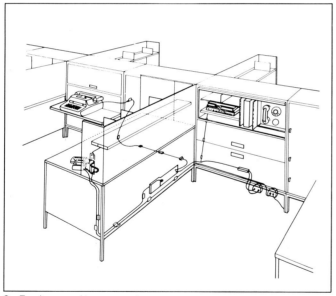

2 Furniture used to carry services

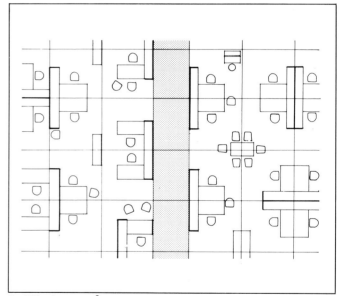

3 Office layout 8 m²/head

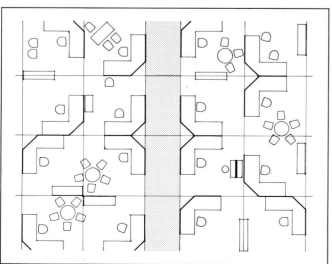

4 Office layout 12 m²/head

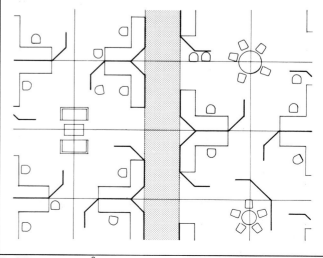

5 Office layout 16 m²/head

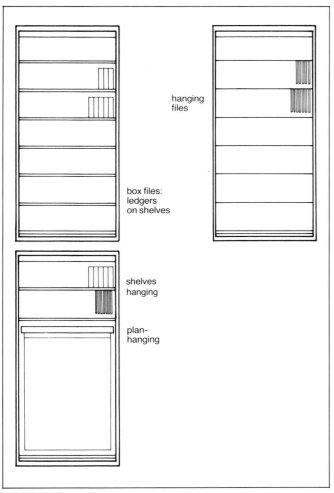

1   Filing

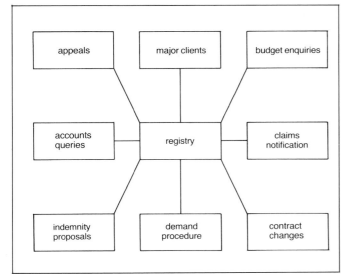

2   Example of relationships with registry in insurance firm

	4-drawer filing cabinet	lateral filing cabinet	open shewing unit
theoretical capacity (linear m)	2.4	4.5	5.4
capacity in use (linear m)	2.0	4.5	5.4
capacity/unit ar (linear m/m^2)	2.7	5.5	6.0

3   Comparison of space requirements of filing systems

STORAGE

Filing cabinets still predominant method of storing office paper: but many other possibilities, including suspended and lateral filing, which can be considerably more efficient in space use →(1).

Microfilm →p7 can be used to reduce bulk of paper held in offices: may not always be acceptable substitute because of:
complexity of information stored
frequency of retrieval
cost
legal requirements to keep original copy

Drawer type filing cabinet still predominant type of sto unit but not always most efficient in space use →p242(1).

Space requirements

Deeper the cabinets, wider the passage required between them. High shelves not easily serviced: time saved because access easier to vertical sto. Hanging files utilise wall area 87% more efficiently than box files →p242(1). Files may have be transported by conveyor; desks in filing rm should have shelves for sorting; provision of small tables and chairs on castors for convenience of clerks desirable.

Registry (document entry) should be centrally situated. Since clear height of 2100 only required, 3 storeys of registry could be fitted into equivalent of 2 normal office storeys. Dry rm essential. Deep registries more economical. Provide writing on reference surfaces next to stacks. Trolleys may be needed for moving files. Moveable registries make possible 20% greater utilisation of space by doing away with intermediate passages. Layouts not standardised but adapted to different needs, such as archives, lib, sto. Paper sto very heavy; can create acute floor loading problems.

Space required and capacity of 3 types of filing system compared →(3)(4). USA dimensions filing cabinets, lockers, sto cabinets →(5)(6) p242(6).

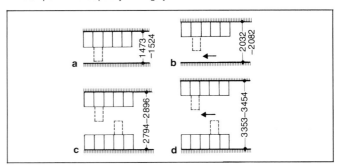

4   Comparison of capacity of filing systems

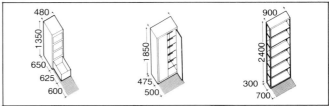

5   USA standard clearances for filing cabinets **a** passage drawers closed only **b** passage drawers open **c** cabinets face to face passage drawers closed only **d** cabinets face to face passage drawers open

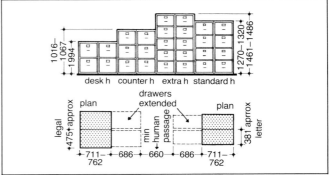

6   Filing cabinet dimensions USA

Commerce

STORAGE

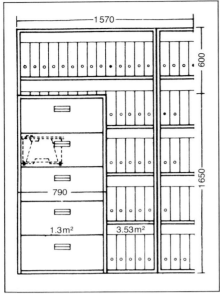

1 Wall space comparison between suspended & box files of same capacity

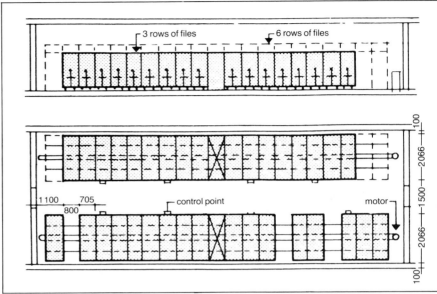

4 Movable registry (document entry)

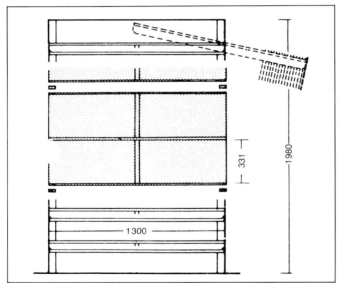

2 Large document chest: section & plan

		flat filing in loose-leaf binder on open shelves 35/200	library filing in index in roll-front cpd 40/125/220	vertical & suspended filing in folders, pigeon-holes 65/78/200
10 000 files approx 2 mm thick without holders; approx 25 sheets	continuous cpd/cabinet floor ar incl operation but excl side passages	7.25 m	11.0 m	2.4 m
		5.92 m²	8.25 m²	3.6 m²

5 Proportion of gangway space to filing cabinet space

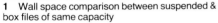

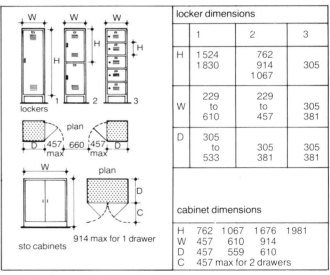

locker dimensions

	1	2	3
H	1524 1830	762 914 1067	305
W	229 to 610	229 to 457	305 381
D	305 to 533	305 381	305 381

cabinet dimensions

H	762	1067	1676	1981
W	457	610	914	
D	457	559	610	
C	457 max for 2 drawers			

6 Locker & sto cabinet dimensions USA

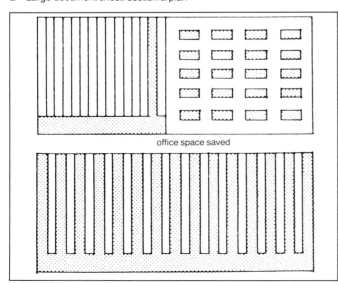

3 Comparison of space required for movable & ordinary registry

OFFICE EQUIPMENT

Office eqp increasing rapidly in complexity and scope as information technology develops. Use of office automation growing rapidly and expected be single most important use of information technology in long term.

	power supply	telephone connexions	heat extract	noise	water supply
el typewriter	•				
telex	•	•	•	•	
word processor	•		•	•	
copier	•		•	•	
terminal	•	•	•	•	
telecopier	•	•	•	•	
micro-computer	•	•	•	•	
microfilm viewer	•		•	•	
telephone	•				
vending machine	•		•	•	
video/tv monitor	•		•	•	•

1 Basic requirements of office eqp in current use

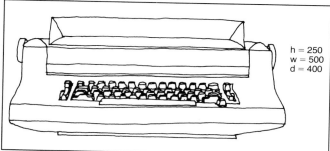

h = 250
w = 500
d = 400

2 El golf ball typewriter

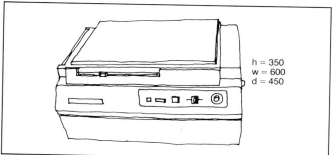

h = 350
w = 600
d = 450

3 Small photocopier

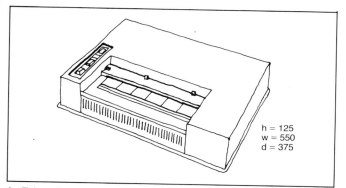

h = 125
w = 550
d = 375

4 Telecopier

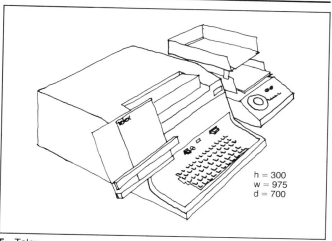

h = 300
w = 975
d = 700

5 Telex

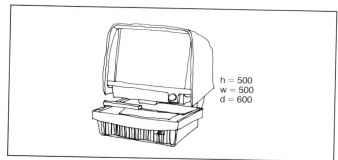

h = 500
w = 500
d = 600

6 Microfilm viewer

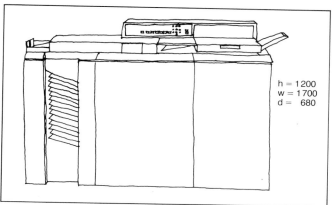

h = 1200
w = 1700
d = 680

7 Large (15 collator) copier

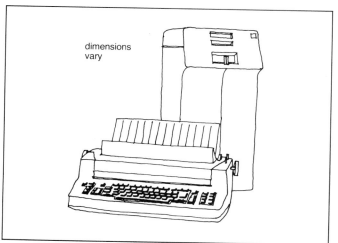

dimensions vary

8 Word processor with hard copy only; visual display unit (VDU) commonly used in addition

Office buildings

OFFICE EQUIPMENT

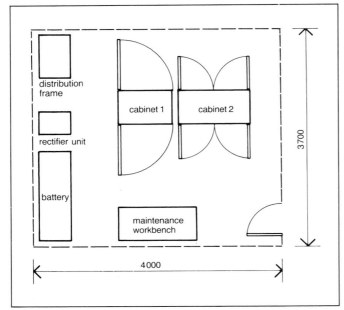

distribution frame

rectifier unit

battery

cabinet 1   cabinet 2

maintenance workbench

3700

4000

1   Private automatic branch exchange (PABX) rm requirements

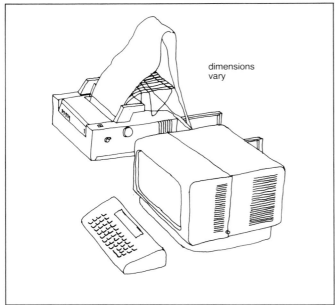

dimensions vary

2   Terminals

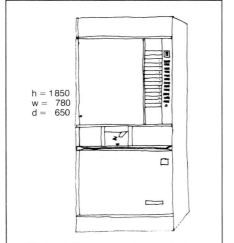

h = 1850
w = 780
d = 650

3   Large free standing vending machine

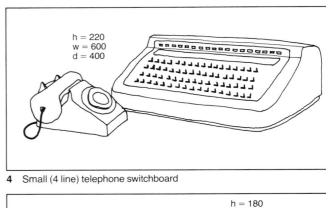

h = 220
w = 600
d = 400

4   Small (4 line) telephone switchboard

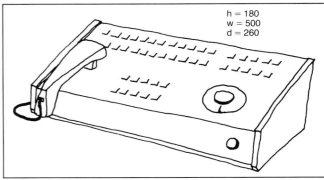

h = 180
w = 500
d = 260

5   Medium sized telephone switchboard (20 lines PABX)

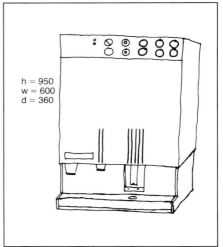

h = 950
w = 600
d = 360

6   Small vending machine

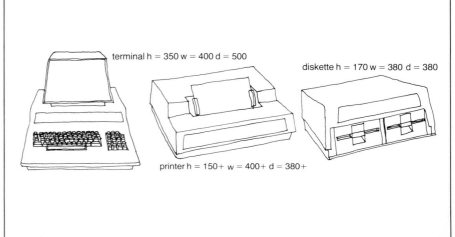

terminal h = 350 w = 400 d = 500

diskette h = 170 w = 380 d = 380

printer h = 150+ w = 400+ d = 380+

7   Micro computer

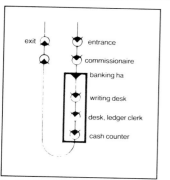

1   Customer's routes in major European banks

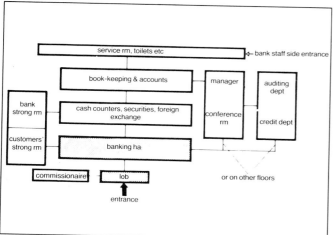

2   Routes to strong rm

Different design requirements according to whether private bank with primarily mercantile interests, major bank, savings bank, mortgage bank; but in general banks places where money paid in or withdrawn by customers. Procedures need be transacted quickly, securely, simply as possible. Mech conveyance and similar systems not necessary or worth while except for really large institutions.

Route followed by customer: from street outside through lobby into banking hall, sometimes fitted with bench seats or chairs for waiting and writing desks for customers, and various positions for paying in, drawing out, security, savings and (in Europe) giro transactions, or 'uniqueue'

Desks for accounts and book-keeping (check on state of drawer's account) usually behind cash counter →(1).

Other offices serving customers, *eg* manager, credit dept, auditing dept, usually next to banking hall with separate ante-rm, or on upper floor →(3).

Route to deposit boxes (often in basement): from banking hall through partition into passage, usually past securities dept and safe custody dept down stairs to protective grille in front of lobby leading to strong rm, where customers' deposit boxes and strong rm door; sizes of boxes: for 1 person 1000×1500 up to 1500×1500, for 2 persons 2000×1500.

Larger institutions normally have separate bank strong rm next to customers' strong rm, while safe custody dept has offices in front of entrance to this, with separate staircase to banking hall or special cash elevators →(3).

Basement reached by separate staircase comprises cloakrm, sto space, heating plant, plant for operating elevators and pneumatic despatch tubes, electromech communications eqp and so on, as well as registry and elevator for documents.

In **mortgage banks** must be possible for all mortgage business be completed conveniently on ground floor.

3   Relationships of rm in big bank

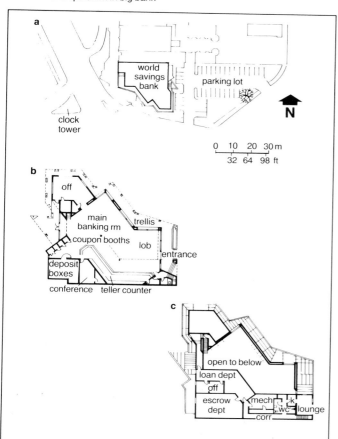

4   World Savings & Loan Association Santa Cruz USA; main banking rm extends upwards through 2 storeys lit by skylights & clerestory windows **a** site plan **b** ground floor **c** first floor   Arch Esherick Homsey Dodge & Davis

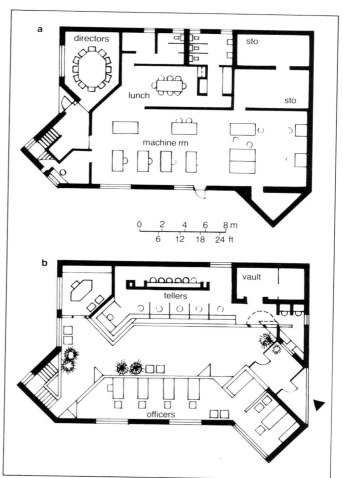

5   Tanners National Bank Woburn USA: conversion of originally square rectangular bldg by addition of 2 corners enclosing respectively staircase & off **a** lower level **b** main level   Arch Architectural Resources

Banks

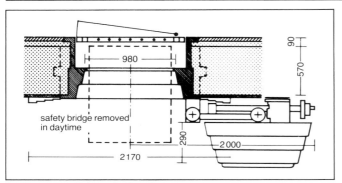

1 Strong rm with inner daytime door

safety bridge removed in daytime

980

2170

2000

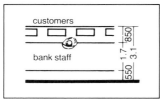

2 Parallel counter arrangement

customers

bank staff

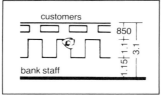

3 As →(2) with desks

customers

bank staff

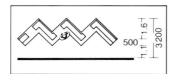

4 Sawtooth counter arrangement with desks at sides

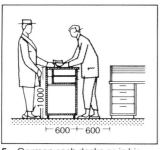

5 German cash desks as in big Berlin banks

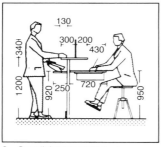

6 Swedish type cash desk

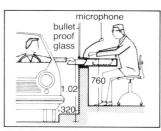

7 Drive-up cash point, no parking

microphone

bullet proof glass

760

1.02

320

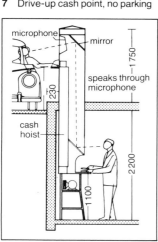

microphone

mirror

speaks through microphone

cash hoist

1750

230

2200

1100

8 Drive-up cash point in kiosk

a-b

b ◁ a

9 Cash point below pavement with shaft for customer service ≥ 3 parking places needed for uninterrupted & smooth service (Snorkel bank)

Strong rm doors and armoured doors pivot gently on steel hinges without dropping; can withstand any attack and fitted with unpierceable, indestructible steel plates, with fire-proof and non-melting reinforcing, with additional fireproof, non-melting and unpierceable compound casting. Total thickness approx 270–300. No keyhole: elaborate locking device (*eg* miracle lock, remote-control lock) and el-operated alarm system, which sounds at slightest vibration of door.

Cashier positions →(2)–(6) nowadays in Europe usually completely protected with bullet-proof reinforced glass, 4 panes ≥ 250 thick. Similar protection over sunken drawers. Alarm system operated by foot or knee. Underneath counter normally standard type steel cabinets.

Exceptions still exist, particularly in USA, in banks wishing foster informal 'non-authoritarian' image. In USA many banks still retain teller positions either behind grille or even open.

Intercommunications system now more usually by means of television instead of by pneumatic tubes, belt conveyors etc.

Drive-in banks: to save time customers do not go into bank but drive up to cash point →(8). No parking problems: cash points can be incorporated in bank bldg →(10)(11), separate islands →(12)(13), or below pavement level, with shaft by kerb containing reflecting mirror, loudspeaker and cash conveyance device →(9). Each cash point can serve up to 250 customers/day. (Each transaction takes approx 60 seconds.) Not all banking transactions can be at drive-up cashier's desk: even where this system operates normal banking ha also needed for lengthier business.

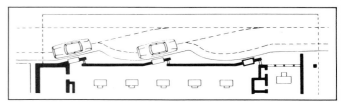

10 Drive-up cash points

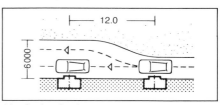

12.0

6000

11 Cash points incorporated in bank bldg

28.0

8.0

16.0

13.0

12 Twin cash points as islands to ease traffic

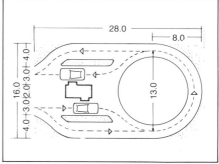

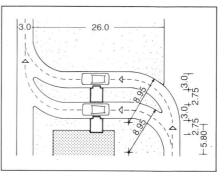

3.0

26.0

8.95

8.95

3.0

2.75

3.0

2.75

5.80

13 Cash points as →(7)(8) for through traffic

EXAMPLES

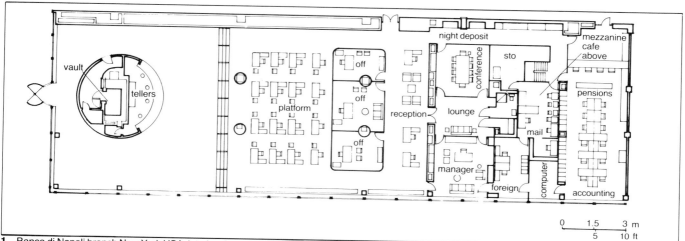

1 Banco di Napoli branch New York USA; interior plan conversion of 1 070 m² ground floor off space in off tower block   Arch Skidmore Owings & Merrill

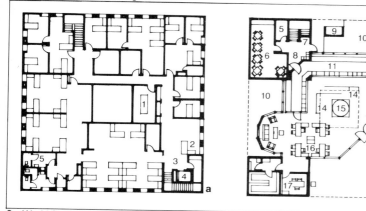

key
1 conference 2 reception 3 lob 4 elevator
5 toilet 6 lunch rm 7 clo 8 lockers 9 refuse
10 planting bed 11 teller counter 12 strong rm
13 safe deposit desk & booths 14 cheque writer
15 fountain 16 new accounts 17 district
manager 18 covered entrance

2 World Savings & Loan Associates Santa Ana USA **a** first floor **b** ground floor   Arch Kamnitzer Cotton Vreeland

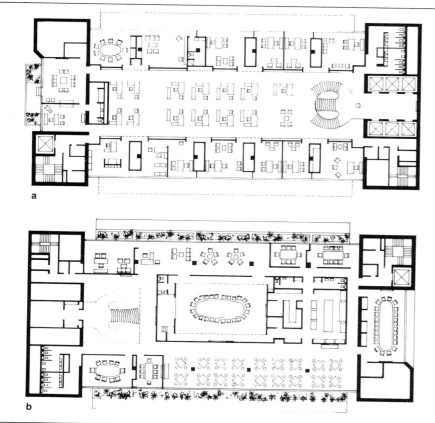

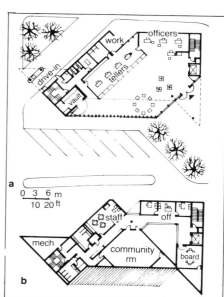

4 Albany Savings Bank: small branch bank New York USA **a** ground floor **b** first floor Arch Feibes & Schmitt

3 Federal Reserve Bank Boston USA, arrangement of **a** executive off 32nd floor **b** executive dining & meeting rm 31st floor Arch Hugh Stubbins

Banks references:
→ Bibliograhpy entries 007 249 254 374 477

Vehicle services

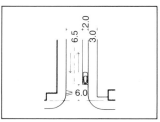

1   Parking lane alongside footway

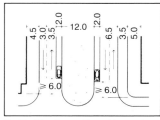

2   Parking lane either side road divide

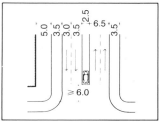

3   Parking lane down middle of roadway

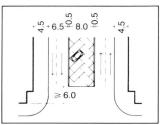

4   Double parking lane down middle of roadway

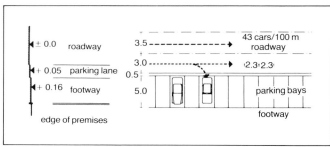

5   Segregated approach & departure

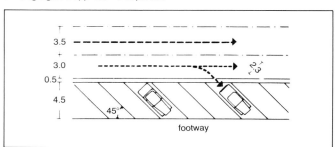

6   Oblique alignment

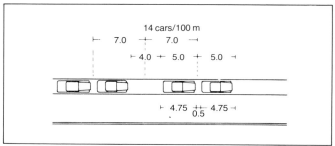

7   Right angled alignment

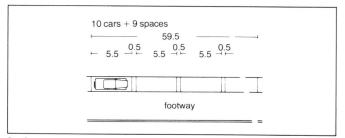

8   Setting down: continuous approach & departure (*eg* theatres, taxis)

CAR PARKS

With growth in motor transport separation of moving and stationary traffic essential.

Results of traffic research suggest different parking layouts on basis of local conditions:

Population: desirable parking area in mid-town = 0.5–1% of population of whole built-up area.

Number of cars: 1 parking space on town centre for every 5–8 cars kept in built-up area.

Visiting traffic: parking space for 7–9% of vehicles regular visitors to town centre.

Parking space needed (including drive in) 20–25 m²/car.

Parking areas within roadway limits
Kerb space requirements for longitudinal parking →(1)–(3)(7)(8).

Parking lanes: oblique or right angle parking lanes for various road widths →(4)(5)(6). Parked vehicles must not restrict vision of moving vehicles at corners; therefore gap between end of parking lane and bldg line ≥ 6000; 10000 preferred →(1)–(4).

Avoid right angle parking (dangerous for passing traffic).

Safety strips 500 wide recommended between parking lanes and moving traffic.

NB diagrams on this page apply to traffic driving on right: data based on German practice

relation to street edge	45°	60°	90°
w	5 000	5 400	5 500
ar required (m²)	18	16	13
cars/100 m	31	38	43

9   Parking lanes for motor cars

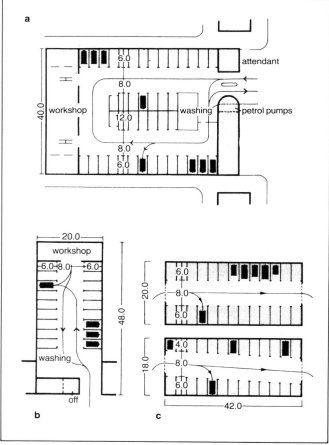

10   Enclosed parking spaces **a** neighbourhood garage **b** arrangement for narrow site **c** road at angle gives economical use of space for different car sizes, saves approx 10% floor ar

Vehicle services

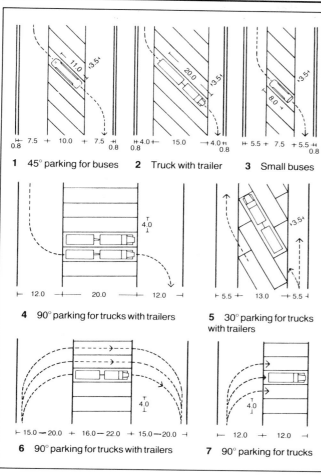

1   45° parking for buses   **2**   Truck with trailer   **3**   Small buses

4   90° parking for trucks with trailers

5   30° parking for trucks with trailers

6   90° parking for trucks with trailers

7   90° parking for trucks

CAR PARKS

USA standards →p250

Off street parking

In permanent car parks, lanes and bays should be clearly marked with safety strips for pedestrians →(10)(13). Enclosed parking spaces also →p248(10).

Space requirements →(8)–(15)

Space/car with driving lanes but without main access and exit:

90° parking approx 20 m²
45° parking approx 23 m²: usually preferred for ease of parking.

Parking bays →(8)–(10)

Space/car (medium–large) 5 000 × 1 800. For car parks larger than 800 m² provide 20% bays for larger cars (6 000 × 2 100) if park attended. Provision for motor cycles, bicycles, disabled according to local requirements.

Truck & bus parking

Fixed bay sizes advisable because vehicle size varies greatly. For trucks with trailers provide for parking without reversing →(1)–(6). For articulated lorries reversing usual.

For long distance traffic provide yards at town approaches with driver accn, workshops, filling stations etc.

NB diagrams on this page apply to traffic driving on right: data based on German practice

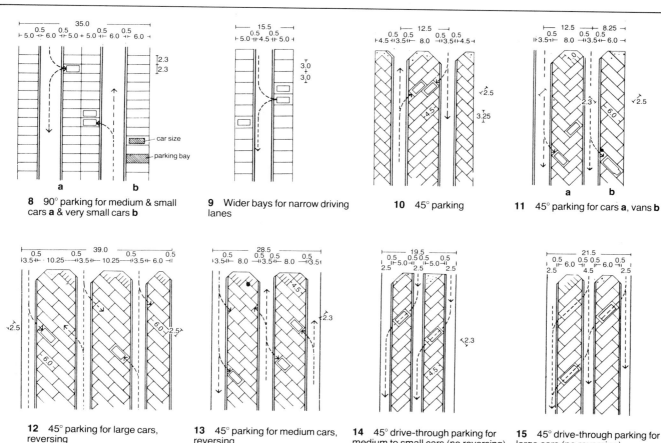

8   90° parking for medium & small cars **a** & very small cars **b**

9   Wider bays for narrow driving lanes

10   45° parking

11   45° parking for cars **a**, vans **b**

12   45° parking for large cars, reversing

13   45° parking for medium cars, reversing

14   45° drive-through parking for medium to small cars (no reversing)

15   45° drive-through parking for large cars (no reversing)

Vehicle services

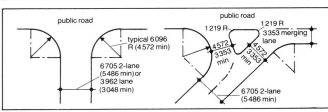

1 Intersections between private & public roads

PARKING: USA STANDARDS

→(2) gives USA recommended (→Bib 594) parking layouts, stall widths and parking dimensions for 2 most typical car sizes. Recommended small car dimensions be used only in car parks designed for small cars or with entrance controls which admit only small cars; putting small cars into standard car layout not recommended: standard dimensions will take all normal passenger vehicles. With large car dimensions parking easier, quicker: recommended for elderly, high turnover, luxury. With parking angle 60° or less may be necessary increase bay width by 75–162 to give room for users walking to and from parked cars. Always consult local zoning reg.

Turning dimensions

→(1) shows USA dimensions at intersection of private with public roads. 'U' drive →(3) illustrates procedure for designating any drive configuration given vehicle's dimensions →p21(1) and turning radii. Tangent (T) dimensions approx min only: may vary with driver's ability and speed.

Roadways →p21

NB: diagrams on this page apply to traffic circulation on right

a

w	2.43	2.74	3.05	3.35
small car use				
all day parker use				
standard car use				
luxury & elderly use				
supermarket & camper use				
handicapped use*				

* min requirements = 1 or 2/100 stalls or as specified by local, state, or federal law; place convenient to destination

b

PW = SW/sine θ

single loaded wall to wall (with bumpers) — double loaded wall to wall (with continuous concrete kerb) — double loaded wall to ₡ (with sawtooth concrete kerb) — double loaded ₡ to ₡ (or ₡ to walk edge) — ₡ of bay or edge of walk

c

SW	w	\u03b8 angle of park								
		45°	50°	55°	60°	65°	70°	75°	80°	85°	90°
2743	1	9.75	9.98	10.36	10.77	11.43	12.09	12.8	13.51	14.07	14.63
	2	15.03	15.54	16.2	16.91	17.63	18.29	18.85	19.61	19.74	20.12
	3	14.12	14.88	15.65	16.41	17.07	17.88	18.59	19.2	19.66	20.12
	4	13.61	14.17	14.94	15.7	16.46	17.37	18.19	18.9	19.56	20.12
2896	1	9.75	9.96	10.36	10.67	11.23	11.84	12.65	13.31	14.02	14.63
	2	14.99	15.39	15.8	16.31	16.87	17.68	18.44	19.1	19.66	20.09
	3	14.33	14.68	15.19	15.7	16.43	17.37	18.19	18.9	19.58	20.09
	4	13.61	13.97	14.48	15.19	16.0	16.99	17.9	18.74	19.46	20.09

NOTE: θ angles greater than 70° have aisle w for 2-way travel

2 Parking **a** recommended stall w **b** layouts **c** parking dimensions

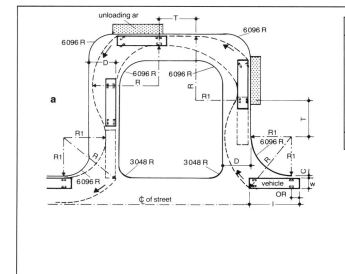

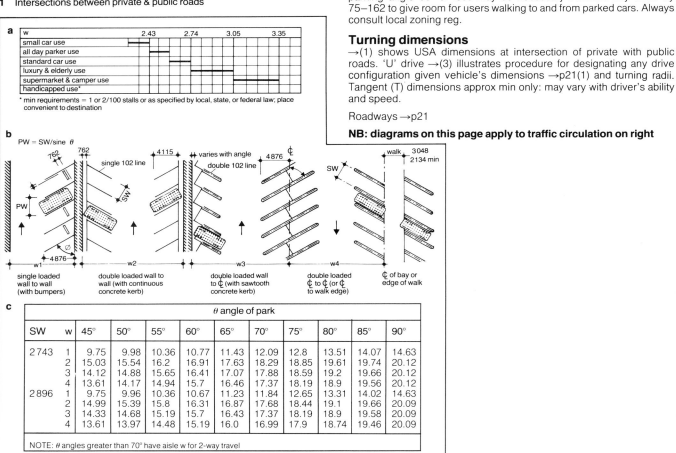

vehicle	R	R1	T	D	C
small car	6.05	3.28	3.7	3.05	0.15
compact car	6.55	3.61	4.57	3.3	0.18
standard car	6.83	3.84	4.57	3.4	0.2
large car	7.01	3.84	4.57	3.66	0.23
intercity bus*	16.76	10.06	9.14	6.86	0.3
city bus	16.3	10.1	9.14	6.86	0.3
school bus	13.26	7.92	9.14	5.92	0.3
ambulance	9.14	5.72	7.62	4.04	0.3

* headroom = 4.62

	small	large
F	15.52	26.59
A	46.71°	35.58°
B	273.42°	251.15°
Ra	9.75	30.48
Rb	11.58	15.24
La	7.95	18.8
Lb	55.27	66.8

NOTE: R values for vehicles intended to use these culs-de-sac should not exceed Rb.

3 **a** 'U' drive diagram with table of turning dimensions **b** cul-de-sac with table of dimensions & angles; large vehicle l →p20a(1)

Multi-storey car parks

DESIGN GEOMETRY

'Standard design car' →(1)

UK 95% of all new vehicle registrations: USA large car dimensions column 2:

l	A	4750	5500
w	B	1800	2030
h	C	1700	1630
door opening clearance	D	500	
wheel base (worst cases)	E	2900	3250
	F	900	890
	G	1100	1350
turning circle (dia)			
kerb	H	13000	6500
wall	J	14000	7010
ground clearance	K	100	1220

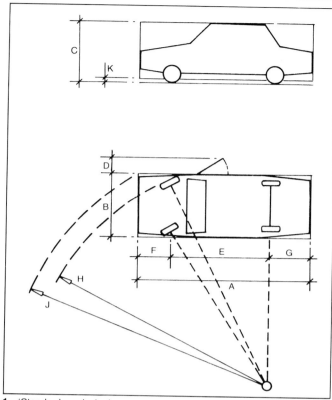

1 'Standard car design'

Recommended parking dimensions (90° layout) →(2)

stall l	L	4750	5500
stall w	M		
standard		2400	2750
short stay		2300	2600
long stay		2500	2750
disabled persons		3000	3050
roadway w	N		
1-way		6000	9150
2-way		6950	10200
standard bin w	P	15500	20100
headroom (min clearance)		2050	2130

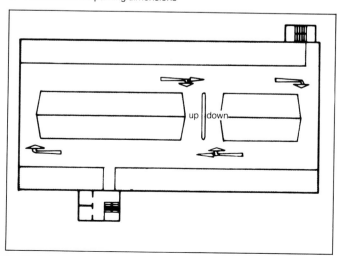

2 Recommended parking dimensions

Recommended ramp design

up to 1500 rise	1 in 7	USA: ramp l < 19.8 m
more than 1500 rise	1 in 10	max slope 1 in 7
used for parking	1 in 20	< 19.8 m ramp l
		max slope 1 in 9

gradients, max, on helical ramps:

up to 3000 rise	1 in 10
more than 3000 rise	1 in 12

w, min, straight ramp, no turning:

between kerbs	3000	4000
clearance, kerb to structure	300	75

w, min, curved ramp, turning traffic:

1-way	3650	5200
2-way	7000	9150
central kerb, 2-way	500	150

turning circle, outer kerb radius:

recommended	12000	6600
min	9000	6600
clearance kerb, to structure	600	460

Use of angled parking layout →(3)

parking angle	bin w mm	av ar/vehicle m²	USA m²
90°	15500	24.0	27.0
80°	15400	25.0	27.9
70°	15300	27.0	28.0
45°	13700	34.0	35.3

Most efficient parking angle 90°; lesser parking angles not normally used in UK.

CAR PARK ARRANGEMENT

2 parallel bins normally used provide circulation arrangement with 1-way traffic flows having upward and downward routes separated; makes possible best traffic capacity. Dynamic capacity reduced if 2-way traffic flows or mixed upwards and downwards circulation used. Cul-de-sac driveways undesirable: should not exceed 6 stalls in length.

Economy achieved by using longest practicable bin lengths. Downward route should be short expedite exit; upwards route devised give best possible search pattern for vacant stalls.

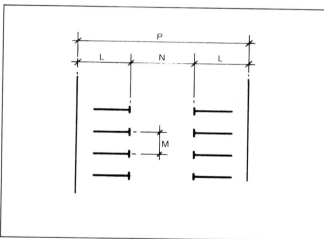

3 Typical car park arrangement

Multi-storey car parks

Split level layout →(1)
Arrangement widely adopted.

2 bins so arranged that adjacent parking levels separated by half storey height.

Short interconnecting ramps used between levels.

Warped slab layout →(2)
Parking levels constructed with uninterrupted horizontal external edge: steady transition of gradients constructed give internal interconnexion of parking levels. Compared with split level layout need for ramps at either end of bldg eliminated, gradients reduced.

Parking ramp layout →(3)
Parking level constructed as long ramp: has significant effect on elevational appearance; to keep to acceptable gradients long bldg required. When necessary exit can be speeded up by adopting external helical ramp.

Flat slab layout →(4)
External ramp used to interconnect level parking areas.

VEHICLE CONTROL

Fee collection
Group A driver payment:
fixed or variable charge payed on exit

Group B pedestrian payment:
fixed or variable charge by purchase of token or ticket
season ticket
pay & display ticket

Barrier capacity
2 barrier types available: rising arm or rising kerb, having recommended capacities:

entry barrier	400 vehicles/hr
exit barrier	
group A	250 vehicles/hr
group B	400 vehicles/hr

LIGHTING

Mean service illumination for public should be (lx):

parking areas	20
driveways	50
ramps	70
roof	20
entrance & exit	150

FIRE PROTECTION & SAFETY

USA: check applicable codes and standards.

Structural fire resistance
Construction of non-combustible materials with structural fr 1 hr. In specified restricted circumstances requirement for structural fr may be waived for bldg less than 15.2 m high.

Means of escape
All parking spaces within 45.7 m of escape stairway having 1 hr fr. Adequate alternative means of escape.

Fire precautions
Adequate fire brigade access, dry rising main, fire points plus any specific requirements of local fire officer.

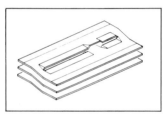

1   Split level layout

2   Warped slab layout

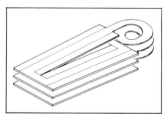

3   Parking ramp layout

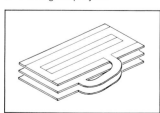

4   Flat slab layout

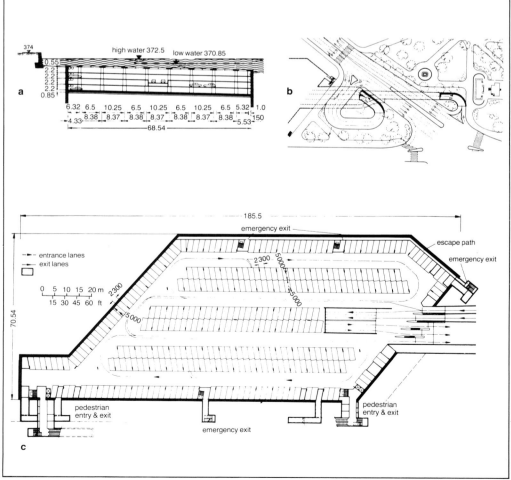

5   Under lake car park Geneva Switzerland a section b site plan c plan of first floor   Design C Zschokke

Vehicle services: petrol stations

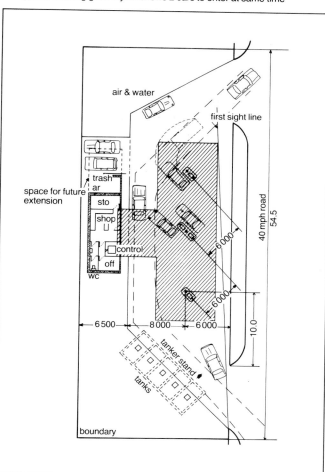

1 Typical 'starting gate' layout allows 2 cars to enter at same time

Self-service station now dominating influence on design, as result partly of high labour costs, partly of availability of new electronic pumping systems with memories for storing pump information at control counter. In UK self-service basis adopted by oil company petrol station networks: approx 75% of petrol sold in UK through self-service. Practice spreading rapidly in continental Europe. Proportion lower in USA but growing; motorway and inter-state stations increasingly self-service operations. Whether self-service or manned petrol stations usually now include shops or selling areas exposing customers to wide range of goods as they pay for petrol.

DESIGN & LAYOUT

Basic principles same whether for self or attended service.

Preliminary
Trading area: detail study will establish need for site.

Road pattern: whether single, dual or three lane roadway will determine ease of entry into site.

Traffic flow: number of vehicles passing site per hour per day to be established.

Vehicle road speed: will influence frequency of customers visiting site.

From these factors estimate number of vehicles/hr/day calling at site and of expected peak periods for which site will have to provide.

Basic
Initial communication: visibility; pole sign visible at least 300 m before site entrance →p254(2).

Visibility: price sign readable 100 m before site entrance.

In and out: easy steering on to site and space for cars to line up while waiting for place at pump; easy steering away from pump with no blocking of exit and good visibility for driving out on to road →p254(3).

Site traffic: 1-way flow only on site.

Pumps: think in terms of filling positions →(1)(2)p254(4):
consider filling at peak periods, usually 2/day, morning and evening; note that car is at pump site before starting filling for 4.5 minutes, and actual filling for 1.5 minutes;
memory system at control counter imperative to allow for quick release of pump;
capacity of 1-hose pump with all grades of fuel available approx 320 l/hr.

Pre-payment: consider whether volume of cars at peak periods or at night warrant money acceptor or card acceptor units to relieve control counter operator.

Shop: commonly 20–40 m² depending on retailing activity envisaged. Control counter area additional 4.5 m²: sited to supervise refuelling area and shop activity.

Air, water: site away from pumps with adequate parking spaces according to size of station.

Other services: should be kept separate from petrol filling area, *eg* derv filling, car wash, sale of liquefied petrol gases.

NB diagrams on this page apply to traffic driving on left

2 Typical echelon layout suits narrower site

Vehicle services: petrol stations

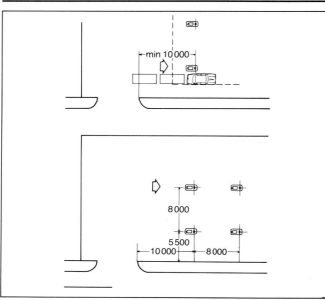

1 Forecourt layout of pump sites with preferred dimensions

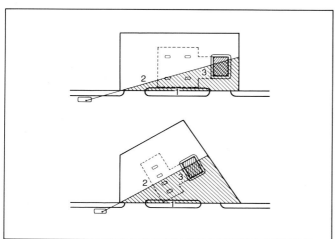

2 Areas of vision: 1 main pole 2 canopy facia signs 3 secondary signs
NB higher road speeds reduce motorist's angle of vision

SITE ESSENTIALS

Accommodation: shop and control counter, office, toilet(s), sto, perhaps staff area →p253(1)(2).

Petrol sto: underground steel tanks cased in sulphate-resisting concrete 1:2:4 mix. Consult local code for thickness of concrete surround. Tank sizes (UK) vary 13000–36000 l, in 4560 l increments.

Supply tanker: easy route to discharge pad on site. Discharging must not obstruct cars. In case of emergency tankers should be able drive direct from site. Lighting required for night deliveries.

Canopy: required to cover all filling positions with approx 3500 projection beyond pumps on both sides: height above filling area 3850. On lighting for night time retailing consult codes; in UK zone 2 type (vapour proof) if fitted to canopy ceiling; zone 1 type (flame proof) if fitted within 750 of pump sight glass; USA requirements similar.

Levels: avoid variation in level beyond 1:80 on filling area and tanker discharging pad.

Drainage: consult codes; in UK from all areas within 4250 of petrol source (*ie* pumps, tanks) vents to be taken to 3-chamber petrol interceptor before processing to main foul sewer.

Site size: dependent on number of filling points and future marketing needs; preferred sizes →(4)p253(1)(2).

NB diagrams on this page apply to traffic driving on left

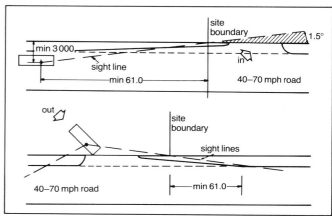

3 Entry & exit sight lines

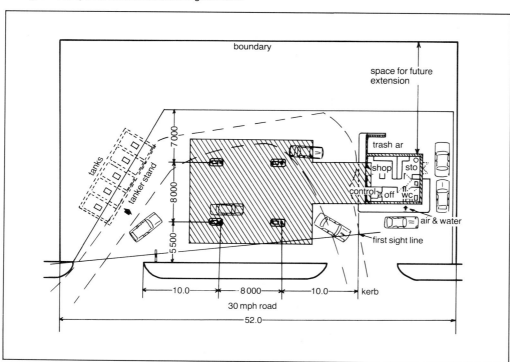

4 Typical foursquare layout suits deeper site

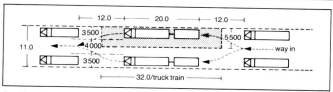

1   Parking ar layout parallel to direction of arrival

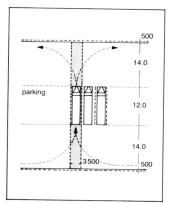

2   Parking places of vehicles with trailers or coaches

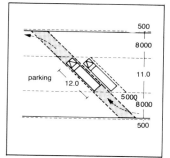

3   Obliquely (45°) to direction of arrival for coaches

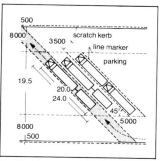

4   Right angles to direction of arrival for coaches

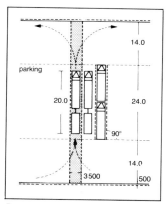

5   For vehicles with trailers or coaches

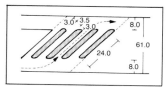

6   Obliquely to direction of arrival

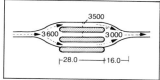

7   Platform alignment parallel with direction of arrival

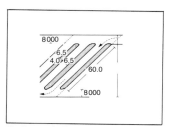

8   Long platform at 45° to direction of arrival

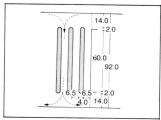

9   At right angles to direction of arrival

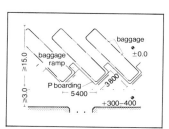

10   Standard vertical interlocking layout (USA)

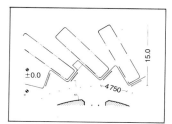

11   Radial layout providing more rm in front (USA)

FORMS OF PLATFORM

Buses increasingly taking over from trains, demand ever increasing attention in relation urban traffic. Need take corners especially wide: turning spread needs special watchfulness →p256(1). Bus parks large and small an essential part of traffic planning. Forms of platform →(1)–(18).

Bus stops should be under cover →(19)(20).

Town centre squares should be designed or adapted serve as bus stations according nature of requirements →p256(10)–(12).

End ramps and convenient boarding steps of 300–400 →(10)–(11) and for loading baggage to floor level.

Service rm needed in connexion with bus stations →p256(10)–(14). Provide space for temporary car parking →p256(9). Keep in mind possibilities of extension →p256(8).

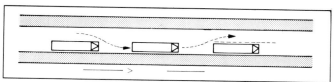

12   Platform alignment with passing lane

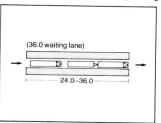

13   Without passing lane   **14**   Oblique platform alignment

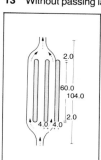

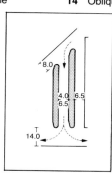

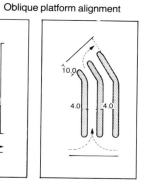

15   Long platforms with passing lanes

16   Departure at right angles; arrival at oblique angle

17   Departure at oblique angle

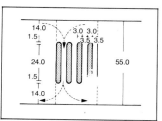

18   Position at right angles to direction of arrival

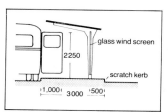

19   Shelter for unilateral loading platform

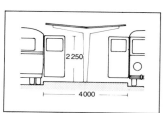

20   For loading both sides

Vehicle services: bus stations

TRAFFIC ORGANISATION

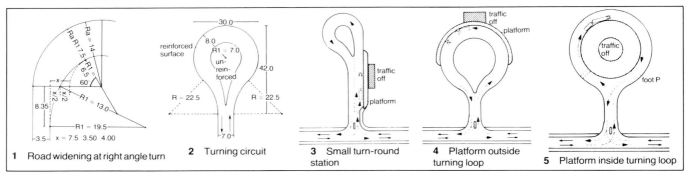

1 Road widening at right angle turn

2 Turning circuit

3 Small turn-round station

4 Platform outside turning loop

5 Platform inside turning loop

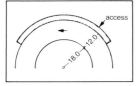

6 Semicircular platform outside loop with no P crossing over roadway

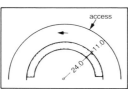

7 Semicircular platform inside loop accessible only by crossing road

platform type	without passing lane			with passing lane		
relation to line of arrival	parallel	at 45°	at 90°	parallel	at 45°	at 90°
platform l (m)	24	24	24	36–60	36–60	36–60
platform w (m)	3	3	3	3.5–4.0	3.5–4.0	3.0–4.0
no of loading points a coaches	2	2	2	2–3	2–3	2–3
b vehicles with trailers	1	1	1	1–2	1–2	1–2
ar of platform & arrival spur (m²) a coaches	138	170	189	293	296	313
b vehicles with trailers	276	340	378	439	444	470

8 Space requirements for platform ar

relation to line of arrival	parallel	at 45°		at 90°	
l each parking place (m)	32	12	24	12	24
parking options	1 vehicle with trailer 2 coaches	1 coach	1 vehicle with trailer 2 coaches	1 coach	1 vehicle with trailer 2 coaches
w each parking place (m)	3.5	3.5	3.5	3.5	3.5
w arrival spur (m)	4.0	8.0	8.0	14	14
parking ar with roadway (m²) a vehicle with trailer	176		178		182
b coach	88	135	89	140	91

9 Space requirements for parking places

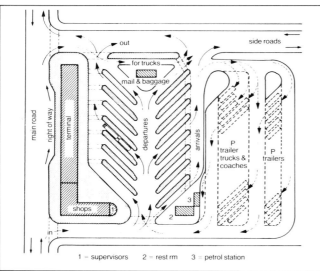

10 Large transit station with parking ar

1 = supervisors   2 = rest rm   3 = petrol station

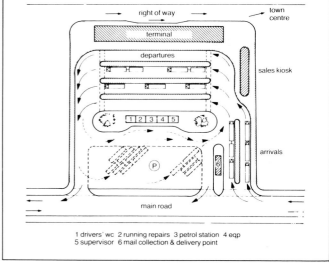

1 drivers' wc 2 running repairs 3 petrol station 4 eqp
5 supervisor 6 mail collection & delivery point

11 Large transit station with separate departure & arrival platforms

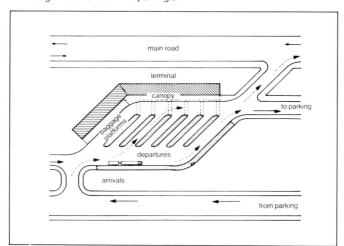

12 Transit station with separate arrival & departure platforms positioned obliquely, parking ar in separate location

1 departure P entrance
2 arrival P exit
3 vestibule
4 baggage despatch
5 arrival P entrance
6 baggage in arrival
7 departure P exit
8 baggage off
9 baggage deposit
10 manager's off
11 off
12 information & air tickets
13 wr

13 Ground floor KLM bus station Arch Brock & Bakema

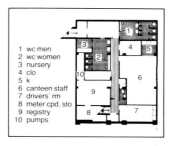

1 wc men
2 wc women
3 nursery
4 clo
5 k
6 canteen staff
7 drivers' rm
8 meter cpd, sto
9 registry
10 pumps

14 Basement KLM

1 to 4   Space taken up by people

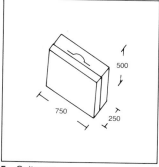

5   Suitcase

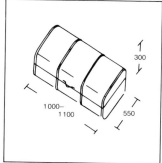

6   Cabin trunk

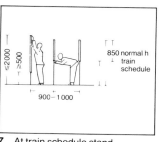

7   At train schedule stand

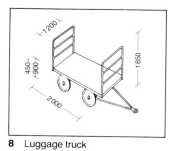

8   Luggage truck

PASSENGER DETAILS

Temp booking hall 12°C
Daylighting ≥ 1/5 surface area
Ticket off from 1 500 × 2 000 upwards
Type of surface: rough, hard sintered clay or granitic tiles
Walling up to 1 750 high with impact-resistant lining: tiles, hard plaster, boards
Baggage deposit: doors for baggage trucks 1 900–2 300 wide; all doors preferably steel to withstand heaviest demands. Opening at deposit counter up to 1 200 high; sliding window or protected by grille.
Baggage despatch cabin 2 000 × 2 250
Arrangements for storing bicycles very simple and space saving: hung up neatly by front wheel →(12)(13)
Easy to hang up if first raised on rear wheel, then lifted up with knee behind saddle

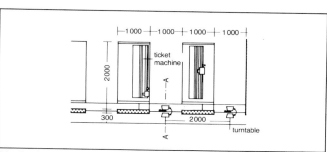

14   Booking off

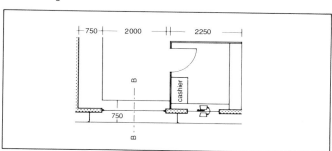

15   Baggage off

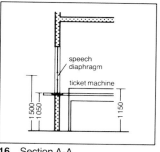

16   Section A-A

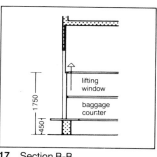

17   Section B-B

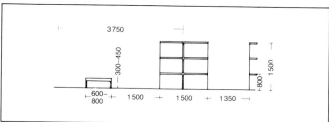

9   Platform steps

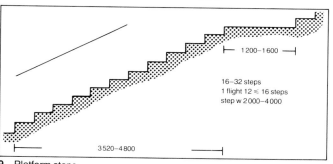

10   Baggage stand   **11**   Baggage rack

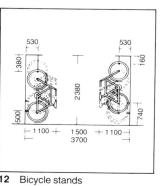

12   Bicycle stands

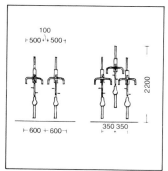

13   Abreast staggered

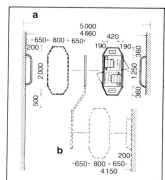

18   **a** Straight barrier **b** oblique barrier

Airports

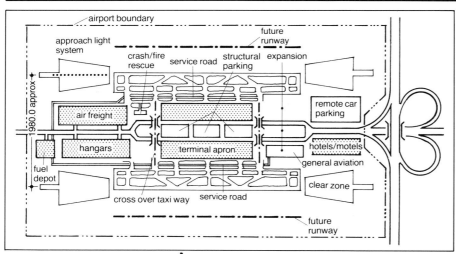

1 Airport layout for parallel runway system

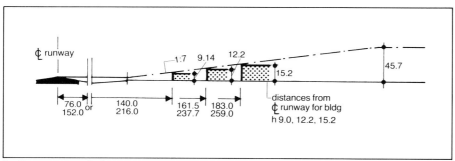

2 Passenger terminal & apron distances from runway centre line for various bldg h; 1:7 = imaginary surface cannot be penetrated by stationary objects (aircraft at gates) or fixed objects (bldg)

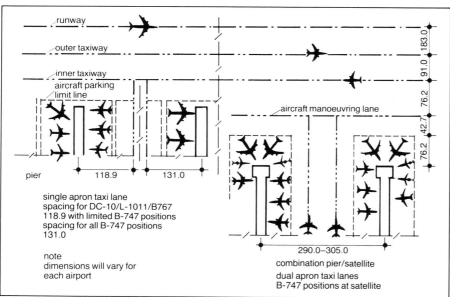

3 Runways & taxiways

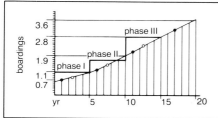

4 Planning & project design schedule: ● start planning 4 yr in advance ○ forecast update: 1 start design & working drawings 2 revise 3 defer

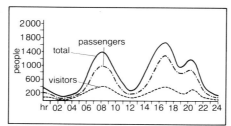

5 Derive pattern departing P av day, peak month, yr & visitor ratios from surveys; prepare similar graphs for arriving P, ground traffic etc: major data for determining size of installations

Prime function provide passenger air transport. During short history has had respond tremendous growth and technological change.

Should be planned and developed progressively meet changes and new demands →(1).

PRELIMINARY WORK

Planning and design of airport should evolve according to sequence:
preliminary study; examine in detail what exists and identify constraints
physical: land boundaries, topography, geology
access: airside and landside
environment: noise, pollution, landscaping
resources: finance, labour, materials
assess economic, demographic characteristics of population: gauge impact on airport; forecast traffic demands 5–10 and 20 years in future, showing annual and day, peak month, peak hr traffic for passenger boarding and aircraft movements →(4)(5)
develop master plan for whole airport
develop plans for each component airside/landside:
airside:
runways, taxiways →(3)
landside:
passenger terminal with apron (2) →p260–1
ground transport
air freight terminal with apron →p262
aircraft maintenance with apron →p262
other components: car rental, hotel, motel, offices
surface access: road systems, fixed guideways

Reg standards, min criteria →Bib391 392 393 394 395 396.

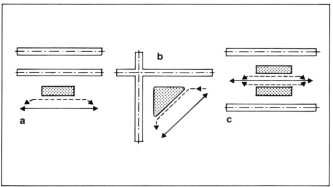

1 Runway configurations (airport boundaries not shown) **a** closely placed parallel runways for small to medium volumes: parallel access road system limits expansion **b** intersecting runways for medium to large volumes: terminal expansion limited within triangular ar **c** parallel runways with simultaneous aircraft operating 1 280 m spacing for large volumes: expansion capabilities along axis (cross over taxiways not shown)

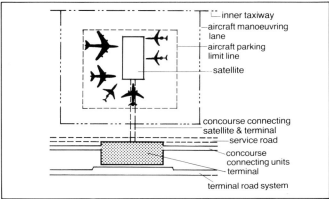

2 Satellite

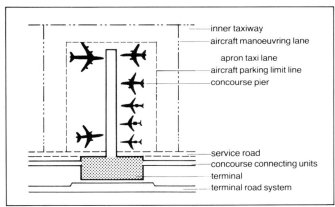

3 Pier

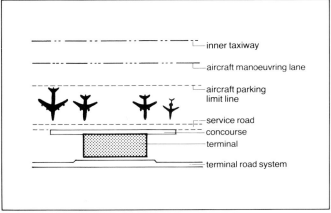

4 Linear

AIRSIDE

Runways & taxiways →(1)
Length of runway depends on prevailing weather, topography, altitude, temp, environmental restrictions, aircraft type and weight expected operate from airport.

Orientation of runway in direction of prevailing wind. Modern aircraft can usually land and take off with cross wind up to 20 knots. Light aircraft seriously affected by wind: if airport to be heavily used by this type additional runway may be justified.

Utilisation: aim should be for airport be usable by all aircraft for min 97% of time.

Single runway can handle up to 39 movement/hr (1 movement = 1 landing or take off), depending on mix of aircraft, when operating under instrument flight rules (IFR). 2 parallel runways 1 280 m apart can accept up to 72 aircraft movements (USA reg) under IFR. Number of movements higher under visual flight rules (VFR). Where large and small aircraft operate to same airport specific separations required in air, at landing, take off and taxiing because trailing vortices from large aircraft will reduce capacity.

Taxiway systems should be designed allow aircraft clear runway soon as possible and provide shortest route betweeen runway and parking aprons.

Layout & design of runways and taxiways: essential consult expert advice.

LANDSIDE

Passenger terminal concepts
Aircraft gate configuration and way aircraft gates connected with one another and with main terminal dominant features of terminal concepts, of which 4 can be distinguished. Concepts nearly always occur in variations and combinations.

Satellite →(2): aircraft parked in cluster surrounding structure connected with main terminal by passenger corridor or concourse positioned below, on or above ground level.

Satellite structure can take several geometrical shapes.

Pier →(3): aircraft parked in line at either side of structure. Passenger corridor or concourse attached to main terminal.
(In both these concepts passenger ticket, inbound and outbound baggage handling usually centralised in main terminal but variations and exceptions occur.)

Linear→(4): aircraft parked in single line at structure, passenger corridor connecting functional elements of terminal. Formerly with aircraft parked in line on apron functions centralised in small terminal. In past 10–15 years linear concept developed provide passenger handling functions and ground transport for individual aircraft positions. In such arrangement terminal functions decentralised.

Transporter →(5): aircraft positions placed at distance from terminal; passengers carried by vehicles between terminal and aircraft. Passenger handling centralised in main terminal.

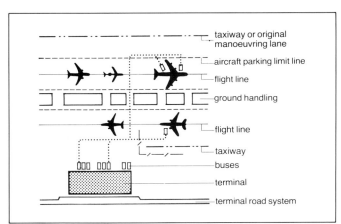

5 Transporter

Airports

FLOW & FUNCTIONS

Flow of aircraft, passengers, baggage and vehicles can be shown in composite and single diagrams, used to identify sequence of functions for preparation of schemes in plan and cross section →(1). Series of diagrams can be developed as graphic model to identify effect of change in events, test different arrangement of functions or sub-fucntions.

Flow in terminal complex takes place in 3 major areas:

apron: area between runway/taxiway system and terminal; serves aircraft flow to and from gates and flow of aircraft ground handling eqp.

terminal: area between aircraft gate positions and vehicular kerb; serves flow of passengers and baggage.

ground transport: area located between terminal and points of access at airport boundaries; serves 2 flows, *ie* passenger vehicles, service vehicles.

Flow of passengers & baggage
Both domestic and international can be divided into 3 categories each requiring sequence of operatings as below (based on USA practice):

outward passengers arrive at terminal by ground transport for which major operations:
kerbside baggage check in for passengers with tickets →(2)
ticket processing at counters with baggage check-in →(2)
outbound baggage →(2)
security check →(2)
passport check for international flights
ticket control at aircraft gates; passenger waiting rm →(3)(4)
aircraft boarding stairs, loading bridge etc →p261(4)

inward passengers arrive at terminal by aircraft; major operations:
aircraft disembarking (stairs, loading bridge etc)
immigration control (international)
customs control (international)
baggage claim
ground transport

transfer passengers from 1 flight to another; inter-line from 1 airline to another or intra-line on same airline; baggage handled by airline except for passengers transferring from international to domestic flight who must claim baggage and pass through immigration and customs inspection.

Outward and inward passenger traffic generates visitor traffic. Visitor/P ratios vary by airport; need be established as part of quantifying passenger flow during pre-determined times of day.

Transfer passengers seldom met by people at point of transfer.

Through passengers continuing on same aircraft domestically rarely disembark except, *eg,* occasionally for telephone calls.

Secondary flow →p262
Air freight flow between freight terminal and aircraft passenger terminal/apron.

Mail flow between mail depot and passenger terminal/apron.

Catering flow between catering service and passenger terminal/apron.

Fuel flow between fuel depot and passenger terminal aircraft apron: takes place increasingly by pipeline (hydrant fuelling), eliminating large fuel trucks and requiring only hydrant pump vehicles on apron.

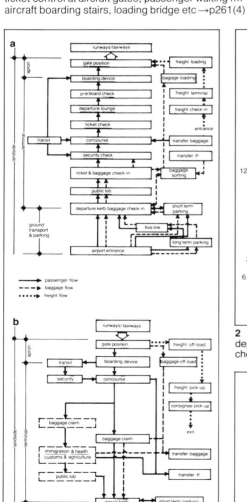

1 Airport flow diagrams based on USA procedures **a** departure **b** arrival: broken boxes indicate international traffic functions

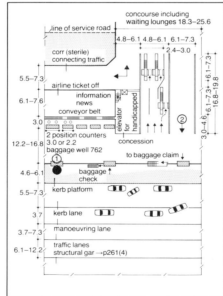

2 Schematic diagram of layout of terminal departure side: ① counter check-in ② security check

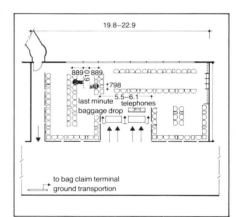

4 P wr at aircraft gates, capacity for 200 seat aircraft, 80% load factor, boarding 10–15 minutes before scheduled departure time: gross ar 180 m² excluding fire stairs, net 150 m²

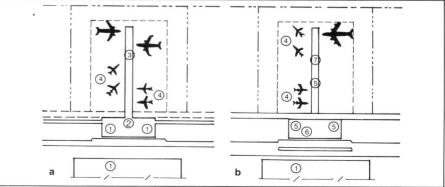

3 Ticket control at aircraft gates **a** second level 1 car parking, kerbside baggage check, ticket lob 2 security 3 P wr 4 aircraft parking at gate positions **b** ground level 5 outwards baggage 6 inwards baggage 7 off, ground handling operation (not detailed)

Baggage handling

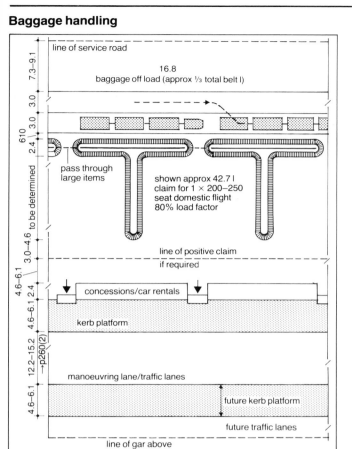

line of service road

16.8
baggage off load (approx ⅓ total belt l)

7.3–9.1

3.0

610

3.0

2.4

pass through
large items

shown approx 42.7 l
claim for 1 × 200–250
seat domestic flight
80% load factor

to be determined

line of positive claim
if required

3.0–4.6

4.6–6.1

concessions/car rentals

4.6–6.1 2.4

kerb platform

4.6–6.1

12.2–15.2

→p260(2)

manoeuvring lane/traffic lanes

4.6–6.1

future kerb platform

future traffic lanes

line of gar above

1 Inward baggage

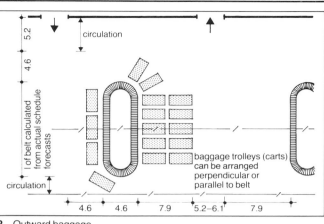

5.2

circulation

4.6

l of belt calculated
from actual schedule
forecasts

baggage trolleys (carts)
can be arranged
perpendicular or
parallel to belt

circulation

4.6   4.6   7.9   5.2–6.1   7.9

2 Outward baggage

Aircraft parking

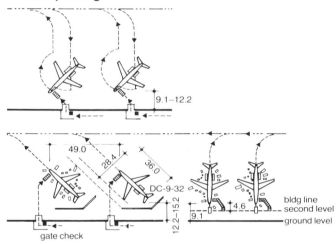

9.1–12.2

49.0

28.4

36.0

DC-9-32

12.2–15.2

gate check

bldg line
second level
9.1   4.6
ground level

3 Aircraft parking

Terminals

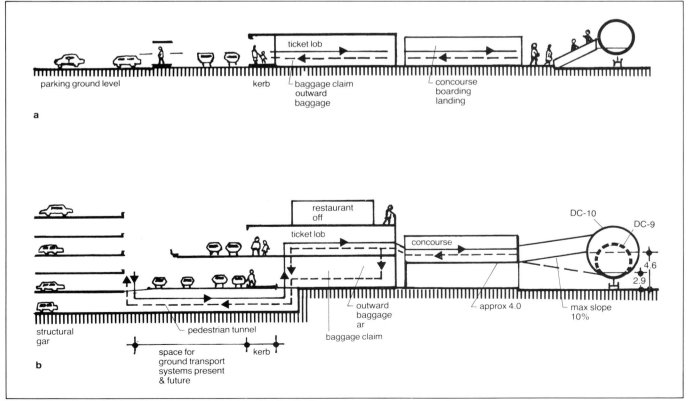

ticket lob

parking ground level

kerb

baggage claim
outward
baggage

concourse
boarding
landing

a

restaurant
off

ticket lob

concourse

DC-10

DC-9

4.6

2.9

outward
baggage
ar

baggage claim

approx 4.0

max slope
10%

structural
gar

pedestrian tunnel

space for
ground transport
systems present
& future

kerb

b

4 Terminal cross sections **a** small 1-level **b** large 2-level

Airports

SECONDARY SERVICES

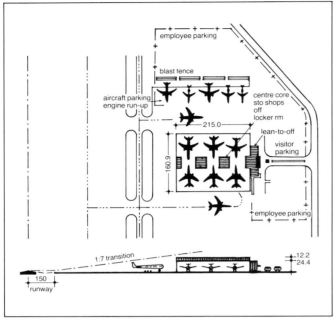

1 Aircraft maintenance

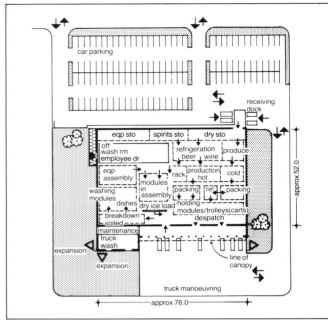

2 Catering bldg

FREIGHT

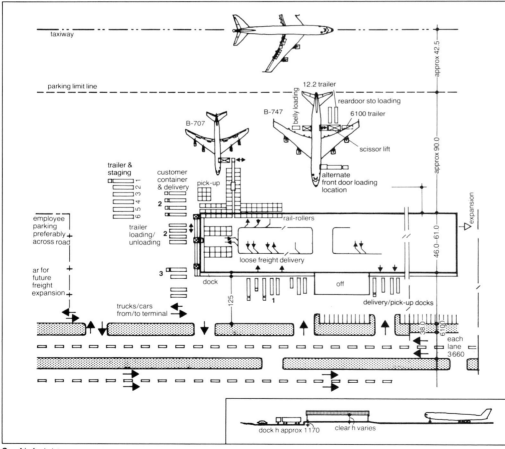

3 Air freight

Freight carried by airline operating both passenger & airfreight aircraft consists mainly of inbound & outbound flow →(3). Freight also transferred from 1 aircraft to another. Handling takes place inside & outside bldg. Procedure varies; to large degree depends on type & volume of freight handled: size, percent loose, percent containerised; type of aircraft in use: single deck, double deck, side door loading, nose loading, tail loading, combinations. Such factors influence degree of mechanisation required. →(3) shows 1 B-747 position, nose-in, push-out, side door loading by trailers, & 1 B-707 position, side door loading mechanised.

Outbound flow →(3) **1** loose freight delivered at truck docks & processed through bldg; **2** containers delivered at truck docks, processed & loaded outside bldg by mech systems; **3** percentage of all freight carried on passenger aircraft (as high as 70%) & dispatched from freight terminal by truck, cart or trolly to air passenger terminal to be loaded at gate position.

Industrial buildings

SITE SELECTION

Assess area requirements from client's brief for factory or warehouse, including:
expansion potential
parking: visitors, employees, trucks
external sto area
landscaping
road, railway or barge access

Check national and local legislation, zoning ordinances and codes for:
permitted site densities
use of public utilities such as (for process and personnel consumption) water, power, gas, effluent disposal
access on public and private roads for employees, goods vehicles and trucks

Assess environmental impact of heavy industry, light manufacturing and warehousing on surrounding community; in USA file environmental impact statement with authority. Consider:
noise: machinery and vehicles (particularly at night)
vibration
light (external circulation, marshalling, shipping and sto areas at night)
fume and dust pollution
effluent into waterways or ground water
hazards of possible explosion or radiation exposure

Investigate assistance for development finance from central government (Assisted Development Areas in UK) and local authorities, city development corporations (State Development Commissions USA) etc.

DEVELOPMENT OPTIONS

Rehabilitate existing site/bldg
Infill + rehabilitate (including in town sites)
New bldg on existing site (including phased redevelopment)
New bldg on new site

Each will be defined by:
Zoning ordinances, reg USA
Suitability of site size/shape; boundaries
Suitability of bldg size/type/shape (as briefed)
Geology
Topography
Public utilities
Statutory permissions
Access for industrial vehicles and work people's cars
Rail or water access
Airport proximity to site
Labour resources of area
Finance: development costs or subsidies, operating costs including taxes/tax relief, loan interests

SITE DEVELOPMENT

Building plot ratio & site coverage

Plot ratio of 1:1 should be regarded as max on all sites inclusive of industrial and ancillary office bldg. Site coverage should not exceed 75% of site at ground level. Likely that site coverage of approx 50–60% can be achieved. Site area for plot ratio calculation purposes excludes any part of adjoining streets (except where these to be closed).

Car & truck parking

Typical car parking requirements for industrial accn (check local standards):

UK		USA
m²	spaces	
less than 92.9	4	a total employees on max shift × 85%
less than 232.26	5	(15% absent × per cent who arrive by
less than 371.61	6	car) divided by av car occupancy =
less than 510.96	7	parking spaces required
less than 656.32	8	b 1 space for every 2 employees during
less than 789.67	9	shift of max employment & 1 for each
less than 929.92	10	truck to be stopped simultaneoulsy
less than 1021.92	11	
less than 1114.83	12	

Lorry parking requirements will depend on needs of particular users and local reg.

1 Locate factories & warehouses on site to allow expansion, preferably in 2 directions: consider vehicle access during phased expansion

Key: 1 manufacturing ar 2 off
3 factory expansion options
4 off expansion options
5 ar of potential planning conflict
6 goods vehicle access

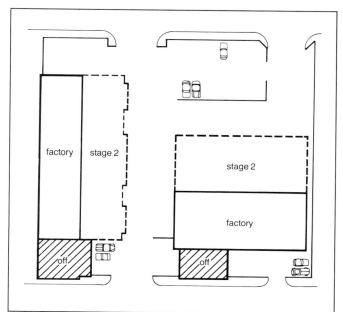

2 'Nursery' unit developments should also allow for expansion but with urban infill sites this may have to be at expense of yard ar

Industrial buildings

BASIC BUILDING TYPE SELECTION

Factories and warehouse bldg types only economically and operationally interchangeable where structural frame has column spans that will not conflict with spacing of pallet racking, clear height permitting use of modern mech handling eqp, roof structure that can accept loading of production and environmental services. This normally only economic for small scale bldg or where company has mixed sto and manufacturing uses on site likely to change.

Key factors in building type selection

Factories →p266–8:
operational flexibility for rapid response to changing production demands: clear height column spacing, roof and floor loading, roof construction for services routing for type of manufacturing process invloved
energy and environmental control: natural or artificial light; environmental needs of/from process: good working conditions for labour
durability and fire control: selection of materials for structure and envelope related to fire risk and any corrosive effects from process
resale potential
promotional value for user company

Warehouses →p269–72:
structure commensurate with sto demands: structural spans to suit rack spacing and height and floor strength to allow more than 1 arrangement
energy and environmental control: to keep stored products in good condition: insulation and cooling in some cases, ventilation in others; good working conditions for labour (*eg* avoiding loading docks facing into prevailing wind)
fire control: compartmentation to minimise fire spread assessed against hindrance to sto and handling and cost of sprinklers

Selection strategy

Single or multi-storey development
modern production and sto techniques make full use of bldg cube with inherent multi-level characteristics
multi-storey development (or conversion) can be efficient for light and high technology industry, particularly where land costly in urban areas: consider personnel circulation and escape, national and local reg, fire control, goods circulation and process, services routing and trucks and private vehicle access and parking, particularly in dense developments
consider cost and environment impact

AREAS FOR SOME INDUSTRIAL OCCUPANCIES

For feasibility studies before detailed brief (program) from user these areas can be used as approximate bldg areas.

Service industries

15 m²/P (smallest) to 30 m² medium size
el repairs
builders
engineering contractors (*eg* machine tool movers)
appliance repairs
instrument repairs
reprographic services
printers
machine tool repairs

Manufacturing industries

Av 28 m²/P; range 22–33 (33 m²/P under 664.5 m²)
anodising
sheet metal work
polishing
furniture manufacture
shop fitting manufacture
clothing
textile (made up)

Distributive trades

Av 80 m²/pp
builders merchants
timber supply
books & magazines
machine spares
electrical goods & spares
antiques/furntiture
upholstery/textile

Average area/worker

	m²
clothing	11
research & development	13
electrical components & assembly	17.5
surgical instruments/appliances, scientific instruments	19.25
miscellaneous manufacture (*eg* plastics products, musical instruments)	23.5
leather work	24.0
metal goods, cutlery, jewellery, forging, small tools	24.25
made up textiles (*eg* bags)	28.75
packaging, stationery, printing	32.5
pottery & glass blowing	36.75
motor repairs, reprographic services	45.5
joinery, furnishing upholstery, shop fitting, timber goods	46.75

Typical area distribution

Includes circulation space

Manufacturing

production	60–70%	(decreases as size increases)
sto	20% & less	(increases as size increases)
off	10–15%	(increases as size decreases)
amenities	5–9%	(increases as size increases)

Distribution

sto	80% +	
off	10–20%	(greater need in some types of distribution)
amenities	0–5%	

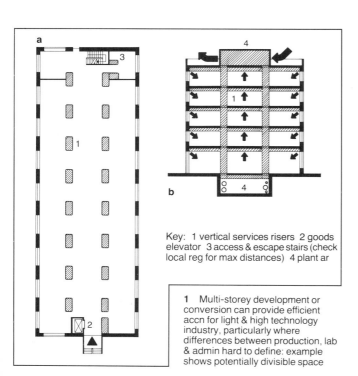

Key: 1 vertical services risers 2 goods elevator 3 access & escape stairs (check local reg for max distances) 4 plant ar

1 Multi-storey development or conversion can provide efficient accn for light & high technology industry, particularly where differences between production, lab & admin hard to define: example shows potentially divisible space

industry

Industrial buildings

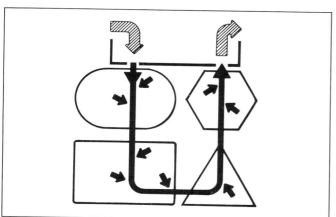

Key: 1 ground level: goods in, despatch, parking 2 production level 3 intermediate process plant level 4 principal environmental plant level

1 Multi-storey factories economic for process-based industries (*eg* food, pharmaceuticals, tobacco) where gravity can be used in process and energy be conserved by compact planning

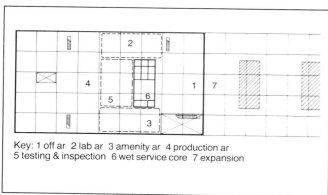

2 Mass production does not usually demand long narrow bldg, *ie* formalisation of flow diagram: typically process is looped between common vehicle access & sto zone

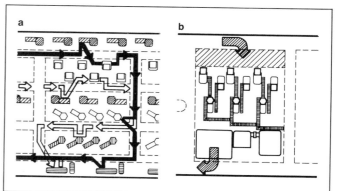

Key: 1 off ar 2 lab ar 3 amenity ar 4 production ar 5 testing & inspection 6 wet service core 7 expansion

3 In light & high technology industry production research & admin ar are becoming less & less distinct: dept will need to expand or contract freely

SELECTION STRATEGY (cont)

Building shape in plan. Selection of plan shape is function of:
demands of production or sto system
climate, size, shape,
topography and geology of site
location of utilities
expansion potential of process in relation to site →p274(1)(2)

Some production processes can demand long, narrow bldg:
intensive line production methods, *eg* metal rolling, paper manufacture
factories using overhead gantry cranes, *eg* heavy engineering
high-bay automated warehouses: function of eqp movement efficiency
multi-storey development, flatted workshops for natural light and ventilation

Majority of other industrial uses can be efficiently installed in rectangular plan with proportions 1:1–1:4, typically 1:2/2:3. Modern mass production methods capitalise on mech handling techniques no longer literally interpreting 'line production'.

Increasing demand for bldg which will not restrict location of production, sto and admin to clearly defined areas, but which permit rapid reallocation within bldg envelope.

Structural bay sizes suited to process and location of access equal shape in importance.

IDENTIFICATION OF BUILDING REQUIREMENT

Factories:
should be designed to serve variety of uses within their life: frequent problem inefficient factory stock through structural obsolescence – insufficient services support capacity of roof structure, insufficient headroom, short spans.
should not be considered merely as weather-proof envelopes round production process. Form and disposition of their structure fundamentally influences essential freedom to optimise production layout and route services equally freely to serve that or any future production layouts without demanding long periods of down time for alteration.
Selection of structure is key factor in providing efficient and flexible operation. There is range of structural types that have proved efficient and adaptable. But technological innovation may add to these types, *eg* stressed skin construction requiring only minimal frame support for envelope.

Assess roof structure for:
service carrying ability in each direction and easy access for relocation ability to accept point loads and flexible location for materials handling eqp, *eg* overhead hoists, conveyors
natural lighting: consider glare and insolation/heat loss
durability and maintenance: performance in fire and need for cleaning/ repainting, particularly in clean areas

Industrial bldg designed to be closely matched to initial process or layout can prove as inflexible and costly to operate in long term as those designed to minimise capital cost (to exclusion of consideration of operating costs and operational flexibility).

4 Factory structures must have spans wide enough in both directions to allow user optimise production layout: traditional batch production lines of similar machines, a, may need to be reorganised into integrated 'cell' to exploit modern mech handling techniques, b

Industrial buildings

FACTORY BUILDING TYPES

Separate bldg types can be identified as most efficient in meeting operational demands of certain methods of production. Spans, type of structure, clear height, roof and floor loadings function of *how* product manufactured or stored rather than what product is. Industrial bldg should be designed to serve broad range of uses within that general production sector.

Basic types to be identified are:

Light duty

Implies small scale (also →p285–90 workshops). Industrial bldg where operational demands of production or sto process place few demands on structural frame or floor. Interchangeable between light production and distribution duties. Typically up to 1860 m². Light metal work, packaging, clothing, consumer durable repairs, small printers. Distribution of el goods, builders' components, sub-depots for local retail distribution.

Medium duty

Principally batch production or sto duties where process and supporting services imply some demands on design of bldg structure, shape and floor, allowing potential flexibility of production and sto layout. Sto and production bldg types not interchangeable unless roof structure designed with production services support capacity.

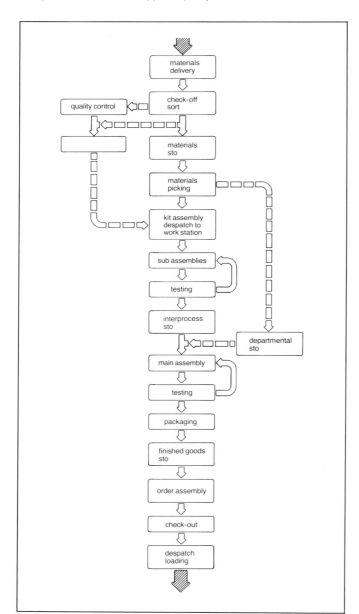

1 Typical process flow diagram for high technology industry, *eg* electronics material

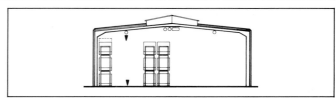

2 Light duty industrial bldg mainly for sto purposes: portal framed structure typically 4.5 m to eaves; spans min 9 m, typical 12 m; roof loading 0.35 kN/m² (no hoisting); floor loading 16 kN/m²

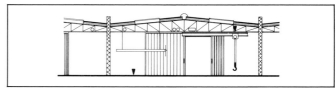

3 Mainly light production: trussed frame; eaves h & spans as →(2); roof structural loading (services) 0.5 kN/m² (up to 2 t hoist loads distributed/structural bay)

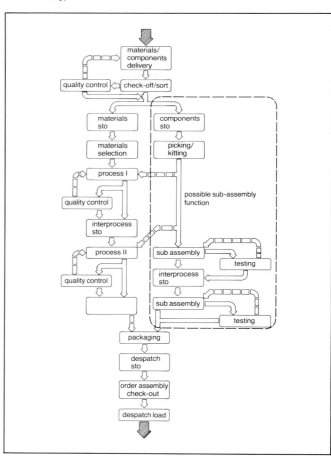

4 Typical process flow diagram for traditional batch production organisation, *eg* engineering components

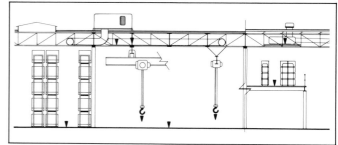

5 Medium duty industrial bldg: 6.5 m preferred eaves h (to allow mezzanine), min 5.5 m; spans typically 12 m × 18 m; roof structural loading: to accept point loads 2 t monorail hoist/bay or up to 5 t suspended crane loads distributed over bay; floor loading 25 kN/m² for stacked sto

Industrial buildings

FACTORY BUILDING TYPES (cont)

Heavy duty

Designed to accept large scale batch or mass production systems, which have intensive demands for overhead production and environmental service and materials handling, and dense floor layouts with some heavy production machinery and inter-process sto areas. May need high bldg to exploit multi-level ability of materials-handling eqp. In heavy engineering sector some special types to exploit heavy lift overhead gantry cranes.

1 Heavy duty industrial bldg: 7 m min general purpose eaves h, 9 m for racked, sto & overhead handling systems **a**; 12 m for bulk processing plant **b**; spans typically 12 m × 18 m but can be less for heavy roof loadings (9 m × 12 m) or greater for lighter loads (20 m); roof structural loading: 5 t point loads & 10 t beam loads distributed over bay; heavier loads need gantry cranes & additional structure; floor loading: 15–30 kN/m² with some special bases for heavy machine tools

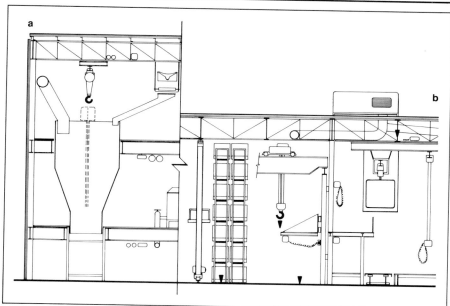

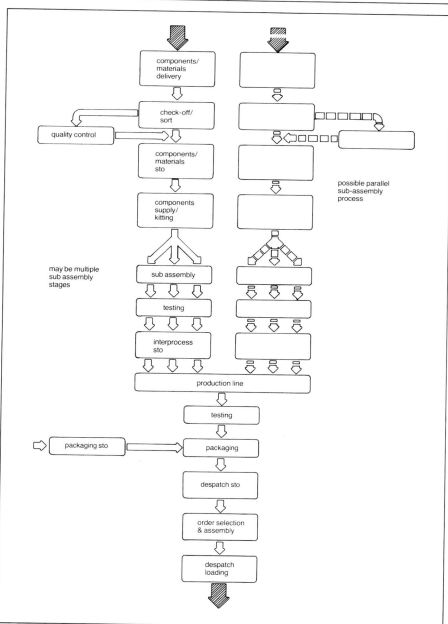

2 Typical process flow diagram for traditional mass production line: modern developments tend to split assembly functions off line into teams

Industrial buildings

FACTORY BUILDING TYPES (cont)

High technology

Demanding high quality process and/or personnel environment. Small or large scale: similar design demands. Provision for intensive services in roof zone; can also be requirement for under floor servicing. High content of bulk handling; powders, liquids, gases. Interchangeability between production, lab and admin areas: rapid change demand with technological innovation and volatile markets.

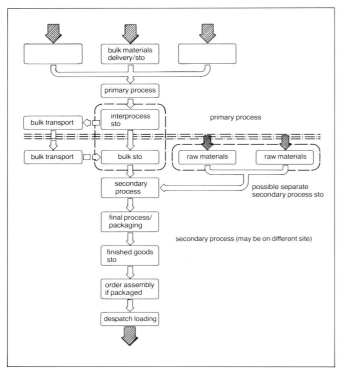

1   Typical process flow diagram for process-based industry, *eg* petrochemical, rubber

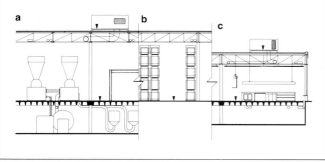

2   High technology industrial bldg: may require undercroft for bulk process access & services routing; 7 m preferred min eaves h over process plant **a** & for palletised sto **b**; 4 m min for high technology assembly environment **c**; roof structural loadings up to 1.2 kN/m², distributed, for services, hoist loads up to 5 t distributed per bay for plant removal; floor loadings 15–20 kN/m² for large plant, 10–15 kN/m² for high labour use assembly

STRUCTURAL SELECTION

Check national and local (state) reg for construction and performance in fire relating to required occupancy and with client's insurance company: this will affect materials choice →p277.

SERVICING STANDARDS; STATUTORY REQUIREMENTS

For general servicing standards in industrial bldg →p383–970.

structural type		1	2	3	4	5	6
factory type	light duty	● CST	● S	● CST	● AS	● AS	● (a) AS
	medium duty	● CS	● S	○ (b) CS	● S	● S	
	heavy duty		● S	○ (b) cS	● S	● S	● (c) AS
	high technology		● S		● CS		● AS
warehouse type	small scale	● CST		● CST			
	general purpose	● CS	● S	● CS	● CS		
	intermediate high bay	● CS	● S	● CS	● CS		● (c) AS

●	appropriate structure
○	appropriate structure in noted case only
A	aluminium
C	concrete
S	steel
T	timber
a	mult-divisible spaces
b	with overhead gantry cranes only
c	wide spans on irregular site

3   Factory structural types

4   Structural types: **a** single axis solid beam, long span purlins **b** single axis castella beam, long span purlins: for service routing **c** portal frame for use where service loading minimal or gantry craneage: typical pitch 6°, roof lights built into pitch or ridge **d** flat or cambered truss, 1 or 2 axes **e** monitor roof, evenly distributed light, single axis **f** space frame: for very wide spans; where columns cannot be at equal spacing; where high degree of servicing freedom required

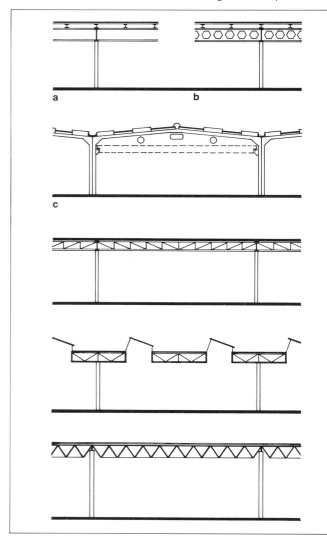

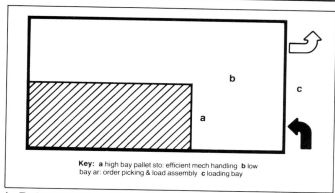

1   Typical proportions of high & low bay ar for distribution warehouse

Key: **a** high bay pallet sto: efficient mech handling **b** low bay ar: order picking & load assembly **c** loading bay

WAREHOUSES

Warehouse bldg selection depends on scale and type of sto operation. Different methods of sto unit loads imply various levels of efficiency in filling bldg volume and accessibility to load. Equally these decisions affect selection of mech handling eqp →p278(3)(4).

Warehousing operation usually involves bulk sto and order selection functions. These tend have dissimilar sto and materials handling demands except when small scale installations: typically high dense sto for bulk stock to exploit handling techniques with lower 'active stock' areas for order picking. Typical proportion divides warehouse: $1/3$ high bay area, $2/3$ lower area for order picking and assembly and loading bay zones →(1), *ie* can combine 2 of bldg types described below. Because of density of stock bulk sto area may not need to expand so rapidly as processing zones.

WAREHOUSE BUILDING TYPES

Small scale
→p266 light duty factory and →p268(3) entries 1 & 2.

General purpose
For fork-lift, reach truck and narrow aisle stacker operation. Bldg acts as weather-proof envelope to sto operation. Important that spans, height, floor strength allow for flexible installation of sto methods →p272 types 3–6, 7a & 8a; also →p266 medium duty factory types and →p272(10).

Intermediate high bay
Independent bldg structure for intermediate height narrow aisle sto systems. Up to 14 m bldg height (12 m sto height). Allows variations in sto layout and possibility of other later uses; also →p267 heavy duty factory.

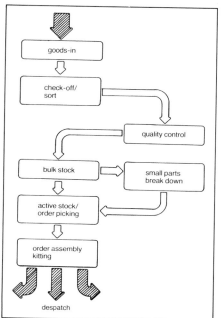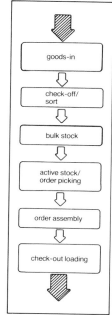

2   Typical sto flow diagram: repository, *eg* cold sto, steel stockholding

3   Typical sto flow diagram: repository, *eg* cold sto, steel stockholding

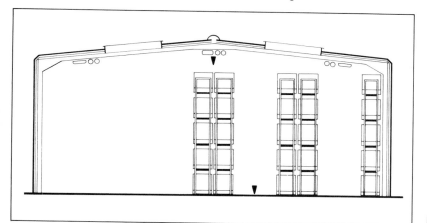

4   General purpose warehouse, typically for 7 500 stack h: 8 000 to eaves; spans 12–18 m; floor loading 25 kN/m² min   *NB* consider also flat roof

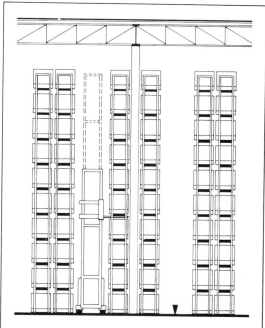

5   Intermediate high bay warehouse, typically 14 m to eaves: spans 11.1–20.5 m depending on aisle w and pallet size; floor loadings 50 kN/m² distributed loads

Industrial buildings

WAREHOUSES

High bay

Integral rack structure: for sto heights to 30 m to exploit automated handling techniques →(2). Economic land cost high, labour cost high, expansion potential limited. Sto racking forms bldg structure, with roof and wall cladding attached to it. Very strong floor and foundations required so poor ground can preclude concept.

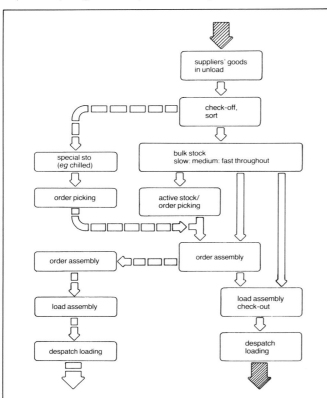

1 Typical sto flow diagram for distribution warehouse, *eg* retail food distribution

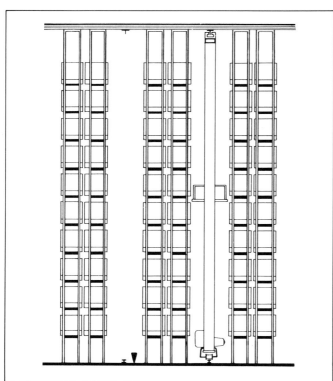

2 High bay warehouse, bldg structure integral with pallet racking; h 30 m; floor loadings can be more than 60 kN/m² distributed

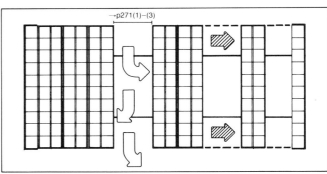

3 Where sto ar limited & throughput speed not top priority intense use of volume can be made with mobile racking; double-sided racking mounted on rail-borne carriers: racks nest face to face, only 1 aisle opening at time; imposes high floor loadings

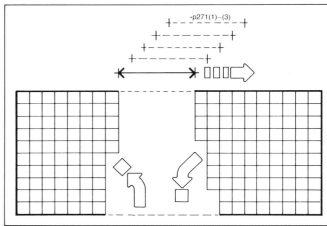

4 Block stacking 3–4 pallets h: aisle moves through stack to provide first-in, first-out rotation; aisle w related to type of truck used →p271

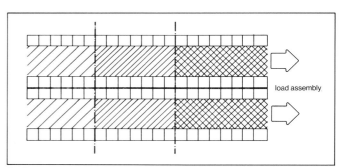

5 For bulk pallet sto in long aisles stock should be arranged in notional ar so that fastest throughput stock closest to assembly ar: note rack orientation at 90° to assembly zone

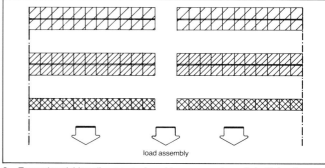

6 For order picking diverse stock racking arranged parallel with load assembly zone with rack ar devoted to stock with various throughput speeds, fastest nearest assembly zone: reduces slow moving picking machinery blocking movement of others

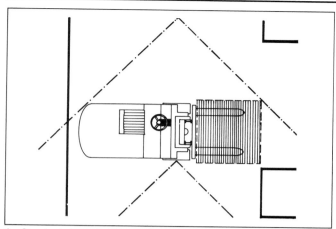

1 Counter-balance forklift capacity 3 000 kg: stacking aisle 90° with 1 220 square pallet 3 670; intersecting aisle (dotted) 2 000; l without pallet 3 150, w 1 100

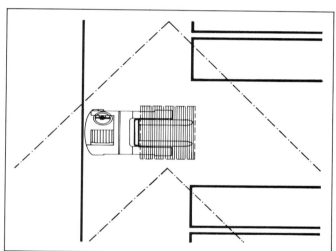

2 Reach fork-lift capacity 1 500 kg, pallet carried within wheel base; stacking aisle 90° with 1 220 square pallet 2 400; intersecting aisle (dotted) 1 900; l without pallet 1 600, w 990

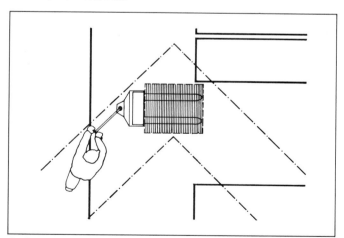

3 Powered P-controlled pallet fork-lift: stacking aisle 90° with 1 220 square pallet 1 750; intersecting aisle (dotted) 1 500; l without pallet 1 820, w 787

WAREHOUSES

Fork-lift dimensions

In design for best use of sto space note interaction between aisle spaces and fork-lift dimensions: decision on stacking may decide size and make of fork-lift, choice of fork-lift may decide stacking. Relevant details for some fork-lift types and pallet sizes →(1)–(6).

type of truck	dimensions	weight kg
counter-balanced fork-lift: load capacity		
2 500 kg at 610 load centre		
l without pallet	3 246	
w without pallet	1 118	
h: mast lowered	2 286	
weight without load		4 500
wheel loads laden[1]: front (drive)		6 000
rear (steer)		750
90° stacking aisle (1 200 pallet)	3 480	
turn-out aisle (1 200 pallet) (dotted) →(1)	2 000	

[1] for distributed rolling loads divide by wheel contact ar, available from trade literature

4 Counter-balanced fork-lift dimensions & weights: pallet sizes USA 1 220 × 1 220, 1 220 × 1 830; some pallets have sides 1 220 h

type of truck	dimensions	weight kg
extending mast reach fork-lift: load capacity		
2 040 kg at 610 load centre		
l without pallet	1 930	
w without pallet	990	
h: mast lowered	2 667	
weight without load		2 722
wheel loads laden[1]: front (mast extended)		4 282
rear (mast extended)		481
90° stacking aisle (1 200 pallet)	2 362	
turn-out aisle (1 200 pallet) (dotted) →(2)	1 905	

[1] for distributed rolling loads divide by wheel contact ar, available from trade literature

5 Extending mast reach truck dimensions & weights

type of truck	dimensions	weight kg
powered P-controlled pallet fork-lift: load		
capacity 1 815 kg		
l without pallet	1 854	
w without pallet	762	
h: mast lowered	not applicable	
w without load		372
wheel loads	not applicable	
90° stacking aisle (1 200 pallet)	1 752	
turn-out aisle (1 200 pallet) (dotted) →(3)	1 498	

6 Powered P-controlled pallet truck dimensions & weight

Industrial buildings

1 Fork-lift in block stack: 3 500 aisle; 3 600 stack h (4.5 m bldg h dotted)

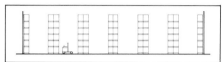

2 Fork-lift in pallet racking: 3 500 aisle; 7 500 stack h

3 Reach fork-lift in block stack: 2 600 aisle; 3 600 stack h (4 500 bldg h dotted)

4 Reach fork-lift in pallet racking: 2 600 aisle; 7 500 stack h

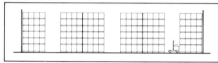

5 Reach fork-lift in drive-in racking, drives into stack between frames: 7 500 stack h

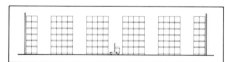

6 Reach fork-lift in double deep racking, has extending fork attachment: 2 600 aisle

7 Narrow aisle stacker, moves parallel with rack: **a** stack h 7 500 **b** stack h dotted 10.5 m

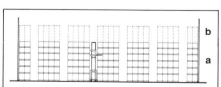

8 Narrow aisle stacker in double deep racking, 1 600 aisle: **a** stack h 7 500 **b** stack h dotted 10.5 m

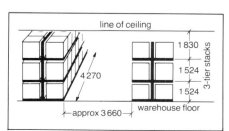

WAREHOUSES

Storage efficiency with various handling methods

Taking typical stacking areas 33 m × 33 m, volume efficiency assessment includes 1 repositioning aisle at end of rack runs; pallet size: 1 200 × 1 000 × 200 tall →(1)–(9); figures in column 2 of (10) relate to numbers of picture captions. USA pallet sizes →(9) and p271(4).

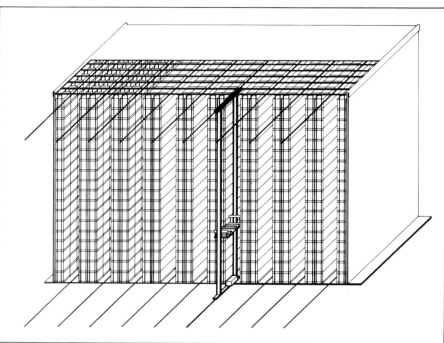

9 Automated fixed path stacker crane: 1 400 aisle; 24 m stack h; integral rack structure

eqp	type of sto	stack h	pallets stored	volume efficiency	access	sto increase over fork-lift equivalent
				%	%	%
fork-lift: bldg h 8 m to underside of structure	1 block stack[1]	3	1 452	24	poor	
	2 beam pallet racking	5	1 200	20	100	
reach fork-lift: bldg h 8 m to underside of structure	3 block stack[2]	3	1 584	28	poor	9
	4 beam pallet racking	5	1 400	35	100	17
	5 drive-in racking	5	2 400	58	1st in last out	
	6 double deep racking	5	2 400	49	50	
narrow aisle stacker:	7a beam pallet racking[3]	5	1 800	46	100	50
	7b beam pallet racking[4]	7	2 520	46	46	110
	8a double deep racking[3]	5	2 400	59	50	
	8b double deep racking[4]	7	3 360	60	50	
automated high bay stacker crane, rail guided: bldg h 24 m to underside of roof structure (can be 30 m+)	9 beam pallet racking	15	5 400	32[5]	100	

[1] volume efficiency increases if lower bldg used (4 500 min)   [2] volume efficiency increases if lower bldg used   [3] bldg h to underside roof structure 8 000   [4] bldg h to underside of roof structure 11 m   [5] as section of longer aisle: typically 100 m+

10 Sto efficiency with various handling methods

11 When using pallets 1 220 × 1 830 (frequent in USA) preferred aisle w 3 600; 4 270 run of rack accommodates 3 pallets 1 220 × 1 220 or 2 pallets 1 220 × 1 830

Industrial buildings

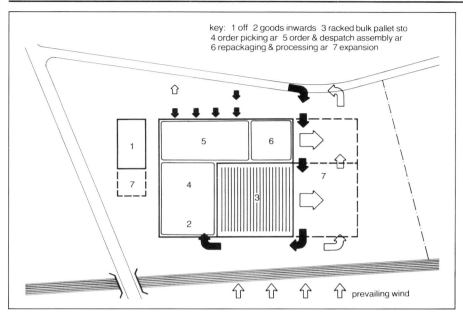

key: 1 off 2 goods inwards 3 racked bulk pallet sto
4 order picking ar 5 order & despatch assembly ar
6 repackaging & processing ar 7 expansion

prevailing wind

1 Option 1: low rise 'conventional' sto; minimal site works

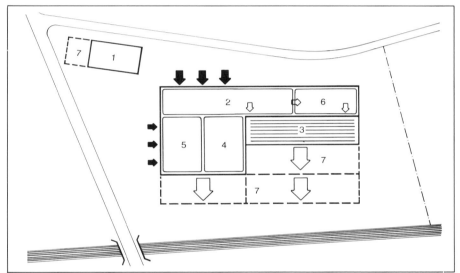

2 Option 2: narrow aisle high bay sto: trade-off = cost of site works against increased operational flexibility & lower energy loss

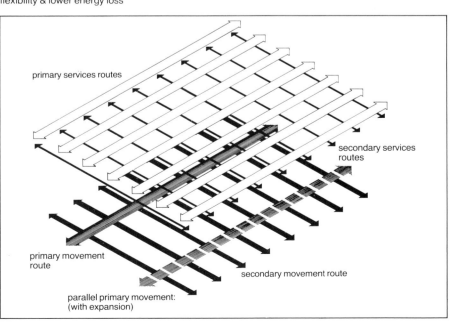

primary services routes

secondary services routes

primary movement route

secondary movement route

parallel primary movement: (with expansion)

SITE LAYOUT

Site layout for factories and warehouses determined by:
shape and size of bldg
expansion potential
services running through site, *eg* gas mains, power cables
topography: affecting access for heavy vehicles and building economics (cut and fill)
energy conservation: exposure to prevailing and storm winds
ground conditions and drainage, *eg* avoiding piling or potential flood areas
surrounding neighbourhood: keeping noisy external plant and loading bays from residential area
vehicle (road and rail) manoeuvring and marshalling area in relation to loading bays →p283–4.

Economics

Comparing alternative site layouts will usually result in trade-off between conflicting factors. Example shows alternatives for siting distribution warehouse: important cost factor involves expansion potential and linked mech handling eqp investment decision

First option →(1) minimises excavation by exploiting fall of land to provide raised loading dock at infeed: distribution vehicles were to be side loaded from ground level. But goods inwards loading bay would face prevailing wind, energy cost, and circulation round site required, needing relocation in event of expansion.
Second option →(2) accepts some excavation for raised dock: in lee and exploits fall of site to sink part of high bay stacking area for less environmental intrusion and increased handling efficiency. Revised axis of bulk sto area allows much increased expansion potential without affecting operation of existing installation. This combined with improved sto and handling economics more than offset any increase in capital cost of construction.

Planning grids

To coordinate building's structure, services and circulation in formulating siting and expansion strategy and to integrate these elements during bldg design, discipline their disposition by employing planning grid.

3 To coordinate structure, services & movement in development strategy work to master grid; not 3-dimensional implications

Industrial buildings

LAYOUT OF MULTIPLE UNIT DEVELOPMENTS & ESTATES

Small scale 'nursery' and 'seedbed' units: meet need to integrate group of units into existing urban or rural community. Illustrations →(1)(2) show small 'seedbed' group combined with landscaped open space and 'nursery' units with expansion capacity with grouped goods access.

Speculative developments for rental: built in various forms of terrace to allow flexible space allocation. Note:
sufficient heavy goods vehicle manoeuvring and parking area (see also loading bays)

car parking for work people and visitors (check local standards)
off and amenity accn: either integral within volume of bldg (where site area restricted) or as attached block (where developer requires max rental from production/sto area)
mixture of sizes of unit in estate can be achieved by variable location of cross walls in terrace or by providing 2 or more groups of bldg of increasing size: decision depends on scale

Trade mart concept may be used to revitalise urban areas: divisible space under common roof allowing high degree of planning flexibility.

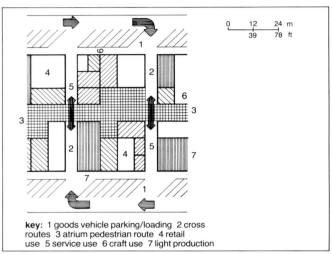

key: 1 goods vehicle parking/loading 2 cross routes 3 atrium pedestrian route 4 retail use 5 service use 6 craft use 7 light production

1 'Nursery' & 'seedbed' industrial units can be integrated into rural community, bring relief to crowded inner city

key: 1 yard 2 public open space

3 'Trade mart' type development, attractive inner city possibility mixing light industrial, craft & retail users to stimulate working community: common envelope provides multi-divisible space

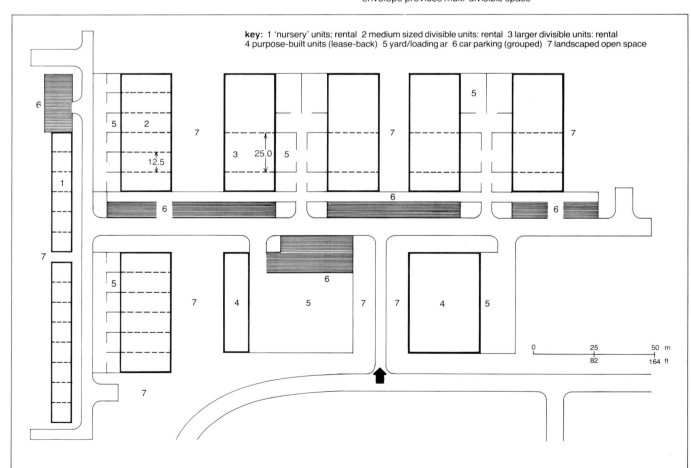

key: 1 'nursery' units; rental 2 medium sized divisible units: rental 3 larger divisible units: rental 4 purpose-built units (lease-back) 5 yard/loading ar 6 car parking (grouped) 7 landscaped open space

2 Typical mixed use industrial estate with range of unit sizes for rental each having expansion options (by extending into adjoining unit); open space & grouped, shielded parking & yards for each property; landscaping improves what can too easily be desolate environment

Industrial buildings

INDUSTRIAL PARKS

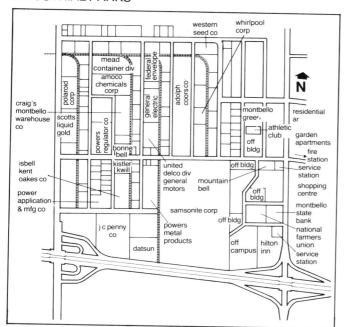

1 Site plan industrial park at Montbello USA

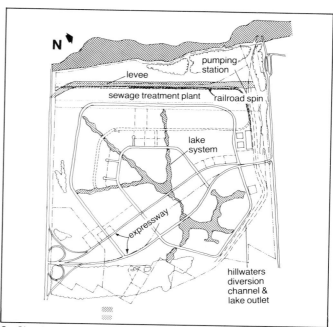

2 Site plan Earth City industrial park St Louis USA: development in flood plain of Missouri river necessitated system of drainage lakes & diversion channel, with levee between Earth City & river

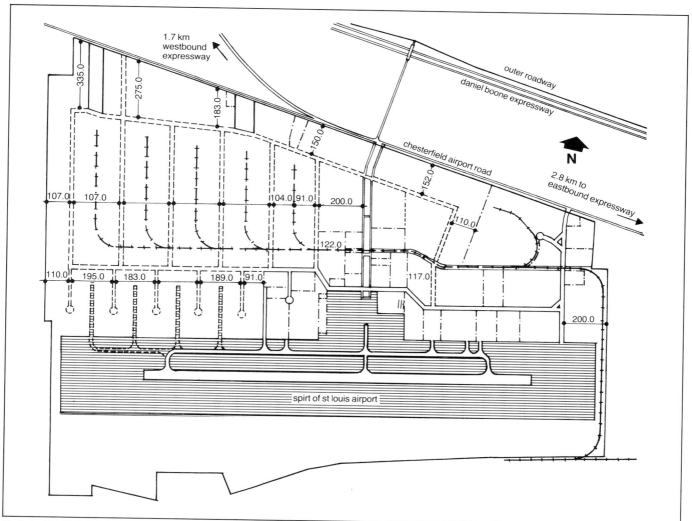

3 Industrial Airpark Spirit West St Louis USA has access from airport to individual sites in park through taxiway easement & also from Chicago-Rock Island railroad

Industrial buildings

BUILDING ENVIRONMENT

Rising energy and labour costs make bldg environment increasingly important contributor to operating costs and productivity. Factors to be considered in providing good conditions at work place include:
dust and fume extraction
ventilation in hot weather
heating in cold weather
natural and artificial lighting
noise control

Ventilation

As rough guide 5 l/s/P: conventional air change rate of 1–1.5 air changes/hr may result in more than 50 times this requirement, wasting much energy.

Heating

sedentary work	19°C	66°F
active (bench) work	16°C	59°F
very active work	13°C	57°F

For many companies with processes involving heat, energy can be recovered and waste heat transferred to contribute to work place requirements: considerable cost savings possible. Warehouses with refrigerated or chilled areas can also benefit, heat being recovered from the chiller's compressors to warm areas where people work.

Heating and ventilation demands also function of standard of insulation and quantity of glazing provided. In UK factory and warehouse bldg must be insulated to 0.7 W/m² °C, with single glazing limited to 20% of roof area and 15% of wall area. These areas still high for energy conservation: 10% of wall and roof area usually considered appropriate.

Natural lighting

Demand for natural roof lighting influences selection of roof structure. Compared with the insulated roof without any openings 20% permitted glazing will increase both heat loss by 4 times and ventilation demand through insolation: in highly serviced environments uncomfortable glare can result from pipe runs crossing bright roof lights. Outdoor illuminance varies from 5000–25000 lux from overcast to sunshine conditions in temperate climates: therefore 3% DF will provide equivalent of 150–750 lux at work place; 10% roof glazing will result in av DF about 5%. Flank glazing must also be carefully designed to avoid glare, particularly at high level. Natural lighting in warehouses can be positive disadvantage, sunlight raising temp and causing package fade.

Artificial lighting

→p398–400; →(1)

Noise control

Noise major pollution and limit on working efficiency: noise damage to hearing, human sensitivity to vibration →p18; max levels in work place →(2).

Reduce noise at source by design of eqp, screening and enclosure.

Reduce vibration at source by mounting machinery on resilient pads or special foundations.

Reduce noise before reaches work place by absorption (walls, roofs and pendant absorbers) and/or by modifying background noise.

Reduce noise effect by isolating workers in noise reducing enclosures.

Escaping noise also troublesome outside bldg: place external plant away from direct lines with surrounding users; screen and suppress source.

place	light requirement lx
engineering machine shops	
manual work	200
bench work	300
careful bench work	500
precision work	1 000
engineering inspection & testing	
medium detail	500
fine detail	1 000
minute detail	1 500
sheet metal	
bench work	750
stamping, pressing	500
spot welding, general	500
precision welds	1 000[1]
assembly	
medium detail	500
small detail	1 000[1]
very fine detail	1 500[1]
stores issue counter	300
paint shops	
paint dips	300
spraying	500
colour matching	1 000
warehousing	
loading bays	150
pallet picking	200
order picking small items	300
packing stations	500

[1] also needs task lighting

1 Artificial lighting: typical requirements

sound pressure level dBA	max exposure time
	hr
85	24
87	16
90	8
93	4
96	2
99	1
	minutes
102	30
105	15
108	7½
111	3¼
continuous levels over 85 dBA should be avoided	

2 Max exposure to noise

PLANNING FOR FIRE CONTROL

Designing factory or warehouse to meet potential fire hazard involves:
measures to limit spread of fire within and outside bldg by compartmentation, detection devices, sprinklers and choice of materials for structure and cladding
providing readily accessible and identifiable means of escape with alternative route in every situation
providing ventilation in roof to reduce heat and smoke build-up to prevent fire 'leap-frogging' under roof cladding and enable fire service rapidly vent smoke: typically 1 vent per structural bay, with curtains of non-inflammable material forming smoke reservoirs in roof space
extinguishing fire or at least controlling seat of fire until brigade can extinguish it, by means of sprinklers, high expansion foam or gas drenching

Fire design decisions involve consultation with:
user: compartmentation may significantly affect layout of process or warehouse
fire chief/officer: local reg and practice, particularly on fire appliance access, water supply and means of escape
user's insurance company: predominant influence on fire control in USA. Insurance company can demand compartmentation on basis of calculated 'maximum forseeable loss' (MFL fire wall). Reduced compartmentation can be negotiated against designing roof structure of greater fr and installation of sprinkler system. Insurance companies usually allow 50% premium reduction for sprinkler system.

Statutory controls
On national or state basis. In UK controls affect max cubic capacity of compartments for single and multi-storey bldg and fr of elements of structure for factory and warehouse bldg of certain floor areas.

Warehouses
Warehouses with pallet racking can provide particular fire hazard, aisles acting as flues. Reg for installation of sprinklers, accounting for frequency of outlet and flow rates based on degree of hazard for stored material. In USA apply rules from National Fire Protection Assocation and client's insurer. In UK Fire Officers' Committee Rules for Automatic Sprinkler Installations should be adhered to.

Site planning
Control of fire spread can also affect location of factory or warehouse on site, particularly in relation to adjoining users. This can affect bldg costs as there are rules set down for materials and fr of walls when adjoining other property at particular distance. For UK →unprotected area requirements in Bldg Reg E5 (Bib592); for USA →state bldg codes and requirements of American Insurance Association (Bib026); in general codes provide fire safety for people and underwriters protect bldg.

BUILDING REGULATIONS

UK bldg reg relating to compartmentation for fire control and cubic capacity of bldg, covering *eg* rules for measurement, periods of fr for elements of structure→Bib480 481 505 590 592 593 594 601 604 608.

In USA areas, construction types, egress or exits, compartmentation and all matters concerning fire safety and fire control are regulated by bldg code administered by city or municipal inspection dept (→Bib027 505 509 510). Matters concerning fire insurance ratings of hazard and bldg covered by standards of National Board of Fire Underwriters.

1 Factories without smoke vents can become rapidly smoke-filled with fire spreading under roof surface

2 With vents & smoke reservoirs fire can be quickly contained & controlled

Industrial buildings

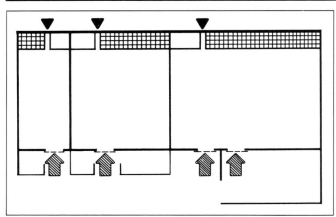

1 In units constructed speculatively for renting off & amenity accn provided in strip for flexible space allocation

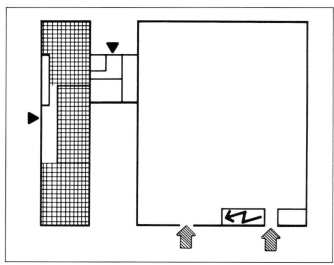

2 Environmental factors can be considered for purpose designed factories: with noisy & dirty processes off and amenity accn can be segregated from production zone

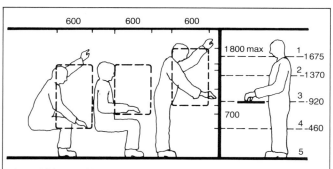

key: 1 light material: low usage, infrequent operation 2 frequent high level controls or light positioning 3 convenient control zone: standing manipulation 4 seated control zone: light & medium-heavy location 5 infrequent zone of heavy material

3 Manual work & sto involve some critical dimensions: most common working & manipulative zone is in 2–4 band

4 Simple handling aids such as scissor lift can improve working conditions & productivity

ENVIRONMENTAL COMPARTMENTATION

Compartmentation, so long as compatible with handling and services demands of production and sto process, can be used reduce both energy loss and certain hostile environments, such as fumes, heat, noise and dust, as well as limiting fire spread.

Hot, dirty processes can be grouped to exploit energy and material recovery techniques. Proportion of area/volume of factory affected by process will indicate strategy; high proportion of area affected, group processes into compartment; low proportion, enclose separate elements of process with local extraction and controls. Alternative increasingly attractive with high energy cost: segregate those who work in production area into environmental enclosure, exploiting automation, and only minimally temper majority of area. Parallel with warehouses: automate main sto section, limiting environmental controls to zones of high labour use for order picking and assembly.

WORK PLACE DESIGN

Design of work place fundamental to achieving high levels of productivity: also influences labour relations and absenteeism. Work place combines:

Ergonomics
Work people's relationship to machinery and work actions to reduce fatigue and increase safety.

Mechanical handling
From most basic, low cost handling devices, scissor lifts, hoists and counterbalanced manipulators, which can revolutionise manual work, to accumulating conveyors, automatically routing mobile work stations and robot assembly machines.

Work organisation
Grouping people for certain tasks. Traditional isolation of machine operators and line assembly organisation under review in several countries in Europe and in USA; team organisation can offer greater communication and production flexibility.

Environment
Positive demands:
temp suited to activity →USA: American Society of Heating, Refrigeration & Air-conditioning Engineers (Bib031), UK: Institution of Heating & Ventilating Engineers (Bib164)
air flow and air cleanliness
lighting: background and task →p398–400

Defence against:
glare
noise
vibration
harmful gaseous or dust products: explosions

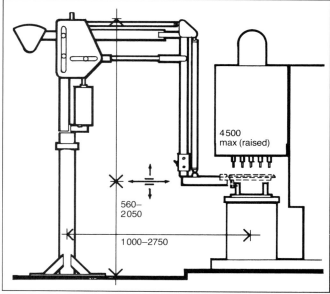

5 Counter-balanced manipulator can enable operator place heavy loads accurately

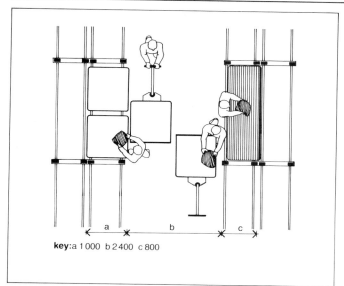

key: a 1 000 b 2 400 c 800

1 Typical manual order picking from pallets & shelf, replenished by reach truck; simultaneous picking from each side for high throughput installation

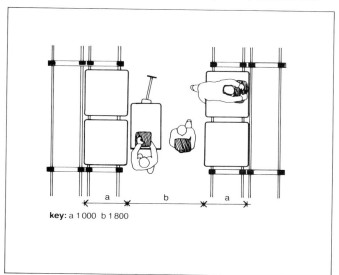

key: a 1 000 b 1 800

2 Slower throughput picking operation with 1-way trolley access: replenished by narrow aisle stacker or from behind rack

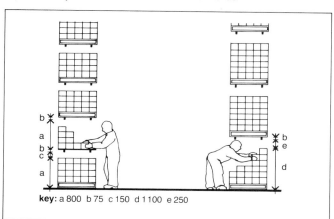

key: a 800 b 75 c 150 d 1 100 e 250

3 Typical rack & shelf h for floor level order picking

WORK PLACE DESIGN

Amenity
Washing, changing, wc and smoke/rest provision related to work place. Location and scale depend on work organisation →(4):

traditional line production will require centralised services accessible to numbers of people

team organisation implies amenity accn close by or local to team operating area; with changes in production organisation depending on manufacturing methods and volume, both are likely to change with increasing frequency.

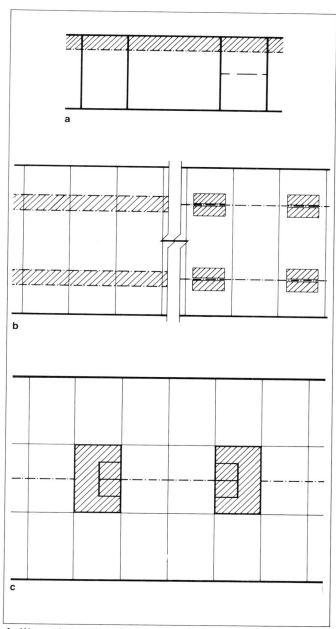

4 Wet services, washing & rest ar: **a** small divisible units as strip along boundary **b** med & large size factory bldg with 2 possible zones for placing wet services, either allowing free location in each zone or grouping into flexibly positioned but distinct wet service units, *eg* for team access **c** for large scale factories another option is island wet service and amenity ar; advantages: single underground services run & accessibility from all sides

Industrial buildings

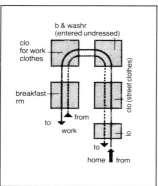

1 Layout of clo, washr, dr in food products firm

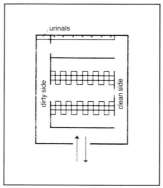

2 Changing rm with strict separation of clean & dirty clothes

HYGIENE

Washing general

UK law requires that adequate and suitable facilities for washing, conveniently accessible, be provided and maintained for use of employed persons in all factories. Where no special order official recommendation not less than 1 washbasin/20P doing clean work, 1/10P doing dirty work, 1/5P handling poisonous substances.

Provision of washbasins →Bib608

Lavatories

UK factory laws do not specify numbers of lavatories: provision considered 'suitable and sufficient' for offices, shops and railways equally relevant for factories →Bib346 347 604.

Lockers

For clean trades 1 locker/P must be provided; for dirty 1 double locker/P to keep work and street clothing separate.

Changing areas

Min changing area 0.5 m²/P

Ambulance rooms

Specification for ambulance rm:
Floor space not less than 9.29 m² with natural light and ventilation. Should contain: glazed sink with hot and cold running water, table with smooth surface, means of sterilising instruments, adequate supply of suitable dressings, bandages and splints, couch, stretcher, separate rm for male and female, qualified nurse always available.

locker sizes

h	w	d
	steel	
1 750	300	300
1 850	300	300
1 850	350	500
	timber	
2 000	400	500
2 000	400	530

3 2-tier row of lockers for multiple shift firm: or lower locker for work clothes upper for street clothes

4 Double row of ventilated clothes lockers: benches in front

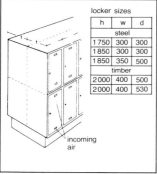

5 Hb with taps and adequate dimensions; washing troughs narrower (up to 940 deep)

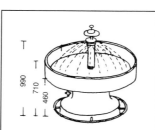

6 Wash fountain (Bradley system): 25% saving in space compared with rows of basins; water consumption 10 P/15–39 l: water pressure ≥ ½ atmosphere

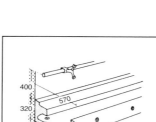

7 Continuous basin: Rotter system

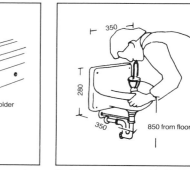

8 Fountain on wall with drinking jet, controlled by lever

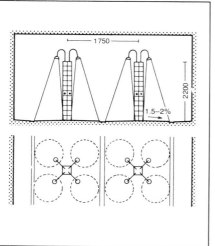

9 Series sho each for 4 P

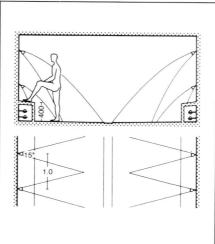

10 Continuous sho along walls with foot sho

11 Sho cubicles with clothes hooks outside

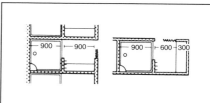

12 Sho cubicles with clothes hooks inside

Industrial buildings

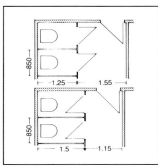

1 Single row closets doors opening outwards (above), inwards (below)

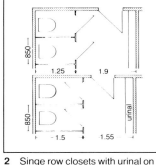

2 Singe row closets with urinal on opposite wall

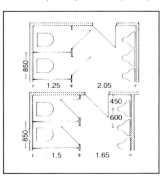

3 Single row closets with bowl urinals opposite

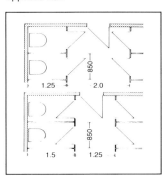

4 Double row closets

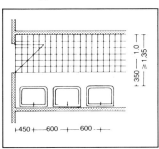

5 Washr with hb

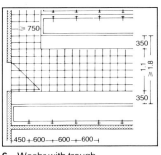

6 Washr with trough

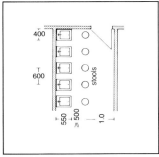

7 Washr with footbaths

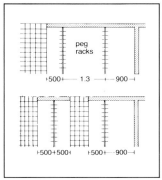

8 Washr with foot-trough

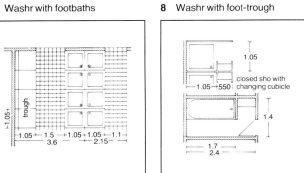

9 Gully drainage, individual drainage for half-open sho compartment

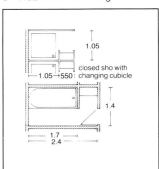

10 Bath cubicle with changing alcove: min dimensions for sho & bath units

SANITARY INSTALLATIONS

Sanitary installations according to German standard given here. 1 floor outlet with smell trap per closet and 1 tap connexion with 1 socket spanner and hose union. Cleaner's sink. Floor surface non-slip, water resistant, easy clean.

Walls washable up to 2000 high. Floor and walls sealed against moisture. Rm temp min 15°C. Wc partitions to ceiling height; space outside well ventilated; 1 washbasin and hand drier per 5 wc. Where soap dispensers fitted 1/2 basins. Min 1 mirror for 2–3 basins.

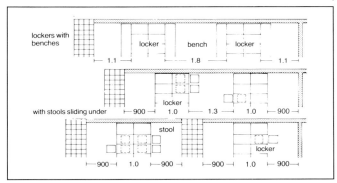

11 Changing ar with simple hook fittings: unattended

12 Changing ar with hanger fittings: unattended

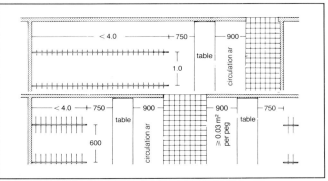

13 Min dimensions for changing rm

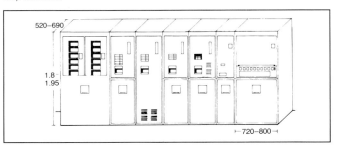

14 Deposit clo, single layout with pegs, dual layout with hangers (theatre clo): attended

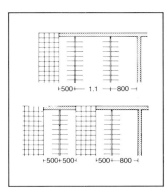

15 Vending machines

Industrial buildings

LOADING BAYS

Link between production or sto process and distribution system. Much effort to reduce production costs can be wasted through delayed vehicle turn-round and increased manning if loading area not carefully designed.

Decisions in loading bay planning

Raised or ground level dock? Generally, for end-loading containers and box bodies vehicles, as in retail distribution, raised; for side-loading curtain sided and flat bed vehicles, ground level.

Separate loading bays for incoming and despatch →(1): separate bays, together with vehicle marshalling areas, where manufacturing system involves different characteristics between raw materials and finished products, with raw materials calling for side handling at ground level and palletised for despatch needing end loading. Similarly for large distri-

bution warehouse: bulk loads of single product delivered, mixed loads of orders despatched in distributors' own vehicles; here segregation for traffic management and materials flow in warehouse, particularly as vehicle handling peaks may coincide.

Number of loading bays, spacing and layout:
loading bays must never be considered in isolation; must be related to circulation and check-off area behind them. Decision on numbers question of throughput patterns and available area next to dock for load preparation. Clearly if vehicles can be handled faster with pre-assembled loads, less loading docks required than for slower turn-round with material being assembled as loading operation continues.
loading bay spacing and layout influenced by depth of manoeuvring area available and depth of load accumulation space behind dock. Choice of which should have more space must be based on assessment of individual throughput demand.

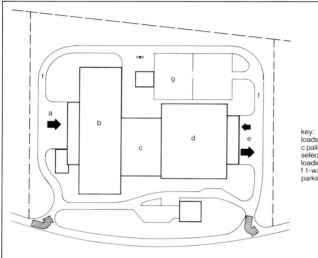

key: a goods inwards: suppliers' bulk loads b high bay bulk stock pallet sto c pallet breakdown & repacking ar d order selection & load assembly e despatch loading bay: users' distribution vehicle f 1-way traffic flow g long term truck parking & users' maintenance ar

1 Large retail distribution centre with separate goods inwards & despatch loading bays

2 Many warehouses can use dock for incoming & despatch goods; in factories sharing type of loading bay may not be possible but goods vehicle manoeuvring ar can be common

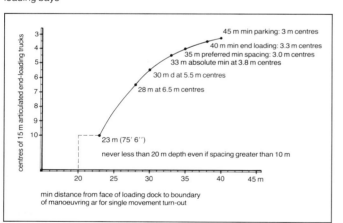

45 m min parking: 3 m centres
40 m min end loading: 3.3 m centres
35 m preferred min spacing: 3.0 m centres
33 m absolute min at 3.8 m centres
30 m d at 5.5 m centres
28 m at 6.5 m centres
23 m (75' 6'')
never less than 20 m depth even if spacing greater than 10 m

centres of 15 m articulated end-loading trucks

min distance from face of loading dock to boundary of manoeuvring ar for single movement turn-out

3 Calculating yard depth & loading bay spacing for 15 m articulated trucks parked at 90° to dock

key:
long wheelbase rigid chassis truck
a 2.8 m b 3.9 m c 4.7 m d 5.5 m
e 5.1 m f 4.6 m g 26.8 m turning circle

15 m articulate truck
a 4.7 m b 5.7 m c 7.3 m d 8.3 m
e 8.8 m f 7.8 m g 27 m turning circle at 90° full lock

4 Typical turning dimensions for rigid chassis & articulated trucks

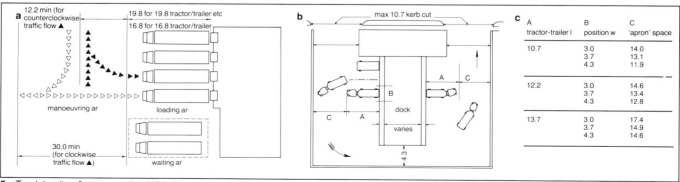

a 12.2 min (for counterclockwise traffic flow ▲)
19.8 for 19.8 tractor/trailer etc
16.8 for 16.8 tractor/trailer
manoeuvring ar
loading ar
30.0 min (for clockwise traffic flow ▲)
waiting ar

b max 10.7 kerb cut
dock varies
4.3

c A	B	C
tractor-trailer l	position w	'apron' space
10.7	3.0	14.0
	3.7	13.1
	4.3	11.9
12.2	3.0	14.6
	3.7	13.4
	4.3	12.8
13.7	3.0	17.4
	3.7	14.9
	4.3	14.6

5 Truck loading & manoeuvring, USA dimensions **a** loading, manoeuvring and waiting ar **b** & **c** apron space required for 1 move into or out of position

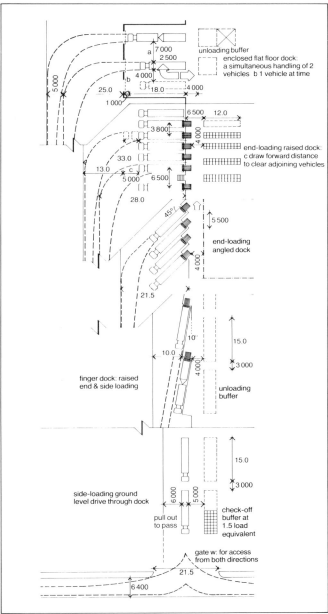

1 The more angle of vehicle from loading dock reduced greater reduction in yard depth but lower number of vehicles handled simultaneously in space

LOADING BAYS (cont)

Spacing
Directly related to yard depth; conditioning factor: distance closely parked vehicles have to pull out before turning →(1). Angled, raised docks reduce yard depth at expense of number of vehicles handled at 1 time: ground level drive-through bays reduce circulation width but increase length. Finger dock compromise for side and end loading where manoeuvring area limited.

Load check-off/accumulation space
Behind cross circulation aisle load handling zone (dock levellers with raised docks). Should have capacity of 1.5 vehicle loads. Remember space for broken pallets, rejected loads, rubbish: at least 1 load area. Cross circulation aisle 4 000 allows 2 fork-lift pass and for turnout from dock levellers. Keep this area clear of columns.

Raised docks
Equip with dock leveller plates accommodate both changes in vehicle bed height as they are loaded and different types of vehicle. Standard loading dock height in USA 1 220, common with 1 200 in Europe: with European vehicles greater variations in bed height. Dock levellers should not exceed gradient of 1 in 10 with highest or lowest vehicle.

Energy
Do not face loading bays into prevailing wind. Raised docks: use dock shelters where vehicle forms hermetic seal with bldg and segmental or roller shutter door closes on to leveller when vehicle leaves. Ground level or finger docks can be completely enclosed (straight through flow or tail in). Alternatively, hot or cold air curtains can be used but these not substitute for enclosure.

Security
Drivers should not be able gain access beyond dock, except in some distribution operations with company's own vehicles where driver arranges order of loading. Generally, raised docks with dock shelters provide inherent security: separate lavatories and access to traffic office should be provided for visiting drivers.

Weather protection
If dock shelters or enclosed dock cannot be installed canopy required over loading area: should allow at least 5 000 clear height.

Gradients
Ground should be flat (except for local drainage fall) for length of vehicle in front of dock or min of length of articulated semi-trailer.

Heavy goods vehicle marshalling & circulation
Segregate light vans from heavy goods vehicles: to use different docks/parts of the dock
Provide heavy vehicle waiting bays before loading bay area and clear of manoeuvring space
Provide parking bay before exit for drivers to check load security
Circulation should be clockwise in right hand drive countries, anti-clockwise in left hand drive: *ie* reversing into loading docks always on driver's side.

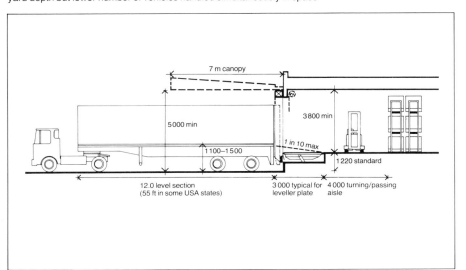

2 Section through raised loading dock fitted with dock shelter for energy retention: canopy (dotted) only needed if shelter omitted

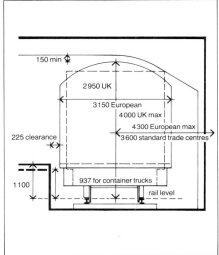

3 Rail wagon section (container dotted): in USA check individual railroad dimensions

Industrial buildings

LOADING BAYS: USA RAIL

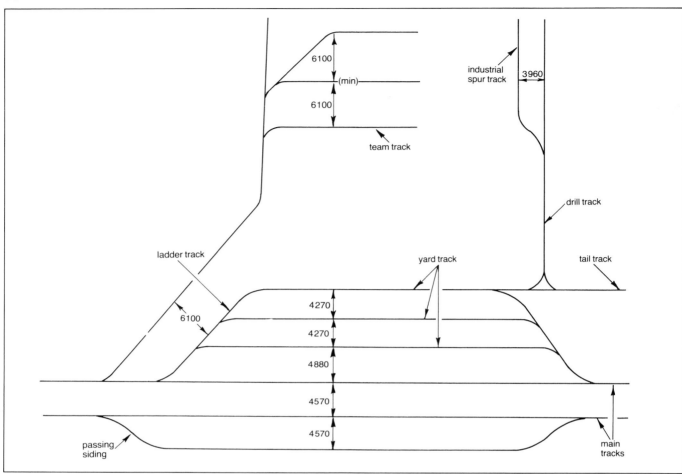

1 Typical rail track spacing requirements USA

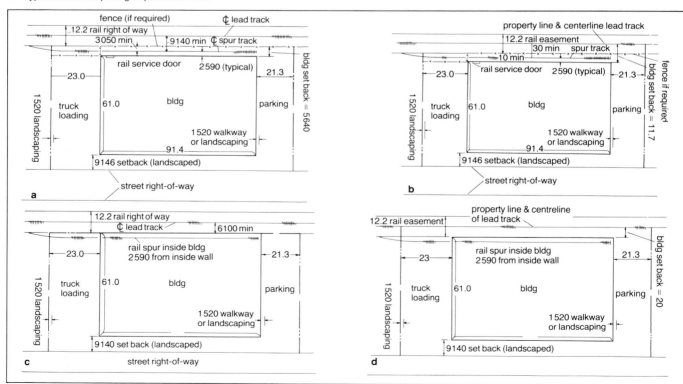

2 Rail served bldg layouts USA **a** rail in right-of-way, bldg set back, spur alongside bldg **b** rail in easement, bldg set back, spur alongside bldg, note: spur layout requires easement on adjacent property: can be eliminated by moving eastward rail service door & consequently point of switch **c** rail in right-of-way, bldg on property line, spur inside bldg **d** rail in easement, bldg set back, spur inside bldg

WORKSHOPS

Great variety in shape and size: workshops classified here by location, circulation requirements →p286, tenancy types →p287, and technology they can accommodate →p288. Most of detailed standards and examples given those required for typical inner city flatted factory (rental unit).

Most common locations →(1)–(5).

Domestic

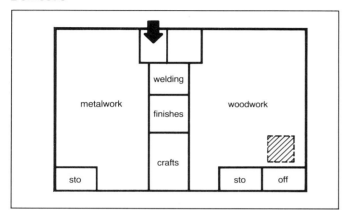

1   1 or 2 people carrying on hobby or part-time occupation in extension of home

Educational institution

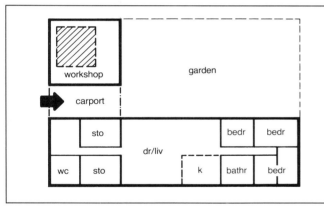

2   Repetitive provision for class or group of 20–40 people

Small industrial estate

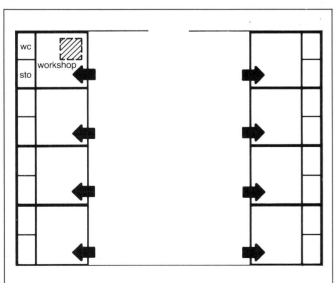

3   Group of non-specific units for range of very small businesses

Rental unit

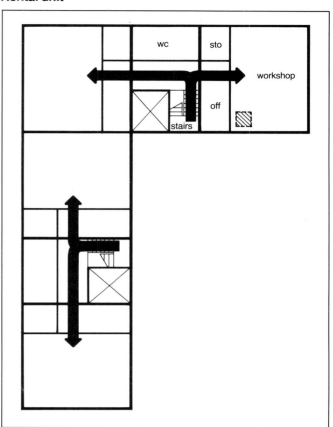

4   Standard units with shared access in multi- storey bldg

Ancillary to large factory

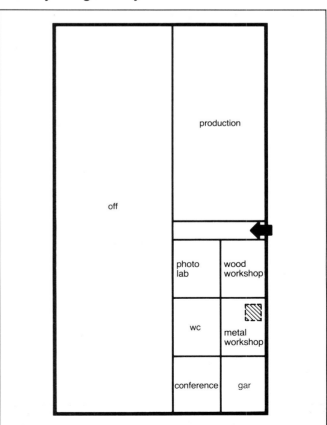

5   Specialist workshops for use by staff maintaining company's plant or bldg itself

Industrial buildings

spaces/floor ar	inner city	suburbs & rural
distribution	m²	m²
heavy goods vehicles	1/1 000	1/500
light commercial vehicles	1/1 000	1/500
cars	1/400	1/1 000
light industry		
heavy goods vehicles	1/4 000	1/2 000
light commercial vehicles	1/1 000	1/500
cars	1/200	1/50
off space		
light commercial vehicles	1/1 000	1/500
cars	1/150	1/30

1 Parking guide lines: USA standards →p263

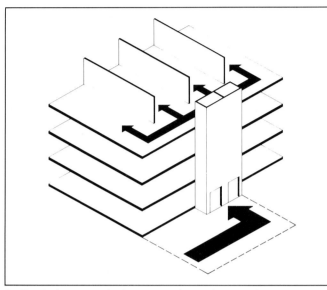

2 Goods elevator serving large group of tenancies: central management may needed to maintain free use of elevators at peak times

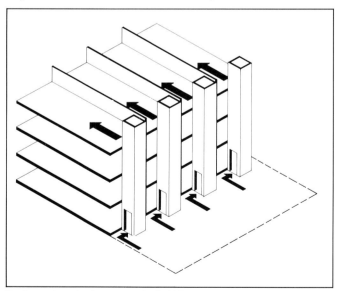

3 Several goods elevators each of which serves several tenants, who must cooperate in its use

WORKSHOP CIRCULATION

Parking outside building
Standards depend on location as well as on type of use →(1).

Elevators inside building
Related to external parking and to tenancies →(2)(3).

Circulation within workshop
Derived from technology used as well as type of tenancy →(4)–(7).

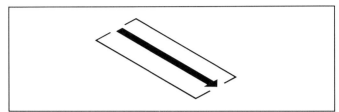

4 Straight line: goods in & out opposite sides of plant; requires bldg with good access both sides: common in medium-sized firms

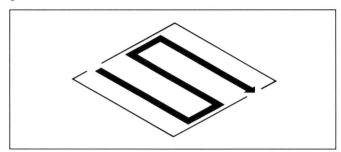

5 Overlapping: similar to **4** but for much larger type of firm

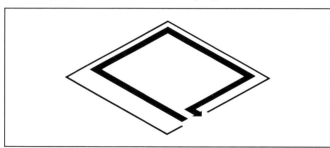

6 U-shape: goods in & out same side of plant; possible in bldg with only limited access: common with very small firms

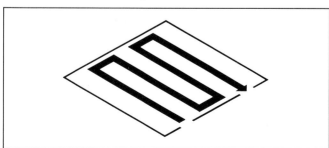

7 Convoluted: goods in & out on same side of plant; sometimes necessary for large firms when accommodated in bldg with restricted access

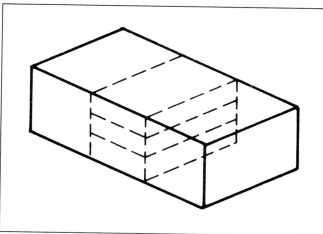

1 Indirect access

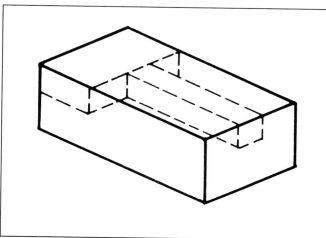

2 Open plan

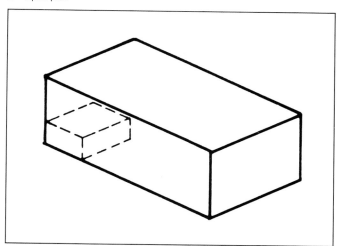

3 Shared space

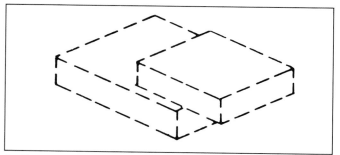

4 Shared space

WORKSHOP TENANCIES: BUILDING TYPE

Indirect access →(1)

Type of bldg: shallow or medium depth with cross walls to create vertical compartments.
Type of management: individual firm's name displayed and each has unit with own services. Management could take 1 unit over for own use.
Type of user: small well established firms requiring own identity.
Subdivision: units have street (or yard) frontage, may receive visitors directly and have own stairs, elevators.
Compartmentation: each bldg contains several tenancies divided by fr walls.
Escape routes: each tenant has fr stairway; if area of high fire risk alternative means of escape required.

Open plan →(2)

Type of bldg: shallow or medium depth with central corridor on each level.
Type of management: common receptionist; lifts/stairs/corridors from intermediate space to be maintained.
Type of user: small firms needing some security but less concerned with presenting individual identity.
Subdivision: units reached through internal stairs or corridors common to several users.
Compartmentation: each tenant separated from adjacent tenants by fr floor.
Escape routes: each individual tenant has door to shared fr escape corridor which leads to fr stairway, second means of escape normally also needed.

Shared space I →(3)

Type of bldg: deep plan.
Type of management: tenants share services and participate in management of accn.
Type of user: small expanding firms with compatible uses: allows for rapid changes in size and staffing.
Subdivision: units as such do not exist but tenants take space within large envelope having single front door.
Compartmentation: each open area surrounded by fr walls and floors.ร.
Escape routes: each compartment has direct access or 2 or more fr stairways: may be necessary protect relevant doorways with fire shutter.

Shared space II →(4)

Type of bldg: any building type.
Type of management: head lessee relinquishes no responsibility for space; may provide telephone, secretarial services on time sharing basis.
Type of user: newly founded tiny firms (1–5 persons) requiring low overheads and min commitments.
Subdivision: space rented from another firm usually on some kind of licence.
Compartmentation: separate subdivision only required if sub-tenant represents high risk of fire or explosion.
Escape routes: considered same as for main tenant unless special fire risk.

Industrial buildings

type	passengers	heavy goods	light goods	machine rm	pit	external fittings	access
el elevators	yes	yes	yes	yes	yes	yes	3 sides
hydraulic lift	yes	yes	yes	no	yes	yes	3 sides
manually operated lift	yes	no	yes	no	yes	yes	3 sides
platform hoist	no	yes	yes	no	no	yes	2 sides
el service lift	no	no	yes	no	no	yes	3 sides
scissors lift	no	yes	yes	no	yes	no	4 sides
dock leveller	no	yes	yes	no	no	yes	2 sides
el belt conveyor	no	yes	yes	no	yes	no	2 sides
gravity conveyors	no	yes	yes	no	no	yes	2 sides
el winch	no	yes	yes	no	no	yes	4 sides
manual winch	no	no	yes	no	no	yes	4 sides
manual floor	no	no	yes	no	no	mobile	mobile

1 Suitable handling eqp for small premises

WORKSHOPS: EQUIPMENT SPACE

→(1) shows requirements for some suitable handling eqp for small premises. →(2)(3) show typical space needed per machine in tightly planned layout: does not necessarily allow for general circulation, process sto or initial installation of machinery. →(4) shows percentage of total area required for operations in various types of workshop.

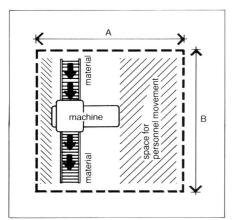

2 Eqp space →(3)

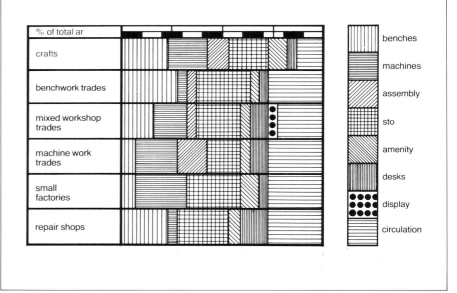

4 Space budgetting by technology types

eqp in common use	A × B →(2) working space per item

metal work

machining centre	6.0 × 4.0
jig boring & milling machine	3.0 × 3.0
turret drill	2.6 × 3.2
surface grinding machine	2.6 × 2.2
capstan lathe	3.0 × 4.0
bar & billet shears	2.5 × 3.0
press brake	3.0 × 6.0
engraver	2.2 × 3.0
die sinker	1.8 × 2.2
welding plant	2.8 × 2.5
tool grinder	1.1 × 1.2
shaper	1.7 × 2.1
power hack saw	4.0 × 1.2
punch press	1.5 × 1.3
slip roll	1.1 × 2.1
nibbler	2.3 × 1.2
shear clamp head	2.1 × 1.5
band saw	2.3 × 3.1
workbench	2.7 × 1.9

plastics

extruder	2.8 × 2.8
vacuum former	2.8 × 2.8
blow moulder	3.0 × 4.5
acrylic saw	3.0 × 5.0
heating oven	0.6 × 1.1

woodwork

band saw	3.0 × 5.0
circular saw	4.8 × 7.9
surface planer	2.6 × 5.0
knot hole drill	2.2 × 4.2
milling machine	4.0 × 5.0
slot boring machine	2.2 × 5.0
dove-tailer	2.2 × 4.3
jointer	1.4 × 8.3
scroll saw	1.6 × 1.9
drill press	1.6 × 1.6
wood shaper	2.9 × 1.6
radial arm saw	6.5 × 1.8
belt sander	4.4 × 4.8
veneer press	5.0 × 4.2
lathe	2.0 × 3.0
polisher	2.2 × 2.6
carpenter's bench	3.0 × 4.5

printing

lithographic press	2.5 × 5.0
plate maker	1.5 × 1.8
folder	1.2 × 1.5
drill	1.2 × 1.5
guillotine	1.5 × 3.0
glueing belt	2.0 × 4.2

photographic

developing tank	2.4 × max length print
enlarger	1.5 × max length print/2

clothing

laying up machine	7.0 × 14.0
sewing machine	1.2 × 2.2
steam press	2.0 × 2.0
ironing bar	2.0 × 2.0
steam boiler	1.2 × 1.2

footwear

nailer	1.5 × 2.2
sole press	1.5 × 2.2
heel press	1.5 × 2.2
shaping machine	2.0 × 2.5
leather cutter	3.0 × 3.5
pattern stamper	1.5 × 1.7

electronics

instrument bench	1.5 × 4.5

motor repairs

each bay	3.0 × 6.0

general

compressor	0.75 × 1.2
dust collector	1.5 × 2.0
furnace	1.5 × 3.0
hot dip tank	1.7 × 2.2
drying cabinet	3.0 × 7.0
upholstery press	2.5 × 3.5
forge	0.9 × 2.1
kiln	0.9 × 2.1
potter's wheel	1.8 × 1.7

3 Typical space required per machine in tightly packed layout

WORKSHOP EXAMPLES

1 Benchwork shop: *fur skins; employs 2; approx 75 m²*

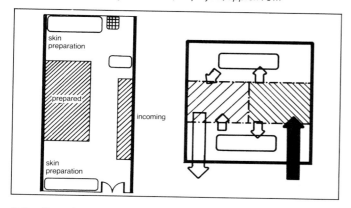

2 Craftwork: *organ building & wood furniture; employs 2; approx 175 m²*

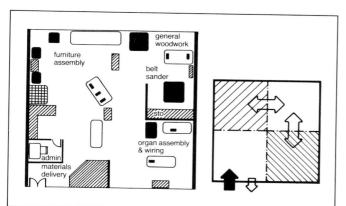

3 Mixed workshop: *die casting; employs 15; approx 150 m²*

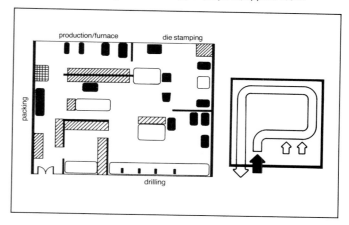

4 Repair shop: *electronics repair; employs 2; approx 47 m²*

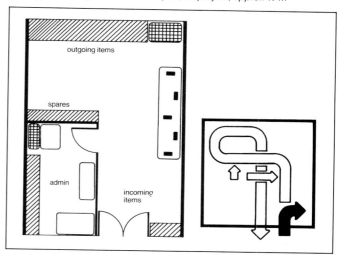

5 Machine workshop:

lithographic printing; employs 3; approx 93 m²

6 Small factory:

women's shoe manufacturer; employs 47; approx 370 m²

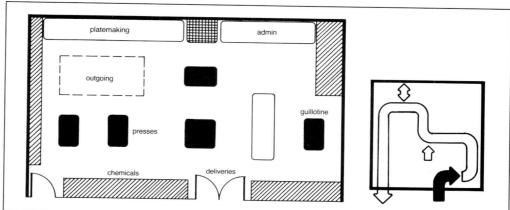

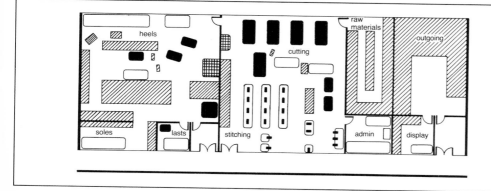

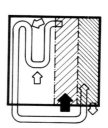

Industrial buildings

Workshop design factors

Factors affecting fabric design and services requirements for representative categories of workshop →(1).

1 Factors affecting fabric design & service requirements for workshops

		factors affecting fabric design — noise produces (or vibration)	process affected by noise from others	normally security	high security	preferred lighting: N light	natural	artificial	preferred plan: self-contained	open plan	partly enclosed	rm sizes 5.0×3.75–5.0×7.5	10.0×3.75–10.0×12.5	15.0×7.5–10.0×12.5	floor loading: up to & incl 3 kN/m²	up to & incl 5 kN/m²	over 5 kN/m²	floor to ceiling h: 2700 (min)	3300 (min)	4200 (min)	cor w: 2000 (min)	2500 (min)	3000 (min)	preferred heating level °C 16–19	19–22	22–25	water services needed: cold	hot	sk cannot be shared	waste disposal	domestic drain	industrial drain	solid material	paper packaging	el: 3-phase needed	gas normally used	telephone: own line needed	could share
A	pottery			•			•			•			•	•			•		•			•			•			•			•			•				•
	glass blowing		•			•				•			•	•			•		•			•			•			•			•			•			•	•
	timber furniture	•		•				•			•		•	•		•			•			•			•			•			•			•				•
	film production			•			•	•		•			•		•			•			•			•				•	•	•		•			•
	furs, skins		•	•			•			•					•			•			•			•		•				•			•				•
B	film processing	•	•	•			•		•				•		•			•			•			•		•		•	•	•	•			•
	electronic recording	•		•	•		•		•				•				•			•			•					•			•	•		•
	engraving	•	•	•			•	•			•			•			•			•			•		•				•		•			•
C	toys, musical instruments	•	•	•			•			•			•				•			•			•		•				•			•			•
	metalwork, plating, casting	•		•			•			•				•			•			•	•		•		•	•	•		•	•	•			•
	clothing	•		•			•			•			•				•			•		•			•				•			•		•	•
	shoes	•		•			•			•			•				•			•			•		•				•			•			•
D	light engineering	•		•			•			•			•				•			•			•						•		•		•	•
	valves, tools	•		•			•			•			•				•			•			•						•			•	•	•
	desk accessories, plastics	•		•			•			•	•			•			•			•			•		•			•	•	•	•		•	•
	food processing	•		•			•			•			•				•			•			•		•	•		•	•	•	•		•	•
E	printing	•	•	•			•	•		•			•	•			•			•	•			•			•			•			•	•	•
	manufacturing stationery	•	•	•			•	•			•			•			•			•	•			•			•			•		•	•	
	brewing	•		•			•	•	•				•				•			•	•			•		•	•	•	•	•			•
	spinning	•		•			•	•			•			•			•			•			•						•			•	•
F	electronic repairs		•	•	•		•			•			•		•			•			•			•		•			•			•	•	•
	motor car repairs	•	•			•			•	•			•	•			•			•			•		•			•	•	•	•		•	•
	bicycle repairs	•		•			•		•	•			•				•			•			•		•				•			•	•	•
	theatrical props	•		•			•	•		•			•				•			•			•		•				•			•		•

SERVICING STANDARDS

Check all applicable bldg codes and municipal plan review requirements. For new industrial bldg following standards apply:

Electricity

UK: Each unit to be provided with separate 415 V 3-phase supply, including, sited normally within production area, main distribution board, of adequate capacity for normally anticipated unit need of about 70 kVA, fitted with fused switchboard. (70 kVA units in range of 1 000 m² and upwards need separate load calculations.) Lighting circuits to be provided within offices and lav in appropriate locations. Power socket outlets to be provided in offices. Fused switch socket outlets to be provided in lav where el sto heaters used. In offices →p234 lighting wiring should follow likely office subdivision and should finish with fluorescent fitting but in lav and clo should be batten ceiling type fitting. Provide external flood lighting at back of bldg over service door wired to each individual unit to illuminate rear service area: may be supplemented by street lighting where layout permits.

Note: no provision to be made in standard specification for lighting trunking or 13 amp ring main in production areas.

USA: current characteristics of service vary with process. El eqp for air conditioning may be required for some processes or locations.

Telephone

Underground service duct to be provided into ground floor to allow easy cable connexion.

Gas/gas central heating

Services to be carried into bldg and sealed off in production area. Supply capacity to be designed to allow provision of central heating to production and office areas to normal working standards. Central heating to be provided only when required at landlord's cost: may be in office areas for larger units using conventional hot water radiator system incorporating provision for hot water for domestic uses. Boiler to be sited in production area.

Water supply/plumbing

Cold water supply for domestic needs only to be carried into bldg; tenants' process or sprinkler requirements not allowed for: supplementary service to be laid if excessive need indicated. Cold and hot water supplies to be connected to all washing installations: hot water supplied from either wall mounted el 3 kW sto heater (capacity 54 l) or if more economic central hot water cylinder having capacity approx 35 l/basin or sink. All sto tanks to be adequately insulated.

Drainage

Surface water drainage down pipes should have traps accessible from ground floor level and be located in positions to avoid accidental damage. Ample external surface water gullies should be provided in service yard to avoid water standing and grid channels should be provided across service yard entrance where levels of yard could allow surface water to run off into bldg. Foul drainage should allow for domestic demand; sealed gully in production area for process effluent. Trade effluent certificate required for individual trade needs.

Ventilation

Mech ventilation to be provided for wc only where layout makes impractical natural ventilation. All offices naturally ventilated. Production areas need only have separate provision for manually controlled roof mounted extractors where chosen form of heating will not achieve this result. Any extractor fans to be completely weather proofed and capable of being serviced at roof level.

Fire alarm

Alarm systems to be installed to each unit throughout office production areas. El operated system with manual initiation. Supplementary brief (program) to advise if provision to be made for sprinklers, smoke detectors or emergency lighting. Hosereel points only to be provided where required by reg or statute.

In USA sprinkler design approved by state insurance commission or fire marshall's office.

Industrial buildings references:
→Bibliography entries 031 036 052 053 164 177 178 257 280 284 305 331 332 333 338 341 346 348 352 354 363 374 382 387 418 456 470 477 480 481 483 486 505 534 539 590 592 597 600 601 602 603 604 605 606 608 616 627 642 651

Laboratories

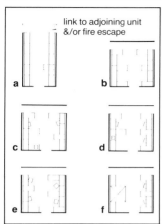

1 Comparison of square & rectangular lab units of equal ar showing greater flexibility offered by square layout **a** rectangular unit (24.8 m²) **b** square unit (24.5 m²) **c** 2 workers & shared eqp **d** 3 workers & shared eqp **e** 4 workers & shared eqp in central ar **f** 2 workers & large rig

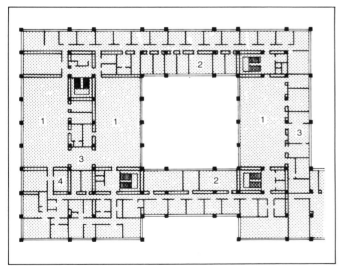

2 a b anthropometric data governing bench spacing for both teaching & research

type	bench h	seat h	min w kneehole	min vertical distance floor to under bench
sitting only	700	425	575	606
sitting & standing: women	850	625	575	800
sitting & standing: men	900	675	575	850

3 Typical range of bench & seat l

4 Typical plan showing flexible lab with grouped central services (pre-clinical sciences Southampton University England) Arch John S Bonnington Partnership
key 1 teaching lab 2 post-graduate & research lab 3 preparation & service rm 4 rm with specialist eqp

5 Typical plan showing relationship of central work space to lab unit (zoology dept Edinburgh University Scotland) Arch Architecture Research Unit University of Edinburgh
key 1 lav 2 sto 3 culture 4 research lab 5 off 6 cold rm 7 lecture lab 8 instruments 9 post-graduate lab 10 chromatology 11 central work space 12 warm rm 13 dark rm 14 secretary 15 lab 16 radioactive rm 17 media preparation rm 18 wash-up

CLASSIFICATION

Lab differ widely in layout and service requirements according to use. Classification categories include type of discipline (*eg* chemistry, physics, biology), level of study (*eg* routine, teaching, research), provision of eqp (*eg* benches, rigs), level of servicing (*eg* wet, dry).

Hospital lab →p176

TRENDS

In past lab designed for specific, fixed use; now growing tendency advocate 'multi-purpose' where worker has permanent station. Rapid changes in technology create new fields of study and demand costly sophisticated eqp which must be fully used: consequent need for adaptable lab spaces which may be changed during life of bldg.

Most difficulties in adapting to change arise because lab benches, sto cupboards and piped services as permanent fixtures can only be moved with considerable effort and disruption. 1 approach is design main structure and standard services as fixed items with more specific variable items, including furniture, movable.

PLANNING PRINCIPLES

Most significant recent developments in planning:

adoption of square rather than rectangular modules →(1) allowing for greater flexibility in bench arrangements with introduction of island bench units and free standing eqp;

use of movable table tops rather than permanent fixed bench units: variations in work top height as well as grouping of tables can be achieved to suit particular needs;

arrangement of heavy eqp, fume cupboards, wash-up etc grouped in central service zones.

INDIVIDUAL SPACE REQUIREMENTS →(2)(3)

Ideally conditioned by critical anthropometric dimensions, *eg* depth of work top being based on max convenient reach; may be some 600 in theory but in practice work top may vary between 610 and 840. Work top length similarly may vary between 2100 and 4600 for research student, depending on discipline and particular research requirements; can be reduced to approx 1500/P where groups of workers share eqp. Work top height may vary between low chemistry benches at 450 above floor level and 900 for benches at which worker stands.

PLANNING MODULE

Working unit (group of work places) forms basic planning bay or module →(2b). Normal work place can be considered as being approx 1600 × 800. Module width may vary from 2600 × 5250; av approx 3000 to 3600, which allows 2 parallel rows of benches with centre gangway giving room to pass between 2 workers.

Module w = 2 work spaces + centre passageway
3000–3600 2 × 800 1400–2000

Typical bldg dimensions include:
module w 3000–3600
module d 5000–8000
corr w 2000–2500
storey h 3600–4200

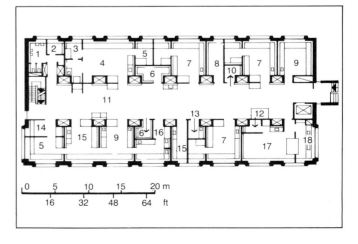

Laboratories

SERVICES DISTRIBUTION →p383–4

Sub-main distribution can be either off vertical ducts serving individual or pairs of lab at every floor or off horizontal ducts serving group of lab on every floor. Vertical ducts can be integrated with main structural frame, provide ready access to services on floor they serve, eliminate problem of fume cupboard ducting; but can prove expensive structurally if service potential not fully utilised. Horizontal distribution of sub-mains usually cheaper initially; but has not same adaptability and requires numerous connexions in floor.

Several methods of servicing individual benches available; need for adaptability led to development of movable and pre-plumbed services connected flexibly to floor points. Central service spine permits back-to-back layout of benches; service bollard allows benching laid out in 2 directions. However, studies of relocatable spine systems show new layout often involves extra cost and disrupts activities in rm below since live supply of services to all possible connexion points prohibitively expensive.

Overhead servicing by mast and/or flexibles more convenient and economic arrangement. Perimeter, peninsular and island layouts can be serviced in any combination and spacing required. Access for main-tenance and adaptation can be achieved with min disruption of furniture and eqp layouts and confined to floor being served. Valuable floor space can be saved since traditional floor-mounted service spine between benches removed. Furthermore, tendency overprovide to compensate for lack of flexibility in layout reduced.

DISPOSAL SYSTEMS

Drainage problem with overhead servicing: gravity rather than pumped or vacuum-assisted systems simplest, with permanent grid of floor points. Lab wastes may carry corrosive agents or be of very high temp. Drip cups, bottle traps in borosilicate glass and chemically resistant ptfe flexible tubing to outlets normal methods of dealing with such requirements. In any case waste runs should be immediately visible and accessble in rm to which they belong.

Solid waste normally put in bins; but in hospital research or animal experiment lab incineration of soiled material or carcasses obligatory.

STORAGE

Growth in project work and use of multi-discipline lab has increased amount and type of sto. Recent developments toward adjustable shelving and trays: movable sto units under tables more adaptable than fixed bench sto.

Pressing need for further space makes organisation and management of sto major consideration. Categories include:

central: special sto often centralised (eg workshop sto, inflammable solvents, explosives, poisons); best for large scale and/or expensive eqp; staff organisation and checking control important;

local: frequent use of items necessitates regular local sto, limited in capacity;

work place: essential for personal eqp and project work material.

1 Flexible lab ar of science block
Wellesley College Massachusetts
USA Arch Perry Dean Stahl Rogers

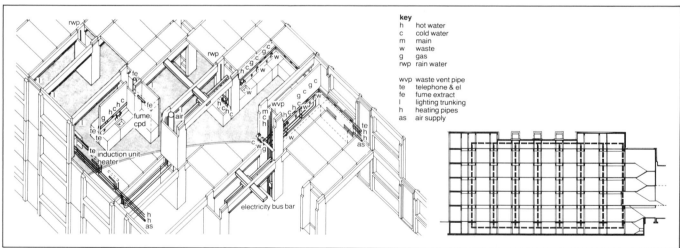

key
h	hot water
c	cold water
m	main
w	waste
g	gas
rwp	rain water
wvp	waste vent pipe
te	telephone & el
fe	fume extract
l	lighting trunking
h	heating pipes
as	air supply

2 3 Zoology dept Edinburgh University Scotland: *left* integration of services and structure *right* section through dept extension showing repetitive vertical sub-mains ducting

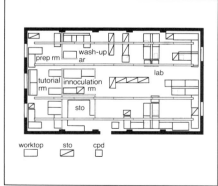

4 Overhead flexible servicing in pilot project Leicester Polytechnic England Arch Leicester Education Authority

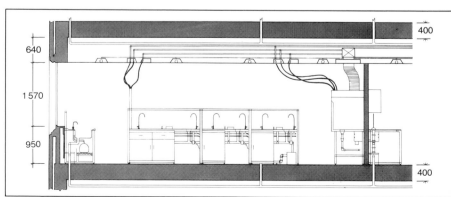

5 Section through sciences lab Polytechnic Sunderland England showing details of overhead servicing & its integration within structure Arch John S Bonnington Partnership

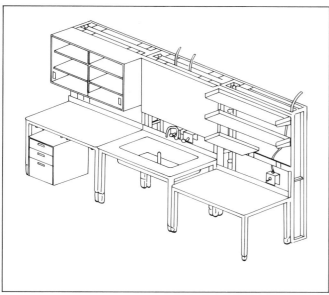

1 Details of lab benches in science block Wellesley College Massachusetts USA

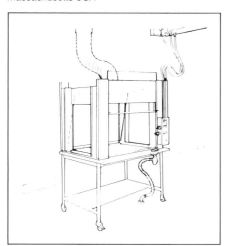

2 Mobile fume cpd showing service connexions

SPECIAL REQUIREMENTS

Some operations need special eqp or techniques calling for particular controlled environment not available or appropriate in general lab areas. These include:

cold sto & lab	temp control important
warm & incubator rm	,,
sterile/dust free rm	air locks & cleansing provision needed
dark rm	entry control needed
fume producing techniques	cupboards usually sufficient: large scale need special rm
chromatography rm	special rm: fume extraction
chemical distillation	,,
steam production	extraction needed
vibration/noisy eqp	structural & plan isolation
animal rm	environment & security control
radiation & x-ray rm	screening & security

RELATED SPACES

Space for related activities needed in addition to general lab provision: staff, seminar, small off, lib, clo, sto, plant, preparation; some or all of such rm will be needed

FINISHES

Floor: durable, easy clean and maintain, resistant to most chemicals likely be spilled; ideally should be jointless or have min joints possible. Such traditional finishes as wood blocks still preferred by users but tend to high cost. Sheet linoleum, pvc or rubber with welded or sealed joints and coved skirtings now more common.

Walls & ceilings: special protection not generally needed. Suspended ceilings provide smooth, light-reflecting surface with acoustic properties to which partitions can be abutted. Walls need to be washed down from time to time: blockwork should be plastered and decorated or sealed with sprayed plastics finish.

Worktops: traditionally solid timber, teak or iroko; laminated plastics faced board cheaper. As with floor multitude of finishes from pvc tiles or sheet to vitreous tiles can be used, depending on type of work being carried out.

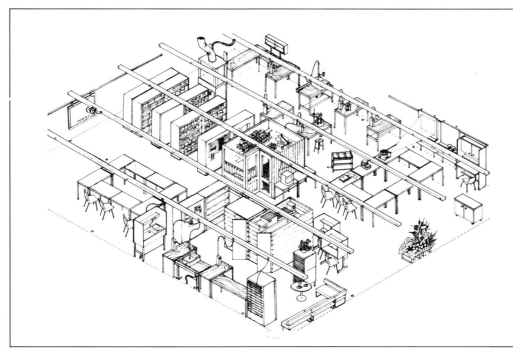

3 Typical teaching ar Teacher Training College Teeside England

Laboratory references:
→Bibliography entries 039 122 206 278 283 336 337 341 349 354 362 524 571

Farm buildings

	parts per million		
	hydrogen sulphide H_2S	carbon dioxide CO_2	ammonia NH_3
upper limit considered acceptable for man to breath during working day	10	5000	25

1   Toxic gas limits

	illumination (lx) →p25
stockyard	20–50*
calf nursery	50
sick animal pen	50
pig/poultry shed	30–50*
milking A	100
dairy	100
vac pump rm	20–50*
barn etc	2050*
tractor implements	20–50*
farm workshop	100

* higher figure applies when no natural lighting

2   Illumination levels

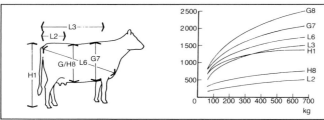

3   Dimensions of Friesian cows

type	age	weight kg	h to withers	body l	neck l
calves	at birth 6 months	35 175	700 1000	650 1100	— —
young females (heifers)	1 year 2 year 3 year	300 450 575	1150 · 250 300	1250 1450 1600	— — —
cows light breeds medium-heavy heavy	mature mature mature	350–450 500–550 600–650	1140–1350 1320–1380 1350–1440	1390–1620 1530–1650 1620–1680	600–620 630–650 650–700

4   Typical dimensions of cattle; recently USA beef cattle reverted to longer back

animal l	reach of mouth for various h of feed table above stance				
	0	100	200	300	400
1100	750	800	840	910	940
1300	800	840	910	960	990
1500	850	880	980	1010	1040
1600	880	900	1020	1030	1070
1700	900	920	1060	1060	1090
1800	930	940	1080	1080	1120

5   Reach of mouth of cattle

PURPOSE

Function of farm bldg to modify effect of climate on livestock, crops, agricultural eqp and man at work. Housing also allows easier handling and storing of feeds, products and waste materials. Decision to erect farm bldg may also be influenced by other considerations, *eg* investment, taxation, personal motives etc.

Design data presented here are based on human and animal requirements, animal housing technology including labour use, crop sto and processing, waste handling and legal controls.

HUMAN WELFARE

Man: environment

Air velocity should be in range 150–130/s (approx 5–12 in/s)
Dust concentration not more than 10 mg/m^3 of air
Toxic gases →(1)
Noise level not more than 90 dB (A) per 8 hr-day exposure
Avoid contact with dirt if possible
Illumination levels →(2)

CATTLE: BASIC DATA

Thermal requirements

Under UK climatic conditions all classes of cattle can be housed at temp equivalent to those prevailing outside. Protection from rain not necessary for older animals (180 kg live weight) if animal performance only criterion. But combination of rain, wind and low temp may lead to fluctuation of food intake. In high rainfall areas rainwater entering waste sto system can be excessive.

USA wide variations in climate mean all classes cattle cannot everywhere be housed at temp equivalent to that prevailing outside. Except in temperate areas milking cows need protection in extremes of cold and heat. In blizzard areas cows calving and beef cattle up to 14–16 months old need shelter.

Animal dimensions

Typical dimensions of Friesian cows shown →(3); other classes of cattle →(4).

Reach of mouth basic criterion for design of feeding barriers and troughs →(5).

Feed & water intake

Cattle in UK consume 30–60 kg of forage or silage depending upon energy and fibre content of ration, and drink 35–60 l of water per day.

In USA wider variation in normal feed and water intake.

CATTLE

Waste production

Cattle defecate and urinate indiscriminately: can only be made to deposit waste in particular places by use of physical restraint, *eg* cubicles. →(1) shows quantities of waste produced by different classes of cattle

HOUSING ELEMENTS

Housing systems can be classified by method of collecting and handling waste products. In slatted floor systems waste passes through perforations in floor to be collected and periodically removed from cellar beneath. In straw-bedded pens dung and some urine absorbed by straw. Resultant farmyard manure must be removed periodically. In cubicle systems use made of inability of cattle to walk backwards up step. Raised cubicles can therefore only be entered head first; dung and urine deposited into cubicle passage, scraped regularly, or may be slatted.

Slatted floor pens

Slatted floor systems eliminate bedding and save labour. Proper space allowances →(2) should be maintained to ensure sufficient animal treading action. Totally slatted floors normally used for beef cattle or suckler cows only. For dairy cows use of slats limited to cubicle passages, feeding stances and circulation areas.

125 slat laid with 40 gap suitable for all stock above 200 kg live weight or 6–8 months →(3). For younger stock quality and condition of slats more critical: 25 or 30 gap preferable.

Slurry cellars should be flat floored with draw-off points or receiving pits for vacuum tankers or pumps at gable ends or perimeter walls. Sluice gates lifted or pushed down allowing slurry to fill receiving pit and overflow lip system →p304(4) also used. Sometimes necessary agitate slurry before emptying. For this purpose slats may have to be removed for access with recirculation/agitation pump. Some designs incorporate suspended central passage with several access points. Some pumps require 10.5 m sump to work efficiently. Examples of slurry draw-off points →(4).

Sto capacities of slurry cellars →(5).

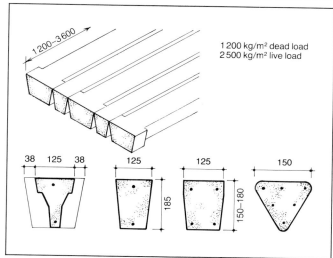

3 Reinforced concrete slats for cattle

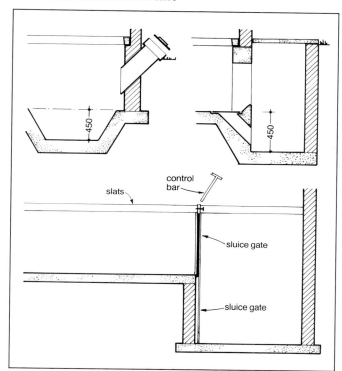

4 Slurry draw-off points

animal	age (month)	waste produced		
		(kg/day)	(m³/day)	
calf	0–3	5	0.005	(0.17 ft³)
calf	3–6	7	0.007	
store (stock)	6–15	14	0.014	
dairy heifer	6–15	14	0.014	
beef	15–24	21	0.021	
dairy heifer	15–24	21	0.021	
beef cow	24+	28	0.028	
dairy cow	24+	45	0.045	(1.6 ft³)

1 Av quantities of waste produced by cattle

weight of animal (kg)	approx age (months)	floor ar (m²/animal)
200	7	1.1
300	12	1.5
400	16	1.8
450	18	1.9
500	20	2.1
550	23	2.2

2 Space allowance for beef cattle on slats

weight of beast (kg)	floor ar (m²/beast)	sto capacity (m³/beast) for various cellar depths (m)							
		0.9	1.2	1.5	1.8	2.1	2.4	2.7	3.0
200	1.1	0.99	1.32	1.65	1.98	2.31	2.64	2.97	3.3
300	1.5	1.35	1.8	2.35	2.7	3.15	3.6	4.05	4.5
400	1.8	1.62	2.16	2.7	3.24	3.78	4.32	4.86	5.4
450	1.9	1.71	2.28	2.85	3.42	3.99	4.56	5.13	5.7
500	2.1	1.89	2.52	3.15	3.78	4.41	5.04	5.67	5.3
550	2.2	1.98	2.64	3.3	3.96	4.62	5.28	5.94	6.6

5 Sto capacities of below-slat cellars

Farm buildings

number of animals	capacity of urine tank required (m³)		
	540 kg beef cows	360 kg beef cattle	450 kg beef cattle
50	22	19	22
100	44	38	44
150	66	57	66
200	88	76	88

1 Tank capacity required for 2 months sto of urine from high level slatted bldg

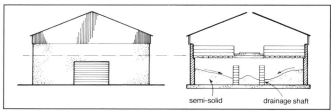

2 High level slats for beef cattle

weight (kg)	approx age (months)	total ar, lying & feeding (m²/animal)
200	7	3.0
300	12	3.4
450	18	4.0
500	20	4.2
550	23	4.4

3 Space allowances for cattle in bedded pens

l of housing period (months)	build-up of muck (m)	
	3.4 m²/beast	4.0 m²/beast
6	2.1	1.8
5	1.75	1.5
4	1.4	1.2
3	1.05	0.9
2	0.7	0.6
1	0.35	0.3

4 Build-up of muck at 2 stocking densities (not USA practice)

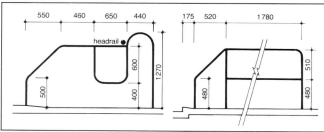

5 Step or ramp on bedded floor

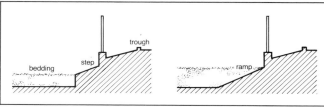

6 Cubicle divisions for cattle

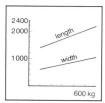

7 l & w cubicles as related to weight

pen type	age (weeks)	min space (m²/calf)
individual	up to 4	1.1 (1.5 × 0.75 m)
	up to 8	1.8 (1.8 × 1.0 m)
group	up to 8	1.1
	up to 12	1.5 min

8 Min space required for calf pens

CATTLE

Build-up of slurry at recommended stocking densities 300–400/month, depending on type and level of feeding. Hay fed animals produce thick slurry difficult handle with pumps. In such systems high-level slats can be installed allowing tractor access for mucking out. Urine drained off through drainage shafts into urine tank. Urine tank capacity for different numbers of animals →(1).

For typical arrangement of high-level slatted systems →(2).

Straw-bedded pens
Resting area bedded with 2–4 kg of straw/animal/day. For space allowance/animal →(3).

Mucking out usually done once during and at end of housing period. Build-up of bedding over housing period →(4).

Walls must be built withstand pressure of muck and stock: 225 blockwork with piers at 3000 centres rising to height of 1400 above max level of muck build-up suitable. Height should preferably be 3700 (min 3000 at eaves to allow tractor headroom for mucking out.

Wherever bedding next to feeding trough step or ramp should be provided allow cattle reach trough comfortably →(5). Floors should preferably be concreted but rammed hardcore may be used.

If liquid to be drained from under bedding concrete floor should have fall of 1:20. Concrete feeding stance above level of bedding area provided in part-bedded pens: saves some straw. Cattle may also be given access concrete area cleaned by scraping in self-feed silage systems. Silo floor should fall 1:30 away from feed face. Open scraped areas should fall 1:30 away from troughs and covered areas. Urine and faeces together with breeding and feed residuals scraped to external slurry sto (midden). Tractor mounted or automatic scraper blades normally used remove slurry into sto.

Cubicles
In this system small quantities bedding (500 g/day chopped straw or sawdust) spread over resting area equipped with cubicles and raised 150 above passage. Cubicle divisions →(6) should not hinder lying or rising movements of animals or allow animal to get trapped or entangled in cubicle frame. Cubicles not often used for beef cattle. Keeping cubicle bed dry more difficult with male animals. Problem accentuated by fact that animals are growing. Cubicle system not suitable for bull beef production.

Cubicle must not be so wide that smallest animal to use it can turn round and dung in it; but must be wide enough allow animal lie comfortably. Cubicles must be short enough ensure dung falls in passage: but cubicles too short will not be used as animal will lie over heelstone or kerb. Adjustable head or knee rail used to reduce effective length of cubicle; adjustable side rails accommodate different sizes of beast.

Cubicle dimensions should be related to animal weight →(7).

Cubicle passage widths (min): slatted 1800, solid scraped 2100. If passage serves also as feed stance, min widths 2500 slatted, 3000 scraped. Cross-passes 1800 should be provided if more than 25–30 cubicles in line.

Calf pens
Min space required →(8).

Divisions for individual pens can be constructed from demountable and adjustable rails, or boards where complete separation required. Divisions should be demountable and easily cleaned and disinfected. Alternative to individual pens tethered feed fence →(9).

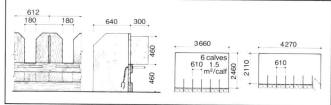

9 Tethered feed fence

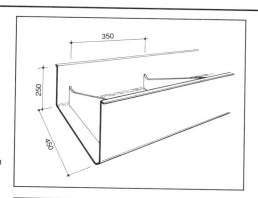

1 Cascade trough for milk feeding calves

weight (kg)	approx age (months)	min trough space (mm/animal)
150	5	360
300	12	520
400	16	600
450	18	620
500	20	640
550	23	660

2 Trough space for restricted feeding

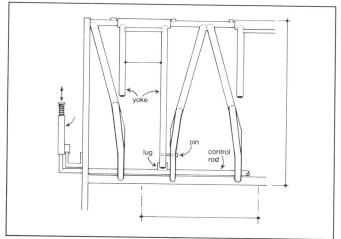

3 Feeding barriers for cattle

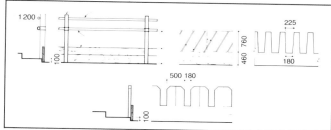

4 Self-feeding barrier

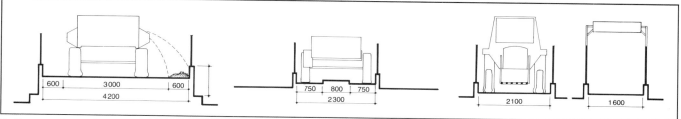

5 Passages for mechanised feeding of cattle

CATTLE

Calf pens (cont)

In group pens with bucket feeding pen front often equipped with simple manual trapping yoke.

Alternative to buckets cascade trough: allows simplified pipeline delivery of milk with individual rationing. →(1) shows details of cascade trough: system suitable for larger scale operations where labour spent on feeding tasks often reduced to min. Self-trapping yoke installed to control calves during feeding reduces subsequent cross-suckling.

'Automatic' feeders mix and supply milk substitute feed to groups of 10–15 calves on *ad lib* basis: allow more flexible labour routines but feed consumption (and hence cost) higher.

Feeding

When feed rationed or restricted sufficient trough space must be provided for all animals feed simultaneously. Trough space requirements →(2).

When feed continuously available (*ad lib* feeding) not all animals require feed at once. Trough-space/animal depends on type of feed as well as size of animal. Less space required for cereal feed than for forage:
grain or concentrates: 75–100/animal
self-feed silage: 100–175/animal
mechanically-filled trough maintained full: 175/animal

Feeding barriers →(3) essential prevent feed wastage.

Self-trapping feeding barriers (yokes) designed prevent animal access to feed, or restrain or release selected animals →(4).

Dimensions of trough and feeding passages for mechanised cattle feeding →(5). Inclined floor trough allows animals reach further; subsequently less secondary handling of feeds required→p294(5). For units housing over 200 animals flat floor feeding passage 4 400 wide preferred: feed left outside reach of cattle can be pushed forward nearer to them using specialised tractor mounted plough or brush attachment. Feed residuals can be also removed using this machine. Feed bankers for complete (mixed) diets →(6). These hold 2–3 days' supply since denser feed deteriorates less rapidly.

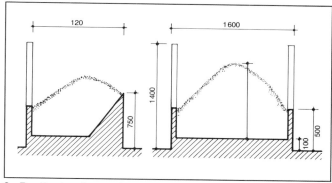

6 Feed bunkers for complete (mixed) diets

Farm buildings

CATTLE

Feeding (cont)

Typical dimensions of mobile feeding eqp →(1); turning space requirements →(2).

Feeding stances should allow space for animals pass behind others feeding. For adult cattle allow 2 400 min for slatted stances, 2 700 min for solid scraped stances.

Watering

Should be 10–30 animals/water bowl. Water troughs should provide 0.02 m² of water surface/animal of 300 of water trough frontage for 40–50 animals. During winter water should be heated to 10°C. Provision to prevent cattle from defecating into water drinker required: install floor curb 200 high or rail about 300 from drinker; or drinkers can be recessed into wall or covered with cattle operated flaps. Water bowls or troughs usually installed at height 700–1 000: should be located where do not obstruct other animals feeding or moving to and from feeding area, and preferably where spillage will not wet bedded lying areas.

Ventilation

Natural ventilation suitable for ventilating all cattle bldg, including calf bldg. Fan-assisted ventilation systems only justified in exceptional circumstances eg USA in heavily fly infested areas to supplement fly spray system; exhaust fan system not continuous running but worked on times. Sizes of openings for natural ventilation based on bldg floor area, weight of cattle and difference in height between air inlet and air outlet. →(3a) used to obtain area/animal of upper opening (outlet) from av weight of animal in bldg and total bldg floor area/animal (including passages). Lower (inlet) area twice this. If difference in height between inlets and outlets different from 1 000, areas multiplied by height factor obtained from →(3b).

Example 1: 30 × 100 kg calves in bldg 750 × 10000 with 2000 h difference between inlets & outlets
floor ar/calf 75/30 = 2.5 m²
outlet ar 0.042 × h factor 0.7 = 0.03 m²/calf
inlet ar double this = 0.06 m²/calf

Example 2: 100 × 400 kg cattle in bldg 10 × 30 m, 2500 h difference between inlets & outlets
floor ar/animal 300/100 = 3 m²
outlet ar 0.087 × h factor 0.57 = 0.05 m²/head
inlet ar double this = 0.1 m²/head

Design procedures also available for bldg with single openings, eg open-fronted bldg, and slotted roofs (→Bib108). Type of ventilation opening can be chosen suit method of construction and size required. Simplest has continuous opening at eaves and open ridge formed by omitting ridge capping →(4).

Mech ventilation should not be needed if natural ventilation designed for in new work or conversions. If required, provide capacity of 1.4 m³/h kg live weight = 0.39 l/s kg live weight. Design openings to provide inlet speed of 0.5–1 m/s.

Animal handling & veterinary systems

Efficient handling systems essential for speedy and safe restriction of animals for veterinary, breeding or management purposes. Important elements of cattle handling and control systems are shown →p299.

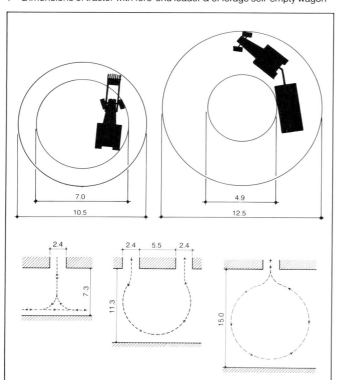

1   Dimensions of tractor with fore-end loader & of forage self-empty wagon

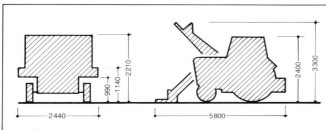

2   Turning spaces for feeding machinery

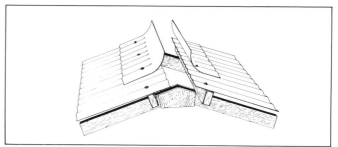

3   **a** ar of ridge opening as determined by weight of animal & stocking density;   **b** h factor for calculation of ventilation openings

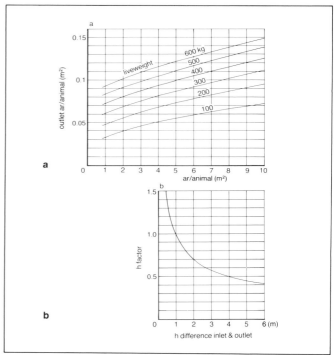

4   Open ridge: USA vented ridge preferred

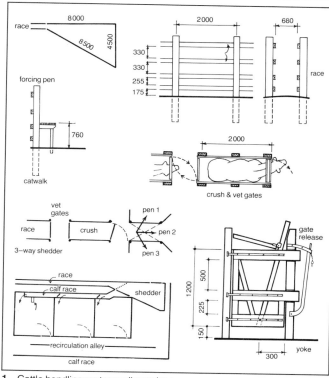

1 Cattle handling systems: dimensions

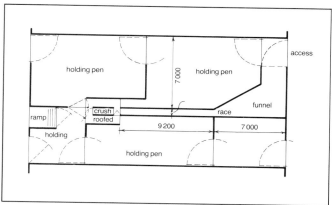

2 Cattle handling systems: typical layout

CATTLE

Animal handling (cont)

Isolation pens for veterinary treatment, disease diagnosis etc should be provided. Pens (3000 × 6000) should be bedded: feed should be delivered to trough from outside pen; for dairy cows milking line should be installed. Drain separately from other animal areas.

Calving pens should be separate from main resting area; floor should be bedded; tractor access for mucking out required. Pen size 4000 × 4000 adequate.

Holding pens space requirements: beef cattle 0.95–1.4 m²/beast min adult cattle 1.7 m²/beast
cows and cattle 1.85 m²/cow and calf

Forcing pen leads from collecting pen to race; should be funnel-shaped and should hold not less than 12 cows plus calves or 15 adult cattle. Single sided splay preferable, with 30° angle.

Race (chute): 18 m long 680 wide internally and 1680 to top rail will hold 10–12 cattle. Catwalks should be provided on both sides of race 760 above ground level and not less than 300 wide.

Crush (squeeze chute): race terminated by crush which may be metal proprietary make or constructed in timber. Weighcrate sometimes used as crush. There should be good access at both sides to head, neck, feet, under flanks and rear of animal. Crush should be under cover with good daylight and artificial light and provision for hosing down whole area.

Shedder gate: should be installed after crush wherever need to sort animals for weighing, separation for pregnancy, loading etc. Gates should be installed at far end of all holding pens allow recirculation of groups or individual animals. Dimensions of cattle handling systems →(1), typical layout →(2).

Milking

In loose housing systems cows milked in parlour. Milking in cowsheds using bucket or pipeline not practised in new dairy units because of hygiene and high labour requirements both in milking and cleaning eqp. Examples of typical milking parlours →(3).

Basic considerations which will determine type and size of milking parlour:
max size of herd (allowing for future expansion)
time allowance for milking (max 2 hours)
max mean peak yield
concentrate feeding policy
use of dairy labour (1 or 2 men)
capital available

Automatic cluster removal essential in 1-man operated rotary parlours to avoid serious overmilking of cows. In UK second operator considered wasteful of labour since not fully occupied during milking. In USA second operator required for hand stripping. Selecting number of milking units complex matter: for advice consult local agricultural advisory service.

Design of parlour pit for operator should respect ergonomic limitations of operators. Location of milking jar should not hinder routine tasks or obscure view of cows.

3 Types of milking parlour

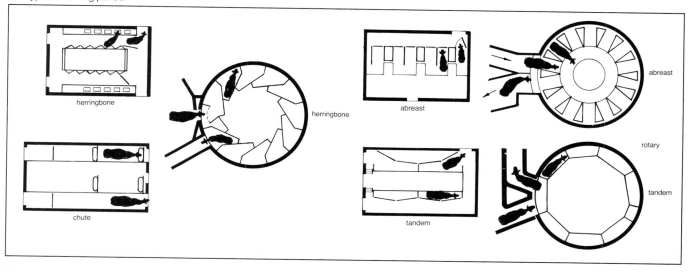

Farm buildings

CATTLE

Milking (cont)

Pit depth →(1)(D) ideally 950 for tall milker, false floor being used for shorter milkers: compromise depth of 750 often used.

Pit width →(1)(C) for 2 stalls/unit min 1515, for 1 stall/unit 1515 min for 1 operator and 1828 min for 2 operators.

Use only high-level jars in pits less than 1515 min.

Parlour length →(1)(A) 3050 + 500/standing.

Rotary parlour dimensions vary between individual manufacturers as well as with type and number of standing. →(2) gives guide; use manufacturer's data for detailed design.

Collecting area: before milking cows moved from resting and feeding area to collecting area next milking parlour. Space allowance in collecting area should be 1.35 m²/cow, but 1.1 m² usually adequate with straight herringbone parlours where initial batch of cows removed almost immediately. In rectangular yards width usually equal that of parlour. Cows should enter at farther end so that all movement in 1 direction. Circular yards make backing gate easier install: usually either full or three-quarter round. Capacity should be coordinated with size of herd or group. When at grazing in summer herd may be grouped differently or not at all.

Dairy: normally attached milking parlour reduce length of pipe runs. Should be sited so that rear of milk tanker can be parked within 3000 of door; adequate tanker turning space must be provided. 900 clear space should be left all round bulk milk tank(s) (min 600). Space must be provided for working and for eqp as required: washing troughs, water heater, cupboard, cleaning products etc. If expansion of herd may take place space should be provided for replacement of tank by larger one, or installation of second tank. 2600 min ceiling height may be required for use of tank dipstick. Wide external doorway (2000–2500) with no astragal should be provided for installation or replacement of tank.

Tank capacity can be calculated by taking av daily yield and adding 40–50% to contain fluctuations and possible future yield increases. Alternatively, work from figures of 18 l as daily yield, to which 20% may be added to allow for all cows reaching peak yield at same time.

Internal finish of dairy must be smooth and easily cleaned *eg* walls cement rendered and painted with chlorinated rubber or epoxy paint to height of at least 1400; non-slip concrete floor draining to trapped gulley; roof lined on underside of joists so that it can be kept free of dust and cobwebs.

Dairy must be light and airy: windows one-tenth of floor area; opening windows or ventilators fly-proof; illumination of 100 lx required. In USA reg require screened openings; lobby type entry also necessary prevent fly spray mist contaminating animals' feed or utensils.

Motor rm should be separate from dairy, area 3.5–4 m². Provision for tractor pto to operate vacuum pump in power emergencies may be required.

Office to accommodate table, wall charts etc should be sited with clear view of parlour and area next to unit. Modern dairy unit should have wc, changing rm and rest rm for staff.

Feeding: concentrate often fed in parlour from automatic dispenser, often feed stored in loft over parlour. Sometimes bulk bin set outside and feeds transported to parlour by auger.

Footbath: provide for footbath far enough away from parlour exit prevent slow flow of cattle leaving parlour. In such situation footbath does not require to be more than 1200 wide but to be effective should be at least 3000 in length and have drain outlet. Possible arrangement of services in 120-cow dairy unit →(3).

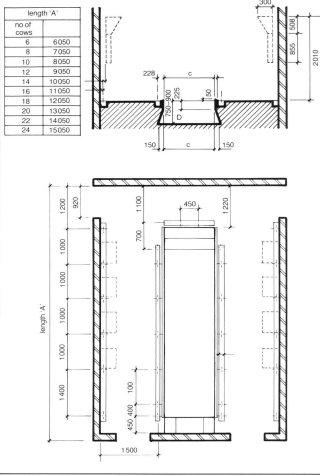

length 'A'	
no of cows	
6	6050
8	7050
10	8050
12	9050
14	10050
16	11050
18	12050
20	13050
22	14050
24	15050

1 Herring-bone milking parlour dimensions

type	number of standings	approx dia (m)
tandem	8	7.6
tandem	16	13.5
herringbone	12	7.0
herringbone	18	9.2
abreast	14	6.1
abreast	20	7.7
abreast	30	11.4

2 Rotary milking parlours: approx dia

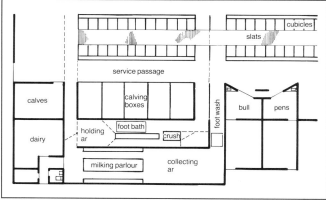

3 Services in 120-cow unit

Farm buildings

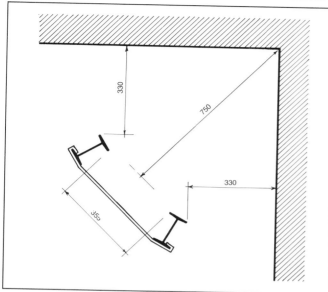

1 Bull pen refuge detail

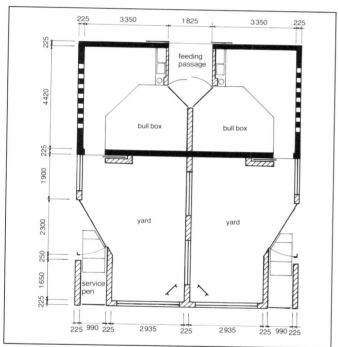

2 Bull pens: typical layout & dimensions

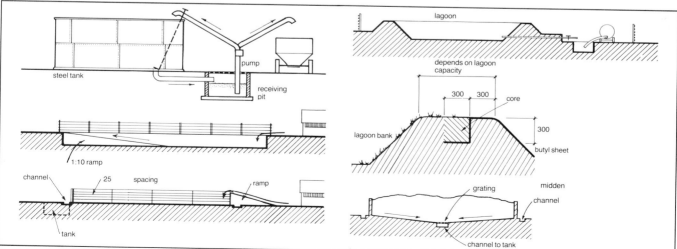

3 External waste sto

CATTLE

Bull pens

Pen can be sited near collecting area so that cows on their way to milking parlour may see bull. Stockman can thus observe cow behaviour and look for manifestation of 'heat' or readiness to mate.

Feeding and watering of bull must be carried out from outside pen. Wall, gates and feeders must be of substantial construction. Cow service area should be incorporated within pen layout. Dry lying area should slope to drain, usually raised by 50 from concrete floor and well bedded with straw or sawdust. Feeder should be provided with strong trapping yoke to restrain animal for routine veterinary treatment or restriction during cleaning. 'Refuge' must be installed in each corner of pen →(1). Tethering ring enables bull tethered independently of yoke.

Exercising yard (unroofed) often provided next to bull pen (20–35 m²).

Service pen should include foot rests to take weight of heavy bull especially when used with young heifers. Foot rests are 2 sloping timber ramps 225–300 wide, fitted to inside of pen walls. Length of rests approx 1 500, height 530 at rear to 900 at cow's shoulder. Typical layout and dimensions for twin bull pens →(2).

External waste storage

Slurry sto →p295–304 required for waste from scraped areas in cubicle units or as extra sto for slatted units with shallow channels. Slurry silos or tanks (above and below ground) lose moisture ony by evaporation. Dungsteads and middens designed drain off excess liquids and used for more solid waste, or help solidify semi-solid wastes (not used USA, where muck collected by contractors). Examples →(3).

Dairy cow housing

Examples of dairy units →(4).

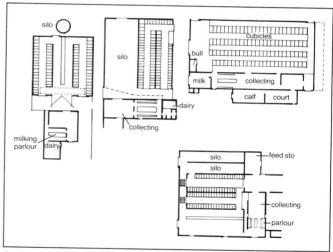

4 Dairy units: typical layouts

Farm buildings

CATTLE

Beef cattle housing

Beef cattle normally housed in slatted, bedded or part-bedded pens, occasionally in cubicles. Linear plans usual, with pens arranged either side feeding passages. Pen depth determined by ratio of floor space →p294(5) 295(2) to feed trough length animal →p297(2). Typical plans →(1).

In some low rainfall areas possible house and fatten cattle in roofless units on sheltered sites or with sheltered wall. These units have slatted pens or sometimes cubicles. Slurry sto must have additional capacity for rain falling on unit.

If entire male cattle (bull beef) kept pens must be robust with divisions at least 1 600 high: cubicles should not be used. For safety of stockmen all fittings, *eg* waterbowls, should be accessible from outside pens and good animal handling and loading arrangements (race (chute) etc) must be provided: example of bull beef housing →(2).

NB: beef cattle not normally housed in USA apart from loafing barns →(6)

Suckler cow housing

Calf production from suckler cows usually relies on small, early maturing cow, well adapted severe environments. Provision of calf creep (nursery) pens (where calves receive food without competition from cows and rest) major design point of difference from other form of beef housing.

Cows housed in cubicles, bedded pens or slatted pens. In slatted pens allow 2.5–3 m²/cow. Cow areas communicate with calf creep pens by creep gate through which only calves can pass. Creep pens dimensioned according av size of calf, which depends on calving date →(3).

Should be visual contact between cows and calves in creep; inspection of and access to creep pen for supervision, feeding, cleaning water-bowls and mucking out (in bedded pens) should be good. Provide 1 water drinker for every 12 calves.

If cows to calve indoors, provide separate calving area, preferably straw bedded pen.

Typical arrangements of suckler cow housing →(4).

Calf housing

General arrangement of calf housing units →(5).

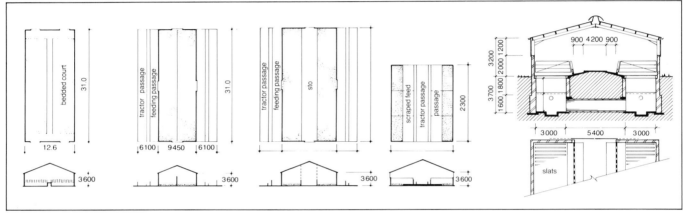

1 Beef housing units: typical layouts

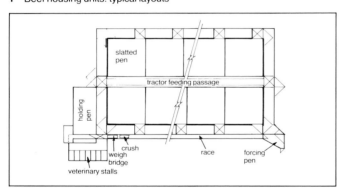

2 Bull beef unit layout

3 Sizes of calf creep pens

calving date	bedded pen (m²/calf)	slatted creep pen (m²/calf)
spring calving	1.1	1.0
continuous calving	1.4	1.2
autumn calving	1.7	1.4

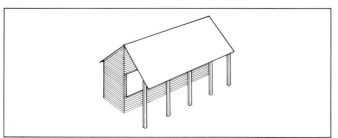

4 Suckler cow bldg: typical layout

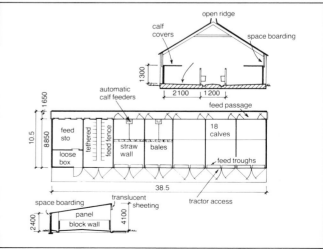

5 Calf housing units: layout

6 Loafing barn

PIGS: BASIC DATA

Thermal requirements

Outside thermoneutral range of temp animals either too hot, or will be wasting feed keeping warm because too cold. Thermoneutral range of different classes of pigs depends on level of feeding, type of flooring, number of pigs/pen and air velocity. →(1) shows ambient air temp related to 3 floor types, 3 times maintenance level of feeding and air velocity not exceeding 0.15 m/s.

Thermoneutral zone of sows pregnant for 112 days, live weight of 140 kg under same conditions as above: 11–25° for thin and 7–25° for fat animals.

Pigs on low feeding levels should be kept at 2–3°C higher air temp than those on high levels. →(2) shows relationships between feed, floor and min air temp for 65 kg pigs.
Thermal insulation →p393–4

Animal dimensions

→(3) gives body dimensions of different classes of pigs.

Behaviour: building implication

Eliminatory: pigs defecate in discriminatory fashion, *ie* within selected area usually determined by location of water drinkers →p304. Every pig tends defecate in own area within eliminatory zone. Important allow enough space in eliminatory zone, so that at least 3 pigs may defecate at same time. Should less space be given likely that some excreta will be deposited elsewhere, *eg* in lying or feeding area.

Sexual: newly weaned sows should be housed near boar in order to encourage sexual behaviour. Partition between sows and boar should be perforated, allowing visual and bodily contact.

Resting, eating & general movements: piglets spend approx 10–20% of time suckling (15–25 times/day). Fattening pigs on dry *ab lib* rations spend 5% of time feeding (8–12 times/day). On wet feeding only 3% of time spent at trough (4–8 times/day). In general fatteners (75 kg) would spend 80–85% of time lying, 15–17% moving about in pen, 3–5% eating.

Abnormal behaviour: aggression amongst growing pigs manifested by tail and ear biting, sometimes cannibalism. Savaging more predominant among adult sows. Bldg designer can influence behaviour pattern by changes in stocking rate, group size or housing systems. Abnormal behaviour can be also caused by nutritional factors, genetic susceptibility, disease states, teething problems etc.

Pig husbandry data-check list:

age at first parturition	403 days
litters/sow/year	2.0
number/litter born alive	10.5
number/litter at 3 weeks	9.0
av weight of piglet at 3 weeks	5.9 kg
number of piglets still alive at 8 weeks	8.7
av weight at 8 weeks	18.2 kg
total weight of weaned pigs/sow/year	300 kg
farrowing index = days between birth of 1 litter & next	
limit to farrowing index	133 days
national av of farrowing index	195 days
10% of UK producers with farrowing index	230 days
length of lactation = any time up to 85 days	

pigs fattened as
porkers   40–90 kg
baconers   90 kg
heavy hogs 120 kg; USA 147–180 kg

Illumination

Keep pigs in dim light: but at least 5 lux →p25 should be provided for management and servicing tasks.

Feeding systems

Pig can be fed wet or dry meal either in *ad lib* or rationed form. Typical systems shown in following scheme:

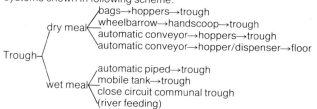

Water consumption

Adequate supplies of fresh water should be available at all times. Following water allowances should be given:

Growing pigs	1 l/day at 15 kg live weight increasing to 5 l/day at 90 kg live weight
sows non-pregnant	5 l/day
sows pregnant	5–8 l/day
sows lactating	15–20 l/day

2 days sto of water should be provided to ensure continuity of supply in emergencies.

floor type	thermoneutral range (°C) for various live weights (kg)				
	1.5	20	40	60	100
concrete	34–5	17–30	13–29	11–29	10–28
perforated	31–5	16–30	13–29	12–29	11–28
bedded	30–5	10–30	7–29	5–29	4–28

1   Thermoneutral zone of pigs

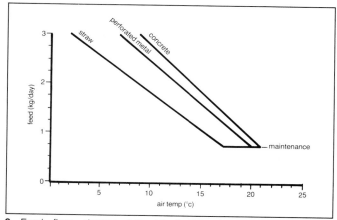

2   Feed – floor – air temp relationships for 65 kg pig

animal	l (m)	w (m)	h (m)	rump to shoulder (m)	approx weight (kg)	breed
boar	1.95	0.32	0.85	1.1	135	large white
sow	1.5	0.35	0.75	1.1	135	landrace
	1.85	0.4	0.85	1.2	158	large white
fattener	1.28	0.3	0.7	0.95	77	large white
weaner	0.9	0.2	0.42	0.7	50	large white 13 weeks old
	0.72	0.17	0.33	0.58	40	large white 11 weeks old
piglet	0.4	0.09	0.22	0.23	2.5	7 days old

3   Approx pig sizes

Farm buildings

PIGS: BASIC DATA

Watering

For various types of drinkers and their respective water wastage →(1).

There should be 2 drinkers/pen in case 1 gets blocked. In general 1 drinker/6 pigs required. Bowl type drinkers should be sited where faeces contamination minimised. Pig-operated flaps can be used prevent contamination.

Variation on trough drinker sometimes used: 50–75 pvc pipe set in raised concrete floor and top cut open, discharging water into shaped concrete within concrete floor: water supply controlled with ballcock valve located at beginning of line.

PIGS: WASTE

Waste production

Pigs fed dry meal with *ad lib* water produce quantities of waste as given →(2).

Waste handling systems

Typical systems →(3).

Solid wastes produced by additions of bedding material, usually straw,

type of drinker	% of water wastage
indirect nipple (bite type)	46
directly operated nipple	56
bowl	6
trough	12

1 Water wastage of drinkers

animal	live weight kg	waste produced kg/day
piglet	15	1.04
weaner	30	1.9
growing – finishing	70	4.4
growing – finishing	90	5.8
dry sow	125	4.03
sow & litter	170	14.9
boar	160	4.9

2 Waste (urine & faeces) produced by pigs

but also sawdust, peat, woodshavings etc, to faeces and urine. In general housing systems based on solid waste (farmyard manure) demand more labour for bedding tasks but no problems should occur where access, sto area and run off drain properly designed.

Bedded systems

Straw bedding often used for pregnant sows (1.0 kg/day), boars and weaners (5 000 g/day).

Bedded pens should be at least 3 000 wide. All internal partitions should be removable to allow tractor access for mucking out.

Floors should be sloped 1 : 20 towards drain leading to sump at side of bldg accessible for slurry tanker.

Some bedded units have chain and paddle manure conveyor including loading elevator at one gable end. Manure removed twice weekly into muck spreader and then to fields or sto (not usual in USA).

Slurry systems

Pigs housed on perforated floors, *eg* slats, expanded metal or mesh; or dunging area only either perforated or regularly scraped to holding tank. Faeces and urine stored in channels below perforated floors. Channels emptied either continuously or once in 3 months into external slurry sto. Channels emptied periodically have sluice gate and receiving pit.

Flushing system where liquid fraction of slurry pumped into tipping buckets holding several hundred l sometimes used. Flow removes solid faeces and feed residuals into external sto. Some slurry channels have sump at end directly emptied with vacuum tanker. This system not recommended as often difficult remove solid sedimented at far end of channel. Continuous emptying of slurry channels into external sto relies on hydrostatic pressure gradient which causes slurry to slide over lip into pit. Only narrow (1 000) channels not longer than 20 m should be used. Depth determined from equation given →(4).

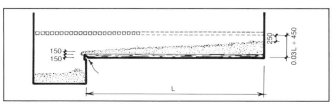

4 Continuous overflow slurry channel

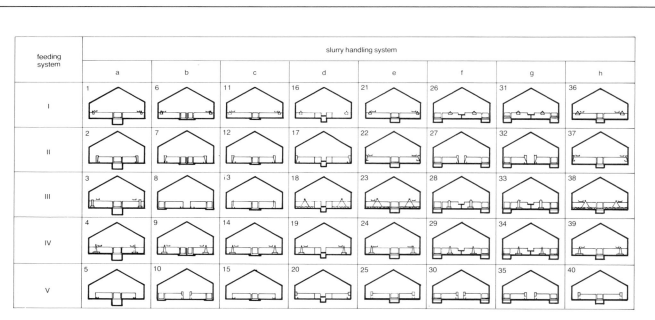

feeding systems: I dry feeding on floor II dry feeding from automatic feeders III liquid feeding from trough & bowls IV dry feeding from bowls V dry feeding from troughs

manure removal systems: a partly slatted floor over slurry channel b double dunging passages with solid floors c central dunging passage with solid floor d service passage over central scraper channel e partly slatted floor (gaps: 25) over central scraper channel f partly slatted floor (gaps: 25) over side scraper channels g partly slatted floor (raised: 100) over side channels h partly slatted floor (raised: 100) over central scraper channel

3 Typical waste handling & feeding systems

PIGS: MANAGEMENT

Ventilation

Forced or fan ventilation should be designed according to min and max ventilation rate required, inlet air speed and subsequent air jet and air distribution pattern within bldg. Free air output of fans can be found from manufacturers' data sheets. Allowance should be made for resistance of ventilation ducts, usually 0.5–0.7 of their free air output. Inlet air speed or jets can be used to determine air movement within house: specialised technique and assistance of specialist should be sought.

Pressurised systems usually blow air into roof space and use false ceiling of glass fibre supported on netting for even distribution of air. Air outlet often below slat level thus removing most air pollutants. In air extraction systems fans housed in central shafts terminating above apex or alternatively in side walls suitably baffled and terminated in neutral pressure area to minimise effect of wind. Location, area and number of air inlets will determine air distribution and air velocities in bldg. Manufacturers of fans who specialise in animal housing applications often provide design assistance.

Min ventilation rate should be 0.000052 m^3/s per kg live weight, summer ventilation rate 0.000312 m^3/s per kg of live weight. Max air velocity at pig level to be 150–200/s.

With natural ventilation systems air inlet area should be twice as large as air outlet area. Air outlet can be either open ridge or several chimney-type extractors with flat capping. Air enters through baffled inlets round wall, at least 1000 above pigs. Ventilation extraction area should be 3.6 cm^2/kg live weight. Air inlet area should be 7.2 cm^2/kg live weight. Typical ventilation systems →(1).

Handling

Pigs, particularly fatteners, regularly weighed, usually by mobile crate/weigher in feed passage. Some arrangements have permanent service area for weighing, cleansing and veterinary tasks with holding area. Pig movement should be controllable by 1 man.

Pigs can walk through 600 wide passage. With 700 baconers will be able turn around. Mature sows and boars require 1250–1450 wide passages to turn round. Corners should be wider (900). Wherever pigs, particularly sows, required reverse round corners passage should be increased by 300 →(2).

For loading and unloading into animal road transporters provide ramp (1:7) with battens or deep grooves to prevent slipping.

Sow & boar housing

→(3)(4) show examples of dry sow housing and service bldg.
Sow stalls:
w: 600–650 (if divisions open to 150 above floor level) or 700–750 (if divisions solid from floor level)
l: 2000, with or without trough according to design
h: 900
gate for entry and exit of sow: usually at rear floor: rear half usually slatted.
Boar pens:
should extend to at least 9 m^2; 1 side of pen should be approx 2500 long; divisions should be verticular tubular railing 1400 high, allowing boar observe other animals and general activities within bldg; vertical arrangement of railing prevents boars from climbing and jumping on to divisions.
Farrowing:
→(5) shows farrowing crate and creep area for piglets. Function of farrowing crate prevent piglets from getting injured or crushed by sow. Creep for piglets of up to 5 weeks of age should be 1.3 m^2 min and from 5 to 8 weeks 1.75 m^2. Most of farrowing accn designed for weaning of piglets at 5 weeks of age. Approx 1.0 m^2 of creep area should be heated. Farrowing house →(6).

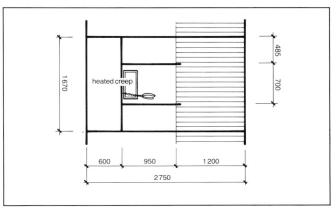

4 Dry sow house with boar pens & food sto

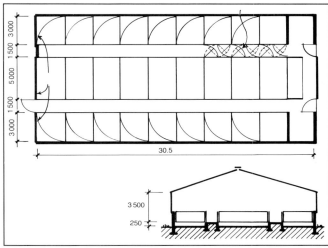

1 Typical ventilation systems for pig housing units

5 Farrowing pens: dimensions & layout

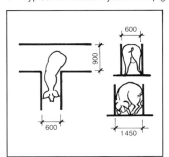

2 w of passages for sows

3 Dry sow house with boar pens

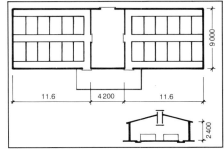

6 Farrowing house

Farm buildings

live weight kg	total ar m²	daily consumption of bedding kg
10–30	0.75	0.3
30–90	1.1	0.5
sows	2.5	1.2

1 Individual space allowances & straw consumption

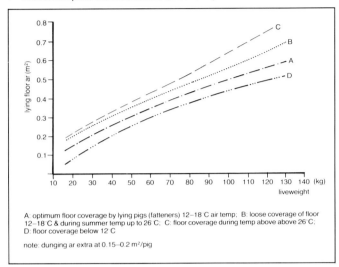

A: optimum floor coverage by lying pigs (fatteners) 12–18°C air temp; B: loose coverage of floor 12–18°C & during summer temp up to 26°C; C: floor coverage during temp above above 26°C; D: floor coverage below 12°C

note: dunging ar extra at 0.15–0.2 m²/pig

2 Space allowances for fattening pigs

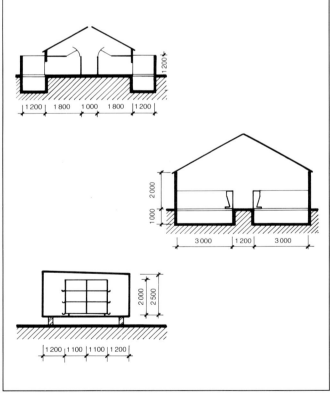

3 Rearing accn

PIGS: REARING & FATTENING

Group size & pen shape

Formation of stable social hierarchy desirable. Fatteners on *ad lib* floor feeding should be kept in groups of 15–20. Pigs lying down should cover floor area, so that excreta will be deposited elsewhere (dunging area). With part-solid, part-slatted floors, pen should be twice as long as wide with approx 900 wide slatted dunging area.

Trough space

Trough space/pig for *ad lib* feeding should be 100 and for rationed feeding 300.

Spatial requirements

→(1) shows individual space allowances for bedded systems, *ie* total floor area divided by number of animals occupying it; →(2) shows space allowances for systems with solid floor and slatted dunging area.

→(3)(4) show examples of rearing and fattening houses.

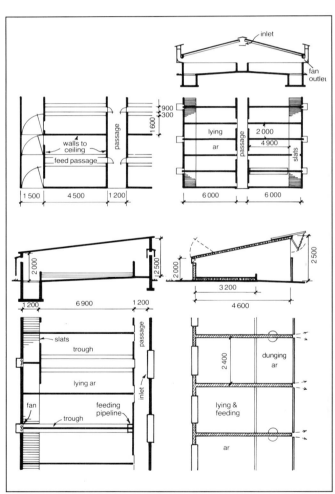

4 Fattening house for pigs

Farm buildings

SHEEP

Housing of sheep prevents poaching of land, allows better management and labour use, can lead to increased stocking rate on land, may release pasture for cropping and can reduce lamb mortality during lambing period. These potential benefits are offset by high cost of housing as well as cost of providing additional feed.

Space requirements
Individual floor space allowances for sheep →(1).

Solid floor
Sheep housed on bedded floor seem to have more foot troubles than those kept on timber slatted floors. Solid floor should be well drained consolidated hardcore with 150 of straw.

Slatted floor
Pressure treated timber slats range from 63 × 32 to 38 × 25 with 20 gap for larger sheep and 16 gap for smaller breeds. Slats usually arranged in removable floor sections 1 200 × 2 400. Slatted panels can be supported on dry blocks for easy removal and so allow easy tractor access for mucking out. Floor panel joists 75 × 50 should be splayed for easier self cleaning and set at 450 centres. Depth of 500 is sufficient for 1 housing season waste sto.

Layout
Ewes prefer lamb in groups rather than individual pens. Creep area for lambs after lambing can be provided. Feeding should be carried out in pen passages. →(2) shows 2 typical layouts.

type	space allotment (mm²)	
	slatted floor	solid floor
large ewe (68–70 kg)	0.95–1.1	1.2–1.4
large ewe & lamb	1.2–1.7	1.4–1.85
small ewe (45–69 kg)	0.75–0.95	1.0–1.3
small ewe & lamb	1.0–1.4	1.3–1.75
ewe hogg	0.45–0.75	0.65–0.95

1 Floor space for sheep

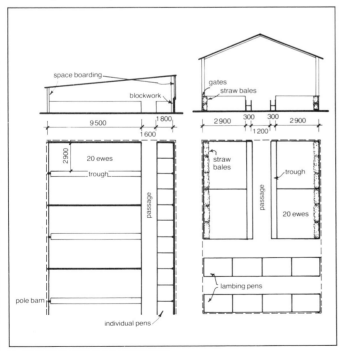

2 Typical layouts for sheep housing

type of sheep	trough l*
large ewes	475–500
small ewes	375–425
hoggs	350–400
* on self-feed silage 100–250 adequate for all sheep	

3 Recommended trough l

Feeding
Hayracks and concentrate troughs required. →(3) shows recommended trough length. Simple wooden trough with hayrack →(4) sufficient.

Water
Sheep prefer running fresh water. This can be provided by trough equipped with overflow to drain: 600 × 300 water trough surface sufficient for up to 80 ewes.

Ventilation
Natural ventilation system based on 450 open ridge and 1 200 deep spaceboarding with 100 boards and 25 gaps satisfactory. Sheep in open-fronted bldg can be protected by straw bales.

Illumination
Illumination of 20 lx →p25 required during lambing period.

Feed storage
Feed sto area at gable end or close by should be provided to minimise handling time.

Sheep housing
Example of slatted pole barn type sheephouse for 320 ewes →(5).

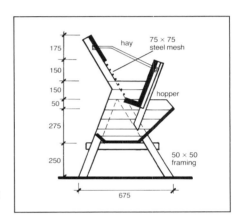

4 Trough for feeding hay & concentrate

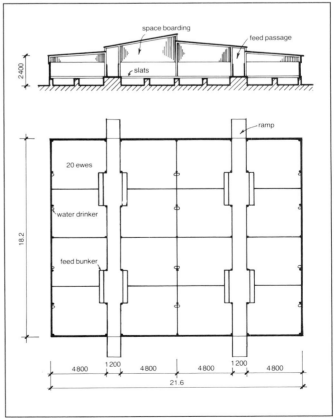

5 Slatted pole barn sheep house for 320 ewes

Farm buildings

SHEEP/POULTRY

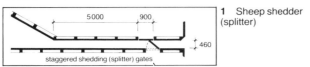

1 Sheep shedder (splitter)

staggered shedding (splitter) gates

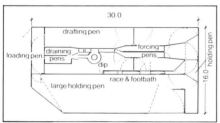

approx capacity(l)	dimensions					
	A	B	C	D	E	F
955	610	1168	381	2743	1219	305
1090	686	1168	381	2743	1219	305
1365	686	1245	381	3200	1372	229

2 Sheep dip

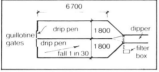

3 Sheep draining pen

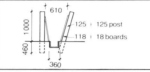

4 Sheep footbath race

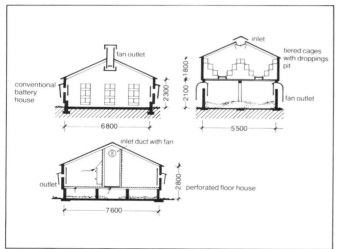

5 Typical sheep handling layout

POULTRY HOUSING

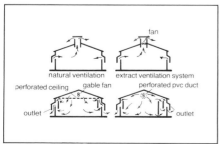

6 Typical designs of poultry houses

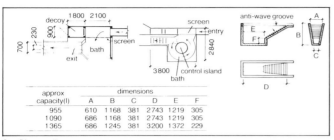

7 Typical ventilation systems, poultry houses

Sheep handling
Handling eqp usually constructed from 950 high, 125 × 125 timber posts set at 1500 centres with either complete dressed boarded sides or 4 × 100 wide timber rails. Should consist of following:
holding pen: space allowance/ewe and lamb 0.65 m²
shedder (splitter): width 460 and length 3000–5000; should have 2 staggered gates →(1).

Sheep dip
Sheep dip bath and swim-around dipper often used when sheep enter bath on side-slide principle and walk out on ramp. →(2) shows dimensions and layout of such dips.

Draining pen
2 draining pens required side by side with shedding entry and guillotine exit gates →(3).

Forcing pen
2 forcing pens or circular pen leading to dip with exit shedder gate required. Forcing pen usually 8000 long and 900 wide with solid sides.

Footbath race (trough)
Footbath race should be 10–12 m long, 900 wide at top and 350 wide at bottom →(4).

Typical layout for handling 200 ewes and lambs →(5).

Poultry houses should be well insulated (0.6 W/m²°C), equipped with fan ventilation, feeding, watering and mechanical waste removal systems. Deep litter houses suitable for all domestic fowl. Layers normally kept in cages. →(6) shows typical designs for poultry houses.

Light requirements
Light levels of 0–20 lx →p25 required; for most poultry control eqp for manipulation of artificial day length required.

Ventilation rates

category	weight kg	max rate m³/h bird	min rate m³/h bird
pullets & hens	1.2	10	0.8–1.3
	2.5	14	1.5
	3.5	15	2
broilers	0.05		0.1
	0.9		0.8
	1.8	10	1.3
	2.2	14	1.7
turkeys	0.5	6	0.7
	2.0	12	1.2
	5.0	15	1.5
	11.0	27	2.7

Ventilation systems & controls
Poultry house ventilation systems consist of light-proofed air inlets, air distribution, outlets, fans and control gear. →(7) shows typical ventilation arrangements.

Farm buildings

POULTRY

Space requirements: hens

deep litter

system	density (live weight per unit of floor ar)	qualifications
rearing birds for laying (age 16–20 weeks)	19.5 kg/m^2	floor ar to include that occupied by feeding & watering eqp
laying birds up to 3.2 kg live weight over 3.2 kg live weight	14.7 kg/m^2 17.1 kg/m^2	floor ar to include that occupied by feeding & watering eqp
broiler production units	34.2 kg/m^2	floor ar to include that occupied by feeding & watering eqp

cages

system	density (live weight per unit of floor ar)	qualifications
rearing birds for laying	39.1 kg/m^2	density relates to cage floor ar
adult battery birds 3 or more lightweight birds/cage 3 or more heavier birds/cage 2 birds/cage single bird cages	39.1 kg/m^2 44 kg/m^2 29.3 kg/m^2 19.5 kg/m^2	densities relate to cage floor ar: min trough space 100/bird

strawyards

system	density (live weight per unit of floor ar)	qualifications
rearing birds for laying	9.8 kg/m^2	floor ar to include that occupied by feeding & watering eqp
laying birds	8.3 kg/m^2	floor ar to include that occupied by feeding & watering eqp

Space requirements: turkeys

rearing

system	density (live weight per unit of floor ar)	qualifications
broiler-type housing	39.1 kg/m^2	floor ar to include any ar occupied by feeding & watering eqp
tier brooders	19.5 kg/m^2	
carry-on cages, hay boxes raised on wire or slats, verandahs	34.2 kg/m^2	
pole barns	24.4 kg/m^2	floor ar to include any ar occupied by feeding & watering eqp
enclosed range ar	10 m^2/bird (987 birds/ha)	

breeding

system	density (live weight per unit of floor ar)	qualifications
on floors hens kept for insemination, hens & males kept together for natural mating	19.5 kg/m^2	floor ar to exclude any floor nest boxes but to include all other eqp
males kept for artificial insemination	0.84 m^2/bird	
in cages hens males	29.3 kg/m^2 0.84 m^2/bird	hens should be housed individually
in enclosed range ar	16.7 m^2/bird (617 birds/ha)	

Farm buildings

SMALL DOMESTIC ANIMALS: DOVES

Specification

space requirements 0.4–0.5 m²/pair
dry and clean
protected from excessive sunshine, wind and rain
safe from predators
demountable for cleaning
good access for keeper

Location

on SE-E facing wall, usually under projecting eaves behind perimeter wall and in roof spaces.

Construction

Dressed T & G boarding with waterproof roof, internally 2 compartments, 1 with nest. Partition between compartments with 40 wide top for roosting. Floor level 100 below entrance to prevent young from falling out. →(1) shows layout and dimensions of dovecots.

RABBITS

Space requirements

breed	space ar (m²)	h of cage
small	0.56	500
medium	0.72	550
large	1.2	650

Design of cages

Depth should be 800 for easy cleaning or catching rabbits. Cages usually arranged in 3 tiers, raised from ground level by 150. Single tier cages should be 800 above ground level. Height of top floor should not exceed 1 600. Floor should be slatted with timber slats, 30 wide with 10 gap: waste collected on sloped floor underneath, urine stored in collecting tank or bucket. →(2) shows details of 2-tier rabbit cages. Cages for nesting should have front half of floor area solid. Frame and walls of rabbit cages usually dressed timber protected with timber preservative. Felted roof should have good overhangs for weather and sun protection.

Feeders & water drinkers

Hay racks with small trough below usually fixed on front gates but should not occupy more than ⅓ of gate area to maintain good lighting and ventilation. To prevent young escaping gaps between wires and hayracks should not exceed 20. Metal or ceramic troughs used for water and grain concentrate: should be fixed to prevent overturning. Trough frontage 50–60/rabbit sufficient.

Pens

Fur rabbits often kept in pens (2 m²/pair) constructed from galvanised netting →(3). Side netting should be sunk about 500 below ground level to prevent rabbits from burrowing out. Pens should have sides about 600 high and be covered over with netting. At 1 corner of pen box consisting of 2 compartments for feeding and nesting. In some instances pens can be raised 800 above ground.

DOGS

Domestic kennels should be roomy enough allow dog stand up and turn round. Construction usually dressed timber with waterproof roofing, eg roofing felt. Kennel should be demountable for easy cleaning. Floor should be raised 60–100 above ground level, often bedded with straw or wood shavings. Floor and roof can project in front of entrance, forming sheltered lying area. →(4) shows typical design for medium size dog.

Professional kennels →p311

SMALL POULTRY HOUSES

Poultry houses for layers should be situated in sheltered locations surrounded by fenced area allowing 15–20 m²/layer.

Internal space of 1 m² sufficient for 3–4 layers. Volume of 0.65 m³ should be provided per hen, with at least 200 of linear space on roosting rail. Rail should be situated about 1 600 high with gaps between rails of 400. Below roosting rail is waste collecting board which is periodically cleaned. Nests should be 300 wide and 350 deep; often located in groups along wall. Nests bedded with straw; if production control required, folding, self-trapping flaps fitted to nests.

Feeders & water drinkers

Hoppers or feeding troughs with wire above trough to prevent hens defecating into feed. Drinkers usually heavy containers 400 high with rail round.

Construction

Hen houses often timber-built with felted roof and resting on concrete base with DPC throughout. Structure should be insulated; provide proper opening for air inlet and outlet for natural ventilation. Typical layout and dimensions of small poultry house →(5).

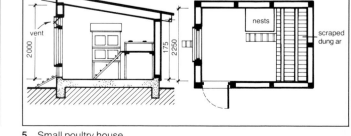

1   Layout of dovecots

2   Tier rabbit cages

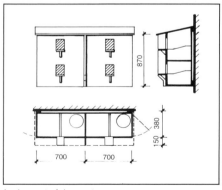

3   Fur rabbit cages

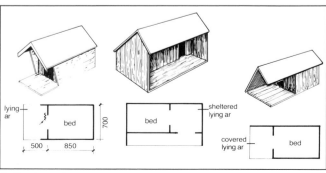

4   Dog kennels

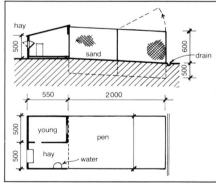

5   Small poultry house

KENNELS

Professional kennels include sleeping quarters in conjunction with adequate exercise runs. Area of individual runs varies according to breed and size of dog.

Where individual independent dog houses used in each run construction should be wood with demountable roof (centre-hinged if large) for sanitary purposes. Floor should be wood min 75 above ground with full ventilation between ground and floor. Burlap bags provide washable bedding and may be stuffed with cedar wood shavings for severe weather protection. Dog house entrance should be baffled against direct wind draughts and driving rain, snow.

Kennels with common shelter bldg, perhaps incorporating grooming and minor med services can be constructed economically of concrete block with poured concrete floor, which should be sloped to gutter and drain, providing easy wash down. Wood pallets with loose washable rugs serve as beds in each enclosure →(1)(2).

Fencing for exercise runs min 1 680 high should be fully fenced across top unless sides 8 440 high. Gravel surface prefered for runs but concrete more easily maintained and offers better sanitation. All exercise runs should have full man gate with patented kennel hardware. Min run 1 070 wide and 3 050 long. Food and water dishes stainless seamless steel mounted on run fencing with steel bands.

BEEHOUSES

Though bees normally kept in hives beehouses equipped with sto and honey extraction and bottling rm sometimes constructed. In general 30 and more bee colonies would justify provision of sto and processing area. Sto area 3 000 × 4 000 should be next to covered loading entrance or patio. Honey processing area (6 000 × 7 000) should have outside door. Layout of work surfaces →(3).

Example of timber beehouse set on stone or concrete foundations for small bee-keeper →(4). Beehouse could be insulated for operator comfort.

DUCKS

Ducks sleep on floors which should be dry and sloped to drain for easy cleaning. Floor should be damp-proofed, lightly bedded with straw and open drain covered with timber slats 40 wide with 20 gaps. Space allowance of 1 m^2 required for 3–4 ducks: 1 duck house should house no more than 20 ducks and 4 drakes. Entrance into house should be 300 wide and 400 high. Ducks must have access to water. Nests should be 450 × 450 with 300 high partitions and placed on floor with no bottom so that ducks do not damage eggs as they enter nest. Good natural ventilation and lighting required. Water trough should be located near slatted drain. Structure may be insulated. Typical layout and dimensions of duck house →(5).

GEESE

Design similar to houses for ducks: space allowance of 0.4 m^2/goose required. Floor should be sloped to drain, damp-proofed and lightly bedded. Nests should be 600 × 650 and nest partitions 300 high. Entrance should be 500 × 500 equipped with doors or curtain. Layout and dimensions of goose house for 30 geese or 3 geese and young →(6).

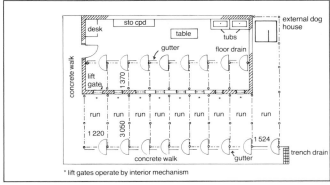

1 Layout plan of kennels with common shelter bldg

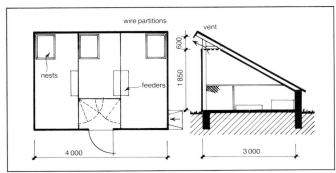

2 Kennels with common shelter bldg **a** elevation **b** section

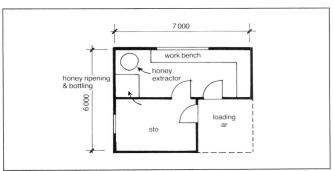

3 Layout of sto & honey processing rm for up to 100 bee colonies

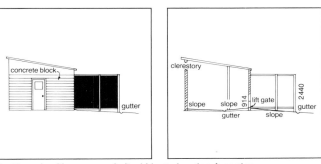

4 Beehouse for 20 bee colonies

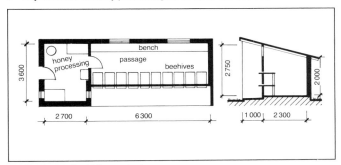

5 House for 20 ducks

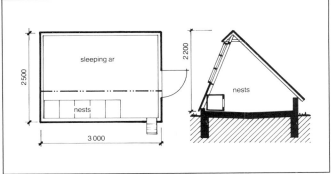

6 House for 30 geese

Farm buildings: crop storage

GRASS

Tower silos

Glass coated steel or concrete, hermetically sealed sto for short chopped (10–12) wilted grass (35–50% moisture content). Rapid filling and emptying possible using blower-loader, cutter unloader, auger and delivery conveyor belt. Av density of silage 1.2 m³/t. Estimated losses 10–15%. Silo dimensions vary from 5500–9000 dia and 12 to 21 m height. Site requirements: adequate soil load-bearing capacity, space for dump-box, access for filling and turning of tractors, trailers and elevator loaders. Animal handling, feeding and waste removal should not be affected by tower filling operating. Space for future expansion may be required.

Clamp silos

Usually open concrete pools with drainage of slurry liquor to pit holding 150 l/t of silage. Walls capable of withstanding lateral pressures of unwilted short or long cut grass. Lateral walls of railway sleepers (or ties) held by vertical steel shores or columns, mass reinforced concrete or sloped timber. Detailed designs should be by structural engineer. Cut grass deposited on concrete apron stacked with tractor mounted loaders and compacted by tractor: compacted density 1.1 m³/t. Silage depth 2000 for self-fed cattle up to 3500 for tractor cut-and-cart to cattle. →(1) shows examples of open clamp and tower silos.

STRAW

Baled straw av volume 1.4 m³/t; bales 1000 × 600 × 500 weight 22–27 kg. Simple open-sided Dutch barns with dry floors positioned near livestock bldg with vehicular access adequate. Sometimes bale stacks or round big bales left outside. Loose straw can be blown into barns with space-boarded open sides. Mechanisation of handling difficult: av volume of loose straw 23 m²/t.

HAY

Bale sizes similar to straw. Av volume 9 m³/t; loose hay 12 m³/t. Dutch barn or pvc heavy duty sheeting required protect hay from rain. Good ventilation and moisture content below 25% required prevent spon-taneous combustion. Mechanisation of hay feeding difficult unless chopped, dried and fed as processed feed with other components of ration.

Barn drying: cold or hot air reducing moisture to 20% used to ensure good quality hay during rainy weather. Hay in bales or blown loose stacked on wooden slats or mesh over main and lateral air ducts (600 × 800). Overall height of dried hay up to 3500 in barns with space boarded sides.

POTATOES

Bulk store

Bldg usually portal frame, 4800 to eaves, insulated to 0.5 W/m² °C with thrust-resistant walls for bulk sto. Concrete floor with DPC strong enough support heavy vehicles; doors normally sliding, insulated (4500 × 4500) with personnel door. Ventilation system based on under-floor lateral ducts (350 × 350) at 2000 centres running at right angles to main air ducts. 75 thick spaced timber slats used to cover ducts. Surface 'A' frame ducts cheaper but inconvenient during unloading. Fans to supply air flow of 0.02 m³/s per t stored including mixing chamber for recirculation and thermostatic control system required. Bulk sto volume 1.5 m³/t; height up to 4000.

Pallet box store

Suitable for sto of different lots, varieties or seed crop potatoes. If potatoes harvested direct into boxes less handling damage to tubers.

Bldg specification similar bulk sto but 6000 high to eaves and of narrower span. Because no thrust on walls, timber frames and panels often used. Ventilation based on floor level ducts for air distribution and extract fans located at 1 gable end opposite air intake fan. Recirculation duct required to maintain air recirculation during periods of low ventilation rate: usually of plywood suspended from ridge, fitted with adjustable apertures. Ventilation rate of 0.01 m³/s per t stored adequate. Pallet box 1200 × 1800 × 900 deep will hold 1 t. Boxes often stacked 6 deep. Allow 3000 free floor space at 1 gable end.

Good sto management required to minimise:
bacterial rot & loss of colour
moisture loss
loss due to sprouting
loss of cooking quality, and
to prevent frost damage

→(2) shows examples of bldg for bulk and pallet methods of sto.

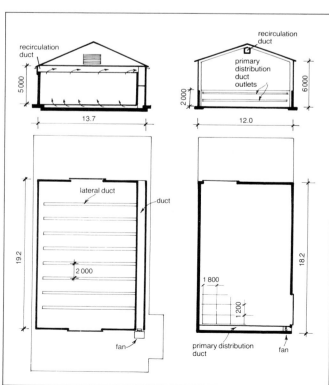

1 Tower & open clamp silos

2 Bulk & pallet box potato sto bldg

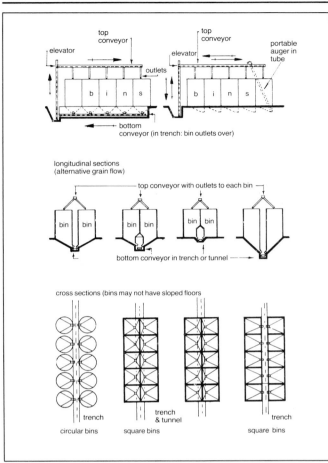

1   Layouts for grain sto bins

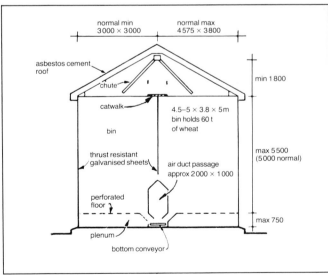

2   Grain drying & sto: nest of bins with roof: section

GRAIN

Sto: wheat 1.3, barley 1.4, oats 2 m³/t.
(i) **bulk:** within thrust-resistant walls, usually steel, approx 2500 high, plus asbestos-cement sheets to eaves 1200; waterproof floor, with grain coned up at 30° to centre of bldg; normal spans 14–18 m; filled by blower-auger or overhead conveyor and emptied by portable auger; uninsulated roof; small gable vents; artificial lighting; doors 3700 × 3700.
(ii) **bins:** (mostly for small quantities of very mechanised units) →(1), square or circular thrust-resistant steel or timber sides set on 3500 grid and 3800 high; usually bins support roof; filled by conveyor under ridge, emptied by gravity and shovel into below ground conveyor or by floor sloped at 35°.
(iii) **hermetically sealed bins:** using glass-fused steel or reinforced plastics rings for wet grain of ≤ 25% moisture content; ≤ 9 dia × 12 m high (sometimes 18 m); reinforced waterproof concrete base; filled by blower through top dome, emptied by bottom outlet auger.

Drying
(i) **in situ:** for bulk, in principle generally as for potatoes →p312; for bins →(2) (more normally predried) ≤ 4500 high; slotted metal floor over plenum chamber approx 600 deep (special slots can blow air to lift grain without manual work into bottom conveyor) connected to fan rm (el or oil fired) by airduct, usually combined with bottom conveyor. Some circular bins have perforated sides and central plenum vertical duct of < 1000 dia →(3).
(ii) **predrying:** mostly by continuous flow or batch driers (el or oil fired) for < 10 t/hr. Former may need 10000 × 3000 × 2500 high plus perimeter access and latter 3000 × 2500 × 4000 high. Intake pit →(4) (from bulk tanker truck) slopes to elevator which raises wet grain to drier (possibly through pre-cleaner) and/or to sto. Work space for drier and eqp may need 80–100 m². Elevator will need ≥ 2000 above top conveyor, probably as penthouse (vented). Driers need dust extract pipe(s); intake doors should be ≥ 3500 × 4500 high.
(iii) **refrigerated:** better quality if grain kept at 4.4°C by means of cold air blown through bulk or bin sto. Most layouts similar to warm air drying: some have lateral ducts at 3000 centres with external mobile refrigerator/blower connected to each in turn.

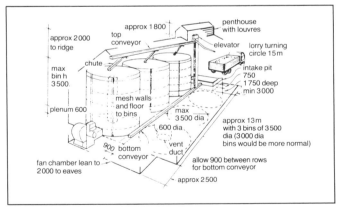

3   Grain drying & sto: radial flow bins in barn

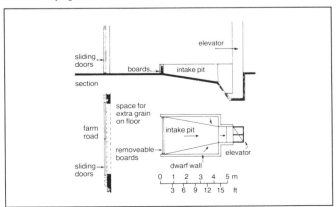

4   Intake pit

Farm buildings

Industry

MACHINERY & IMPLEMENT STORAGE

Circulation round stationery machines

automotive machinery	space allowance	to side	1 000
high machinery	''	''	to side	600
low machinery	''	''	to side	500
all machinery	''	''	to front	500
all machinery	''	''	to front	500

Static space requirements of farm machinery

description	h	w	l
tractor	2 600–3 000	1 800	3 200
trailer	1 400	2 200	4 000–6 000
manure spreader	1 800	2 200	5 500
crawler	2 300	2 300	3 800
combine harvester	4 000	3 500	9 500
lorry	2 900	2 500	8 600
slurry spreader	2 200	1 800	3 600
baler	2 600	2 800	6 000
drill	2 000	3 200	2 800
mounted plough	1 200	1 400	2 400
disc harrows/roller	800	4 300	2 400
hay turner	1 200	2 800	2 500

Machinery sheds

Open-fronted sheds adequate for simple implement sto. Tractor, combine harvester and self-propelled machinery requiring some daily maintenance should be kept in sheds equipped with sliding door, el light, water source and preferably concrete floor.

Workshop

Fully enclosed, insulated bldg 4 000 to eaves, equipped with sliding door, water source, el light and power points, forge with chimney or point for el forge, operating pit with gantry beam over, racks above work benches. Outside concreted drained turning area and floodlight

Fuel store

Oil-tanks to workshop and turning area, raised on concrete walls to allow gravity filling of machinery. Catchpit holding content of tanks desirable. Fuel stored in separate sto complying with conditions of reg and codes. →(1) shows example of machineryshed and workshop.

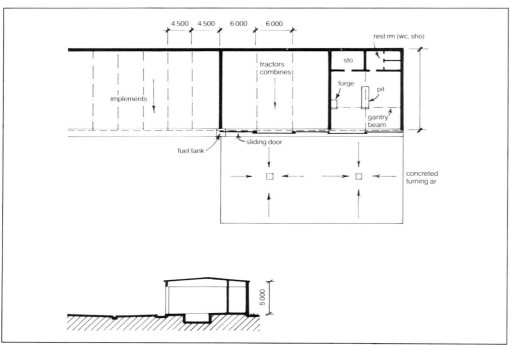

1   Sto for tractor & implements with workshop

Farm buildings references:
→Bibliography entries 108 115 118 137 288 325 333 334 335 340 341 347 348 351 352 356 357 358 359 360 363 364 365 415 582 589 601 646

STADIA: GENERAL DESIGN

Sports data on following pages compiled with help of British Sports Council Technical Unit for Sport: basic technical information gathered from governing bodies of sports and games covered.

Activities divided into 3 categories: outdoor; those which can be played in common spaces indoors; those which essentially need separate or exclusive space. Governing bodies commonly specify dimensions for 3 standards of play: international and national; county and club; recreational. In some instances standard dimensions available for olympic competition and for sports for disabled: for these dimensions for all standard have not been included; unless specified they are inadequate for national standards.

Several sports subject to statutory requirements for lighting, temp, playing surfaces and eqp: always refer to governing body.

Combined soccer pitch with running track round it conforming to recognised international athletics standards may determine size of sports area: basic shape ellipse →(6).

Stadium usually part excavated: earth so gained built up all round. Combination of grandstand with changing rm, shower, first aid rm and provision for police, fire service, admin, press, broadcasting now usually avoided (economy and hygiene). Dormitories for training courses in separate bldg.

Town planning: stadia should be well integrated with surroundings, with easy access for traffic and supplies (rail station, bus stops, car parks etc). Neighbouring industries with smoke, smell and noise undesirable.

Group together covered and open-air installations for different sports: if possible in town's green belt.

1 USA: segmental

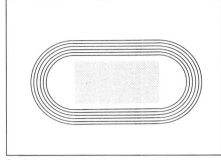

2 Amsterdam: semicircular

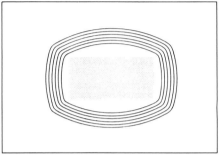

3 Rotterdam: sides & corners curved; for football only

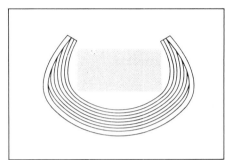

4 U-shaped plan

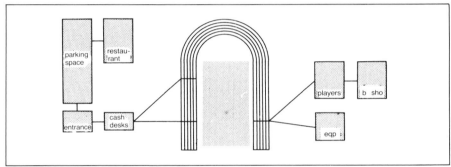

5 Budapest: horseshoe shape about transverse axis

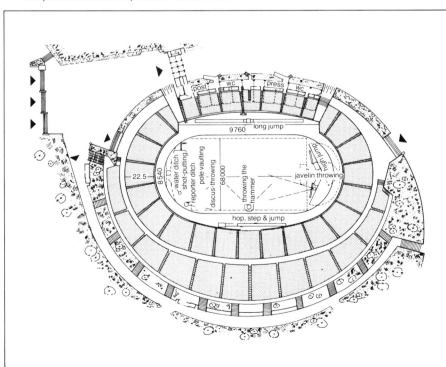

6 Stadium at Hanover   Arch Hillebrecht Goesmann

Sport: stadia

SIGHT LINES

In Europe axes of stadia usually NE-SE →(1) ensure most spectators have sun behind them. According to Vitruvius (1st century BC) rows of seats and standing terraces should rise at steady rate 1:2 for acoustic reasons also. Today use of amplifiers makes good view only criterion for tiering. For staggered seat arrangement every other back row should look over heads of corresponding front rows: gives parabolic curve →(3) starting with rise of ≥ 380 and ending with rise of ≤ 480. Best views on long sides within segment; hence stadia of this shape, first built by Hadden (USA), which give new and convincing impression.

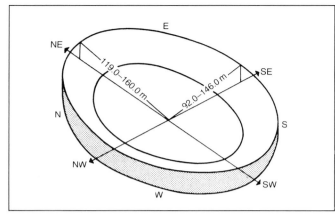

1   Visibility determines size of stadium

2   Design for grandstand of stadium for 100 000 spectators (Nervi) **a** section **b** construction of sight lines

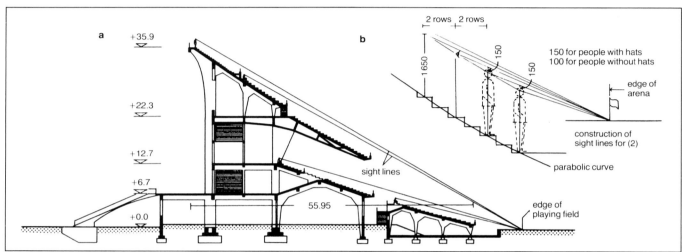

TRAFFIC

Stadia should be near traffic arteries, accessible by road and rail, with projecting turnstiles so that spectators can divide into streams for different entrances. These usually at half height of grandstand, giving access to rows higher and lower by ramps or stairs →(2). Calculate widths of passages and stairs according number of spectators leaving stadium as all leave at same time in contrast to gradual arrival. According van Eestern's investigations 5000 spectators at Amsterdam stadium need 420 s to leave by 9500 stairways (Los Angeles 720 s Turin 540 s).

1 spectator occupies 1 000 stair w in $\frac{9500 \times 420\,s}{5000} = 0.8\,s$ or

in 1 s $\frac{5000}{9500 \times 420\,s} = 1.25$ spectators occupy 1 000 of stairway w.

To determine stair w to evacuate given number of spectators from stadium within given time: stair $w = \dfrac{\text{number of spectators}}{\text{departure time in s} \times 1.25}$

Stairs and corridors flow times →p407–8

Check applicable codes and standards.

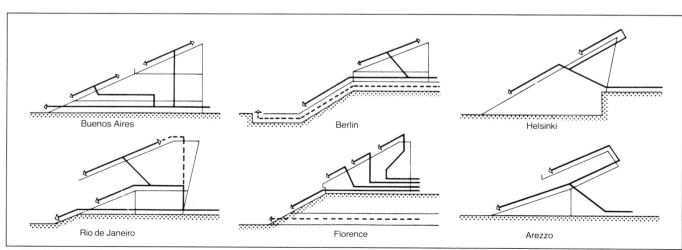

3   Circulation routes in stadia

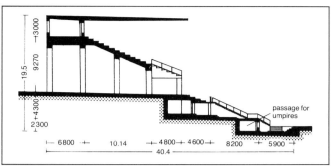

1 Section through Olympic stadium Berlin   Arch March Brothers

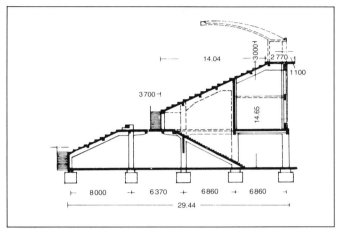

2 Section through Vienna stadium

STANDING TERRACES

Standing terraces: proportion w : h 400 : 200 →(4)–(9)

Seating terraces: proportion w : h from 800 : 480→(11)–(17)

After 5 steps firm railings (crush barrier)

Lower passageway all round ⩾ 1 250 wide

Double and treble standing terraces no longer built

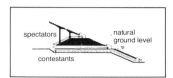

3 Section through stadium with partial excavation, earth mound & superstructure

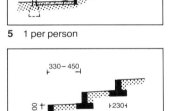

4 Steps with timber reinforcement   **5** 1 per person

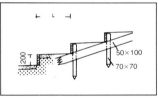

6 Angle steps   **7** Movable concrete units

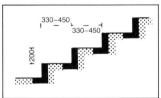

8 Reinforced concrete with falls to drain   **9** Prefabricated RC units on steel joists

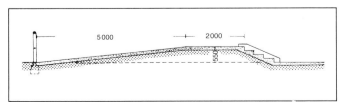

10 Standing ramp, slope ⩽ 10%, 6 P/1 000 mm²

SEATING TERRACES

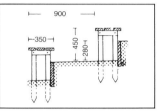

11 Wooden benches with plank step

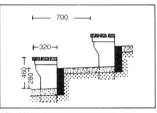

12 Wooden seats on concrete uprights   **13** Sloping RC deck with steps in concrete topping

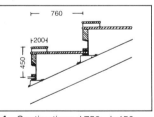

14 Seating tiers: d 750 h 450 w 500   **15** On timber frame as at Stuttgart

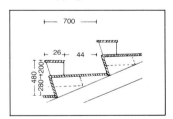

16 On metal brackets set in concrete   **17** Seating with backs

GRANDSTAND SECTIONS

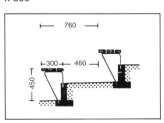

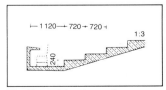

18 Normal rise, upper steps   **19** Normal rise, lower steps
USA risers 152–460, treads 610–762 (660 usually satisfactory)

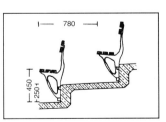

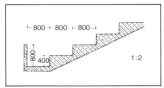

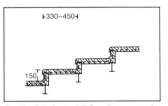

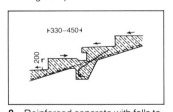

Sport centres

ORGANISATION

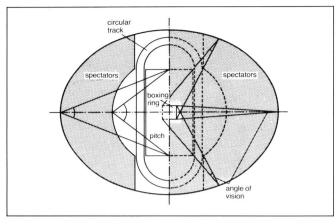

1 Disposition of spectators

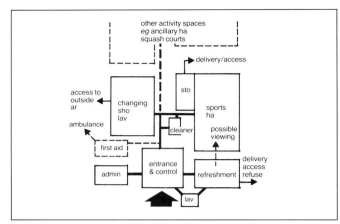

2 Spatial patterns & circulation in dry sports centre

	large scale sports & leisure/rec centre	large scale sports centre (wet & dry)	medium scale wet & dry sports/rec centre	medium scale dry only sports/rec centre	small sports centre	small community provision
pools	●●	●●	●●			
50 m	○	○				
25 m	●	●	○			
20 m			○			
free shape	○					
learner	●	●	○			
diving	●	●	○			
sports hall(s)	●●	●●	●●	●●	●●	●●
large	●	●	○	○		
medium		○	●	●		
small	○	○			●	
small community						●
ancillary indoor sports accn	●●	●●	●●	●●	○	
practice ha	●	●	●	●	○	
weight training/conditioning rm	●	●	○	○		
projectile ha	○	○	○	○		
squash courts	●	●	●	●	●	●
climbing wall	○	○	○	○		
indoor bowls	●	○				
billiards/snooker	○	○				
ice rink	○					
theatre/multi-purpose ha	○					
ancillary accn	●●	●●	●●	●●	●●	●●
changing	●●	●●	●●	●●	●●	●●
spectator seating: fixed	○	○				
occasional	●	●	●	●	●	●
informal viewing	●	●	●	●	●	●
club meeting rm	○	○				○
first aid	●●	●●	●●	○		
first aid eqp	●	●●	●●	●●	●●	●●
creche sto	●	○	○			
creche (alternative use, sto)		○	○	○		
sauna suite	○	○				
refreshments	●●	●●	●●	●●	●	●
cafeteria	●	●	●	●	○	
bar	●	●	●	●	○	○
vending machine	○	○	○	○	○	●
staff & management	●●	●●	●●	●●	●●	●●
reception						
off	●●	●●	●●	●●	●	●
staff rest rm	●●	●●	○	○		
staff changing	●	●	○	○		
outdoor grounds						
grass pitches	○	○	○	○		
hard porous/synthetic pitches	○	○	○	○		
floodlit pitches	○	○	○	○		
tennis courts	○	○	○	○		

key: ●● essential ● typical/desirable
○ possible

3 Main features required for 6 sizes of sports bldg: general recommendations only all bldg being influenced by ar served, population & other resources available

Sport centres

EXAMPLES

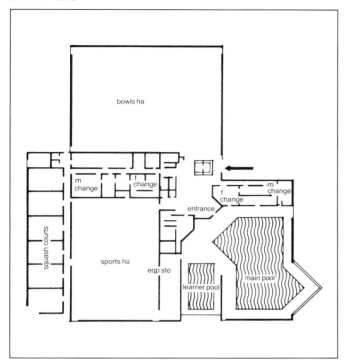

1   Dry & wet leisure centre on school site Dunstable England

Sports centres for disabled →Bib639

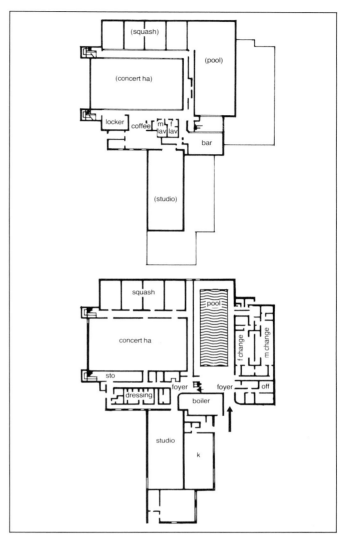

2   Sports centre Bridgnorth England: circulation & social spaces spatially well conceived *eg* in entrance ha glazed screen allows views into swimming pool, between sports ha & squash courts glazed bridge offers view into either ar

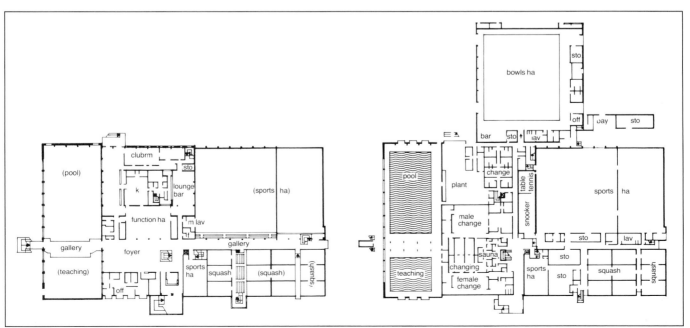

3   Large complex Harrow England comprises indoor & outdoor sports centre, with pool alongside & outdoor bowls ground

Sport halls

USE OF UNDIVIDED SPACE

→(1) shows number of sport playing courts or other spaces which fit into various sizes of sports or community halls. Number of spaces given for each sport optimum will fit into undivided hall space for 3 standards of play: N international and UK national; C UK county or club; R recreational. Required min space allowed for each takes into account not only actual playing area but: necessary run-out or safety margins, team bench and officials' space round playing space which amount to overall areas used for assessment; where practical some overlap of margin between parallel courts of same kind; critical heights which in some instances degrade standard for which otherwise floor space adequate; need for some additional free circulation space inside hall entrance.

For most sports possible provide spaces for mix of 3 standards; in practice several different activities may be programmed at same time.

Fire: check fr reg and max component value; in UK halls 7000 m³ or over need DoE waiver; 'volume' can include unenclosed structural roof space.

sports	large ha 36.5 × 32 × 9.1 1168 m² (120 × 105 × 30 ft) 12600 ft²		medium ha 32 × 26 × 7.6–9.1 832 m² (105 × 85 × 25–30 ft) 8925 ft²		29 × 26 × 7.6–9.1 754 m² (96 × 85 × 25–30 ft) 8175 ft²		32 × 23 × 6.7–9.1 736 m² (105 × 75 × 25–30 ft) 7770 ft²		small ha 32 × 17 × 6.7–7.6 554 m² (105 × 56 × 22–25 ft) 5880 ft²		29.5 × 16.5 × 6.7–7.6 486.7 m² (97 × 54 × 22–25 ft) 5238 ft²		26 × 16.5 × 6.7–7.6 429 m² (85 × 54 × 22–25 ft) 4590 ft²		22.5 × 16.5 6.7–7.6 371.25 m² (92 × 54 × 22–25 ft) 3995 ft²		community ha 17.0–20.0 × 15.6 × 6.7 265.2–321 m² (56–65 × 41 × 22 ft) 2850–3455 ft²		17.0 × 8.5 6.7 144.5 m² (56 × 28 × 22 ft) 1555 ft²	
	no standard		no standard		no standard		no standard		no standard		no standard		no standard		no standard		no standard		no standard	
aikido	4 6	N C	4	N	4	N	2 +3(1*)	C R	2 3(1*)	N R	2	N	2	N	1 2	N R	1	N	—	—
archery (l of shoot)	¹30 m 25 m 18 m 20 yd		¹25 m 18 m 20 yd			18 m 20 yd	¹25 m	18 m 20 yd	¹25 m 18 m 20 yd			18 m 20 yd		18 m 15 yd		18 m 15 yd	—	—	—	—
badminton	8	N	5 6(2*)	N† R	3/4 4	N†/C R*	4 6	N† R	4	C**	3 4	C** R*	3	C**	3	R	2	R†	1	R†²
basketball	2	N	1 2	N C*/R	1 2	N R*	1	N	1	C**	1	C**	1	C**	1 1	R* mini BB	1	mini BB	—	—
bowls (portable non-competitive rinks)	7	R	5	R	5	R*	4	R	3	N	3	R*	—		—		—		—	
boxing (training rings)	9 12	N R	6 12	N R	4 9	N R	6 8	N R	3 6	C R	3 5	C R	2 5	C R	2 4	C R	2 4	C R	2	R
⁽¹⁾cricket 6-a-side pitches	1 2	N C	1	C	—	—	1	C	1	R	—		—		—		—		—	
cricket nets	8	N	6	N	6	C	5	N	4	C	4	C	4	R	—		—		—	
fencing (pistes)	12 14	N C	8(3*) 9	N C	7 8	N C	6 8	N C	3/4 2/3	N/C R*	3/4* +2	N/C R*	3/4* +1	N/C R	3 4	N C*	3	C	2	R
5-a-side football	1 2	N R*	1 2	C R*	1	R*	1	C	1	R*	1	R*	1	R*	1	R*	1	R*	—	
gymnastics (olympic)	—	N	—	C	—	P	—	C	—	P	—	P	—	P	—	P	—	P	—	
handball mini-handball	1	N*	1	C	1	R*	1	C	1	R	1 1	R* C	1	C	1	C	1	R*	1	R*
hockey	1	C*	1	R	1	R	1	R	1	R	1	R	1	R	1	R	—		—	
judo	4 6	N R	2 4	N C	1 4	N C	2 4	N R	2 3	N R	1 2	N C	1 2	N R	1 2	N R	1/2	R	—	
karate	4 12	N R	2/4 6	N/C R	2 4/6	N* C/R	2 6	N R	2 6	N R*	2 3	N*/C R	1/2 3	N/C R	1 2	N R	1 2	N R	2	R*
⁽¹⁾keep fit movement & dance; Yoga		✓		✓		✓		✓		✓		✓		✓		✓		✓		✓
kendo	4 6	N R*	2 4	N C	2 4	N* C	2 4	N R	2	N	2 2	N* C	1 2	N C	1 2	N R*	1	R	—	
lacrosse female	1	N	1	C*	1	R	1	C*	1	C*	1	R	—	P	—	P	—		—	
lawn tennis	1 2	N* R	1	R*	—	—	1	R*	1	R*	—		—		—		—		—	
micro korfball	1	C	1	C	1	C	1	C	1	R*	—		—		—		—		—	
netball	1 2	N C*/R	1	R	—	—	1	R	1	R	—		—		—		—		—	
table tennis c/c	10 15/21	N C/C	6 10/15	N C/C	6 10/12	N C/C	6 10/12	N C/C	7/9 14	C/C R	7 12	C/C R	6/7 10	C/C R	4 8	C/C R	3–6 6–8	C/C R	4	R*
trampolining	12	N	8 12	N† R	8	N†	4 8	N† C*/R	4 6	C** R	—	R	4	C**	4	R	2	R	1	R
tug-of-war	—	N	—	C	—	R	—	C	—	C	—	R	—		—		—		—	
volleyball	2 3	N R	1 2 3	N† C R*	1 2	N† R	2* 2	N†/C R	1	C**	1	C**	1	C**	1*	C**	1	R*	—	

1 Definition of scales: max number of courts related to standards of play: (for key & footnotes →p321(1))

USE OF UNDIVIDED SPACE (cont)

	large ha	medium ha			small ha				community ha	
	36.5 × 32 × 9.1 1168 m² (120 × 105 × 30 ft) 12600 ft²	32 × 26 × 7.6–9.1 832 m² (105 × 85 × 25–30 ft) 8925 ft²	29 × 26 × 7.6–9.1 754 m² (96 × 85 × 25–30 ft) 8175 ft²	32 × 23 × 6.7–9.1 736 m² (105 × 75 25–30 ft) 7770 ft²	32 × 17 × 6.7–7.6 554 m² (105 × 56 × 22–25 ft) 5880 ft²	29.5 × 16.5 × 6.7–7.6 486.7 m² (97 × 54 × 22–25 ft) 5238 ft²	26 × 16.5 × 6.7–7.6 429 m² (85 × 54 × 22–25 ft) 4590 ft²	22.5 × 16.5 6.7–7.6 371.25 m² (92 × 54 × 22–25 ft) 3955 ft²	170–20.0 × 15.6 × 6.7 265.2–321 m² (56–65 × 41 × 22 ft) 2850–3455 ft²	17.0 × 8.5 6.7 144.5 m² (56 × 28 × 22 ft) 1555 ft²
weight lifting contests	— N	— N	— N	— N	— C	— C	— C	— C	— C	— —
wrestling	4 N 12 C	2 N 6 C	6 C	2 N 6 C	2 N* 3 C	3 C 8 R	2 C 6 R	2 C 6 R*	2 C 4 R	2 R

Key:
N   international/national standard
C   county/club standard
R   recreational standard
P   practice ar only
C/C for table tennis 2 grades of min space allowances for inter-county/inter-club standards of play
ns   no standards have yet been laid down
S   ar behind shooting line below safety standard recommended; acceptable space can be provided by slight lengthening of ha; or existing spaces may be used for practice
*   below min space standard recommended by governing body concerned but capable of providing purposeful & enjoyable activity
**   recreational standard where ha is less than 7600 clear h for badminton & trampolining or less than 7000 for basketball & volleyball; 6700 h suitable for mini-basketball & mini-volleyball
†   county/club standard where ha less than 9000 clear h

1   Continuation of →p320(1) definition of scales

STORAGE

Inadequate sto space for sport halls very common fault. Allow for full range of eqp needed. As eqp must be accessible sto must be shallow (say 5000 max) and ideally placed along side of hall. Recommended min requirements for 3 categories of hall →(2).

ha	sto ar m²	h access	w access
large	112	7000	4500
medium	75	2700	4500
small	50	2250	3600

2   Min sto requirements for 3 categories ha

sports ha	fixed	movable
ceiling		
protection for lighting	●	
climbing ropes & trackway	●	
climbing poles & trackway	●	
speakers	●	
track system for division nets	●	
cricket		●
golf		●
archery		●
volleyball		●
5-a-side-soccer		●
basketball		
ceiling mounted backboards & goals (manual or el operation)	●	●
wall mounted backboards & goals (manual or el operation)	●	●
gymnastics		
asymmetric bars	●	●
pommel horse	●	●
vaulting buck	●	●
vaulting horse	●	●
horizontal bars	●	●
rings	●	●
trampoline spotting rig	●	●
parallel bars	●	●
springboards, floors		●
boxing		
ring	●	●
games apparatus		
tennis		●
volleyball		●
badminton		●
5-a-side soccer		●
indoor hockey		●
handball		●
netball		●

sports ha	fixed	movable
walls		
scoreboard		●
wall protection/padding	●	●
seating fixings/recesses		●
fire eqp	●	
protection to services/heating	●	
wall speakers		●
floors		
court markings	●	
sockets & plates (fixed to floor or sub-floor)		●
ancillary ha		
ceiling		
track system for curtains	●	
lighting systems		
activities		
judo & martial arts (mats, wall padding)	●	●
snooker	●	
table tennis		●
fencing		●
boxing		●
boxing training	●	●
weight/fitness training	●	●
weight lifting	●	
wrestling	●	●
movement & dance (barre, mirrors)	●	
floor		
sockets/fixings	●	
markings	●	
movable floors/platforms		●

3   Sports eqp check list

Sport: outdoor

PITCHES

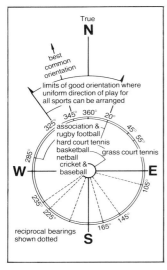

2 Archery, target

1 Orientation diagram: for purposes of this chart seasons for various games taken to be as follows (southern hemisphere excepted): association football & rugby football 1 Sep–30 Apr; hard court tennis, basketball, netball all year round; cricket, baseball, grass court tennis 1 May–15 Sep; pavilions should avoid SW-NW aspect (225°–315°)

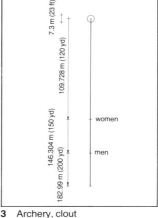

3 Archery, clout

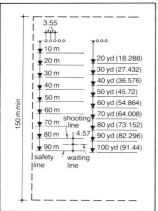

4 Baseball (Little league ⅔ size)

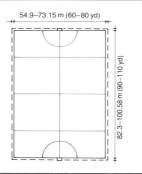

5 Bicycle polo

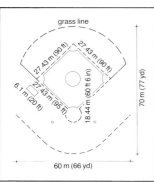

6 Camogie

7 Football, association: National Playing Fields Association recommends sizes: senior pitches 96–100 × 60–64 (105–109 × 66½–70 yd); junior pitches 90 × 46–55 (98½ × 50–60 yd); international 100–110 × 64–75 (109–120 × 70–82 yd)

8 Football, Australian

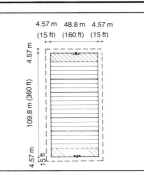

9 Football, American

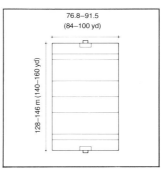

10 Football, Gaelic

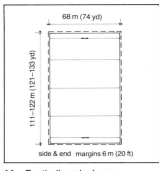

11 Football, rugby league

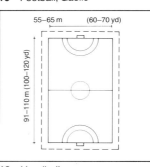

12 Handball

13 Hockey: for county & club matches recommended pitch 90 × 55 (98½ × 60 yd), overall space 95 × 60 (104 × 66½ yd)

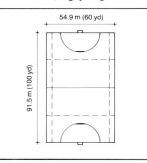

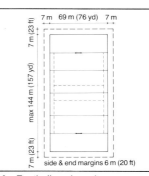

14 Football, rugby union

15 Football, Canadian

16 Hurling

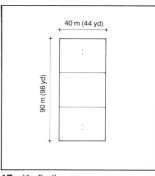

17 Korfball

Sport: outdoor

PITCHES

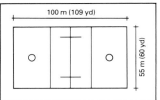

1 Lacrosse, men

100 m (109 yd)
55 m (60 yd)

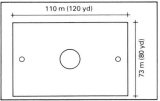

2 Lacrosse, women: ground has no measured or marked out boundaries

110 m (120 yd)
73 m (80 yd)

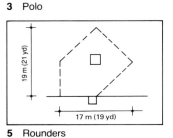

3 Polo

27.5 m (30 yd) 275 m (300 yd) 27.5 m
18.5 m (20 yd)
183 m (200 yd)
18.5 m

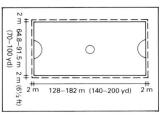

4 Netball

30.48 m (33 yd)
18 m (20 yd)
15.25 m (17 yd)
33 m (35 yd)

5 Rounders

19 m (21 yd)
17 m (19 yd)

6 Shinty

2 m (6½ yd)
64.8–91.5 m (70–100 yd)
2 m
2 m 128–182 m (140–200 yd) 2 m

7 Tug-of-war

46 m (50 yd)
5 m (16½ ft)
rope off

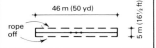

8 Curling

42.1 m (46 yd)
4.27

9 Cricket

160 m (175 yd)
20 m (22 yd)
22 m (24 yd)
3.66 m (4 yd)
142 m (155 yd)

10 Croquet

25.56 m (28 yd)
31.95 m (35 yd)

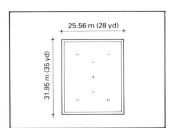

11 Bowls, crown

27.43–54.86 m (30–60 yd)
usually about 36.6 m (40 yd)
rises in middle 203–457 mm

12 Bowls

38.4 m square (42 yd)
6 rink
ditch 200–380 mm
path 1.2–1.8 m (4–5¾ ft)
41.2–42.8 m (45–46 yd) square

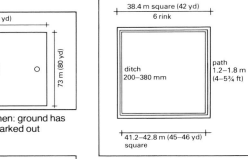

13 Cycling 333 ⅓ track

144.35 m (158 yd)
71.42 m (78 yd)

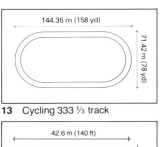

14 Roller hockey

42.6 m (140 ft)
21 m (70 ft)

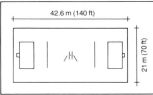

15 Basketball

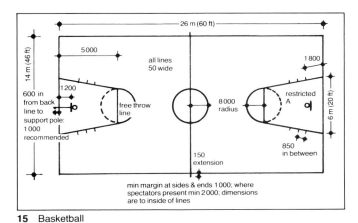

26 m (60 ft)
14 m (46 ft)
5 000
all lines 50 wide
1 800
600 in from back line to support pole: 1 000 recommended
1 200
free throw line
8 000 radius
restricted A
6 m (20 ft)
150 extension
850 in between
min margin at sides & ends 1 000; where spectators present min 2 000; dimensions are to inside of lines

16 Mini-hockey

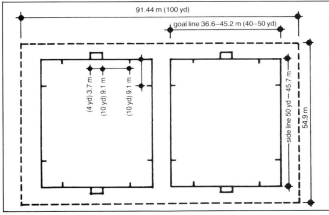

91.44 m (100 yd)
goal line 36.6–45.2 m (40–50 yd)
(4 yd) 3.7 m
(10 yd) 9.1 m
(10 yd) 9.1 m
side line 50 yd – 45.7 m
54.9 m

17 6-man football

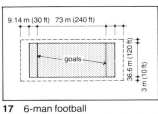

9.14 m (30 ft) 73 m (240 ft)
36.6 m (120 ft)
goals
3 m (10 ft)

18 Soft ball

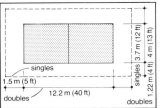

18.3 m (60 ft)
min 7.6 m (25 yd)
14 m (46 ft) men
10 m (33 ft) women

19 Deck tennis

9.14 m (30 ft) 73 m (240 ft)
singles 3.7 m (12 ft)
4 m (13 ft)
1.5 m (5 ft)
singles 1.22 m (4 ft)
12.2 m (40 ft)
doubles
doubles

20 Paddle tennis

6 m (20 ft)
5.8 m (19 ft)
13.4 m (44 ft)
11.9 m (39 ft)
junior: 3.2 m (10 ft 6 in)
senior: 4 m (13 ft)
senior: 1.8 m (6 ft)
junior: 1.8 m (6 ft)

Sport: outdoor

ATHLETICS

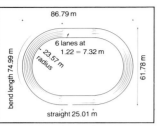

1 200 m running track

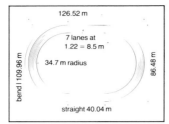

2 300 m running track

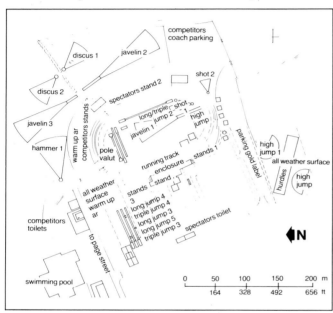

3 Plan of Copthall sports centre London England Borough of Barnet

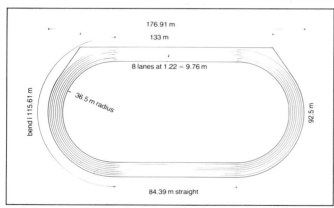

4 400 m standard 7-lane club running track: for 6-lane all-weather surfaces reduce overall dimensions by 2 440 (approx overall size 179 × 106 m (193 × 116 yd)); major competition & regional tracks require 8 all-weather lanes with 10-lane sprint straight: increase overall dimensiosns by 2 440 (approx overall size 181 × 111 m (198 × 121 yd))

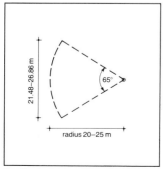

5 Shot

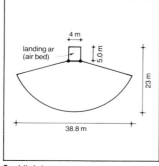

6 High jump

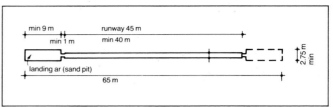

7 Long jump: NB landing ar at both ends to avoid adverse wind

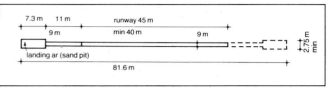

8 Triple jump (senior & junior)

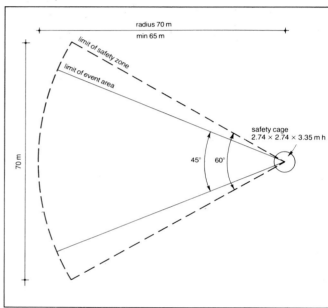

9 Discus & hammer: discus base 2 500 hammer base 2 135

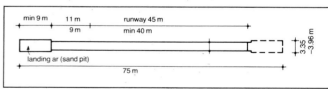

10 Combined triple & long jump

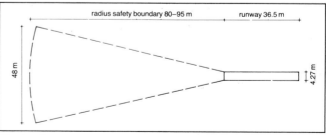

11 Javelin

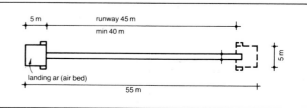

12 Pole vault

PITCHES

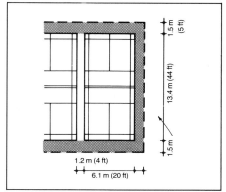

1 Badminton: min h 7 600 (25 ft)

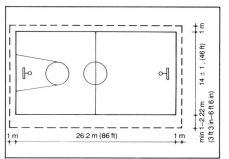

2 Basketball: min h 7 000 (23 ft)

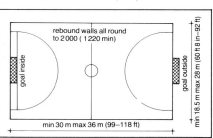

3 5-a-side football

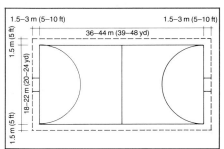

4 Gymnastics, male: min h 7 600 (25 ft)

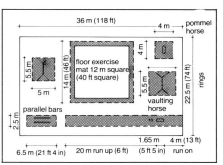

5 Hockey: team sizes adjusted according to size of pitch available

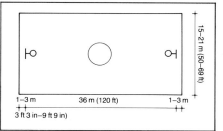

6 Lacrosse, female: pitch for male game (not shown) 46–48 × 18–24 m (151–158 ft × 60–79 ft)

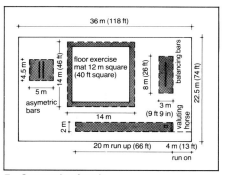

7 Gymnastics, female

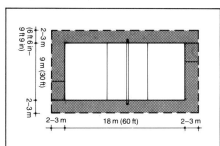

8 Volleyball

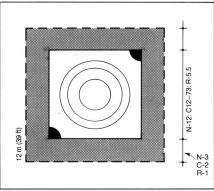

9 Wrestling (N national C club R recreation)

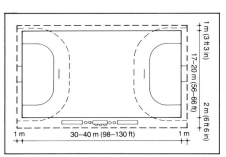

10 Handball, 7-a-side

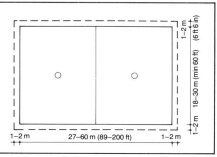

11 Micro-korfball

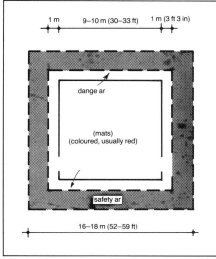

12 Judo

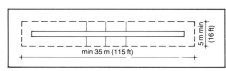

13 Tug-of-war

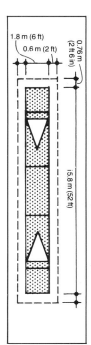

14 American bowling alley (may have any number lanes: usual min 8)

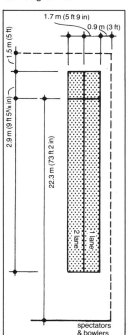

15 Shuffle board

Sport: indoor

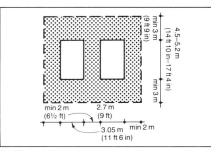

1 Tennis

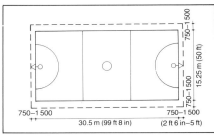

2 Netball

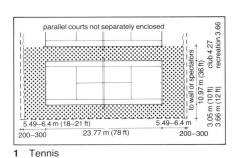

3 Trampoline

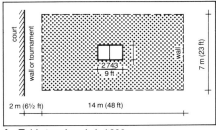

4 Table tennis: min h 4200

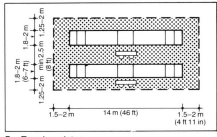

5 Fencing pistes

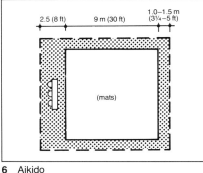

6 Aikido

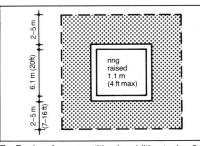

7 Boxing: for competition in addition to ring & spectator accn following needed: med exam rm, weighing rm, gloving-up rm, admin, lighting above ring, water supply to each corner

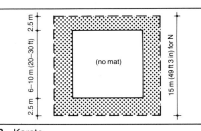

8 Karate

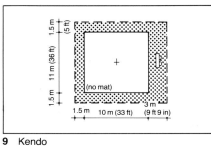

9 Kendo

ATHLETICS TRACKS

Resources for indoor athletics fall into 2 main categories:

competition: provide for full range of competitive disciplines; will provide for spectators
training: (a) with some limited competitive use; (b) purpose built; (c) adaptations of existing sports halls.

In USA National Collegiate Athletic Association (NCAA) rules for college athletics, for other amateur events Amateur Athletic Union (AAU); some track and field events still measured in yards, feet and inches; many present tracks still in such measurements; new layouts generally in metres or other SI units.

European Athletic Association (EAA) specifies for indoor events:

Arena
Shall be covered and heated and shall consist of track circuit, sprint straight, runways for 4 jumps, site for shot putt.

Nature of tracks
Tracks and runways surfaced with wood or such other material as allows normal use of spiked shoes; number of spikes shall comply with International Amateur Athletics Federation rule 142 (4).

Circular track
1 lap of track shall measure ≥ 160 m ≤ 200 m in length. Each bend shall be ≥ 35 m in length and banked at an angle ≥ 10° ≤ 18°. Each straight ≥ 35 m. Where no raised border, measurement shall be taken 200 outward from inner edge of track. Track shall be ≥ 4000 ≤ 6100 wide; shall include ≥ 4 lanes.

Sprint track
Sprint straight shall have ≥ 6 lanes: width of each 1220; extension beyond finishing line ≥ 15 m.

Hurdle races
Male: 50 m hurdles shall include 4 hurdles, h 1060. There shall be 13.72 m from start line to first hurdle; 9140 between hurdles; 8860 from last hurdle to finish line.

60 m hurdles shall include 5 hurdles, h 1060; 13.72 m from start line to first hurdle; 9140 between hurdles; 9720 from last hurdle to finish line.

Female: 50 m hurdles shall include 4 hurdles, h 844; 13.0 m from start line to first hurdle; 8500 between hurdles; 11.5 m from last hurdle to finish line.

60 m hurdles shall include 5 hurdles, h 844; 13.0 m from start line to first hurdle; 8500 between hurdles; 13.0 m from last hurdle to finish line.

Events
Runways for long & triple jump & pole vault: ≥ 40 m long and 1220 wide.

Landing area for jumps: in high jump and pole vault landing areas shall be in accordance with IAAF rules 201 (e) and 3 (d). In long jump and triple jump they shall measure ≥ 6000 long and 2500 wide and shall consist of ≥ 300 in depth of wet sand on synthetic track base.

Putting the shot: sector shall be 45° but may be reduced by technical delegate if necessary to meet local conditions.

Other technical installations: all other technical installations shall be strictly in accordance with IAAF rules.

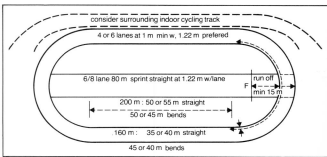

10 Requirements for indoor track

Sport: indoor

ATHLETICS TRAINING

Provision for athletes training indoors, with limited competitive use, need not include expensive 200 m banked tracks. Many events can be simulated if brief thought out in advance with consideration of needs of athletes.

Needs of athletes should be considered at planning stage of sports centres so that this major spectator and participant sport can gain some of benefits from indoor provision other sports have received →(1)

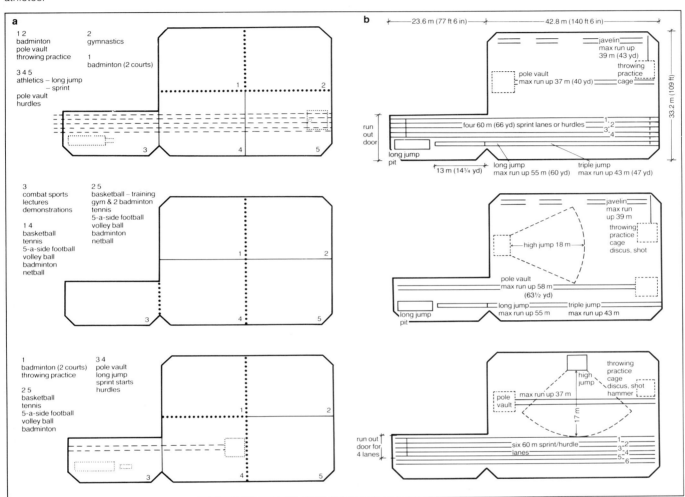

1 Sports stadium training ha Gateshead England: **a** permutations of possible activities **b** permutations of possible athletics training

WEIGHT & FITNESS TRAINING

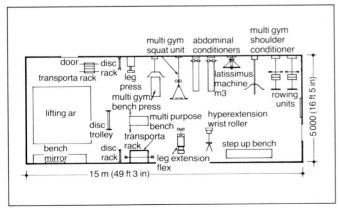

2 Fitness rm at leisure centre Cramlington England

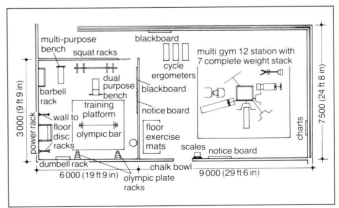

3 Conditioning & weight training rm Bunyan recreation centre Bedford England

Sport: indoor

SPORT NEEDING OWN PITCHES/SPACES

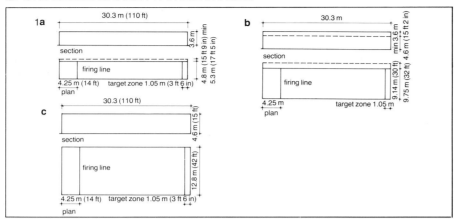

1 Projectile ha section & plan **a** small **b** medium **c** large

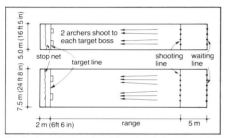

2 Archery: international & national shoots require ranges of 30 25 & 18 m & 20 yd; for club & recreational shoots 13. 716 (15 yd) will do: min ceiling h 3000

3 Bowling: single rink in projectile hall

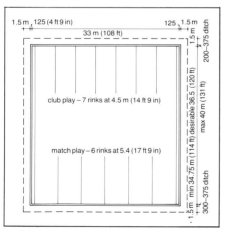

4 Bowling: 4 rinks min for recreation, 6 for tournaments

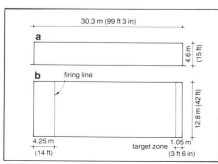

5 Shooting, target, small bore **a** section **b** plan

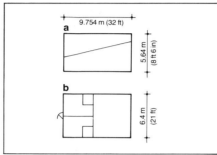

6 Squash **a** section **b** plan: dimensions & surface finishes critical; refer to governing bodies

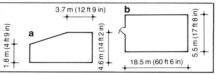

7 Rugby fives **a** section **b** plan

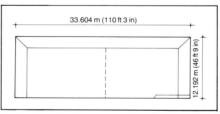

8 Real tennis: dimensions of court at Hampton Court England

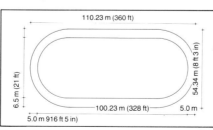

9 Cycling

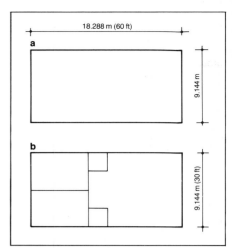

10 Rackets **a** section **b** plan

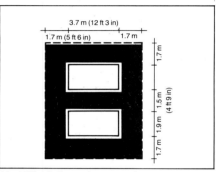

11 Billiards & snooker, agreed standards table: 3500 playing ar

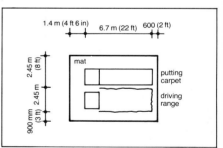

12 Golf practice

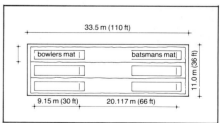

13 Cricket practice nets

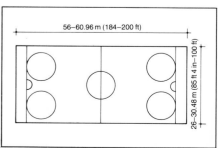

14 Ice skating

INDOOR POOLS

Location: central, good public transport connexions. Rough guide to provision: dispersed population (rural areas) 20–25 × 11–13 m within 25 minutes travel of 30000 people; partially concentrated (surburban areas and free standing towns) 25 × 11 m pool + learner pool within 15–20 minutes travel of 30000 people; concentrated population 25 × 13 m pool + learner pool within 12 minutes walking time of 30000 people. Usage/head of population: medium and small towns 3.5 times/year; cities 1.3–2.5/year.

Water area →(1)

Changing rm →p336–7: accessible from hall, separated by sex; not inside pool area; 1 clo unit/1–1.5 m² pool area; common changing rm as extra space.

Pre-cleanse: barefoot passage past wc to showers; 1 sho/8 clo spaces: sho space required 1.35–2.15 m²; in some countries (*eg* Switzerland USA) use of cleaning passages with sho activated by floor contact or light beam. Through sho rm to swimming and teaching pools →p335.

Toilets: min 2 wc; male 1/15–20 female 1/7–10; urinals 1/15–20 male.

type of b	covered space	
	changing rm 2 floors	changing rm 1 floor
small av large	m³ 30–40 40–55 50–70	m³ 40–50 50–65 60–80

1 Ratio of enclosed space to 1 m²

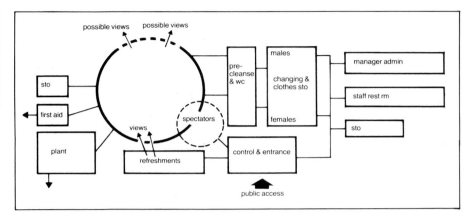

2 Circulation & grouping of elements

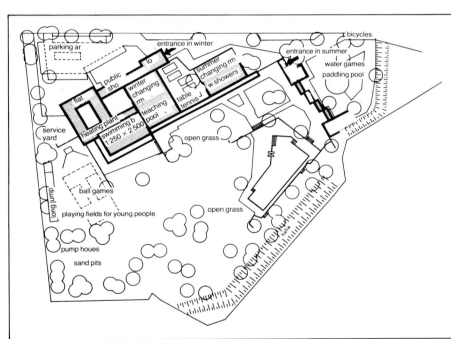

3 Baths at Hanover-Linden Germany (design Hochbauamt Hanover): indoor b separated from outdoor b by 3 submersible doors with footbasins and 6 sh in front
indoor swimming b:
pool 12.5 × 25 m
training pool 6 × 12.5 m
open air swimming b:
free-shape general purpose pool 20 × 25 m
diving pool with 10 m stage 20 × 20 m
changing: indoor 49 change-over cubicles, 600 clo & 5 group changing rm; outdoor 36 change-over cubicles & 1 320 clo

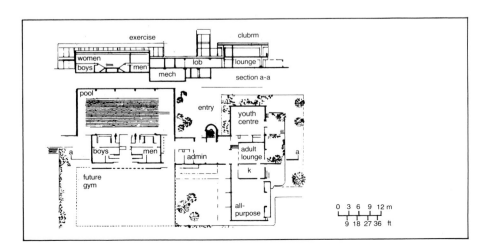

4 Leisure & pool complex Roxbury YMCA USA Arch The Architects Collaborative

Sport: swimming

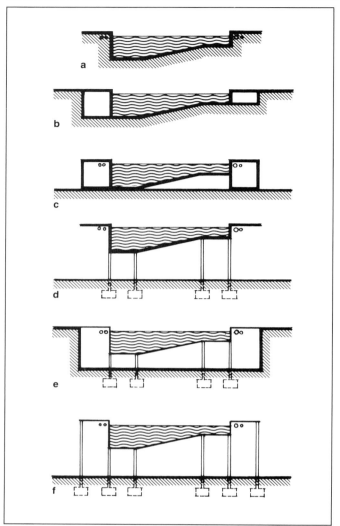

1 Typical pool profiles: **a** & **b** for 'in ground' pools **c** & **d** for 'above ground' pools **e** 'in ground' steel tank **f** 'above ground' steel tank

	international pool	national/ regional pool	local pool	recreational/ leisure pool
pool water ar				
50 m main pool	●	●		
25 m main pool		○	●	
free form shape pool			○	●
separate deep water diving pool	●	●		
separate teaching/training pool	●	●	○	○
1 000 springboard main pool			○	
recreational diving chutes			○	●
wave machine			○	○
spectator seating				
fixed raked spectator seating	●	●		
occasional spectators at poolside	○	○	●	●
informal viewing				
viewing ar overlooking pool	○	○	○	○
refreshments				
cafeteria	●	●	○	●
bar	○	○		○
vending machines	●	●	○	●
first aid rm	●	●	●	●
sauna suite	○	○		○

● definite provision
○ possible provision

2 Pool features

INDOOR POOLS (cont)

Heating & ventilation: water temp recreational pools 27°C, learner pools 28°–30°, diving pool 28°; air temp 1–2° above water temp: changing rm, pre-cleanse, clothes sto not less than pool water; air changes: volume flow rate of 15 mm³/m²/s of pool water plus set surround.

Water purification plant for heating, filtering, disinfection. Water circulation: main pool ≤ 3 hr (if very shallow with heavy bathing load every 2 hr); learner pool ≤ 1½ hr; diving pool 6 hr; pH near as possible 7.7 or 7.6, never outside range 7.2–8.0.

Pool: width, length →(3); water depth: non-swimmers 800–1250, swimmers 1250–3500, learner pool 500–900. Min depth for swimming 900.

Internal finishes: floors easy-grip and slip-resistant finish, glazed ceramic tiles, small size mosaic; pool surrounds slip-resistant flooring; pool bottom and walls tiles; wall surround up to 2000 tiles or waterproof paint; upper wall areas and ceiling sound absorbent materials. Metal parts rust and condensation proof encased, no heat transmission bridges. Plastics generally suitable. All fixings and fittings ideally made from corrosion resistant metals, *eg* stainless steel, bronze, certain aluminium alloys.

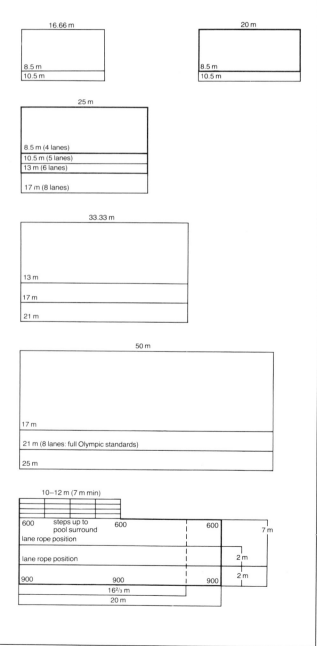

3 Main pool sizes: most common sizes shown in heavier lines

INDOOR POOLS (cont)

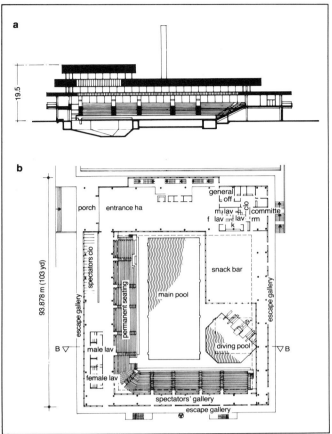

1 Commonwealth pool Edinburgh Scotland **a** section **b** plan Arch Robert Matthew Johnson Marshall & Partners

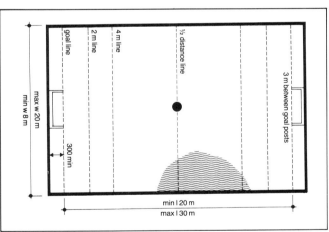

2 Dimensions for water polo

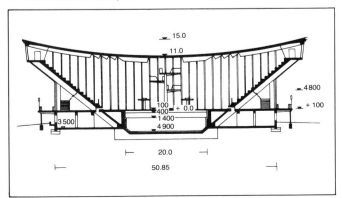

3 Indoor b Wuppertal Germany: section Arch Hetzelt

Water polo

Playing area: for national/international events 1800 deep; district/county events 1500 min; club/Amateur Swimming Association events in UK 1200 min. Dimensions →(2).

Swimming pools for disabled →Bib639

Pools for leisure

Main features of pools specifically created for indoor leisure and recreational swimming: lively, warm, gay interior; good quality materials; shallow water with beach edges; wave machines; water chutes; artificial sun bathing; plants, trees, seating, refreshment areas for swimmers.

Private indoor pools →p115–6

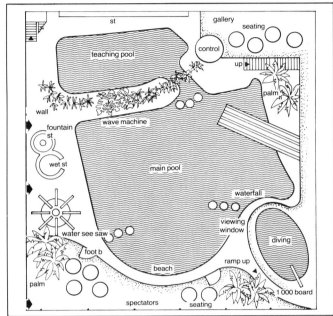

4 Typical 'leisure' free form pool Whitley Bay England; plan Arch Gillinson Barnett & Partner

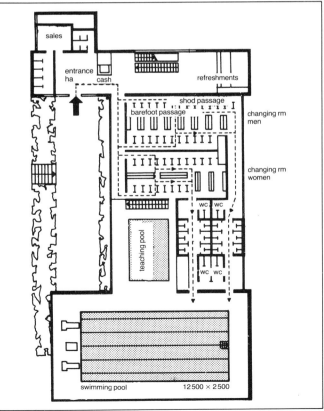

5 Indoor pool Bottrup Germany Arch Heinz Kisler

Sport: swimming

INDOOR POOLS

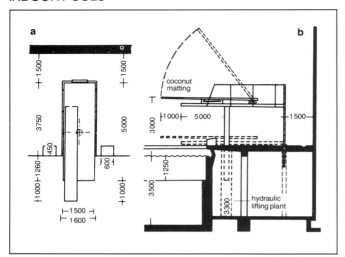

1   Spring board hydraulically adjustable 1 000–3 500   **a** plan **b** section

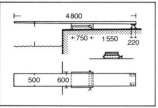

2   Spring board detail

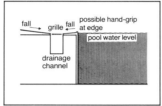

3   Deck-level pool: edge section

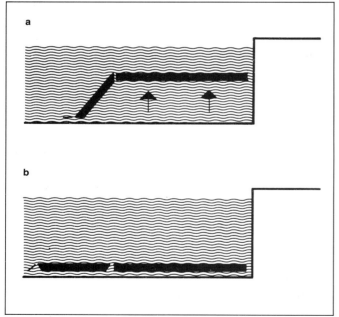

4   Moveable floors typical installation **a** in raised position **b** lowered

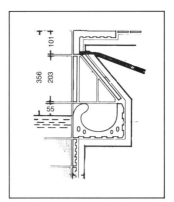

7   Pool edge detail

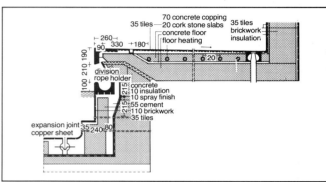

8   Pool edge with Wiesbaden type overflow: resting ledge & gangway in multi-purpose pool

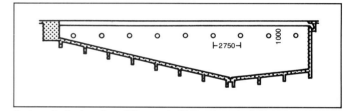

9   Longitudinal section of 25 m pool with 9 underwater lights

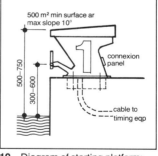

10   Diagram of starting platform: cable to timing eqp only built-in in major pool centres

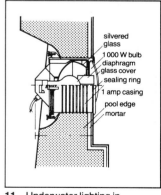

11   Underwater lighting in swimming, diving & multi-purpose pool

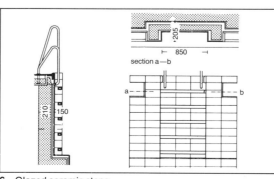

5   Recessed shaped steps

6   Glazed ceramic steps

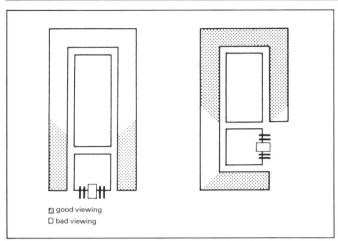

good viewing
bad viewing

1 Viewing conditions for end & side position diving boards

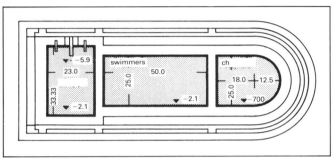

2 D'Albaro open air b at Genoa Italy

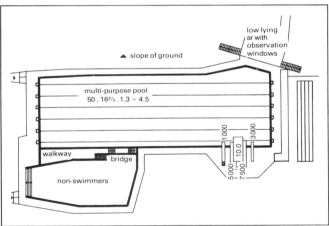

3 Layout of alpine b Gloggnitz Austria

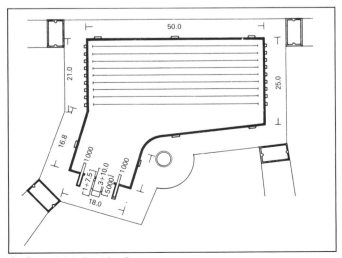

4 Open air b in Frankfurt Germany

OPEN AIR POOLS

Location: sunny, not down wind of industrial plants, nuisance from smoke or noise.

Season: depends on climate. For NW Europe:
100–120 visits/year, of which
40–60 busy days, of which
10–15 peak days

Per head of population (depending on climate):
1.5–3 visits/year.
1–2 m² overall site area
0.1–0.2 m² water area

Per visitor 0.6–1 m² water area

Changing rm for 5–8% of population

Non-swimmers pool: separate in large installations; depth 800–1 250; easy-grip steps for sitting at shallow end; floor surface of pool not too slippery.

Paddling pool: access by gently falling ramp; free shape; depth 100–400; floor surface of pool not too slippery.

Water chute: →p337(5)

Pool construction: dense vibrated concrete or RC; inside finish frost resistant tiles, paint (epoxy resin or other).

Expansion joints depending on construction

Steps (a) corrosion resistant metal in 600–1000 wide recesses (b) special shaped ceramic glazed units built in →p332.
Distance apart of steps ≤ 10 m; distance from diving tower ≤ 8000

Starting platforms: →p332

Guide line: vertical below starting platforms.

Diving line: on pool floor, 250–300 wide.

Walk-through pool: 3 000 × 4 000–4 000 × 6 000; depth 300–400 with overflow.

Walkway round pool: ≥ 2 000; ≥ 5 600 near diving stages and pool access.

Water circulation: 6 hr turnover when bathing load infrequent; 3 hr turnover when load heavy. Water cleaning →p337.

Ancillaries:
entrance with cash desk, centrally situated
laundry issue & sto
swimming instructors' rm
first aid rm (or doctor's rm)
staff rm, separate for men & women
eqp, swimming & sports gear, deckchairs etc, possibly with issuing counter
changing rm, separate for men & women (communal changing rm, changing cubicles, separate rm for clubs & schools); family change
wc sited conveniently to changing rm & pool
pre-cleanse showers hand & foot wash basins
plant rm: water circulation & purification; boilers
telephone, loudspeaker & clock systems with signal device
adequate parking space
admin off

Showers, lavatories →p335; changing rm →p336

Desirable: roofed rest rm, sales rm, manager's flat, broadcasting system.

Garden swimming pools →p114

Sport: swimming

DIVING POOL DIMENSIONS

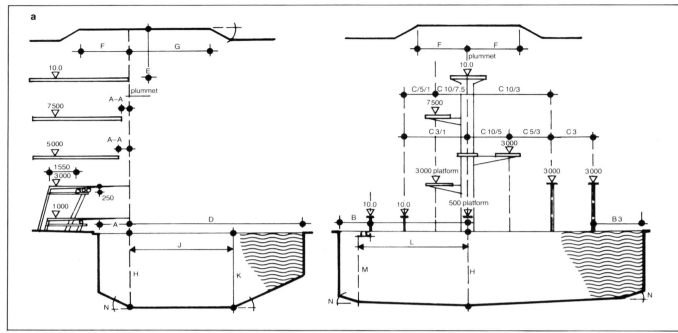

a

1 Fédération Internationale de Natation Amateur (FINA) international standards of diving: diagrams **a** longitudinal section **b** cross section

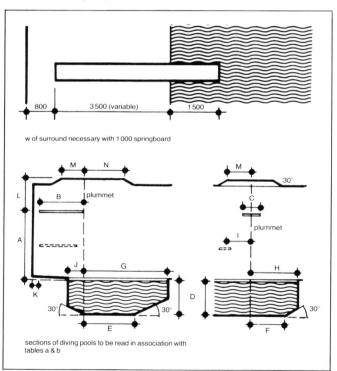

w of surround necessary with 1 000 springboard

sections of diving pools to be read in association with tables a & b

2 Standards for diving boards approved by Amateur Swimming Association (UK) table **a** competitive diving table **b** recreational diving (from boards)

a

		springboards		fixed boards		
A	board h from water	1 m	3 m	5 m	7.5 m	10 m
B	board l	4.8	4.8	5.0	6.0	6.0
C	board w	0.5	0.5	2.0	2.0	2.0
D	d of water at plummet	3.0	3.5	3.8	4.1	4.5
E	distance d D maintained forward	5.3	6.0	6.0	8.0	10.5
F	distance d D maintained to sides	2.2	2.7	3.0	3.0	3.0
G	clearance forward	7.5	9.0	10.25	11.0	13.5
H	clearance to sides	2.5	3.5	3.8	4.5	4.5
I	distance to adjacent board	2.5	2.5	2.5	2.5	2.5
J	clearance behind	1.5	1.5	1.25	1.5	1.5
L	clearance overhead	4.6	4.6	3.0	3.2	3.4
M	clearance overhead maintained to sides	2.75	2.75	2.75	2.75	2.75
N	clearance overhead maintained forward	5.0	5.0	5.0	5.0	6.0

Notes: 1 table incorporates latest dimensions recommended by ASA; includes column of dimensions for 7 500 platform h (considered useful for high board training) 2 ± 100 tolerance permissible on nominal board h: all dimensions should relate to central point at front end of diving board(s) 3 platform thickness should not be ≤ 200 at its front 4 designers should consider current standards specified by FINA if pool to be used for national/international standard events; recommended that diving pool be separate from main pool: where not possible board h of springboard should be confined to 1 000 and when in use ar concerned should be roped off to avoid swimmers causing safety hazard

b

A	board h from water	1 m	1 m	2 m	2 m	3 m	3 m	5 m
B	board l	0.75	1.75	0.75	1.75	0.75	1.75	5.0
C	board w	0.75	0.75	0.75	0.75	0.75	0.75	2.0
D	d of water at plummet	2.6	2.6	3.0	3.0	3.25	3.25	3.8
E	distance d D maintained forward	3.0	4.0	3.0	4.0	3.5	4.5	6.0
F	distance d D maintained to sides	2.2	2.2	2.4	2.4	2.6	2.6	3.0
G	clearance forward	4.5	5.5	5.5	6.5	6.5	7.5	10.25
H	clearance to sides	2.5	2.5	3.0	3.0	3.5	3.5	3.8
I	distance to adjacent board	2.5	2.5	2.5	2.5	2.5	2.5	2.5
J	clearance behind	1.25	1.25	1.25	1.25	1.25	1.25	1.25
K	clearance behind board to wall	0.8	0.8	0.8	0.8	0.8	0.8	0.8
L	clearance overhead	3.0	3.0	3.0	3.0	3.0	3.0	3.0

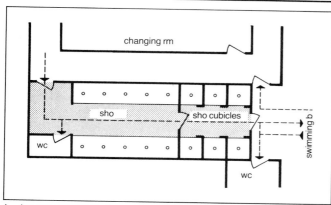

1 Arrangement of sho & wc with circulation routes

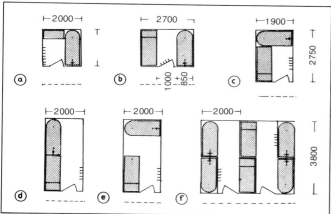

2 3 Sho passage section & plan

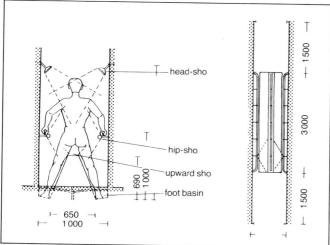

4 Cubicle sizes

5 Standard Finnish sauna stove with boiler (also suitable for washing clothes)

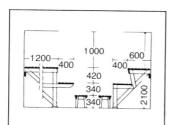

6 Bench types for steam b according to Finnish standards: l 2 000; steps & benches of wooden battens nailed from below so that body does not touch hot nail heads

SLIPPER BATHS, SHOWERS

Slipper baths: in separate units; number approx 0.1 × pool size (m²); sizes according to demand and number of visitors →(4); space required →(8).

Centre passage width 3 000.

Side passage width 1 600.

Clothes hooks inside on free wall or inside door.

Window cill above bath ≥ 1 300 above floor level.

Washable walls ≥1 800 above floor level.

Hard finish on solid floor with drainage; all corners and skirtings coved; all metal parts heavily galvanised; all timber painted 3 undercoats and 1 finishing coat.

Steam baths: individual cubicles, box baths or shared baths (steam baths), separate for men and women, or used at different times. Separate rest rm 22°C, massage rm 30°, sho rm 25° with warm bath 22° and cold bath 10°. Shapes of benches for lying on →(6).

Turkish bath →(7): warm air rm 45–50°C, hot air rm 55–60° and sweat rm 65–70°, adjoining rest, sho and massage rm as above. Outer walls double with heated air cavity; ceiling slopes towards outside to drain off condensation. All fittings rustproof. Windows with treble glazing. El fittings water tight.

Saunas →(5)(6) →p117 338

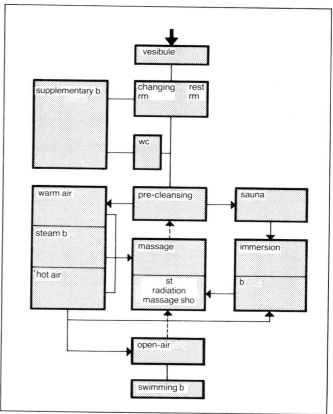

7 Functional analysis of health b

bathr layout →(4)	− vesitibule mm²	+ vestibule (1 000) mm²
a b & bench	3 800	5 600
b b & couch	5 120	7 800
c b as above	5 220	7 120
d–e as above	7 600	9 600
f as above	7 600	9 600

8 Space needed for bath cubicles →(4)

Sport: swimming

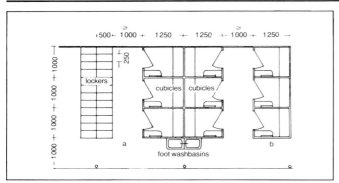

1 Cubicles without separate shod & barefoot passages: **a** interchangeable with locker **b** individual

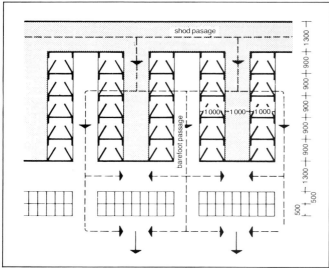

2 Interchangeable cubicles with lockers

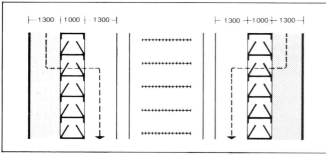

3 Interchangeable cubicles with central attended clo

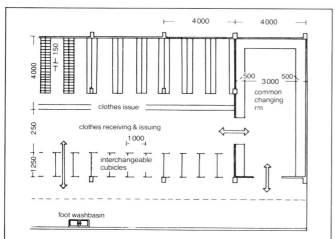

4 Interchangeable cubicles & common changing rm with central supervised clo

POOL CHANGING ROOMS

Individual cubicles →(1b): 1/visitor; size 1 000 × 1 000–1 200; gross area of changing rm/cubicle 3–4 m².

Cubicles to be used in turn: (a) with locker →(1a)(2) 3–4 lockers/ cubicle; (b) with supervised central clo →(3)(4); size and area as for individual cubicle; desirable ratio approx 53%. (Very economical: if few visitors cubicles can be used singly.)

Bath cubicles →p335(4)(8)

Common changing rooms: (a) with central handing-in clo →(4); space required/place 0.5–0.8 m²; (b) with locker →(5b); space requirement as (a) + locker area, 3–4 lockers/seat; locker size: 300 × 500– 400 × 600 desirable ratio approx 26%; (c) without locker, with clothes hooks →(5a); for groups supervision desirable; space requirement as (a); desirable ratio approx 14%.

Height of changing rm ≥ 2 800.

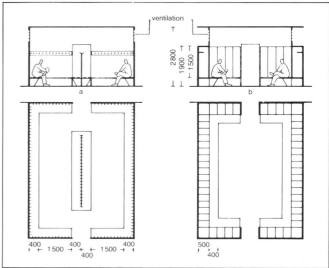

5 Common changing rm: **a** with clothes hooks **b** with lockers

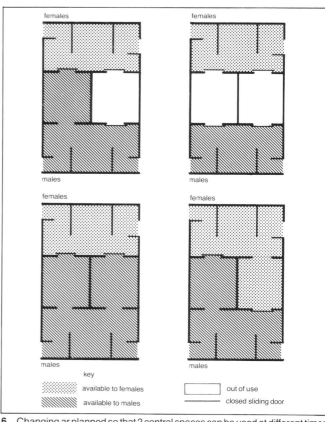

key

available to females   out of use
available to males   closed sliding door

6 Changing ar planned so that 2 central spaces can be used at different times by either sex

Sport: swimming

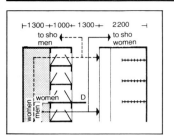

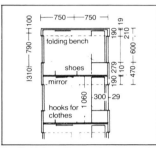

1   Cubicle with supervised clo; interchangeable cubicles for men & women; indicator board D can be switched according to demand

2   Coat stands for interchangeable cubicle clo

3   Cubicles with proprietary panels in baths at Nordeney Germany

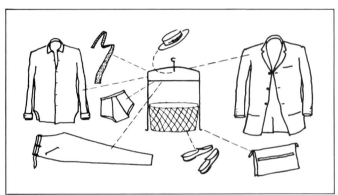

4   Basket coathanger with shoebag for interchangeable cubicles

capacity/hr m³	ar of filter rm m²	clear h of filter rm m
20–40	20–30	3.5
60	40	3.5
80–100	50	3.5
150–200	60	3.5
250	65	3.5
300	70	3.5
400	80	4.5

6   Space required for filter installation; for open air add 50%

POOL CHANGING ROOMS (cont)

For public bldg essential find most economic staffing solution. Division of interchangeable sections by sex can be varied by use of sliding partitions →p336(6) or by switching notice boards.

Av visitors 60–70% men 30–40% women

Clothes sto: individual lockers or attendant supervised basket →(4) sto →p336(3)(4).

Space requirements →(2)(3):

500 bench/adult

400 bench/child

bench h 375; bench w 300

In open-air baths per changing rm 40 users per section or area 20 coat hooks on run of board for coat hooks 3000.

Ratio of total changing/clothes sto space per user approx 1.75 m².

Cubicles and clothes stand of timber or corrosion resistant metal with proprietary panels →(3).

Include changing needs of disabled users: 2000 × 2000 cubicle.

WATER CLEANING

Purification, flocculation and disinfection of swimming pool water: hygienically essential turnover period for indoor public pools:
swimming pool 3 hr
learner pool ½ hr
diving pool 6 hr

Purification of river, surface and pool water chemically by flocculation of organic substances to induce coagulation followed by filtration. Filter rm sizes →(6).
Disinfection usually by chlorination.

In asymmetrical pools arrange outlets so that complete through flow possible and no water can stagnate in corners. For cleaning pool floor, specially in open-air pools, remove sediment with brushes and suction sediment pump.

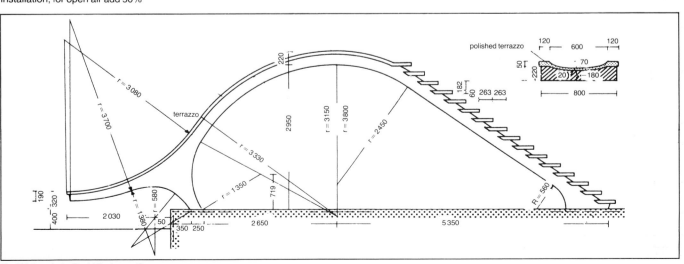

5   Water chute Bad Kissingen Germany

Sport

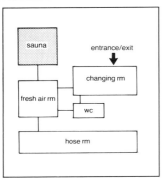

1 Private sauna diagram

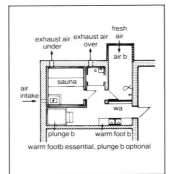

warm footb essential, plunge b optional

2 Domestic sauna →p117

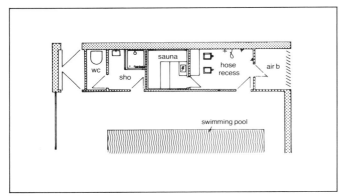

3 Sauna in swimming ha

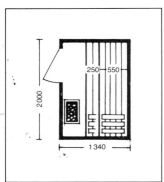

4 Plan 1–3 P

5 2–4 P

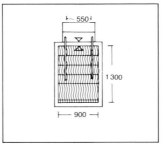

6 3–5 P

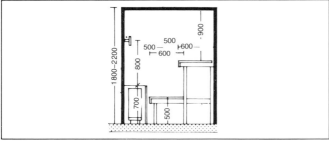

7 Sauna for 1–3 P: section

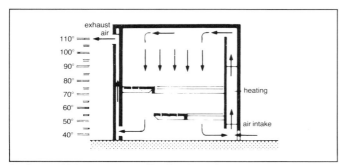

8 Sauna with indirect heating (Bemberg): section

SAUNA PLANNING

Domestic saunas →p117

Bathing time: 3 × 8–12 minute sessions, total for 1 bath 120 minutes. Rm for cooling (sho, hose, plunge) →(2)(3)(9)(10) and air bath →(3)(12). Natural cold water pleasanter: lake or sea inlet (or snow).

Air bath: breathing in fresh cool air as offset to hot air, cooling down body. Provide protection against peeping; seating; water cooling by hose without rose or/and plunge of approx 1 000 m³. Warm footb with seating required.

Changing area: cubicles (or open) for twice number of visitors at peak times →(13); also ancillary rest and massage rm →(12) for approx 30 visitors, 2 massage points; 1 rest rm for ⅓ bathers apart from staff.

Room temp: undressing 20–22°C; pre-cleanse ≥ 24–26°; cooling (cold water) rm ≤ 18–20°; massage rm 20–22°.

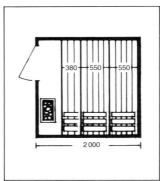

9 Plunge b

10 Section →(9)

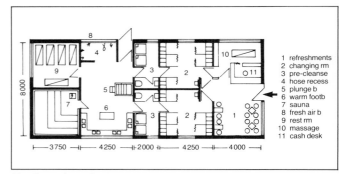

11 Public sauna suite Ashton-under-Lyne pool England Arch Technical Unit for Sport

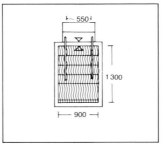

12 Sauna for 30 P: plan

1 refreshments
2 changing rm
3 pre-cleanse
4 hose recess
5 plunge b
6 warm footb
7 sauna
8 fresh air b
9 rest rm
10 massage
11 cash desk

A/P		rm sizes *eg* for 30 P	
changing rm	0.8–1.0 m²/P	changing rm	24–30 m²
pre-cleanse & wc	0.3–0.5 m²/P	pre-cleanse	9–15 m²
sauna	0.5–0.6 m²/P	sauna	15–18 m²
cooling rm	1.0–1.5 m²/P	cooling rm	30–45 m²
rest rm	0.3–0.6 m²/P	massage	12–18 m²
		rest rm	9–18 m²
fresh air	≥ 0.5 m²/P		
		lob, lav, corr	99–144 m²
massage	6–8 m²		+21–35 m²
		air b	20–50 m²
		bench	120–179 m²

13 Ar required per P & rm sizes

Sport: tennis

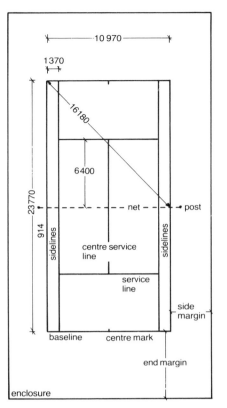

1 Playing space needed for courts of different standards according to requirements of (UK) Lawn Tennis Association

enclosure dimensions relating to standards of play	international & national official championships	county & club recommended	recreational
min end margin	6400	6400	5490
min side margin	3660	3660	3050
min enclosure size for 1 court	36580 × 18290	36580 × 18290	34750 × 17070
w for courts in 1 enclosure		33530	31700
w added for each additional court		15240	14630

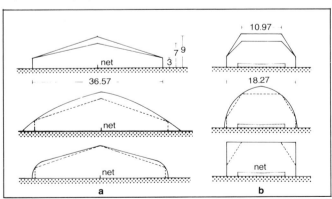

2 Drainage plans for tennis courts

COURT REQUIREMENTS

Playing space needed for court →(1): h of net at centre 915, at posts 1060; netting enclosure h 4000; 2.5 wire 40 mesh. Artificial lighting 10 m h at long sides. Scale of courts to population: regular players av 2% of total; ratio courts/players 1:30 to 1:35 very good, 1:45 or over poor; new courts 1:30. Additional space amounting to 25% of playing space needed for car park, children's play area, paths, bldg etc.

Surface: exceptionally smooth, hard and pervious to rain: must attract very little dust and be dazzle free; materials: grass, cinders, plastics.

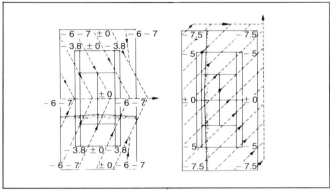

3 Dimensions & shapes for covered courts →(4) sections **a** longitudinal **b** cross

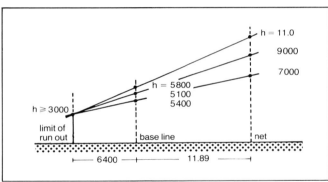

4 Covered court h

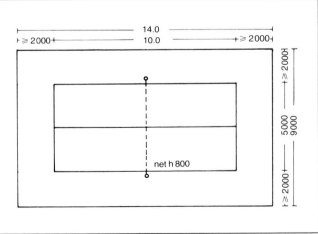

5 Children's court

Sport

SKI JUMPING SLOPES

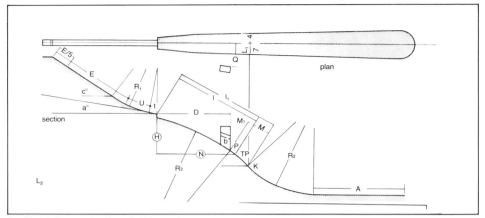

1 Sketch for construction of ski jump slopes

Following symbols should be used:

P   datum point
TP   table point
10K   critical point (end of slowing down section & start of run out slope)
B   end of landing run for vaulting
M   slowing-down section (distance from P to K)
M1   distance from P to B
L   distance from edge of slope to P
L1   distance from edge of slope to K
H   vertical projection of L
N   horizontal projection of L
H:N   ratio of verticals to horizontals
a   slope of platform
b   slope of jump-off track at datum point (P) up to critical point (K)
c   run up slope
R1   radius of bend from run up to platform
R2   radius of bend from jump-off to run out
R3   radius of bend from platform to jump-off track
T   l of platform
U   part of run up in which speed no longer increases
E   part of run up in which speed increases
F   overall l of run up (F = U + E + T)
A   l of run out
Vo   speed at platform edge in m/s
D   horizontal distance from platform edge to lower part of referee's tower
Q   distance from jump off track access to referee's tower front edge

Standards for chief parts of platform:
H:N 0.48–0.56

Datum point of platform can be determined:
P   L1 − M, where standards for M are:
M   0.5–0.8 Vo for platforms up to P = 70 m
M   0.7–1.1 Vo for platforms up to P = 90 m
M1   0–0.2 Vo
R1   0.12 Vo²–0.12 Vo² + 8 m
R2   0.14 Vo²–0.14 Vo⁰ + 20 m
R3   profile selected for front structure which best meets angle of flight
T   0.22 Vo
U   0.02 Vo²   D   0.5–0.7 × L1 to lower edge of tower
A   4–5 Vo on horizontal run out   Q   0.25–0.50 × L1

Distance from parapet of lower referee's cabin of horizontal 'd' beneath edge of platform: D × tg 16°–20°. Cabins should be located stepped along diagonals formed by line from platform edge to end of point 'D'. Upper side of floor of individual cabins lies 1 000–1 200 beneath parapet. Diagonal of tower to access of track should be 7°–10° so that referee can properly observe entire flight and landing.

As many starting points as possible should be located on run up distributed evenly along length E/5 whose distance should amount to about 1 000 vertically. Bottom starting point: E − E/5.

Min width of jump-off track at K: L1/7 + 4 m.

Remarks
All slopes given in old grading (360°). If transfers parabolic, then R1 and R2 smallest curves on those parabolas.

With natural run up, sections mainly used should be marked every 2 000 to help locate starting point precisely. Gradients on platform and several points in curve between run up and platform end should be recorded on both sides by fixed built-in profiles so that even non-experts can determine correct and precise profile when jump being worked.

Profile markings should be applied along jump-off profile both sides down to run-out, allowing exact snow profile to be determined particularly in deep snow. Jumps with L more than 50 m should not normally be built with Vo of less than 21 m/s. Jumps with L over 90 m not approved by Fédération internationale de ski (FIS) (except for aerial ski jumps).

small jumps

E			L									
c	c	c		8–10°		7–9°		6–8°			−a	
30°	25°	40°	U	T	Vo	H:N=0.5	0.48	0.46	0.44	0.42	0.4	0.38	b	l
25	23	21	4.5	3.3	15	20.0	19.5	19.0	18.5	18.0	17.5	17.0	30–34°
32	28	25	5.1	3.5	16	25.5	24.8	24.0	23.3	22.5	21.8	21.0	30–35°
39	32	28	5.8	3.7	17	31.0	30.0	29.0	28.0	27.0	26.0	25.0	33–36°
46	37	32	6.5	4.0	18	36.5	35.3	34.0	32.8	31.5	30.3	29.0	33–36°
52	43	37	7.2	4.2	19	42.0	40.5	39.0	37.5	36.0	34.5	33.0	34–37°
59	49	42	8.0	4.4	20	47.5	45.8	44.0	42.3	40.5	38.8	37.0	34–37°

2 Dimensions small slopes

medium & large jumps

E			L									
c	c	c				9–12°			8–10°		−a	
30°	35°	40°	U	T	Vo	H:N=0.56	0.54	0.52	0.5	0.48	b	l
62	52	44	8.8	4.6	21				53.0	51.0	35–37°
71	58	49	9.7	4.8	22	65.3	63.0	60.8	58.5	56.2	
80	65	54	10.6	5.1	23	71.5	69.0	66.5	64.0	61.5	36–38°
89	72	60	11.4	5.3	24	77.7	75.0	72.2	69.5	66.7	
99	80	67	12.5	5.5	25	84.0	81.0	78.0	75.0	72.0	37–39°
111	90	74	14.0	5.7	26	90.2	87.0	83.7	80.5	77.2	
124	100	81	15.0	5.9	27	96.3	93.0	89.5	86.0	82.5	38–40°
137	110	88	16.0	6.2	28			91.5	87.7		

3 Dimensions larger slopes
Example: according to terrain following data apply to LI & H:N eg H/N = 0.54; c = 35°; L = 87 m; in table you will find L = 87 & in column to left Vo = 26; at some level beneath c = 35°, E = 90 m, U = 14 & T = 5.7; F = E + U + T = 90 + 14 + 5.7 = 109.7 m: ski jump with dimensions differing from above can be approved by FIS but in such cases designer must give written reasons

SKI JUMPING SLOPES

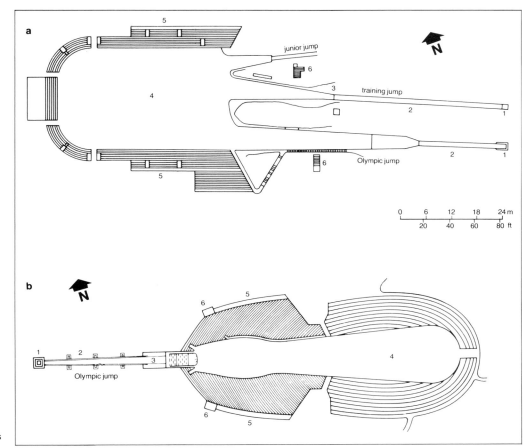

1 Ski jumps at **a** Garmisch-Partenkirchen Germany **b** Holmenkollen Norway: 1 start 2 run up 3 take-off platform 4 run out 5 grandstand 6 umpires' towers

ICE RINKS

Hosed ice rinks in some countries on tennis courts, roller skating rinks and similar large areas (surrounding wall h approx 100–150); water layer 20; drainage for letting out water.

Artificial ice rinks with refrigeration system 25 below screed. Pump system with deep freeze salt solution or cold air chambers (usually ammonia compression method) →(3)–(5). Sometimes combination of roller skating rink summer (Mar–Nov) and ice rink winter (Dec–Feb). Refrigeration system 25–50 below top of rink surface (not possible on terrazzo).

Standard race track: l 300 m, 333.3 m, standard 400 m: measured 500 in from edge of track →(2). In double track system each track w ≥ 3 000 ≤ 5 000. Ice hockey →p342.

Bobsleigh runs with pronounced camber made of ice blocks at curves. Spectators preferably on inside curves, otherwise protective mounds of snow or straw bales.

Toboggan runs situated on N-NW-NE slopes, preferably in hollow: l 1 500–2 500 m; incline 15–25% w ≥ 2 000. Flat finish or rise in opposite direction, camber at curves, obstacles protected with straw bales or snow mounds. Walk-up alongside not on run.

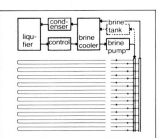

2 Standard race track 400 m l

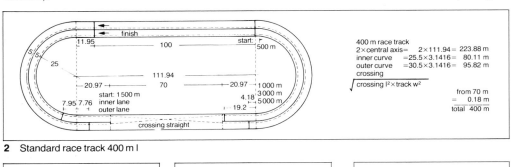

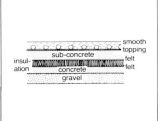

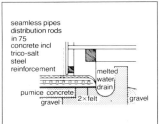

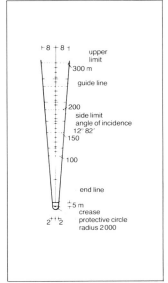

3 Artificial ice rink: layout of refrigeration system (brine)

4 Detail of surface pipes

5 Detail of embedded pipes

6 Long curling ground

Sport

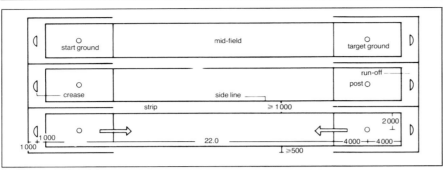

1 German curling rink

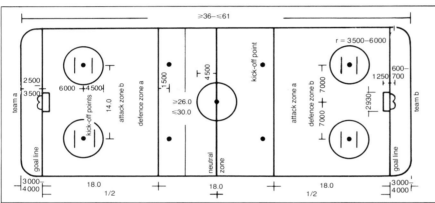

2 Scottish curling rink

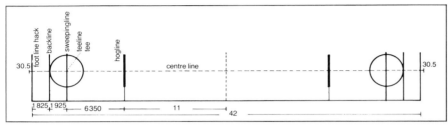

3 Ice hockey

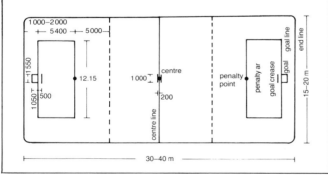

4 Roller skating hockey

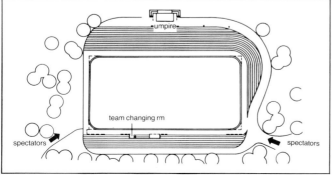

5 Artificial ice & roller skating track

ICE RINKS (cont)

Curling →(1): ground l 42 m; w 4000 (30 × 3000 also possible); intermediate tracks (strips) 1 m; pitch ends ≥ 600. Starting and aiming areas surrounded with easily crossed wooden barrier on 3 sides.

Scottish curling →(2): field l 42 m; target area (tee) ∅ 3650. To centre point of tee 38.35 m. If ice poor, reduce to 29.26 m. Curling stone: weight ≤ 19.958 kg, circumference ≤ 914, h ≥ ¹/₈ of circumference.

Ice hockey →(3): ground ≥ 26 × 56 m, ≤ 30 × 61 m. Goal 1830 w, 1220 h; may be played around back. Pitch requires wooden barrier 1200 h →(3).

Figure skating: rectangular rink ≥ 26 × 53 m ≤ 30 × 60 m. Combination of roller skating rink in summer (Mar–Nov) and ice rink in winter (Dec–Feb). Cold pipe system 25–50 beneath track surface →p341(5).

ROLLER SKATING RINKS

1 Sports tracks
   roller skating hockey →(4)15 × 30–
                                    20 × 40 m
   figure skating   25 × 50 m
2 Play tracks   10 × 10–
                          20 × 20 m.

Impact board 250 h, 30 above track, 800 parapet along all sides, 2000 chain-link grid at narrow end (to catch ball), surrounding walking areas 1200; 50–100 deeper. Joints ≤ 5–6, slope ≤ 0.2%. Surface water in gutters or ditches, frost protection layer ≥ 200 →(4).

Construction

Asbestos cement panels 15; laid on squared timber or on sand bed. Concrete tracks, 100–150 according to type of bed, jointless if possible, but imitation joints may be incised 2–3 wide. Space joints every 25–30 m, gap width ≥ 15.

Hard concrete screed, ≥ 8 on fresh concrete base (20 mortar if possible to take up stress between screed and concrete base).

Cement screed with additives 1–10.

Terrazzo, polished, ≥ 15, joint rails of brass, metal alloy or plastics, only for indoor tracks.

Cast asphalt tracks on fixed base, as normal.

Sport: golf

SITE

Courses generally cover between 40 and 60 ha. Most popular those among sand dunes or on heath land, neither hilly nor flat. Well-drained arable land generally suitable; in UK government grants may enable more expensive works be considered if derelict or tipped land reclaimed.

Golf holes need proper safety margin: should not pass close roads or through narrow tongues between houses.

LAYOUT →(1)

Normally 18 holes: often prudent start with 9 holes while providing future extension.

Site round club house 1st and 10th tee, 9th and 18th green (preferably in full view), putting green, practice ground, car parks, members entrance and service access. If professional's shop separate, place on way to first tee.

Area dictates total length absolutely; contour, natural features and obstacles affect it marginally.

Expect about 5 300 m from 40 ha
6 220 m from 60 ha

Par is rating of av professional performance and yardstick by which measure skill, errors and course difficulty: applied to each hole and totalled for 18 →(2).

Tees

May be combined on av length course but may be separated into championship, medal, club, ladies at progressively shorter distances. Allow 300 m² (400 m² at par 3 holes).

Greens →(4)

Size to suit approach shot and need to spread wear by changing holes: say 400 m² to 600 m².

Fairways

Width normally 30–40 m. Start 100 m from men's tee. Playing width/hole: 60 m (90 m on boundaries).

Rough

Carry rough: tee to fairway

Marginal rough: to either side of fairway, generally with mown band of 'semi-rough' of approx 10 m before trees, shrubs etc.

Bunkers

Sand areas averaging perhaps 100 m² but of all shapes and sizes. To influence play determine optimum line, provide options and penalise mistakes.

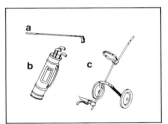

3   a golf club **b** golf bag
c golf trolley

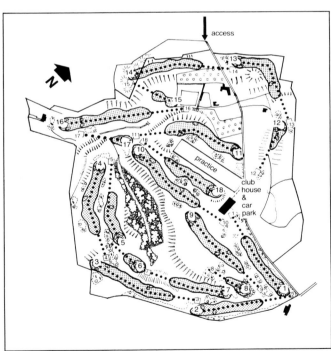

1   Golf course layout (Golf Development Council)

par/hole	usual l m	strokes			par				
		tee	fairway	green	75	72	71	67	67
3	110–192	1	–	2	3	4	5	4	4
4	290–410	1	1	2	9	11	13	12	10
5	440–500	1	2	2	6	3	0	1	4
	av m				6310	5580	5120	5120	6760

2   Par values

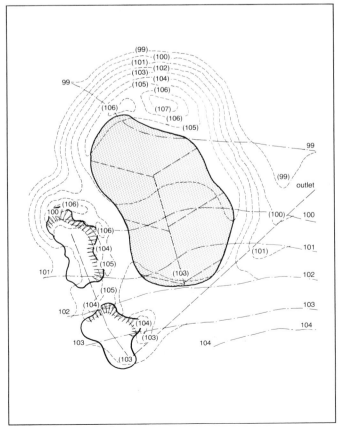

4   Typical green: 59 m²

Sport: equitation

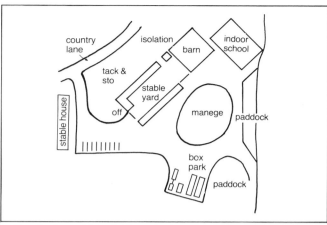

1 Country livery stables & riding school

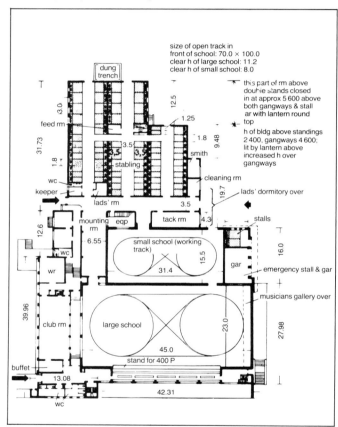

size of open track in
front of school: 70.0 × 100.0
clear h of large school: 11.2
clear h of small school: 8.0

this part of rm above
double stands closed
in at approx 5 600 above
both gangways & stall
ar with lantern round
top

h of bldg above standings
2 400, gangways 4 600;
lit by lantern above
increased h over
gangways

dung
trench

feed rm

stabling

smith

wc

keeper

lads' rm

cleaning rm

lads' dormitory over

mounting
rm

eqp

tack rm

stalls

wc

wr

small school (working
track)

gar

emergency stall & gar

musicians gallery over

club rm

large school

buffet

stand for 400 P

wc

2 Riding grounds Essen-Stadtwald Germany   Arch J Fischer

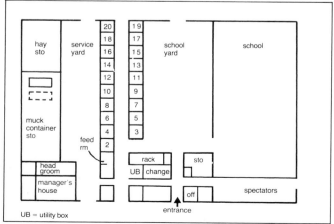

3 Plan of Lea Bridge riding school London Lee Valley Regional Park
Authority   J M V Bishop M G Quinton

UB = utility box

INDOOR SCHOOLS

Location
Preferably at town edges directly connected by bridlepath to woodland, pasture, heath-land or other hacking-out →(1).

In past riding schools usually grew round existing bldg, *eg* adding to stables of old house, building asbestos-clad barn structure over riding area to provide all-weather teaching.

Siting & access
Essential requirements for any site:
good access for heavy vehicles as well as cars
access to open country and/or bridlepaths
adequate el supply
adequate water supply, possibly including fire hydrants
loose boxes should be protected from prevailing winds
low-lying sites which catch water and are usually frosty in winter to be avoided
stable smells sited away from adjacent houses
turning space for horsebox trailers and for lowering ramps side and rear, with space to load and unload difficult horses; turning space also required for muck lorry →p345(1)(2)
access for fire appliances; requires roads min 3 600 wide capable of supporting pumping appliance laden weight approx 10 t, with min turning circle 17 m dia
min clearance height 3 600, for hay lorries 4 500: all gate openings min width 3 000 clear
space to convert barn or erect purpose-designed indoor school; min land requirement with outdoor installations →p345 4 ha.

Planning & layout
Planning of installations breaks down into 3 main groups: instruction, horse management, admin →p345.

Traditional plan usually arranges loose boxes looking inwards to courtyard with only covered way in front of each box. Later development: totally enclosed loose boxes arranged either side of corridor enabling them to be serviced by tractor and trailor circulating through block →(3): disadvantage extra cost, including extra fire precautions; horses can become bored without outside view. However, better working conditions for stable girls; ventilation can be controlled to eliminate draughts; easier to maintain even temp; quieter conditions can be advantage if site near road or railways.

Other general principles:
preferable school not so near stables that voice of command from instructors can be heard and so disturb horses at rest;
risk of fire in stables necessitates special planning consideration: straw sto requires min 1 hr fr from other parts of bldg, or fire break at least 4 500 recommended.

Consult relevant codes and standards.

Space required
Size of indoor school dictated by ability of fast moving horse turn 10.0–11.0 mØ. Many different standards of covered school. UK National Equestrian Centre has riding area 61 × 24.4 m, large enough contain international size arena and hold dressage and show jumping events, with seating for 300 along 1 side. At other end of scale possible provide suitable area under Dutch barn, of which sides only clad for 3 000 from eaves, with wattle hurdles enclosing floor. Whatever standard of bldg essential indoor riding space be ≥ 42 × 22 m to give 40 × 20 m clear floor space required for elementary dressage, allowing for tilted kicking-board surrounding walls.

w of school floor for single circuit accordingly: 12.0 m
w of school floor for groups: 15.25 preferably 20.117 m
l of school floor ratio 2 : 1 to w *eg* 40.0 : 20.0
l can be increased: 20.0 × 60.0–80.0
military school: 18.29 × 54.86 m
h of bldg: 4 000–5 000

Information based on requirements of British Horse Society (BHS), British Show Jumping Association (BSJA) and Fédération d'Equitation Internationale (FEI)

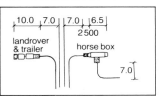

1 Clearance required for manoeuvring horses into trailer or box

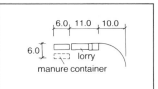

2 Clearance required for manoeuvring large container truck

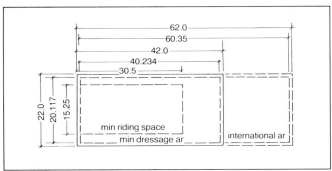

3 Riding school ar: min h needed for jumping 4 000, ≥ 5 000 preferable; door w 2 300 in twin sliders; if spectator seating needed will be additional to riding ar; judges box & collection/mounting ar also needed

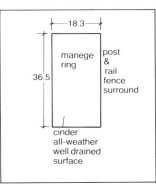

4 Manege ring

5 Indoor show jumping arena with collecting ring, warm-up & practice jump space: for mounting/collecting ar allow for 20–30 horses at 3.5–5 m² each

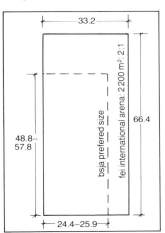

a

b

c

6 Typical layout for loose box: min internal dimensions ponies 3 000 × 3 000, horses below 16 hands high 3 000 × 3 500, horses above 16 hh 3 500 × 4 000; recommended h approx 3 000–4 000; if internal corr needed min w 3 000 recommended for use by servicing vehicles & as means of fire escape; stalls min l 2 700, min w 1 800; min passage between stalls 1 800 **a** section **b** elevation **c** plan

RIDING CENTRE PREMISES

Vehicle and loading areas →(1)(2)

Instructional: indoor school and areas →(3)(4); outdoor manege →(5); grass paddocks (min 8 000 m²); outdoor show jumping ring; outdoor dressage area; cross country training area; club rm/lecture rm/canteen; sto for jumps, cavaletti etc (approx 5% activity area).

Horse management: stables (loose boxes →(6) and stalls); utility box: grooming, clipping, shoeing, washing, treatment of cuts etc (size as loose box but without fittings except tie rings); sick box (approx 3 500 × 4 500): should be away from other boxes but within sight of other horses; door should be in 2 leaves for horse to look out or be enclosed if requires complete quiet; sling suspended from beam with block and chain may be needed: 1 250 kg max loading (for heavy draught horse); larger establishments may need completely isolated box for infectious diseases.

Feed sto →(7), feed rm, tack rm →(8)(9), tool sto; hay and straw sto: Dutch-barn type structure; size depends on number of horses and method of buying: year's supply of hay most economic way to buy as price rises steeply during winter; straw price not affected so much therefore sto less critical. Data to determine size required: for 1 horse approx 9 kg hay/day, ½ bale straw/day; weight: 1 bale hay approx 23 kg, 1 bale straw approx 18 kg; bale size approx 900 × 450 × 450: approx 10% extra volume should be allowed on total sto required for air circulation and remaining stock when new load arrives.

Muck sto: traditionally open bunkers with brick or block walls on 4 sides with opening approx 900 wide on 1 side: concrete floor should drain towards this opening with gully outside. Size depends on number of horses and management. Allow approx 5.6 m³/horse/week. After month volume reduced approx two-thirds. Skip-type containers recommended: various sizes depending on number of horses and frequency of removal.

Veterinary sto: bandages may be kept in cupboards or pigeon-hole racks. Leg bandage measures 127 wide and approx 75 dia. Medicines and poisons should be kept in separate cupboards and clearly labelled.

Smithy: possibly 10–15 m² in large centres otherwise space to park mobile blacksmith.

Administration; reception off; manager's off; staff rm; first aid rm; lavatories; changing rm; garaging for horse boxes, tractors and trailers; resident accn for manager; resident accn for grooms and/or stable girls; plant rm (boilers, el switchgear etc); workshop.

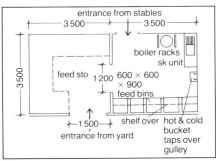

7 Feed sto: size depends on number of horses & method of buying feed (sacks or bulk); each bin capable of holding 101 kg oats, 76 kg bran, 178 kg cubes

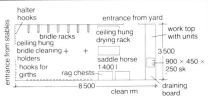

8 Plan of typical tack & clean rm; in larger establishments separate cleaning rm desirable; BHS recommends 1 track rm/15 horses; value of tack requires rm specially secure from burglars (barred windows etc)

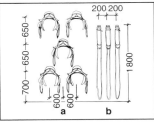

9 Eqp stored in tack rm includes: saddles on racks **a** not lower than 700 from floor nor higher than 1 800, 600 centres; stirrups & leathers; bridles on racks **b** 1 600 above floor; head collars, girths on hooks ≥ 1 800 above floor; blankets, rugs, sheets usually stored in galvanised steel chests (may be kept in general sto)

Sport: marinas

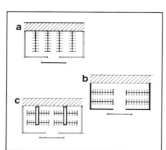

1 Land to water relationship: **a** land-locked **b** built-in **c** semi-recessed **d** offshore **e** island

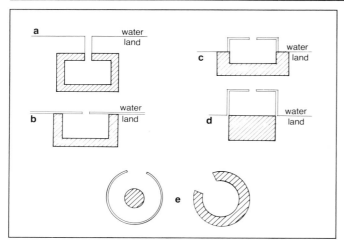

2 Energy-absorbing slopes inside Hantsholm harbour Denmark

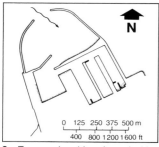

3 Pontoon layouts: **a** stretching from land **b** stretching from breakwaters **c** stretching from floating elements

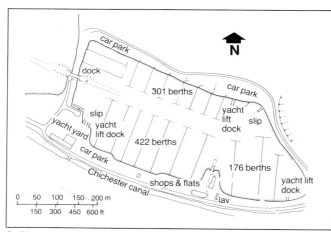

4 Yacht basin Chichester England: land locked, 1 000 berths

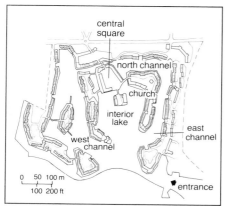

5 Marina Port Grimaud France built on reclaimed marshland: 900 flats each with berth

DEFINITION

Marina's main role provide shelter from wind, waves and swell of passing craft; access to moorings at all states of tide with space for manoeuvre; tieing-up points for boats with services, *eg* water, el, telephone, television, refuse collection, fire fighting, sanitation, public address system; sanitary needs and amenities for yachtsmen, *eg* wc, sho, changing and drying rm, entertaining, sporting activities, shopping; car parking; eqp for launching, lifting, manoeuvring, repairing, maintaining boats; other bldg directly related to boating.

TYPES OF DEVELOPMENT

Land to water relationship →(1): land locked →(4), built-in →(5), semi-recessed, offshore, island (constructed in open water: special case).

Tidal situation:

non-tidal: variations of water level ≤ 1 000; usually easy for people and trolleys and simple connexions between onshore and offshore service systems;

tidal: substantial changes of water level; difficult connexion between pontoons and land for people and services; construction difficulties almost inevitable.

Site selection factors: legal problems; transport systems; potential for future extension; construction options and methods; geological, hydraulic, climatic; soil and sub-soil; orientation, physical features, erosion, possibility of flooding; engineering network on shore; materials stability; tides, currents, navigational requirements; pollution control; labour sources; effect of marina on existing environment during construction period and after completion.

OFFSHORE BOAT HARBOUR COMPONENTS

Area needed: craft sizes vary: l 4.8–21.3 m (USA 4.3–24.4 m), beam 1.8–6.0 m (USA 2–6 m); areas of water calculated on basis of planned number and size of craft moored, pontoon layout, types of berth.

Depth of water: min 600 (USA 610) plus max draft of vessel at lowest astronomical tide, 300 reserved for stilting, 300 for clearance. If too shallow at lowest tide dredging necessary.

Channel: leading to entrance ≥ 20–30 m wide; main channel within harbour area depends on number and sizes of craft passing through at any 1 time, min w 18 m.

Entrance: protection required from ingress (wave energy to be absorbed before choppy conditions arise in yacht basin) →(2); suitable protection: spending beaches, rocks or concrete blocks moulded to appropriate shapes, piles.

Pontoon layouts: well selected layout very important; main choice limited to pontoons stretching from a land, b breakwaters, c floating elements →(3).

Berth types →(6): a stern to quay, jetty or pontoon bows to piles (poor for embarking); b same but bows moored to anchors or buoys (not for tidal marinas); c alongside finger piers or catwalks, 1 craft each side (convenient for embarking); d alongside quays, jetties or pontoons, single banked; e same up to 3 or 4 abreast (disadvantage of yachtsmen on outer climbing over inner craft); f star finger.

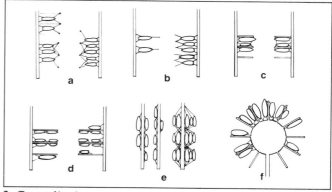

6 Types of berth

Sport: marinas

COMPONENTS (cont)

Locks: often have more than 1 compartment; should maintain constant water level on 1 side, other side varying with tide; capacity decided by peak use; waiting pontoons either side lock recommended.

Pontoon design: often used to carry services and to support lighting units, lockers, refuse collection points, fire fighting devices; service bollards often provided: boats/bollard 2–6; sewage collection points for boats recommended either as holding tanks or as outlets connected with vacuum sewage system leading to onshore network. Min w main access pontoons 2000 with fingers ⩾ 500 wide; if total pier l over 100, 2500 w more appropriate; min w floating pontoon 2500.

Pontoon types: fixed: for non-tidal marinas; fixed deck (timber, aluminium, plastics decking) resting on structural supports (piles most common); service ducts usually under deck;

floating: for tidal marinas or where structural difficulties occur and supports on bed not feasible (eg deep water, geological conditions); deck fixed to floating units and so kept at required level above water; floats of steel, plastics, timber, concrete, polystyrene, filled with lightweight material (eg polystyrene) or left hollow; pontoons held in position by dolphins; in exceptional cases may be anchored to bed; connexion to land by hinged bridge, ramps, lifts, hoists, collapsible steps.

Breakwaters: rubble mound: mainly for sites with relatively small tidal variations; alternative concrete blocks moulded to shape: not appropriate for more extensive structures; with relatively shallow slope (1:2 to 1:3) rubble mound occupies large water area otherwise available for craft or other essential uses;

vertical face: concrete walls (constructed in open sea conditions as mass concrete or buttress structures): efficient when built, difficult to construct and maintain;

caisson type: precast concrete cylinders (either hollow or filled with sand) resting on sea bed; circular shaped cusps between units, positive contribution to wave energy absorption;

floating: usually considered for sites with great depth of water and relatively mild conditions; sometimes act as secondary protection or primary barrier, reducing sea impact before waves reach main sea defence.

Fuelling points: considered desirable but not required by authorities (UK); floating tanks not usually accepted. **NB** fire risk prevention at points of flexible connexions between tanks and floating pumps.

Pollution control: in non-tidal marinas water circulation certainly required but hard to achieve. Sanitary accn for yachtsmen essential (travelling distance ⩽ 100 m); provide refuse disposal units close to craft as possible; pollution culverts may also be needed.

Onshore elements:

car parking: ratio cars: boats 1:1–1:2; not too far from craft for yachtsmen and their eqp;

sanitary accn; recommended min either 1 wc and 1 sho each sex per 20 berths or 1 wc, 1 urinal, 1 hb, 1 sho per 25 men, 1 wc, 1 hb, 1 sho per 25 women (max occupancy of harbour estimated 60%; suggested ratio men to women 2:1);

yacht clubs: floor ar/P 1.0–5.0 m²: club rm, lav, drying rm, bars, restaurants, meeting rm, indoor sports, off, information centre, sleeping accn, caretaker's flat:

hard standing, boat sto, repair shop and other elements related to boat maintenance and handling; should have suitable device for boat lifting and launching and easy connexion to roads; free areas for manoeuvring; fuel tanks often sited close to boatyards;

ancillaries may include customs, coastguards, lock keepers, insurance brokers, car hire, travel agent off.

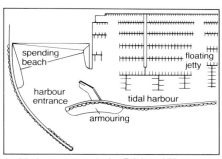

1 Marina entrance design Brighton UK

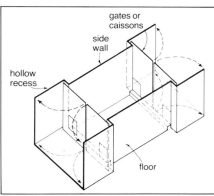

2 Main components of lock

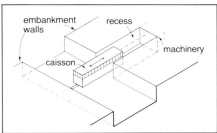

3 Sliding caisson & dock entrance

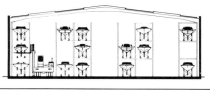

4 Boat sto with hoist

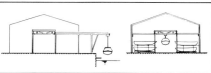

5 Sto for small motor boats

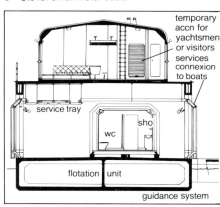

6 Floating jetty with housing superstructure Brighton marina: section

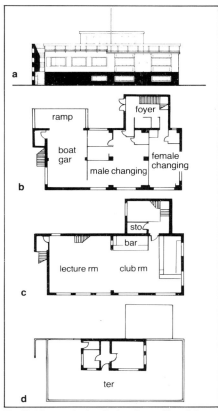

7 Clubhouse design Stokes Bay sailing club Gosport UK: **a** W elevation **b** ground floor **c** first floor **d** second floor

Sport references:
→Bibliography entries 003 006 046 083 183 205 212 297 355 384 388 475 514 515 516 517 537 538 549 585 586 587 588 639

Leisure

Theatres

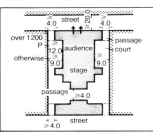

1 Distance to adjoining bldg if theatre ⊥ to street

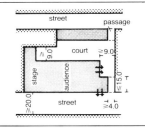

2 Distance if theatre parallel to street

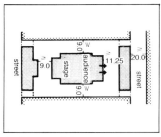

3 Distance if theatre lies between blocks

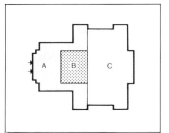

4 Layout of Vienna State Opera

	concert opera	review	cinema
P waiting in booking ha	6%	10%	—
P booking within 20 min before performance	8%	20%	100%
queuing for advance booking	2–15 min	2–15 min	—
ticket control	1 min	1 min	1 min
time, if arriving by car	4–12 min	6–9 min	2–5 min
seating	4 min		
% of P leaving seats at interval	75	50	—
time required for leaving seat to foyer	4 min	4 min	
time in toilet	1 min	6 min	—
time from seat to drive, excluding clo	5 min	6 min	—
waiting for taxis or transport	1–15 min	1–15 min	—

5 Table after Burris-Meyer & Cole (→Bib152) giving % of P & time in min needed reach or leave seats, as measured in USA

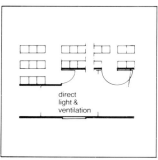

6 Corr w: 1 100 for up to 100 P, 1 600 for up to 250 P

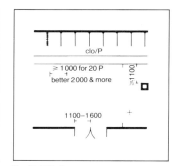

7 Exit & clo

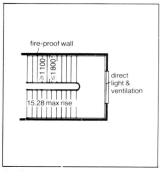

8 Stairs: 1 100 for up to 100 P; 1 600 for up to 250 P; centre handrail required over 1 800 w

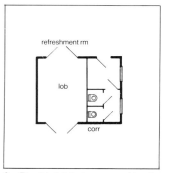

9 Provide lob between smoking & non-smoking ar: doors to open in direction of exit

REGULATIONS

Reg concerning theatre and cinema bldg and schemes not rigid in UK or USA: concern public safety; must be complied with to obtain necessary licence; should be discussed with licensing authority at earliest stage. Principles applicable world wide; main task of architect achieve balance between commercial, artistic and spectator requirements, and design scheme which complies with 'means of escape' and differential detail safety reg.

For consents required in UK in addition to theatre or cinematograph licence →Bib 300 301 328 329 346 347 361 363 591 598 599

For USA → local bldg codes

Organisation

Theatres may be divided into 3 parts →(4):

reception: entrance, booking hall, foyer, cloaks etc
auditorium
stage: main stage, wings, back of stage, scenery sto, workshops, dressing rm, rehearsal rm etc

Parts vary in content and size depending on type of theatre: opera, drama, review or cinema.

Situation: Bldg for public entertainment must be sited allow audience leave area more rapidly than required leave premises. Check requirements at earliest stage.

→(1)(2)(3) for typical dimensions.

Audience arrival times →(5) extend from 15–30 minutes, departures 5–20 minutes.

Car parks →p248–50. Capacities usually determined by planning authority. Site vehicle entrance away from theatre entrance. Include covered area for setting down passengers.

Exits must all open outwards and comply with requirements for numbers and travel distance. General rule for numbers (UK) 1 600 width for 250 visitors or part thereof with min of 2 exits →(6)(7). Ramps not to exceed 10% in UK; can be limited to 5% in continental Europe.

Cloakrooms →(7) Modern systems include self-service lockable coathangers or limited length counters with min number attendants.

Stairs →(8) →p408 Must comply with exit widths requirements. If width more than 1 800 should be designed as double stairs with central handrail, 2 × 1 100 ie 2 200 wide. Risers not exceed 150, treads min 280.

Foyers for theatres can be 100–500 m²/P; for cinemas space required for circulation and exit only, unlikely be more than 100 m²/P.

Toilets in accordance with licensing requirements; also →Bib092.

USA reg for exits, stairs etc vary: example →(10).

	max travel distance within assembly space (m)		capacity (P/unit of w¹)				ramps corr, safe ar, exit passageways
			aisle & cross aisle	from assembly space	doors or openings		
occupancy group classification	primary	secondary			from safe ar	stairs & escalators	
f-1a	26	38	80	50	100	60	80
f-1b	30	38	90	80	125	80	100
f-2	53	76	400	400	500	320	425

¹unit: 560

f-1a: enclosed theatres with stages that may have scenic elements; f-1b: enclosed theatres which prohibit use of scenic elements on or above stage; f-2: outdoor assembly spaces

10 Determination of exit & access requirements: extract from New York City bldg code

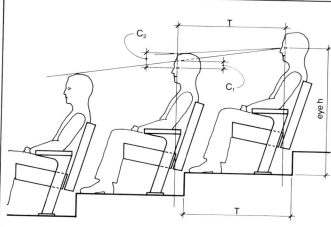

1 Typical seated spectator

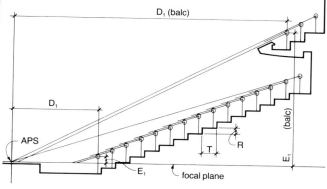

2 Constant rise floor slopes

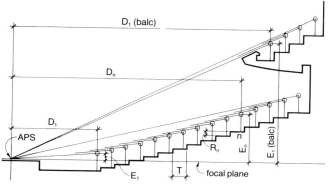

3 Iscidomal floor slopes

SIGHT LINES

Typical seated spectator →(1)
Eye height: 1120 ± 100
Tread of seating tier (row spacing) T: 800–1150
Head clearance C:
$C_1 = 65$: min clearance/row, assuming spectator will see between heads row in front (every-other-row vision)
$C_2 = 130$ allows av spectator see over head av specator in front (every-row vision)
Rise R →(2): difference in height between adjacent seating platforms
Floor slope:
Arrival point of sight (APS) →(2)(3): intersection of highest sightline at focal plane positioned 50 above stage platform
Distance: horizontal distance from eye of seated spectator to APS
D_1 = distance from eye of first row to APS
D_n = distance from eye of given row n to APS
Elevation: vertical height of eye of seated spectator above focal plane
E_1 = vertical height of eye of first row above focal plane
E_n = vertical height of eye of given row n above focal plane
$E_1 = 0$ establishes max stage height allowable, *ie* 1060

Constant rise floor slope →(2): sight lines from rows parallel; APS determined by intersection of sight line from last or highest row at focal plane:

$$R = \frac{T}{D_1}\left[E_1 + (N-1) + C\right] \qquad D_1 = \frac{T}{R-C}\left[E_1 + (N-1)C\right]$$

$$E_1 = \frac{D_1}{T}(R-C) - C(N-1)$$

N = number of rows in seat bank.

Iscidomal floor slope →(3): exponential shape of floor slope results from generation of sight lines from single focal point or APS; iscidomal floor slope makes more efficient use of given total rise:

$$E_n = D_n\left[\frac{E_1}{D_1} + C\left(\frac{1}{D_1} + \frac{1}{D_2} + \frac{1}{D_3} + \ldots + \frac{1}{D_{n-1}}\right)\right] \qquad R_n = E_n = E_{n-1}$$

Type and scale of performance will dictate range of performing area sizes →(4). May be desirable enable performing space accommodate variety of performing area sizes. Containment of audience within 130° angle peripheral spread of vision from performer at point of command will help promote max visual and aural communication between performer and spectator.

Largest performing area should fall within boundary defined by 130° angle of peripheral spread of vision from seats at ends of front rows →(5). Limit of centre of action defined by 60° angle of normal, accurate, polychromatic vision from seats at ends of front rows. Point of command should logically fall within centre of action.

Boundary limit of seating area of auditorium might be defined by given constant angle of peripheral spread of vision to sides of given stage opening. Limits of both 30° and 60° angles of peripheral spread of vision to various openings illustrated →(6).

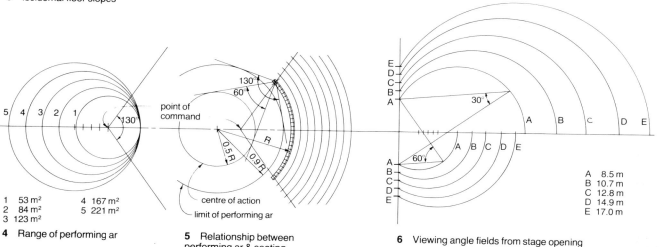

1	53 m²	
2	84 m²	
3	123 m²	
4	167 m²	
5	221 m²	

4 Range of performing ar

5 Relationship between performing ar & seating

6 Viewing angle fields from stage opening

A 8.5 m
B 10.7 m
C 12.8 m
D 14.9 m
E 17.0 m

Theatres

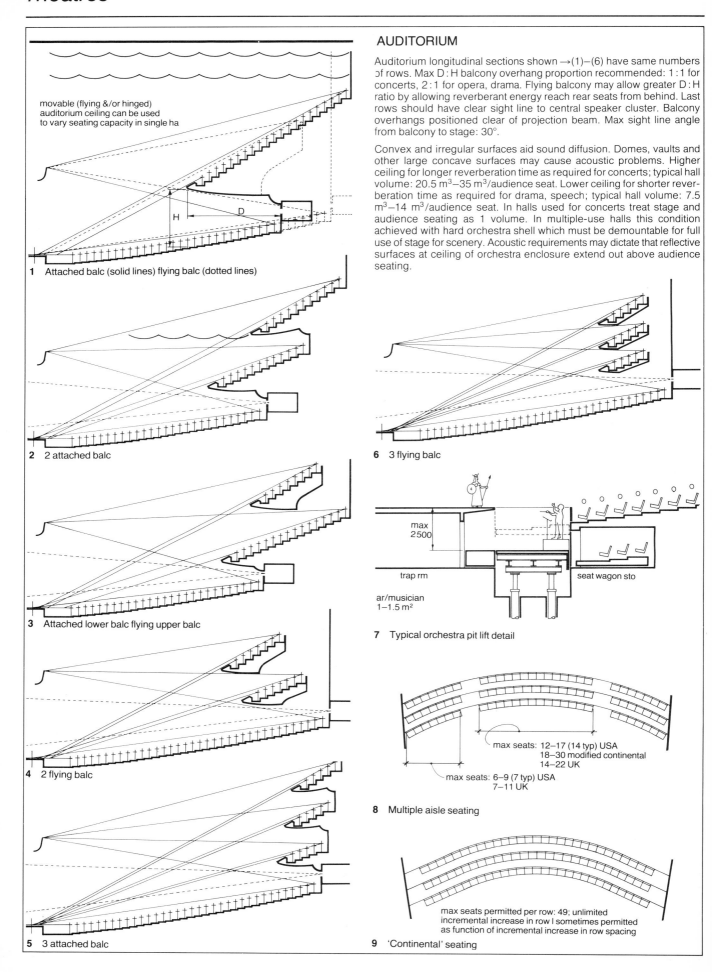

movable (flying &/or hinged)
auditorium ceiling can be used
to vary seating capacity in single ha

1 Attached balc (solid lines) flying balc (dotted lines)

2 2 attached balc

3 Attached lower balc flying upper balc

4 2 flying balc

5 3 attached balc

AUDITORIUM

Auditorium longitudinal sections shown →(1)–(6) have same numbers of rows. Max D : H balcony overhang proportion recommended: 1 : 1 for concerts, 2 : 1 for opera, drama. Flying balcony may allow greater D : H ratio by allowing reverberant energy reach rear seats from behind. Last rows should have clear sight line to central speaker cluster. Balcony overhangs positioned clear of projection beam. Max sight line angle from balcony to stage: 30°.

Convex and irregular surfaces aid sound diffusion. Domes, vaults and other large concave surfaces may cause acoustic problems. Higher ceiling for longer reverberation time as required for concerts; typical hall volume: 20.5 m^3–35 m^3/audience seat. Lower ceiling for shorter reverberation time as required for drama, speech; typical hall volume: 7.5 m^3–14 m^3/audience seat. In halls used for concerts treat stage and audience seating as 1 volume. In multiple-use halls this condition achieved with hard orchestra shell which must be demountable for full use of stage for scenery. Acoustic requirements may dictate that reflective surfaces at ceiling of orchestra enclosure extend out above audience seating.

6 3 flying balc

max
2500

trap rm

seat wagon sto

ar/musician
1–1.5 m^2

7 Typical orchestra pit lift detail

max seats: 12–17 (14 typ) USA
18–30 modified continental
14–22 UK

max seats: 6–9 (7 typ) USA
7–11 UK

8 Multiple aisle seating

max seats permitted per row: 49; unlimited
incremental increase in row l sometimes permitted
as function of incremental increase in row spacing

9 'Continental' seating

Theatres

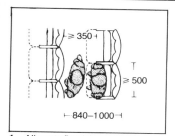

1 All seats fixed tip-up chairs (except in boxes); armchair seating needs 1400 × 750 spaces

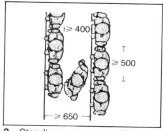

2 Standing room, unusual in modern theatres

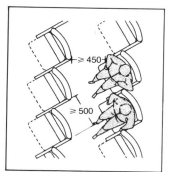

3 Angled tip-up seats give elbow room

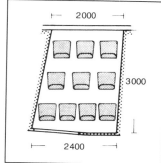

4 Boxes may have 10 chairs & clear way to exit

SEATING

Sizes depend on type of chair and determine chair spacing. Decide on chair style at outset. Traditional chairs require min spacing at 840 and are 500 wide →(1); most common USA dimension 530. Modern chairs vary considerably: can need 1400 spacing and width of 750. Standing space →(2) formerly normal not usual in modern theatres. Seating usually laid out in straight or curved rows; in some theatres angled seating tried →(3). Seating radius centre point best established by trying alternative positions. Short radius enables whole audience face centre of stage but this must be drawn to ensure adequate circulation space at front stalls sides.

BALCONIES

Theatres with 1 balcony (frequent in USA) →(5) can give better sight lines than multiple →p349, reduce staff requirements, simplify exits, increase spectator convenience. Sometimes movable ceiling. Very deep stalls under balcony →(5) tend to limit upward sight line. Multiple auditoria have become common →(7). Containment of sound in each auditorium major problem.

FLEXIBLE SEATING →also p136

Division of auditoria into smaller rm by sliding folding partitions common in conference centres; more difficult in theatres with stepped floors. Consider closing off areas of seating to provide smaller capacity; to provide full flexibility folding seating areas can slide away to expose level floor →p136(4). Loose seating used on flat floor gives very poor sight lines: must have temporary fixing. Sto accn for loose seating must be provided; 1000 folding chairs need 20–36 m² sto space.

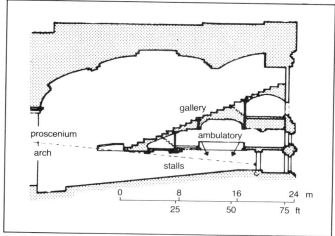

5 Section through auditorium of American 1-balcony theatre with ambulatory & view into rear stalls: equal seat value so standard prices possible

6 Hamilton Place Ontario Canada **a** orchestra floor **b** 1st balcony floor Arch Garwood-Jones

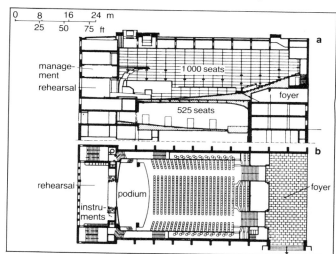

7 Concert ha Helsingborg Finland with 2 ha 1 above other **a** longitudinal section **b** plan of large ha   Arch S Markelius

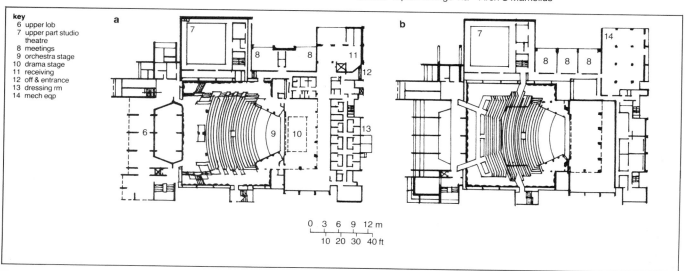

key
6 upper lob
7 upper part studio theatre
8 meetings
9 orchestra stage
10 drama stage
11 receiving
12 off & entrance
13 dressing rm
14 mech eqp

Theatres

	min	normal	max
	m	m	m
drama	8	10	12
review	10	11	14
musical	10	12	15
opera	12	18	25

1 Stage w

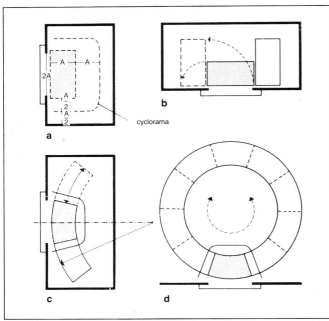

2 Diagrams showing various ways of setting & handling scenery

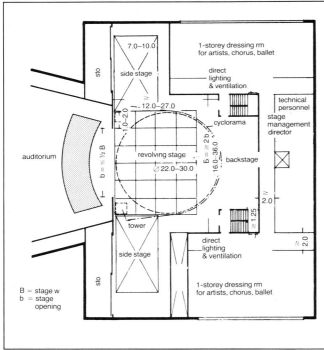

B = stage w
b = stage opening

3 Diagrammatic plan of stage tower with typical dimensions

STAGE TOWER

Dimensions governed by stage machinery, increasingly complex to speed scenery handling and changes. Small stage without side and backstage →(2a). Shifting scenery by hand with trained staff ≥ 3 min; with 'jacknife' trolleys 15 sec →(2b); if side and backstage with traverse trolleys 10 sec →(3).

Revolving stage
Disc with 2–3 sets →(3)
2 discs with contact at stage centre
Reciprocating segments →(2c)
Ring stage with centre upstage →(2d)
Ring stage with centre in house →p353

Stage tower
Width of stage ≥ twice stage opening →(3).
Depth of stage from fire curtain ≥ ¾ stage width, height to rigging loft underside ≥ medium height of auditorium + height of stage opening →(4).
Fireman's rm ≥ 800 wide, 2200 high scenery at each side of stage, with view and exit to stage; escape route also required.
Width of corridor at stage level ≥ 2200, otherwise ≥ 1500. If stage (without side and backstage) larger than 350 m² width of corridors increases by 150/50 m².

Exits from stage areas should be planned provide ready egress from all parts. Include at least 2 exits of which 1 must lead to open air through unventilated lobby. Min widths should comply with reg. Exit requirements from basement and dressing rm areas similar, 1 to be independent of stage area and 1 from dressing rm should also lead direct to open air.

Workshops (locksmith, carpenter, paint shop) connected by fire lobbies to corridors.
Scenery sto at stage level ≥ 10% of stage area.
Height of scenery sto approx 6000–10000.

Rigging loft: space over stage used for hanging scenery and lighting eqp. Between loft and roof construction allow ≥ 2100 head room. Adequate ventilation equal to 10% stage area to be provided by haystack lantern above loft. Varies from code to code USA.

Fire curtain: stage must be separated from auditorium by fire proof curtain of wire-woven asbestos cloth stretched between top and bottom steel pipes, asbestos plates fixed to fire proof steel frame or sheet metal fixed to fire proof steel frame. Hand release to operate fire curtain and drencher system over. Both automatic and hand release usually required in USA.

Curtain must be in 1 piece; should move vertically and should close completely in 30 seconds.

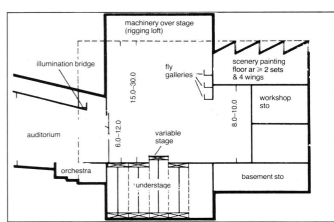

4 Diagrammatic section of stage tower with typical dimensions

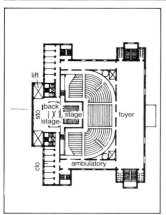

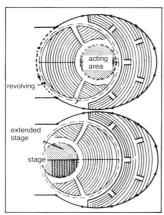

1 Arena stage: ground floor plan
Arch Kreislinger & Rosenbaum

2 'Total theatre' with revolving centre: plan shows both positions: after Gropius

MULTI-FORM THEATRE

Ring stage with centre in house →(1)–(5) Aims at intimate connexion of audience and actor; brings play amongst audience in contrast to 'peep-show' stage. These methods call for modern stagecraft. Actor plays surrounded by his audience →(2)(4)(5) without curtain and with little scenery. Auditorium may be round, square or rectangular →(4). Instead of scenery use can be made of film projection. Revolving stages →(2)(3). Revolving auditorium →(2)(3). 'Theatre in the round' (arena type) where common stage omitted →(5).

Combined 'arena' & 'peep-show' stage As arena theatre side walls of auditorium have rolling or sliding out panels which line up with cyclorama and thus enclose space. As 'peep-show' theatre proscenium arch put between auditorium and stage.

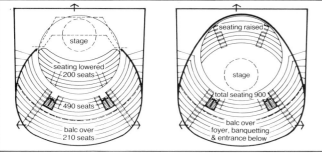

3 New London Theatre Drury Lane London: revolving stage & front stalls with adjustable h seating; can be either in the round or proscenium Arch Tvrtkovic & Kenny Chew & Percival

Theatre references:
→Bibliography entries 015 034 113 114 152 266 298 309 340 343 350 351 352 361 408 409 413 475 556 572 626

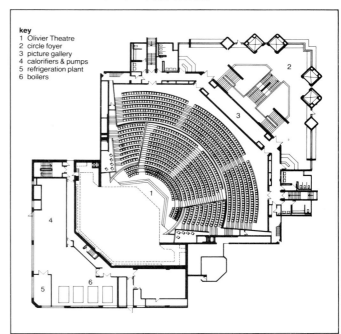

key
1 Olivier Theatre
2 circle foyer
3 picture gallery
4 calorifiers & pumps
5 refrigeration plant
6 boilers

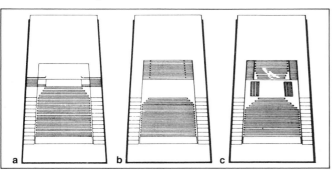

4 Kleines Haus Theater Mannheim (Germany) with adjustable seating
a 'peep-show' stage with orchestra **b** double-sided arena stage **c** arena stage all round   Arch G Weber

6 Circle level Olivier auditorium National Theatre London England   Arch Denys Lasdun

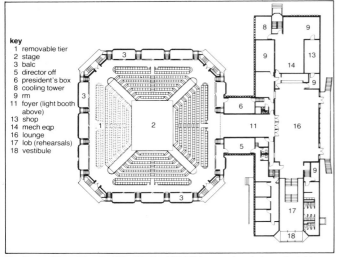

key
1 removable tier
2 stage
3 balc
4 director off
5 president's box
7 cooling tower
8 rm
11 foyer (light booth above)
13 shop
14 mech eqp
16 lounge
17 lob (rehearsals)
18 vestibule

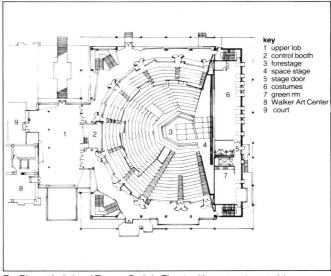

key
1 upper lob
2 control booth
3 forestage
4 space stage
5 stage door
6 costumes
7 green rm
8 Walker Art Center
9 court

5 Arena Stage Theater Washington DC USA upper level plan   Arch Harry Weese

7 Plan at balc level Tyrone Guthrie Theater (three-quarter arena) Minneapolis USA   Arch Ralph Rapson

Cinemas

→also theatres p348–53

Techniques & regulations

Very similar to theatres. Old requirements (UK) for open space round cinemas still applicable →(1)(2); architect must discuss requirements at earliest stage. Use of court or mall access becomes more common in comprehensive schemes, but unless court fully fire protected may not count as exit →(3).

Consult relevant codes and standards for all details.

Doors & corridors

Widths must match exit requirements. Doors to open outwards against exit flow in corridor and to be free of fastenings except panic bolts. Projections for handrails up to 75 allowed into exit widths but doors must provide clear exit dimension measured from door face to frame when standing open. Doors generally required to be fr and self closing →(5).

Staircases

Must also match exit requirements →p348, clear width being measured between walls or wall and balustrade →(6). Not less than 3 risers permitted; not more than 16 risers in straight flights. Max of 2 successive flights without turn allowed provided number of risers reduced to 12. Landings at top, bottom and between flights should equal width required. Stair risers (UK code) not to exceed 150, treads at least 280; USA codes vary.

Stairs →p408

Seating

Layouts similar to theatres →p349–50, except seat blocks do not normally exceed 14 chairs. Spectator convenience improved for continuous performances; sales of confectionery improve when access from seating increased. Modern chairs, some of which have not tip-up seats, need greater spacing, Distance from screen to front row of seats determined by max allowable angle between sightline from first row to top of screen and perpendicular to screen at that point: max angle 30°–35° recommended. Limit to sight angle of 35° above horizontal produces distance to screen on centre line of 1.43 × height from front row eye level to top of picture →p357(4).

Seat sizes finally determine layout dimensions →p350–1. Vertical sight lines determined in similar way as for theatres →p349 except that each spectator should have clear view to bottom of picture. Side seating at front limited by angles of sight to screen →p354(6).

Access to auditorium

In stepped seating can be from beneath through vomitory or from rear, each to crossover aisle. Side and rear aisles add to ease of access and supervision of audience.

Multiple auditorium

Now often considered necessary in commercial cinemas. Various theories used to divide total seats needed. Ratios of 1 : 2 or 2 : 3 for dual cinemas; ratios of 1 : 2 : 3 for triple cinemas; progression of seat totals for larger multiples. Basic requirement: give visitor choice of programmes and enable operator judge business potential of each film so as show it in auditorium of capacity to match public demand. If film playing to half capacity audiences can be transferred to smaller auditorium or vice versa.

Seating capacities vary between 100–600 chairs: generally regarded (UK) as min and max auditorium sizes →(7).

Sales, staff, projection and service arrangements can be as for single cinema →p355–7.

Ventilation and acoustic separation must be provided. Single projection rm to link all auditoria preferred but automation and closed circuit tv to monitor programmes make possible separate eqp in conversion of old properties.

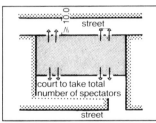

1 Cinemas with more than 2000 seats should have exits on more than 1 public road, or be situated in courts

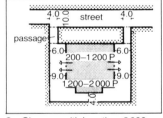

2 Cinemas with less than 2000 seats should have exits on public road; may be in courts →(3); for passages →(4)

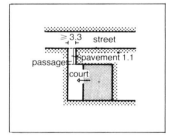

3 Cinemas can be situated off street but may require alternative exits

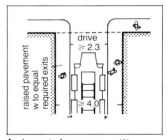

4 Layout of passages →(2)

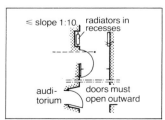

5 Door & corr w to comply with reg →p341: doors to open against exit flow

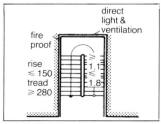

6 W of stairs to equal exit w →p341: flights not less than 3 risers not more than 16, 12 if 2 flights without turn

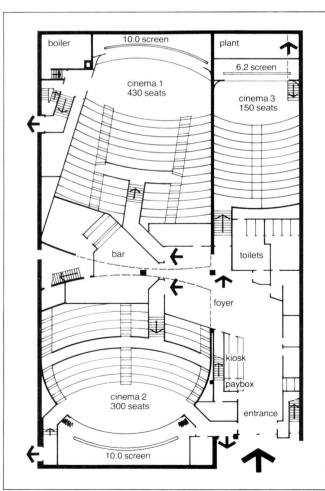

7 Cinema Putney London: multiple auditoria; part of commercial bldg, with high level common projection rm

Cinemas

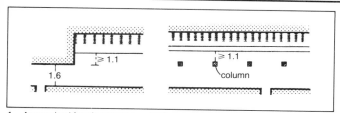

1 Ar required for clo counter →p348: not usual in modern cinemas

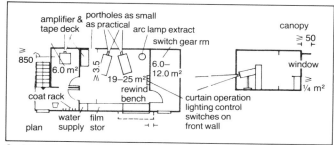

2 Diagram of projection rm; if window installed ensure daylight cannot reach screen **a** plan **b** section

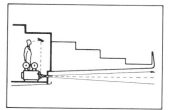

3 Projection rm in gallery structure, observation through mirrors: with 35 mm also project through mirrors

4 Internal projection rm with mech ventilation

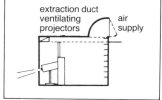

1:1.37 normal
1:1.66 paramount
1:1.75 mgm
1:1.85 columbia
1:2.2 todd ao (70 mm)
1:2.34 cinemascope
1:3.25 cinerama

5 Common film ratios: use adjustable screen masking to screen to suit picture sizes

Cloakrooms

Not standard requirement in UK cinemas: if provided should be planned not to obstruct exits or normal circulation →(1) →p348.

Projection rooms

Used to be divided into separate compartments for rewinding and projecting film with dimmer rm, battery rm, switch rm, spotlight rm, workshop and staff and sto rm, each 6–10 m² forming suite →(2)(3).

Modern automated systems take about same space and require rewind bench to give operational flexibility.

Type of eqp to be used should be established at outset to finalise detail dimensions. Provided non-inflammable (safety) film only used exits can be internal →(4): if inflammable fim used 1 exit must lead to open air and haystack lantern must be provided, with opening area of 0.19 m² for each 640 m of film used and stored in rm. Exit to public area must be through ventilated protected lobby. Circulation space for servicing and access must be provided round eqp; front wall length of 5500 × rm depth of 3500 is av size. Plan staircase and door widths to allow for access of eqp; risers should not exceed 190 treads at least 250.

Mirror projections and observation used where space limited, and before automation became available →(3). With mirrors 1 projection rm can serve multiple cinemas located vertically; but as general rule better avoid mirror projection. Picture ratios vary with film systems: operator must decide what required →(5). Advance techniques employ variable height and width pictures; as size of arc lamp used determined by picture area max effect obtained by using different ratios of equal areas.

Using 70 film makes possible bigger areas screens. Normally accepted max screen widths: for 70 film 20 m, for 35 film 13 m.

Screen size should be large as possible up to these maxima or width of seating whichever least; ratios of width to max viewing distance should be from 1 : 2 to 1 : 3 →(6). Advisable in very small cinemas accept ratio of 1 : 2 to enable standard local length lenses to be used and avoid very small pictures. Wider pictures would require special lenses. To calculate picture width obtainable from given lens:

$$w = \frac{\text{film frame apperture w} \times \text{throw}}{\text{focal l of lens}}$$

In anamorphic (Cinemascope) projection same formula used multiplied by 2.

Curved directional screens originally developed to overcome dispersion of reflected light from flat screen. Modern cinema with better screen material able to use curve of screen to reduce amount of apparent distortion to side sight lines. Too much rise on chord can give problems with focus over whole picture area. Screen radius usually between 75–100% of projection throw; rise on chord should not exceed 10–12% of chord width.

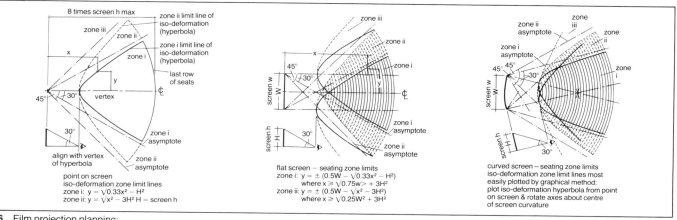

6 Film projection planning:
viewing point on screen: line of iso-deformation = boundary of seating ar for which spectators will see same apparent distortion: hyperbola shape defined in plan by asymptotes from point on screen; zone I distortion exists but not noticed from seats falling within hyperbola: min horizontal distance from vertex of hyperbola to screen determined by limitation of vertical angle from eye of first row to top of screen to max of 30°–35°; zone II distortions noticed but tolerated from seats falling outside zone I; zone III (seating placed beyond limit of zone II) distortions of projected image not tolerated & viewer will refuse

seat placed here:
viewing flat screen: seating ar represented by ar common to space within 2 hyperbolas; ar in zone I for wide projected images less than zone I for point on screen; seating ar for zone II for wide image on flat screen may correspond approx to zone I point on screen
viewing curved screen: zone I ar for given screen w can be increased by curving screen; appropriate curving will cause overlap of hyperbolas drawn from sides of projected image so as to define greater common seating ar

Cinemas

General layout

In addition to public areas must include staff and service areas:

	m²		m²
boiler house	25–30	plenum chamber	20
el substation	28–38	kiosk stock rm	10–15
ice-cream sto	20	manager off suite	38
staff rm	45	3 sto rm	28
projection rm	19–25	switch, battery, workshop & staffrm	40

Lighting systems

Provide in accordance with detail licensing requirements:

decorative lighting and any required spotlights to auditorium dimmed to show film, other public areas maintained while spectators use bldg;

cleaner's lighting to auditorium and foyers: auditorium system used as emergency lighting under management control; USA emergency lighting operates automatically if main fails;

maintained lighting to auditorium and exit boxes throughout bldg: designed provide illumination of seating areas and gangways during film programme (no light to fall on screen or walls); New York City code requires aisles and crossings have min 5.35 lx at all times;

safety lighting to all public, key staff areas and exit boxes throughout bldg: must be kept on as part of maintained system; should main el supply fail safety system must be able provide sufficient light allow public and staff leave bldg safely; N American and continental Europe practice provide separate emergency lighting system which only illumines on failure of main supply: not permitted in UK.

other el systems include fire and burglar alarms, speaker wiring, internal telephones, induction systems for both deaf-aids and management call, closed circuit tv, emergency public address and main switchgear for control of heating, ventilation, projection and stage eqp.

Heating →p16 385–9

Ventilation & air conditioning →p15–16 392–4

Heating and ventilation for public entertainment bldg developed as licensing authorities required higher ventilation standards. In UK fresh air ventilation requirement based on number of persons accommodated and varies from 70–93 m³/hr/P in auditorium and extract system for 75% of input air. Where air-conditioning installed at least half this quantity must be fresh air, with up to 50% filtered and recirculated.

Foyer and toilet systems based on normally accepted standards →Bib347. Toilets affected by licensing requirements.

Incoming air must be heated; plenum system generally used with air supply at screen end and extract divided in auditorium rear corners to avoid vitiated air being illuminated by projection light ray. General parts of bldg can be heated by low pressure hot water system.

Film display

In schools, universities, hotels and other bldg 16 eqp used; when approved this does not require separate projection rm, provided clear space maintained round eqp. Regulations for space requirement vary from 900 to 2000. Picture widths up to 6000 possible with suitable light source; anamorphic (Cinemascope) ratio varies from 35 to 1:2.66. Commercial cinemas in USA and UK have used 16 eqp but in UK picture and print quality not good enough.

→also lecture theatres p135

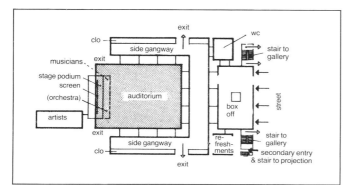

1 Circulation diagram: stage accn not normally needed; exits to suit seating capacity

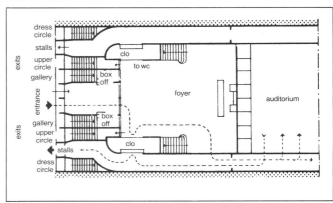

2 Cinema in Oslo: ground floor plan showing circulation in lateral arrangement with double-sided clo   Arch Blackstad & Dunker

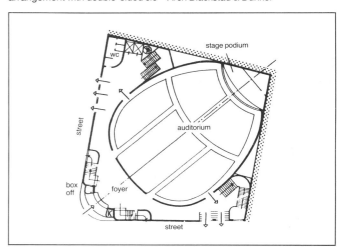

3 Cinema in Madrid: diagonally situated in corner bldg with most economic use of space & good shape of auditorium; ground floor plan   Arch Gutierrez Soto

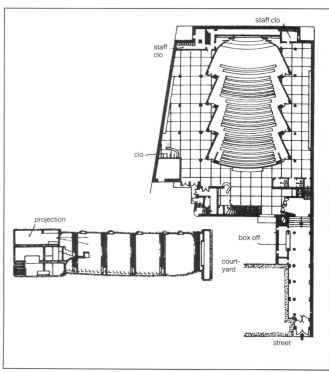

4 Cinema in Turku Finland: 590 seats   Arch Bryggman

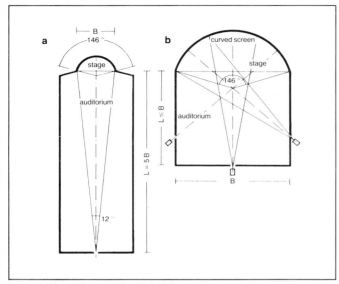

1 **a** traditional cinema **b** for original Cinerama system

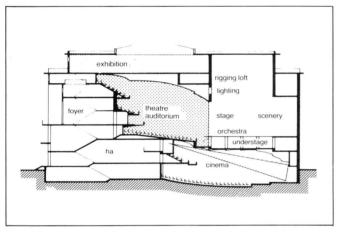

2 Civic centre in central restricted position forces placing of ha for various uses (cinema, concert, exhibition, museum, theatre) above one another: spacious central lob, foyer & stairs shared   Arch Cassandra Athens

Screen systems

Cinema screen in past fitted into adapted theatre; today increased picture size (Cinemascope, Cinerama, Todd AO, Circarama, IMAX, for small cinemas closed circuit tv) determines interior design. Traditional cinemas →(1a) had small pictures whereas 3-projector original Cinerama system →(1b) involved spectator with 30.5 m screen. This surpassed by new single projector IMAX system with 70 film used horizontally to enlarge frame size and provide 36.5 m picture, seating being placed close screen preventing whole picture being seen without both vertical and horizontal movement of head; calls for special projector and auditorium; used in Canada and USA.

Circarama system using 11 projectors gives full involvement but no seating practical and handrails necessary prevent audience falling over →(3): used very successfully at Disneyland.

Further development used in theme parks and now in Experience theatres world wide: audio-visual technique of automated multiple projection of still pictures with auditorium effects and multi-track magnetic sound systems. Closed circuit projection tv system feasible with electronic line enhancement; gives pictures of 2430 × 1830. With 'Eidophor' screen sizes up to 9 m × 12 m possible. Development in progress in USA and UK.

Sound systems

Have developed considerably; problems of handling magnetic sound recordings on film being answered by Dolby encoding optical system. Stereo across screen and to front and rear provided on 70 film with 5 rear screen speaker tracks and 6th track for auditorium speakers. Wide screens and side sound sources can produce acoustic problems: generally for cinemas reflected sound paths should not exceed direct paths by more than 15 m →p18 395–7.

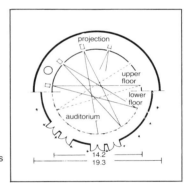

3 Circarama: screen circular (370°); 11 synchronised projectors produce coherent picture; example; Expo Brussels

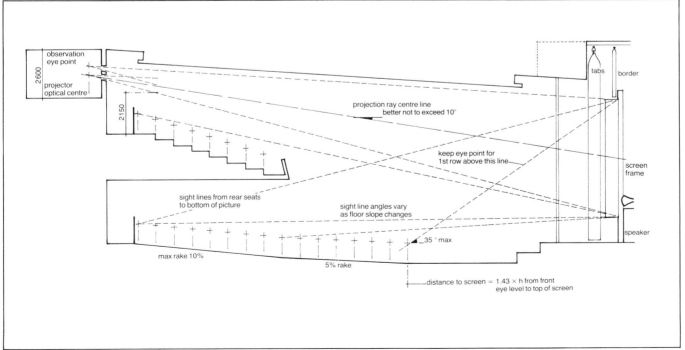

4 Basic requirements for auditorium levels; rake not necessarily limited to 10% & 5% in USA

Drive-in cinemas

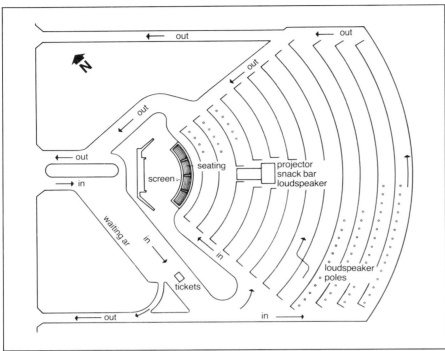

1 Drive-in cinema in fan shape with single ramp, shown for right-hand drive traffic; projection bldg obstructs view from 2 rows to rear

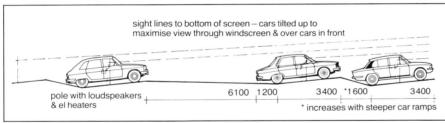

2 Dimensions for double ramp layout: single ramps common in USA

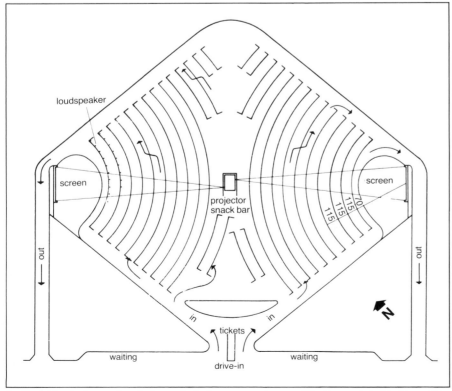

3 Dual drive-in cinema: 1 projection rm for both screens makes possible staggered starting times; all other services (eg ticket off, bar, lav) used jointly

Curved layouts give max of 360 car spaces and individual screens for each car. Usual layouts on principle of amphitheatre for both individual and multiple schemes. →(1)(3).

Sizes over 1000 cars unusual. Multiple schemes more acceptable to operators. Some original situations in N America rebuilt to include dual, triple or quadruple layouts.

Situation on highways usually away from residential areas. Should be sited so that lights from passing traffic do not disturb spectators or throw light on screen.

Layout should provide view of picture at not more than 45° from screen centre; ramps should be designed so that spectators can see over cars in front →(2). Distance from screen to front row with large screen often more than 50 m. Car holding areas avoid traffic jams on highway. 2 double ticket booths normal min: 500 cars need min 20 minutes to enter. Exits should be away from entrance. Cars may leave and enter simultaneously between programmes.

Screen size varies with overall capacity: 30.4 × 13 m normal max, 20% of distance to rear cars normal min. Should face between E and S, making possible earlier evening performances. Height above ground depends on site profile, determines angles of car ramps.

Children's playground and outside seating provided in N America. Surface water drainage catchment pool often sited in front of screen.

Projection bldg in centre or at rear, includes workshop, sto, switchrm, sound and projection system. Can include public toilets, restaurant and office. Max projection throw ≤ 137 m nor less than 2 × screen width.

Sound reproduction best with speaker taken into car from poles spaced at 5000 centres. El fan heaters may also be on poles. Some N American operators also have air-conditioning by underground ducts with flexible car connexions.

Floodlighting provided for intermission; hooded roadway lighting maintained through performance.

Cinema references:
→Bibliography entries 084 098 099 113 114 129 328 329 339 426 598 599

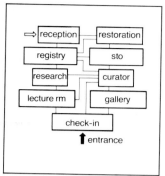

1 Layout diagram

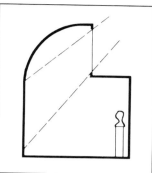

2 Section of gallery lit from 1 side only, bottom part indirectly, attenuated lighting

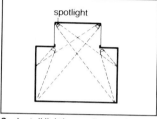

3 Install lighting so that angles of incidence correspond with natural light

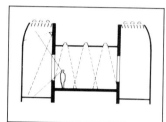

4 Typical cross-section for museum of natural history

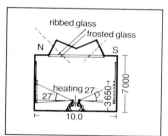

5 Well-lit exhibition ha based on Boston experiments

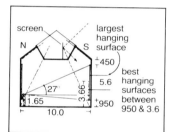

6 Ideally lit rm with uniform lighting from both sides, as worked out by S Hurst Seager (→Bib561)

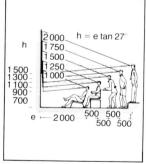

7 Field of vision: h & distance

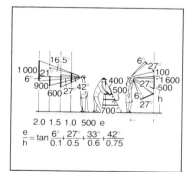

8 Size & distance

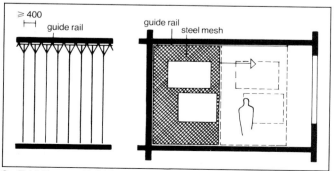

9 Exhibition rm with folding screens (design K Schneider) allows great variety of rm arrangements

ROOMS

For showing works of art and objects of cultural and scientific interest rm must:

ensure protection against damage, theft, fire, damp, aridity, strong sunlight and dust;

show works in best light (in both senses of term): normally achieved by dividing collection into

objects for study (eg engravings, drawings) kept in portfolios and stored in cupboards (with drawers) about 800 deep and 1600 high;

objects for display (eg paintings, frescoes, statuary, ceramics, furniture)

Exhibits must be so placed as to be seen without effort: calls for selective and spacious arrangement, with variety and suitable rm shape and sequence.

So far as possible each group of pictures in 1 rm or sequence of rm and each picture a wall to itself: ie number of small rm. These also provide more wall space in relation to ground area than large rm, necessary for big pictures: rm size depends on picture size. Normal human angle of vision (54° or 27° up from eye level) achieved with well lit pictures 10 m away = hanging height of 4900 above eye level and about 700 below it →(5). Only with large pictures is there need for eye to travel from bottom of frame up above angle of vision. Best hanging position for smaller pictures: point of emphasis (level of horizon in picture) at eye level →(7)(8).

space/picture	3–5 m² hanging surface
space/sculpture	6–10 m² ground surface
space/400 coins	1 m² cabinet space

Calculations for museum lighting highly theoretical: quality of light what matters. Experiments carried out in America therefore more important (→Bib561). In recent times continuous increase in use of artificial lighting, instead of constant variations of light experiences even with N lighting →p360.

GENERAL LAYOUT

No continous circular itinerary but wings leading out from entrance. Side rm for packing, despatch, transparency section, restoration workshops, lecture rm. Museums sometimes in bldg originally designed for other purposes.

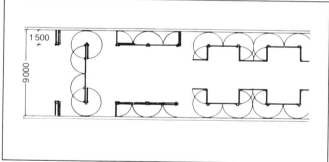

10 Painting sto with detachable steel mesh frames on which pictures can be hung as required & be ready for removal at any time for study

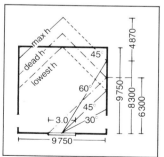

11 Exhibition rm with side lighting: suitable hanging surface between 30° & 60° with rm h of 6700 & cill h 2130 for pictures or 3040–3650 for sculpture, as calculated from Boston experiments

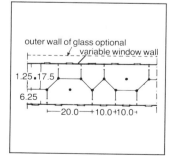

12 Exhibition rm with successful use of available space: panels between central pillars can be rearranged between supports as needed; if outer side-wall of glass installed window arrangement of inner wall can also be varied

Museums

LIGHTING

Daylight as light source gives min overheads.

Overhead lighting: advantages, independent of orientation, not affected by overhanging trees or neighbouring bldg, easily regulated (lamella ceiling), little reflection, light more widely spread over exhibit area; disadvantages, strong heat build-up, risk of damage from water and condensation, only diffused light.

Window lighting: view out (relaxing), rm easily aired and kept at even temp, better light on groups and individual exhibits, illumination of showcases from back.

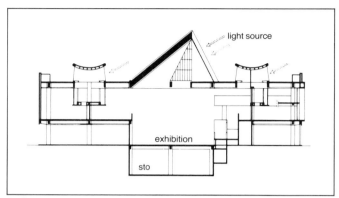

1 Section & light sources Museum of Western Art Tokyo Japan Arch Le Corbusier

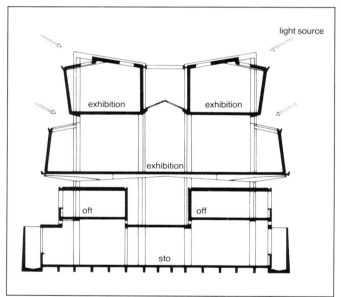

2 Section & light sources Museo Civico Turin Italy Arch Bassi & Boschetti

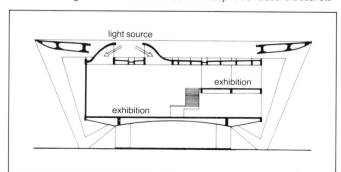

3 Section & light sources Museum of Modern Art Rio de Janeiro Brazil Arch Reidy

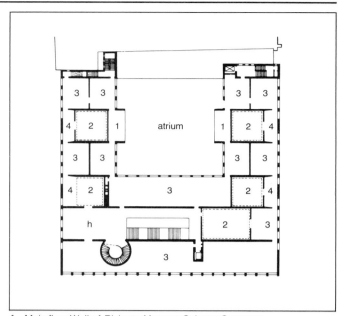

4 Main floor Wallraf-Richartz-Museum Cologne Germany Arch R Schwartz & Bernard
key 1 rest rm 2 rm reaching to overhead light in upper storey 3 side-lit rm 4 side-lit recess

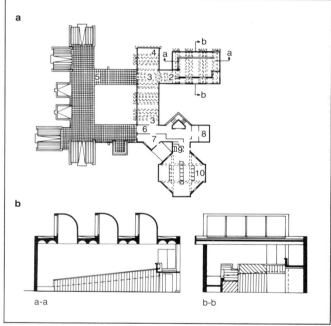

5 Joan Miro Foundation Barcelona Spain has ramp extending round all 4 sides of sculpture rm allowing works to be viewed from varying heights and aspects; note use of skylights →section **a** first floor plan **b** sections Arch Sert Section
key 1 sculpture rm 2 ha 3 print rm 4 balc over ground floor 5 ter with sculptures 6 ha 7 off 8 director's off 9 rest rm 10 print archives

EXAMPLES

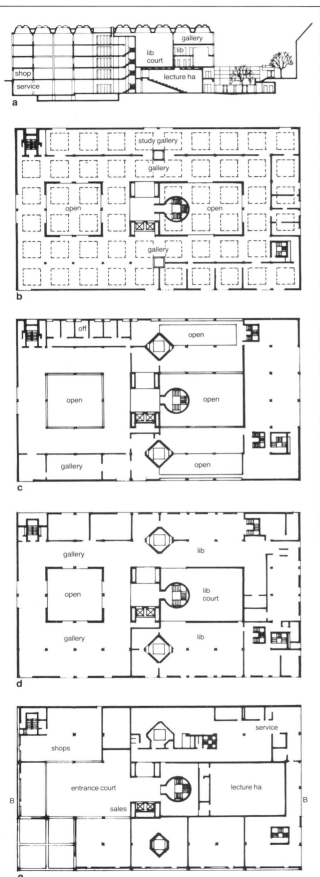

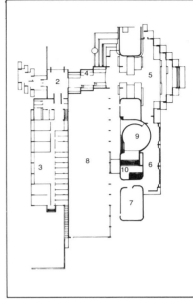

2 Vancouver Museum
Canada   Arch Arthur Erickson
key
1 entrance
2 lob
3 off/seminar rm
4 ramped gallery
5 great ha
6 small object gallery
7 theatre
8 visible sto ar
9 lounge
10 outdoor court

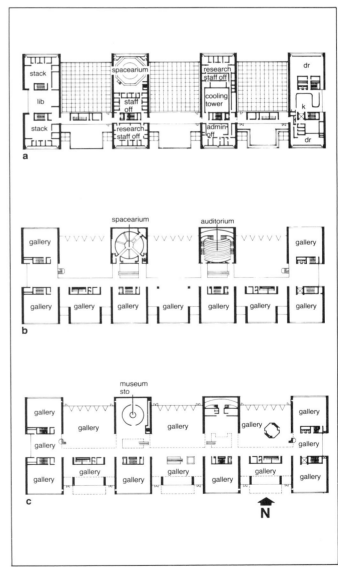

1   Center for British Art Yale USA **a** section at B→le **b** third floor **c** second floor **d** first floor **e** ground floor   Arch Kahn

3   Air & Space Museum Washington USA **a** second floor **b** first floor **c** ground floor   Arch Hok

Museums references
→Bibliography entries 040 318 385 476 612

INTRODUCTION

Components brings together various categories of construction data intended as an aid to the user of *Architects' Data* in applying the principles and examples given throughout the body of the book. Under the general heading 'Services' are guidelines on the spaces needed to install, operate and maintain systems of distribution, heating, ventilation, thermal and sound insulation, lighting. Thereafter follow practical criteria for certain components: doors, windows, corridors and ramps, stairs, escalators, elevators.

Data here presented are based on the latest British and European research and are not directly applicable by those working in non-metric units of measurement. The material presented and the approach to its presentation are thought to be of general interest to architects in America as in other continents; but USA practices differ in some respects from what is given here. Such practices are presented in detail in Ramsey & Sleeper/American Institute of Architects *Architectural Graphic Standards* →Bib 549.

Conversions

As an aid to readers who do not work in metric units of measurement a list of conversion factors and a set of 42 conversion tables introduce the pages on services systems.

Materials

Values to be given to physical characteristics of common building materials have been brought together in a table which follows the conversion tables and precedes 'Services' →p384(1).

Conversions

FACTORS

metric	'imperial'/US
length	
1.0 mm	0.039 in
25.4 mm (2.54 cm)	1 in
304.8 mm (30.48 cm)	1 ft
914.4 mm	1 yd
1000.0 mm (1.0 m)	1 yd 3.4 in (1.093 yd)
20.117 m	1 chain
1000.00 m (1 km)	0.621 mile
1609.31 m	1 mile
area	
100 mm² (1.0 cm²)	0.155 in²
645.2 mm² (6.452 cm²)	1 in²
929.03 cm² (0.093 m²)	1 ft²'
0.836 m²	1 yd²
1.0 m²	1.196 yd² (10.763 m²)
0.405 ha (4046.9 m²)	1 acre
1.0 ha (10000 m²)	2.471 acre
1.0 km²	0.386 mile²
2.59 km² (259 ha)	1 mile²
volume	
1000 mm³ (1.0 cm³; 1.0 ml)	0.061 in³
16387 mm³ (16.387 cm³; 0.0164 l; 16.387 ml)	1 in³
1.0 l (1.0 dc³; 1000 cm³)	61.025 in³ (0.035 ft³)
0.028 m³ (28.32 l)	1 ft³
0.755 m³	1 yd³
1.0 m³	1.308 yd³ (35.314 ft³)
capacity	
1.0 ml	0.034 fl oz US
1.0 ml	0.035 fl oz imp
28.41 ml	1 fl oz imp
29.57 ml	1 fl oz US
0.473 litre	1 pint (liquid) US
0.568 litre	1 pint imp
1.0 litre	1.76 pint imp
1.0 litre	2.113 pint US
3.785 litre	1 gal US
4.546 litre	1 gal imp
100.0 litre	21.99 gal imp
100.0 litre	26.42 gal US
159.0 litre	1 barrel US
164.0 litre	1 barrel imp
mass	
1.0 g	0.035 oz (avoirdupois)
28.35 g	1 oz (avoirdupois)
454.0 g (0.454 kg)	1 lb
1000.0 g (1 kg)	2.205 lb
45.36 kg	1 cwt US
50.8 kg	1 cwt imp
907.2 kg (0.907 t)	1 ton US
1000.0 kg (1.0 t)	0.984 ton imp
1000.0 kg (1.0 t)	1.102 ton US
1016.0 kg (1.016 t)	1 ton imp
mass/unit length	
0.496 kg/m	1 lb/yd
0.564 kg/m (0.564 t/km)	1 ton US/mile
0.631 kg/m (0.631 t/km)	1 ton imp/mile
1.0 kg/m	0.056 lb/in (0.896 oz/in)
1.116 kg/m	1 oz/in
1.488 kg/m	1 lb/ft
17.86 kg/m	1 lb/in
length/unit mass	
1.0 m/kg	0.496 yd/lb
2.016 m/kg	1 yd/lb

metric	'imperial'/US
mass/unit area	
1.0 g/m²	0.003 oz/ft²
33.91 g/m²	1 oz/yd²
305.15 g/m²	1 oz/ft²
0.011 kg/m²	1 cwt US/acre
0.013 kg/m²	1 cwt imp/acre
0.224 kg/m²	1 ton US/acre
0.251 kg/m²	1 ton imp/acre
1.0 kg/m²	29.5 oz/yd²
4.882 kg/m²	1 lb/ft²
703.07 kg/m²	1 lb/in²
350.3 kg/km² (3.503 kg/ha; 0.35 g/m²)	1 ton US/mile²
392.3 kg/km² (3.923 kg/ha; 0.392 g/m²)	1 ton imp/mile²
density (mass/volume)	
0.593 kg/m³	1 lb/yd³
1.0 kg/m³	0.062 lb/ft³
16.02 kg/m³	1 lb/ft
1186.7 kg/m³ (1.187 t/mkg/m³)	1 ton US/yd³
1328.9 kg/m³ (1.329 t/m³)	1 ton imp/yd³
27680.0 kg/m³ (27.68 t/m³; 27.68 g/cm³)	1 lb/in³
specific surface (area/unit mass)	
0.823 m²/t	1 yd²/ton
1.0 m²/kg	0.034 yd²/oz
29.493 m²/kg	1 yd²/oz
area/unit capacity	
0.184 m²/l	1 yd²/gal
1.0 m²/l	5.437 yd²/gal
concentration	
0.014 kg/m³	1 grain/gal imp
0.017 kg/m³	1 grain/gal US
1.0 kg/m³ (1.0 g/l)	58.42 grain/gal US
1.0 kg/m³ (1.0 g/l)	70.16 grain/gal imp
6.236 kg/m³	1 oz/gal imp
7.489 kg/m³	1 oz/gal US
mass rate of flow	
0.454 kg/s	1 lb/s
1.0 kg/s	2.204 lb/s
volume rate of flow	
0.063 l/s	1 gal US/minute
0.076 l/s	1 gal imp/minute
0.472 l/s	1 ft³/minute
1.0 l/s (86.4 m³/day)	13.2 gal imp/s
1.0 l/s	0.264 gal US/s
1.0 l/m	0.22 gal imp/min
1.0 l/m	0.264 gal US/min
3.785 l/s	1 gal US/sec
4.546 l/s	1 gal imp/sec
28.32 l/s	1 ft³/s
0.0045 m³/(m².d) (0.000052 mm/s)	1 gal US/(yd².day)
0.0054 m³/(m².d) (0.000062 mm/s)	1 gal imp/(yd².day)
0.0005 m³/(m³.d)	1 gal US/(yd³.day)
0.0006 m³/(m³.d)	1 gal imp/(yd³.day)
velocity	
0.005 m/s	1 ft/minute
0.025 m/s	1 in/s
0.305 m/s	1 ft/s
1.0 m/s	3.28 ft/s
1000.0 m/hr (1 km/hr)	0.621 mile/hr
1609.0 m/hr (0.447 m/s)	1 mile/hr

metric	'imperial'/US	metric	'imperial'/US
fuel consumption		**refrigeration**	
1.0 l/km	0.354 gal imp/mile	3.517 kW	12000 Btu/hr = 'ton of
1.0 l/km	0.425 gal US/mile		refrigeration'
2.352 l/km	1 gal US/mile		
2.824 l/km	1 gal imp/mile	**illumination**	
		1 lx (1 lumen/m²)	0.093 ft-candle (0.093 lumen/ft²)
acceleration		10.764 lx	1.0 ft-candle (1 lumen/ft²)
0.305 m/s²	1 ft/s²		
1.0 m/s²	3.28 ft/s²	**luminance**	
9.806 m/s² = g (standard	g = 32.172 ft/s²	0.3183 cd/m²	1 apostilb
acceleration		1.0 cd/m²	0.000645 cd/ft²
due to gravity)		10.764 cd/m²	1 cd/ft²
		1550.0 cd/m²	1.0 cd/in²
temperature			
X°C	($\frac{9}{5}$X + 32) °F	**force**	
$\frac{5}{9}$ × (X − 32) °C	X°F	1.0 N	0.225 lbf
		1.0 kgf (9.807 N; 1.0 kilopond)	2.205 lbf
temperature interval		4.448 kN	1.0 kipf (1000 lbf)
0.5556 K	1°F	8.897 kN	1.0 tonf US
1 K = 1°C	1.8°F	9.964 kN	1.0 tonf imp
energy		**force/unit length**	
1.0 J	0.239 calorie	1.0 N/m	0.067 lbf/ft
1.356 J	1 ft lbf	14.59 N/m	1.0 lbf/ft
4.187 J	1.0 calorie	32.69 kN/m	1.0 tonf/ft
9.807 J (1 kf m)	7.233 ft lbf	175.1 kN/m (175.1 N/mm)	1.0 lbf/in
1055.06 J	1 Btu		
3.6 MJ	1 kilowatt-hr	**moment of force (torque)**	
105.5 MJ	1 therm (100000 Btu)	0.113 Nm (113.0 Nmm)	1.0 lbf in
		1.0 Nm	0.738 lbf ft
power (energy/time)		1.356 Nm	1.0 lbf ft
0.293 W	1 Btu/hr	113.0 Nm	1.0 kipf in
1.0 W	0.738 ft lbf/s	253.1 Nm	1.0 tonf in
1.163 W	1.0 kilocalorie/hr	1356.0 Nm	1.0 kipf ft
1.356 W	1 ft lbf/s	3037.0 Nm	1.0 tonf ft
4.187 W	1 calorie/s		
1 kgf m/s (9.807 W)	7.233 ft lbf/s)	**pressure**	
745.7 W	1 horsepower	1.0 Pa (1.0 N/m²)	0.021 lbf/ft²
1 metric horsepower (75 kgf	0.986 horsepower	1.0 kPa	0.145 lbf/in²
m/s)		100.0 Pa	1.0 millibar
		2.99 kPa	1 ft water
intensity of heat flow rate		3.39 kPa	1 in mercury
1 W/m²	0.317 Btu/(ft² hr)	6.9 kPa	1.0 lbf/in²
3.155 W/m²	1.0 Btu/(ft² hr)	100.0 kPa	1.0 bar
		101.33 kPa	1.0 standard atmosphere
thermal conductivity		107.25 kPa	1.0 tonf/ft²
0.144 W/(m.K)	1 Btu in/(ft² hr °F)	15.44 MPa	1.0 tonf/in²
1.0 W/(m.K)	6.933 Btu in/(ft² hr °F)		
thermal conductance			
1.0 W/(m².K)	0.176 Btu/(ft² hr °F)		
5.678 W/(m².K)	1.0 Btu/(ft² hr °F)		
thermal registivity			
1.0 m K/W	0.144 ft² hr °F/(Btu in)		
6.933 m K/W	1.0 ft² hr °F/(Btu in)		
specific heat capacity			
1.0 kJ/(kg.K)	0.239 Btu/(lb °F)		
4.187 kJ/(kg.K)	1.0 Btu/(lb °F)		
1.0 kJ/(m³ K)	0.015 Btu/(ft³ °F)		
67.07 kJ/(m³ K)	1.0 Btu/(ft³ °F)		
specific energy			
1.0 kJ/kg	0.43 Btu/lb		
2.326 kJ/kg	1.0 Btu/lb		
1.0 kJ/m³ (1 kJ/l)	0.027 Btu/ft³		
1.0 J/l	0.004 Btu/gal		
232.1 J/l	1.0 Btu/gal		

Conversions

TABLES

List of tables

TABLES

Length

1
millimetres to inches

mm	0	1	2	3	4	5	6	7	8	9
	in									
0		0.04	0.08	0.11	0.16	0.2	0.24	0.28	0.31	0.3
10	0.39	0.43	0.47	0.51	0.55	0.59	0.63	0.67	0.71	0.7
20	0.79	0.83	0.87	0.91	0.94	0.98	1.02	1.06	1.1	1.1
30	1.18	1.22	1.25	1.3	1.34	1.38	1.41	1.46	1.5	1.5
40	1.57	1.61	1.65	1.69	1.73	1.77	1.81	1.85	1.89	1.9
50	1.97	2.00	2.05	2.09	2.13	2.17	2.21	2.24	2.28	2.3
60	2.36	2.4	2.44	2.48	2.52	2.56	2.6	2.64	2.68	2.7
70	2.76	2.8	2.83	2.87	2.91	2.95	3.0	3.03	3.07	3.1
80	3.15	3.19	3.23	3.27	3.31	3.35	3.39	3.42	3.46	3.5
90	3.54	3.58	3.62	3.66	3.7	3.74	3.78	3.82	3.86	3.9
100	3.94	3.98	4.02	4.06	4.09	4.13	4.17	4.21	4.25	4.2
110	4.33	4.37	4.41	4.45	4.49	4.53	4.57	4.61	4.65	4.6
120	4.72	4.76	4.8	4.84	4.88	4.92	4.96	5.0	5.04	5.0
130	5.12	5.16	5.2	5.24	5.28	5.31	5.35	5.39	5.43	5.4
140	5.51	5.55	5.59	5.63	5.67	5.71	5.75	5.79	5.83	5.8
150	5.91	5.94	5.98	6.02	6.06	6.1	6.14	6.18	6.22	6.2
160	6.3	6.34	6.38	6.42	6.46	6.5	6.54	6.57	6.61	6.6
170	6.69	6.73	6.77	6.81	6.85	6.89	6.93	6.97	7.01	7.0
180	7.09	7.13	7.17	7.21	7.24	7.28	7.32	7.36	7.4	7.4
190	7.48	7.52	7.56	7.6	7.64	7.68	7.72	7.76	7.8	7.8
200	7.87	7.91	7.95	7.99	8.03	8.07	8.11	8.15	8.19	8.2
210	8.27	8.31	8.35	8.39	8.43	8.46	8.5	8.54	8.58	8.6
220	8.66	8.7	8.74	8.78	8.82	8.86	8.9	8.94	8.98	9.0
230	9.06	9.09	9.13	9.17	9.21	9.25	9.29	9.33	9.37	9.4
240	9.45	9.49	9.53	9.57	9.61	9.65	9.69	9.72	9.76	9.8
250	9.84									

in	0.000	0.001	0.002	0.003	0.004	0.005	0.006	0.007	0.008	0.009
	mm									
0.0		0.0254	0.0508	0.0762	0.1016	0.127	0.1524	0.1778	0.2032	0.2286
0.01	0.254	0.2794	0.3048	0.3302	0.3556	0.381	0.4064	0.4318	0.4572	0.4826
0.02	0.508	0.5334	0.5588	0.5842	0.6096	0.635	0.6604	0.6858	0.7112	0.7366
0.03	0.762	0.7874	0.8128	0.8382	0.8636	0.889	0.9144	0.9398	0.9652	0.9906
0.04	1.016	1.0414	1.0668	1.0922	1.1176	1.143	1.1684	1.1938	1.2192	1.2446
0.05	1.27	1.2954	1.3208	1.3462	1.3716	1.397	1.4224	1.4478	1.4732	1.4986
0.06	1.524	1.5494	1.5748	1.6002	1.6256	1.651	1.6764	1.7018	1.7272	1.7526
0.07	1.778	1.8034	1.8288	1.8542	1.8796	1.905	1.9304	1.9558	1.9812	2.0066
0.08	2.032	2.0574	2.0828	2.1082	2.1336	2.159	2.1844	2.2098	2.2352	2.2606
0.09	2.286	2.3114	2.3368	2.3622	2.3876	2.413	2.4384	2.4638	2.4892	2.5146
0.1	2.54									

2
decimals of inch to millimetres

in	$^1/_{16}$	$^1/_8$	$^3/_{16}$	$^1/_4$	$^5/_{16}$	$^3/_8$	$^7/_{16}$	$^1/_2$	$^9/_{16}$	$^5/_8$	$^{11}/_{16}$	$^3/_4$	$^{13}/_{16}$	$^7/_8$	$^{15}/_{16}$
	mm														
	1.6	3.2	4.8	6.4	7.9	9.5	11.1	12.7	14.3	15.9	17.5	19.1	20.6	22.2	23.8
1	25.4	27.0	28.6	30.2	31.8	33.3	34.9	36.5	38.1	39.7	41.3	42.9	44.5	46.0	47.6	49.2
2	50.8	52.4	54.0	55.6	57.2	58.7	60.3	61.9	63.5	65.1	66.7	68.3	69.9	71.4	73.0	74.6
3	76.2	77.8	79.4	81.0	82.6	84.1	85.7	87.3	88.9	90.5	92.1	93.7	95.3	96.8	98.4	100.0
4	101.6	103.2	104.8	106.4	108.0	109.5	111.1	112.7	114.3	115.9	117.5	119.1	120.7	122.2	123.8	125.4
5	127.0	128.6	130.2	131.8	133.4	134.9	136.5	138.1	139.7	141.3	142.9	144.5	146.1	147.6	149.2	150.8
6	152.4	154.0	155.6	157.2	158.8	160.3	161.9	163.5	165.1	166.7	168.3	169.9	171.5	173.0	174.6	176.2
7	177.8	179.4	181.0	182.6	184.2	185.7	187.3	188.9	190.5	192.1	193.7	195.3	196.9	198.4	200.0	201.6
8	203.2	204.8	206.4	208.0	209.6	211.1	212.7	214.3	215.9	217.5	219.1	220.7	222.3	223.8	225.4	227.0
9	228.6	230.2	231.8	233.4	235.0	236.5	238.1	239.7	241.3	242.9	244.5	246.1	247.7	249.2	250.8	252.4
10	254.0	255.6	257.2	258.8	260.4	261.9	263.5	265.1	266.7	268.3	269.9	271.5	273.1	274.6	276.2	277.8

3
inches & fractions of inch to millimetres

ft \ in	0	1	2	3	4	5	6	7	8	9	10	11
	m											
0		0.0254	0.0508	0.0762	0.1016	0.127	0.1524	0.1778	0.2032	0.2286	0.254	0.2794
1	0.3048	0.3302	0.3556	0.381	0.4064	0.4318	0.4572	0.4826	0.508	0.5334	0.5588	0.5842
2	0.6096	0.635	0.6604	0.6858	0.7112	0.7366	0.762	0.7874	0.8128	0.8382	0.8636	0.889
3	0.9144	0.9398	0.9652	0.9906	1.016	1.0414	1.0668	1.0922	1.1176	1.143	1.1684	1.1938
4	1.2192	1.2446	1.27	1.2954	1.3208	1.3462	1.3716	1.397	1.4224	1.4478	1.4732	1.4986
5	1.524	1.5494	1.5748	1.6002	1.6256	1.651	1.6764	1.7018	1.7272	1.7526	1.778	1.8034
6	1.8288	1.8542	1.8796	1.905	1.9304	1.9558	1.9812	2.0066	2.032	2.0574	2.0828	2.1082
7	2.1336	2.159	2.1844	2.2098	2.2352	2.2606	2.286	2.3114	2.3368	2.3622	2.3876	2.413
8	2.4384	2.4638	2.4892	2.5146	2.54	2.5654	2.5908	2.6162	2.6416	2.667	2.6924	2.7178
9	2.7432	2.7686	2.794	2.8194	2.8448	2.8702	2.8956	2.921	2.9464	2.9718	2.9972	3.0226
10	3.048											

4
feet & inches to metres

Conversions

5
metres to feet

m	0	1	2	3	4	5	6	7	8	9
	ft									
0		3.28	6.56	9.84	13.12	16.40	19.69	22.97	26.25	29.53
10	32.8	36.09	39.37	42.65	45.93	49.21	52.49	55.77	59.06	62.34
20	65.62	68.9	72.17	75.45	78.74	82.02	85.3	88.58	91.86	95.14
30	98.43	101.7	104.99	108.27	111.55	114.82	118.11	121.39	124.67	127.95
40	131.23	134.51	137.8	141.08	144.36	147.63	150.91	154.2	157.48	160.76
50	164.04	167.32	170.6	173.89	177.17	180.45	183.73	187.01	190.29	193.57
60	196.85	200.13	203.41	206.69	209.97	213.25	216.54	219.82	223.1	226.38
70	229.66	232.94	236.22	239.5	242.78	246.06	249.34	252.63	255.91	259.19
80	262.46	265.75	269.03	272.31	275.59	278.87	282.15	285.43	288.71	292.0
90	295.28	298.56	301.84	305.12	308.4	311.68	314.96	318.24	321.52	324.8
100	328.08	331.37	334.65	337.93	341.21	344.49	347.77	351.05	354.33	357.61
110	360.89	364.17	367.45	370.74	374.02	377.3	380.58	383.86	387.14	390.42
120	393.7	396.98	400.26	403.54	406.82	410.1	413.39	416.67	419.95	423.23
130	426.51	429.79	433.07	436.35	439.63	442.91	446.19	449.48	452.76	456.04
140	459.32	462.6	465.88	469.16	472.44	475.72	479.0	482.28	485.56	488.85
150	492.13	495.41	498.69	502.0	505.25	508.53	511.81	515.09	518.37	521.65
160	524.93	528.22	531.5	534.78	538.06	541.34	544.62	547.9	551.18	554.46
170	557.74	561.02	564.3	567.59	570.87	574.15	577.43	580.71	583.99	587.27
180	590.55	593.83	597.11	600.39	603.68	606.96	610.24	613.52	616.8	620.08
190	623.36	626.64	629.92	633.2	636.48	639.76	643.05	646.33	649.6	652.89
200	656.17	659.45	662.73	666.01	669.29	672.57	675.85	679.13	682.42	685.7
210	688.98	692.26	695.54	698.82	702.1	705.38	708.66	711.94	715.22	718.5
220	721.79	725.07	728.35	731.63	734.91	738.19	741.47	744.75	748.03	751.31
230	754.59	757.87	761.16	764.44	767.72	771.0	774.28	777.56	780.84	784.12
240	787.4	790.68	793.96	797.24	800.53	803.81	807.09	810.37	813.65	816.93
250	820.21									

7
metres to yards

m	0	1	2	3	4	5	6	7	8	9
	yd									
0		1.09	2.19	3.28	4.37	5.47	6.56	7.66	8.75	9.84
10	10.94	12.03	13.12	14.22	15.31	16.4	17.5	18.59	19.69	20.78
20	21.87	22.97	24.06	25.15	26.25	27.34	28.43	29.53	30.62	31.71
30	32.8	33.9	35.0	36.09	37.18	38.28	39.37	40.46	41.56	42.65
40	43.74	44.84	45.93	47.03	48.12	49.21	50.31	51.4	52.49	53.59
50	54.68	55.77	56.87	57.96	59.06	60.15	61.24	62.34	63.43	64.52
60	65.62	66.71	67.8	68.9	69.99	71.08	72.18	73.27	74.37	75.46
70	76.55	77.65	78.74	79.83	80.93	82.02	83.11	84.21	85.3	86.4
80	87.49	88.58	89.68	90.77	91.86	92.96	94.05	95.14	96.24	97.33
90	98.43	99.52	100.61	101.71	102.8	103.89	104.99	106.08	107.17	108.27
100	109.36	110.46	111.55	112.64	113.74	114.83	115.92	117.02	118.11	119.2
110	120.3	121.39	122.49	123.58	124.67	125.74	126.86	127.95	129.05	130.14
120	131.23	132.33	133.42	134.51	135.61	136.7	137.8	138.89	139.99	141.08
130	142.17	143.26	144.36	145.45	146.54	147.64	148.73	149.83	150.92	152.01
140	153.1	154.2	155.29	156.39	157.48	158.57	159.67	160.76	161.86	162.95
150	164.04	165.14	166.23	167.32	168.42	169.51	170.6	171.7	172.79	173.89
160	174.98	176.07	177.17	178.26	179.35	180.45	181.54	182.63	183.73	184.82
170	185.91	187.0	188.1	189.2	190.29	191.38	192.48	193.57	194.66	195.76
180	196.85	197.94	199.04	200.13	201.23	202.32	203.41	204.51	205.6	206.69
190	207.79	208.88	209.97	211.07	212.16	213.26	214.35	215.44	216.53	217.63
200	218.72	219.82	220.91	222.0	223.1	224.19	225.28	226.38	227.47	228.57
210	229.66	230.75	231.85	232.94	234.03	235.13	236.22	237.31	238.41	239.5
220	240.56	241.69	242.78	243.88	244.97	246.06	247.16	248.25	249.34	250.44
230	251.53	252.63	253.72	254.81	255.91	257.0	258.09	259.19	260.28	261.37
240	262.47	263.56	264.65	265.75	266.84	267.94	269.03	270.12	271.22	272.31
250	273.4									

9
kilometres to miles

km	0	1	2	3	4	5	6	7	8	9
	mile									
0		0.62	1.24	1.86	2.49	3.11	3.73	4.35	4.98	5.59
10	6.21	6.84	7.46	8.08	8.7	9.32	9.94	10.56	11.18	11.81
20	12.43	13.05	13.67	14.29	14.91	15.53	16.16	16.78	17.4	18.02
30	18.64	19.29	19.88	20.5	21.13	21.75	22.37	22.99	23.61	24.23
40	24.85	25.47	26.1	26.72	27.34	27.96	28.58	29.2	29.83	30.45
50	31.07	31.69	32.31	32.93	33.55	34.18	34.8	35.42	36.04	36.66
60	37.28	37.9	38.53	39.15	39.77	40.39	41.01	41.63	42.25	42.87
70	43.5	44.12	44.74	45.36	45.98	46.6	47.22	47.85	48.47	49.09
80	49.7	50.33	50.95	51.57	52.2	52.82	53.44	54.06	54.68	55.3
90	55.92	56.54	57.17	57.79	58.41	59.03	59.65	60.27	60.89	61.52
100	62.14									

ft	0	1	2	3	4	5	6	7	8	9
	m									
0		0.31	0.6	0.91	1.22	1.52	1.83	2.13	2.44	2.74
10	3.05	3.35	3.66	3.96	4.27	4.57	4.88	5.18	5.49	5.79
20	6.1	6.4	6.71	7.01	7.31	7.62	7.92	8.23	8.53	8.84
30	9.14	9.45	9.75	10.06	10.36	10.67	10.97	11.28	11.58	11.89
40	12.19	12.5	12.80	13.1	13.41	13.72	14.02	14.36	14.63	14.94
50	15.24	15.54	15.85	16.15	16.46	16.76	17.07	17.37	17.68	17.98
60	18.29	18.59	18.9	19.2	19.58	19.81	20.12	20.42	20.73	21.03
70	21.33	21.64	21.95	22.25	22.56	22.86	23.16	23.47	23.77	24.08
80	24.38	24.69	24.99	25.3	25.6	25.91	26.21	26.52	26.82	27.13
90	27.43	27.74	28.04	28.35	28.65	28.96	29.26	29.57	29.87	30.18
100	30.48	30.78	31.09	31.39	31.7	32.0	32.31	32.61	32.92	33.22
110	33.53	33.83	34.14	34.44	34.75	35.05	35.37	35.67	36.0	36.3
120	36.58	36.88	37.19	37.49	37.8	38.1	38.41	38.7	39.01	39.32
130	39.62	39.93	40.23	40.54	40.84	41.15	41.45	41.76	42.06	42.37
140	42.67	42.98	43.28	43.59	43.89	44.2	44.5	44.81	45.11	45.46
150	45.72	46.02	46.33	46.63	46.94	47.24	47.55	47.85	48.16	48.46
160	48.77	49.07	49.38	49.68	49.99	50.29	50.6	50.9	51.21	51.51
170	51.82	52.12	52.43	52.73	53.04	53.34	53.64	53.95	54.25	54.56
180	54.86	55.17	55.47	55.78	56.08	56.39	56.69	57.0	57.3	57.61
190	57.91	58.22	58.52	58.83	59.13	59.44	59.74	60.05	60.35	60.66
200	60.96	61.26	61.57	61.87	62.18	62.48	62.79	63.09	63.4	63.7
210	64.01	64.31	64.62	64.92	65.23	65.53	65.84	66.14	66.45	66.75
220	67.06	67.36	67.67	67.97	68.28	68.58	68.89	69.19	69.49	69.79
230	70.1	70.41	70.71	71.02	71.32	71.63	71.93	72.24	72.54	72.85
240	73.15	73.46	73.76	74.07	74.37	74.68	74.98	75.29	75.59	75.9
250	76.2									

6
feet to metres

yd	0	1	2	3	4	5	6	7	8	9
	m									
0		0.91	1.83	2.74	3.65	4.57	5.49	6.4	7.32	8.23
10	9.14	10.06	10.97	11.89	12.8	13.71	14.63	15.54	16.46	17.37
20	18.29	19.2	20.12	21.03	21.95	22.86	23.77	24.69	25.6	26.52
30	27.43	28.35	29.26	30.18	31.09	32.0	32.92	33.83	34.75	35.66
40	36.58	37.49	38.4	39.32	40.23	41.15	42.06	42.98	43.89	44.81
50	45.72	46.63	47.55	48.46	49.38	50.29	51.21	52.12	53.04	53.95
60	54.86	55.78	56.69	57.61	58.52	59.44	60.35	61.27	62.18	63.09
70	64.0	64.92	65.84	66.75	67.67	68.58	69.49	70.41	71.32	72.24
80	73.15	74.07	74.98	75.9	76.81	77.72	78.64	79.55	80.47	81.38
90	82.3	83.21	84.12	85.04	85.95	86.87	87.78	88.7	89.61	90.53
100	91.44	92.35	93.27	94.18	95.1	96.01	96.93	97.84	98.76	99.67
110	100.58	101.5	102.41	103.33	104.24	105.16	106.07	106.99	107.9	108.81
120	109.73	110.64	111.56	112.47	113.39	114.3	115.21	116.13	117.04	117.96
130	118.87	119.79	120.7	121.61	122.53	123.44	124.36	125.27	126.19	127.1
140	128.02	128.93	129.85	130.76	131.67	132.59	133.5	134.42	135.33	136.25
150	137.16	138.07	138.99	139.9	140.82	141.73	142.65	143.56	144.48	145.39
160	146.3	147.22	148.13	149.05	149.96	150.88	151.79	152.71	153.62	154.53
170	155.45	156.36	157.28	158.19	159.11	160.02	160.93	161.85	162.76	163.68
180	164.59	165.51	166.42	167.34	168.25	169.16	170.08	170.99	171.9	172.82
190	173.74	174.65	175.57	176.48	177.39	178.31	179.22	180.14	181.05	181.97
200	182.88	183.79	184.71	185.62	186.54	187.45	188.37	189.28	190.2	191.11
210	192.02	192.94	193.85	194.77	195.68	196.6	197.51	198.43	199.34	200.25
220	201.17	202.08	203.0	203.91	204.83	205.74	206.65	207.57	208.48	209.4
230	210.31	211.23	212.14	213.06	213.97	214.88	215.8	216.71	217.63	218.54
240	219.46	220.37	221.29	222.0	223.11	224.03	224.94	225.86	226.77	227.69
250	228.6									

8
yards to metres

mile	0	1	2	3	4	5	6	7	8	9
	km									
0		1.61	3.22	4.83	6.44	8.05	9.66	11.27	12.87	14.48
10	16.09	17.7	19.31	20.92	22.53	24.14	25.75	27.36	28.97	30.58
20	32.19	33.8	35.41	37.01	38.62	40.23	41.84	43.45	45.06	46.67
30	48.28	49.89	51.5	53.11	54.72	56.33	57.94	59.55	61.16	62.76
40	64.37	65.98	67.59	69.2	70.81	72.42	74.03	75.64	77.25	78.86
50	80.47	82.08	83.69	85.3	86.9	88.51	90.12	91.73	93.34	94.95
60	96.56	98.17	99.78	101.39	103.0	104.61	106.22	107.83	109.44	111.05
70	112.65	114.26	115.87	117.48	119.09	120.7	122.31	123.92	125.53	127.14
80	128.75	130.36	131.97	133.58	135.19	136.79	138.4	140.01	141.62	143.23
90	144.84	146.45	148.06	149.67	151.28	152.89	154.5	156.11	157.72	159.33
100	160.93									

10
miles to kilometres

Conversions

Area

11
square centimetres
to square inches

cm²	0	1	2	3	4	5	6	7	8	9
	in²									
0		0.16	0.31	0.47	0.62	0.78	0.93	1.09	1.24	1.4
10	1.6	1.71	1.86	2.02	2.17	2.33	2.48	2.64	2.79	2.95
20	3.1	3.26	3.41	3.57	3.72	3.88	4.03	4.19	4.34	4.5
30	4.65	4.81	4.96	5.12	5.27	5.43	5.58	5.74	5.9	6.05
40	6.2	6.36	6.51	6.67	6.82	6.98	7.13	7.29	7.44	7.6
50	7.75	7.91	8.06	8.22	8.37	8.53	8.68	8.84	9.0	9.15
60	9.3	9.46	9.61	9.77	9.92	10.08	10.23	10.39	10.54	10.7
70	10.85	11.01	11.16	11.32	11.47	11.63	11.78	11.94	12.09	12.25
80	12.4	12.56	12.71	12.87	13.02	13.18	13.33	13.49	13.64	13.8
90	13.95	14.11	14.26	14.42	14.57	14.73	14.88	15.04	15.19	15.35
100	15.5	15.66	15.81	15.97	16.12	16.28	16.43	16.59	16.74	16.9
110	17.05	17.21	17.36	17.52	17.67	17.83	17.98	18.14	18.29	18.45
120	18.6	18.76	18.91	19.07	19.22	19.38	19.53	19.69	19.84	20.0
130	20.15	20.31	20.46	20.62	20.77	20.93	21.08	21.24	21.39	21.55
140	21.7	21.86	22.01	22.17	22.32	22.48	22.63	22.79	22.94	23.1
150	23.25	23.41	23.56	23.72	23.87	24.03	24.18	24.34	24.49	24.65
160	24.8	24.96	25.11	25.27	25.42	25.58	25.73	25.89	26.04	26.2
170	26.35	26.51	26.66	26.82	26.97	27.13	27.28	27.44	27.59	27.75
180	27.9	28.06	28.21	28.37	28.52	28.68	28.83	28.99	29.14	29.3
190	29.45	29.61	29.76	29.92	30.07	30.23	30.38	30.54	30.69	30.85
200	31.0	31.16	31.31	31.47	31.62	31.78	31.93	32.09	32.24	32.4
210	32.55	32.71	32.86	33.02	33.17	33.33	33.48	33.64	33.79	33.95
220	34.1	34.26	34.41	34.57	34.72	34.88	35.03	35.19	35.34	35.5
230	35.65	35.81	35.96	36.12	36.27	36.43	36.58	36.75	36.89	37.05
240	37.20	37.36	37.51	37.67	37.82	37.98	38.13	38.29	38.44	38.6
250	38.75									

13
square metres to
square feet

m²	0	1	2	3	4	5	6	7	8	9
	ft²									
0		10.76	21.53	32.29	43.06	53.82	64.58	75.35	86.11	96.88
10	107.64	118.4	129.17	139.93	150.66	161.46	172.22	182.97	193.75	204.51
20	215.29	226.01	236.81	247.57	258.33	269.1	279.86	290.63	301.39	312.15
30	322.92	333.68	344.45	355.21	365.97	376.74	387.5	398.27	409.03	419.79
40	430.56	441.32	452.08	462.85	473.61	484.38	495.14	505.91	516.67	527.43
50	538.2	548.96	559.72	570.49	581.25	592.02	602.78	613.54	624.31	635.07
60	645.84	656.6	667.36	678.13	688.89	699.65	710.42	721.18	731.95	742.71
70	753.47	764.24	775.0	785.77	796.53	807.29	818.06	828.82	839.59	850.35
80	861.11	871.88	882.64	893.41	904.17	914.93	925.7	936.46	947.22	957.99
90	968.75	979.52	990.28	1 001.04	1 011.81	1 022.57	1 033.34	1 044.1	1 054.86	1 065.63
100	1 076.39	1 087.15	1 097.92	1 108.68	1 119.45	1 130.21	1 140.97	1 151.74	1 162.5	1 173.27
110	1 184.03	1 194.79	1 205.56	1 216.32	1 227.09	1 237.85	1 248.61	1 259.38	1 270.14	1 280.91
120	1 291.67	1 302.43	1 313.2	1 323.96	1 334.72	1 345.49	1 356.25	1 367.02	1 377.78	1 388.54
130	1 399.31	1 410.07	1 420.84	1 431.6	1 442.36	1 453.13	1 463.89	1 474.66	1 485.42	1 496.18
140	1 506.95	1 517.71	1 528.48	1 539.24	1 550.0	1 560.77	1 571.53	1 582.29	1 593.06	1 603.82
150	1 614.59	1 625.35	1 636.11	1 646.88	1 657.64	1 668.41	1 679.17	1 689.93	1 700.7	1 711.46
160	1 722.23	1 732.99	1 743.75	1 754.52	1 765.28	1 776.05	1 786.81	1 797.57	1 808.34	1 819.1
170	1 829.86	1 840.63	1 851.39	1 862.16	1 872.92	1 883.68	1 894.45	1 905.21	1 915.98	1 926.74
180	1 937.5	1 948.27	1 959.03	1 969.8	1 980.56	1 991.32	2 002.09	2 012.85	2 023.62	2 034.38
190	2 045.14	2 055.91	2 066.67	2 077.43	2 088.2	2 098.96	2 109.73	2 120.49	2 131.25	2 142.02
200	2 152.78	2 163.55	2 174.31	2 185.07	2 195.84	2 206.6	2 217.37	2 228.13	2 238.89	2 249.66
210	2 260.42	2 271.19	2 281.95	2 292.71	2 303.48	2 314.24	2 325.0	2 335.77	2 346.53	2 357.3
220	2 368.06	2 378.82	2 389.59	2 400.35	2 411.12	2 421.88	2 432.64	2 443.41	2 454.17	2 464.94
230	2 475.7	2 486.46	2 497.23	2 507.99	2 518.76	2 529.52	2 540.28	2 551.05	2 561.81	2 572.57
240	2 583.34	2 594.1	2 604.87	2 615.63	2 626.39	2 637.16	2 647.92	2 658.69	2 669.45	2 680.21
250	2 690.98	2 701.74	2 712.51	2 723.27	2 734.03	2 744.8	2 755.56	2 766.32	2 777.09	2 787.85
260	2 798.62	2 809.38	2 820.14	2 830.91	2 841.67	2 852.44	2 863.2	2 873.96	2 884.73	2 895.49
270	2 906.26	2 917.02	2 927.78	2 938.55	2 949.31	2 960.08	2 970.84	2 981.6	2 992.37	3 003.13
280	3 013.89	3 024.66	3 035.42	3 046.19	3 056.95	3 067.71	3 078.48	3 089.24	3 100.01	3 110.77
290	3 121.53	3 132.3	3 143.06	3 153.83	3 164.59	3 175.35	3 186.12	3 196.88	3 207.65	3 218.41
300	3 229.17	3 239.94	3 250.7	3 261.46	3 272.23	3 282.99	3 293.76	3 304.52	3 315.28	3 326.05
310	3 336.81	3 347.58	3 358.34	3 369.1	3 379.87	3 390.63	3 401.4	3 412.16	3 422.92	3 433.69
320	3 444.45	3 455.22	3 465.98	3 476.74	3 487.51	3 498.27	3 509.03	3 519.8	3 530.56	3 541.33
330	3 552.09	3 562.85	3 573.62	3 584.38	3 595.15	3 605.91	3 616.67	3 627.44	3 638.2	3 648.97
340	3 659.73	3 670.49	3 681.26	3 692.02	3 702.79	3 713.55	3 724.31	3 735.08	3 745.84	3 756.6
350	3 767.37	3 778.13	3 788.9	3 799.66	3 810.42	3 821.19	3 831.95	3 842.72	3 853.48	3 864.24
360	3 875.01	3 885.77	3 896.54	3 907.3	3 918.06	3 928.83	3 939.59	3 950.36	3 961.12	3 971.88
370	3 982.65	3 993.41	4 004.17	4 014.94	4 025.7	4 036.47	4 047.23	4 057.99	4 068.76	4 079.52
380	4 090.29	4 101.05	4 111.81	4 122.58	4 133.34	4 144.11	4 154.87	4 165.63	4 176.4	4 187.16
390	4 197.93	4 208.69	4 219.45	4 230.22	4 240.98	4 251.74	4 262.51	4 273.27	4 284.04	4 294.8
400	4 305.56	4 316.33	4 327.09	4 337.86	4 348.62	4 359.38	4 370.15	4 380.91	4 391.68	4 402.44
410	4 413.2	4 423.97	4 434.73	4 445.49	4 456.26	4 467.02	4 477.79	4 488.55	4 499.31	4 510.08
420	4 520.84	4 531.61	4 542.37	4 553.13	4 563.9	4 574.66	4 585.43	4 596.19	4 606.95	4 617.72
430	4 628.48	4 639.25	4 650.01	4 660.77	4 671.54	4 682.3	4 693.06	4 703.83	4 714.59	4 725.36
440	4 736.12	4 746.88	4 757.65	4 768.41	4 779.18	4 789.94	4 800.7	4 811.47	4 822.23	4 833.0
450	4 843.76	4 854.52	4 865.29	4 876.05	4 886.82	4 897.58	4 908.34	4 919.11	4 929.87	4 940.63
460	4 951.4	4 962.16	4 972.93	4 983.69	4 994.45	5 005.22	5 015.98	5 026.75	5 037.51	5 048.27
470	5 059.04	5 069.8	5 080.57	5 091.33	5 102.09	5 112.86	5 123.62	5 134.39	5 145.15	5 155.91
480	5 166.68	5 177.44	5 188.2	5 198.97	5 209.73	5 220.5	5 231.26	5 242.02	5 252.79	5 263.55
490	5 274.32	5 285.08	5 295.84	5 306.61	5 317.37	5 328.14	5 338.9	5 349.66	5 360.43	5 371.19
500	5 381.96									

in²	0	1	2	3	4	5	6	7	8	9
	cm²									
0		6.45	12.9	19.36	25.81	32.26	38.71	45.16	51.61	58.06
10	64.52	70.97	77.41	83.87	90.32	96.77	103.23	109.68	116.13	122.58
20	129.03	135.48	141.94	148.39	154.84	161.29	167.74	174.19	180.65	187.1
30	193.55	200.0	206.45	212.9	219.35	225.8	232.26	238.71	245.16	251.61
40	258.06	264.52	270.97	277.42	283.87	290.32	296.77	303.23	309.68	316.13
50	322.58	329.03	335.48	341.94	348.4	354.84	361.29	367.74	374.19	380.64
60	387.1	393.55	400.0	406.45	412.91	419.35	425.81	432.26	438.71	445.16
70	451.61	458.06	464.52	470.97	477.42	483.87	490.32	496.77	503.23	509.68
80	516.13	522.58	529.03	535.48	541.93	548.39	554.84	561.29	567.74	574.19
90	580.64	587.1	593.55	600.0	606.45	612.91	619.35	625.81	632.26	638.71
100	645.16	651.61	658.06	664.51	670.97	677.42	683.87	690.32	696.77	703.22
110	709.6	716.13	722.58	729.03	735.48	741.93	748.39	754.84	761.29	767.74
120	774.19	780.64	787.1	793.55	800.0	806.45	812.9	819.35	825.81	832.26
130	838.71	845.16	851.61	858.06	864.51	870.97	877.42	883.87	890.32	896.77
140	903.22	909.68	916.13	922.58	929.03	935.48	941.93	948.39	954.84	961.29
150	967.74	974.19	980.64	987.1	993.55	1 000.00	1 006.45	1 012.9	1 019.35	1 025.8
160	1 032.26	1 038.71	1 045.16	1 051.61	1 058.06	1 064.51	1 070.97	1 077.42	1 083.87	1 090.32
170	1 096.77	1 103.22	1 109.68	1 116.13	1 122.58	1 129.03	1 135.48	1 141.93	1 148.38	1 154.84
180	1 161.29	1 167.74	1 174.19	1 180.64	1 187.09	1 193.55	1 200.0	1 206.45	1 212.9	1 219.35
190	1 225.8	1 232.26	1 238.71	1 245.16	1 251.61	1 258.06	1 264.51	1 270.97	1 277.42	1 283.87
200	1 290.32	1 296.77	1 303.22	1 309.67	1 316.13	1 322.58	1 329.03	1 335.48	1 341.93	1 348.38
210	1 354.84	1 361.29	1 367.74	1 374.19	1 380.64	1 387.09	1 393.55	1 400.0	1 406.45	1 412.9
220	1 419.35	1 425.8	1 432.26	1 438.71	1 445.16	1 451.61	1 458.06	1 464.51	1 470.96	1 477.42
230	1 483.87	1 490.32	1 496.77	1 503.22	1 509.67	1 516.13	1 522.58	1 529.03	1 535.48	1 541.93
240	1 548.38	1 554.84	1 561.29	1 567.74	1 574.19	1 580.64	1 587.09	1 593.55	1 600.0	1 606.45
250	1 612.9									

12
square inches
to square
centimetres

ft²	0	1	2	3	4	5	6	7	8	9
	m²									
0		0.09	0.19	0.28	0.37	0.46	0.56	0.65	0.74	0.84
10	0.93	1.02	1.11	1.21	1.3	1.39	1.49	1.58	1.67	1.77
20	1.86	1.95	2.04	2.14	2.23	2.32	2.42	2.51	2.6	2.69
30	2.79	2.88	2.97	3.07	3.16	3.25	3.34	3.44	3.53	3.62
40	3.72	3.81	3.9	3.99	4.09	4.18	4.27	4.37	4.46	4.55
50	4.65	4.74	4.83	4.92	5.02	5.11	5.2	5.3	5.39	5.48
60	5.57	5.67	5.76	5.85	5.95	6.04	6.13	6.22	6.32	6.41
70	6.5	6.6	6.69	6.78	6.87	6.97	7.06	7.15	7.25	7.34
80	7.43	7.53	7.62	7.71	7.8	7.9	7.99	8.08	8.18	8.27
90	8.36	8.45	8.55	8.64	8.73	8.83	8.92	9.01	9.1	9.2
100	9.29	9.38	9.48	9.57	9.66	9.75	9.85	9.94	10.03	10.13
110	10.22	10.31	10.41	10.5	10.59	10.68	10.78	10.87	10.96	11.06
120	11.15	11.24	11.33	11.43	11.52	11.61	11.71	11.8	11,89	11.98
130	12.08	12.17	12.26	12.36	12.45	12.54	12.63	12.73	12.82	12.91
140	13.01	13.1	13.19	13.29	13.38	13.47	13.56	13.66	13.75	13.84
150	13.94	14.03	14.12	14.21	14.31	14.4	14.49	14.59	14.68	14.77
160	14.86	14.96	15.05	15.14	15.24	15.33	15.42	15.51	15.61	15.7
170	15.79	15.89	15.98	16.07	16.17	16.26	16.35	16.44	16.54	16.63
180	16.72	16.82	16.91	17.0	17.09	17.19	17.28	17.37	17.47	17.56
190	17.65	17.74	17.84	17.93	18.02	18.12	18.21	18.3	18.39	18.49
200	18.58	18.67	18.77	18.86	18.95	19.05	19.14	19.23	19.32	19.42
210	19.51	19.6	19.7	19.79	19.88	19.97	20.07	20.16	20.25	20.35
220	20.44	20.53	20.62	20.72	20.81	20.9	21.0	21.09	21.18	21.27
230	21.37	21.46	21.55	21.65	21.74	21.83	21.93	22.02	22.11	22.2
240	22.3	22.39	22.48	22.58	22.67	22.76	22.85	22.95	23.04	23.13
250	23.23	23.32	23.41	23.5	23.6	23.69	23.78	23.88	23.97	24.06
260	24.15	24.25	24.34	24.43	24.53	24.62	24.71	24.81	24.9	24.99
270	25.08	25.18	25.27	25.36	25.46	25.55	25.64	25.73	25.83	25.92
280	26.01	26.11	26.2	26.29	26.38	26.48	26.57	26.66	26.76	26.85
290	26.94	27.03	27.13	27.22	27.31	27.41	27.5	27.59	27.69	27.78
300	27.87	27.96	28.06	28.15	28.24	28.34	28.43	28.52	28.61	28.71
310	28.8	28.89	28.99	29.08	29.17	29.26	29.36	29.45	29.54	29.64
320	29.73	29.82	29.91	30.01	30.1	30.19	30.29	30.38	30.47	30.57
330	30.66	30.75	30.84	30.94	31.03	31.12	31.22	31.31	31.4	31.49
340	31.59	31.68	31.77	31.87	31.96	32.05	32.14	32.24	32.33	32.42
350	32.52	32.61	32.7	32.79	32.89	32.98	33.07	33.17	33.26	33.35
360	33.45	33.54	33.63	33.72	33.82	33.91	34.0	34.1	34.19	34.28
370	34.37	34.47	34.56	34.65	34.75	34.84	34.93	35.02	35.12	35.21
380	35.3	35.4	35.49	35.58	35.67	35.77	35.86	35.95	36.05	36.14
390	36.23	36.33	36.42	36.51	36.6	36.7	36.79	36.88	36.98	37.07
400	37.16	37.25	37.35	37.44	37.53	37.63	37.72	37.81	37.9	38.0
410	38.09	38.18	38.28	38.37	38.46	38.55	38.65	38.74	38.83	38.93
420	39.02	39.11	39.21	39.3	39.39	39.48	39.58	39.67	39.76	39.86
430	39.95	40.04	40.13	40.23	40.32	40.41	40.51	40.6	40.69	40.78
440	40.88	40.97	41.06	41.16	41.25	41.34	41.43	41.53	41.62	41.71
450	41.81	41.9	41.99	42.09	42.18	42.27	42.36	42.46	42.55	42.64
460	42.74	42.83	42.92	43.01	43.11	43.2	43.29	43.39	43.48	43.57
470	43.66	43.76	43.85	43.94	44.04	44.13	44.22	44.31	44.41	44.5
480	44.59	44.69	44.78	44.87	44.97	45.06	45.15	45.24	45.34	45.43
490	45.52	45.62	45.71	45.8	45.89	45.99	46.08	46.17	46.27	46.36
500	46.45									

14
square feet to
square metres

Conversions

15
square metres to
square yards

m²	0	1	2	3	4	5	6	7	8	9
	yd²									
0		1.2	2.39	3.58	4.78	5.98	7.18	8.37	9.57	10.76
10	11.96	13.16	14.35	15.55	16.74	17.94	19.14	20.33	21.53	22.72
20	23.92	25.12	26.31	27.51	28.7	29.9	31.1	32.29	33.49	34.68
30	35.88	37.08	38.27	39.47	40.66	41.86	43.06	44.25	45.45	46.64
40	47.84	49.04	50.23	51.43	52.62	53.82	55.02	56.21	57.41	58.6
50	59.8	61.0	62.19	63.39	64.58	65.78	66.98	68.17	69.37	70.56
60	71.76	72.96	74.15	75.35	76.54	77.74	78.94	80.13	81.33	82.52
70	83.72	84.92	86.11	87.31	88.5	89.7	90.9	92.09	93.29	94.48
80	95.68	96.88	98.07	99.27	100.46	101.66	102.86	104.05	105.25	106.44
90	107.64	108.84	110.03	111.23	112.42	113.62	114.82	116.01	117.21	118.4
100	119.6	120.8	121.99	123.19	124.38	125.58	126.78	127.97	129.17	130.36
110	131.56	132.76	133.95	135.15	136.34	137.54	138.74	139.93	141.13	142.32
120	143.52	144.72	145.91	147.11	148.31	149.5	150.7	151.89	153.09	154.28
130	155.48	156.68	157.87	159.07	160.26	161.46	162.66	163.85	165.05	166.24
140	167.44	168.64	169.83	171.03	172.22	173.41	174.62	175.81	177.01	178.2
150	179.34	180.59	181.79	182.99	184.18	185.38	186.57	187.77	188.97	190.16
160	191.36	192.55	193.75	194.95	196.14	197.34	198.53	199.73	200.93	202.12
170	203.32	204.51	205.71	206.91	208.1	209.3	210.49	211.69	212.89	214.08
180	215.28	216.47	217.67	218.87	220.06	221.26	222.45	223.65	224.85	226.04
190	227.24	228.43	229.63	230.83	232.02	233.22	234.41	235.61	236.81	238.0
200	239.2	240.39	241.59	242.79	243.98	245.18	246.37	247.57	248.77	249.96
210	251.16	252.35	253.55	254.75	255.94	257.14	258.33	259.53	260.73	261.92
220	263.12	264.31	265.51	266.71	267.9	269.1	270.29	271.49	272.69	273.88
230	275.08	276.27	277.47	278.67	279.86	281.06	282.25	283.45	284.65	285.84
240	287.04	288.23	289.43	290.63	291.82	293.02	294.21	295.41	296.61	297.8
250	299.0	300.19	301.39	302.59	303.78	304.98	306.17	307.37	308.57	309.76
260	310.96	312.15	313.35	314.55	315.74	316.94	318.13	319.33	320.53	321.72
270	322.92	324.11	325.31	326.51	327.7	328.9	330.09	331.29	332.49	333.68
280	334.88	336.07	337.27	338.47	339.66	340.86	342.05	343.25	344.45	345.64
290	346.84	348.03	349.23	350.43	351.62	352.82	354.02	355.21	356.41	357.6
300	358.78	359.99	361.19	362.39	363.58	364.78	365.97	367.17	368.37	369.56
310	370.76	371.95	373.15	374.35	375.54	376.74	377.94	379.13	380.33	381.52
320	382.72	383.91	385.11	386.31	387.5	388.7	389.89	391.09	392.29	393.48
330	394.68	395.87	397.07	398.27	399.46	400.66	401.85	403.05	404.25	405.44
340	406.64	407.83	409.03	410.23	411.42	412.62	413.81	415.01	416.21	417.4
350	418.6	419.79	420.99	422.18	423.38	424.58	425.77	426.97	428.16	429.36
360	430.56	431.75	432.95	434.14	435.34	436.54	437.73	438.93	440.12	441.32
370	442.52	443.71	444.91	446.11	447.3	448.5	449.69	450.89	452.08	453.28
380	454.48	455.67	456.87	458.06	459.26	460.46	461.65	462.84	464.04	465.24
390	466.44	467.63	468.83	470.02	471.22	472.42	473.61	474.81	476.0	477.2
400	478.4	479.59	480.79	481.98	483.18	484.38	485.57	486.77	487.96	489.16
410	490.36	491.55	492.75	493.94	495.14	496.34	497.53	498.73	499.92	501.12
420	502.32	503.51	504.71	505.9	507.1	508.3	509.49	510.69	511.88	513.08
430	514.28	515.47	516.67	517.86	519.06	520.26	521.45	522.65	523.84	525.04
440	526.24	527.43	528.63	529.82	531.02	532.22	533.41	534.61	535.8	537.0
450	538.2	539.39	540.59	541.78	542.98	544.18	545.37	546.57	547.76	548.96
460	550.16	551.35	552.55	553.74	554.94	556.14	557.33	558.53	559.72	560.92
470	562.12	563.31	564.5	565.71	566.9	568.1	569.29	570.49	571.68	572.88
480	574.08	575.27	576.47	577.66	578.86	580.06	581.25	582.45	583.64	584.84
490	586.04	587.23	588.43	589.62	590.82	592.02	593.21	594.41	595.6	596.8
500	598.0									

17
hectares to acres

ha	0	1	2	3	4	5	6	7	8	9
	acre									
		2.47	4.94	7.41	9.88	12.36	14.83	17.3	19.77	22.24

ha	0	10	20	30	40	50	60	70	80	90
	acre									
0		24.71	49.42	74.13	98.84	123.55	148.26	172.97	197.68	222.4
100	247.11	271.82	296.53	321.24	345.95	370.66	395.37	420.08	444.8	469.5
200	494.21	518.92	543.63	568.34	593.05	617.76	642.47	667.19	691.9	716.61
300	741.32	766.03	790.74	815.45	840.16	864.87	889.58	914.29	939.0	963.71
400	988.42	1 013.13	1 037.84	1 062.55	1 087.26	1 111.97	1 136.68	1 161.4	1 186.11	1 210.82
500	1 235.53	1 260.24	1 284.95	1 309.66	1 334.37	1 359.08	1 383.79	1 408.5	1 433.21	1 457.92
600	1 482.63	1 507.34	1 532.05	1 556.76	1 581.47	1 606.18	1 630.9	1 655.61	1 680.32	1 705.03
700	1 729.74	1 754.45	1 779.16	1 803.87	1 828.58	1 853.29	1 878.0	1 902.71	1 927.42	1 952.13
800	1 976.84	2 001.55	2 026.26	2 050.97	2 075.69	2 100.4	2 125.11	2 149.82	2 174.53	2 199.24
900	2 223.95	2 248.66	2 273.37	2 298.08	2 322.79	2 347.5	2 372.21	2 396.92	2 421.63	2 446.34
1 000	2 471.05									

yd²	0	1	2	3	4	5	6	7	8	9
	m²									
0		0.84	1.67	2.51	3.34	4.18	5.02	5.85	6.69	7.53
10	8.36	9.2	10.03	10.87	11.71	12.54	13.38	14.21	15.05	15.89
20	16.72	17.56	18.39	19.23	20.07	20.9	21.74	22.58	23.41	24.25
30	25.08	25.92	26.76	27.59	28.43	29.26	30.1	30.94	31.77	32.61
40	33.45	34.28	35.12	35.95	36.79	37.63	38.46	39.3	40.13	40.97
50	41.81	42.64	43.48	44.31	45.15	45.99	46.82	47.66	48.5	49.33
60	50.17	51.0	51.84	52.68	53.51	54.35	55.18	56.02	56.86	57.69
70	58.53	59.37	60.2	61.04	61.87	62.71	63.55	64.38	65.22	66.05
80	66.89	67.7	68.56	69.3	70.23	71.07	71.9	72.74	73.5	74.4
90	75.25	76.09	76.92	77.76	78.6	79.43	80.27	81.10	81.94	82.78
100	83.61	84.45	85.29	86.12	86.96	87.79	88.62	89.47	90.3	91.14
110	91.97	92.81	93.65	94.48	95.32	96.15	96.99	97.83	98.66	99.5
120	100.34	101.17	102.0	102.84	103.68	104.52	105.35	106.19	107.02	107.86
130	108.7	109.53	110.37	111.21	112.04	112.88	113.71	114.55	115.39	116.22
140	117.06	117.89	118.73	119.57	120.41	121.24	122.08	122.91	123.75	124.58
150	125.42	126.26	127.09	127.93	128.76	129.6	130.44	131.27	132.11	132.94
160	133.78	134.62	135.45	136.29	137.13	137.96	138.8	139.63	140.47	141.31
170	142.14	142.98	143.81	144.65	145.49	146.32	147.16	148.0	148.83	149.67
180	150.5	151.34	152.18	153.01	153.85	154.68	155.52	156.36	157.19	158.03
190	158.86	159.7	160.54	161.37	162.21	163.05	163.88	164.72	165.55	166.39
200	167.23	168.06	168.9	169.73	170.57	171.41	172.24	173.08	173.91	174.75
210	175.59	176.42	177.26	178.1	178.93	179.77	180.61	181.44	182.28	183.11
220	183.95	184.78	185.62	186.46	187.29	188.13	188.97	189.80	190.64	191.47
230	192.31	193.15	193.98	194.82	195.65	196.49	197.33	198.16	199.0	199.83
240	200.67	201.51	202.34	203.18	204.02	204.85	205.69	206.52	207.36	208.2
250	209.03	209.87	210.7	211.54	212.38	213.21	214.1	214.89	215.72	216.56
260	217.39	218.3	219.07	219.9	220.74	221.57	222.41	223.25	224.08	224.92
270	225.75	226.59	227.43	228.26	229.1	229.94	230.77	231.61	232.44	233.28
280	234.12	234.95	235.79	236.62	237.46	238.3	239.13	239.97	240.81	241.64
290	242.48	243.31	244.15	244.99	245.82	246.66	247.49	248.33	249.17	250.0
300	250.84	251.67	252.51	253.35	254.18	255.02	255.86	256.69	257.53	258.36
310	259.2	260.04	260.87	261.71	262.54	263.38	264.22	265.05	265.89	266.73
320	267.56	268.4	269.23	270.07	270.91	271.74	272.58	273.41	274.25	275.09
330	275.92	276.76	277.59	278.43	279.27	280.11	280.94	281.78	282.61	283.45
340	284.28	285.12	285.96	286.79	287.63	288.46	289.3	290.14	290.97	291.81
350	292.65	293.48	294.32	295.15	295.99	296.83	297.66	298.5	299.33	300.17
360	301.0	301.84	302.68	303.51	304.35	305.19	306.02	306.86	307.7	308.53
370	309.37	310.2	311.04	311.88	312.71	313.55	314.38	315.22	316.06	316.89
380	317.73	318.57	319.4	320.24	321.07	321.91	322.75	323.58	324.42	325.25
390	326.09	326.93	327.76	328.6	329.43	330.27	331.11	331.94	332.78	333.62
400	334.45	335.29	336.12	336.96	337.8	338.63	339.47	340.31	341.14	341.98
410	342.81	343.65	344.48	345.32	346.16	346.99	347.83	348.67	349.51	350.34
420	351.17	352.01	352.85	353.68	354.52	355.35	356.19	357.03	357.86	358.7
430	359.54	360.37	361.21	362.04	362.88	363.72	364.55	365.39	366.22	367.06
440	367.9	368.73	369.57	370.41	371.24	372.08	372.91	373.75	374.59	375.42
450	376.26	377.09	377.93	378.77	379.6	380.44	381.27	382.11	382.95	383.78
460	384.62	385.46	386.29	387.13	387.96	388.8	389.64	390.47	391.31	392.14
470	392.98	393.82	394.65	395.49	396.32	397.16	398.0	398.83	399.67	400.51
480	401.34	402.18	403.01	403.85	404.69	405.52	406.36	407.19	408.03	408.87
490	409.7	410.54	411.38	412.21	413.05	413.88	414.72	415.56	416.39	417.23
500	418.0									

16
square yards to
square metres

acre	0	1	2	3	4	5	6	7	8	9
	ha									
		0.4	0.81	1.21	1.62	2.02	2.42	2.83	3.23	3.64

18
acres to hectares

acre	0	10	20	30	40	50	60	70	80	90
	ha									
0		4.05	8.09	12.14	16.19	20.23	24.28	28.33	32.37	36.42
100	40.47	44.52	48.56	52.6	56.66	60.71	64.75	68.8	72.84	76.89
200	80.94	84.98	89.03	93.08	97.12	101.17	105.22	109.26	113.31	117.36
300	121.41	125.46	129.5	133.55	137.59	141.64	145.69	149.73	153.78	157.83
400	161.87	165.92	169.97	174.02	178.06	182.11	186.16	190.20	194.25	198.3
500	202.34	206.39	210.44	214.48	218.53	222.58	226.62	230.67	234.71	238.77
600	242.81	246.86	250.91	254.95	259.0	263.05	267.09	271.14	275.19	279.23
700	283.28	287.33	291.37	295.42	299.47	303.51	307.56	311.61	315.66	319.7
800	323.75	327.8	331.84	335.84	339.94	343.98	348.03	352.07	356.12	360.17
900	364.22	368.26	372.31	376.36	380.41	384.45	388.5	392.55	396.59	400.64
1 000	404.69									

Conversions

Volume

19
cubic centimetres to cubic inches

cm³	0	1	2	3	4	5	6	7	8	9
in³										
		0.06	0.12	0.18	0.24	0.31	0.37	0.43	0.49	0.55

cm³	0	10	20	30	40	50	60	70	80	90
in³										
0		0.61	1.22	1.83	2.44	3.05	3.66	4.27	4.88	5.49
100	6.1	6.71	7.32	7.93	8.54	9.15	9.76	10.37	10.98	11.59
200	12.2	12.82	13.43	14.04	14.65	15.26	15.87	16.48	17.09	17.7
300	18.31	18.92	19.53	20.14	20.75	21.36	21.97	22.58	23.19	23.8
400	24.41	25.02	25.63	26.24	26.85	27.46	28.07	28.68	29.29	29.9
500	30.51	31.12	31.73	32.34	32.95	33.56	34.17	34.78	35.39	36.0
600	36.61	37.22	37.83	38.45	39.06	39.67	40.28	40.89	41.5	42.11
700	42.72	43.38	43.94	44.55	45.16	45.77	46.38	46.99	47.6	48.21
800	48.82	49.43	50.04	50.65	51.26	51.87	52.48	53.09	53.7	54.31
900	54.92	55.53	56.14	56.75	57.36	57.97	58.58	59.19	59.8	60.41
1 000	61.02									

21
cubic metres to cubic feet

m³	0	1	2	3	4	5	6	7	8	9
ft³										
0		35.31	70.63	105.94	141.26	176.57	211.89	247.2	282.52	317.83
10	353.15	388.46	423.78	459.09	494.41	592.72	565.04	600.35	635.67	670.98
20	706.29	741.61	776.92	812.24	847.55	882.87	918.18	953.5	988.81	1 024.13
30	1 059.44	1 094.75	1 130.07	1 165.38	1 200.7	1 236.01	1 271.33	1 306.64	1 341.96	1 377.27
40	1 412.59	1 447.9	1 483.22	1 518.53	1 553.85	1 589.16	1 624.47	1 659.79	1 695.1	1 730.42
50	1 765.73	1 801.05	1 836.36	1 871.68	1 906.99	1 942.31	1 977.62	2 012.94	2 048.25	2 083.57
60	2 118.88	2 154.19	2 189.51	2 224.82	2 260.14	2 295.45	2 330.77	2 366.08	2 401.4	2 436.71
70	2 472.03	2 507.34	2 542.66	2 577.97	2 613.29	2 648.6	2 683.91	2 719.23	2 754.54	2 789.86
80	2 825.17	2 860.49	2 895.8	2 931.12	2 966.43	3 001.75	3 037.06	3 072.38	3 107.69	3 143.01
90	3 178.32	3 213.63	3 248.95	3 284.26	3 319.58	3 354.89	3 390.21	3 425.52	3 460.84	3 496.15
100	3 531.47	3 566.78	3 602.1	3 637.41	3 672.73	3 708.04	3 743.35	3 778.67	3 813.98	3 849.3
110	3 884.61	3 919.93	3 955.24	3 990.56	4 025.87	4 061.19	4 096.5	4 131.82	4 167.13	4 202.45
120	4 237.76	4 273.07	4 308.39	4 343.7	4 379.02	4 414.33	4 449.65	4 484.96	4 520.28	4 555.59
130	4 590.91	4 626.22	4 661.54	4 696.85	4 732.17	4 767.48	4 802.79	4 838.11	4 873.42	4 908.74
140	4 944.05	4 979.37	5 014.68	5 050.0	5 085.31	5 120.63	5 155.94	5 191.26	5 226.57	5 261.89
150	5 297.2	5 332.51	5 367.83	5 403.14	5 438.46	5 473.77	5 509.09	5 544.4	5 579.72	5 615.03
160	5 650.35	5 685.66	5 720.98	5 756.29	5 791.61	5 826.92	5 862.23	5 897.55	5 932.86	5 968.18
170	6 003.49	6 038.81	6 074.12	6 109.44	6 144.75	6 180.07	6 215.38	6 250.7	6 286.01	6 321.33
180	6 356.64	6 391.95	6 427.27	6 462.58	6 497.9	6 533.21	6 568.53	6 603.84	6 639.16	6 674.47
190	6 709.79	6 745.1	6 780.42	6 815.73	6 851.05	6 886.36	6 921.67	6 956.99	6 992.3	7 027.62
200	7 062.93	7 098.25	7 133.56	7 168.88	7 204.19	7 239.51	7 274.82	7 310.14	7 345.45	7 380.77
210	7 416.08	7 451.39	7 486.71	7 522.02	7 557.34	7 592.65	7 627.97	7 663.28	7 698.6	7 733.91
220	7 769.23	7 804.54	7 839.86	7 875.17	7 910.49	7 945.8	7 981.11	8 016.43	8 051.74	8 087.06
230	8 122.37	8 157.69	8 193.0	8 228.32	8 263.63	8 298.95	8 334.26	8 369.58	8 404.89	8 440.21
240	8 475.52	8 510.83	8 546.15	8 581.46	8 616.78	8 652.09	8 687.41	8 722.72	8 758.04	8 793.35
250	8 828.67									

23
litres to cubic feet

litre	0	1	2	3	4	5	6	7	8	9
ft³										
0		0.04	0.07	0.11	0.14	0.18	0.21	0.25	0.28	0.32
10	0.35	0.39	0.42	0.46	0.49	0.53	0.57	0.60	0.64	0.67
20	0.71	0.74	0.78	0.81	0.85	0.88	0.92	0.95	0.99	1.02
30	1.06	1.09	1.13	1.17	1.2	1.24	1.27	1.31	1.34	1.38
40	1.41	1.45	1.48	1.52	1.55	1.59	1.62	1.66	1.7	1.73
50	1.77	1.8	1.84	1.87	1.91	1.94	1.98	2.01	2.05	2.08
60	2.12	2.15	2.19	2.22	2.26	2.3	2.33	2.37	2.4	2.44
70	2.47	2.51	2.54	2.58	2.61	2.65	2.68	2.72	2.75	2.79
80	2.83	2.86	2.9	2.93	2.97	3.0	3.04	3.07	3.11	3.14
90	3.18	3.21	3.25	3.28	3.32	3.35	3.39	3.42	3.46	3.5
100	3.53									

in³	0	1	2	3	4	5	6	7	8	9
cm³										
		16.39	32.77	49.16	65.55	81.94	98.32	114.71	131.1	147.48

20
cubic inches to
cubic centimetres

in³	0	10	20	30	40	50	60	70	80	90
cm³										
0		163.87	327.74	491.61	655.48	819.35	983.22	1 147.09	1 310.97	1 474.84
100	1 638.71	1 802.58	1 966.45	2 130.32	2 294.19	2 458.06	2 621.93	2 785.8	2 949.67	3 113.54
200	3 277.41	3 441.28	3 605.15	3 769.02	3 932.9	4 096.77	4 260.64	4 424.51	4 588.38	4 752.25
300	4 916.12	5 079.99	5 243.86	5 407.73	5 571.6	5 735.47	5 899.34	6 063.21	6 227.08	6 390.95
400	6 554.83	6 718.7	6 882.57	7 046.44	7 210.31	7 374.18	7 538.05	7 701.92	7 865.79	8 029.66
500	8 193.53	8 357.4	8 521.27	8 685.14	8 849.01	9 012.89	9 176.76	9 340.63	9 504.5	9 668.37
600	9 832.24	9 996.11	10 160.0	10 323.9	10 487.7	10 651.6	10 815.5	10 979.3	11 143.2	11 307.1
700	11 470.9	11 634.8	11 798.7	11 962.6	12 126.4	12 290.3	12 454.2	12 618.0	12 781.9	12 945.8
800	13 109.7	13 273.5	13 437.4	13 601.3	13 765.1	13 929.0	14 092.9	14 256.7	14 420.6	14 584.5
900	14 748.4	14 912.2	15 076.1	15 240.0	15 403.8	15 567.7	15 731.6	15 895.5	16 059.3	16 223.2
1 000	16 387.1									

ft³	0	1	2	3	4	5	6	7	8	9
m³										
0		0.03	0.06	0.08	0.11	0.14	0.17	0.2	0.23	0.25
10	0.28	0.31	0.34	0.37	0.4	0.42	0.45	0.48	0.51	0.54
20	0.57	0.59	0.62	0.65	0.68	0.71	0.74	0.77	0.79	0.82
30	0.85	0.88	0.91	0.93	0.96	0.99	1.02	1.05	1.08	1.1
40	1.13	1.16	1.19	1.22	1.25	1.27	1.3	1.33	1.36	1.39
50	1.42	1.44	1.47	1.5	1.53	1.56	1.59	1.61	1.64	1.67
60	1.7	1.73	1.76	1.78	1.81	1.84	1.87	1.9	1.93	1.95
70	1.98	2.01	2.04	2.07	2.1	2.12	2.15	2.18	2.21	2.24
80	2.27	2.29	2.32	2.35	2.38	2.41	2.44	2.46	2.49	2.52
90	2.55	2.58	2.61	2.63	2.66	2.69	2.71	2.75	2.78	2.8
100	2.83	2.86	2.89	2.92	2.94	2.97	3.01	3.03	3.06	3.09
110	3.11	3.14	3.17	3.2	3.23	3.26	3.28	3.31	3.34	3.37
120	3.4	3.43	3.46	3.48	3.51	3.54	3.57	3.6	3.62	3.65
130	3.68	3.71	3.74	3.77	3.79	3.82	3.85	3.88	3.91	3.94
140	3.96	4.0	4.02	4.05	4.08	4.11	4.13	4.16	4.19	4.22
150	4.26	4.28	4.3	4.33	4.36	4.39	4.42	4.45	4.47	4.51
160	4.53	4.56	4.59	4.62	4.64	4.67	4.7	4.73	4.76	4.79
170	4.81	4.84	4.87	4.9	4.93	4.96	4.99	5.01	5.04	5.07
180	5.1	5.13	5.15	5.18	5.21	5.24	5.27	5.3	5.32	5.35
190	5.38	5.41	5.44	5.47	5.49	5.52	5.55	5.58	5.61	5.64
200	5.66	5.69	5.72	5.75	5.78	5.8	5.83	5.86	5.89	5.92
210	5.95	5.98	6.0	6.03	6.06	6.09	6.12	6.14	6.17	6.2
220	6.23	6.26	6.29	6.31	6.34	6.37	6.4	6.43	6.46	6.48
230	6.51	6.54	6.57	6.6	6.63	6.65	6.69	6.71	6.74	6.77
240	6.8	6.82	6.85	6.88	6.91	6.94	6.97	6.99	7.02	7.05
250	7.08									

22
cubic feet to
cubic metres

ft³	0	1	2	3	4	5	6	7	8	9
litre										
0		28.32	56.63	84.95	113.26	141.58	169.9	198.21	226.53	254.84
10	283.16	311.48	339.79	368.11	396.42	424.74	453.06	481.37	509.69	538.01
20	566.32	594.64	622.95	651.27	679.59	707.9	736.22	764.53	792.85	821.17
30	849.48	877.8	906.11	934.43	962.75	991.06	1 019.38	1 047.69	1 076.01	1 104.33
40	1 132.64	1 160.96	1 189.27	1 217.59	1 245.91	1 274.22	1 302.54	1 330.85	1 359.17	1 387.49
50	1 415.8	1 444.12	1 472.43	1 500.75	1 529.07	1 557.38	1 585.7	1 614.02	1 642.33	1 670.65
60	1 698.96	1 727.28	1 755.6	1 783.91	1 812.23	1 840.54	1 868.86	1 897.18	1 925.49	1 953.81
70	1 982.12	2 010.44	2 038.76	2 067.07	2 095.39	2 123.7	2 152.02	2 180.34	2 208.65	2 236.97
80	2 265.28	2 293.6	2 321.92	2 350.23	2 378.55	2 406.86	2 435.18	2 463.5	2 491.81	2 520.13
90	2 548.44	2 576.76	2 605.08	2 633.39	2 661.71	2 690.03	2 718.34	2 746.66	2 774.97	2 803.29
100	2 831.61									

24
cubic feet to litres

Conversions

25
litres to gallons
imperial

litre	0	1	2	3	4	5	6	7	8	9
	gal imp									
0		0.22	0.44	0.66	0.88	1.1	1.32	1.54	1.76	1.98
10	2.2	2.42	2.64	2.86	3.08	3.3	3.52	3.74	3.96	4.18
20	4.4	4.62	4.84	5.06	5.28	5.5	5.72	5.94	6.16	6.38
30	6.6	6.82	7.04	7.26	7.48	7.7	7.92	8.14	8.36	8.58
40	8.8	9.02	9.24	9.46	9.68	9.9	10.12	10.34	10.56	10.78
50	11.0	11.22	11.44	11.66	11.88	12.1	12.32	12.54	12.76	12.98
60	13.2	13.42	13.64	13.86	14.08	14.3	14.52	14.74	14.96	15.18
70	15.4	15.62	15.84	16.06	16.28	16.5	16.72	16.94	17.16	17.38
80	17.6	17.82	18.04	18.26	18.48	18.7	18.92	19.14	19.36	19.58
90	19.8	20.02	20.24	20.46	20.68	20.9	21.12	21.34	21.56	21.78
100	22.0									

27
litres to gallons US

litre	0	1	2	3	4	5	6	7	8	9
	gal US									
		0.26	0.53	0.79	1.06	1.32	1.59	1.85	2.11	2.38
10	2.64	2.91	3.17	3.43	3.7	3.96	4.23	4.49	4.76	5.02
20	5.28	5.55	5.81	6.08	6.34	6.61	6.87	7.13	7.4	7.66
30	7.93	8.19	8.45	8.72	8.98	9.25	9.51	9.78	10.04	10.3
40	10.57	10.83	11.1	11.36	11.62	11.89	12.15	12.42	12.68	12.95
50	13.21	13.47	13.74	14.0	14.27	14.53	14.8	15.06	15.32	15.59
60	15.85	16.12	16.38	16.64	16.91	17.17	17.44	17.7	17.97	18.23
70	18.49	18.76	19.02	19.29	19.55	19.82	20.08	20.34	20.61	20.87
80	21.14	21.4	21.66	21.93	22.19	22.46	22.72	22.96	23.25	23.51
90	23.78	24.04	24.31	24.57	24.83	25.1	25.36	25.63	25.89	26.16
100	26.42									

Mass

29
kilograms to pounds

kg	0	1	2	3	4	5	6	7	8	9
	lb									
0		2.21	4.41	6.61	8.82	11.02	13.23	15.43	17.64	19.84
10	22.05	24.25	26.46	28.66	30.86	33.07	35.27	37.47	39.68	41.89
20	44.09	46.3	48.5	50.71	52.91	55.12	57.32	59.52	61.73	63.93
30	66.14	68.34	70.55	72.75	74.96	77.16	79.37	81.57	83.78	85.98
40	88.18	90.39	92.59	94.8	97.0	99.2	101.41	103.61	105.82	108.03
50	110.23	112.44	114.64	116.85	119.05	121.25	123.46	125.66	127.87	130.07
60	132.28	134.48	136.69	138.89	141.1	143.3	145.51	147.71	149.91	152.12
70	154.32	156.53	158.73	160.94	163.14	165.35	167.55	169.76	171.96	174.17
80	176.37	178.57	180.78	182.98	185.19	187.39	189.6	191.8	194.01	196.21
90	198.42	200.62	202.83	205.03	207.24	209.44	211.64	213.85	216.05	218.26
100	220.46	222.67	224.87	227.08	229.28	231.49	233.69	235.9	238.1	240.3
110	242.51	244.71	246.92	249.12	251.33	253.53	255.74	257.94	260.15	262.35
120	264.56	266.76	268.96	271.17	273.37	275.58	277.78	279.99	282.19	284.4
130	286.6	288.81	291.01	293.22	295.42	297.62	299.83	302.03	304.24	306.44
140	308.65	310.85	313.06	315.26	317.47	319.67	321.88	324.08	326.28	328.49
150	330.69	332.9	335.1	337.31	339.51	341.72	343.92	346.13	348.33	350.54
160	352.74	354.94	357.15	359.35	361.56	363.76	365.97	368.17	370.38	372.58
170	374.79	377.0	379.2	381.4	383.6	385.81	388.01	390.22	392.42	394.68
180	396.83	399.04	401.24	403.45	405.65	407.86	410.06	412.26	414.47	416.67
190	418.88	421.08	423.29	425.49	427.68	429.9	432.11	434.31	436.52	438.72
200	440.93	443.13	445.33	447.54	449.74	451.95	454.15	456.36	458.56	460.77
210	462.97	465.18	467.38	469.59	471.79	473.99	476.2	478.4	480.61	482.81
220	485.02	487.22	489.43	491.63	493.84	496.04	498.25	500.45	502.65	504.86
230	507.06	509.2	511.47	513.6	515.88	518.0	520.29	522.4	524.7	526.9
240	529.1	531.31	533.5	535.72	537.9	540.13	542.3	544.54	546.7	548.9
250	551.16	553.36	555.57	557.77	559.97	562.18	564.38	566.59	568.79	571.0
260	573.2	575.41	577.61	579.82	582.02	584.23	586.43	588.63	590.84	593.04
270	595.25	597.45	599.66	601.86	604.07	606.27	608.48	610.68	612.89	615.09
280	617.29	619.5	621.7	623.91	626.11	628.32	630.52	632.73	634.93	637.14
290	639.34	641.55	643.75	645.95	648.16	650.36	652.57	654.77	656.98	659.18
300	661.39	663.59	665.8	668.0	670.21	672.41	674.62	676.82	679.02	681.23
310	683.43	685.64	687.84	690.05	692.25	694.46	696.66	698.87	701.07	703.28
320	705.48	707.68	709.89	712.09	714.3	716.5	718.71	720.91	723.12	725.32
330	727.53	729.73	731.93	734.14	736.34	738.55	740.75	742.96	745.16	747.37
340	749.57	751.78	753.98	756.19	758.39	760.6	762.8	765.0	767.21	769.41
350	771.62	773.82	776.03	778.23	780.44	782.64	784.85	787.05	789.26	791.46
360	793.66	795.87	798.07	800.28	802.48	804.69	806.89	809.1	811.31	813.51
370	815.71	817.92	820.12	822.32	824.53	826.73	828.94	831.14	833.35	835.55
380	837.76	839.96	842.17	844.37	846.58	848.78	850.98	853.19	855.39	857.6
390	859.8	862.0	864.21	866.41	868.62	870.8	873.03	875.2	877.44	879.64
400	881.85	884.05	886.26	888.46	890.67	892.87	895.08	897.28	899.49	901.69
410	903.9	906.1	908.31	910.51	912.71	914.92	917.12	919.33	921.53	923.74
420	925.94	928.15	930.35	932.56	934.76	936.97	939.17	941.37	943.58	945.78
430	947.99	950.19	952.4	954.6	956.81	959.01	961.22	963.42	965.63	967.83
440	970.03	972.24	974.44	976.65	978.85	981.06	983.26	985.47	987.67	989.88
450	992.08	994.29	996.49	998.69	1 000.9	1 003.1	1 005.31	1 007.51	1 009.72	1 011.92
460	1 014.13	1 016.33	1 018.54	1 020.74	1 022.94	1 025.15	1 027.35	1 029.56	1 031.76	1 033.97
470	1 036.17	1 038.38	1 040.58	1 042.79	1 044.99	1 047.2	1 049.4	1 051.6	1 053.81	1 056.01
480	1 058.22	1 060.42	1 062.63	1 064.83	1 067.04	1 069.24	1 071.45	1 073.65	1 075.86	1 078.06
490	1 080.27	1 082.47	1 084.67	1 086.88	1 089.08	1 091.29	1 093.49	1 095.7	1 097.9	1 100.11
500	1 102.31									

gal imp	0	1	2	3	4	5	6	7	8	9
	litre									
0		4.55	9.09	13.64	18.18	22.73	27.28	31.82	36.37	40.91
10	45.46	50.0	54.55	59.1	63.64	68.19	72.74	77.28	81.83	86.38
20	90.92	95.47	100.01	104.56	109.1	113.65	118.2	122.74	127.29	131.83
30	136.38	140.93	145.47	150.02	154.56	159.1	163.66	168.21	172.75	177.3
40	181.84	186.38	190.93	195.48	200.02	204.57	209.11	213.66	218.21	222.75
50	227.3	231.84	236.39	240.94	245.48	250.03	254.57	259.12	263.67	268.21
60	272.76	277.3	281.85	286.4	290.94	295.49	300.03	304.58	309.13	313.67
70	318.22	322.76	327.31	331.86	336.4	340.95	345.49	350.04	354.59	359.13
80	363.68	368.22	372.77	377.32	381.86	386.41	390.95	395.5	400.04	404.59
90	409.14	413.68	418.23	422.77	427.32	431.87	436.41	440.96	445.5	450.05
100	454.6									

26
gallons imperial to litres

gal US	0	1	2	3	4	5	6	7	8	9
	litre									
0		3.79	7.57	11.36	15.14	18.93	22.71	26.5	30.28	34.07
10	37.85	41.64	45.42	49.21	52.99	56.78	60.56	64.35	68.13	71.92
20	75.7	79.49	83.27	87.06	90.84	94.63	98.41	102.2	105.98	109.77
30	113.55	117.34	121.12	124.91	128.69	132.48	136.26	140.05	143.83	147.62
40	151.40	155.19	158.97	162.76	166.54	170.33	174.11	177.9	181.68	185.47
50	189.25	193.04	196.82	200.61	204.39	208.18	211.96	215.75	219.53	223.32
60	227.1	230.89	234.67	238.46	242.24	246.03	249.81	253.6	257.38	261.17
70	264.95	268.74	272.52	276.31	280.09	283.88	287.66	291.45	295.23	299.02
80	302.81	306.59	310.37	314.16	317.94	321.73	325.51	329.3	333.08	336.87
90	340.65	344.44	348.22	352.01	355.79	359.58	363.36	367.14	370.93	374.72
100	378.51									

28
gallons US to litres

lb	0	1	2	3	4	5	6	7	8	9
	kg									
0		0.45	0.91	1.36	1.81	2.27	2.72	3.18	3.63	4.08
10	4.54	4.99	5.44	5.9	6.35	6.8	7.26	7.71	8.16	8.62
20	9.07	9.53	9.98	10.43	10.89	11.34	11.79	12.25	12.7	13.15
30	13.61	14.06	14.52	14.97	15.42	15.88	16.33	16.78	17.24	17.69
40	18.14	18.6	19.05	19.5	19.96	20.41	20.87	21.32	21.77	22.23
50	22.68	23.13	23.59	24.04	24.49	24.95	25.4	25.85	26.31	26.76
60	27.22	27.67	28.12	28.58	29.03	29.48	29.94	30.39	30.84	31.3
70	31.75	32.21	32.66	33.11	33.57	34.02	34.47	34.93	35.38	35.83
80	36.29	36.74	37.19	37.65	38.1	38.56	39.01	39.46	39.92	40.37
90	40.82	41.28	41.73	42.18	42.64	43.09	43.54	44.0	44.45	44.91
100	45.36	45.81	46.27	46.72	47.17	47.63	48.08	48.53	48.99	49.44
110	49.9	50.35	50.8	51.26	51.71	52.16	52.62	53.07	53.52	53.98
120	54.43	54.88	55.34	55.79	56.25	56.7	57.15	57.61	58.06	58.51
130	58.97	59.42	59.87	60.33	60.78	61.24	61.69	62.14	62.6	63.05
140	63.5	63.96	64.41	64.86	65.32	65.77	66.22	66.68	67.13	67.59
150	68.04	68.49	68.95	69.4	69.85	70.31	70.76	71.21	71.67	72.12
160	72.57	73.03	73.48	73.94	74.39	74.84	75.3	75.75	76.2	76.66
170	77.11	77.56	78.02	78.47	78.93	79.38	79.83	80.29	80.74	81.19
180	81.65	82.1	82.55	83.01	83.46	83.91	84.37	84.82	85.28	85.73
190	86.18	86.64	87.09	87.54	88.0	88.45	88.9	89.36	89.81	90.26
200	90.72	91.17	91.63	92.08	92.53	92.99	93.44	93.89	94.35	94.8
210	95.25	95.71	96.16	96.62	97 07	97.52	97.98	98.43	98.88	99.34
220	99.79	100.24	100.7	101.15	101.61	102.06	102.51	102.97	103.42	103.87
230	104.33	104.78	105.23	105.69	106.14	106.59	107.05	107.5	107.96	108.41
240	108.86	109.32	109.77	110.22	110.68	111.13	111.58	112.04	112.49	112.95
250	113.4	113.85	114.31	114.76	115.21	115.67	116.12	116.57	117.03	117.48
260	117.93	118.39	118.84	119.3	119.75	120.2	120.66	121.11	121.56	122.02
270	122.47	122.92	123.38	123.83	124.28	124.74	125.19	125.65	126.1	126.55
280	127.01	127.46	127.91	128.37	128.82	129.27	129.73	130.18	130.64	131.09
290	131.54	132.0	132.45	132.9	133.36	133.81	134.26	134.72	135.17	135.62
300	136.08	136.53	136.99	137.44	137.89	138.35	138.8	139.25	139.71	140.16
310	140.61	141.07	141.52	141.97	142.43	142.88	143.34	143.79	144.24	144.7
320	145.15	145.6	146.06	146.51	146.96	147.42	147.87	148.33	148.78	149.23
330	149.69	150.14	150.59	151.05	151.5	151.95	152.41	152.86	153.31	153.77
340	154.22	154.68	155.13	155.58	156.04	156.49	156.94	157.4	157.85	158.3
350	158.76	159.21	159.67	160.12	160.57	161.03	161.48	161.93	162.39	162.84
360	163.29	163.75	164.2	164.65	165.11	165.56	166.02	166.47	166.92	167.38
370	167.83	168.28	168.74	169.1	169.64	170.1	170.55	171.0	171.46	171.91
380	172.37	172.82	173.27	173.73	174.18	174.63	175.09	175.54	175.99	176.45
390	176.9	177.36	177.81	178.26	178.72	179.17	179.62	180.08	180.53	180.98
400	181.44	181.89	182.34	182.8	183.25	183.71	184.16	184.61	185.07	185.52
410	185.97	186.43	186.88	187.33	187.79	188.24	188.69	189.15	189.6	190.06
420	190.51	190.96	191.42	191.87	192.32	192.78	193.23	193.68	194.14	194.59
430	195.05	195.5	195.95	196.41	196.86	197.31	197.77	198.22	198.67	199.13
440	199.58	200.03	200.49	200.94	201.4	201.85	202.3	202.76	203.21	203.66
450	204.12	204.57	205.02	205.48	205.93	206.39	206.84	207.29	207.75	208.2
460	208.65	209.11	209.56	210.01	210.47	210.92	211.37	211.83	212.28	212.74
470	213.19	213.64	214.1	214.55	215.0	215.46	215.91	216.36	216.82	217.27
480	217.72	218.18	218.63	219.09	219.54	219.99	220.45	220.9	221.35	221.81
490	222.26	222.71	223.17	223.62	224.08	224.53	224.98	225.44	225.89	226.34
500	226.8									

30
pounds to kilograms

Conversions

Density (mass/volume)

31
kilograms per cubic metre to pounds per cubic foot

kg/m³	0	10	20	30	40	50	60	70	80	90
	lb/ft³									
0		0.62	1.25	1.87	2.5	3.12	3.75	4.37	5.0	5.62
100	6.24	6.87	7.49	8.12	8.74	9.36	9.99	10.61	11.24	11.86
200	12.49	13.11	13.73	14.36	14.98	15.61	16.23	16.86	17.48	18.11
300	18.73	19.35	19.98	20.61	21.23	21.85	22.47	23.1	23.72	24.35
400	24.97	25.6	26.22	26.84	27.47	28.09	28.72	29.34	29.97	30.59
500	31.21	31.84	32.46	33.09	33.71	34.33	34.96	35.58	36.21	36.83
600	37.46	38.08	38.71	39.33	39.95	40.58	41.2	41.83	42.45	43.08
700	43.7	44.32	44.95	45.57	46.2	46.82	47.45	48.07	48.7	49.32
800	49.94	50.57	51.19	51.82	52.44	53.06	53.69	54.31	54.94	55.56
900	56.19	56.81	57.43	58.06	58.68	59.31	59.93	60.56	61.18	61.81
1 000	62.43									

Velocity

33
metres per second to miles per hour

m/s	0	1	2	3	4	5	6	7	8	9
	mile/hr									
0		2.24	4.47	6.71	8.95	11.18	13.42	15.66	17.9	20.13
10	22.37	24.61	26.84	29.08	31.32	33.55	35.79	38.03	40.26	42.51
20	44.74	46.96	49.21	51.45	53.69	55.92	58.16	60.4	62.63	64.87
30	67.11	69.35	71.58	73.82	76.06	78.29	80.53	82.77	85.0	87.24
40	89.48	91.71	93.95	96.19	98.43	100.66	102.9	105.13	107.37	109.61
50	111.85	114.08	116.32	118.56	120.8	123.03	125.27	127.5	129.74	131.98
60	134.22	136.45	138.69	140.93	143.16	145.4	147.64	149.88	152.11	154.34
70	156.59	158.82	161.06	163.3	165.53	167.77	170.0	172.24	174.48	176.72
80	178.96	181.19	183.43	185.67	187.9	190.14	192.38	194.61	196.85	199.09
90	201.32	203.56	205.8	208.04	210.27	212.51	214.75	216.98	219.22	221.46
100	223.69									

Pressure, stress

35
kilograms force per square centimetre to pounds force per square inch

kgf/cm²	0.0	0.1	0.2	0.3	0.4	0.5	0.6	0.7	0.8	0.9
	lbf/in²									
0		1.42	2.84	4.27	5.6	7.11	8.53	9.96	11.38	12.8
1	14.22	15.65	17.07	18.49	19.91	21.34	22.76	24.18	25.6	27.02
2	28.45	29.87	31.29	32.71	34.13	35.56	36.98	38.4	39.83	41.25
3	42.67	44.09	45.51	46.94	48.36	49.78	51.2	52.63	54.05	55.47
4	56.9	58.32	59.73	61.16	62.58	64.0	65.43	66.85	68.27	69.69
5	71.12	72.54	73.96	75.38	76.81	78.23	79.65	81.07	82.5	83.92
6	85.34	86.76	88.18	89.61	91.03	92.45	93.87	95.3	96.72	98.14
7	99.56	100.99	102.41	103.83	105.25	106.68	108.1	109.52	110.94	112.36
8	113.79	115.21	116.63	118.05	119.48	120.9	122.32	123.74	125.17	126.59
9	128.01	129.43	130.86	132.28	133.7	135.12	136.54	137.97	139.39	140.81
10	142.23									

37
kilonewtons per square metre to pounds force per square inch

kN/m² (k Pa)	0	10	20	30	40	50	60	70	80	90
	lbf/in²									
0		1.45	2.9	4.35	5.8	7.25	8.7	10.15	11.6	13.05
100	14.50	15.95	17.40	18.85	20.30	21.75	23.21	24.66	26.11	27.56
200	29.01	30.46	31.91	33.36	34.81	36.26	37.71	39.16	40.61	42.06
300	43.51	44.96	46.41	47.86	49.31	50.76	52.21	53.66	55.11	56.56
400	58.01	59.46	60.91	62.36	63.81	65.26	66.71	68.17	69.62	71.07
500	72.52	73.97	75.42	76.87	78.32	79.77	81.22	82.67	84.12	85.57
600	87.02	88.47	89.92	91.37	92.82	94.27	95.72	97.17	98.62	100.07
700	101.52	102.97	104.42	105.87	107.32	108.77	110.22	111.68	113.13	114.58
800	116.03	117.48	118.93	120.38	121.83	123.28	124.73	126.18	127.63	129.08
900	130.53	131.98	133.43	134.88	136.33	137.78	139.23	140.68	142.13	143.58
1 000	145.03									

lb/ft³	0	1	2	3	4	5	6	7	8	9
	kg/m³									
0		16.02	32.04	48.06	64.07	80.09	96.11	112.13	128.15	144.17
10	160.19	176.2	192.22	208.24	224.26	240.28	256.3	272.31	288.33	304.35
20	320.37	336.39	352.41	368.43	384.44	400.46	416.48	432.5	448.52	464.54
30	480.55	496.57	512.59	528.61	544.63	560.65	576.67	592.68	608.7	624.72
40	640.74	656.76	672.78	688.79	704.81	720.83	736.85	752.87	768.89	784.91
50	800.92	816.94	832.96	848.98	865.0	881.02	897.03	913.05	929.07	945.09
60	961.11	977.13	993.15	1 009.16	1 025.18	1 041.2	1 057.22	1 073.24	1 089.26	1 105.27
70	1 121.29	1 137.31	1 153.33	1 169.35	1 185.37	1 201.38	1 217.4	1 233.42	1 249.44	1 265.46
80	1 281.48	1 297.5	1 313.51	1 329.53	1 345.55	1 361.57	1 377.59	1 393.61	1 409.62	1 425.64
90	1 441.66	1 457.68	1 473.7	1 489.72	1 505.74	1 521.75	1 537.77	1 553.79	1 569.81	1 585.83
100	1 601.85									

32
pounds per cubic foot to kilograms per cubic metre

mile/hr	0	1	2	3	4	5	6	7	8	9
	m/s									
0		0.45	0.89	1.34	1.79	2.24	2.68	3.13	3.58	4.02
10	4.47	4.92	5.36	5.81	6.26	6.71	7.15	7.6	8.05	8.49
20	8.94	9.39	9.83	10.28	10.73	11.18	11.62	12.07	12.52	12.96
30	13.41	13.86	14.31	14.75	15.2	15.65	16.09	16.54	16.99	17.43
40	17.88	18.33	18.78	19.22	19.67	20.12	20.56	21.01	21.46	21.91
50	22.35	22.8	23.25	23.69	24.14	24.59	25.03	25.48	25.93	26.38
60	26.82	27.27	27.72	28.16	28.61	29.06	29.5	29.95	30.4	30.85
70	31.29	31.74	32.19	32.63	33.08	33.53	33.98	34.42	34.87	35.32
80	35.76	36.21	36.66	37.1	37.55	38.0	38.45	38.89	39.34	39.79
90	40.23	40.68	41.13	41.57	42.02	42.47	42.92	43.36	43.81	44.26
100	44.7									

34
miles per hour to metres per second

lbf/in²	0	1	2	3	4	5	6	7	8	9
	kgf/cm²									
0		0.07	0.14	0.21	0.28	0.35	0.42	0.49	0.56	0.63
10	0.7	0.77	0.84	0.91	0.98	1.05	1.12	1.2	1.27	1.34
20	1.41	1.48	1.55	1.62	1.69	1.76	1.83	1.9	1.97	2.04
30	2.11	2.18	2.25	2.32	2.39	2.46	2.53	2.6	2.67	2.74
40	2.81	2.88	2.95	3.02	3.09	3.16	3.23	3.3	3.37	3.45
50	3.52	3.59	3.66	3.73	3.8	3.87	3.94	4.01	4.08	4.15
60	4.22	4.29	4.36	4.43	4.5	4.57	4.64	4.71	4.78	4.85
70	4.92	4.99	5.06	5.13	5.2	5.27	5.34	5.41	5.48	5.55
80	5.62	5.69	5.77	5.84	5.91	5.98	6.05	6.12	6.19	6.26
90	6.33	6.4	6.47	6.54	6.61	6.68	6.75	6.82	6.89	6.96
100	7.03									

36
pounds force per square inch to kilograms force per square centimetre

lbf/in²	0	1	2	3	4	5	6	7	8	9
	kN/m² (k Pa)									
0		6.9	13.79	20.68	27.58	34.48	41.37	48.26	55.16	62.06
10	68.95	75.84	82.74	89.64	96.53	103.42	110.32	117.22	124.11	131.0
20	137.9	144.8	151.69	158.58	165.48	172.38	179.27	186.16	193.06	199.96
30	206.85	213.74	220.64	227.54	234.43	241.32	248.22	255.12	262.01	268.9
40	275.8	282.7	289.59	296.48	303.38	310.28	317.17	324.06	330.96	337.86
50	344.75	351.64	358.54	365.44	372.33	379.22	386.12	393.02	399.91	406.8
60	413.7	420.6	427.49	434.38	441.28	448.18	455.07	461.96	468.86	475.76
70	482.65	489.54	496.44	503.34	510.23	517.12	524.02	530.92	537.81	544.7
80	551.6	558.5	565.39	572.28	579.18	586.08	592.97	599.86	606.76	613.66
90	620.55	627.44	634.34	641.24	648.13	655.02	661.92	668.82	675.71	682.6
100	689.5									

38
pounds force per square inch to kilonewtons per square metre

Conversions

Refrigeration

39
watts to British
thermal units
per hour

W	0	1	2	3	4	5	6	7	8	9
	Btu/hr									
0		3.41	6.82	10.24	13.65	17.06	20.47	23.89	27.3	30.71
10	34.12	37.53	40.95	44.36	47.77	51.18	54.59	58.01	61.42	64.83
20	68.24	71.66	75.07	78.5	81.89	85.3	88.72	92.13	95.54	98.95
30	102.36	105.78	109.12	112.6	116.01	119.43	122.76	126.25	129.66	133.07
40	136.49	139.91	143.31	146.72	150.13	153.55	156.96	160.37	163.78	167.2
50	170.61	174.02	177.43	180.84	184.26	187.67	191.08	194.49	197.9	201.31
60	204.73	208.14	211.55	214.97	218.38	221.79	225.2	228.61	232.03	235.44
70	238.85	242.26	245.68	249.09	252.5	255.91	259.32	262.74	266.15	269.56
80	272.97	276.38	279.8	283.21	286.62	290.03	293.45	296.86	300.27	303.68
90	307.09	310.51	313.92	317.33	320.74	324.15	327.57	330.98	334.39	337.8
100	341.22									

Thermal conductance

41
watts per square
metre kelvin to
British thermal units
per square foot hour
degree F

W/(m²K)	0.0	0.1	0.2	0.3	0.4	0.5	0.6	0.7	0.8	0.9
	Btu/(ft²hr°F)									
0.0		0.018	0.035	0.053	0.074	0.088	0.106	0.123	0.141	0.158
1.0	0.176	0.194	0.211	0.229	0.247	0.264	0.282	0.299	0.317	0.335
2.0	0.352	0.370	0.387	0.405	0.423	0.440	0.458	0.476	0.493	0.511
3.0	0.528	0.546	0.564	0.581	0.599	0.616	0.634	0.652	0.669	0.687
4.0	0.704	0.722	0.740	0.757	0.775	0.793	0.810	0.828	0.845	0.863
5.0	0.881	0.898	0.916	0.933	0.951	0.969	0.986	1.004	1.021	1.039
6.0	1.057	1.074	1.092	1.110	1.127	1.145	1.162	1.180	1.198	1.215
7.0	1.233	1.250	1.268	1.286	1.303	1.321	1.34	1.356	1.374	1.391
8.0	1.409	1.427	1.444	1.462	1.479	1.497	1.515	1.532	1.550	1.567
9.0	1.585	1.603	1.620	1.638	1.656	1.673	1.691	1.708	1.726	1.744
10.0	1.761									

Btu/hr	0	1	2	3	4	5	6	7	8	9
	W									
0		0.29	0.59	0.88	1.17	1.47	1.76	2.05	2.34	2.64
10	2.93	3.22	3.52	3.81	4.1	4.4	4.69	4.98	5.28	5.57
20	5.86	6.16	6.45	6.74	7.03	7.33	7.62	7.91	8.21	8.5
30	8.79	9.09	9.38	9.67	9.97	10.26	10.55	10.84	11.14	11.43
40	11.72	12.02	12.31	12.6	12.9	13.19	13.48	13.78	14.07	14.36
50	14.66	14.95	15.24	15.53	15.83	16.12	16.41	16.71	17.0	17.29
60	17.59	17.88	18.17	18.47	18.76	19.05	19.34	19.64	19.93	20.22
70	20.52	20.81	21.1	21.4	21.69	21.98	22.28	22.57	22.86	23.15
80	23.45	23.74	24.03	24.33	24.62	24.91	25.21	25.5	25.79	26.09
90	26.38	26.67	26.97	27.26	27.55	27.84	28.14	28.43	28.72	29.02
100	29.31									

40
British thermal units per hour to watts

Btu/(ft². hr°F)	0.00	0.01	0.02	0.03	0.04	0.05	0.06	0.07	0.08	0.09
	W/(m²K)									
0.0		0.057	0.114	0.17	0.227	0.284	0.341	0.397	0.454	0.511
0.1	0.568	0.624	0.681	0.738	0.795	0.852	0.908	0.965	1.022	1.079
0.2	1.136	1.192	1.249	1.306	1.363	1.42	1.476	1.533	1.59	1.647
0.3	1.703	1.76	1.817	1.874	1.931	1.987	2.044	2.101	2.158	2.214
0.4	2.271	2.328	2.385	2.442	2.498	2.555	2.612	2.669	2.725	2.782
0.5	2.839	2.896	2.953	3.009	3.066	3.123	3.18	3.236	3.293	3.35
0.6	3.407	3.464	3.52	3.577	3.634	3.691	3.747	3.804	3.861	3.918
0.7	3.975	4.031	4.088	4.145	4.202	4.258	4.315	4.372	4.429	4.486
0.8	4.542	4.599	4.656	4.713	4.77	4.826	4.883	4.94	4.997	5.053
0.9	5.11	5.167	5.224	5.281	5.337	5.394	5.451	5.508	5.564	5.621
1.0	5.678									

42
British thermal units per square foot hour degree F to watts per square metre kelvin

Materials

PHYSICAL CHARACTERISTICS OF COMMON BUILDING MATERIALS

In selecting building materials architect needs take into account their significant physical characteristics. This knowledge helps him assess how manufactured products specified and constructions designed perform in use. Precise values influenced by such factors as temp, moisture content, surface condition, internal structure. These usually determined by means of standard tests, which may take into account conditions of use. Handbooks issued by professional and other independent organisations give precise values for many common materials, with details on conditions under which values were determined. Manufacturers' literature may also give values.

→(1) brings together values from many sources: devised as aid for architects at early stages of design. In most instances range of values given. Designer must judge which appropriate to his need. However, in some instances contractual or regulatory reasons may impose standardised values, or values determined by standard tests.

Manufactured products may be combinations of different materials, chosen and placed to give desired performance. Innumerable combinations available, some proprietary. Not possible give their values here. For many values may be calculated using recognised procedures. For others information must be sought from manufacturers or obtained experimentally.

Characteristics

Table gives following characteristics:

Density (kg/m³): enables mass of material be calculated; gives indication of many other properties, eg generally light weight material when dry gives good thermal insulation and sound absorption but poor sound insulation

Modulus of elasticity (kN/mm²) and **Tensile and impressive strength** (MN/m²) give indications of structural performance, modulus of elasticity indicating stiffness

Moisture movements expressed as percentages. Generally lightweight and fibrous and some cement-based materials show dimensional changes when wet or dry; such need be accommodated in design; movement may be reversible or only happen on first use

Coefficient of thermal expansion (per °C × 10^{-6}): changes in temp cause materials expand or contract; such movement again may need be accommodated: expressed by coefficient

Thermal conductivity →p393(2) expressed as Wm/m2°C, conventionally W/m°C. For some materials values greatly influenced by moisture content

Sound apsorption coefficients →p397(2)

material	density (kg/m³)	E-modulus (kN/mm²)	tensile strength (MN/m²)	moisture movement (%)	thermal movement (per °C × 10⁻⁶)	thermal conductivity (W/m°C)
masonry: natural stone, clay bricks, terracotta blocks, calcium silicate bricks, concrete (block, slab or cast): dense or light weight (aerated, cellular, or light weight aggregate); physical characteristics depend on density, shape, geometrical arrangement, mortar, reinforcement; lighter weight materials: better thermal insulation, sound absorption, absorb moisture & show dimensional change on wetting & lower thermal resistivity; non-combustible						
natural stone						
granite	2600	20–60		slight	8–10	2.5
limestone	2000–2000	10–80		0.01	3–4	1.5
marble	2500	35		slight	4–6	2–2.5
sandstone	2000–2200	3–80		0.07	7–12	1.3
slate	2700	10–35		slight	9–11	1.9–2.0
dense concrete						
gravel aggregate	1800–2500	15–36		0.02–0.06¹	12–14	0.8–2.0
limestone aggregate	1800–2500	20–36		0.02–0.03¹	7–8	0.8–2.0
other rock aggregate	1800–2500	15–36		0.03–0.1¹	10–13	0.8–2.0
no fines	1750					
light weight concrete						
clinker aggregate	1400–1600	8–10		0.03–0.06¹	8–12	0.5–0.7
sintered aggregate	1100–1400	8–10		0.03–0.06¹	8–12	0.35–0.7
vermiculite	400–500			0.1–0.2¹	6–8	0.15–0.18
aerated (auto-claved)	400–900	1.4–3.2		0.02–0.03¹	8	0.15–0.3
bricks						
calcium silicate		14–18		0.0–0.05¹	8–14	0.5–1
load-bearing clay	1500–1800	4–26		0.02²	5–8	0.5–1
engineering	1800–2200			slight	4–6	0.7–1.3
cement screeds	1400–1500	20–35		0.02–0.06	10–13	0.5–0.6
asbestos cement	1400–1600	14–26		0.1–0.25	8–12	0.25–0.4
gypsum: as plaster or slabs, blocks & paper-covered boards; may be reinforced with fibrous materials, be foamed or incorporate light weight aggregate; low strength when wet; non-combustible						
dense plaster	1100–1200	16			18–21	0.4–0.45
foamed plaster	850–900					0.25
plasterboard	950	16			18–21	0.16
metals & glass: dense materials as sheets or thin sections; physical characteristics depend on composition, shape & geometrical arrangement; strong but may be brittle; no significant effect of change in moisture content						
cast iron	7000	80–120	70–280	negligible	10	40
mild steel	7800	210	400	negligible	12	50
aluminium & alloys	2300–2800	70–75	70–550	negligible	24–29	160–230³
copper & alloys	8400–8900	95–130	120–400	negligible	17–21	130–200³
lead	11350	14		negligible	30	
zinc	7000	140–220		negligible	23–33	113
glass	2500	70	30–170	negligible	9–11	0.7–1.1
wood: natural material with considerable variations in physical characteristics according to species & condition, particularly moisture content						
balsa	100–250					0.05–0.06
soft wood	300–600	5.5–12.5		considerable	4.6 with grain	0.1–0.13
hard wood	550–900	7–21		considerable	30–70 across grain	0.14–0.17
(very heavy woods over 1000)						
plastics: synthetic organic polymers: thermosetting remain hard on hardening; thermoplastic softened on reheating; physical characteristics depend on composition, modified by fillers & plasticisers; natural & synthetic rubbers similar; combustible, giving off smoke & toxic combustion products; high coefficient of expansion						
acrylic	1440	2.5–3.3		negligible	50–90	0.2
polycarbonate	1150	2.2–2.5		negligible	50–70	0.23
polyethylene (low density)	920	0.1–0.25		negligible	160–200	0.35
polyethylene (high density)	960	0.51–1		negligible	110–140	0.5
polyproplyene	915	0.9–1.6		negligible	80–110	0.24
polystyrene	1050	1.7–3.1		negligible	60–80	0.17
nylon	1100			negligible	100–120	0.3
rubber	930	0.007		negligible		0.16
asphalt	2300			negligible	30–80	1.2
thermal insulating materials: light weight, fibrous or cellular in composition giving good thermal insulation & sound absorbtion but poor sound insulation; low resistance to crushing; readily absorb moisture, with increase in density & thermal conductivity; most combustible except mineral based; improved by chemical additives						
mineral based						
expanded perlite	65					0.04–0.07
expanded vermiculite	100					0.7–0.1
glass fibre	25–100					0.04–0.07
mineral wool	50–150					0.04–0.07
asbestos or substitute insulating board	750–900	2.6–3.6		0.16–0.25	2.5–7.2	0.12–0.16
cellular glass	175	5–8			8.5	0.06
organic						
wood-wool slab	400–700	0.6–0.7		0.15–0.4		0.08–0.13
chipboard	500–800	2–2.8		0.35		0.15–0.2
fibreboard	250–350			0.4		0.05–0.07
corkboard	130–160					0.04–0.05
expanded						
polystyrene bead	15–25				14–45	0.035
pvc	40–70				35–50	0.035–0.045
foamed						
urea-formaldehyde	8–15				9	0.03–0.04
polyurethane	30				2–7	0.03–0.07

notes: ¹ initial irreversible shrinkage ² initial irreversible expansion ³ low emissivity/high reflectivity of bright surface of these metals against heat radiation

Distribution system for services needs careful planning ensure system economical in both builders and specialist work. System starts at point of entry of service to bldg or from boiler and plant rm to all spaces being served. Points of entry of services and plant rm location should be determined at early stage.

DISTRIBUTION MEDIUM

Heating distribution may be by hot water, steam, or warm air. Water may be at low pressure under boiling point or at high pressure above boiling point depending on quantity of heat to be distributed. Air inefficient means of distribution but required for ventilation or air conditioning.

Example: in 100 tube transfer capacities are:
low velocity air   0.72 kW
high velocity air   2.16 kW
low pressure hot water   525 kW
high pressure hot water   2 385 kW

DISTRIBUTION LAYOUTS

In multi-storey bldg distribution pattern may be:
(a) primarily horizontal with secondary distribution up or down through floors;
(b) primarily vertical with secondary distribution along floors.

(a) more common especially for low bldg or those with dissimilar flow plans but system may occupy greater building volume by increasing floor to floor height of all floors.
(b) more suitable for high bldg with repetitive floor plans.

PRIMARY HORIZONTAL DISTRIBUTION

Whether primary distribution at ground level or roof level will depend on location of boiler or plant rm. At ground level may be in walkways or crawlways under ground slab provided these do not conflict with foundations.

At roof level distribution may be in pitched roof void or in extra deep ceiling void. Horizontal distribution above roof level difficult protect from weather, complicates roof drainage.

PRIMARY VERTICAL DISTRIBUTION

Primary vertical distribution is by vertical duct spaces through bldg. Direction of horizontal connexion at floor slab level should not be limited by adjacent stairwells, lift shafts, or flues. Trimming beams may also limit horizontal connexions.

INTERCONNEXION VERTICAL & HORIZONTAL

Interconnexion between vertical and horizontal duct critical: ducts should not be in same vertical plane and vertical duct should be long side on to horizontal duct to give greatest common interconnecting area.

ACCESS TO DUCTS

Access to ducts should be adequate for maintenance work and for renewal of pipes etc, which have shorter life than that of bldg. Access either through duct – walkways, crawlways and large vertical ducts – or through access panels in side or top of duct.

FIRE PRECAUTIONS

Either firestops at floor level or fr construction and access panels.

SOUND TRANSMISSION

Floor construction carried through at or near floor level. All pipe penetrations sealed airtight. Access panels of adequate sound reduction and sealed airtight.

VENTILATION

Some ducts may require ventilation to limit temp rise or because of service contained, eg natural gas. Where floor construction carried through, vent each floor top and bottom. If duct continuous, vent at ends (→Bib111).

WALKWAYS →(1)(2)

Retain clear working space 700 wide × 2000 high after all services installed. Large takeoffs and expansion loops may require additional width. Access from ends – boiler rm or plant rm. Intermediate access to changes of direction and junctions by removable covers min 450 × 600. Access openings should allow length of pipe (6000) be installed or removed.

CRAWLWAYS →(3)

Clear working space 700 wide × 1000 high after all services installed. Access by covers min 450 × 600 at intervals of 10–15 m.

heat loss up to kW	heating f & r size	A w		B h	
		6 pipes on 1 side	6 pipes on both sides	with hangers	with rollers
35	40	1 065	1 430	2 010	2 000
64	50	1 140	1 580	2 055	2 000
153	65	1 180	1 660	2 130	2 000
255	80	1 235	1 770	2 230	2 000
423	100	1 330	1 960	2 370	2 000
956	125	1 425	2 150	2 515	2 000
1 432	150	1 505	2 310	2 665	2 000

1 Walkways: dimensions (f & r = flow & return)

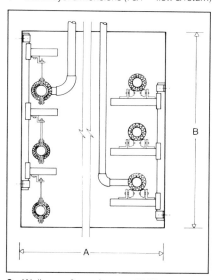

2 Walkways & crawlways →(1)(3)

heat loss up to kW	heating f & r size	3 pipes on each side		
		A w	B h	
			with hangers	with rollers
35	40	1 430	1 070	1 000
64	50	1 580	1 095	1 000
153	65	1 660	1 140	1 000
255	80	1 770	1 205	1 000
423	100	1 960	1 280	1 000
956	125	2 150	1 360	1 000
1 432	150	2 310	1 435	1 020

3 Crawlways: dimensions

Services: distribution

heat loss up to kW	heating f & r size	A w	B h without crossover	h with crossover
3	15	1350	230	320
6	20	1360	235	345
13	25	1395	240	375
24	32	1430	250	410
35	40	1475	255	445
64	50	1520	265	520
153	65	1600	285	560
255	80	1680	295	615
423	100	1780	320	710
956	125	1920	345	805
1432	150	2070	375	885

1 Trench ducts: dimensions (f & r = flow & return)

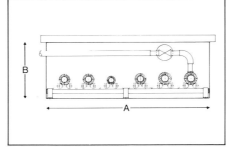

2 Trench duct

heat capacity up to kW	heating f & r size	A w	B h
3	15	605	300
6	20	615	305
13	25	650	315
24	32	685	325
35	40	730	330
64	50	775	340
153	65	855	380
255	80	935	425
423	100	1035	475
956	125	1175	555
1432	150	1320	625

3 Space requirements for horizontal duct at ceiling level (containing heating flow & return, hot water flow & return, cold water service & cold water main)

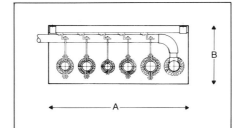

4 Horizontal duct at ceiling level

heat loss up to kW	pipe size	A 1 pipe	A 2 pipes	B d	C dia of hole required for connexion
1.5	10	100	150	54.5	46.5
3	15	100	150	59.0	51.0
6	20	100	150	64.5	56.5
13	25	100	150	71.5	64.0
24	32	100	150	80.0	73.5

5 Screed ducts: dimensions

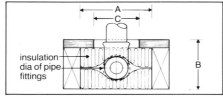

6 Screed duct

heat loss up to kW	heating f & r size	w A with or without crossover	d B without crossover	d B with crossover
3	15	605	115	205
6	20	615	120	230
13	25	650	125	260
24	32	685	135	295
35	40	730	140	330
64	50	775	150	405
153	65	855	170	445
255	80	935	180	500
423	100	1035	205	595
956	125	1175	230	690
1432	150	1320	260	770

7 Space requirements for vertical ducts (containing heating flow & return, hot water flow & return, cold water service & cold water main)

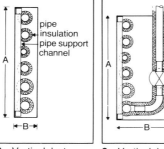

8 Vertical duct **9** Vertical duct with crossover

heat loss up to kW	heating f & r size	A w 75 soil pipe	A w 100 soil pipe	A w 150 soil pipe	B d without crossover 75 soil pipe	B d without crossover 100 soil pipe	B d without crossover 150 soil pipe	B d with crossover 75 soil pipe pvc waste	75 soil pipe copper waste	100 soil pipe pvc waste	100 soil pipe copper waste	150 soil pipe pvc waste	150 soil pipe copper waste
3	15	815	840	895	173	205	255	295	350	320	375	370	425
6	20	825	855	905	173	205	255	295	350	320	375	370	425
13	25	860	885	940	173	205	255	295	350	320	375	370	425
24	32	895	920	975	173	205	255	295	350	320	375	370	425
35	40	940	965	1020	173	205	255	295	350	320	375	370	425
64	50	985	1015	1065	173	205	255	295	350	320	375	370	425
153	65	1060	1090	1140	173	205	255	295	350	320	375	370	425
255	80	1145	1170	1225	180	205	255	295	350	320	375	370	425
423	100	1245	1270	1325	205	205	255	295	350	320	375	370	425
956	125	1385	1415	2875	230	230	255	295	350	320	375	370	425
1432	150	1530	1555	1610	260	260	260	295	350	320	375	370	425

10 Space requirements for vertical duct including soil pipe (containing heating flow & return, hot water flow & return, cold water service, cold water main & soil & waste pipes)

TRENCH DUCTS →(1)(2)

Pipe supports should be below pipes or on sides to allow lengths of pipe be installed or removed. Allow space under pipe supports and slight fall for draining. Access through continuous covers or covers at junctions and changes of direction and break out screed cover when required. Pipes on rollers allow expansion movement.

HORIZONTAL DUCTS AT CEILING LEVEL →(3)(4)

Pipe supports above pipes for pipework to be installed or removed from below. Crossovers may be above or below depending on venting of pipework. Continuous access from below through ceiling or panel. Add extra depth of ceiling support system, recessed light fittings etc. Drop rods allow expansion movement.

SCREED DUCTS →(5)(6)

Chase formed by omitting floor screed. Useful for local hot and cold water connexions to sanitary fittings and local heating pipework. Floor finish carried over plywood cover *nailed* to battens. Access by cutting floor finish and prising up cover. Pipe size usually limited to 20–22, otherwise screed of uneconomic thickness. Oversized hole required for connexion for expansion of pipework.

VERTICAL DUCTS →(11)(12)

One row pipes to allow installation and removal from front without removing other pipework except crossovers. Access through removable panels or doors full floor height on long side.

Crossovers and clearance for valves increase depth considerably. Diagonal takeoffs with 45° bend reduce depth but increase width by increasing spacing of vertical pipes.

ESTIMATING VENTILATION/ AIR-CONDITIONING SIZES

For preliminary planning purposes ventilation/ air-conditioning ducts may be calculated from:

Low velocity: cross sectional ar of duct m² = $\dfrac{\text{floor ar served m}^2}{750}$

High velocity: cross sectional ar of duct m² = $\dfrac{\text{floor ar served m}^2}{2250}$

Ducts should not exceed 1:4 short to long side and best square. High velocity ducts should be circular. Allow space for insulation, flanges and supports: 100 on all sides.

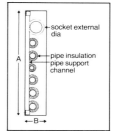

11 Vertical duct with soil pipe

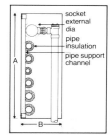

12 Vertical duct with soil pipe & crossover

Services: Methods of heating

angle valves, side connexions, top & bottom			
size mm	A	B	C
15	115	115	
20	125	120	25
25	140	135	
straight valves, bottom connexions			
15	130		130
20	150		140
25	160		155

If radiator under shelf, clearance of twice d from face of radiator to wall required above radiator; clearance of 1½ times d required under radiator

1   Space for radiator valves→(2)(3)

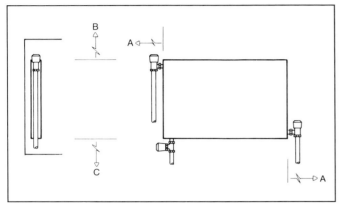

2   Space for radiator valves →(1)

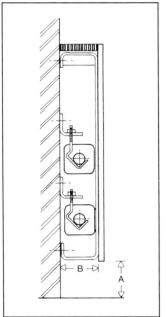

3   Builders work natural convector →(1)

type of heat emitter	order of thermal comfort under steady conditions	approx order of response
floor heating	1	5
medium temp radiant panels	2	4
panel radiators	3	3
natural convectors	4	2
fan convectors or ducted warm air	5	1

thermal comfort requirement of surface temp than air temp can only be met with some radiant emission; proportion of radiation required will depend on thermal insulation

4   Order of thermal comfort & speed of response from heating emitters

Decision on type of heating emission in individual spaces depends on requirements of thermal comfort in relation to thermal response of bldg.

THERMAL COMFORT →(4)

→p16

High standard of thermal comfort requires:
surrounding surface temp higher than air temp
air temp at head lower than at floor level: low temp gradient
air movement just perceptible but variable and with no draughts
hum not very important except at temp above 21°C: should not exceed 70% nor be less than 30%

THERMAL RESPONSE OF BUILDING

Thermal response of bldg depends on:
area and orientation of glazing: large areas of glazing facing sun give quick response
reflectivity of external surfaces where exposed to sun: high reflectivity reduces heat gain from sun and reduces response
mass of bldg structure and position of thermal insulation: mass inside insulation gives long response time; lightweight bldg have short response time
Quick response bldg will give economy in heating cost but be hotter in summer and more difficult heat comfortably.

TYPES OF HEAT EMITTERS

Low temperature radiant panels: heated by embedded el cables or heating water pipework. Surface preferably floor for low temp gradient but wall or ceiling surfaces can be used.
Floor surface temp limited to 29°C.
Emission: 50% radiation 50% convection.

Medium temp radiant panels: flat steel or cast iron plates with water-ways cast in or welded to back of plate. Surface temp generally 75°C.
Emission: 50% radiation 50% convection.

Radiators: generally made from sheet steel; may be 1, 2 or 3 panel or with fins on back to increase output for given face area. Surface temp 75°C.
Radiant: convection emission depends on number of panels, fins etc; single panel approx 25% radiation 75% convection.
If radiators in corner or recess allow space for valves and for air flow →(1).

Natural convectors: may be continuous casing or individual casing of pressed steel containing finned tube heater. Heat output depends on size of finned tube and height of convector.
Surface temp lower than radiator: about 35°C. Safer with young children or disabled people.
Emission: 10% radiation 90% convection.
Natural convector cases often made of builders work for better appearance and robustness →(2). Opening at bottom A should not be less than width of finned tube. Inside depth of casing B should only allow min clearance (6) for finned tube. Grille at top should have at least 70% open area.

Fan convectors: similar to natural convectors except that air circulation by fan. High output for small size and independent of height of casing. Heat output easily controlled by fan speed. May be positioned overhead if fan adequate to blow hot air down.
Emission: 100% convection.

Ducted warm air: for heating similar to fan convectors. Difference is in method of heat distribution and in space occupied in rm. Used in domestic installations but in large bldg only when mech ventilation required.
Emission: 100% convection.

Services: Heating systems

In choosing heating system 3 decisions to make:
fuel to be used
means of distributing heat from central source
method of heat emission in individual spaces

CAPACITY OF INSTALLATION

Approx capacity of installation can be calculated (→Bib593).
Example: 4-storey bldg 13 × 70 × (shallow plan bldg)
ventilation rate 2 air changes

ground floor 13 × 70 × 79 =	71890
intermediate floors 2 × 13 × 70 × 72 =	131040
top floor 13 × 70 × 86 =	78260
total heat loss =	281190
=	280 kW

Bldg with intermittent heating need overload capacity: this depends on heat up time. Normally 20% but may be 100% excess capacity.

	small bldg			shallow plan bldg			deep plan bldg		
number of air changes	2	4	6	2	4	6	2	4	6
ground floor	102	146	192	79	121	167	62	104	150
intermediate floor	92	135	181	72	115	161	57	100	146
top floor	106	148	194	86	128	174	71	113	159
single storey	117	159	205	92	134	180	75	117	163

1 Heat loss W/m^2

GAS SUPPLIES

Distribution
Gas distributed through high pressure national grid system to all regions.

The main: provision and maintenance of main gas supply in UK responsiblity of British Gas Corporation.

Service pipe: where laid in public ground, British Gas Corporation responsible for provision and maintenance of service pipe between main and inlet side of meter. Where part of service pipe laid in private land provision and maintenance usually responsibility of user.

Internal installation pipes from meter to appliances responsibility of bldg owner. No service pipe may be installed in unventilated void space or duct.

Protection of pipes: gas pipes must be protected against condensation, damp, freezing and corrosion.
Flues and air supply for gas appliances (→Bib119).

The meter
Primary meters should be situated close as possible point of entry of service pipe and allow easy access without disturbing consumer. Meters should not be exposed to:
possibility of physical damage
continuous damp or wet
excessive changes of temp
possibility of contact with flame or el sparks.

Gas meters must be separated from el meters by fr partition.
Domestic meters require space 330 wide, 360 deep, 660 high.

Gas meters in larger installations require separate rm →(2).

meter size kW	w	d	h	door w	door h
373	1980	1170	1530	1220	1450
560	2060	1220	1680	1370	1520
933	2290	1370	1830	1680	1680
1400	2590	1450	1830	1680	1830
1867	2750	1450	2220	1680	1830
2800	2900	1710	2360	1830	1830
3733	3050	1730	2520	1830	1830

ventilation required: up to 1867 kW ventilation ar to be 4% of floor ar of meter rm divided between high & low level; over 2800 kW ventilation ar to be 6% of floor ar

2 Gas meter rm min dimensions

ELECTRICITY TARIFFS

2 basic types of tariff for el heating: restricted hours tariff, with el available at night only at cheap rate; normal tariffs, with el available at any time but at 2–3 times restricted hours rate.

With restricted hours tariff heat generated must be stored during night for use next day. Heat may be stored in structure of bldg, particularly concrete floors, in vessels containing water under pressure, or in well-insulated high-density cores of thermal sto units. Storing heat in form of hot water most flexible arrangement.

Direct el heating by radiant or convective emitters, often in form of individual portable appliances.

OIL STORAGE

4 main types of oil sto tanks for industrial and commercial oil fuels:
mild steel welded
mild steel sectional
cast iron sectional
reinforced concrete

Most widely used: mild steel welded; usually horizontal, cylindrical or rectangular. If ground space limited vertical cylindrical tanks may be used.

CAPACITIES

Min net sto capacity (→Bib130) can be calculated in 2 ways (use largest):
3 weeks supply at max rate of consumption
2 weeks supply at max rate of consumption plus usual quantity ordered for 1 delivery.

If max weekly offtake less than 900 l, sto capacity still should not be less than 2950 l to accept 2270 l deliveries.

Desirable provide more than 1 tank in many circumstances, each of capacity accept at least full delivery, each tank having separate filling pipe, unless situated next each other where common filling point can be used, with isolating valves. Different grades must be stored in separate tanks.

SITING

Should if possible be installed above ground. Site should not be subject extremes of temp and not be intrusive. Clearance should be allowed for withdrawal of fittings such as steam coils and immersion heaters.

If underground installation unavoidable, should be in specially constructed brick or concrete chamber, with access to drain valve etc: dry ground and finished structure made watertight.

Sump must be provided in floor at 1 end and floor must slope towards sump.

Buried tanks should not be in direct contact with soil: almost impossible avoid corrosive attack.

Services: Heating systems

OIL STORAGE (cont)

Supports

Horizontal tanks on brick or reinforced concrete cradles. Downward slope of 1:50 from drawoff towards drain. Cradles should not be under joints or seams of tank plates; layer of bitumenised felt between cradle and tank. Height of tank supports should provide at least 400 space between drain valve and ground level to allow access for draining and painting.

Vertical tanks

Up to 2750 dia may be directly erected on RC foundation. Base of tank with bitumen-based seal between tank and concrete. Larger dia tanks to be assembled on site should be erected on self-draining foundation with base plated on bitumen and sand or bitumen-macadam base.

Catchpit

Where overfilling or leakage would be fire hazard or contaminate drains catchpit required. Made of brick or concrete with oil-tight lining and sealed to concrete base under tank supports. Capacity should be 10% greater than capacity of tank or tanks. Catchpit should have facility to remove water but no permanent drain.

Manholes →p13

Every sto tank should have manhole in accessible position, preferably at top. Circular: not less than 460 dia; oval or rectangular: not less than 460 long, 410 wide. Vertical tanks over 3650 high should have additional manhole at base for maintenance and cleaning.

Storage temp

oil class	BS classification	min temp sto °C	min temp at outflow from sto & for handling °C
light fuel oil	E	10	10
medium fuel oil	F	25	30
heavy fuel oil	G	35	45

1 Oil sto temp

SOLID FUEL

Delivery

About 7 to 8 t capacity. Delivery vehicle dimensions similar to 7 t long wheelbase tipping vehicle. Conveyor delivery vehicles can stack to 2500 above load level: ordinary delivery 1400. Factors:
bulk delivery for economy
sto capacity min 1½ × capacity of delivery vehicle
good sto height saves space
plan for min manual handling eg gravity feed for delivery point to sto

Where boiler fired from front fuel should be stored in front or gravitate to front from sto at higher level. Magazine type boilers should be fed from fuel sto above hopper at top of boiler.

Calorific Value & Density

fuel	calorific value MJ/kg	density kg/m³
anthracite	35	330
bituminous		
coal	30	800
coke	28	400

2 Calorific value & density

capacity l	length A	dia B	capacity	length A	dia B
1140	1655	990	18185	5260	2135
2275	1705	1375	22730	5870	2290
2730	2010	1375	27280	6175	2440
3410	2165	1375	31825	5590	2745
4550	3150	1375	36370	6505	2745
5455	3760	1375	40915	7420	2745
6820	2900	1830	45460	8030	2745
9095	3305	1985	54555	9550	2745
11365	3940	1985	68190	12195	2745
13640	3965	2135	81230	12195	3050
15915	4880	2135	90920	13720	3050

3 Oil sto: dimensions of cylindrical tanks →(4)

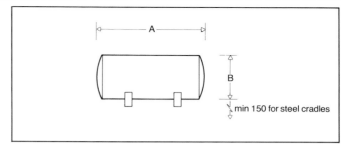

4 Cylindrical oil sto tank →(3)

BOILER ROOMS

Space round eqp required for making pipe and el connexions and dismantling eqp for servicing. Good maintenance of all plant essential for proper performance, fuel economy and max life.

Boilers and associated eqp heavy and noisy. Generally best position on ground slab. Boiler rm should not be next spaces that are to remain cool or quiet.

Access from road to boiler house must be adequate for largest piece of eqp to be replaced. Boilers require air for combustion and boiler houses need good ventilation reduce internal temp. In large boiler houses separate flue desirable for each boiler, rising directly to highest part of bldg.

For size of boiler rm, access and ventilation requirements →p388(1)–(4). Dimensions allow all layouts. Solid fuel boilers may need larger boiler house for fuel handling eqp. If pressurisation eqp or chillers to be included boiler rm must be larger.

load kW	l	w	clear h	access door w	access door h	ventilation louvres inlet (low level) m²	ventilation louvres outlet (high level) m²
up to 200	7900	5300	3500	1500	2000	0.48	0.422
200–600	9800	7900	4300	1700	2300	1.44	1.22
600–1800	16900	12200	5300	3400	3000	4.32	3.709
1800–6000	19100	18200	7300	3400	4200	14.4	11.646
6000–20000	26800	26000	9300	4400	5800	48.0	36.68

5 Boiler rm data

Services: heating systems

BOILER ROOMS (cont)

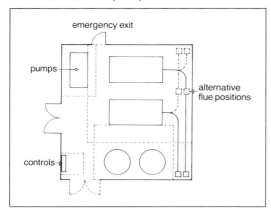

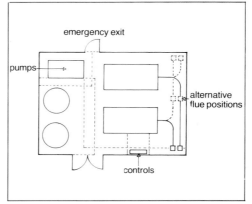

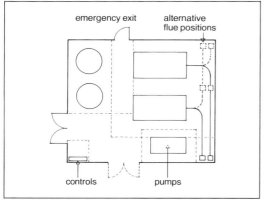

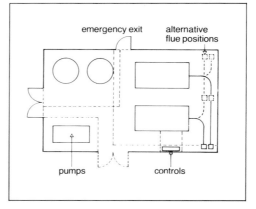

1 to 4 Boiler house layouts; technical data →p387(5)

CALORIFIER ROOMS

Calorifier rm is heating substation where heat in water (or steam) at high pressure and temp changed to heat at low pressure and temp. Several calorifier rm may be fed from 1 boiler house in large installation.

In district heating schemes with distribution at high pressure and temp, calorifier rm required at intake.

Calorifier rm should not be next to spaces that are to remain cool.

Access required from road through bldg to calorifier rm for largest piece of eqp to be replaced.

Calorifier rm must be ventilated to reduce internal temp.

Calorifier rm →(5) contain 2 hot water sto calorifiers, 2 water to water non-sto calorifiers, pumps and controls.

ATMOSPHERIC GAS BOILERS

Smaller gas boilers burn gas at low pressure, do not have forced draught; quieter than pressure jet boilers but less efficient.

Boilers up to about 35 kW capacity available with either balanced flue or conventional flue.

Space must be allowed at front for withdrawal of burners and at side and back for connexions →(6)(7)p389(1)–(4).

load kW	l	w	clear h	access door		ventilation louvres	
				w	h	inlet (low level) m²	outlet (high level) m²
up to 200	6900	4800	3500	1100	1950	0.422	0.422
200–600	10100	6500	4300	1500	1950	1.22	1.22
600–1800	12000	7000	5300	1600	1950	3.709	3.709

5 Calorifier rm data

rating	A h	B w	C d	D space at front	E space at back	F space on left side	G space on right side	H space above	weight full kg	flue I/D
up to 35	915	500	535	610	10	75	75	500	115	102
35	915	500	600	610	10	150	150	680	220	150
35– 100	1020	560	840	610	155	160	160	810	270	178
100	1320	845	1130	960	250	160	160	840	680	225
100– 300	1605	775	1525	960	510	200	510	900	980	254
300	1605	1640	1525	1180	510	200	510	990	1750	2 × 254
300– 900	1605	2230	1525	1180	510	200	510	990	2520	460
900	1765	2230	1885	1550	510	200	510	990	3350	2 × 356

6 Atmospheric gas boiler data: dimensions for top & bottom of range of each rating; I/D = internal dia

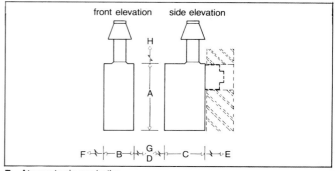

7 Atmospheric gas boiler

Services: heating systems

rating kW	A h	B w	C d with burner	D space at front	E space at back	F space on left side	G space on right side	H space above	weight full kg	flue I/D
35–100	1195	640	1450	610	500	160	460	540	890	200
	1470	1310	2005	940	1310	400	560	765	1690	200
100–300	1550	1310	3060	940	1310	700	1210	765	2915	254
	1780	1465	3160	1100	1400	700	1210	800	2915	432
300–900	2060	1830	3520	1000	1500	1425	1210	1000	4850	432
	2490	2080	3890	1415	1500	1425	1210	1000	6095	432
900–3000	2490	2080	4350	2290	1640	1505	1230	1500	6095	432
	3560	2770	5645	3250	3835	1655	1375	1500	30990	660
3000–10000	3785	2980	7040	2760	4370	1655	1375	2000	30990	710
	5095	4115	8435	4130	6225	1655	1380	2000	49490	1016

1 Pressure jet gas boilers data: dimension for top & bottom of each heating range →(3)

rating kW	A h	B w	C d with burner	D space at front	E space at back	F space on left side	G space on right side	H space above	weight full kg	flue I/D
up to 35	950	550	845	800	400	150	205	200	185	152
	950	550	925	800	400	150	205	200	230	152
35–100	1195	640	1005	800	500	150	205	200	260	203
	1470	1310	2005	1215	1310	155	355	200	1380	204
100–300	1550	1265	2930	1215	1310	700	1000	1000	2915	254
	1780	1465	2930	1220	1320	700	1000	1000	4675	255
300–900	2060	1830	3150	1220	1320	700	1425	1000	4675	350
	2490	3170	3945	1450	1415	700	1505	1000	6100	400
900–3000	2820	3170	3965	2290	1415	1505	1505	1000	9755	400
	3655	3180	6535	3050	3535	1655	1550	2000	30990	710
3000–10000	3950	3180	7045	2880	4370	1655	1550	2000	30990	710
	5250	4115	8435	3695	6225	1655	1550	2000	63100	1016

2 Pressure jet oil-filled boilers data: dimension for top & bottom of each heating range →(3)

PRESSURE JET GAS OR OIL BOILERS

On pressure jet boilers burner forced-draught fan assembly projects considerably from front. Assembly often hinged for access to boiler shell for maintenance.

In larger sizes considerable space required at back for easy bend flue connexion →(1)(2)(3).

Domestic hot water cylinders

Domestic hot water cylinders must be installed with enough space make and unmake connexions to fit or remove cylinder →(4)–(6) p390(1). In rectangular cupboard connexions on diagonal save space →(7).

Large indirect cylinders

Indirect cylinders need only low primary circulation pressure and will operate with gravity flow if correctly placed in relation to boiler.

Large indirect cylinders have bolted head to allow internal annular heater to be withdrawn and replaced. For withdrawal space required →p390(3). Indirect cylinders may be vertical or horizontal →p390(2)–(5). Horizontal useful if headroom limited but vertical more efficient in preventing mixing of incoming cold water with remaining hot.

Inspection opening often provided in side of cylinder.

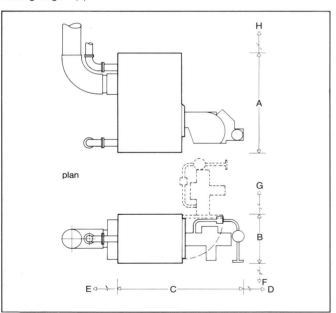

plan

3 Pressure jet gas & oil-filled boiler →(1)(2)

capacity l	A h with insulation	B dia with insulation	C space for connexions opposite sides	D space above for connexions	D space above to withdraw immersion heater	E space round over insulation for hand access
78	990	510	115	115	840	100
101	990	560	115	115	840	100
119	1145	560	115	115	995	100
91	765	610	115	115	615	100
103	840	610	115	115	690	100
115	915	610	115	115	765	100
127	990	610	115	115	840	100
151	1145	610	140	140	995	100
175	1295	610	140	140	1145	100
238	1295	685	140	140	1145	100
307	1295	760	155	155	1145	100
414	1675	760	155	155	1525	100

4 Domestic vertical direct cylinders data →(6)(7)

capacity l	A h with insulation	B dia with insulation	C space for connexions opposite sides	D space above for connexions	D space above to withdraw immersion heater	E space round over insulation for hand access
114	1145	560	115	115	995	100
100	840	610	115	115	690	100
123	990	610	115	115	840	100
145	1145	610	140	140	995	100
170	1295	610	140	140	1145	100
215	1345	660	155	155	1195	100
255	1550	660	155	155	1400	100
332	1450	760	185	185	1300	100
418	1830	760	185	185	1680	100

5 Domestic vertical indirect cylinders data →p390(1)

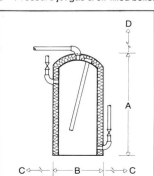

6 Domestic vertical direct cylinder →(4)

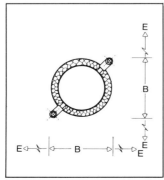

7 Domestic vertical cylinder: connexions on diagonal →(4)

Services: heating systems

STORAGE CYLINDERS (cont)

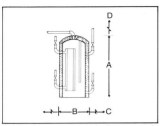

1 Domestic vertical indirect cylinder →p389(5)

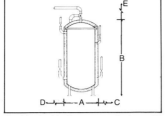

2 Vertical indirect sto cylinder →(3)

capacity l	A dia with insulation	B h with insulation	C space for connexions	D space for connexions	E space above for connexions	F space above for connexions
100	600	940	115	115	385	465
150	600	1255	115	115	385	700
200	650	1335	115	155	455	760
250	650	1590	115	155	455	950
300	750	1415	115	155	455	820
350	750	1590	115	185	485	950
400	750	1765	115	185	485	1080
450	750	1945	140	185	485	1215
500	850	1685	140	185	485	1020
600	850	1945	140	185	485	1215
700	900	1925	140	215	540	1200
800	900	2205	155	215	540	1410
900	1000	1995	155	249	595	1252
1000	1000	2185	155	240	595	1395
1200	1050	2305	185	240	595	1485
1350	1050	2535	185	240	595	1660
1500	1200	2185	185	240	595	1395
1800	1200	2535	185	240	595	1660
2100	1300	2505	215	240	595	1635
2500	1350	2705	215	240	595	1785
3000	1350	3145	215	305	660	2115
3500	1500	2995	215	305	660	2005
4000	1500	3335	215	305	660	2260
4500	1600	3285	215	305	660	2220

note: space of 300 required for general access & 500 for access to inspection opening

3 Vertical indirect sto cylinders data →(2)

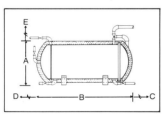

4 Horizontal indirect sto cylinder →(5)

capacity l	A h with insulation	B l with insulation	C front space for withdrawal	D back space for connexions	E space above for connexions
100	630	865	465	80	385
150	630	1180	700	80	385
200	680	1260	760	95	455
250	680	1515	950	95	455
300	790	1340	820	95	455
350	790	1515	950	115	485
400	790	1690	1080	115	485
450	790	1870	1215	115	485
500	890	1610	1202	115	485
600	890	1870	1215	115	485
700	955	1850	1200	140	540
800	955	2130	1410	140	540
900	1080	1920	1255	155	595
1000	1080	2110	1395	155	595
1200	1130	2230	1485	155	595
1350	1130	2460	1660	155	595
1500	1280	2110	1395	155	595
1800	1280	2460	1660	155	595
2100	1380	2430	1635	155	595
2500	1430	2630	1785	155	595
3000	1430	3070	2115	185	660
3500	1590	2920	2005	185	660
4000	1590	3260	2260	185	660
4500	1690	3210	2220	185	660

note: a space of 300 required for general access & 500 for access to inspection opening

5 Horizontal indirect sto cylinders data →(4)

STORAGE CALORIFIERS

Sto calorifiers serve same purpose as indirect cylinders except that heater is tubular battery in side requiring pumped primary circulation. Vertical withdrawal space not required. Sto calorifiers may be vertical →(6)(8) or horizontal →(7)(9). Vertical more efficient.

capacity l	A dia with insulation	B h with insulation	C front space for connexions	C front space for withdrawal	D back space for connexions	E space above for connexions
200	715	1335	315	720	155	455
250	715	1590	315	720	155	455
300	815	1415	315	820	155	455
350	815	1590	315	820	185	485
400	815	1765	315	820	185	485
450	815	1945	340	820	185	485
500	915	1685	340	920	185	485
600	915	1945	340	920	185	485
700	965	1925	340	970	215	540
800	965	2205	355	970	215	540
900	1065	1995	355	1070	240	595
1000	1065	2185	435	1150	240	595
1200	1115	2305	47-	1200	240	595
1350	1115	2535	470	1200	305	595
1500	1265	2185	470	1350	305	595
1800	1265	2535	470	1350	305	595
2100	1365	2505	520	1470	305	595
2500	1415	2705	520	1520	305	595
3000	1415	3145	560	1560	305	660
3500	1565	3075	560	1710	305	660
4000	1565	3415	560	1710	305	660
4500	1565	3365	560	1710	305	660

note: a space of 300 required for general access & 500 for access to inspection opening

6 Vertical sto calorifiers data →(8)

capacity l	A h with insulation	B l with insulation	C front space for connexions	C front space for coil withdrawal	D back space for connexions	E space above for connexions
200	745	1325	315	1330	85	455
250	745	1580	315	1585	85	455
300	855	1405	315	1410	85	455
350	855	1580	315	1585	85	485
400	855	1755	315	1760	85	485
450	855	1935	340	1940	85	485
500	955	1675	340	1680	85	485
600	955	1935	340	1940	85	485
700	1005	1915	340	1920	85	540
800	1005	2195	355	2200	85	540
900	1120	1985	355	1990	125	595
1000	1120	2175	435	2260	125	595
1200	1170	2295	470	2380	125	595
1350	1170	2525	470	2610	125	595
1500	1345	2260	470	2260	125	595
1800	1345	2580	470	2610	125	595
2100	1445	2510	520	2600	160	595
2500	1495	3040	520	2800	160	595
3000	1495	3135	560	3280	190	660
3500	1645	3220	560	3130	190	660
4000	1645	3325	560	3470	190	660
4500	1645	3540	560	3420	190	660

note: a space of 300 required for general access & 500 for access to inspection opening

7 Horizontal sto calorifiers data →(9)

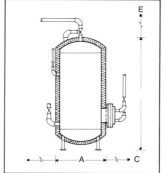

8 Vertical sto calorifier →(6)

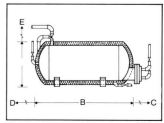

9 Horizontal sto calorifier →(7)

kW	A h with insulation	B dia with insulation	C space for pipework on 2 opposite sides	space for pipework on 3rd side	D space for withdrawal
100	880	395	160	85	575
125	1390	395	160	85	1185
150	1940	420	215	160	1490
175	2550	420	215	160	2105
225	1725	470	280	215	1220
400	2640	470	280	215	2135
500	2100	525	375	280	1540
725	2710	525	375	280	2150
800	2225	575	480	375	1560
1125	2835	575	480	375	2170
1250	2590	615	580	375	1880

note: calorifiers may be vertical or horizontal: space of 500 required for access on sides with pipe connexions and 300 for access on side without connexions

1   Non-sto water to water calorifiers data →(2)

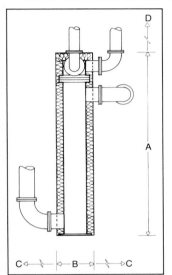

l capacity to water line	tank dimensions		
	l	w	d
18	475	305	305
36	610	305	371
54	610	406	371
68	610	432	432
86	610	457	482
114	686	508	508
159	736	559	559
191	762	584	610
227	914	610	584
264	914	606	610
327	1220	610	610
336	965	686	686
423	965	762	787
491	1090	864	736
709	1170	889	889
841	1520	914	813
1230	1520	1140	914
1730	1830	1220	1020
2140	1830	1220	1220
3360	2440	1520	1220

2   Non-sto water to water calorifier →(1)

3   Cold water tanks, open top rectangular, data

boiler or water heater rating kW	nominal capacity	tank dimensions		
	l	l	w	d
up to 20	40	475	305	305
20–45	70	610	305	371
45–60	90	610	406	371
60–75	110	610	432	432
75–150	170	686	508	508
150–225	220	736	559	559
225–300	260	762	584	610
300–375	300	914	610	584
375–450	350	914	660	610
450–600	430	1220	610	610
600–750	550	965	762	787
750–1200	880	1170	889	889
1200–1500	1000	1520	914	813

4   Feed & expansion tanks data

NON-STORAGE CALORIFIERS

Non-sto calorifiers used to change heating water temp or pressure without mixing. Horizontal calorifiers more usual than vertical but in smaller sizes may take up more space. Interior may have to be withdrawn annually for inspection and space must be allowed →(1)(2).

TANK ROOMS

In all but smallest bldg should be at least 2 cold water sto tanks →(3) to allow for draining down and maintenance without interrupting supply. More than 2 tanks may be necessary for sto required by water authority (→Bib145).

Feed and expansion tank for heating system also generally installed in tank rm →(4). Tank rm should be well above highest distribution pipework and outlets to give adequate head and flow rate.

A clear space of 500 round and above all tanks necessary for access, with additional space at entrance to tank rm. Min dimension over tank less than 450 l capacity 300. Access allow installation of replacement tanks desirable. Otherwise old tank may be cut up, removed in pieces and replaced with sectional tank. Cold water sto tanks may produce condensation on outside of tank unless insulated with vapour barrier.

Drip tray often provided prevent condensation damaging ceilings below.

Tanks larger than those listed →(3) either purpose-made or built up from plate sections 1000 square or 1200 square. Sectional tanks require 500 clear space under tank and bearers shaped allow bolts be tightened under joints between plates.

Services: Ventilation

ESTIMATING CAPACITY OF AIR HANDLING PLANT

Quality of air →p15

For preliminary estimates of space required for ductwork and air handling plant rate of 8 air changes adequate to carry heating and cooling loads of most bldg:

Air handling unit capacity will be approx
$$\frac{\text{floor ar of bldg}}{150} \times \text{m}^3\text{s}^{-1}$$

Where other air change rates required capacity will be approx
$$\frac{\text{floor ar of bldg}}{1\,200} \times n\,\text{ACH m}^3\text{s}^{-1}$$
where n = number of air changes

AIR HANDLING PLANT ROOMS

Air handling plant bulky but relatively light; considerable additional space required in plant rm for duct connexions. Large fresh air inlet and exhaust openings required: for economy should lead directly to outside. With internal air handling plant rm large duct connexions to outside air will be necessary in addition to duct distribution system to individual spaces.

Fresh air inlet and exhaust openings noisy; fresh air should be taken from well above street level to be free from dust and fumes.

Air handling plant rm generally positioned on top of bldg to reduce these problems. Connexion to boiler and chiller rm by heating and chilled water pipework.

Interconnexion between extract fan and fresh air inlet of air handling unit partly determines size of air handling plant rm. Generally extract fan is separate from air handling unit →(2). Alternative is for extract fan to be part of air handling unit; this avoids interconnecting ductwork but complicates fresh air inlet and exhaust outlet connexions to outside →(3). Silencers generally necessary on supply and extract ductwork to reduce fan noise in distribution ductwork. Silencers should ideally be halfway through plant rm wall or floor to reduce flanking sound transmission.

Provide adequate space in plant rm to withdraw individual components of air handling unit: this requires space alongside unit slightly wider than unit. Elsewhere min 500 access space should be provided →(4)(5).

Access route from road to air handling plant rm should allow for removal and replacement of fan section and should be same clear dimensions as door opening →(1)−(3).

air volume	l air-conditioning	l ventilation	w	h	ar of fresh air & exhaust openings	ar of main ducts	access door	
							w	h
m³s⁻¹	mm	mm	mm	mm	m²	m²	mm	mm
0.5	9 300	7 200	3 500	2 400	0.4	0.067	1 300	1 600
1.0	10 000	7 900	3 900	2 400	0.8	0.13	1 300	1 600
1.5	10 800	8 700	3 900	2 600	1.2	0.2	1 300	1 600
2	11 500	9 700	4 400	2 900	1.6	0.27	1 500	1 800
3	11 700	9 700	4 700	3 300	2.4	0.4	1 700	2 000
4	13 100	11 000	5 500	3 700	3.2	0.53	2 000	2 300
5	13 100	11 000	6 000	4 000	4.0	0.67	2 000	2 300
6	14 700	12 500	6 500	4 300	4.8	0.8	2 300	2 600
7	15 000	12 800	6 800	4 600	5.6	0.93	2 300	2 600
9	16 400	14 100	7 200	4 800	7.2	1.2	2 400	2 700
11	16 800	14 500	7 300	5 300	8.8	1.47	2 500	2 800
13	18 400	16 100	7 900	5 800	10.4	1.73	2 700	3 000
16	19 600	17 400	8 700	6 400	12.8	2.13	3 000	3 300
20	20 400	18 200	9 900	6 700	16.0	2.67	3 200	3 500

1 Air handling plant rm data

air volume₁ m³s⁻¹	l air-conditioning	l ventilation	w	h	l of mix box + fan section²
0.5	4 330	2 220	1 200	1 090	1 470
1.0	4 530	2 420	1 500	1 090	1 670
1.5	4 530	2 420	1 500	1 090	1 815
2	4 805	3 005	1 700	1 280	2 125
3	5 030	3 005	1 900	1 480	2 125
4	5 330	3 220	2 280	1 780	2 410
5	5 330	3 220	2 635	1 780	2 410
6	6 430	4 220	2 650	2 080	3 110
7	6 430	4 220	2 890	2 080	3 110
9	6 910	4 640	3 200	2 200	3 515
11	6 910	4 640	3 200	2 255	3 515
13	7 350	5 080	3 600	2 520	3 955
16	7 530	5 320	4 000	2 730	4 210
20	7 730	5 520	4 600	2 930	4 410

¹ based on coil face velocity of 2.5 m/s⁻¹
² to be added to l of AHU if extract fan to be in unit

4 Air handling units data

2 Air handling plant rm with separate fan

3 Air handling plant rm with extract fan in handling unit

air volume m³s⁻¹	l	w	h
0.5	785	655	775
1.0	850	775	915
1.5	850	775	915
2	1 100	1 010	1 220
3	1 180	1 125	1 375
4	1 295	1 240	1 525
5	1 850	1 540	1 890
6	1 850	1 540	1 890
7	1 850	1 540	1 890
9	1 915	1 650	1 975
11	2 070	1 880	2 255
13	2 220	2 110	2 480
16	2 680	2 350	2 820
20	2 850	2 580	3 080

5 Extract fans data

Services: Thermal insulation

element	resistance m² °C/W
internal surface of wall	0.123
internal surface of ceilings & floors (downward heat flow)	0.15
internal surface of ceilings & floors (upward heat flow)	0.106
outside surface of wall sheltered exposure	0.08
outside surface of wall normal exposure	0.055
outside surface of wall severe exposure	0.03
outside surface of roof sheltered exposure	0.09
outside surface of roof normal exposure	0.045
outside surface of roof severe exposure	0.02
unventilated air space 5 thick	0.11
unventilated air space 20 thick or more	0.18
loft space below unsealed, tiled pitched roof	0.11
loft space below unsealed, tiled pitched roof with felt below tiles	0.18
air space behind tiles on tile hung wall	0.12
air space in cavity wall	0.18

1 Surface & air resistances

material	thermal conductivity (k) W/m °C	material	thermal conductivity (k) W/m °C
aerated concrete	0.21	gypsum plaster	0.46
aluminium	160	hardboard	0.08
asbestos cement	0.4	lightweight plaster	0.2
asphalt	0.43	limestone	1.5
brickwork, common	0.7	linoleum	0.22
carpet	0.05	plasterboard	0.16
composition flooring	0.44	roofing felt	0.19
dense concrete	1.5	sand cement	0.53
expanded polystyrene	0.035	slate	2.0
fibreboard	0.057	steel	50
glass	1.05	thatch	0.09
glassfibre	0.035	timber	0.15
granite	2.5	wood chipboard	0.15
granolithic	1.16	woodwool	0.1

2 Thermal conductivities of common bldg materials

construction	U value W/m² °C
solid 225 brick wall unplastered	2.3
solid 225 brick wall plastered	2.1
cavity wall 2 × 105 plastered on inside	1.5
cavity wall 105 brick outer leaf 100 aerated concrete block inner leaf plastered on inside	0.96
cavity wall 105 brick outer leaf 100 aerated concrete block inner leaf plastered on inside with 13 polystyrene in cavity	0.7
150 concrete	3.5
150 concrete with 50 woodwool as permanent shuttering, plastered	1.1
weatherboarding on timber framing with 10 plasterboard lining & 50 glass fibre in cavity	0.62
19 asphalt on 150 dense concrete roof	3.4
19 asphalt on 150 aerated concrete slab roof	0.88
3 layer felt on prescreeded 50 woodwool slabs with plasterboard ceiling	0.9
3 layer felt on prescreeded 50 woodwool slabs with plasterboard ceiling & 25 glass fibre between joists	0.6
3 layer felt on 13 fibreboard on metal decking	2.2
3 layer felt on 25 polystyrene on metal decking	1.1
pitched roof, tiles on felt on boarding with plasterboard ceiling	1.3
pitched roof, tiles on felt on boarding with plasterboard ceiling with 50 glass fibre	0.5
internal 20 timber boarded floor on joists with plasterboard ceiling	1.6
internal 150 concrete floor with 50 screed	2.4
single glazing any weight timber frame	4.3
single glazing metal frame	5.6
double glazing any weight timber frames	2.5
double glazing metal frames with thermal break	3.2

3 U values for common bldg structures

HEAT TRANSFER

Conduction: direct transfer of heat through a material.

Thermal conductivity (k): property of material alone.

Convection: transport of heat through fluids by circulation: affects heat transfer through air spaces and air movement over surfaces.

Radiation: transfer of heat between bodies at distance by electro-magnetic radiation.

Resistance of wall to passage of heat through it made up from resistance of each element of wall, eg resistance of brick wall will be sum of resistance caused by conduction through brick and resistance through convective and radiative transfer at outside surface. Plastered cavity brick wall will include resistance of air space and plaster etc.

Thermal transmittance (or U value) of bldg element: reciprocal of resistance ie

$$U = \frac{1}{R} = \frac{1}{R_{si} + R_1 + R_2 + \cdots + R_a + R_{so}}$$

where R_{si} = internal surface resistance
R_{so} = outside surface resistance
R_a = air space resistance
R_1, R_2, etc = resistance of components $= \dfrac{L}{K}$

where L = thickness of component layer (m)
K = thermal conductivity W/m °C

Units of U are W/m² °C and heat flow through composite structure is given by U A($t_1 - t_0$) where A is area and t_1 and t_0 are inside and outside temp.

Values of inside and outside surface resistances and air space resistances →(1) and values of conductivity (k) for common bldg materials →(2).

Example: Calculate U value of cavity wall consisting of 105 brick outer leaf with 25 render, 50 air space, internal leaf of 150 aerated concrete block with 10 plasterboard lining on 25 battens:

inside surface resistance →(1) = 0.123
resistance of 10 plasterboard →(2) = 0.01/0.16 = 0.063
resistance of air space →(1) = 0.18
resistance of 150 aerated concrete →(2) = 0.150/0.21 = 0.714
resistance of air space →(1) = 0.18
resistance of 105 brick →(2) = 0.105/0.7 = 0.15
resistance of render →(2) = 0.025/0.53 = 0.047
outside surface resistance →(1) (normal) = 0.055
total resistance R = 1.1512 m² deg C/W
U = 1/R = 0.66 W/m² °C

U values of some common structures for normal exposure →(3).

Condensation →p394

Services: Thermal insulation

CONDENSATION

Moisture inside bldg arises from such sources as external air, breath of occupants, cooking, washing, flueless gas and oil heaters. Warm air can hold more moisture than cold air →(1). Warm air cooled becomes saturated at temp called *dew point,* which depends on amount of moisture initially in warm air. *Condensation* occurs on surfaces with temp below dew point.

Condensation prevented by (a) ventilation: introduction of outdoor air with low moisture content; (b) heating: raises surface temp: (c) insulation: indirectly by increasing temp for heat output available.

Calculation of condensation risk requires knowledge of temp and moisture differences between inside and outside air.

Example:
Unheated bedr at 6°C, outside air − 1°C, wall U value = 0.6 W/m²°C. Ventilation rate 1 airchange/hr, rm volume 35 m³.

moisture content of saturated air at − 1°C = 0.0035 kg/kg
outdoor air in winter approx 90% saturated moisture content = 0.90 × 0.0035 = 0.0032 kg/kg
indoor air moisture = outdoor air moisture + added moisture
assume moisture input from 2 occupants at 0.040 kg/hr:
outdoor air added = airchange rate × volume = 35 m² = 35 × 1.2 = 42 kg;

moisture added $= \dfrac{2 \times 0.040}{42} = 0.0019$ kg/kg

indoor air moisture = 0.0032 + 0.0019 = 0.0051 kg/kg.
→(1), indoor air dew point = 4.2°C
temp distribution through wall in proportion to resistances: U value 0.6

gives resistance $\dfrac{1}{0.6} = 1.7$, inside surface resistance = 0.123, temp

difference inside to out = 7°C, surface is $\dfrac{0.123}{1.7} = 0.5°C$ below rm temp

ie 5.5°C. Condensation will not take place

Cold bridges
Wall of previous example bridged by concrete lintel U value 3.5 W/m² °C:

resistance $= \dfrac{1}{3.5} = 0.286$

surface is $\dfrac{0.123}{0.286} \times 7 = 3°C$ below rm temp,

ie 3°C: condensation will take place

Interstitial condensation
Assume wall with U value = 0.6 W/m² °C consists of 19 weatherboarding on timber studs, 9 plasterboard on studs with 50 glass fibre between. Temp through wall obtained by proportioning total temp drop according to resistances →(2): moisture contents of inside and outside air taken as previous example. Within partition moisture varies but will be constant through air space and porous insulation. Dew point corresponding to moisture content is above temp in air space and condensation occurs. Vapour barrier on rm side of insulant reduces moisture content in cold side of wall to that of outdoor air, temp in wall will always be above dew point of outside air so condensation cannot occur.

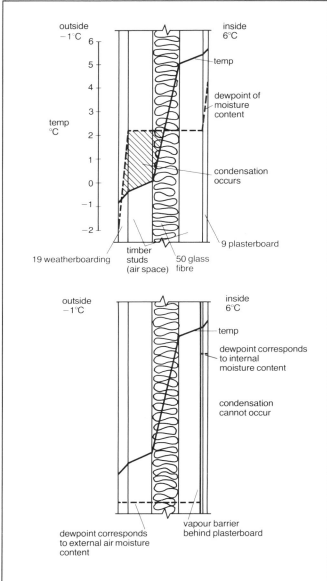

2 Occurrence of interstitial condensation & its prevention by vapour barrier on warm side of insulation

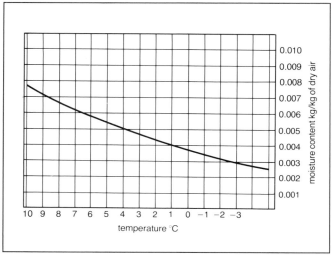

1 Moisture content of saturated air

Services: Sound insulation

Sound measured in decibels (dB); increase of 10 dB gives approx doubling in loudness. Sounds of equal level in dB but at different frequencies (frequency roughly equivalent to pitch) not equally loud: always necessary make frequency analysis of sound; 'overall' levels or single figure measurements not related frequency little use.

SOUND REDUCTION INDEX (SRI)

Measure of sound insulation against airborne sound: difference in noise levels between 2 spaces separated by wall or floor corrected for acoustical conditions in quiet rm. Conversely, subtracting SRI of 1 element from noise level in 1 rm gives after correction noise level to be expected in second rm caused by sound transmitted by that element.

$SIR = L_1 - L_2 - \log S/A$ where L_1 and L_2 are noise levels in rm 1 & 2, S is partition area, A is total sound absorption in rm 2

SRI depends on weight and will vary with frequency. Values for 1-leaf homogeneous solid partitions can be calculated →(1).

Method of calculation:
enter figure at surface weight of panel and draw horizontal line in lower part of figure
draw vertical lines through intersections of this line with frequency scale into upper part of figure
read off SRI at intersections with graph for appropriate material: lower parts of graph identical for panels of same weight; graphs change from initial slope to flat 'plateau' at points indicated for each material

Example:
SRI of 100 concrete: surface weight = 230 kg/m²

frequency Hz	63	125	250	500	1000	2000	4000	8000
SRI db	37	38	38	46	56	62	68	74

For more complex structures SRI can be estimated →p396(1).

From →(1) can be seen that weight of partition must be doubled to increase SRI by 6dB below plateau regions. If SRI too low for application because of plateau, increase only possible without massive increase in weight by changing material, eg from breeze block to brick.

Composite structure consisting of 2 elements of different SRI (eg wall with window) will have SRI closer to weakest element as found from →(2).

Method of calculation:
1 calculate ratio of areas of 2 elements and difference between values of SRI at each frequency
2 enter graph on horizontal scale at difference in SRI
3 draw vertical line to intercept curve appropriate to area ratio
4 read off reduction in SRI on vertical scale
5 subtract from high SRI to give SRI of composite
repeat steps 2–5 for each frequency

Example:
from →(1) SRI of 100 concrete (surface weight 230 kg/m²) is 46 dB; SRI of 9 plywood (surface weight 4.5 kg/m²) is 19 dB
difference between values of SRI is 27 dB; ratio of areas is 0.01
from →(2) reduction is SRI: 8 dB
SRI of composite: 46 − 8 = 38 dB

Effect of small holes and gaps in and round partitions can be found using →(2) and taking SRI of hole as 0 dB: eg if composite partition in previous example with SRI dB at 500 Hz has gaps of 1.5 wide down edges, ar of gaps = 2 × 0.0015 × 3 = 0.009 m²; ratio of ar = 0.001; difference between values of SRI = 38 − 0; so reduction in SRI partition will from →(2) be 9 dB, giving a total of 38 − 9 = 29 dB: gaps, though small, more significant than plywood infill panel. All structures intended give sound insulation must be sealed airtight to eliminate holes and gaps. Joints between different materials and round pipes and ducts etc must be filled with resilient sealant to eliminate opening of gaps from shrinkage, differential thermal expansion, structural movement etc.

Adding sound absorbent tile or panel to wall or floor will have no effect on SRI except through negligible increase in weight. Sound absorption will affect final levels in receiving rm through factor log S/A while sound absorption in source rm will limit build-up of reflected sound and therefore levels that have to be designed against. Rm level is only reduced 3 dB for doubling in absorption. Principal use of sound absorption is to control character of sound in rm.

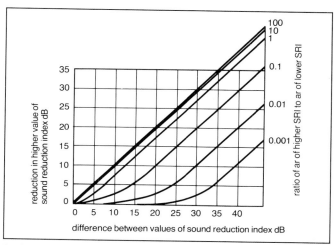

2 SRI of a 2 A composite structure

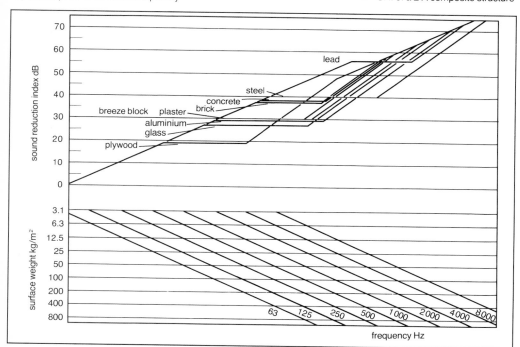

1 Calculation of sound reduction of 1-leaf partitions of common materials

Services: sound insulation

SOUND REDUCTION INDICES

→p395

material & construction	thickness	weight kg/m²	31	63	125	250	500	1000	2000	4000	8000
1. single sheet materials											
1.1 aluminium, corrugated	0.9	2.44	—	—	33	31	33	33	42		
1.2 asbestos insulation board on wood frame	6	8.4	2	8	13	16	24	29	33		
1.3 chipboard on wood frame	0.9	16	4	11	17	18	25	30	26		
1.4 fibreboard on wood frame	12	3.9	—	—	13	17	21	25	30		
1.5 steel sheet 1000 × 2000	1.6	12.9	6	10	16	20	27	32	37		
steel sheet 1000 × 2000 with stiffeners	1.6	12.9	6	14	17	18	23	30	36		
1.6 plasterboard on wood frame 400 centres	9	9.5	3	8	15	19	25	28	31		
1.7 T & G wood, joints sealed	25	14	5	12	21	17	22	24	30	36	
2. laminated sheet materials											
2.1 gypsum wallboard 2 × 12 thick	25	22	12	18	24	29	31	32	30	35	
2.2 9 plywood panel 1000 × 2000	9	4.5	—	2	7	13	19	25	19	22	32
2.3 2 no 9 plywood panels as 2.2 bolted together	18	9.0	—	5	15	18	22	24	30	30	43
2.4 9 asbestos board faced 1.2 steel sheet	12	37	14	20	22	25	31	27	37	38	
2.5 laminated insulation board faced both sides with 3 hardboard	32	13	4	10	17	14	20	23	19	20	
3. masonry											
3.1 brickwork: plain	115	190	26	32	36	37	40	46	54	56	
3.2 plastered 1 side	125	210	26	32	36	36	38	48	57	59	
3.3 plastered both sides	140	260	30	32	34	36	41	51	58	60	
3.4 plastered both sides	255	465	35	40	41	45	48	56	58	60	
3.5 clinker concrete blocks, 50 with 9 plaster both sides	76	96	25	28	30	35	30	40	46	51	
3.6 reinforced concrete	100	230	30	35	38	38	41	48	57	65	
3.7 cellular concrete, plastered 1 side	220	220	20	22	22	34	43	51	56	58	
3.8 hollow clay blocks plastered 1 side	90	75	20	25	30	33	32	33	37	41	
3.9 dense concrete	150	300	38	38	48	58	65	71	78	85	
4. single partitions of complex panels											
4.1 2 × 12 skins of plaster joined by honeycomb web of plaster	70	47	—	24	26	24	24	26	28	34	
4.2 ditto with cells filled with foamed plaster	100	58	—	18	18	25	28	29	33	38	
4.3 2 skins of plasterboard 9 joined by cardboard egg-crate	58	19	—	18	18	24	30	32	30	32	
4.4 ditto with 12 plasterboard	65	29	—	23	23	26	30	34	30		
4.5 25 polystyrene faced each side with 3 hardboard on 9 plasterboard	50	23	—	20	21	24	27	27	27	30	—
4.6 12 plasterboard faces to core of parallel packed straws	50	14	—	15	17	19	25	30	35	40	—
4.7 wood chipboard with vertical cylindrical holes 15 dia at 38 centres	30	11	—	14	15	21	25	28	26	30	—
5. stud partitions											
5.1 lead plywood 12 core 20 kg/² on 50 × 100 studs at 400 centres	125	49	—	28	38	34	41	46	50	54	58
5.2 plasterboard 9.5 on 50 × 100 studs at 400 centres	120	25	—	12	15	31	35	37	45	46	48
5.3 as above but plasterboard 12.7	125	29	—	20	25	32	34	47	39	50	52
5.4 as above, 12.7 boards & with 25 mineral wool blanket between studs	125	29	—	20	25	37	42	49	46	59	63
5.5 6 plywood on 50 × 50 studs at 600 centres	65	7.2	—	10	10	14	22	28	42	42	44
6. double masonry											
6.1 115 brick with 50 cavity no ties	280	380	—	39	43	45	55	55	79	87	—
6.2 as above but plastered both sides to 12	300	420	—	43	39	48	58	57	77	86	—
6.3 as above but with 9 3.7 butterfly ties	300	420	—	30	28	40	45	62	73	82	—
7. double partitions of sheet materials											
7.1 asbestos board, 6, on separate 50 × 25 studs, at 300 centres spaced 12 apart, studs outermost		15	—	22	16	18	31	36	46	50	—
7.2 as above but filled with fine sand between leaves		42	—	26	27	25	34	35	34	42	—
7.3 9 plywood, 1 leaf on 50 × 50 studs other leaf on 25 × 50 studs at 1200 centres spaced 50 apart	168	15	—	10	9	13	22	29	42	42	
8. double partitions of complex panels											
8.1 plaster, 2 leaves as 4.1 with 20 slag wool blanket in cavity	300	310	36	40	38	45	50	56	61	61	62
8.2 plasterboard, 2 leaves as 5.2 spaced 50 apart with 25 glass wool in cavity	290	50	25	28	28	38	44	49	52	56	58
8.3 12 asbestos wallboard on 30 timber frame spaced 200 apart	282	32	20	21	22	36	45	49	58	64	64
8.4 as 8.3 but 50 spacing	134	32	13	15	18	32	42	49	58	64	64
9. typical floor constructions											
9.1 concrete, 130	130	245	32	40	38	38	48	58	64	70	82
9.2 as above but with 50 floating screed			32	34	38	43	48	54	61	68	75
9.3 25 T & G boarding on joists at 400 centres, 12 plaster ceiling			10	14	18	25	37	39	45	48	48
9.4 as 9.3 with 50 sand on ceiling			28	32	35	40	45	50	60	64	68
9.5 as 9.4 with boards 'floating' on 25 glass wool blanket across joists			28	32	37	42	47	53	64	68	74
10. typical window constructions											
10.1 3 glazing in usealed openable frames	3	7.3	—	16	15	17	19	22	18	22	—
10.2 ditto in weatherstripped openable frames	—	—	—	16	18	16	23	26	21	23	—
10.3 3 + 3 thermal glazing units in weatherstripped openable frames	—	—	—	18	23	19	21	25	24	25	—
10.4 6 glazing in frames as 10.1	—	—	—	30	22	23	28	30	23	29	—
10.5 as 10.1 with additional frame 150 away glazed with 4 glass, reveals lined with absorbent	4	9.7	—	27	25	28	50	51	45	42	—
10.6 as 10.5 but with 4 glass in both frames & sealed	—	—	—	25	38	35	41	54	48	38	—
10.7 as 10.6 but 6 glass & 200 air space	212	30	—	35	38	41	49	56	49	40	—
10.8 6 glazing in sealed frame	6	15	6	12	17	24	30	28	24	28	38
10.9 12 glazing in sealed frame	12	30	12	18	24	27	27	27	29	41	48

1 Typical SRI in dB

Services: Sound insulation

SOUND ABSORBENT TREATMENTS

Surfaces of rm partly reflect and absorb sound according to nature and construction of surface. Proportion will vary with frequency. Result of reflection is reverberant sound which merges with direct sound and affects its character. Period of sustained sound known as reverberation time. Suitable reverberation time depends on purpose of rm and is established from experience →(1).

Reverberation time

Can be calculated from $T = \dfrac{0.16V}{A}$

where V is rm volume m^3 and A is total absorption in rm. A is found at each frequency by multiplying area (in m^2) of each type of surface treatment by its absorption coefficient and summing over all different surfaces of rm.

Absorbent materials

May be classified into 3 types:
(a) porous materials: absorb sound over whole frequency range, efficiency depends on thickness;
(b) panel absorbents: panels over airspace absorb sound over narrow frequency range according to panel weight and airspace depth; useful for low frequency absorption: too much absorption may be introduced by inadvertent use of seemingly solid materials which can only be fixed over an air space;
(c) cavity resonators can be 'tuned' to give selective absorption over narrow frequency range; of little practical importance as absorption obtained more efficiently using (a) or (b) but can be made from 'non-acoustic' materials, *eg* concrete: design not easy.

Absorption coefficients

For common materials given →(2), for use in calculation of reverberation times. For absorption coefficients of proprietary acoustic tiles refer manufacturers' literature; but make sure method of mounting of tiles same for test data as for intended application. Surface finish and treatment as well as subsequent redecoration will also affect absorption. Painting porous acoustic tile will destroy absorption at middle and high frequencies.

Absorption of people and seats in auditoria taken into account using absorption units/item, and air/cm^3 of rm volume.

Services references:
→Bibliography entries 111 119 124 130 133 143 145 150 151 246 377 390 416 489 490 503 593

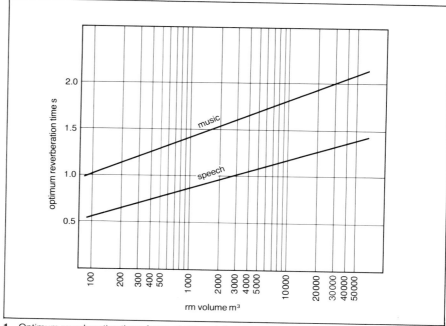

1   Optimum reverbaration times for rm of different sizes & uses

	125 Hz	500 Hz	2000 Hz	4000 Hz
boarding (match) 15 thick over air space on solid wall	0.3	0.1	0.1	0.1
brickwork: plain or painted	0.02	0.02	0.04	0.05
breeze block: unplastered, plain	0.2	0.6	0.5	0.4
pile carpet + underfelt on solid floor	0.1	0.3	0.5	0.6
pile carpet + underfelt on board & batten floor	0.2	0.3	0.5	0.6
pile carpet on impervious backing on concrete floor	0.1	0.2	0.3	0.4
felted or woven carpet on impervious backing on concrete floor	0.05	0.1	0.2	0.2
concrete, plain or tooled or granolithic finish	0.01	0.02	0.02	0.02
cork, linoleum or wood block floor (or wall)	0.05	0.05	0.1	0.1
curtains (medium fabrics) hung straight & close to wall	0.05	0.25	0.3	0.4
curtains (medium fabrics) double widths in folds spaced away from wall	0.1	0.4	0.5	0.6
25 thick hair felt, covered by scrim cloth on solid backing	0.1	0.7	0.8	0.8
fibreboard (soft) on solid backing, 12 nominal thickness	0.05	0.15	0.3	0.3
ditto painted	0.05	0.1	0.15	0.15
fibreboard (12) over air space on solid wall	0.3	0.3	0.3	0.3
ditto painted	0.3	0.15	0.1	0.1
floor tiles, plastics or linoleum	0.03	0.03	0.05	0.05
glass windows glazed up to 4	0.2	0.1	0.05	0.02
glass 6 or thicker in large sheets	0.1	0.04	0.02	0.02
glass or glazed tiles as wall finish	0.01	0.01	0.01	0.01
glass fibre or mineral fibre 25 thick on solid backing	0.02	0.7	0.9	0.8
ditto 50 thick	0.3	0.8	0.95	0.9
glass or mineral fibre 25 thick over air space on solid backing	0.4	0.8	0.9	0.8
plaster, lime or gypsum on solid backing	0.02	0.02	0.04	0.04
plaster on lath & plasterboard on joists, or studs, air space & solid backing	0.3	0.1	0.04	0.04
plasterboard on cellular core partition	0.15	0.07	0.04	0.05
plywood mounted solidly	0.05	0.05	0.05	0.05
plywood panels mounted over air space on solid backing	0.3	0.15	0.1	0.05
ditto with porous material in air space	0.4	0.15	0.1	0.5
water, as in swimming baths	0.01	0.01	0.01	0.01
wood boards on joists or battens	0.15	0.1	0.1	0.1
woodwool slabs, unplastered, 25 thick on solid backing	0.1	0.4	0.6	0.6
woodwool slabs ditto 75 thick	0.2	0.8	0.8	0.8
woodwool slabs, ditto 50 thick	0.2	0.8	0.7	0.7
empty fully upholstered seats (per seat)	0.12	0.28	0.31	0.33
empty plastics + metal chairs (per chair)	0.07	0.14	0.14	0.14
adults in fully upholstered seats (per P)	0.18	0.46	0.51	0.46
adults in plastics + metal chairs (per P)	0.16	0.4	0.43	0.4
proscenium opening with av stage set (per m^3)	—	—	0.007	0.02

audience or seating in any rm causes shading of floor: should be allowed for in calculating reverberation times; suggested suitable adjustments in floor absorption in consequence of this shading are: reduce by 20% 40% 60% 80%

2   Absorption coefficients

Lighting

type of interior & illuminance	lamp circuit efficacy (lm/W)					
	35	45	50	60	70	90
heavy industry						
av service illuminance 200 lux/R I 5	—	—	7.0	6.0	5.0	4.0
/R I 2	—	—	8.0	7.0	6.0	4.5
av service illuminance 500 lux/R I 5	—	—	18.0	15.0	13.0	10.0
/R I 2	—	—	20.0	16.5	14.0	11.0
light industry						
av service illuminance 200 lux/R I 5	12.0	9.5	8.5	7.0	—	—
/R I 2	13.0	10.5	9.5	8.0	—	—
av service illuminance 500 lux/R I 5	30.0	23.0	21.0	17.5	—	—
/R I 2	34.0	26.5	24.0	20.0	—	—
commercial						
av service illuminance 200 lux/R I 5	14.5	11.0	10.0	8.5	—	—
/R I 2	17.0	13.5	12.0	10.0	—	—
av service illuminance 500 lux/R I 5	36.0	28.0	25.0	21.0	—	—
/R I 2	42.5	33.0	30.0	25.0	—	—

1 Target wattage loading: boxed numbers indicate restricted range when most efficient source with compatible other parameters chosen

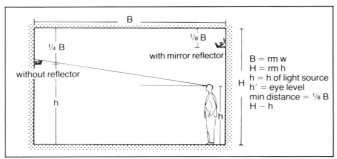

2 Cornice lighting

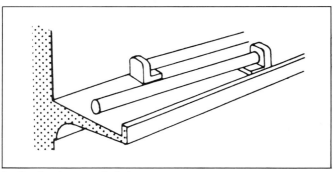

3 Overlapping prevents dark ar

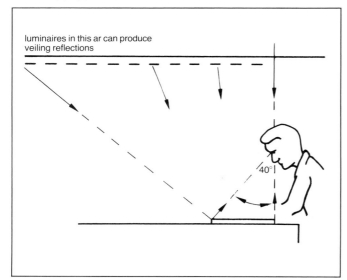

4 Offending zone within which reflections from light source will degrade contrast of flat task (about 85% office tasks viewed between 0° and 40° from vertical)

GENERAL LIGHTING

→also p25–6

Loading required to produce given av illuminance on horizontal plane from general lighting may be calculated from 'lumen formula'.

If E_s is service illuminance required in lux over working place area A m^2

lamps flux (L) $= \dfrac{E_s \times A}{MF \times UF}$ lumens where UF is utilisation factor described above.

Wattage $= \dfrac{L}{\text{lamp circuit efficacy}}$

Sources and luminaires with highest practical efficacy shoud be selected in conjunction with light decoration so that wattage loading is in line with targets given →(1).

If light output of each lamp is L^1 then number of lamps required to produce $L = \dfrac{L}{L^1}$

Magnetic programmes available from RIBA and CIBS for performing these calculations on programmable hand calculators.

BUILDING LIGHTING

High degree of uniformity of lighting can be provided by indirect lighting from cornices →(2): inefficient in terms of power but may be desirable to display ceilings of particular architectural interest.

Edge of masking cornice should be high enough conceal lamps. To avoid dark areas between lamps tubes should be staggered or over-lapped →(3). High reflectances on upper walls and ceiling essential to redirect light on working plane.

More efficient overall lighting given by fluorescent lamps fitted above 'egg-crate' or other forms of louvred false ceiling. Specially contoured plastics metallised louvre grids concentrate light downwards with low brightness appearance of ceiling.

In air-conditioned bldg extract air should be drawn through 'air-handling' luminaires so that heat can be removed from lamps and control gear before enters rm. This heat may often be usefully recovered for use in perimeter areas.

Glare

Excessive brightness contrast in field of view can cause glare →p17 32. If source, *eg* window or unshaded desk lamp, seen close to visual task it can cause disability glare and reduce task visibility; can also be cause of discomfort; this can occur even when source is well away from task, *eg* luminaires on ceiling, and is much more common danger. IES code gives recommendations for upper limit of discomfort glare index, which is related to luminance and size of light sources, their number and position in field of view and luminance of their surroundings. Calculation of this glare index can be performed as described →Bib382.

Contrast

Objects are seen by contrast, either contained contrast or contrast with their background: higher the contrast the more visible the object. Visibility of printed or written matter depends on contrast of marking material with paper. This can be markedly dependent on lighting and viewing angles even if materials used not obviously glossy. Light sources should be kept out of 'forbidden zone' indicated →(4): best position is to one side of worker rather than in front.

Uniformity

Variation of illuminance over working area should not normally be such that min is less than 0.8 of av. To ensure this manufacturer's recommended spacing/h ratio (ratio of horizontal distance apart, S, to mounting height above working plane, H_m) should not be exceeded.

Lighting

TASK LIGHTING

Calculations of power required for task lighting usually made on basis of direct intensity.

For filament lamp desk lights with diffusing reflectors inverse square law can be assumed to hold and it will be found that 500 lux can be obtained at about 600 to 650 directly below 60 watt lamp in usual type of reflector. For fluorescent lamps use has to be made of 'aspect factor' method as described →Bib383. This gives distances for 500 lux according to →(1).

lamp wattage	lamp l m	distance d (for offset 0.5 h) m
40	1.2	1.0
65	1.5	1.3
85	1.8	1.5

1 Values of direct distance of fluorescent lamps in typical dispersive metal reflector luminaire to give 500 lux at point opposite centre of lamp →(2)

LIGHT SOURCES

Incandescent tungsten filament lamps still used extensively in home and in display lighting where ease and cheapness of replacement, provision for limited areas of warm colour light and very small effect on life of frequent switching required. Standard life 1000 hr and 'efficacy', *ie* efficiency of light production, varies from 10–18 lumens per watt (lm/W); some manufacturers offer lamp lasting 2000 hr for use where concomitant drop in light output can be accepted as price of less frequent maintenance.

Lamps with bulbs silvered for use as integral spotlight or floodlight available; but better optical control and higher efficacy obtainable from tungsten lamps with small quartz bulbs and halogen gas filling.

Fluorescent lamps suitable for concealed lighting in home →(3)(4), for kitchen lighting and for most industrial and commercial interiors of moderate ceiling height. They can have efficacy up to 5 times that of filament lamp with reasonably acceptable colour rendering properties and up to 3 times where particularly accurate colour rendering needed. Their normal life is 7500 hr.

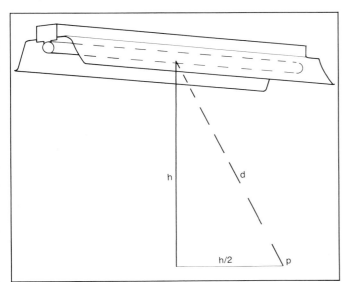
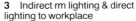

2 Task lighting with fluorescent lamp in dispersive metal reflector: →(1) gives values of d to get 500 lux at P from various lamp wattages

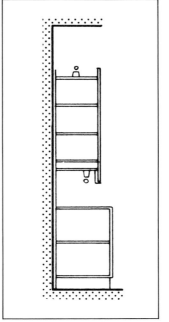
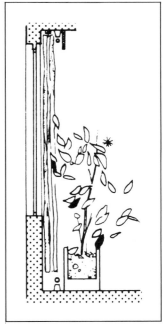

3 Indirect rm lighting & direct lighting to workplace

4 Illuminated curtain

Mercury discharge lamps, colour corrected by use of fluorescent bulbs (commonly designated MBF type) and/or introduction of metal halide into arc tube (MBI and MBIF), acceptable for achieving high illuminances in shops and in high-ceiling industrial areas. MBF lamps are available in wattages low as 50, which offers possibility of use to highlight small areas. Efficacy can be 35–70 lm/W including ballast losses or nearly 6 times that of filament lamps, with life 7000–10000 hr (to 70% of initial output).

Low pressure sodium lamps (SOX or SLI) only suitable for outdoor lighting because of monochromatic nature of light emitted; but operation at higher pressure (SON) broadens spectrum so that light is suitable for industrial applications (in high bays) and some comemrcial uses. SON lamps have efficacies 55–110 lm/W, or up to 9 times those of filament lamps, and SOX lamps up to 10 times, with lives of 10000 hours (to 70% of initial light output).

Colour appearance of light source not good guide to appearance of colours illuminated by it. For classification of lamps into three grades of appearances independently of colour rendering properties →p25(3).

All discharge lamps require control gear for starting and limiting current and capacitor for power factor correction. Mercury and sodium lamps take several minutes to reach full light output and from 1 to 20 minutes to restrike after interruption of supply: some fluorescent or filament lighting should be provided in any interior where light is needed immediately power is restored.

100 cycle per second (Hz) fluctuation of light output from discharge lamps on 50 Hz AC mains not normally disturbing, but if problems encountered, *eg* with moving machinery lit by high pressure discharge lamps at low mounting height, measures such as dividing lamps between three phases, or locally lighting critical points by incandescent filament lamps, may be taken. Fluorescent lamps may be mounted in pairs with 'lead lag' control gear.

EMERGENCY LIGHTING

Provision of emergency lighting legal requirement for many bldg; consult →Bib112.

OUTDOOR LIGHTING

Architect will often be required make provision for lighting exterior environment: may range from floodlighting whole bldg or feature to amenity lighting of city precincts, car parks and gardens, or functional lighting of railway, bus or air terminals. Wide variety of specialised techniques is involved; guidance given →Bib386.

Lighting

INTEGRATION OF ELECTRIC LIGHTING & DAYLIGHTING

Even in well daylit rm, el light has to be used on winter afternoons when daylight fades. When side-lit rm deep enough for work requiring illuminance 500 lx to be carried out at distance from window greater than height of window head above working plane, el light required for more than 15% of working year as DF will probably be less than 10% →p27–30. This requirement increases to about 50%, at depth of 1½–2 window head height and to practically 100%, even with fully glazed wall, if depth greater than 5 × that height. If tinted glazing used these depths greatly reduced.

Therefore arrange general lighting luminaires in rows parallel to window wall, each row switched separately. Switches should be located so that they can be conveniently operated by occupants as required and so that it is clear which rows they operate. Often possible provide pendant switches controlling individual luminaires with thin light cords which can be reached from standing position.

Fluorescent lamps should be chosen from 'intermediate' colour range →p25(3) compatible with colour rendering requirements and with warmth of lighting required at night. El lighting should be designed to provide illuminance recommended for particular tasks carried out in interior, but not less than 30 lx on av over working plane.

For max conservation of energy automatic control should be installed in new bldg to switch off, or preferably dim, those rows of luminaires lighting the working area (usually first 2 or 3) which are not required when daylight rises to provide illuminance at that depth such that full el lighting not necessary →(1).

Under these conditions windows need not be designed to achieve max penetration of daylight; more attention can be paid to any requirements for obtaining max benefit from exterior view, *eg* by providing wide uninterrupted windows rather than high and narrow ones. Opportunity can be taken to reduce contrast of wall above or between windows with exterior seen through them by maintaining light colour and arranging for some wall washing by artificial lighting.

In top-lit interiors with sufficient glazing to provide an average DF of 10% over working area el lighting will similarly be required for 15% of working year for tasks on which 500 lx required, and for longer than this where higher illuminance required or lower DF provided. If there is difference between activities carried out in different areas, requiring different illuminances or different periods of occupation, el lighting may be switched by areas. Otherwise whole installation can be linked to 1 controller. This may be photo-electric switch or photo-electric dimming control where fluorescent lighting is used; but at the date of writing there is little experience of application of such control to other types of discharge lamps.

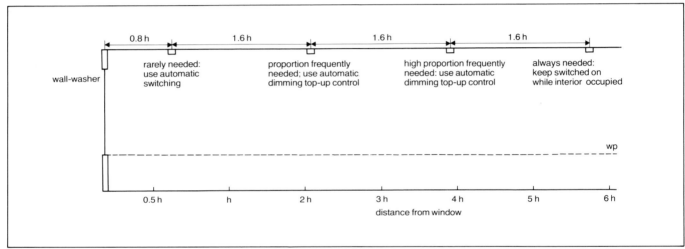

1   Daytime control of luminaires in relation to depth of interior space

Lighting references:
→Bibliography entries 112 124 202 271 367 380 381 382 383 384 385 386 387 397 449 457 523

Doors

DIMENSIONS

Recommended dimensions for wood internal and external door leaves and frames →Bib145: doors to these dimensions cheaper than units built to special sizes. Dimensions for steel frame doors and windows for domestic purposes →Bib138 →(1)(2).

	internal doors	external doors
coordinating h of doorset	2100 2300 2350 2400 2700 3000	2100 2300 2400 2700 3000
h of opening	2027	1982
coordinating w of doorset (L)→(2) s single d double	600 s 700 s 800 s & d 900 s & d 1000 s & d 1200 d 1500 d 1800 d 2100 d	 900 s 1000 s 1200 d 1500 d 1800 d 2100 d

1 Size of wood doors (→Bib145)

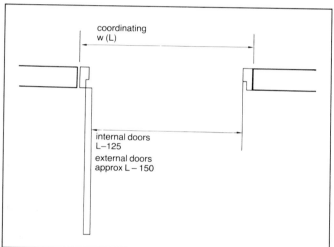

2 Opening w of doors (→Bib145)

coordinating w (L)

internal doors L−125

external doors approx L − 150

FIRE SAFETY

This may affect design of doorways both in need to maintain fr of partition and provision of means of escape.

fr doors described in E11 of bldg reg. In general fr door must be self-closing; hinges must be neither combustible nor of metal that softens at low temp; rebates to frame generally larger than standard (25). For some cases directions of swing of double doors specified in reg.

Means of escape from fire covered in Section II of Part E of Bldg reg: contains no detail on doorways but refers to code of practice. CP3: Chapter IV. Part 1: 1971 (Flats and maisonettes in blocks over two storeys) contains recommendations on main entrance doors to dwellings and on type and location of internal doors to bedr, living rm and kitchens. Section 4.3 lists requirements of fr doors. Part 2: 1968 (Shops and dept stores) gives dimensions for exit openings: 1070 for up to 200 users with additional 152 for each 30 persons over 200. Number of persons found by dividing total occupants of floor by number 1 less than number of exits. Part 3: 1968 (Office buildings) gives requirement of min opening width of exit doors in multi-staircase bldg as 765 for doorway serving up to 230 m² gross floor area, 1070 up to 1860 m² plus an additional 76 for each additional 140 m² served.

In general all doors which are fire escapes must open in direction of escape; doors which open into corridor must not cause obstruction within corridor; width of final exit doorway must not be less than min width of stairs, corridors or lobbies which it serves. Exit doors must be labelled; in certain instances sign must have emergency illumination.

FLOW CAPACITY

Where pedestrian traffic heavy rate at which people move through doorway determined by type of people (old/young, whether carrying baggage etc) and by degree of congestion on each side of doorway. Total rate at which people can move through doorway in both directions far less than capacity with flow in 1 direction only; for heavy 2-way traffic, 2 separate openings should be provided →(3).

	(P/min)
gateways & other clear openings	60–110/m w
single swing door (900)	40–60 increased by 50% if fastened open
revolving door	25–35 1 direction: this is doubled if leaves collapse to give 2 openings

waist-high turnstile:
  with free admision
  with cashier
  operated with single coin
	
	40–60
	12–18
	25–50

3 Capacity of doorways with unidirectional pedestrian flow

DISABLED PERSONS

Standard door sizes: min convenient width for ambulant disabled 800 doorset (opening width 675, internal door). This too narrow for wheelchair users: 900 doorset usually adequate. Wider doors not necessarily better for wheelchairs provided adequate space to position chair beside door.

Location of doors: corridors should be not less than 1200 wide for wheelchair users to position themselves to open doors in end wall of corridor or at side. At end door should be offset to give max space beside handle. Similarly when located in corner of rm door should be hinged at side nearer corner →(4)(5).

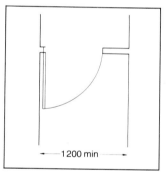

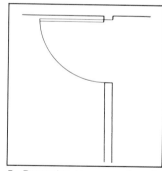

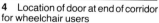
1200 min

4 Location of door at end of corridor for wheelchair users

5 Doorswing in corner of rm for wheelchair users

In small rm, such as wc cubicles, side-hung doors should open outwards or sliding doors should be used. Designer should check whether doors swinging outwards into corridors or public areas such as washrm likely to be hazardous. Doorswings should not conflict with each other and should not extend over steps.

Self-closing doors can cause difficulty to disabled; if essential, action should be as light as possible. In bldg for blind, self-closing doors required in some locations. Automatically-opening doors can be advantage to handicapped in public bldg but must not be of type that closes after predetermined delay.

Lever handles preferable to knobs and usually satisfactory at standard height of 1040. Glazed doors should be used where possible. For adult users base of glazed panel should not be over 1010 from floor and it should be down to kick-plate level in bldg used by handicapped children. Fully-glazed doors must carry some marking as hazard cue.

Sliding doors slightly easier than side-hung doors for wheelchair users to operate; but may be less robust and give significantly poorer sound and thermal insulation. In general their use should be limited to locations where space inadequate for a satisfactory side-hung door.

Also →p85–7

Doors

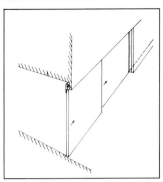

1 Sliding door

2 Telescopic sliding door

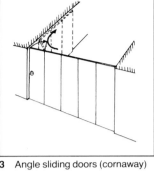

3 Angle sliding doors (cornaway)

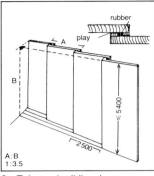

4 Folding doors (foldaway)

5 Folding doors (centafold)

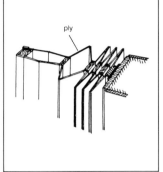

6 Concertina folding doors (plywood)

7 Concertina folding doors (plastics fabrics)

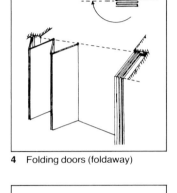

8 Power-operated folding door

9 Roll shutter door over corner or with sectional supports (h reach possibilities)

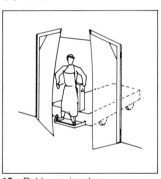

10 Rubber swing door

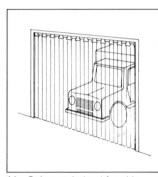

11 Strip curtain (pvc) for wide access

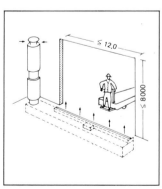

12 Air curtain system

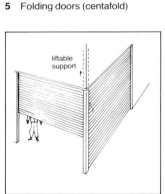

13 Air curtain for small doors

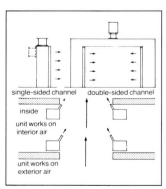

14 Rubber edging door seal

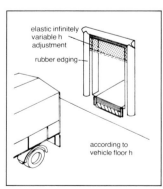

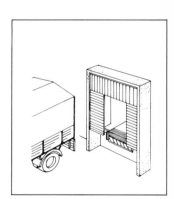

15 Wired rubber segments door seal

INDUSTRIAL TYPES

For large openings (partitions) sliding, sliding-folding, concertina-folding →(1)–(8).

Private garage doors (folding, sectional, roller) →p101(7)–(10).

For very large and high bldg (*eg* aircraft hangers) special design with lifting corner or section supports →(9).

Access way doors of impact resistant plastics →(10); also plastics strip curtain →(11).

Air doors: injection of spanning air curtain →(12)–(13).

Door frames of weather-proof rubber edging →(14); all-round wired rubber segments →(15).

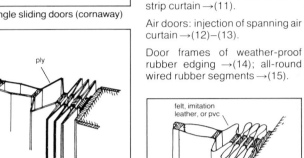

Door references:
→Bibliography entries 138 145 401 628

COORDINATING SIZES

To suit matrices of basic spaces in PO 6444 Pt 1 (→Bib103)

Ranges of steel windows to BS 990 Pt 2 & to 'Module 100 Metric Range' as given by Steel Window Association

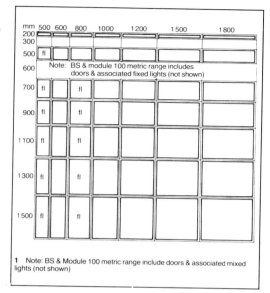

1   Note: BS & Module 100 metric range include doors & associated mixed lights (not shown)

Metric preferred range of W20 steel windows as specified by Steel Window Association

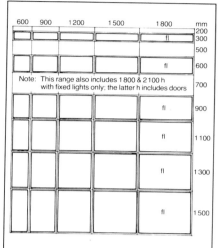

2   Note: this range also includes 1 800 & 2 100 h with fixed lights only: 2 100 h include doors

Ranges of aluminium windows to BS 4873: wide range of windows including vertically & horizontally sliding types

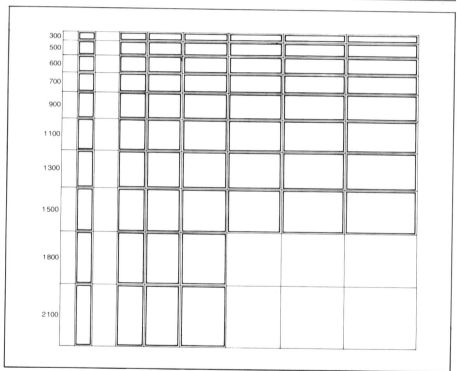

Window Sizes

For fitting windows into basic openings 3 options
window tailor-made to fit completed opening
window used as template for forming opening: traditional method in UK
basic openings coordinated with specified range of windows and other components: success depends on accuracy with which openings are built, dimensional compatibility of joints and dimensional accuracy of windows

On more general aspects of modular coordination →BS 4011, BS 4330, PD 6426 and PD nation →Bib104 105.

Range of sizes in steel windows can be extended by coupling members, by use of pressed steel box mullions and by use of wood surrounds. Aluminium window size limits in each range vary with type of window, *eg* whether horizontal or vertical sliders.

Work sizes

Steel windows (→Bib138) 6 less than coordinating size, permissible deviation 1.5. Aluminium windows (→Bib091) as specified by manufacturers, permissible deviation 1.5. Wood windows in metric range 6 less than coordinated size.

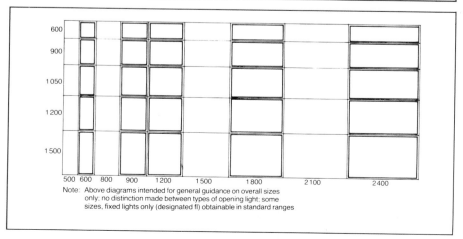

Note: Above diagrams intended for general guidance on overall sizes only; no distinction made between types of opening light; some sizes, fixed lights only (designated fl) obtainable in standard ranges

Dimensionally coordinated metric sizes for wood windows as recommended by British Wood-working Federation

Windows

POSITION RELEVANT TO DAYLIGHT PENETRATION

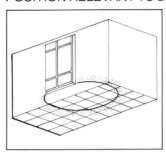

1 Tall windows can give good daylight penetration towards back of rm

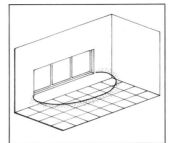

2 Long horizontal windows can give good lateral spread of daylight close to window

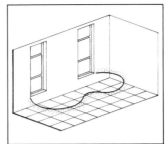

3 As →(1) can give good daylight penetration but if windows widely separated lighting can be uneven

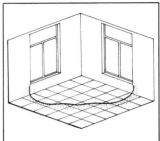

4 Can give good spread of daylight & useful light on wall surrounding opposing window

POSITION RELEVANT OT VIEW OUT & ACTIVITY

5 Where panoramic views & balc provided, windows down to floor level take full advantage of view

6 In liv where extensive views over country or townscape low cills may be provided if compatible with safety

7 In liv on upper floors, for safety, cill h should be not less than 1 020 or guard rails provided

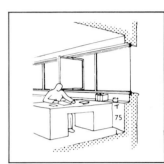

8 In off long windows often preferred but in deep rm on upper floors lower part of view obscured to people at back of rm

SAFETY & ACCESS FOR CLEANING

9 In k, cills often h to provide splash-back but in domestic k can give awkward shadows & restricted view-out

10 In off filing spaces cill usually fixed by filing cpd dimensions

11 In clo same considerations as →(10): in 1-storey bldg roof lights may be better solution

eqp	max h of facade (m)	max l of facade (m)
ladders		
ordinary ladders	9	any
travelling ladders	any[1]	any
suspension systems		
portable eqp	45	12
permanent eqp		
manually-operated cradles	45[2]	any
power-operated cradles	any	any
walkways	any	any

[1] but limited to ladder l of 9 m
[2] but wire ropes should be used above 30 m

12 Recommended ranges of external means of access to windows for cleaning & maintenance (based on CP 153 (5) →Bib146)

POSITION & SIZE OF WINDOWS

Additional considerations

Positioning of windows in bldg facade, and their overall sizes determined usually by daylighting considerations →(1)–(4), admission of sunlight and importance given to view out →(5)–(8). Constraints on positioning and selection of window sizes may be imposed by activities of occupants and positions of fixed furniture, fittings and plant →(9)–(11). Energy conservation, protection against external noise and security against unauthorised entry may also impose constraints. With reference to conservation of fuel and power in bldg and restriction of total area of window openings for buildings other than dwellings →Bib593. Fire precautions with particular reference to heat radiation hazards on escape routes may impose constraints. Bldg standards reg for Scotland (→Bib594 595 596) limit amount of unprotected area of external wall, *ie* area comprising windows, doors or other openings.

Windows

BASIC TYPES OF WINDOW

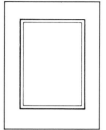

1 Fixed light

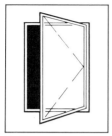

2 Casement – side hung

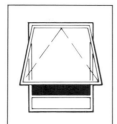

3 Casement – top hung

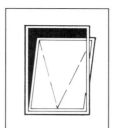

4 Casement – bottom hung

5 Horizontally pivoted

6 Vertically pivoted

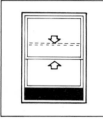

7 Vertically sliding

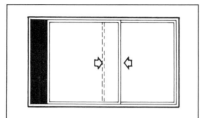

8 Horizontally sliding

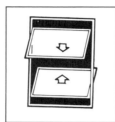

9 Linked hopper

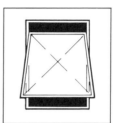

10 Projected top hung

11 Louvred

VENTILATION

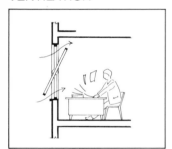

12 Trouble from ventilation in high winds at desk h

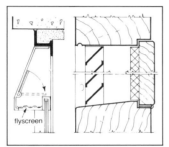

13 Adjustable devices to give minimal ventilation can be fitted or obtained incorporated in window: some types include optional flyscreen

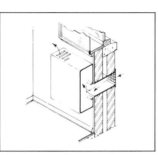

14 Fan-operated acoustic ventilation unit associated with double-glazed window

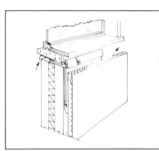

15 Scandinavian-type sub-cill ventilator associated with radiator to admit warmed air

DOUBLE GLAZING & DOUBLE WINDOWS

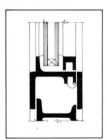

16 Factory-sealed double glazing unit in steel window

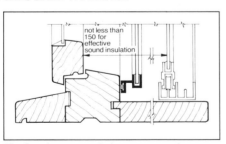

17 Supplementary window types: proprietary hinged & fixed panels available for fitting to frame or sliding types in separate light frame

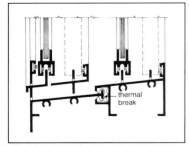

18 Proprietory horizontally sliding type in aluminium with two pairs of sashes

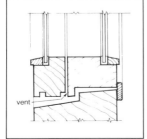

19 Horizontally pivoted type in wood with coupled sashes

Cost: if main consideration use standard windows

Performance: check against reports of tests in strength, air-leakage & resistance to water penetration

Fixed windows: do conditions justify? in particular:
will there be access to outside for cleaning?
will they inhibit fire-fighting & escape from fire?
are fixed windows required for security?
will additional indirect costs outweigh potential savings?

Openable windows: what types of opening light should be used?
is easy maintenance & cleaning from inside required? if so, consider reversible pivoted, inward opening casement, or projected top hung
are projecting opening lights to be avoided? if so, consider vertically or horizontally sliding types
when should multiple louvre windows be considered? where full opening with limited projection is desired

Double glazing (sound insulation):
is protection against outdoor noise essential?
can double glazing with wide gap be afforded?
will it cause ventilation & solar heat problems?

Double glazing (heat insulation):
if air-conditioning, double glazing may be essential?
if desired mainly for amenity is someone prepared to pay?
is double glazing to be used for both sound & heat insulation? if so, form with wide gap essential

Further details →Bib058

Windows

Retractable types

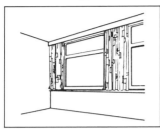

1 Curtains give flexible control for low level sun: for other than domestic use laundering can be problem

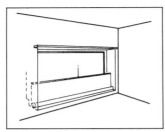

2 Spring roller fabric blinds, easy maintain: some fabrics too dense allow diffuse daylight through, but open weave materials better

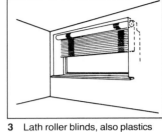

3 Lath roller blinds, also plastics louvred sheeting type, which allows venting through small louvres

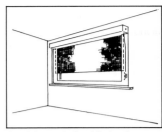

4 Light-excluding blinds where complete black-out needed in lab & dark rm: require light-proof casings; ventilated box heads available

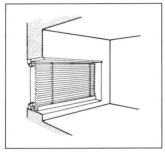

5 Venetian blinds give flexible control of sunlight & ventilation: wide range available, including external types & for use in space in double glazing

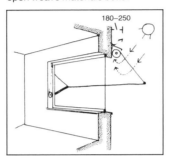

6 External awnings give good sun control: motorised versions available for commercial use

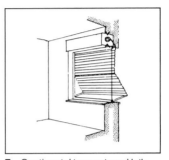

7 Continental type external lath awning: Norwegian variant available with aluminium slats

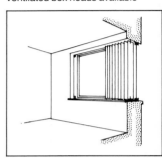

8 Internal vertically pivoted louvre blinds with impregnated cotton or extruded white pvc louvres: allow good penetration of daylight; useful for low angle sun facing E or W; retractable on top, or top & bottom tracks

Practical considerations

Internal shades fixed on or behind windows less effective than external shades for reducing solar heat gains because proportion heat they absorb released to rm: have advantage of protection against weather and accessible for control and maintenance; when not required during sunless periods can be easily retracted; when fully drawn at night can improve interior illumination. Curtains can be used with most window designs but pivoted windows can cause problems. Costs vary widely depending on materials. Fabric roller blinds simple operate but tend restrict ventilation unless of open weave: can be automated. Venetian blinds easy install and maintain: manually-operated types relatively inexpensive but susceptible misuse; full automation available with photocell solar controls. Vertical louvre blinds →(8) can be set exclude sunlight over wide range of conditions but for S facing windows may need frequent adjustment follow sun path: can be automated; but this tends be expensive.

In general external solar shading devices more effective than their internal counterparts.

Folding awnings and roll sun blinds often combine solar shading with decorative function. External vertical roller blinds, as also horizontally louvred types, usually provided with guides at sides give protection against winds. For neatness banks of louvred types often controlled together, either manually by rod control through gear box or by electric motors housed in head member. Provision need be made in window heads house retracted louvres.

Fixed external shading devices less flexible than retractable and adjustable shades for dealing with sunlight; as rule more appropriate for climates with predictably continuous sunlight than for Britain: cost high for benefit received. In temperate climates, canopy type probably most useful for S facing windows when desired exclude summer sun but admit winter sunlight. Fixed vertical louvres →(11) can be used for effective screening of windows mainly facing E or W if slats inclined towards N. Fixed horizontal louvre systems can give protection against direct sunlight over wide range of conditions depending on setting of louvres but reduction in diffuse daylight can be quite severe →(13)(14).

Performance of fixed types can be checked against sun path diagrams →p34−6 by using shading masks →(9)−(14).

Properties of materials used for blinds and louvre systems can be related to proportion of solar radiation they reflect, absorb and transmit; but in practice solar heat transfer complicated by number of factors. Some comparative data →Bib164.

Fixed external types

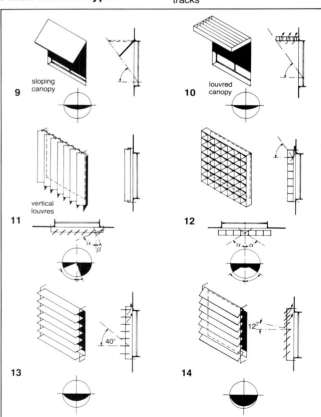

9 sloping canopy

10 louvred canopy

11 vertical louvres

12

13 40°

14

Fixed external canopies, louvres & screens with shading masks; for examples given windows assumed face SW & sun's rays as at approx 1400 hr midsummer lat 51.5°N.

Window references:
→Bibliography references 019 058 091 103 138 146 170 375 380 381 434 459 467 520 536 543 567 610

WALKING SPEEDS

On level walkways, within bldg and outside, rate of movement affected by: purpose of journey; age and sex of individuals; whether walking alone or in group (groups slower); air temp (people walk more quickly in cold); floor surface (soft surfaces associated with slower pace); carrying of baggage; crowd density; overall flow pattern of crowd.

Within any crowd considerable variation of walking speed found; even in homogeneous sample, *eg* women shoppers, range between highest speed observed and lowest equals mean value.

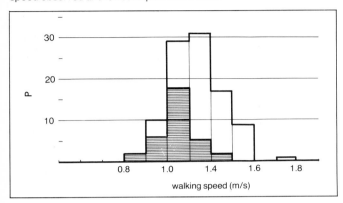

1 Observed walking speeds in indoor shopping mall: shaded ar indicates P walking with 1 or more others

Short length of slope in otherwise level corridor may have little effect on walking speeds. Longer ramps of low gradient, 5% or less, may similarly have little effect. On steeper ramps walking pace can be reduced from level rate by 20% with 10% gradient, 40% with 15% gradient (gradient % = vertical distance/horizontal distance × 100). Some people, particularly elderly and disabled, walk more slowly down ramp than up.

CORRIDOR CAPACITY

Limit of free flow conditions about 0.3 P/m². At greater densities individuals not able always walk at their natural speed or overtake slower pedestrians. Commonly-adopted max density for design of circulation areas: 1.4 P/m. At this crowding most people will walk at less than their natural speed and be aware of some discomfort. For short distances along route, up to about 3000, tighter crowding permissible provided significantly wider spaces occur before and after obstruction. With corridors wider than about 1200 flow capacity proportional to width; in narrower passages 2 people unable pass each other with ease. Corridor dimensions given →(2) for unobstructed routes; static people or fixtures reduce effective width →(3).

RAMPS FOR DISABLED

Except for very short ramps gradient should not exceeed 8½% (1:12) and should not be greater than 5% (1:20) when more than 6000 long →(4). Level platform 1800 long should be provided at top; in long ramps rest-platforms desirable at changes of direction. No changes of gradient along ramp. Bldg reg H4 specifies max gradient of 1:12min widths 800 within dwellings, 900 for common ramps to 2 or more dwellings, 1000 in institutional and other bldg. Handrail required by reg when total rise exceeds 600.

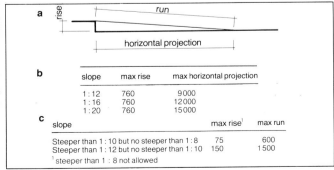

4 **a** components of single ramp run **b** sample ramp dimensions in existing sites **c** allowable ramp dimensions for construction in existing sites & bldg (USA standards)

WAITING AREAS

Linear queues

Width of queue can be reduced to 600 when barriers or other constraints used. Unconstrained queue, such as at bus stop or ticket office window, typically has av width of 1200. Form of queue can be affected by heavy flows of pedestrians nearby. Down length of queue av distance between persons is 400–500 under normal circumstances.

Bulk queues

Crowd of 2 P/m² seems dense to those within it but much higher crowding (up to 6 P/m²) possible in elevator cars and similar situations. Most people feel comfortable in crowd of 1 P/m²: useful design figure for waiting areas off main circulation routes. In foyers and other areas which combine waiting and circulation density of 0.4 P/m² good overall design value.

	free flow: mean density 0.3 P/m² or less		full design capacity 1-way flow: 1.4 P/m²	
	walking speed (m/s)	limit of corr capacity with free flow (P/min per m w)	walking speed (m/s)	corr capacity (P/min per m w)
commuters, working population	1.5	27	1.0	84
individual shoppers	1.3	23	0.8	67
family groups: shoppers with high proportion of young children or with bulky packages; tourists in circulation ar indoors, or outside near places of interest	1.0	18	0.6	50
school children	1.1–1.8 increasing with age	18–32	0.7–1.1	59–92

under free flow conditions range of speed in any group may extend, typically, from 0.6 m/s below mean to 0.6 m/s above: with crowding & all pedestrians moving in one direction range is very small

2 Approx mean walking speeds on level walkways; approx corr capacities

single queue along side of corr	1200
persons seated on bench along wall	1000
coin-operated machines	depth of machine plus 600 for first person and 400 for each additional user
waiting pedestrian with baggage	600
shop windows	500–800, varying with the interest shown in the goods, and with their size
small fire-fighting appliances	200–400
wall-mounted radiator	200
rough or dirty bldg surface	200

3 Approx reductions from effective w of walkway

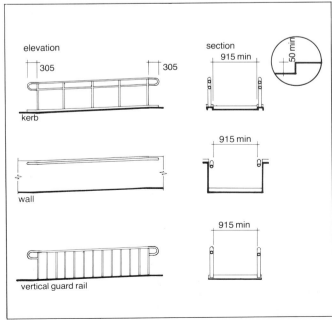

5 Examples of ramp edge protection & handrail extensions

Stairs

TREAD & RISE PROPORTIONS

Following rule-of-thumb based on assumption of adult pace of 300 in ascending stair: going + twice rise = 600 →(1).

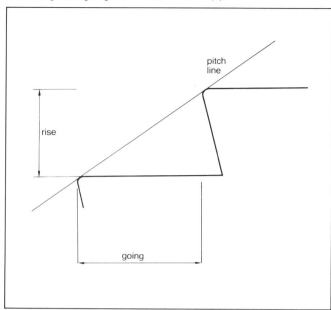

1 Definition of terms

No scientific ground for exactness in achieving this although some codes of practice specify particular proportions. Bldg reg H3 gives requirement that going and twice rise should add up to between 550 and 700.

Other criteria of stair proportions: energy expenditure and freedom from accidents. Total amount of energy used can become smaller as stairs increase in steepness but rate of energy expenditure increases. More accidents occur in descending than in climbing stairs; number of mis-steps increases as size of tread reduced. Generally satisfactory proportions can vary from 100 rise and 360 going to 180 rise and 280 going. Private stairs in dwellings may be satisfactory up to steepness of 210 rise and 240 going.

WALKING SPEEDS & FLOW CAPACITY

Short flights of stairs rarely climbed at speed which minimises energy expenditure (as people tend to do when walking on level) but av walking speeds on stairs lower than in corridors. When alone most people walk faster downwards than upwards but in dense crowd reverse can be true.

For fire safety codes flow capacity of 1.3 P/s/m width has often been used as basis of recommendations but this is greater than normally acceptable in general use →(2).

	free flow: mean plan density 0.6 P/m² or less		full design capacity 1-way flow: plan density 2 P/m²	
	speed along slope (m/s)	limit of stair capacity with free flow (P/min/m w)	speed along slope (m/s)	stair capacity (P/min/m w)
young & middle-aged men	0.9	27	0.6	60
young & middle-aged women	0.7	21	0.6	60
elderly people, family groups	0.5	15	0.4	40

2 Approx mean speeds of movement up stairways; approx stair capacities

BUILDING REGULATIONS

General requirements for stairs in UK in Part H of Bldg reg:

i Must be landing at top and bottom with going not less than width of stair (except at top of steps to an inward-opening external door where total rise does not exceed 600). Landing must be unobstructed and, if internal, level; if external may slope at gradient up to 1:12.
ii Max of 16 risers allowed in each flight. With very long stairways must be change of direction of 30° or more at landing after not more than 36 rises in consecutive flights. Landings between flights must be level and unobstructed, with going not less than width of stair.
iii Clear headroom of 2000 must be maintained, measured vertically from pitch line (line of nosings).
iv Treads must be level, extend to complete width of stair, and be either parallel or tapered (except that lowest 2 of stairway may be rounded). All parallel treads must have same going; tapered treads must have same rate of taper, narrow ends at same side, and same going when measured in centre.
v Rises must be same throughout stairway.
vi Projection of nosings not exceed 15.
vii Continuous handrails required on any flight rising more than 600. Height must be 800–1000 above pitch line. Rails required at both sides on stairs wider than 1000.
viii Sum of going and twice rise must not be less than 550 and not more than 700.
ix Except in dwellings, stairs wider than 1800 must be divided by handrails into sections not less than 1000 and not more than 1800 wide.

FIRE ESCAPE STAIRS

Requirements for escape stairs in UK given in number of statutory documents. These include London Building Acts, Building Standards (Scotland), Bldg Reg (England & Wales) and Fire Precautions Act 1971. Requirements given also in statutes covering specific uses of bldg, such as Factories Act 1961 and Offices, Shops & Railway Premises Act 1963.

In general, fire escape stairs must be built within enclosed shaft with walls of given fire resistance and fr self-closing doors. Doors must open into shaft at all floors except final exit level; doorswings must not obstruct flow of people already on staircase. Stairs from upper floors must not continue in unobstructed flight past ground floor to basement. Winders generally not permitted. In most other aspects requirements given in recent British codes of practice related to those in bldg reg. Section II of Part E of reg covers dwellings, office bldg and shops, and refers to Code of Practice CP3: Chapter IV for all instances except certain single-staircase bldg. Staircase widths for specified numbers of occupants given in code.

STAIRS FOR DISABLED

External stairs particularly dangerous for elderly and disabled in bad weather. On internal stairs splayed treads should be avoided. There should be no open risers; splayed risers with slightly-rounded nosings preferable to undercut square nosings. Handrails should be provided on both sides of staircase; section of rail that is gripped should be rounded, with width about 50. Rails should be continuous at landings and extend at least 300 beyond top of stairs; height should be about 850 above pitch line. Max gradient should be 40°; 35° or less better. Preferred going 250; rise should not exceed 190 and preferably be 170 or less.

	stairs serving only 1 dwelling	stairs common to 2 or more dwellings	stairs in institutional bldg, except those used solely by staff	all other stairs
min w	600 if serving 1 rm (except k or liv) or to bathr and wc 800 otherwise	900	1000	800 if serving part of bldg capable of being used by not more than 50 P 1000 otherwise
max pitch	42°	38°	—	—
number of rises per flight: max / min	16 / 2	16 / 2	16 / 3	16 / 3
rise: max / min	220 / 75	190 / 75	180 / 75	190 / 75
parallel treads: min going	220	240	280	250
tapered treads: min going	75	—	—	75
max angle between adjacent risers	—	15°	15°	—
min going 270 from ends of tread or in centre if wider than 1000	220	240	280	250

3 Extract from table to Bldg reg H3

DIMENSIONS

UK reg limits angle of elevation to 35° when rise does not exceed 6 m and speed along line of slope not greater than 0.5 m/s. In all other instances angle must not exceed 30°. This most common, although some manufacturers produce escalators to lower angle. BS allows max tread width of 1 050 and min 600. Manufacturers have ranges of standard escalators cheaper than eqp built to special sizes →(1).

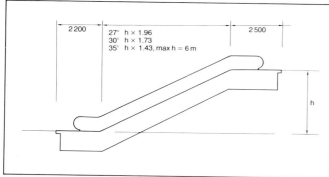

27° h × 1.96
30° h × 1.73
35° h × 1.43, max h = 6 m

1 Dimensions of escalators for initial planning

Structure of escalator: steel truss supported at upper and lower landings, and usually at intermediate point when rise exceeds 6000. Steps are carried on 2 sets of rails and drawn by steel chains. Motor and driving mechanism usually within truss below upper landing.

TRAFFIC CAPACITY

Dependent on rate at which people step on to escalator which, in turn, depends on
width of escalator
speed of escalator: up to about 0.75 m/s increasing speed results in greater capacity; higher speeds tend deter passengers stepping on
type of passenger and location: capacity of escalators in dept stores etc can be significantly less than those used by commuters in underground stations

→(2) gives approx capacities with escalators used by commuters or in

tread w m	max w between balustrades m	overall w m	approx capacity (P/min)		
			speed (m/s)		
			0.45	0.6	0.75
0.6	0.85	1.25	65	90	95
0.8	1.05	1.45	95	120	125
1.0	1.25	1.65	125	150	155

2 Approx w & traffic capacity of escalators

bldg with regular users. For other instances useful figure for preliminary planning 60 P/min, regardless of width and speed →(2).

PLANNING

For escalators serving several storeys in 1 direction of travel superimposed flights occupy least plan area but require passengers to walk between successive rises. Crossover arrangement eliminates this; double crossover is common in large dept stores, for movement in both directions →(3).

When escalators extend through fire compartment boundaries, selfclosing shutters required. Escalators not normally acceptable as means of escape from fire →Bib117.

PASSENGER CONVEYORS

Passenger conveyors →Bib123. Restrictions on width same as for escalators: min tread width 600, max 1 050. At angles of slope from 0° to 8° max permissible speed 0.90 m/s; above 8° to 12° 0.75 m/s; angles of slope greater than 12° not permitted.

Traffic capacity same as that of escalators of equivalent width under most conditions; with commuters, not carrying baggage, slightly higher values may be observed.

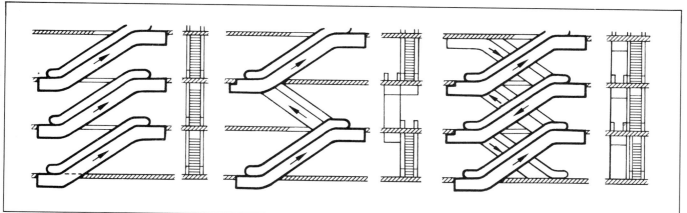

3 Superimposed, crossover & double crossover arrangements of escalators

Stairs references:
→Bibliography entries 117 123 300 338 340 346 501 591 594 613 628

Elevators

DIMENSIONS

Dimensions for 7 classes of electric elevators →Bib123:

Light traffic passenger & perambulator/passenger
Stretcher/passenger
General purpose passenger
Intensive traffic passenger
Bed/passenger
General purpose goods
Heavy duty goods

Tables for classes 1, 3 and 6 →(2)(3)(4)

Eqp to manufacturers' standard specifications less expensive than elevators to special dimensions or with special finishes.

Electro-hydraulic elevators an alternative to el traction elevators. Maximum travel approx 25 m and max speed 1.0 m/s. Motor rm need not be at top shaft and may be remote. Initial cost slightly greater than that of equivalent traction elevator but maintenance costs can be lower.

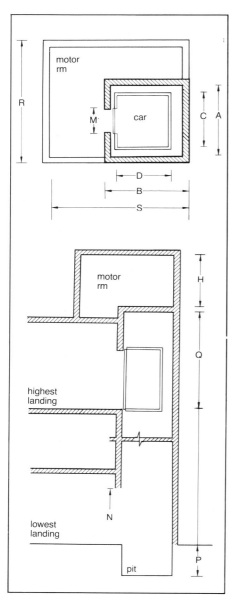

1 Lettered distances refer to →(2)(3)(4) which give dimensions in mm of elevators to BS 2655 (→Bib123)

number of P			4	6	8	10
load in kg			300	450	600	750
well w	A		1800	1800	2000	2000
d	B		1300	1600	1900	1900
car internal w	C		1100	1100	1100	1300
internal d	D		800	1100	1400	1400
internal h			2200	2200	2200	2200
landing doors clear w	M		700	700	800	800
clear h	N		2000	2000	2000	2000
pit d V = 0.5 m/s	P		1400	1400	1400	1500
V = 0.75 m/s	P		—	1500	1500	1600
V = 1.0 m/s	P		—	1500	1500	1600
free h V = 0.5 m/s	Q		3900	3900	4000	4000
top terminal V = 0.75 m/s	Q		—	3900	4000	4000
V = 1.0 m/s	Q		—	4000	4000	4000
machine rm w	R		1800	2300	2000	2000
d	S		3700	4000	4400	4400
min h	H		2300	2300	2600	2600

2 Light traffic P & perambulator elevators

number of P			8	10	12	16	20
load in kg			600	750	900	1200	1500
well w	A		1800	2000	2100	2600	2600
d	B		1900	1900	2100	2200	2500
car internal w	C		1100	1300	1600	2000	2000
internal d	D		1400	1400	1400	1400	1700
internal h			2200	2200	2200	2200	2200
landing doors clear w	M		800	800	800	1100	1100
clear h	N		2000	2000	2000	2000	2000
pit d V = 0.75 m/s	P		1500	1600	1600	1700	1700
V = 1.0 m/s	P		1700	1700	1800	1900	1900
V = 1.5 m/s	P		1700	1700	1800	1900	1900
free h V = 0.75 m/s	Q		4000	4000	4000	4100	4100
top terminal V = 1.0 m/s	Q		4000	4000	4200	4200	4200
V = 1.5 m/s	Q		4200	4200	4200	4300	4300
machine rm w	R		3100	3100	3300	3500	3500
d	S		4800	5000	5100	5300	5600
min h	H		2600	2600	2700	2700	2700

3 General purpose P elevators

max number of P			6	13	20	26	26	40	40
load in kg			500	1000	1500	2000	2000	3000	3000
well w	A		1800	2100	2500	2500	2800	3000	3500
d	B		1500	2100	2300	2800	2400	3300	2700
car internal w	C		1100	1400	1700	1700	2000	2000	2500
internal d	D		1200	1800	2000	2500	2100	3000	2400
internal h			2000	2000	2300	2300	2300	2300	2300
landing doors clear w	M		1100	1400	1700	1700	2000	2000	2500
clear h	N		2000	2000	2300	2300	2300	2300	2300
pit V = 0.25 m/s	P		—	—	1500	1500	1500	1500	1500
V = 0.5 m/s	P		1400	1500	1700	1700	1700	1700	1700
V = 0.75 m/s	P		1500	1500	1800	1800	1800	1800	1800
V = 1.0 m/s	P		1500	1500	1800	1800	1800	1800	1800
free h V = 0.25 m/s	Q		—	—	3800	4000	4100	4100	4200	4200
top terminal V = 0.5 m/s	Q		3800	3800	4100	4300	4300	4400	4400
V = 0.75 m/s	Q		3800	3800	4200	4500	4500	4500	4500
V = 1.0 m/s	Q		3800	3800	4200	4500	4500	—	—
machine rm w	R		2000	2100	2500	2500	2800	3000	3500
d	S		3700	4300	4500	5100	4700	5600	5000
min h	H		2400	2400	2700	2900	2900	2900	2900

4 General purpose goods elevators

TRAFFIC CAPACITY

With intensive traffic detailed analysis of flow pattern required. Selection of elevators and of control system requires specialist advice. Preliminary design can be made with aid →(2)(3); →(1) gives typical values of elevator traffic flow and acceptable interval between successive departures of elevators.

Example: multi-storey office bldg in several tenancies of similar type with 600 people occupying 10 storeys above ground level. Number of people arriving in peak 5 min period: 600 × 15% = 90. Rate of flow 90/5 = 18 P/min. From →(2) will be seen that 4 × 1.5 m/s elevators can carry 21 P/min with 30 s interval; for 18 P/min car size required 900 kg. From →(3) 3 × 1.5 m/s elevators would give interval of 45 s.

number of P arriving in 5 min, given as % occupants above ground floor level		interval(s)
single occupancy off bldg, industrial bldg	15–20%	25–35
multiple tenancy off bldg	11–15%	25–35
hotels	10–15%	30–60
housing	5–7%	60–90
leisure bldg, multi-storey car parks, dept sto	individual assessment required	40–50

an interval at lower end of each range associated with bldg having high standard of finishes & fittings

1 Peak period elevator demand & acceptable intervals between elevator departures

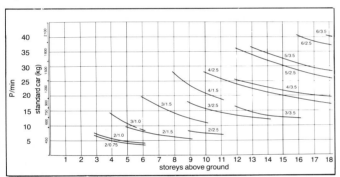

2 Elevator systems with mean interval of 30 s: unidirectional traffic, 3 300 storey h (3/1.0 represents system with 3 cars of max speed 1.0 m/s)

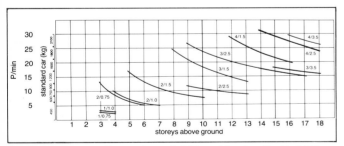

3 Elevator system with mean interval of 45 s: unidirectional traffic, 3 800 storey

PATERNOSTER ELEVATORS

Dimensions

For paternoster elevators →BSI 1970. Car dimensions limited to min clear height of 2 200; width and depth to between 900 and 1 000 with max floor area 0.93 m². Landing entrances must be same width as open sides of cars with height between 2 600 and 2 800. Max permissible speed 0.4 m/s. Stringent recommendations on safety devices →(4)(5).

Traffic capacity

Paternosters appropriate for random interfloor traffic with able-bodied users, having total traffic capacity significantly greater than that of conventional elevators of similar plan area. With random interfloor traffic evenly distributed through bldg total of about 30 P/min can be carried with little waiting when installation serves 5 floors, 35 P/min when 11 floors served and approx 42 P/min with 16 floors. If queues tolerated capacity can be about 60% more. With traffic emanating from 1 floor flow capacity significantly less: for upward traffic only from ground floor max approx 12 P/min. In real conditions interfloor traffic not usually even over all storeys: intermediate figure should be adopted.

Long journeys slow: if dominant traffic pattern flow to and from ground conventional elevators should be used. Paternosters generally inappropriate in bldg used by general public, by children and by disabled.

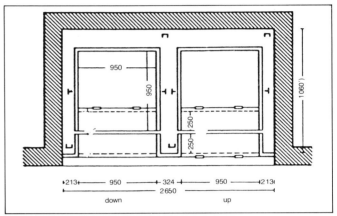

4 Paternoster elevator: typical plan dimensions

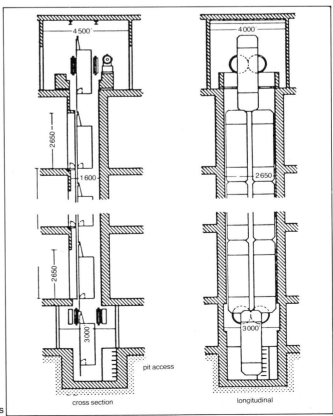

5 Paternoster: typical shaft dimensions

Elevators

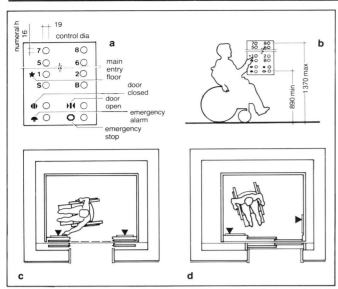

1 Elevator car controls for wheelchair users ANSI standards **a** panel detail
b control h **c** alternative placing of panel with centre opening door
d alternatives with side opening door

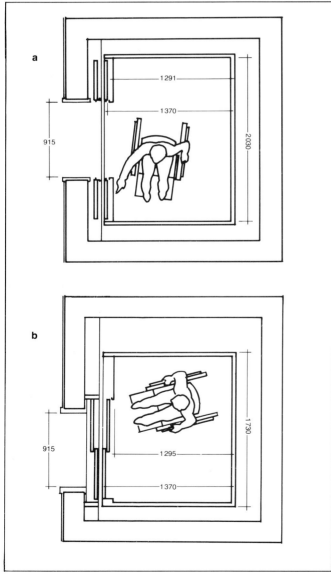

2 Min dimensions elevator cars ANSI standards **a** centre opening doors
b side opening doors   NB cars with min w less than shown but not less than
1 370 can be used for elevators of less capacity than 900 kg

ELEVATORS FOR DISABLED

In multi-storey bldg elevators are principal means of vertical circulation for those confined to wheelchairs and for others with difficulty in walking.

Min dimensions of elevator car to accommodate standard wheelchair: 1100 internal depth, 900 width, 700 clear door opening: 6-person light traffic passenger elevator →Bib123 just meets these dimensions but larger cars preferable. In public bldg there should be sufficient space for another person to accompany chair-bound: 1400 min depth, 1100 width. In special residential homes large wheelchairs need to be accommodated; dimensions for these: 1800 depth, 1000 width, 800 door opening. ANSI standards →(1)(2).

Elevator cars must be accurate in levelling at landings; must not accelerate or brake with jerk, requirements which dictate use of either variable-voltage traction motors or electro-hydraulic elevators. Doors should close slowly (0.3 m/s residential homes, 0.5 m/s elsewhere); photo-electric devices to prevent premature closing desirable.

Control buttons should light to operate. For general purposes normal vertical layout is best, with buttons at 30 centres min spacing. Mean height should be 1400, max 1600. In bldg used by unaccompanied wheelchair users controls should not be higher than 1300. In residential homes horizontal arrangement of control buttons in cars can be desirable, at height 1050 and set in wall at least 600 back from door.

At landings floor numbers should be very clearly indicated. To position wheelchairs there should be clear space at least 1500 × 1500 before each lift door.

PLANNING

Elevators serving single zone of upper floor should be grouped in plan with interlinked controls. Arrangement of lobbies should allow waiting passenger move rapidly to whichever car arrives first. No more than 4 elevator entrances should be alongside each other; facing entrances should be 2500–3500 apart. Elevator entrances should not lie on opposite sides of circulation route →(1).

In large bldg lobby area tends to be 5–6 m² per elevator on upper floors and 15–20 m² per elevator at ground floor with single group of elevators.

For efficient performances under heavy flows of traffic numbers of stops made by elevator cars should be kept to min. In large bldg there should be single main loading floor; passengers entering bldg at other levels should be brought by secondary circulation to main lobby at ground level. Use of elevators for mail deliveries or for other interfloor traffic at peak arrival or departure periods should be discouraged.

In residential bldg and hotels noise to be generated by elevators must be considered at early planning stage. Bedr should be remote from machine rm and walls carrying landing door eqp should not be adjacent to them. Risk of noise carried through structural continuity should be examined.

Total volume of elevator shafts in very tall bldg reduced when different groups of elevators serve separate zones of upper floors. Generally justified only in bldg higher than 15 storeys but normal practice in commercial bldg of 30 storeys or more.

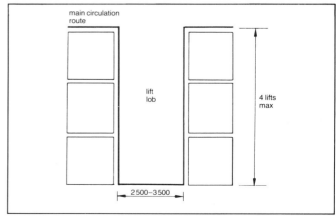

3 Lift lob dimensions

Elevator references:
→Bibliography entries 053 123 504 613 628

ARRANGEMENT
The bibliography has 3 parts:
basic complete list of publications, numbered consecutively
extracted from that a list of codes, guides, reg, standards and statutes
reference numbers of publications listed under topics

Initials are used for the following:

AIA	American Institute of Architects
AJ	*Architects Journal*
ANSI	American National Standards Institute
AR	*Architectural Record*
BRE	Building Research Establishment
BSI	British Standards Institution
CIB	International Council for Building Research, Studies & Documentation
CIBS	Chartered Institute of Building Services
CIRIA	Construction Industry Research & Information Association
DES	Dept of Education & Science
DHSS	Dept of Health & Social Services
DoE	Dept of the Environment
IES	Illuminating Engineering Society
ISO	International Organization for Standardization
HMSO	Her Majesty's Stationery Office
PSA	Property Services Agency
RIBA	Royal Institute of British Architects

Sources
In addition to publications listed in the bibliography some general sources of information may be found useful:

BRE information directory BRE Garston England annually
British Architectural Library *Architectural periodicals index* RIBA Publications London England quarterly
Building Centre/CIRIA *Guide to sources of information* Building Centre Group London England every second year
Building Centre Group *Books for the construction industry* annual list

HMSO Government publications section list 61: Building
HMSO Government publications section list 65: Scottish Development Dept
RIBA Book list RIBA Publications London England annual

BASIC LIST
Reference numbers of publications in this list are used for in-text references throughout the book

001   Abraben E *Resort hotels, planning & management* Reinhold New York USA 1965

002   Abraham G *The green thumb book of fruit & vegetable gardening* Prentice-Hall Englewood Cliffs N J USA 1970

003   Ackroyd P *Sports pavilions* National Playing Fields Association London England 1970

004   Adams R & M & Willens A & A *Dry lands: man & plants* Architectural Press London England 1978

005   Addleshaw G W O & Etchells F *The architectural setting of anglican worship* Faber & Faber London England 1948

006   Adie D *Marinas: a working guide to their development & design* Architectural Press London England 2nd edn 1977

007   A4 Publications *Office planner* A4 Publications Edenbridge England 1976

008   *AJ Handbook of building structure* (Hodgkinson A (ed)) Architectural Press London England 1974

009   *AJ Legal handbook* (Davey P & Freeth E (ed)) Architectural Press London England 2nd edn 1978

010   *AJ New metric handbook* (Tutt P & Adler D (ed)) Architectural Press London England 1979

011   *AJ Principles of hotel design* Architectural Press London England 1970

012   *AJ Urban landscape handbook* (Tandy C (ed)) Architectural Press London England 1972 reprinted 1978

013   *AJ/MoH Hospital planning & design guide* Architectural Press London England 1967

014   Allen R W *Hospital planning handbook* John Wiley & Sons New York USA 1976

015   Aloi R *Architetture per lo spettacolo* Hoepli Milan Italy 1964

016   Aloi R *Ristoranti* Hoepli Milan Italy 1972

017   Aloi R & Bassco C *Ospedali: hospitals* Hoepli Milan Italy 1973

018   Alpern A *Apartments for the affluent* McGraw-Hill New York USA 1975

019   Aluminium Window Association *Aluminium window edge profiles* (Technical report 1) London England 1976

020   American Association of Hospital Consultants (Mills B (ed)) *Functional planning of general hospitals* McGraw-Hill New York USA & Maidenhead England 1969

021   American Federation of Arts *Fountains in contemporary architecture* distributed by October House New York USA 1965

022   American Hospital Association *The extended care unit in a general hospital: a guide to planning, organization & management* AHA Chicago USA 1973

023   American Hospital Association *Hospital engineering handbook* AHA Chicago USA 1974

024   American Hospital Association *The practice of planning in health care institutions* AHA Chicago USA 1973

025   American Hospital Association (committee on infections within hospitals) *Infection control in the hospital* AHA Chicago USA 3rd edn 1974

026   American Insurance Association *Fire prevention code* AIA New York USA latest edition

027   American Insurance Association *National building code* AIA New York USA latest edition

028   ANSI *Specifications for making buildings & facilities accessible to & usable by the physically handicapped people* ANSI New York USA 2nd edn 1979

029   ANSI *Standards* ANSI New York USA latest edition

030   American Society of Heating Refrigerating & Air-Conditioning Engineers *ASHRAE standard 90–75; energy conservation in new building design* ASHRAE New York USA 1975

031   American Society of Heating Refrigerating & Air-Conditioning Engineers *ASHRAE handbook of fundamentals* ASHRAE New York USA 1977

032   American Society of Landscape Architects *Handbook of landscape* ASLA McLean Va USA 1973

033   American Society for Testing Materials *Standards* ASTM Philadelphia USA latest editions

034   Amery C *The National Theatre: an architectural guide* Architectural Press London England 1977

035   Annett F *Elevators* McGraw-Hill New York USA 3rd edn 1960

036   Anton T J *Occupational safety & health management* McGraw-Hill New York USA 1979

037   *AR Apartments, townhouses & condominiums* McGraw-Hill New York USA 1975

038   *AR The Architectural Record book of vacation houses* McGraw-Hill New York USA 2nd edn 1977

039   *AR Buildings for research* F W Dodge New York USA 1958

040   *AR Buildings for the arts* McGraw-Hill New York USA 1978

041   *AR Campus planning & design* McGraw-Hill New York USA 1972

042   *AR Great houses for view sites, beach sites, wood sites, meadow sites, small sites, sloping sites, steep sites, flat sites* McGraw-Hill New York USA 1976

043   *AR Hotels, motels, restaurants & bars* F W Dodge New York USA 2nd edn 1960

044   *AR Houses, architects design for themselves* McGraw-Hill New York USA 1974

045   *AR Places for people; hotels, motels, restaurants, bars, clubs, community recreation facilities, camps, parks, plazas, playgrounds* (Davern J (ed)) McGraw-Hill New York USA 1976

046   Arlott J (ed) *The Oxford companion to sports & games* Oxford University Press Oxford England 1975

Bibliography

BASIC LIST

047 Aronin J E *Climate & architecture* Reinhold New York USA 1953

048 Ashford N & Wright P *Airport engineering* John Wiley & Sons New York USA 1979

049 Atkins W W & Adler J *Interiors book of restaurants* Whitney Library of Design New York USA 1960

050 Baker G & Funaro B *Motels* Reinhold New York USA 1955

051 Banham R *Architecture of the well-tempered environment* Architectural Press London England 1969

052 Barron I & Curnow R *The future with microelectronics* Francis Pinter London England 1979

053 Bates W *Introduction to the design of industrial buildings* Constrado London England 1978

054 Baynes K Langslow B & Courtenay C C *Evaluating new hospital buildings* King Edward's Hospital Fund London England 1969

055 Bays K & Franklin S *Designing for the handicapped* George Goodwin London England 1971

056 Beazley E *Design & detail of the space between buildings* Architectural Press London England 1960

057 Beazley E *Designed for recreation: a practical handbook for all concerned with providing leisure facilities in the countryside* Faber & Faber London England 1969

058 Beckett H E & Godfrey A J *Windows: performance, design & installation* RIBA/Crosby Lockwood Staples London England 1974

059 Beckman W A Klein S A & Duffie J A *Solar heating design by the f-chart method* John Wiley & Sons New York USA 1977

060 Bedhar M (ed) *Barrier-free environments* Dowden Hutchinson & Ross Stroudsburg Pa USA 1977

061 Bellis H & Schmidt W *Architectural drafting* McGraw-Hill New York USA 2nd edn 1971

062 Bengtsson A *Adventure playgrounds* Crosby Lockwood London England 1972

063 Beranek L L *Music, acoustics & architecture* John Wiley & Sons New York USA 1962

064 Beranek L L *Noise & vibration control* McGraw-Hill New York USA 1971

065 Berriman S G & Harrison K C *British public library buildings* Grafton/Deutsch London England 1966

066 Bishop M L (ed) *Fountains in contemporary architecture* American Federation of Arts New York USA 1965

067 Blankenship E G *The airport* Praeger New York USA Pall Mall London England 1974

068 Bockrath J T *Environmental law for engineers, scientists & managers* McGraw-Hill New York USA 1977

069 Boje A *Open-plan offices* Business Books London England 1971

070 Borchardt S *Religious architecture in America 1632–1979* St John's Church Washington D C USA 1976

071 Boswell D M & Wingrove J M *The handicapped person in the community* Tavistock Publications/Open University Press London England 1974

072 Bower J *The evolution of church buildings* Whitney Library of Design New York USA 1977

073 Brawne M *Libraries: architecture & equipment* Praeger New York USA 1970

074 BRE *Availability of sunshine* (Ne'eman E & Light W) (Current Paper 75/75) Garston England 1975

075 BRE *Co-ordinating working drawings* (Crawshaw D T) (Current Paper 60/76) BRE Garston England 1976

076 BRE *Estimating daylight in buildings* (Digests 41 42) HMSO London England 1970

077 BRE *Information directory* BRE Garston England annual

078 BRE *Noise abatement zone* Parts 1 & 2 BRE Garston England 1977

079 BRE *Smoke control methods in enclosed shopping complexes of one or more storeys: a design summary* (Morgan H P) HMSO London England 1979

080 BRE *Ventilation requirements* (Digest 206) HMSO London England 1977

081 BRE *Working drawings* (Digest 172) HMSO London England 1973

082 BRE *Working drawings in use* (Daltry C D & Crawshaw D T) (Current Paper 18/73) BRE Garston England 1973

083 British Horse Society *Basic requirements of a riding centre* BHS Kenilworth England 1947

084 British Industrial-Scientific Film Association *Film guide for the construction industry* Construction Press Lancaster England 1979

085 Broadbent G & Ward A (ed) *Design methods in architecture* Lund Humphries London England 1969

086 Brock G *Road width requirments of commercial vehicles when cornering* Transport & Road Research Laboratory DoE London1973

087 Brooks J *The small garden* Marshall Cavendish London England 1977

088 BSI BS CP 96 *Access for the disabled to buildings Part 1 General recommendations* BSI London England 1967

089 BSI BS 5606 *Accuracy in building* BSI London England 1978

090 BSI BS 5440 Part 2 *Air supply* BSI London England 1976

091 BSI BS 4873 *Aluminium alloy windows* BSI London England 1972

092 BSI BS CP3 *Basic data for the design of buildings, code of* see Fire precautions Loading Sunlight Thermal insulation

093 BSI British Standards Handbook 3 vol 1–4 *Summaries of British standards of building* BSI London England latest edition

094 BSI *British standards yearbook* BSI London England annual

095 BSI BS 1192 *Building drawing practice (metric units), recommendations* BSI London England 1969 (revision in progress)

096 BSI BS 4104 *Catering equipment burning liquefied petroleum gases* BSI London England 1967

097 BSI BS 2512 *Catering equipment, gas heated* BSI London England 1963

098 BSI BS CP 1007 *Cinemas, maintained lighting for* BSI London England 1955

099 BSI BS 5382 *Cinematograph screens, specification* BSI London England 1976

100 BSI BS 5252 *Colour co-ordination for building purposes, framework for* BSI London England 1976

101 BSI BS LP 110 *Concrete, structural use of*
Part 1 1972 *Design materials & workmanship*
Part 2 1972 *Design charts for singly reinforced beams & rectangular columns*
Part 3 1972 *Design charts for circular columns & prestressed beams*
BSI London England 1972

102 BSI BS 350: Part 1 *Conversion factors, basis of tables* BSI London England 1974

103 BSI PD 6444 Part 1 *Co-ordination of dimensions in building, recommendations: Basic spaces for structure, external envelope & internal sub-divisions* BSI London England 1969

104 BSI BS 4330 *Co-ordination of dimensions in building, recommendations: Controlling dimensions* BSI London England 1968

105 BSI BS 4011 *Co-ordination of dimensions in building, recommendations: Co-ordinating sizes for building components & assemblies* BSI London England 1966

106 BSI BS 2900 *Co-ordination of dimensions in building, recommendations: Glossary of terms* BSI London England 1970

107 BSI BS CP3: Ch 1: Part 1 *Daylighting* BSI London England 1964

108 BSI 5502 *Design of buildings & structures for agriculture, code of practice* BSI London England 1978

109 BSI BS 5619 *Design of housing for the convenience of disabled people, code of practice* BSI London England 1978

BASIC LIST

110   BSI DD 51 *Dimensional co-ordination in buildings, guidance on* BSI London England 1977

111   BSI BS CP 413 *Ducts for building services* BSI London England 1975

112   BSI BS 5266 Part 1 *Emergency lighting for premises other than cinemas & certain other specified premises used for entertainment, code of practice* BSI London England 1975

113   BSI BS 2560 *Exit signs, internally illuminated* BSI London England 1976

114   BSI BS 4218 *Exit signs, self-luminous* BSI London England 1978

115   BSI BS 2053 *Farm buildings of framed construction, general purpose* BSI London England 1972

116   BSI BS 5588 *Fire precautions in the design of buildings, code of practice* Part 4 *Smoke control in protected escape routes using pressurisation* BSI London England 1978

117   BSI BS CP 3: Chap iv: *Fire, precautions against*
Part 1 1971 *Flats & maisonettes (in blocks over two storeys)*
Part 2 1968 *Shops & department stores*
Part 3 1968 *Office buildings*
BSI London England 1968 & 1971

118   BSI BS 2505 *Fixed equipment for cowsheds*
Part 1 1965 *Imperial units*
Part 2 1972 *Metric units*
BSI London England 1965 & 1972

119   BSI BS 5440 Part 1 *Flues* Part 2 *Air supply* BSI London England 1976 & 1978

120   BSI CP 2004 *Foundations, general* BSI London England 1972

121   BSI CP 101 *Foundations & sub-structure for non-industrial buildings of not more than four storeys* BSI London England 1972

122   BSI BS 3202 *Laboratory furniture & fittings* BSI London England 1959

123   BSI BS 2655 Parts 1–10 *Lifts, escalators, passenger conveyors & paternosters* BSI London England 1969–71

124   BSI BS 4727: Part IV: Group 03 *Lighting technology terminology: Glossary of electrotechnical, power, telecommunication, electronics, lighting & colour terms* BSI London England 1972

125   BSI BS CP 3: Chap v: *Loading*
Part 1 1967 *Dead & imposed loads*
Part 2 1072 *Wind loads*
BSI London England 1967 & 1972

126   BSI BS 5628 *Masonry, structural use code of practice* Part 1 *Universal masonry* BSI London England 1978

127   BSI PD 6031 *Metric system in the construction industry, use of* BSI London England 2nd edn 1968

128   BSI BS 5536 *Micro-filming, preparation of technical drawings for* BSI London England 1978

129   BSI BS 5550: Part V: Section 5. 1: Subsection 5.1.1 *Motion-picture safety film, definition testing & marking* BSI London England 1978

130   BSI BS 799: Part V *Oil storage tanks* BSI London England 1975

131   BSI BS 3178 *Playground equipment for parks* BSI London England various dates

132   BSI BS CP 114 *Reinforced concrete, structural use in buildings* BSI London England 1969

133   BSI BS 5572 *Sanitary pipework, code of practice* BSI London England 1978

134   BSI BS 3030 *School furniture*
Part 1 1959 *Materials, workmanship & finish*
Part 2 1959 *Performance tests*
Part 3 1972 *Pupils' chairs & tables*
Part 4 1959 *Chalkboards*
BSI London England 1959 & 1972

135   BSI PD 5686 *SI units, use of* BSI London England 1978

136   BSI BS 5709 *Specification for stiles, bridle gates & kissing gates* BSI London England 1979

137   BSI BS 1754 *Steel barns with covered roofs* BSI London England 1961

138   BSI BS 990 *Steel windows generally for domestic & similar buildings* Part 2 *Metric units* BSI London England 1972

139   BSI BS CP 117 *Structural steel & concrete, composite structures in* Part 1 *Simply supported beams in buildings* BSI London England 1965

140   BSI BS 449 *Structural steel in buildings, use of* Part 2 1969 *Metric units* BSI London England 1969

141   BSI BS CP 3: Chap i(B) *Sunlight (houses, flats & schools only)* BSI London England 1945

142   BSI PD 6479 *Symbols & other graphic conventions for building production drawings, recommendations* BSI London England 1976

143   BSI BS CP 3: Chap ii *Thermal insulation in relation to the control of the environment* BSI London England 1970

144   BSI BS CP 112 *Timber, structural use of*
Part 2 1971 *Metric units*
Part 3 1973 *Trussed rafters for roofs of dwellings*
BSI London England 1971 & 1973

145   BSI BS 4787 Part 1 *Wood doorsets, door leaves & frames* BSI London England 1972

146   BSI BS CP 153 *Windows & roof lights* Part 1 *Cleaning & safety* BSI London England 1969

147   Buchanan R D *et al The anatomy of foods service design 1* Cahners Books Boston USA 1975

148   Building Officials & Code Administrators International *Basic building code* BOCA Chicago USA triennial 7th edn 1978

149   Burberry P *Building for energy conservation* Architectural Press London England 1977 Halsted Press John Wiley & Sons New York USA 1978

150   Burberry P *Environment & services* Batsford London England 2nd end 1975

151   Burberry P & Aldersley-Williams A *A guide to domestic heating installations & controls* Architectural Press London England 1977

152   Burris-Meyer H & Cole E C *Theatres & auditoriums* Reinhold New York USA 2nd edn 1964

153   Busche-Sievers U *Kneipen, pubs & restaurants* Callwey Munich Germany 1973

154   Butcher E G & Parnell A C *Smoke control in fire safety design* E & F N Spon London England 1979

155   Campbell C S *Water in landscape architecture* Van Nostrand Reinhold New York USA 1978

156   Casson H *Inscape* Architectural Press London England 1968

157   Cheshire County Council *Architect's brief: day centre for physically handicapped* C C C Chester England 1975

158   Cheshire County Council *Design aid housing: roads* C C C Chester England 1976

159   Cheshire County Council *Made to measure: domestic extensions & adaptations for handicapped persons* C C C Chester England 1974

160   Christ-Janer A & Foley M M *Modern church architecture* McGraw-Hill New York USA 1962

161   Church T D *Gardens are for people* Reinhold New York USA 1955

162   CIB *Directory of building research information & development organizations* International Council for Building Research Studies & Documentation Rotterdam Netherlands 4th edn 1979

163   CIBS *Design notes for the Middle East* (Technical memorandum 4) CIBS London England 1979

164   CIBS *Institution of heating & ventilation engineers guide* (vol A B & C) CIBS London England 1970

165   Civil Aviation Authority *Licensing of aerodromes* CAP 168 CAA London England 1978

Bibliography

BASIC LIST

166   Clay G (ed) *Water & the landscape* McGraw-Hill New York USA 1979

167   Clouston B (ed) *Landscape design with plants* Heinemann London England 1978

168   Coates D S *Industrial catering management* Business Books London England 1971

169   Cochrane A & Brown J (ed) *Landscape design for the Middle East* RIBA Publications London England 1978

170   Collins I D & Collins E J *Window selection* Newnes-Butterworth London England 1977

171   Colvin B *Trees for town & country* Lund Humphries London England 4th edn 1972

172   Considine D M (ed) *Energy technology handbook* McGraw-Hill New York USA 1977

173   Constructional Steel Research & Development Organisation *Steel Designer's manual* Crosby Lockwood London England 4th edn 1972

174   Construction Industry Research & Information Assocation *Index of technical publications* CIRIA London England 1970

175   Correale W H & Parker H W *A building code primer* McGraw-Hill New York USA 1979

176   Cottam D J *Technical planning manual for hotels, restaurants, grill & snack bars, industrial restaurants, universities, schools, hospitals, cook/freeze reheat & convenience food kitchens* Stotts Oldham England 5th edn 1973

177   Cullingworth J B *Town & country planning in Britain* Allen & Unwin London England 7th edn 1972

178   Cusworth G R N *The health & safety at work etc act 1974* Butterworth London England 1975

179   Cutler L S & Cutler S S *Handbook of housing systems for designers & developers* Van Nostrand Reinhold New York USA 1974

180   Dattner R *Design for play* Van Nostrand Reinhold New York USA 1975

181   Davis B & E *Spon's architect's & builder's price book* E & F N Spon London England 105th edn 1980

182   Davis B & E *Spon's mechanical & electrical services price book* E & F N Spon London England 1979

183   Dawes J *Designing & planning of swimming pools* Architectural Press London England 1979

184   De Breffney B *The synagogue* Macmillan New York USA 1978

185   De Chiara J & Callender J H *Time-saver standards for building types* McGraw-Hill New York USA 1973

186   De Neufville R *Airport systems planning* MIT Press Cambridge Mass USA 1976

187   Department of Housing & Urban Development *Barrier-free site design* HUD Washington DC USA 1975

188   Department of Industry *Technical services for industry* DoI London England latest edn

189   DES *Access for the physically disabled to educational buildings* (DN 18) HMSO London England 1979

190   DES *Acoustics in educational buildings* (BB 51) HMSO London England 1976

191   DES *Boarding school for maladjusted children* (BB 27) HMSO London England 1965

192   DES *British school population: dimensional survey* (BB 46) HMSO London England 1971

193   DES *Colour in school buildings* (BB 9) HMSO London England 4th edn 1969

194   DES *Energy conservation in educational buildings* (BB 55) HMSO London England 1977

195   DES *Energy conservation in two Oxfordshire schools* (DN 16) DES London England 1944

196   DES *Fire & the design of schools* (BB 7) HMSO London England 5th edn 1975

197   DES *Furniture & equipment dimensions: further & higher education* (BB 44) HMSO London England 1970

198   DES *Furniture & equipment: working heights & zones for practical activities* (BB 50) HMSO London England 1973

199   DES *Guidelines for environmental design & fuel conservation in educational buildings* (DN 17) DES London England 1974

200   DES *JDPCLASP system building for higher education* (BB 45) HMSO London England 1970

201   DES *The design of school kitchens* (BB 11) HMSO London England 1955

202   DES *Lighting in schools* (BB 33) HMSO London England 1967

203   DES *New problems in school design – middle schools* (BB 35) HMSO London England 1966 revised 1973

204   DES *Nursery education in converted space* (BB 56) HMSO London England 1978

205   DES *Playing fields & hard surface areas* (BB 28) HMSO London England 1966 reprinted 1973

206   DES *Safety in science laboratories* (Safety series 2) HMSO London England 1976

207   DES *School furniture dimensions: standing & reaching* (BB 38) HMSO London England 2nd edn (metric) 1974

208   DES *School furniture: standing & sitting postures* (BB 52) HMSO London England 1976

209   DES *Secondary school design: designing for arts & crafts* (BB 34) HMSO London England 1967 reprinted 1972

210   DES *Secondary school design: drama & music* (BB 30) HMSO London England 1966

211   DES *Secondary school design: modern languages* (BB 43) HMSO London England 1966

212   DES *Secondary school design: physical education* (BB 26) HMSO London England 1965

213   DES *Secondary school design: sixth form & staff* (BB 25) HMSO London England 1965

214   DES *Secondary school design: workshop crafts* (BB 31) HMSO London England 1966 reprinted 1969

215   DES *Village schools* (BB 3) HMSO London England 1975

216   DHSS *Building for the health & social services: a bibliography of guidance material* DHSS London England 1978

217   DHSS *Clean catering: a handbook on hygiene in catering establishments* HMSO London England 4th edn 1972

218   DHSS *Hospital building notes* (various subjects) HMSO London England 1963

219   DHSS *Planning, design & construction of hospital buildings for the national health service* (Cruickshank H J) DHSS London England 1973

220   DHSS *Residential accommodation for mentally handicapped adults* (Local authority building note 8) HMSO London England 1973

221   DHS/Nuffield Orthopaedic Centre *Equipment for the disabled* (10 parts) Oxford Regional Health Authority Oxford England 1974/8 (continuously revised)

222   Dickens A *Structural & service systems in office buildings: a background review* (Land use & built form studies working paper 35) University School of Architecture Cambridge England 1970

223   Dodge F W *Motels, hotels, restaurants & bars* F W Dodge New York USA 2nd edn 1966

224   DoE *Building legislation: a guide to sources of information* DoE/ PSA Croydon England 1978

225   DoE *Cars in housing 2* (DB 12) HMSO London England 1971

226   DoE *Catering installations data* DoE London England 1971

227   DoE *Children at play* (DB 27) HMSO London England 1973

228   DoE *Co-ordination of components in housing: metric dimensional framework* (DB 16) HMSO London England 1968 reprinted 1974

BASIC LIST

229　DoE　*The countryside problems & polices*　HMSO　London England　1976

230　DOE　*District heating: an annotated bibliography*　DoE/PSA Croydon England　2nd edn 1977

231　DoE　*The estate outside the dwelling: reactions of residents to aspects of housing layout* (DB 25)　HMSO　London England　1972

232　DoE　*Grouped flatlets for old people: a sociological study* (DB 2)　HMSO　London England　metric edn 1969

233　DoE　*Homes for today & tomorrow* ('Parker Morris report': MHLG 1961)　HMSO　London England　reprinted 1975

234　DoE　*House planning: a guide to user needs with a checklist* (DB 14)　HMSO　London England　1976

235　DoE　*Housing for the elderly: the size of grouped schemes* (DB 31)　HMSO　London England　1975

236　DoE　*Housing the elderly*　MTP Construction　Lancaster England 1974

237　DoE　*Housing the family*　MTP Construction　Lancaster England 1974

238　DoE　*Housing single people: a design guide with a description of a scheme at Leicester* (DB 29)　HMSO　London England　1975

239　DoE (Countryside review committee)　*Leisure & the countryside* HMSO　London England　1977

240　DoE　*New housing & road traffic noise: a design guide for architects* (DB 26)　HMSO　London England　1972 reprinted 1974

241　DoE　*Planned open offices, a cost benefit analysis*　DoE　London England　1971

242　DoE　*Residential roads & footpaths: layout considerations* (DB 32)　HMSO　London England　1977

243　DoE　*Restaurant design: a reading list*　DoE/PSA　Croydon England　1979

244　DoE　*Roads in urban areas*　HMSO　London England　1966 metric supplement 1974

245　DoE　*Safety in the home* (DB 13)　HMSO　London England metric edn 1971 reprinted 1976

246　DoE　*Services for housing: sanitary plumbing & drainage* (DB 30)　HMSO　London England　1974

247　*DoE Some aspects of designing for old people* (DB 1)　HMSO London England　metric edn 1969

248　DoE　*Spaces in the home* (DB 24)
Part 1 *Bathrooms & wc's*
Part 2 *Kitchens & laundering spaces*
HMSO　London England　1972

249　DoE/PSA　*Office space: a primer for users & designers*　HMSO London England　1976

250　DoE/PSA　*Solar energy: an annotated bibliography*　DoE Croydon England　2nd edn 1979

251　DoE/Welsh Office　*Daylight indicators*　HMSO　London England 1971

252　DoE/Welsh Office　*Sunlight & daylight: planning criteria & the design of buildings*　HMSO　London England　1971

253　DoE/Welsh office　*Sunlight indicators*　HMSO　London England 1971

254　DoE & Travers Morgan & Partners　*The calculation of road traffic noise*　HMSO　London England　1975

255　Doswell R　*Towards an integrated approach to hotel planning* New University Education　London England　1970

256　Dreyfuss H　*The measure of man: human factors in design* Whitney Library of Design　New York USA　2nd edn 1967

257　Dubin F S　*How to save energy & cut costs in existing industrial & commercial buildings: an emergency conservation manual*　Noyes Data Corp　Park Ridge NJ USA　1976

258　Dubin F S & Long C G　*Energy conservation standards: for building design, construction & operation*　McGraw-Hill　New York USA 1978

259　Duffy F　Cave C　& Worthington J (ed)　*Planning office space* Architectural Press　London England　1976

260　Duffy F & Wankum A　*Office landscaping*　Anbar　London England　1966

261　Duncan C J　*Modern lecture theatres*　Oriel Press　Newcastle England　1962

262　Dyck R G　*Comprehensive health planning bibliography*　Council of Planning Librarians　Monticello Ill USA　1973

263　Eckbo G　*The art of home landscaping*　McGraw-Hill　New York USA　1956

264　Eckbo G　*Home landscape: the art of home landscaping* McGraw-Hill　New York USA　1978

265　Educational Facilities Laboratories　*Five open plan high schools: a report*　EFL　New York USA　1973

266　Educational Facilities Laboratories　*New places for the arts: a report*　EFL　New York USA　1976

267　Educational Facilities Laboratories　*Rich Township high school, Olympia Fields campus, Rich Township, Illinois; a report*　EFL　New York USA　1976

268　Egan M D　*Concepts in architectural acoustics*　McGraw-Hill New York USA　1972

269　Egan M D　*Concepts in building firesafety*　John Wiley & Sons New York USA　1978

270　Elder A J　*Guide to the building regulations 1976*　Architectural Press　London England　1979

271　Electricity Council & Lighting Industry Federation　*Interior lighting design*　Electricity Council & LIF　London England　1977

272　End H　*Hotels & motor hotels*　Whitney Library of Design　New York USA　1963

273　End H　*Interiors book of hotels & motor hotels*　Whitney Library of Design　New York USA　1963

274　End H　*Interiors 2nd book of hotels*　Whitney Library of Design New York USA　Home Office　London England　1978

275　Englehardt N L　*Complete guide for planning new schools* Parker Publishing Company　West Nyack NY USA　1970

276　Essex County Council　*Design guide for residential areas*　ECC Chelmsford England　1973

277　Everett A　*Materials* (Mitchell's building construction series) Batsford　Stroud England　1978

278　Everett K & Hughes D A　*Guide to laboratory design* Butterworth　London England　1975

279　Fairbrother N　*The nature of landscape design*　Architectural Press　London England　1974

280　Falconer P & Drury J　*Building & planning for industrial storage & distribution*　Architectural Press　London England　1975

281　Farrant J & Subiott A　*Planning for disabled people in the urban environment*　Central Council for the Disabled　London England　1969

282　Fengler M　*Restaurant architecture & design, an international survey of eating places*　Universe Books　New York USA　1971

283　Ferguson W R　*Practical laboratory planning*　John Wiley & Sons New York USA　1973

284　Fire Officers' Committee　*Rules for automatic sprinkler installations*　FOC　London England　1970

285　Flora S D　*Tornadoes of the United States*　University of Oklahoma Press　Norman USA　1953

286　Fokus　*Principles of the Fokus housing units for the severely disabled*　Fokus Society　Gothenburg Sweden　1968

287　Foott S　*Handicapped at home*　Disabled Living Foundation London England　1977

288　Foss E W　*Construction & maintenance for farm & home*　John Wiley & Sons　New York USA　1960

289　Foster J　*Structure & fabric Part 1* (Mitchell's building construction series)　Batsford　Stroud England　1973

290　French T & Vierck C J　*The manual of engineering drawing for students & craftsmen*　McGraw-Hill　New York USA　8th edn 1974

Bibliography

BASIC LIST

291 Fry E M & Drew J *Tropical architecture in the dry & humid zones* Batsford London England 1964

292 Gage M & Kirkbride K *Design in blockwork* Architectural Press London England 2nd edn 1976

293 Gage M & Vandenburg M *Hard landscape in concrete* Architectural Press London England 1976

294 Gainsborough H & Gainsborough J *Principles of hospital design* Architectural Press London England 1964

295 Gelwicks L E & Newcomer R J *Planning housing environments for the elderly* National Council on the Aging Washington DC USA 1974

296 Goldsmith S *Designing for the disabled* RIBA Publications London England 3rd edn 1976

297 Gooch R B & Escritt J R *Sports ground construction: specifications* National Playing Fields Association/Sports Turf Research Institute London England 1975

298 Graubner G *Theaterbau: Aufgabe und Planung* Callwey Munich Germany 1968

299 Greater London Council *An introduction to housing layout* Architectural Press London England 1978

300 Greater London Council *London building (constructional) by-laws* GLC London England 1972

301 Greater London Council *Means of escape in case of fire* (code of practice) GLC London England 1974

302 Green I et al *Housing the elderly: the development & design process* Van Nostrand Reinhold New York USA 1975

303 Green J R B *Health service facilities planning & design: a guide book* University of New South Wales Health Administration Kensingen New South Wales 1974

304 Griffin C W *Energy conservation in buildings – techniques for economical design* Construction Specifications Institute Washington DC USA 1974

305 Grube O W *Industrial buildings & factories* Praeger New York USA Architectural Press London England 1971

306 Gruen V & Smith L *Shopping towns – USA* Reinhold New York USA 1960

307 Halacy D S Jr *Earth, water, wind & sun – our energy alternatives* Harper & Row New York USA 1977

308 Halprin L *Freeways* Reinhold New York USA 1966

309 Ham R (ed) *Theatre planning* Architectural Press London England 1972

310 Hamilton R N D *A guide to development & planning* Oyez London England 6th edn with supplement 1976

311 Hammond P *Liturgy & architecture* Barrie & R London England 1960

312 Hammond P *Towards a new church architecture* Architectural Press London England 1962

313 Handyside C C *Everyday details* Architectural Press London England 1976

314 Hannigan J A & Estes G E (ed) *Media center facilities design* American Library Association Chicago USA 1978

315 Hardy O B & Lammers L P *Hospitals: the planning & design process* Aspen Systems Corporation Germantown Md USA 1977

316 Harington R *Structure & fabric Part II* (Mitchell's building construction series) Batsford Stroud England 1975

317 Harkness S P & Groom J N Jr *Building without barriers* Whitney New York USA 1976

318 Harrison R O *The technical requirements of small museums* Canadian Museums Association Ottawa Canada 1975

319 Hattrell W S & Partners *Hotels, restaurants & bars* Batsford Stroud England 1962

320 Hay R & Synge P M *The colour dictionary of flowers & plants for home & garden* Crown New York USA 1969

321 Heap D (ed) *Encyclopedia of planning law & practice* 4 vol Sweet & Maxwell London England 1962

322 Hepler D & Wallach P *Architecture – drafting & design* McGraw-Hill New York USA 2nd edn 1975

323 Hicks W B *Developing multi-media libraries* R R Bowker Co New York USA 1970

324 HMSO *Guide to fire precautions Act 1971: hotels & boarding houses* HMSO London England 1972

325 HoC *Agriculture (miscellaneous provisions) act 1968: codes of recommendations for the welfare of livestock* HMSO London England 1968

326 HoC *Agriculture (safety, health & welfare) act 1956* HMSO London England 1956

327 HoC *Chronically sick & disabled persons act 1970* HMSO London England 1970

328 HoC *Cinematograph act 1909* HMSO London England 1909

329 HoC *Cinematograph act 1952* HMSO London England 1952

330 HoC *Civil amenities act 1967* HMSO London England 1967

331 HoC *Clean air act 1956* HMSO London England 1956

332 HoC *Clean air act 1968* HMSO London England 1968

333 HoC *Control of pollution act 1974* HMSO London England 1974

334 HoC *Countryside act 1968* HMSO London England 1968

335 HoC *Countryside (Scotland) act 1967* HMSO London England 1967

336 HoC *Dangerous drugs act 1965* HMSO London England 1965

337 HoC *Dangerous drugs act 1967* HMSO London England 1967

338 HoC *Factories act 1961* HMSO London England 1961

339 HoC *Films act 1960* HMSO London England 1960

340 HoC *Fire precautions act 1971* HMSO London England 1971

341 HoC *Health & safety at work etc act 1974* London England 1974

342 HoC *Insulation act 1972* HMSO London England 1972

343 HoC *London building act 1930* HMSO London England 1930

344 HoC *London building (amendment) act 1935* HMSO London England 1935

345 HoC *London building (amendment) act 1939* HMSO London England 1939

346 HoC *Offices, shops & railway premises act 1963* HMSO London England 1963

347 HoC *Offices, shops & railway premises act 1971* HMSO London England 1971

348 HoC *Petroleum (consolidation) act 1928* HMSO London England 1928

349 HoC *Pharmacy & poisons act 1933* HMSO London England 1933

350 HoC *Public health act 1936* HMSO London England 1936

351 HoC *Public health act 1961* HMSO London England 1961

352 HoC *Public health act (recurring nuisances) 1969* HMSO London England 1969

353 HoC *Public libraries & museums act 1964* HMSO London England 1964

354 HoC *Radioactive substances act 1960* HMSO London England 1960

355 HoC *Riding establishments act 1934* HMSO London England 1934

356 HoC *Rivers (prevention of pollution) act 1951* HMSO London England 1951

357 HoC *Rivers (prevention of pollution) act 1961* HMSO London England 1961

358 HoC *Rivers (prevention of pollution) (Scotland) act 1951* HMSO London England 1951

359 HoC *Rivers (prevention of pollution) (Scotland) act 1965* HMSO London England 1965

BASIC LIST

360 HoC *Sewerage (Scotland) act 1968* HMSO London England 1968

361 HoC *Theatres act 1968* HMSO London England 1968

362 HoC *Therapeutic substances act 1956* HMSO London England 1956

363 HoC *Town & country planning act 1971* HMSO London England 1971

364 HoC *Town & country planning (Scotland) act 1972* HMSO London England 1972

365 HoC *Water resources act 1963* HMSO London England 1963

366 Hohl R *Office buildings: an international survey* Praeger New York USA Architectural Press London England 1968

367 Hopkinson R G *Architectural physics: lighting* HMSO London England 1963

368 Hopkinson R G Petherbridge P & Longmore J *Daylighting* Heinemann London England 1966

369 Hornbeck J S (ed) *Stores & shopping centres* McGraw-Hill New York USA 1962

370 Horonjeff R *Planning & design of airports* McGraw-Hill New York USA London England 1975

371 Houghton E L *Wind forces on buildings & structures – an introduction* John Wiley & Sons New York USA 1976

372 Housing Press *The house & home kitchen planning guide* McGraw-Hill New York USA 1978

373 Howell J D E *Notes on the need for planning permission* Oyez London England 1976

374 Hoyt K (ed) *Buildings for commerce & industry* McGraw-Hill New York USA 1978

375 Hunt W D Jr *The contemporary curtain wall –its design fabrication & erection* F W Dodge New York USA 1958

376 Hunter M K & Hunter E H *The indoor garden – design, construction & furnishing* John Wiley & Sons New York USA 1978

377 Hurst R *Services & maintenance for hotels & residential establishments* Heinemann London England 1971

378 Hutton G & Rostron M *The international directory of computer programs for the constructional industry* Architectural Press London England 1979

379 ICB →CIB

380 IES *Control of discomfort sky glare from windows* (supplement to Technical report 4) CIBS London England 1972

381 IES *Daytime lighting in buildings* (Technical report 4) CIBS London England 2nd edn 1972

382 IES *Evaluation of discomfort glare* (Technical report 10) CIBS London England 1967 supplement 1972

383 IES *The IES Code: recommendations for lighting building interiors* CIBS London England 1977

384 IES *Lighting guide: sports* CIBS London England 1974

385 IES *Lighting of art galleries & museums* (Technical report 14) CIBS London England 1970

386 IES *The outdoor environment* (Lighting guide 6) CIBS London England 1975

387 IES(USA) *Lighting handbook* IES New York USA 1972

388 Institute of Baths Management *Swimming pools* (Design guide I) IoBM London England 1966

389 Institute of Directors *Better offices* IoD London England 1974

390 Institution of Electrical Engineers *Regulations for the electrical equipment of buildings* IEE London England latest edition

391 International Air Transport Association *Airport Terminal reference manual* IATA Montreal Canada 6th edn 1976

392 International Civil Aviation Organisation *Aerodrome design manual*
Part 2 *Taxiways, aprons & holding bays*
Part 3 *Pavements*
ICAO Montreal Canada 1977

393 International Civil Aviation Organisation *Airport planning manual*
Part 1 *Master planning*
Part 2 *Land use & environmental control*
ICAO Montreal Canada 1977

394 International Civil Aviation organisation *Heliport manual* ICAO Montreal Canada 1979

395 International Civil Aviation Organisation *International standards, recommended practices: aerodromes. Annex 14 to the convention on international aviation* IACO Montreal Canada 1976

396 International Civil Aviation Organisation *Stolport manual* ICAO Montreal Canada 1976

397 International Commission on Illumination *International recommendations for the calculation of natural daylight* (publication 16) CIE Paris France 1970

398 International Conference of Building Officials *Uniform building code* ICBO Whittier Calif USA latest edition

399 International Federation of Library Associations *Standards for public libraries* Verlag Dokumentation Munich Germany FLR The Hague Netherlands 1973

400 ISO *Modular co-ordination: basic module* (ISO 1006: 1973) ISO Geneva Switzerland 1973

401 ISO *Modular co-ordination: co-ordinating sizes for door-sets, external & internal* (ISO 2776:1974) ISO Geneva Switzerland 1974

402 ISO *Modular co-ordination: multimodules for horizontal co-ordinating dimensions* (ISO 1040:1973) ISO Geneva Switzerland 1973

403 ISO *Modular co-ordination: principles & rules* (ISO 2848:1974) ISO Geneva Switzerland 1974

404 ISO *Modular co-ordination: reference lines of horizontal controlling co-ordinating dimensions* (ISO R 1970:1970) ISO Geneva Switzerland 1970

405 ISO *Modular co-ordination: storey heights & room heights for residential buildings* (ISO 1789:1973) ISO Geneva Switzerland 1973

406 ISO *Modular co-ordination: vocabulary* (ISO 1791:1973) ISO Geneva Switzerland 1978

407 ISO *Standard for the functional sizes of school furniture* (ISO/DIS 5970:1978) ISO Geneva Switzerland 1978

408 International Symposium on Architectural Acoustics Heriot-Watt University 1974 *Auditorium acoustics; proceedings* John Wiley & Sons New York USA 1975

409 Izenour G C *Theater design* McGraw-Hill New York USA 1977

410 Jellicoe S & Allen M *Town gardens to live in* Harmondsworth Penguin London England 1977

411 Jellicoe S & Jellicoe G *Water: the use of water in landscape architecture* St Martin's Press New York USA 1971

412 Jensen R *Fire protection for the design professional* Cahners Books Boston USA 1975

413 Jewell D *Public assembly facilities: planning & management* John Wiley & Sons New York USA 1978

414 Joedicke J *Office & administration buildings* Karl Kramer Verlag Stuttgart Germany 1975

415 Kauffman H J *The American farmhouse* Hawthorn Books New York USA 1975

416 Kell J R & Martin P L *Heating & air conditioning of buildings* Architectural Press London England 6th edn 1979

417 Kepes G *Module, symmetry, proportion* Studio Vista London England 1966

418 Kidney W C *Working places: the adaptive use of industrial buildings* Ober Park Associates Pittsburgh USA 1976

419 King Edward's Hospital Fund for London *An evaluation of New Guy's House* King Edward's Hospital Fund London England 1963

420 King Edward's Hospital Fund for London *Hospital research & briefing problems* (Baynes K (ed)) King Edward's Hospital Fund London England 1971

Bibliography

BASIC LIST

421   King Edward's Hospital Fund for London *Hospital traffic & supply problems* (Holroyd W A H (ed)) King Edward's Hospital Fund London England 1968

422   King H & Everett A *Components & finishes* (Mitchell's building construction series) Batsford Stroud England 1971

423   Kliment S A *Into the mainstream – a syllabus for a barrier-free environment* AIA Washington USA 1974

424   Klose D *Multi-storey car parks & garages* Architectural Press London England 1965

425   Knight T L *Illustrated introduction to brickwork design* Brick Development Association London England 1975

426   Knopp L *The cinematograph regulations 1955* Cinema Press London England 1955

427   Knowles R L *Energy & form: an ecological approach to urban growth* MIT Press Cambridge Mass USA 1974

428   Knudsen V O & Harris C M *Acoustical designing in architecture* John Wiley & Sons New York USA 1950

429   Kraemer S & Partners *Open-plan offices: new ideas, experience & improvements* McGraw-Hill London England 1977

430   Kramer J *Container gardening indoors & out* Doubleday New York USA 1971

431   Kramer J *Water gardening – pools, fountains & plants* Charles Scribner's Sons New York USA 1971

432   Kuldschun H & Rossmann E *Planen und bauen für Behinderte* Deutsche Verlages-Anstalt Stuttgart Germany 1974

433   Lacy R E *Climate & building in Britain* HMSO London England 1977

434   Lacy R E *Driving-rain index* HMSO London England 1976

435   Lancashire County Council *Car parking standards* Lancs CC Preston England 1976

436   Landon-Thames G J *Fire safety in buildings* A C Black London England 1972

437   Langmead S & Beckman M *New library design: guidelines to planning academic library buildings* John Wiley & Sons Toronto Canada New York USA 1979

438   Larsson N *Housing the elderly, & housing the handicapped* Central Mortgage & Finance Corporation Ottawa Canada 1972

439   Lawson F *Designing commercial food service facilities* Whitney Library of Design New York USA 1974

440   Lawson F *Hotels, motels & condominiums – design, planning & maintenance* Cahners Boston USA Architectural Press London England 1976

441   Lawson F *Principles of catering design* Architectural Press London England 2nd edn 1978

442   Lawson F *Restaurant planning & design* Van Nostrand Reinhold New York USA Architectural Press London England 1973

433   Lawson F & B & Bovy M *Tourism & recreation development: a handbook of physical planning* Architectural Press London England 1978

444   Lawton M *Planning & managing housing for the elderly* John Wiley & Sons New York USA 1975

445   Le Corbusier *Le modulor* Faber & Faber London England 1954

446   Leggett S Brubacker W C Cohodes A Shapiro A C *Planning flexible learning spaces* McGraw-Hill New York USA 1977

447   Lewis M J *Libraries for the handicapped* Library Assocation London England 1969

448   Liebing R W & Paul M F *Architectural working drawings* John Wiley & Sons New York USA 1977

449   Lighting Industry Federation & Electricity Council *Interior lighting design* LIF London England metric edn 1969

450   Lion E *Shopping centers – planning, development & administration* John Wiley & Sons New York USA 1976

451   London County Council Education Department *School furniture* Staples London England 1958

452   Longmore J *BRS daylight protractors* HMSO London England 1968

453   Lovejoy D (ed) *Landuse & landscape planning* Leonard Hill London England 2nd edn 1979

454   Lovejoy D & Partners *Spon's landscape handbook* E & F N Spon London England 1978

455   Lushington N & Mills W N *Libraries designed for users: a planning handbook* Gaylord Professional Publications Syracuse NY USA 1979

456   Lynch K *Site planning* MIT Press Cambridge Mass USA 1979

457   Lynes J A *Principles of natural lighting* Elsevier London England 1968

458   McCoy E *Case study houses, 1945–1962* Hennessey & Ingalls Los Angeles USA 2nd edn 1977

459   Macdonald A J *Wind loading on buildings* John Wiley & Sons New York USA 1975

460   McGraw-Hill *Encyclopedia of energy* McGraw-Hill New York USA 1976

461   McGuinness W J & Stein B *Mechanical & electrical equipment for buildings* John Wiley & Sons New York USA 5th edn 1971

462   McHarg I L *Design with nature* Natural History Press New York USA 1969

463   McHugh R C *Working drawing handbook: a guide for architects & builders* Van Nostrand Reinhold New York USA 1977

464   Macsai J Holland E P Nachman H S Yacker J Y *Housing* John Wiley & Sons New York USA 1976

465   Manning P (ed) *Office design: a study of environment* Liverpool University Liverpool England 1965

466   Marlow O C *Outdoor design: a handbook for the architect & planner* Granada Publishing/Crosby Lockwood Staples St Albans England 1977

467   Marsh P *Air & rain penetration of buildings* Construction Press London England 1977

468   Martin D (ed) *Specification 79/80* Architectural Press London England 1980

469   May E E *et al* *Independent living for the handicapped & the elderly* Houghton Mifflin Boston USA 1974

470   Mecklenburgh J C *Plant layout: a guide to the layout of process plants & sites* John Wiley & Sons New York USA 1973

471   Metcalf K D *Library lighting* Association of Research Librarians Washington DC USA 1970

472   Metcalf K D *Planning academic & research library buildings* McGraw-Hill New York USA 1965

473   Metrication Board *How to write metric: a style guide to teaching and using SI units* HMSO London England no date

474   Millard P *Modern library equipment* Crosby Lockwood London England 1966

475   Mills E D (ed) *Planning: building for administration, entertainment & recreation* Newnes-Butterworth London England 1976

476   Mills E D (ed) *Planning: building for education, culture & science* Newnes-Butterworth London England 9th edn 1976

477   Mills E D (ed) *Planning: building for habitation, commerce & industry* Newnes-Butterworth London England 1976

478   Mills E D (ed) *Planning: building for health, welfare & religion* Newnes-Butterworth London England 9th edn 1976

479   Ministry of Housing & Local Government *Metrication of housing building* (circular 1/68) HMSO London England 1968

480   Ministry of Labour *Cloakroom accommodation & washing facilities* (Health & safety at work booklet 5) HMSO London England 1968

481   Ministry of Labour *First aid in factories* (Health & safety at work booklet 36) HMSO London England 1966

482   Mitchell A *A field guide to the trees of Britain & northern Europe* Collins London England 1974

BASIC LIST

483   Mobbs N *Industrial investment. A case study in factory buildings* Slough Estates Slough England 1979

484   Morisseau J J *Designing & planning: the new schools* Van Nostrand Reinhold New York USA 1972

485   Mullins W & Allen P G *Student housing* Crosby Lockwood London England 1970

486   Munce J F *Industrial architecture – an analysis of international building practice* F W Dodge New York USA 1960

487   National Building Agency *Damp protection* (Easiguide) NBA London England 1979

488   National Building Agency *The disabled in rehabilitated housing: guidance for housing associations* NBA London England 1978

489   National Building Agency *Drainage & water installation* (Easiguide) NBA London England 1979

490   National Building Agency *Electrical installations* (Easiguide) NBA London England 1979

491   National Building Agency *External works detail sheets* Architectural Press London England 1977

492   National Building Agency *Fire protection* (Easiguide) NBA London England 1979

493   National Building Agency *Gas heating* (Easiguide) NBA London England 1979

494   National Building Agency *Metric house shells: one-storey plans* NBA London England 1969

495   National Building Agency *Metric house shells: two-storey plans* NBA London England 1970

496   National Building Agency *Open space & ventilation* (Easiguide) NBA London England 1980

497   National Building Agency *Refuse* (Easiguide) NBA London England 1980

498   National Building Agency *Safety & materials* (Easiguide) NBA London England 1979

499   National Building Agency *Sheltered housing for the elderly: design criteria for category 1 dwellings* NBA London England 1977

500   National Building Agency *Solid fuel & oil heating* (Easiguide) NBA London England 1979

501   National Building Agency *Stairs & means of escape* (Easiguide) NBA London England 1979

502   National Building Agency *Structure* (Easiguide) NBA London England 1979

503   National Building Agency *Thermal & sound insulation* (Easiguide) NBA London England 1979

504   National Elevator Industry *Elevator engineering standards* National Elevator Industry Inc New York USA 5th edn 1979

505   National Fire Protection Association *Designing buildings for fire safety* NFPA Boston USA 1975

506   National Fire Protection Association *Fires in high-rise buildings* NFPA Boston USA 1974

507   National Fire Protection Association *High-rise building fires & fire safety* NFPA Boston USA 1973

508   National Fire Protection Association *Life safety code* NFPA Boston USA latest edition

509   National Fire Protection Association *National Fire codes* NFPA Boston USA 16 vol 1976

510   National Fire Protection Assocation *National fire prevention code* NFPA Boston USA latest edition

511   National House Builders Council *Guide to internal planning* (Advisory note 1) NHBC London England 1975

512   National House Builders Council *Registered house builders handbook* NHBC London England 1974

513   National Parking Association/Parking Consultants Council *The dimensions of parking* Urban Land Institute National Parking Association Washington DC USA 1979

514   National Playing Fields Association *Revised drawings of outdoor pitches & courts* NPFA London England 1979

515   National Swimming Pool Institute Technical Council *Minimum standards for public spas* NSPI Washington DC USA 1978

516   National Swimming Pool Institute Technical Council *Minimum standards for public pools* NSPI Washington DC USA 1974

517   National Swimming Pool Institute Standards Codes Committee *Suggested minimum standards for residential swimming pools* NSPI Washington DC USA 1974

518   Nellist I *Planning buildings for handicapped children* Crosby Lockwood London England 1970

519   Nelson G & Wright H *Tomorrow's house – a complete guide for the homebuilder* Simon & Schuster New York USA 1945

520   Newburry C W & Eaton K J *Wind loading handbook* HMSO London England 1974

521   Newman O *Defensible space; crime prevention through urban design* Macmillan New York USA 1972

522   Northwood T D (ed) *Architectural acoustics* Dowden Hutchinson & Ross Stroudsburg Pa USA 1977

523   Nuckolls J L *Interior lighting – for environmental designers* John Wiley & Sons New York USA 1976

524   Nuffield Foundation, Division of Architectural Studies *The design of research laboratories* Oxford University Press Oxford England 1961

Nuffield Orthapaedic Centre →DHSS

525   Nuffield Provincial Hospital Trust *Studies in the functions & design of hospitals* Oxford University Press Oxford England 1955

526   O'Connor J W *A study in school & university building design* Vantage Press New York USA 1974

527   Olgyay V *Design with climate: bioclimatic approach to architectural regionalism* Princeton University Press Princeton USA 1963

528   Olgyay V *Solar control & shading devices* Princeton University Press Princeton USA 1957

529   Oliver J E *Climate & man's environment – an introduction to applied climatology* John Wiley & Sons New York USA 1973

530   Organisation for Economic Cooperation & Development (Programme on educational building) *School furniture* OECD Paris France 1980

531   Page C H & Vigaureux P (ed) *SI: the international system of units* National Physical Laboratory HMSO London England 3rd edn 1977

532   Parkin P H Humphreys H R & Cowell J R *Acoustics, noise & buildings* Faber & Faber London England 1979

533   Paul S *Apartments: their design & development* Reinhold New York USA 1967

534   Pemberton A W *Plant layout & materials handling* Macmillan London England 1974

535   Penton J & Barlow A (ed) *A handbook of housing for disabled people* (London Housing Consortium West Group) RIBA London England 1980

536   Penwarden A D Wise A *Wind environment round buildings* HMSO London England 1975

537   Perkins P H *Swimming pools* Applied Science Publishers London England 2nd edn 1978

538   Perrin G A *Indoor reception centres* National Playing Fields Association London England 1973

539   Peters P (ed) *Design & planning – factories* Van Nostrand Reinhold New York USA 1970

540   Pile J F *Interiors second book of offices* Whitney Library of Design New York USA 1969

541   Pile J *Interiors third book of offices* Whitney Library of Design New York USA Architectural Press London England 1976

542   Pile J *Open office planning; a handbook for interior designers & architects* Whitney Library of Design New York USA Architectural Press London England 1978

Bibliography

BASIC LIST

543 Pilkington Brothers Ltd Environmental Advisory Service *Windows & environment* Pilkington Brothers Limited St Helens England 1969

544 Porges G *Applied acoustics* John Wiley & Sons New York USA 1977

545 Propst R & Wodka M *The action office: acoustics handbook* Herman Miller Research Corporation Ann Arbor USA 1975

546 Prztak L *Standard details for fire resistive building construction* McGraw-Hill New York USA 1977

547 Pütsep E *Modern hospitals: international planning practice* Lloyd-Luke London England 1979

548 Rabb J & Rabb B *Good shelter; a guide to mobile, modular & prefabricated houses, including domes* Quadrangle/New York Times Book Co New York USA 1975

549 Ramsey & Sleeper/American Institute of Architects *Architectural graphic standards* (Packard R T (ed)) John Wiley & Sons New York USA 7th edn 1980

550 Readers' Digest *Encyclopedia of garden plants & flowers* Readers' Digest London England 1971

551 Redstone L G *Hospitals & health care facilities* McGraw-Hill New York USA 1978

552 Redstone L G *New dimensions in shopping centers & stores* McGraw-Hill New York USA 1973

553 RIBA *CI/SfB construction indexing manual* RIBA Services Ltd London England 1976

554 Ripnen K *Office space administration* McGraw-Hill New York USA 1974

555 Ritter P *Planning for man & motor* Macmillan New York USA 1964

556 Robinson H W *Architecture for the educational theatre* University of Oregon Eugene Ore USA 1970

557 Robinson J *Highways & our environment* McGraw-Hill New York USA 1971

558 Rogers T S *Thermal design of buildings* John Wiley & Sons New York USA 1964

559 Rosenfield I & Rosenfield Z *Hospital architecture & beyond* Van Nostrand Reinhold New York USA 1969

560 Rosenfield I & Rosenfield Z *Hospital architecture: integrated components* Van Nostrand Reinhold New York USA & London England 1971

561 Rosenfield J 'Light in museum planning' *Architectural Forum* 619/1932 New York USA

562 Rubenstein H M *Central city malls* John Wiley & Sons New York USA 1968

563 Rubenstein H M *A guide to site & environmental planning* John Wiley & Sons New York USA 2nd edn 1980

564 Salmon G *The working office* Design Council London England 1979

565 Saphier M *Office planning & design* McGraw-Hill New York USA 2nd edn 1978

566 Saphier M *Planning the new office* McGraw-Hill New York USA 1978

567 Schaal R *Curtain walls – design manual* Reinhold New York USA 1959

568 Schild E & Oswald R *Structural failures in residential buildings* vol 1 Granada Publishing St Albans England 1978

569 Schmertz M F (ed) *Campus planning & design* McGraw-Hill New York USA 1972

570 Schmertz M F (ed) *Office building design* McGraw-Hill New York USA 2nd edn 1975

571 Schramm W *Chemistry & biology laboratories: design, construction, equipment* Pergamon Press Oxford England 1965

572 Schubert H *The modern theater; architecture, storage design, lighting* Praeger New York USA 1971

573 Scottish Development Department *Scottish Housing Handbook part 3 Housing Development layout, roads & services* HMSO Edinburgh Scotland 1977

574 Scottish Development Department *Scottish Housing Handbook part 6 Housing for the disabled* HMSO Edinburgh Scotland 1979

575 Scottish Education Department *School kitchens* (Educational building note 14) HMSO Edinburgh Scotland 1976

576 Scottish Home & Health Department *Inpatient accommodation* (Hospital planning note 1) HMSO Edinburgh Scotland revised edn 1977

577 Scottish Hospital Centre *Upgrading of wards* SHC Edinburgh Scotland 1967

578 Scottish Hospital Centre *Ward conversion for geriatric patients* SHC Edinburgh Scotland 1974

579 Shear J K (ed) *Religious buildings for today* F W Dodge New York USA 1957

580 Shoshkes L *Space planning: designing the office environment* Architectural Record Books New York USA 1976

581 Simmonds M F *Accommodation standards for educational buildings* BRE Garston England revised edn 1977

582 Sloane E *An age of barns* Ballantine Books New York USA 1967

583 Smith D *Hotel & restaurant design* Van Nostrand Reinhold New York USA Design Council Publications London England 1978

584 Southern Building Code Congress *Standard building code* SBCC Birmingham Ala USA latest edition

585 Sports Council *Facilities for squash rackets* (Technical unit for sport bulletin 2) Sports Council London England 1975

586 Sports Council *Provision for swimming* Sports Council London England 1978

587 Sports Council *Specification for artificial sports surfaces* (technical report prepared by the Rubber & Plastics Research Association of Great Britain) Sports Council London England 1978

588 Sports Council *Sports halls: a new approach to their dimensions & use* Sports Council London England 1975

589 Statutory instruments 1959:428 *Agriculture (safeguarding of work places) regulations 1959* HMSO London England 1959

590 Statutory instruments 1966:99 *Building operations, construction health & welfare regulations* HMSO London England 1966

591 Statutory instruments 1976:1676 *The building regulations* HMSO London England 1976

592 Statutory instruments 1976:1676 *The building regulations Part*

E Safety in fire

E3 *Rules for measurement*

E4 *Provision of compartment walls & compartment floors*

E5 *Fire resistance of elements of structure*

HMSO London England 1976

593 Statutory instruments 1978:723 *The building (first amendment) regulations* HMSO London England 1978

594 Statutory instruments 1971:2052 *The building standards (Scotland) (consolidation) regulations* HMSO London England 1971

595 Statutory instruments 1973:794 *The building standards (Scotland) amendment regulations 1973* HMSO London England 1973

596 Statutory instruments 1975:404 *The building standards (Scotland) amendment regulations 1975* HMSO London England 1975

597 Statutory instrument: Statutory regulations & orders 1922:73 (as amended by SI 1961:2435) *Chemical works regulations* HMSO London England 1961

598 Statutory instruments 1955:1129 *Cinematograph safety regulations* HMSO London England 1955

599 Statutory instruments 1959:282 *Cinematograph safety regulations* HMSO London England 1959

600 Statutory instruments 1948:1547 *Clay works welfare special regulations* HMSO London England 1948

BASIC LIST

601   Statutory instruments 1976:2010 *Fire precaution (non-certified factory, office, shop & railway premises) regulations* HMSO London England 1976

602   Statutory instruments: Statutory rules & orders 1917:1067 *Metal works* as amended by SR&O 1926:864 & SI 1961:2434 HMSO London England 1917 1926 & 1961

603   Statutory instruments: Statutory rules & orders 1929:534 *Oil cake welfare order* HMSO London England 1929

604   Statutory instruments 1964:966 *Sanitary convenience regulations* HMSO London England 1964

605   Statutory instruments: Statutory rules & orders 1925:864 *Saw mills & wood working factories welfare (ambulance & first aid)* as amended by SI 1961:2434 HMSO London England 1925 & 1961

606   Statutory instruments 1960:1932 *Ship building & ship repairs regulations* HMSO London England 1960

607   Statutory instruments 1972:2051 *Standards for school premises regulations* HMSO London England 1972

608   Statutory instruments 1964:965 *Washing facilities regulations* HMSO London England 1964

609   Steele F *Physical settings & organizational development* Addison-Wesley Reading Mass USA 1973

610   Steel Window Association *Specification for the metric preferred range W20 steel windows SWA 201* SWA London England 1972

611   Stein R G *Architecture & energy* Doubleday Garden City NY USA 1977

612   Stewart H M & Griffin B (ed) *American architecture for the arts* vol 1 Handel & Sons Dallas USA 1978

613   Strakosch G R *Vertical transportation – elevators & escalators* John Wiley & Sons New York USA 1967

614   Sykes C A *Office planner* A4 Publications London England 1976

615   Szokolay S V *Solar energy & building* John Wiley & Sons New York USA 2nd edn 1977

616   Tandy C *Landscape of industry* John Wiley & Sons New York USA 2nd edn 1977

617   Tannehill I R *Hurricanes, their nature & history, particularly those of the West Indies & the southern coasts of the United States* Princeton University Press Princeton USA 9th edn 1956

618   Tansley A G *The British islands & their vegetation* Cambridge University Press Cambridge England 1939

619   Taylor J & Cooke G *The fire precautions act in practice* Architectural Press London England 1970

620   Thiry P Bennett R M & Kamphoefner H *Churches & temples* Reinhold New York USA 1953

621   Thomas M L *Architectural working drawings: a professional technique* McGraw-Hill New York USA 1978

622   Thompson A *Library building of Britain & Europe* Butterworth London England 1963

623   Thompson E K *Apartments, townhouses & condominiums* McGraw-Hill New York USA 1975

624   Thompson E K *Houses of the west* McGraw-Hill New York USA 1979

625   Thompson G *Planning & design of library buildings* Nicols Publishing Co New York USA Architectural Press London England 2nd edn 1977

626   Tidworth S *Theatres: an architectural & cultural history* Praeger New York USA 1973

627   Townroe P *Planning industrial location* Leonard Hill Books London England 1976

628   Tregenza P R *The design of interior circulation* Crosby Lockwood Staples London England 1976

629   United Nations Educational Scientific & Cultural Organization (UNESCO) *Planning buildings & facilities for higher education* Architectural Press London England UNESCO Press Paris France 1975

630   University Grants Committee *Planning norms for university buildings* HMSO London England 1974

631   Urban Land Institute *Residential development handbook* ULI Washington DC USA 1978

632   US Congress *Architectural barriers act* US Superintendent of Documents Washington DC USA 1968

633   US Congress *National environment policy act* US Superintendent of Documents Washington DC USA 1970

634   US Congress *Occupational safety & health act* US Superintendent of Documents Washington DC USA 1971

635   US Federal Aviation Agency *The apron & terminal building: planning manual* 3 vol National Technical Information Service Springfield Va USA 1975

636   Vahlefeld R & Jacques F *Garages & service stations* Leonard Hill London England 1960

637   Wagner W F (ed) *A treasury of contemporary houses* McGraw-Hill New York USA 1978

638   Wakita O A & Linde R M *The professional practice of architectural detailing* John Wiley & Sons New York USA 1977

639   Walter F *Sportsf centres & swimming pools – a study of their design with particular reference to the needs of the physically disabled* Disabled Living Foundation London England 1971

640   Ward C (ed) *Vandalism* Architectural Press London England 1973

641   Ward H (ed) *Better library buildings* 1967–8 Library Association London England 1970

642   Webb J D (ed) *Noise control in industry* Sound Research Laboratories Sudbury Suffolk England 1976

643   Weddle A E (ed) *Landscape techniques* Heinemann for Landscape Institute London England 1979

644   Weiss J *Better buildings for the aged* McGraw-Hill New York USA 1971

645   Weisskamp H *Hotels: an international survey* Architectural Press London England 1968

646   Weller J *Modern agriculture & rural planning* Architectural Press London England 1967

647   Wheeler E T *Hospital modernization & expansion* McGraw-Hill New York USA 1971

648   White B *The literature & study of urban & regional planning* Routledge & Kegan Paul London England 1974

649   Whittaker C Brown P & Monahan J *The handbook of environmental powers* Architectural Press London England 1976

650   Whyte W S & Powell-Smith V *The building regulations explained & illustrated* Crosby Lockwood Staples London England 5th edn 1978

651   Wild F *Factories* Van Nostrand Reinhold New York USA 1972

652   Wild F *Libraries for schools & universities* Van Nostrand Reinhold New York USA 1972

653   Williams C H *Guide to European sources of technical information* Francis Hodgson Guernsey CI 1970

654   Wozniak S J *Solar heating systems for the UK: design, installation & economic aspects* HMSO London England 1979

655   Yerges L F *Sound, noise & vibration control* Van Nostrand Reinhold New York USA 2nd edn 1978

Bibliography

CODES

This list cites

a the principal codes, guides, reg, standards and statutes thought likely to be most often needed

b some less known which are thought likely to be useful

Because USA and UK practices differ UK codes predominate in this list. In the UK most such standards and reg are produced by government bodies or by national institutions. In the USA some are produced by such national bodies as ANSI but far more originate with state and municipal authorities: these are too many and too various to list.

Titles of some BSI publications are cited on a key word instead of with the formal title, *eg* BS CP 114 *The structural use of reinforced concrete in buildings* is given as BS CP 114 *Reinforced concrete, structural use in buildings*, BS 5572 is given as *Sanitary pipework, code of practice*. It is hoped that this will make things easier for the user.

013 AJ/MoH *Hospital planning & design guide* Architectural Press London England 1967

023 American Hospital Association *Hospital engineering handbook* AHA Chicago USA 1974

026 American Insurance Association *Fire prevention code* AIA New York USA latest edition

027 American Insurance Association *National building code* AIA New York USA latest edition

028 ANSI *Specifications for making buildings & facilities accessible to & usable by the physically handicapped people* ANSI New York USA 2nd edn 1979

029 ANSI *Standards* ANSI New York USA latest edition

030 American Society of Heating Refrigerating & Air-Conditioning Engineers *ASHRAE standard 90–75; energy conservation in new building design* ASHRAE New York USA 1975

031 American Society of Heating, Refrigerating & Air-Conditioning Engineers *ASHRAE handbook of fundamentals* ASHRAE New York USA 1977

033 American Society for Testing Materials *Standards* ASTM Philadelphia USA latest editions

084 British Industrial-Scientific Film Association *Film guide for the construction industry* Construction Press Lancaster England 1979

088 BSI BS CP 96 *Access for the disabled to buildings* Part 1 *General recommendations* BSI London England 1967

089 BSI BS 5606 *Accuracy in building* BSI London England 1978

090 BSI BS 5440 Part 2 *Air supply* BSI London England 1976

091 BSI BS 4873 *Aluminium alloy windows* BSI London England 1972

092 BSI BS CP3 *Basic data for the design of buildings, code of* see Fire precautions Loading Sunlight Thermal insulation

093 BSI British Standards Handbook 3 vol 1–4 *Summaries of British standards of building* BSI London England latest edition

094 BSI *British standards yearbook* BSI London England annual

095 BSI BS 1192 *Building drawing practice (metric units), recommendations* BSI London England 1969 (revision in progress)

096 BSI BS 4104 *Catering equipment burning liquefied petroleum gases* BSI London England 1967

097 BSI BS 2512 *Catering equipment, gas heated* BSI London England 1963

098 BSI BS CP 1007 *Cinemas, maintained lighting for* BSI London England 1955

099 BSI BS 5382 *Cinematograph screens, specification* BSI London England 1976

100 BSI BS 5252 *Colour co-ordination for building purposes, framework for* BSI London England 1976

101 BSI BS LP 110 *Concrete, structural use of*
Part 1 1972 *Design materials & workmanship*
Part 2 1972 *Design charts for singly reinforced beams & rectangular columns*
Part 3 1972 *Design charts for circular columns & prestressed beams*

BSI London England 1972

102 BSI BS 350 Part 1 *Conversion factors, basis of tables* BSI London England 1974

103 BSI PD 6444 Part 1 *Co-ordination of dimensions in building, recommendations: Basic spaces for structure, external envelope & internal sub-divisions* BSI London England 1969

104 BSI BS 4330 *Co-ordination of dimensions in building, recommendations: Controlling dimensions* BSI London England 1968

105 BSI 4011 *Co-ordination of dimensions in building, recommendations: Co-ordinating sizes for building components & assemblies* BSI London England 1966

106 BSI BS 2900 *Co-ordination of dimensions in building, recommendations: Glossary of terms* BSI London England 1970

107 BSI BS CP3: Ch 1: Part 1 *Daylighting* BSI London England 1964

108 BSI BS 5502 *Design of buildings & structures for agriculture, code of practice* BSI London England 1978

109 BSI BS 5619 *Design of housing for the convenience of disabled people, code of practice* BSI London England 1978

110 BSI DD 51 *Dimensional co-ordination in buildings, guidance on* BSI London England 1977

111 BSI BS CP 413 *Ducts for building services* BSI London England 1975

112 BSI BS 5266 Part 1 *Emergency lighting for premises other than cinemas & certain other specified premises used for entertainment, code of practice* BSI London England 1975

113 BSI BS 2560 *Exit signs, internally illuminated* BSI London England 1976

114 BSI BS 4218 *Exit signs, self-luminous* BSI London England 1978

115 BSI BS 2053 *Farm buildings of framed construction, general purpose* BSI London England 1972

116 BSI BS 5588 *Fire precautions in the design of buildings, code of practice* Part 4 *Smoke control in protected escape routes using pressurisation* BSI London England 1978

117 BSI BS CP 3: Chap iv: *Fire, precautions against*
Part 1 1971 *Flats & maisonettes (in blocks over two storeys)*
Part 2 1968 *Shops & department stores*
Part 3 1968 *Office buildings*
BSI London England 1968 & 1971

118 BSI BS 2505 *Fixed equipment for cowsheds*
Part 1 1965 *Imperial units*
Part 2 1972 *Metric units*
BSI London England 1965 & 1972

119 BSI BS 5440 Part 1 *Flues* BSI London England 1978

120 BSI CP 2004 *Foundations, general* BSI London England 1972

121 BSI CP 101 *Foundations & sub-structure for non-industrial buildings of not more than four storeys* BSI London England 1972

122 BSI BS 3202 *Laboratory furniture & fittings* BSI London England 1959

123 BSI BS 2655 Parts 1–10 *Lifts, escalators, passenger conveyors & paternosters* BSI London England 1969–71

124 BSI BS 4727: Part IV: Group 03 *Lighting technology terminology: Glossary of electrotechnical, power, telecommunication, electronics, lighting & colour terms* BSI London England 1972

125 BSI BS CP 3: Chap v: *Loading*
Part 1 1967 *Dead & imposed loads*
Part 2 1972 *Wind loads*
BSI London England 1967 & 1972

126 BSI 5628 *Masonry, structural use code of practice* Part 1 *Universal masonry* BSI London England 1978

127 BSI PD 6031 *Metric system in the construction industry, use of* BSI London England 2nd edn 1968

128 BSI 5536 *Micro-filming, preparation of technical drawings for* BSI London England 1978

CODES

129   BSI BS 5550: Part V: Section 5. 1: Subsection 5.1.1
Motion-picture safety film, definition testing & marking BSI London England 1978

130   BSI BS 799: Part V *Oil storage tanks* BSI London England 1975

131   BSI BS 3178 *Playground equipment for parks* BSI London England various dates

132   BSI BS CP 114 *Reinforced concrete, structural use in buildings* BSI London England 1969

133   BSI 5572 *Sanitary pipework, code of practice* BSI London England 1978

134   BSI 3030 *School furniture*
Part 1 1959 *Materials, workmanship & finish*
Part 2 1959 *Performance tests*
Part 3 1972 *Pupils' chairs & tables*
Part 4 1959 *Chalkboards*
BSI London England 1959 & 1972

135   BSI PD 5686 *SI units, use of* BSI London England 1978

136   BSI BS 5709 *Specification for stiles, bridle gates & kissing gates* BSI London England 1979

137   BSI BS 1754 *Steel barns with covered roofs* BSI London England 1961

138   BSI BS 990 *Steel windows generally for domestic & similar buildings* Part 2 *Metric units* BSI London England 1972

139   BSI BS CP 117 *Structural steel & concrete, composite structures in* Part 1 *Simply supported beams in buildings* BSI London England 1965

140   BSI BS 499 *Structural steel in buildings, use of* Part 2: 1969 *Metric units* BSI London England 1969

141   BSI BS CP 3: Chap i(B) *Sunlight (houses, flats & schools only)* BSI London England 1945

142   BSI PD 6479 *Symbols & other graphic conventions for building production drawings, recommendations* BSI London England 1976

143   BSI BS CP 3: Chap ii *Thermal insulation in relation to the control of the environment* BSI London England 1970

144   BSI BS CP 112 *Timber, structural use of*
Part 2 1971 *Metric units*
Part 3 1973 *Trussed rafters for roofs of dwellings*
BSI London England 1971 & 1973

145   BSI BS 4787 Part 1 *Wood doorsets, door leaves & frames* BSI London England 1972

146   BSI BS CP 153 *Windows & roof lights* Part i *Cleaning & safety* BSI London England 1969

148   Building Officials & Codes Administrators International *Basic building code* BOCA Chicago USA triennial 7th edn 1978

164   CIBS *Institution of heating & ventilation engineers guide* (vol A B & C) CIBS London England 1970

173   Constructional Steel Research & Development Organisation *Steel designer's manual* Crosby Lockwood London England 4th edn 1972

197   DES *Furniture & equipment dimensions: further & higher education* (BB 44) HMSO London England 1970

198   DES *Furniture & equipment: working heights & zones for practical activities* (BB 50) HMSO London England 1973

199   DES *Guidelines for environmental design & fuel conservation in educational buildings* (DN 17) DES London England 1974

217   DHSS *Clean catering: a handbook on hygiene in catering establishments* HMSO London England 4th edn 1972

233   DoE *Homes for today & tomorrow* ('Parker Morris report': MHLG 1961) HMSO London England reprinted 1975

234   DoE *House planning: a guide to user needs wtih a checklist* (DB 14) HMSO London England 1976

271   Electricity Council & Lighting Industry Federation *Interior lighting design* Electricity Council & LIF London England 1977

276   Essex County Council *Design guide for residential areas* ECC Chelmsford England 1973

284   Fire Officers' Committee *Rules for automatic sprinkler installations* FOC London England 1970

300   Greater London Council *London building (constructional) by-laws* GLC London England 1972

301   Greater London Council *Means of escape in case of fire* (code of practice) GLC London England 1974

324   HMSO *Guide to fire precautions Act 1971: hotels & boarding houses* HMSO London England 1972

325   HoC *Agriculture (miscellaneous provisions) act 1968: codes of recommendations for the welfare of livestock* HMSO London England 1968

326   HoC *Agriculture (safety, health & welfare) act 1956* HMSO London England 1956

327   HoC *Chronically sick & disabled persons act 1970* HMSO London England 1970

328   HoC *Cinematograph act 1909* HMSO London England 1909

329   HoC *Cinematograph act 1952* HMSO London England 1952

330   HoC *Civil amenities act 1967* HMSO London England 1967

331   HoC *Clean air act 1956* HMSO London England 1956

332   HoC *Clean air act 1968* HMSO London England 1968

333   HoC *Control of pollution act 1974* HMSO London England 1974

334   HoC *Countryside act 1968* HMSO London England 1968

335   HoC *Countryside (Scotland) act 1967* HMSO London England 1967

336   HoC *Dangerous drugs act 1965* HMSO London England 1965

337   HoC *Dangerous drugs act 1967* HMSO London England 1967

338   HoC *Factories act 1961* HMSO London England 1961

339   HoC *Films act 1960* HMSO London England 1960

340   HoC *Fire precautions act 1971* HMSO London England 1971

341   HoC *Health & safety at work etc act 1974* HMSO London England 1974

342   HoC *Insulation act 1972* HMSO London England 1972

343   HoC *London building act 1930* HMSO London England 1930

344   HoC *London building (amendment) act 1935* HMSO London England 1935

345   HoC *London building (amendment) act 1939* HMSO London England 1939

346   HoC *Offices, shops & railway premises act 1963* HMSO London England 1963

347   HoC *Offices, shops & railway premises act 1971* HMSO London England 1971

348   HoC *Petroleum (consolidation) act 1928* HMSO London England 1928

349   HoC *Pharmacy & poisons act 1933* HMSO London England 1933

350   HoC *Public health act 1936* HMSO London England 1936

351   HoC *Public health act 1961* HMSO London England 1961

352   HoC *Public health act (recurring nuisances) 1969* HMSO London England 1969

353   HoC *Public libraries & museums act 1964* HMSO London England 1964

354   HoC *Radioactive substances act 1960* HMSO London England 1960

355   HoC *Riding establishments act 1934* HMSO London England 1934

356   HoC *Rivers (prevention of pollution) act 1951* HMSO London England 1951

357   HoC *Rivers (prevention of pollution) act 1961* HMSO London England 1961

Bibliography

CODES

358 HoC *Rivers (prevention of pollution) (Scotland) act 1951* HMSO London England 1951

359 HoC *Rivers (prevention of pollution) (Scotland) act 1965* HMSO London England 1965

360 HoC *Sewerage (Scotland) act 1968* HMSO London England 1968

361 HoC *Theatres act 1968* HMSO London England 1968

362 HoC *Therapeutic substances act 1956* HMSO London England 1956

363 HoC *Town & country planning act 1971* HMSO London England 1971

364 HoC *Town & country planning (Scotland) act 1972* HMSO London England 1972

365 HoC *Water resources act 1963* HMSO London England 1963

383 IES *The IES Code: recommendations for lighting building interiors* CIBS London England 1977

387 IES(USA) *Lighting handbook* IES New York USA 1972

390 Institution of Electrical Engineers *Regulations for the electrical equipment of buildings* IEE London England latest edtion

391 International Air Transport Assocation *Airport Terminal reference manual* IATA Montreal Canada 6th edn 1976

392 International Civil Aviation Organisation *Aerodrome design manual*
Part 2 *Taxiways, aprons & holding bays*
Part 3 *Pavements*
ICAO Montreal Canada 1977

393 International Civil Aviation Organisation *Airport planning manual*
Part 1 *Master planning*
Part 2 *Land use & environmental control*
ICAO Montreal Canada 1977

394 International Civil Aviation Organisation *Heliport manual* ICAO Montreal Canada 1979

395 International Civil Aviation Organisation *International standards, recommended practices: aerodromes. Annex 14 to the convention on international aviation* IACO Montreal Canada 1976

396 International Civil Aviation Organisation *Stolport manual* ICAO Montreal Canada 1976

397 International Commission on Illumination *International recommendations for the calculation of natural daylight* (publication 16) CIE Paris France 1970

398 International Conference of Building Officials *Uniform building code* ICBO Whittier Calif USA latest edition

399 International Federation of Library Associations *Standards for public libraries* Verlag Dokumentation Munich Germany FLR The Hague Netherlands 1973

400 ISO *Modular co-ordination: basic module* (ISO 1006:1973) ISO Geneva Switzerland 1973

403 ISO *Modular co-ordination: principles & rules* (ISO 2848:1974) ISO Geneva Switzerland 1974

406 ISO *Modular co-ordination: vocabulary* (ISO 1791:1973) ISO Geneva Switzerland 1973

407 ISO *Standard for the functional sizes of school furniture* (ISO/DIS 5970:1978) ISO Geneva Switzerland 1978

473 Metrication Board *How to write metric: a style guide to teaching and using SI units* HMSO London England no date

504 National Elevator Industry *Elevator engineering standards* National Elevator Industry Inc New York USA 5th edn 1979

505 National Fire Protection Association *Designing buildings for fire safety* NFPA Boston USA 1975

508 National Fire Protection Association *Life safety code* NFPA Boston USA latest edition

509 National Fire Protection Association *National Fire codes* NFPA Boston USA 16 vol 1976

510 National Fire Protection Association *National fire prevention code* NFPA Boston USA Latest edition

512 National House Builders Council *Registered house builders handbook* NHBC London England 1974

515 National Swimming Pool Institute Technical Council *Minimum standards for public spas* NSPI Washington DC USA 1978

516 National Swimming Pool Institute Technical Council *Minimum standards for public swimming pools* NSPI Washington DC USA 1974

517 National Swimming Pool Institute Standards Codes Committee *Suggested minimum standards for residential swimming pools* NSPI Washington DC USA 1974

549 Ramsey & Sleeper/American Institute of Architects *Architectural graphic standards* (Packard R T (ed)) John Wiley & Sons New York USA 7th edn 1980

553 RIBA *CI/SfB construction indexing manual* RIBA Services Ltd London England 1976

573 Scottish Development Department *Scottish Housing Handbook part 3 Housing development layout, roads & services* HMSO Edinburgh Scotland 1977

574 Scottish Development Department *Scottish Housing Handbook part 6 Housing for the disabled* HMSO Edinburgh Scotland 1979

581 Simmonds M F *Accommodation standards for educational buildings* BRE Garston England revised edn 1977

584 Southern Building Code Congress *Standard building code* SBCC Birmingham Ala USA latest edition

587 Sports Council *Specification for artificial sports surfaces* (technical report prepared by the Rubber & Plastics Research Association of Great Britain) Sports Council London England 1978

589 Statutory instruments 1959:428 *Agriculture (safeguarding of work places) regulations 1959* HMSO London England 1959

590 Statutory instruments 1966:99 *Building operations, construction health & welfare regulations* HMSO London England 1966

591 Statutory instruments 1976:1676 *The building regulations* HMSO London England 1976

592 Statutory instruments 1976:1676 *The building regulations Part E Safety in fire*
E3 *Rules for measurement*
E4 *Provision of compartment walls & compartment floors*
E5 *Fire resistance of elements of structure*
HMSO London England 1976

593 Statutory instruments 1978:723 *The building (first amendment) regulations* HMSO London England 1978

594 Statutory instruments 1971:2052 *The building standards (Scotland) (consolidation) regulations* HMSO London England 1971

595 Statutory instruments 1973:794 *The building standards (Scotland) amendment regulations 1973* HMSO London England 1973

596 Statutory instruments 1975:404 *The building standards (Scotland) amendment regulations 1975* HMSO London England 1975

597 Statutory instruments: Statutory regulations & orders 1922:73 (as amended by SI 1961:2435) *Chemical works regulations* HMSO London England 1961

598 Statutory instruments 1955:1129 *Cinematograph safety regulations* HMSO London England 1955

599 Statutory instruments 1959:282 *Cinematograph safety regulations* HMSO London England 1959

600 Statutory instruments 1948:1547 *Clay works welfare special regulations* HMSO London England 1948

601 Statutory instruments 1976:2010 *Fire precaution (non-certified factory, office, shop & railway premises) regulations* HMSO London England 1976

602 Statutory instruments: Statutory rules & orders 1917:1067 *Metal works* as amended by SR&O 1926:864 & SI 1961:2434 HMSO London England 1917 1926 & 1961

603 Statutory instruments: Statutory rules & orders 1929:534 *Oil cake welfare order* HMSO London England 1929

CODES

604 Statutory instruments 1964:966 *Sanitary conveniences regulations* HMSO London England 1964

605 Statutory instruments: Statutory rules & orders 1925:864 *Saw mills & wood working factories welfare (ambulance & first aid)* as amended by SI 1961:2434 HMSO London England 1925 & 1961

606 Statutory instruments: 1960:1932 *Ship building & ship repairs regulations* HMSO London England 1960

607 Statutory instruments 1972:2051 *Standards for school premises regulations* HMSO London England 1972

608 Statutory instruments 1964:965 *Washing facilities regulations* HMSO London England 1964

610 Steel Window Association *Specification for the metric preferred range W20 steel windows SWA 201* SWA London England 1972

629 United Nations Educational Scientific & Cultural Organization (UNESCO) *Planning buildings & facilities for higher education* Architectural Press London England UNESCO Press Paris France 1975

630 University Grants Committee *Planning norms for university buildings* HMSO London England 1974

631 Urban Land Institute *Residential development handbook* ULI Washington DC USA 1978

632 US Congress *Architectural barriers act* US Superintendent of Documents Washington DC USA 1968

633 US Congress *National environment policy act* US Superintendent of Documents Washington DC USA 1970

634 US Congress *Occupational safety & health act* US Superintendent of Documents Washington DC USA 1971

635 US Federal Aviation Agency *The apron & terminal building: planning manual* 3 vol National Technical Information Service Springfield Va USA 1975

REFERENCE BY TOPICS

Access
056 086 088 136 158 189 231 242 244 276 557

Acoustics
063 064 190 254 268 408 428 503 522 532 544 545 642 655

Air conditioning →ventilation

Airports
048 067 165 186 341 370 391 392 393 394 395 396 635

Apartments
018 037 464 533 623 628

Auditoriums
063 408 413

Banks
007 249 259 374 477

Building services
111 119 124 130 133 143 150 151 246 377 390 416 461 489 490 503 593

Canteens →refectories

Car parks
086 308 424 435 513 555 557

Cinemas
084 098 099 113 114 129 328 329 339 426 598 599

Climate
047 285 291 433 434 467 520 527 529 536 617

Colleges
039 040 041 063 096 097 113 114 147 168 176 200 217 226 261 377 413 437 441 446 472 476 485 526 556 569 581 612 629 630 652

Construction
008 089 092 101 120 121 125 126 132 139 140 144 173 175 200 228 277 288 289 316 341 371 375 378 422 445 467 491 494 495 498 502 553 568 590

Daylighting also →lighting sunlight
047 059 074 076 107 251 252 291 367 368 375 380 381 382 383 397 452 457 527 528 529 567

Design
085 163 169 173 179 185 209 210 211 212 213 214 247 276 279 292 294 302 303 313 322 375 417 425 445 462 549 567 628 638

Dining rooms
096 097 147 168 176 217 226 439 441

Disabled also →old people
028 055 060 071 088 109 157 187 189 191 220 221 281 286 287 296 317 327 423 432 438 447 469 488 518 535 574 628 632 639

Doors
138 145 401 628

Drawing practice
061 075 081 082 095 128 142 290 322 448 463 553 621 638

Elderly →old people

Elevators also →stairs
035 123 504 613 628

Energy conservation also →climate heating
030 059 149 172 194 195 199 250 257 258 304 427 460 558 611 615

Equitation →sport

Escalators →stairs

Factories →industrial buildings

Farm buildings
108 115 118 137 288 325 326 333 334 335 340 341 347 348 351 352 356 357 358 359 360 363 364 365 415 582 589 601 646

Fire precautions
026 079 116 117 154 196 269 284 301 324 340 412 436 492 501 505 506 507 508 509 510 546 592 601 619

Flats →apartments

Garages
225 276 348 424 636 650

Gardens
002 021 032 066 087 155 161 166 167 171 263 264 320 376 410 411 430 431 466 482 550 562 563

Bibliography

( ) indicates an illustration

Index

Index